SEPARATE AND UNEQUAL

By the Same Author

The Foundations of Local Self-Government in India, Pakistan and Burma

The Union of Burma: a study of the first years of independence

India and Pakistan: a political analysis

Bellot Box and Bayonet: people and government in emergent Asian countries

Reorientations: studies on Asia in transition

South Asia: a short history

Experiment with Freedom: India and Pakistan, 1947

A New System of Slavery: the export of Indian labour overseas, 1830-1920

A Narrative of the Mission to the Court of Ava in 1855 (a new, expanded, version of Henry Yule's Narrative)

Separate and Unequal

INDIA AND THE INDIANS
IN THE BRITISH COMMONWEALTH
1920—1950

HUGH TINKER

UNIVERSITY OF BRITISH COLUMBIA PRESS
VANCOUVER

Published 1976 by the
University of British Columbia Press
For sale only in North America

© 1976 by Hugh Tinker

Canadian Shared Cataloguing in Publication Data

Tinker, Hugh.
 Separate and Unequal: India and the Indians in the British Commonwealth, 1920-1950

 1. Alien labor, East Indian - History. 2 Labor and laboring classes - Great Britain - Colonies - History. 3. East Indians in foreign countries. I. Title
HD8398.E3T551   331.6'2'54
ISBN 0-7748-0046-1

Printed in Great Britain

Contents

		Page
	Introduction	7
	Table: The Rulers	12
	Important Events Concerning the Indians Overseas	14
1.	Prologue: the Helots of the Empire	21
2.	The Claim for Equality (1921-23)	43
3.	The Separation of White, Black and Brown (1924-29)	78
4.	Separation Questioned and Affirmed (1929-35)	106
5.	A Pattern of Inequality (1935-39)	136
6.	Coercion and Conflict (1939-43)	175
7.	Equality: the Claim Asserted (1943-45)	219
8.	Equality: the Claim Vindicated (1945-47)	264
9.	The Test of Independence (1947-50)	313
10.	The Moment of Equality	355
	Notes	395
	A Personal Note	432
	A Note on Sources	436
	Select Bibliography	444
	Index	451

For Peter Lyon and W. H. Morris-Jones
Friends in Need

Introduction

This study of Indian communities overseas in the Colonies and Dominions of the British Commonwealth during three decades is concerned with a transitional phase linking the age of British imperial dominance (which effectively came to an end in 1914) with the present, post-imperial era, which awoke into startled awareness of its condition in the 1950s, when Dean Acheson observed that Britain had lost an empire and not yet found a role. The 1920s, 1930s, and 1940s, were the imperial eventide; though at that time this was anything but obvious. The British Empire, ruling a quarter of the world's population, still appeared to be firmly based and permanent. For India, these three decades formed the era of the Freedom Struggle; a heroic era. For Britain the same decades were marked by the great slump and the era of appeasement — unheroic memories — though the period ended with the Second World War and in 1940 Britain's defiance of the Nazi hegemony with only the nations of the Commonwealth as comrades in the fight. For India and Britain both, then, these were momentous decades in which (to use a simile employed by Lord Zetland at the start of World War II) there was a grand 'churning of the ocean of thought', and a churning up of accepted ways in politics and social usage.

These decades were of vital importance to the overseas Indians. In the 1920s they made political demands, and had demands made of them, in an atmosphere of crisis and tension for their future. The 1930s formed a kind of interlude, while the weight of the world depression pressed down, but then in the 1940s the political challenge reached a new level of intensity. Thereafter, the Indians overseas were almost constantly being called to account, until in the 1960s and 1970s their actual survival is in question in certain places.

The period 1920-50 was the time during which the Indians shook off the bonds which had kept them in a state of servitude, almost, during the long years in which they had laboured on tropical plantations as indentured labourers and in other forms of bondage. During these three decades, as they stepped out of the shadow of indenture, the Indians began to move into new economic activities, and into towns and cities and to become a part of the modern, urban, tropical or sub-tropical world.

Though Indians overseas acquired a social component which could be called middle class — entrepreneurs, professional people, with a coherently middle-class way of life, leading to middle-class demands in housing, education and other facilities — most of the

Indians were managers of small workshops, petty traders, market gardeners, artisans, street vendors, peasants and labourers. This miscellaneous collection of trades and occupations reflected a fragmented society, lacking organization and strength. There were certain groups endowed with internal solidarity and order, such as the Sikhs, the Ismailis (followers of the Aga Khan) and some Gujarati caste-groups, like the Patels. But these groups drew their organic strength from their original places in Indian society. The great mass of the Indians overseas were illorganized, deculturated, and in their transplanted state spoke Creole dialects or other forms of lingua-franca. When they retained their own languages, as the Tamils did in Ceylon and Malaya, this was a doubtful strength as the educated, the middle class, the enterprising moved away into the English-speaking stream. Many of the overseas Indians were creolised, bastardised in some respects, and almost everywhere fragmented and weak in leadership.

Even amongst those who emerged as the leaders of the overseas Indians there was a perpetual tendency to factionalism and defection. The political history of every overseas Indian community was a story of internal conflict — between the prosperous and the less well-off, between conservatives and modernists, between those looking to India as their source of strength and those wanting to take their place in the land of their adoption, between activists and quietists. Compared to the group-solidarity of Jewish or Chinese communities, the overseas Indians were divided and often helpless.

Yet the stereotype which others applied to them was of a clannish, secretive community, constantly acting against the interests of others. From this popular stereotype of a monolithic overseas Indian community there followed semi-scientific explanations of a political, economic and sociological nature which posited the existence of a 'Plural Society' in South-East Asia, Africa, the Caribbean, the Pacific and elsewhere. In the form originally advanced by J. S. Furnivall, the concept of the Plural Society was a relatively neutral one: Furnivall argued that the nature of colonialism was such as to leave different racial groups isolated and unrelated, brought together only in the contacts of the market place. Out of Furnivall's simple comment on the colonial situation has emerged a school of thought which explains all developments, social and political, by assuming that society is stratified vertically into monolithic racial groups. The politicians have taken over this theory of society and have applied it to post-colonial situations. The extreme example is that of Guyana where, on the eve of independence, Duncan Sandys saddled the country with a constitution which accentuated and perpetuated racial divisions.

Others are much more clever at the game of divide and rule than the overseas Indians, though it is they who always stand accused of creating racial politics, and it is they who invariably suffer from its application. However, in the present study the post-colonial situation is not examined in detail. The purpose of this inquiry is to investigate the conditions of the overseas Indians in the British Empire at eventide.

Both their British colonial masters, and the 'Sons of the Soil' they had been brought in to supplant, regarded the Indians as interlopers and middle men. The British brought the Indians with them to perform services which were needed to make their empire work, and which they were not prepared to have performed by a slow process of training and educating the sons of the soil. The British wanted clerks, policemen, tax collectors, post office employees, railway workers, jailers, vaccinators and all the other miscellaneous agents of government and the public services and public works. They also needed agents of economic growth — shopkeepers, technicians, brokers, providers of credit. And finally they needed people to do the hard work — to unload ships, shift loads, remove filth, and perform all the tasks of labour.

The African, the Malay, Burmese or Sinhalese saw the Indian as the man in authority: they confronted an Indian booking clerk at the railway station or an Indian tally-clerk weighing their produce: they could not see the European manager who was really controlling their affairs. So the Indian was feared and envied as the man in authority. He was also despised as the pariah: for it was the Indian who performed the most menial jobs to keep towns and cities clean, and it was the Indian who sweated in the docks and on the plantations at the coolie work which the sons of the soil were too proud to do themselves.

The mass of the Indians overseas carried out their necessary tasks and asked for little more than to be left alone to live their own lives and to recreate something of Mother India in the far country to which they had been sent. They knew that they were little people, lacking power as the British masters knew power. For the British their empire was a vast private preserve in which, as of right, they paraded and exercised authority. There were some exercising this authority with wisdom and mercy; they were Guardians of a Trust which they had been given to exercise until the sons of the soil were fully qualified to take over. But the driving force of this empire was, of course, the motive of exploitation. The lasting achievements of this empire were the gold mines of South Africa, the rubber and tin of Malaya, the sugar and tea of Guiana and Ceylon. In this achievement of exploitation the Indians who were taken overseas as the agents and servants of the British were among the most thoroughly exploited. Yet, to Africans, Malays, Burmese and others they could appear as the exploiters. They were visible; the British were less visible — and the commercial masters in London, Liverpool and Glasgow were invisible.

During the period covered in this study, India, and the leaders of the overseas Indians strove to free themselves from the separate racial compartment into which they were confined by the workings of the plural society. They claimed equality with the Whites. Their claim was based upon the advance of India towards full self-government and full equality within the British Empire. Their critics say that they made this claim on their own behalf: they failed to assert the claim for the Africans. This charge is levelled especially at the Indians in South Africa. Some go on to charge the Indians with having failed to assimilate with the Africans and other sons of the soil by means of inter-marriage, the sharing of social activities, and mingling in mixed neighbourhoods.

This charge is scarcely ever directed at either the Whites or the Blacks. It seems probable that Indians intermarried to a greater extent than Whites did with Blacks in Africa, or with Burmese, Malays and other indigenous peoples. The most that can be said against the Indians is that in a social and political environment which encouraged the concept of social distance the Indians remained equi-distant from both Whites and Blacks. This did not make any appeal: the British Empire was a white empire and the Whites made the rules and were the judges.

This is a story of the Indian claim to equality in the British Empire or British Commonwealth: for the 1920s and 1930s were the time when the formal equality of the United Kingdom and the white Dominions was signified by the Statute of Westminster. It is designed as an overall view. There are a number of works which provide detailed accounts of the Indian communities in the different territories (listed in the bibliographical note at the end). In this book there is no detailed treatment of the internal development of the various Indian communities and of the ways in which their economic situation changed during this period. The main focus is upon the impact of imperial government and politics upon the Indians. This is just as much a study of the British in their imperial role as it is of the Indians.

The political environment of the overseas Indians was largely shaped by the British and the white Dominions. For this reason there are passages in this book devoted to the debate at Westminster and the arguments between departments of the United Kingdom government, especially between the India Office and the Colonial Office. The study opens when Lord Milner and Winston Churchill were in control at the Colonial Office and closes with the regime of Creech Jones. Throughout the intervening years the Colonial Office was antipathetic — and sometimes hostile — to the overseas Indians: as a report by the Royal Institute of International Affairs observed: 'In any dispute concerning the status of Indians in the Colonies, the Colonial Office...has always had the better of the India Office'.[1]

During the thirty years covered by this narrative there were a few British statesmen who were big enough in their own right to rise above the bureaucratic dialectic. Among the viceroys, Irwin— perhaps Linlithgow, and certainly Wavell — made a personal impact upon conditions for the Indians overseas. Among the Secretaries of State for India, only Montagu — and perhaps Wedgwood Benn— were strong enough (or concerned enough) to override official arguments.

Within the Indian national movement there was little more than a rhetorical concern for the communities overseas. Gandhi, previously their champion, had become immersed in his effort to transform the moral and political face of India. Among other outstanding Congress leaders only Jawaharlal Nehru made the condition of the Indians in neighbouring lands his own personal concern. It was left to the Indian Liberals — Sastri, Sapru, Maharaj Singh and Kunzru— to take up this cause.

During the 1920s and '30s an ever-widening gulf opened between the British and the Indians. No-one did more to bridge this gulf than C. F. Andrews; and in the original text of this book he occupied a prominent place. Subsequently, it was decided to make him the subject of a full-length biography, and so his work for Indians overseas has been related only in outline in the present book.

Now that the records of government have been opened to research upon this period, both in London and New Delhi, we can establish how far the overseas Indian communities had their role and their future conditioned for them by the decisions of their rulers, in Britain, India, and the British colonies, in the last years before independence came to India and Pakistan — and then in the brief interval before the overseas Indians found themselves faced with the dilemmas of trying to participate in others' independence in the new nations of Southern Asia and Africa.

The starting point for this study comes with the first major bid for equality for the overseas Indians made at the Imperial Conference of 1921; before that encounter can be assessed it is necessary, briefly, to look back at the origins of the Indian communities round the world to perceive what effects the nineteenth and early twentieth centuries had upon them.

---

1. Richard Frost, ed., *The British Commonwealth and World Society; Proceeding of the Third Unofficial Conference on British Commonwealth Relations* .... London, 1947, p. 25.

The Rulers, 1920-1947

	Great Britain			India	
	Prime Minister	Secretary for the Colonies	Secretary for India	Viceroy	Member for Indians Overseas
1920	Lloyd George	Lord Milner	Edwin Montagu	Lord Chelmsford	Sir George Barnes
1921		Winston Churchill		Lord Reading	Sir C. A. Innes
1922	Bonar Law	Duke of Devonshire	Viscount Peel		
1923	Stanley Baldwin				
1924	Ramsay MacDonald	J. H. Thomas	Lord Olivier		
	Stanley Baldwin	L. S. Amery	Lord Birkenhead		
(November) 1925					Sir Muhammad Habibullah
1926				Lord Irwin	
1928			Lord Peel		
1929	MacDonald	Lord Passfield	Wedgwood Benn		
1930					Sir Fazl-i-Husain

THE RULERS, 1920-1947

Year	Prime Minister	Secretary of State for Dominions	Secretary of State for India	Viceroy	Member
1931 (November)	(National Government)	J. H. Thomas	Sir S. Hoare	Lord Willingdon	
1935	Baldwin	Sir P. Cunliffe-Lister			
(November)		Malcolm MacDonald			
1936		Thomas	Marquess of Zetland		Sir Jagdish Prasad
1937	Neville Chamberlain	W. Ormsby-Gore		Lord Linlithgow	
1938		Malcolm MacDonald			
1940	Winston Churchill	Lord Lloyd	L. S. Amery		Sir G. S. Bajpai
1941		Lord Moyne			
1942		Lord Cranborne			M. S. Aney
		Oliver Stanley			
(November) 1943				Lord Wavell	Dr. N. B. Khare
1945	C. R. Attlee	G. Hall	Lord Pethick-Lawrence		
1946 (July-Sept.)		A. Creech Jones			Sir Gurunath Bewoor
1947			Lord Listowel	Lord Mountbatten	Jawaharlal Nehru

Important Events Concerning the Indians Overseas

	Page
1920 *India:* Indian National Congress demands status for Indians in Dominions and Colonies equal to that of other peoples	36
Fiji: system of indenture of Indian plantation labour abolished	40
Kenya: first elections on all-White franchise	34
1921 *London:* Imperial Conference recognises claim for equality on behalf of Indians in the Dominions	52
Kenya: despatch from Winston Churchill promises Indians 'equal rights for civilised men'	57
1922 *Kenya:* Wood-Winterton agreement: a common roll to enfranchise Indians	59
Fiji: report by Government of India deputation discourages emigration	61
Australia-New Zealand-Canada: goodwill tour by Srinivasa Sastri to obtain equal rights for the resident Indians	61
1923 *Kenya:* Devonshire memorandum destroys Indian hopes	67
London: Imperial Conference declines to revise policies on Indians overseas	74
1924 *South Africa:* Class Areas Bill threatens to restrict Indians; fall of Smuts government; entry of Hertzog and Malan	75
British Guiana: Indian plantation protest	91
London: Colonies Committee on future of Indians in East Africa and Fiji	78
1926 *Fiji:* common franchise for all communities rejected by Colonial Office	90
South Africa: round table conference with Indian delegation, Cape Town, December-January 1927	87
1927 *South Africa:* Sastri appointed first Agent of Government of India	89
India: Jawaharlal Nehru produces draft foreign policy for Congress urging Indians overseas to identify with adopted countries	93

IMPORTANT EVENTS

Page

1928 *East Africa:* Hilton Young Commission recommends federation; majority recommend common roll as the goal; Government of India ask Colonial Office for appointment of Agent, similar to Sastri   99
Ceylon: Donoughmore Commission recommends universal franchise: to be extended to permanent Indian population   116
1929 *India:* Congress sets up overseas department   93
East Africa: visits by Sir Samuel Wilson (Colonial Office) and by Sastri to assess Hilton Young Commission recommendations   101
1930 *Ceylon:* Colonial Office announces rights of Indian population will not be eroded under new constitution   120
Burma: anti-Indian riots, Rangoon; start of movement for separation from India   123
East Africa: British government White Paper accepts common roll as objective in Kenya   110
1931 *East Africa:* Joint Committee of parliament (Westminster) votes down common roll proposal   114
South Africa: second Cape Town conference; proposals for emigration by South African Indians to colonies for resettlement   128
World Slump: Indian emigrants to East Africa, Ceylon and South-East Asia return to India   115, 125
1933 *South Africa:* Indian Colonisation Enquiry Committee   131
1934 *Ceylon:* 'Ceylonisation' policy to exclude Indians from recruitment to all public services   156
Zanzibar: decrees restricting Indian traders   134
1935 *Burma:* Government of Burma Bill (Westminster) includes assurances for Indians in Burma   150
British Guiana: strikes and commission of inquiry   163
1936 *Fiji:* new communal representation in legislature   162
Kenya: delimitation of white highlands   134
Malaya: formation of Indian Central Association; inquiry by Sastri into labour conditions (December)   153
1937 *Burma:* separation from India; visit by Nehru   151
Malaya: Sastri report recommends better labour conditions; visit by Nehru   154
Mauritius: strikes, casualties; commission of inquiry   170
India: Congress boycott committee fights Zanzibar decrees; Government of India asks for Agents in East Africa and Fiji   142,144

IMPORTANT EVENTS

Page

1938 *Zanzibar:* compromise over restrictions on Indian traders — 147
Kenya: immigration controls introduced — 148
Ceylon: Jackson report on Indian immigration and employment — 157
Burma: anti-Muslim riots injure Indian lives and property in Rangoon, Mandalay, etc; riot inquiry committee with Indian members — 151
Mauritius: strikes, leaders penalised — 171
Malaya: employers lower wages; Government of India ban on labour emigration — 155
West Indies: Moyne Commission investigates economic conditions; Government of India deputes observer — 168

1939 *Ceylon:* retrenchment of Indians in public services; visit by Nehru, on behalf of Congress; ban on labour emigration by Government of India — 159
British Guiana: strikes, commission of inquiry — 167
South Africa: Bill restricting Indian trading and settlement; withdrawn by Smuts, with assurance no further legislation directed at Indians during wartime — 174

1940 *Aden, Somaliland, Hong Kong, Gibraltar:* evacuation of some Indian residents — 175
South Africa: India's representative designated High Commissioner — 177
Mauritius: visit by Indian Government representative; report on Indians — 178
Ceylon: shooting of Indians on Mooloya estate — 179

1941 *Ceylon:* revised electoral rolls reduce Indian voters; anti-Indian Bills disallowed by Governor; draft agreement with India defining citizenship for Ceylon Indians (not confirmed) — 182
Malaya: riots and shooting of Indians in Klang District; leaders jailed and deported; Government of India demand inquiry; Governor Shenton Thomas successfully resists demand — 184
Burma: Baxter report on Indian emigration; draft agreement with India on future of Indians in Burma; agreement repudiated after outcry by Indian public — 193
South Africa: first Broome Commission on Indian settlement or 'penetration' — 220
Malaya and Burma: Japanese invasion (December) — 197

1942 *India:* refugees from Malaya, Burma and Ceylon struggle home — 201

	Page
Malaya: formation of Indian National Army (INA)	207
1943 *Malaya, Burma:* Subhas Chandra Bose heads Free Indian Government	208
Fiji: strike by Indian farmers; sugar cane unharvested	213
Mauritius: strikes and shooting of Indians; commission of inquiry	215
South Africa: second Broome Commission finds evidence of Indian 'penetration'; 'Pegging Act' restricts settlement	222
India: Reciprocity Act allows Government to impose penalties on countries discriminating against Indian residents	222
1944 *South Africa:* Smuts and the leaders of the Indians conclude Pretoria Agreement: later repudiated by Natal Whites	229
India: symbolic retaliation against South Africans introduced	232
East Africa: immigration controls reinforced	241
Mauritius: internment of labour leaders	255
Trinidad: introduction of universal franchise includes all Indians	253
1945 *Burma, Malaya:* British forces return; INA disbanded	290
South Africa: third Broome Commission suggests modified common roll including some Indians with White voters	252
Ceylon: Soulbury Report recommends self-government and assimilation of Indian population	259
East Africa: White Papers on land policy in Kenya and inter-territorial organisation alarm both Whites and Indians	277
London: unofficial Commonwealth conference discusses emigration and hears Indian demand for equality and common citizenship	261
1946 *Burma, Malaya:* visit by Nehru	290
East Africa: Maharaj Singh mission examines immigration controls	281
Ceylon: new constitution boycotted by Indian community	286
South Africa: legislation to confine urban Indians ('Ghetto Act') and to provide Indians with White representatives in parliament; satyagraha campaign against Ghetto Act	294
India: cancellation of trade agreement with South	

IMPORTANT EVENTS

		Page
	Africa in reply to Ghetto Act; Nehru—Minister in Interim Government—asks for appointment of Agents in Colonies where Indians reside	295 309
	United Nations: India arraigns South Africa; vote by Assembly requires the two countries to consult about the Indians of South Africa	297
1947	*India:* Asian Relations Conference discusses race and migration; end of British rule; discussion by Nehru and Senanayake on future of Indians in Ceylon (December)	301 339
	Burma: Emergency Immigration Act; Indian Government protest rejected	307
	Fiji: immigration ordinance restricts entry	334
	Malaya: labour disputes; Indian leaders jailed; introduction of new federal constitution with reduced Indian participation; Indians join in boycott	308
	Canada: domiciled Indians enfranchised	304
	London: Commonwealth conference of experts on citizenship laws	362
	United Nations: Indian resolution on South Africa rejected	321
1948	*India:* appointment of Agents in Mauritius, Fiji, East Africa and the West Indies; Congress resolution on India and the Commonwealth	318
	East Africa: immigration controls applied by all three territories; Indian immigration reduced	327
	Ceylon: end of British rule; Citizenship Act excludes most Indians	339
	Burma: end of British rule; few Indians register for citizenship	341
	Malaya: Communist insurgency; Emergency declared; banishment of British subjects (Indians) under Emergency	345
	Mauritius: general election under extended franchise gives Indians 11 seats in legislature (total =19)	335
	Fiji: demand for non-official majority in legislature rejected	334
	South Africa: Smuts defeated; Malan announces removal of Indians from franchise	323
	London: at India's request, British Nationality Act introduces 'Commonwealth citizenship' as alternative to status of British subject	377

IMPORTANT EVENTS

Page

1949 *London:* Commonwealth prime ministers accept India as a member though a republic; Indian plan for common citizenship shelved — 386
South Africa: riots in Durban between Indians and Africans — 324
Ceylon: legislation excludes Indian population from franchise — 339
India: strict control on entry from Pakistan — 391
United Nations: resolution calling for round table conference of South Africa, India and Pakistan — 324

1950 *South Africa:* Group Areas Act further restricts Indian settlement — 325
India, Pakistan: cancel round table conference with South Africa — 325
Kenya: general strike in Nairobi; Indian leader deported — 330
Trinidad: general election, Indians win 5 seats (total =18) — 332
Malaya: less than half Indian community register for Malayan citizenship — 352
India: new constitution takes effect; extends citizenship option to most overseas Indians — 391

1
Prologue: the Helots of the Empire

From the earliest times, Indians made their way across the seas to settle in South-East Asia, Arabia and East Africa. Perhaps some travelled to even more distant shores, in the Pacific Ocean and beyond. Except for the movement of Tamils from the extreme south of India into Ceylon, this emigration was conducted on a relatively small scale. Those who settled round the bounds of the Indian Ocean included wise men — scholars, scribes, priests, astrologers— but most of the overseas Indians were merchants and traders, with some artisans and serving men and also slaves. It was not until the beginning of the nineteenth century that a mass migration was organised to meet the demands of imperial trade and development throughout the British Empire in the aftermath of African slavery.

The Indian labourers exported under the indenture system, and other forms of recruitment for the plantations, were known as coolies, and they laboured under penalties not dissimilar to those of slavery. Their sole advantage over the slaves, their predecessors, was that their bondage was not permanent: most obtained release from their penal contract after five or ten years. Thereafter, between one-quarter and one-third returned to India, and the remainder settled down in the colony as 'free' labourers or as smallholders or hucksters.

In the tropical colonies, they formed an element in plural societies, alongside the indigenous people—Ceylonese, Burmese, or Malays— or else they took their place beside other immigrants (bond or free) in a Creole society of White, Black and Brown. But there were other sub-tropical or temperate colonies in which the accepted pattern was for white settlement. These colonies varied between Canada, Australia and New Zealand — where the indigenous peoples were totally subordinated, and partially extinguished by white penetration—and South Africa, Southern Rhodesia, and Kenya, where white dominance rested upon a work-force which was black and brown.

Opposition to the migration of Indians and other Asians emerged in the colonies of white settlement by the mid-nineteenth century. In Australia, the landlord 'squatters' of New South Wales attempted to persuade the government to import Indian workers, while the sugar planters of Queensland were even more anxious to obtain their labour. However, the urban working class was already well-organised by this time, and determined to preserve living standards against the threat of cheap labour. The first opposition was directed against Chinese immigrants, arriving to work in the goldfields, and local legislatures passed laws to prohibit their entry.[1] The home government, in London, refused to agree to the royal assent being given to most of this legislation, because it discriminated upon race lines. In 1899, the New Zealand parliament adopted an Immigration Restriction Bill which prescribed that any new arrival could be declared a prohibited immigrant if he could not pass a literacy test: this applied to a person 'who fails to write and sign...in any European language the prescribed application for admission'. This measure was deemed non-discriminatory and received the royal assent in 1900. The formula was adopted as a means of regulating entry by Australia and Canada shortly afterwards, though the literacy test was not required in the case of British (United Kingdom) entrants.

Natal, in South Africa, was even more divided over the issue of Indian immigration. The big employers, especially the sugar planters, desperately needed field labour, and demanded the import of indentured Indians. The smaller employers, shopkeepers, and artisans strongly opposed the growth of a community who, they said, would swamp the white population. The big employers were sufficiently powerful to keep open the door to indentured immigration, but the white electorate was also strong enough to place restrictions upon their residence, and to exclude all Indians — not just the indentured labourers — from rights of citizenship, and many of the ordinary social and economic facilities enjoyed by the whites.

The British Government tried to avert policies of exclusion based on race, but gradually, as the self-governing white colonies moved forward to fully responsible government, the principle of local control over immigration policy was conceded. However, it was insisted that all persons resident in the different parts of the British Empire should be eligible for full local citizenship once they had served their apprenticeship under indenture. The claim to equality was first enunciated in a despatch issued on 24 March 1875 when Lord Salisbury was Secretary of State for India. Looking to the future: 'The colonial laws and their administration will be such that Indian settlers... will be in all respects free men, with privileges no whit inferior to those of any other class of Her Majesty's subjects resident in the colonies.'[2] This despatch was thereafter cited as a kind of Magna Carta for Indians overseas, but in actuality it achieved very little. Few Indians gained acceptance within white colonial society, and those few gained their place by assuming a form of disguise: they succeeded in acquiring an English-style education, and perhaps embraced an English-style religion, with an English name. These few passed, as 'brown sahibs'; the rest were excluded and regarded as inferior.

The British Government's request to the white self-governing colonies to admit the 'respectable' or 'educated' Indian was not at all acceptable to them. A few distinguished individuals might be accepted, but the emergence of a brown middle-class was feared: a class which would take the rightful place of the white man. The Indians overseas did not appreciate their futile position. For many years, the Indians in Natal, with Gandhi as their adviser, wasted their energies in petitions addressed to their British rulers asserting that their community was becoming 'civilised': that, in effect, they were becoming brown Englishmen, and should be treated as white Englishmen. Gandhi, at length, realised the futility of this claim, and the futility of the middle-class Indians attempting to 'pass for white' at the price of accepting that the mass of Indian workers might be exploited and repressed because they remained 'uncivilised'.

It was Gandhi who brought the plight of the Indians overseas to the notice of Indian national opinion. Previously, politically conscious Indians had comfortably assumed that emigration was advantageous to their countrymen. Gandhi succeeded in gaining the interest of G. K. Gokhale, and in 1901 the Congress passed a resolution on South Africa, demanding recognition of the rights of the Indians, though Gandhi was vexed at the perfunctory interest that was shown on that occasion. It was in South Africa that Gandhi evolved the philosophy and technique of *satyagraha*, at first described as passive resistance and later as non-violence. From the evidence of Gandhi's autobiography, *My Experiments with Truth*, it appears as though he experienced a spiritual transformation in 1906, when his own vows of dedication merged with a commitment to sacrifice by the Indian community in South Africa. At any rate, the movement which Gandhi led during the next eight years was unlike any Indian political campaign before or after in the impact it made upon the local Indians, upon white South Africa, upon Britain and most of all upon India.[3]

Gandhi's campaign awakened the conscience of the British people to the wrongs inflicted upon Indians overseas and to the institutionalised inequality which had been fastened upon them. John Morley, Secretary for India, was able to foresee the philosophical implications of Gandhi's struggle, without attempting to do very much about it. He told Lord Minto, the Viceroy (3 January 1908) 'The great topic of the hour is the question of Asiatics in the

Transvaal — only a part, however, of one of the largest questions concerning the Empire as a whole and indeed not only the Empire but all white governments against all yellow, brown and black immigrants. It is and will grow to be more and more a World question, if ever there was one.'[4]

Humanitarian organisations such as the Anti-Slavery and Aborigines Protection Society adopted the cause of the Indian labourers, but more important to Gandhi's cause was the involvement of two men in particular: Henry Saloman Leon Polak, and Charles Freer Andrews. Polak, an Anglo-Jewish lawyer, became the propagandist and publicist of the overseas Indians. He was later to provide the main link with India, and all the colonies where Indians settled, from his London office in the Strand (where he managed the Indians Overseas Association). While still in South Africa he exposed the plight of the indentured labourers in his booklet, *The Indians of South Africa: helots within the Empire, and how they are treated* (1909). The Anglican clergyman, C. F. Andrews, was already beginning to identify with Indian cultural and political ideals when he was sent by Gokhale to work alongside Gandhi. He, too, played a major part in telling the world about the condition of the overseas Indians, but his special contribution was to approach those in authority with a personal appeal which they found difficult to shrug off. Andrews knew and was known by politicians, clergy, intellectuals; and though they might consider him emotional and sensational in his appeals, they could not ignore him.

The Gandhian campaign also caused the spokesmen for the British Empire to re-evaluate their principles and policies. South Africa, and the reconstruction of the Transvaal after the Peace of Vereeniging, brought together a group of young imperialists who were also intellectuals. They were called Milner's 'Kindergarten' in the Transvaal, and later they were intimately associated with *The Round Table*, an Arthurian dream of a new Camelot as the focus for a dedicated British Empire. Almost all became famous — Patrick Duncan, future Minister and Governor-General of South Africa, Leopold Amery, future Secretary of State for the Colonies and for India, Geoffrey Dawson, future editor of *The Times*, Philip Kerr, future Minister and Ambassador to the United States — but their recognised leader, who the others came to call 'The Prophet', was a man who eschewed public office for the influence which he believed could be exercised from an Oxford college: Lionel Curtis. As an administrator in the Transvaal, Curtis was directly responsible for the application of policies towards the Indians, until the province was returned to self-government. He applied a series of measures designed to restrict the Indians and keep them apart from the

Whites, who Curtis insisted must develop the Transvaal as a white man's country.

When Botha and Smuts took over, and the Kindergarten went home, they gave expression to their ideas in the new quarterly *Round Table*, and the first issue (November 1910) included an article 'India and the English' with the following elliptic comment:

South Africa and British Columbia have indeed made it plain how they regard the presence of certain Indians in their midst, and it may be that from the heat which their action has aroused will be derived some of the energy which one day will be applied to pull the Empire into shape.

Philip Kerr, who subsequently contributed an article 'India and the Empire' was more explicit: he told Curtis 'Educated Indians must be allowed temporary entry to travel, study or to promote trade' but the white Dominions 'should have the right to exclude coolies altogether and to prevent any native-born Indian from becoming a permanently settled resident'.[5]

Most of the *Round Table* group were Conservatives, or like Milner imperialists above party; but Kerr was attracted to the new Liberalism of Lloyd George and Winston Churchill. This new Liberalism had discarded the anti-colonialism which had split the party during the Boer War. Campbell-Bannerman appeared to have found the answer in South Africa: reconciliation, between Boer and Briton, even if it meant acceptance of white supremacy. How far did these Liberals realise that their attitude did not accord with the Liberalism of Gladstone and John Bright? Churchill, at any rate, was not aware of the ambiguities in his attitude. He made an extended tour through East Africa and wrote about his experience in *My African Journey* (1908) in which he applauded the pioneer efforts of the Indians in opening up the interior: soldiers, traders, labourers, he saluted them all. Yet, in January 1908 he cabled the High Commissioner in South Africa, Lord Selborne: 'Please tell Botha I am going to support his government most strongly on the Indian question as I thoroughly understand the views of white South Africa.'

Churchill was then in his first important government post: Under Secretary for the Colonies. His chief was the dull, elderly Lord Elgin. The combination of an ageing aristocratic nonentity as Secretary of State, and a thrusting, ambitious young politician as Under Secretary was to be tried more than once at the Colonial Office. They were no longer directly responsible for South Africa at the Colonial Office, but they had recently assumed a very worrisome responsibility for East Africa from the Foreign Office. In what were becoming known as the 'White Highlands', a motley collection of Europeans were beginning to own farms: and were beginning to claim also to own the whole country. Elgin was very much afraid of 'the risk in multiplying what we call white men's countries where there are a very small number of Whites in the midst of an overwhelming majority of Blacks'. But Churchill favoured white settlement: 'I cannot feel the slightest sympathy with a policy which tends to preserve the East African Protectorate to officials, capitalists, and Big Game,' he said.

The new white settlers demanded that London recognise their exclusive right to farm in the white highlands: in particular they wanted an assurance that Indian farmers would be excluded. Elgin demurred, and replied to Governor Sadler (17 July 1906): 'It would not be in accordance with the policy of His Majesty's Government to exclude any class of His Majesty's subjects from holding land in any part of a British Protectorate, but that in view of the comparatively limited area in the Protectorate suitable for European colonisation, a reasonable discretion will be exercised in dealing with applications for land on the part of the natives of India and other non-Europeans.' The white riff-raff were stiffened by leaders used to getting their own way and especially Hugh Cholmondeley, third Baron Delamere, owner of 150,000 African acres. Lord Elgin told his successor at the Colonial Office, Lord Crewe, that their fellow peer had 'taken the extreme settler side and actually headed restive mobs'. So Elgin was pressed to reconsider his ruling, and on 19 March 1908 he informed Governor Sadler 'It is not consistent with the views of His Majesty's Government to impose *legal* restrictions on any particular section of the community, but as a matter of administrative convenience, grants in the upland area should not be made to Indians.'

This was the Elgin undertaking, the Elgin pledge, which it was claimed committed British governments, for all eternity, to reserve the white highlands for the white settlers. Even so, the foothold of the white farmers was precarious; in 1909, there were so many failures and bankruptcies that the new Under Secretary for the Colonies, Colonel Seely, was urging that they should forcibly terminate the whole experiment by the repatriation of the white farmers en bloc: Crewe agreed, but when this was put to Sadler he replied that it was not yet necessary (February 1909); so the moment for deliberate choice was allowed to pass.[6]

Indian nationalists did not yet understand the significance of the emergence of a white minority in East Africa; their gaze was fixed upon the struggle in South Africa. In the first decade of the twentieth century, Indian nationalism was divided between the forces of the 'Moderates' and those of the 'Extremists'. Factional disputes split the Indian National Congress apart, but they combined, if only temporarily, in support of Gandhi's campaign in South Africa. Both factions were aroused to an intense awareness that they were stigmatised as an inferior race, 'hewers of wood and drawers of water'. It was the Moderates who cared most about equality and citizenship within the British Empire (the Extremists rejected the conception of partnership with their British rulers) and it was Gokhale, the Liberal, the Moderate, who summoned the Government of India to stand up for Indians overseas. His call for the termination of indentured emigration to South Africa was accepted by the government, but his subsequent demand for the abolition of all indentured emigration was resisted. When the Government voted down his motion by means of the official majority in the central legislature, Gokhale stated that his motion 'will be brought forward again and again till we carry it to a successful issue'.

The Viceroy, Lord Hardinge, was moved by this demonstration of Indian feeling, and when the government of Botha and Smuts retaliated against Gandhi's campaign by mass arrests, Hardinge spoke out. He told a mass audience in Madras in November 1913 that Indians in South Africa 'have violated, as they intended to violate, those laws with full knowledge of the penalties involved.... In all this they have the sympathy of India — deep and burning — and not only of India but of all those who like myself... have feelings of sympathy for the people of this country.' The Viceroy's speech — which was virtually a call to the South African Indians to defy the law of South Africa — was received with consternation by the home government, and by a demand for the Viceroy's recall from Smuts. But Hardinge did not recant; he had established the point that though the Government of India might be the ruler, the custodian, the warden in its internal behaviour towards the people of India, in its approach to the Indians overseas it was the champion, the challenger, the defier.

However, the rulers of India spoke with two voices. One was the voice of the Government of India, which though remote from reality, at Simla or in the new Delhi, was at any rate conscious of the forces of Indian national feeling; the other was the India Office in Whitehall, at the centre of British politics and government. At this critical time, the India Office — led first by the crabbed radical philosopher, Morley, and then the benign aristocrat, Lord Crewe — was not under dynamic direction. The officials, conscious of the community of interests of Whitehall administration, were deaf to the aspirations of India. When another imperial conference gathered in 1911 to mark the accession of George V, the India Office assented to the following declaration on the position of Indians overseas:

> His Majesty's Government fully accept the principle that each of the Dominions must be allowed to decide for itself which elements it desires to accept in its population. The extreme contention urged by some Indians... that membership of the British Empire shall entitle any British subject to reside wherever he chooses is disposed of by acknowledged political facts.

The Government of India had to accept these acknowledged political facts, and asked only that the policies of the white Dominions should be framed 'so as to avoid wanton injury to the self-respect of non-European British subjects', with emphasis put upon exclusion on educational grounds, not on grounds of race.

A blunt demonstration of political facts was now to be given by the Dominion of Canada. A party of Indian soldiers, Sikhs, who had paraded through London for Victoria's first Jubilee in 1887, were sent back home via Canada. The Sikhs saw that it was a good land, and in the following years, adventurous individuals turned up in North America. The waves of emigration were described by Sir Harry Johnston, who met 'Reserve soldiers of the Indian Army who have served with the Malay police or the Hong Kong police, who are Sikhs'. Johnston described how 'In a spirit of adventure they drifted across to the Philippine islands and engaged themselves in the service of the Americans, . . . from there they found their way across to Hawaii and then to the [United] States, and some of them have stayed in California and others come on'.[7] They found well-paid jobs in the lumber industry of British Columbia, and also in railway construction and farming, and news of their good fortune filtered back to the Punjab. Between 1905 and 1908 about 5,000 Indians, overwhelmingly Sikhs, arrived in British Columbia. At first they encountered no opposition, but in 1907 and 1908 unemployment appeared among the Indians (called 'Hindus' as distinct from the North American Indians) and also white workers. The unemployment was ascribed to the arrival of the 'Hindus', and anti-oriental feeling rose high.

Racism broke into song, with the anthem "White Canada for Ever":

> To oriental grasp and greed
> We'll surrender, no never,
> Our watchword the 'God save the King',
> White Canada for ever.[8]

A series of ingenious Orders in Council were drafted under the Canadian Immigration Act. Entry into Canada was refused to persons who had not come from their country of origin by a continuous journey, and who could not produce a through ticket. In addition, arrivals had to be in possession of $200. As a result only twenty-seven Indians (or 'Hindus') were able to enter Canada between 1909 and 1913. The Government of India appealed against these measures, but without result; consequently, the Sikh ex-soldiers and policemen swung violently away from the loyalty they had previously professed to the Crown and to their British commanders. They listened to Lala Lajpat Rai, the Punjabi Extremist politician, and to Hardayal, an Indian lecturer at Stanford University. A new journal was published in San Francisco, *Ghadr*, 'Revolution', and rapidly acquired a wide circulation amongst discontented Indian readers in Canada, British Guiana, Trinidad, South and East Africa, Hong Kong, Japan, and the Philippines. The journal gave its name to an underground movement, *Ghadr*, confined mainly to northern Indians, especially intellectuals. The movement spread back to the Punjab and was condemned by the British authorities who associated its teachings with violence.

In May 1914, a determined effort was made to break through the web of the Canadian regulations. A Sikh businessman chartered a Japanese ship, *Komagata Maru*, and collected Sikh passengers from India, Hong Kong, and Shanghai. With 376 Indians on board, *Komagata Maru* arrived off Vancouver on 23 May. The Immigration Department prevented all but a few from landing, and despite strenuous efforts — including legal proceedings — the local Sikhs could not force open the door for their countrymen. Eventually, escorted by H.M.C.S. *Rainbow*, the *Komagata Maru* turned for home. By the time the travellers reached India the world was at war. On landing they were met by the police, and in resisting arrest the Sikhs suffered casualties. Some were interned back in the Punjab. The incident played a large part in transforming Sikh cultural nationalism into political forms.

The Sikhs were an unusual group in the Indian emigration: they were prepared to fight for their rights. The mass of poor labourers, mainly from Madras, and the traders and shopkeepers from Gujarat, who formed the bulk of the emigrants were not prepared or organised for struggle. Gandhi gave leadership in South Africa which temporarily turned coolies and traders into freedom fighters. And he brought back to India a consciousness of racial inequality within the British Empire which could affect provincial lawyers, schoolmasters, and all the other supporters of the Indian National Congress. Another important voice was that of Benarsi Das Chaturvedi, editor and publicist, whose narrative of the life of an indentured labourer in Fiji — *Fiji Dwip Men Mere Ikkis Varsh* — was published in 1914. Written in Hindi, it reached a wide public throughout northern India, and for the first time urban, middle class people realised how the poor labourers were treated. Benarsi Das followed up this story of one Indian by more general accounts: *Fiji Men Bharatiya* (Indians in Fiji) an adaptation of a report by C. F. Andrews, and *Prabasi Bharatiya* (Indians Overseas). The subject became a scandal to India.

The Viceroy and the more imaginative British administrators in India sensed the depth of Indian feeling. Lord Carmichael of Skirling, Governor of Bengal, addressed the Government of India (2 November 1915) in response to a request for his province's attitude to indentured emigration. He said there was 'indignation' in Bengal; it was 'degrading' and 'a source of danger' to the government. The Government of India 'should disassociate itself entirely' from the indenture system. But the two official members of his Executive Council, Messrs. P. C. Lyon and D. N. Beatson Bell, dissented from the governor's recommendation. An understanding of the burden of racial inequality was not universal among the British administrators of India.

Nor was Britain itself a non-racial society. There were less than five thousand Indians in Britain in the early years of the twentieth century, and most of these were transients: students of law and medicine, aspirants for the Indian Civil Service. Yet even these few were sometimes resented. Lionel Curtis told Lord Chelmsford, the Viceroy (2 November 1916), that in the Oxford of twenty years before there had been only one or two Indian students, and they had been regarded as no different from the rest; but 'Today racial feeling is sadly evident in [the] university'; he added: 'The mixture of any considerable number of Asiatics with a European community is the certain precursor of trouble.'[9] Without fuss, the authorities in the United Kingdom took steps to ensure that the population was not augmented by unwanted Indians or other coloured people. Occasionally, Indian seamen, lascars, were discharged at British ports, while circus people and other entertainers (such as the traditional snake-charmers) found themselves abandoned in England. An official enquiry was held, and administrative arrangements were drafted so that all such waifs and strays should be shipped back to their country of origin.[10]

India's status in the British Empire was affected by India's part in the Great War, in which the military contribution was second only to that of the United Kingdom. In the first weeks of war, two Indian infantry divisions and two cavalry divisions joined the British Expeditionary Force in France, representing between one-quarter and one-third of the British fighting strength. The Indians remained in the line throughout the bitter winter of 1914-15, and subsequently served at Gallipoli, in the Palestine campaigns, in East Africa and in Iraq. Altogether one and a quarter million Indian troops served overseas.

The outbreak of war saw a remarkable demonstration of solidarity with the Imperial cause, not only amongst rajas and those traditionally regarded as 'loyal', but also from the urban middle classes. Gandhi's great prestige was placed behind the recruiting campaign. Yet the British rulers seemed unable to cope with this unexpected support from the politically conscious. Despite this British reserve, Indian support was sustained to a remarkable extent throughout the war: on 29 April 1918, Gandhi was still writing to Lord Chelmsford 'It is clear to me that we should give the Empire every available man for its defence.'[11]

One British statesman understood the vital importance of making a generous gesture to India. In July 1917, Edwin Montagu became Secretary of State for India, and he at once moved the British Cabinet to give an undertaking concerning India's future. Shortly after, there followed the famous announcement of 29 August 1917 promising 'the progressive realisation of responsible government in India as an integral part of the British Empire'. Montagu believed that it was important to symbolise and dramatise India's new status within the empire. India was accorded representation in the Imperial War Cabinet, a somewhat uncoordinated assembly, and also at the Imperial War Conferences of 1917 and 1918. An Indian appeared as India's representative at the 1917 conference, in place of the British, India Office civil servants who had been deputed to attend the previous imperial gatherings. Sir Satyendra Sinha was a Moderate Congress leader who had been the first Indian member of the Viceroy's Executive Council. With considerable dexterity, Sinha moved to advance the position of Indians overseas by introducing a memorandum asking for reciprocity of treatment between the Dominions and India, as regards migration.

Any hope that this could lead to India negotiating severally with the Dominions for better treatment of their Indian settlers was dampened by what happened at the next Imperial Conference, held in July 1918. This gathering also affirmed its acceptance of the reciprocity principle, but interpreted the principle in terms of the perceptions of the white Dominions and not of India: 'It is an inherent function of the Governments of the several communities of the British Commonwealth, including India, that each should enjoy complete control of the composition of its own population by means of restrictions on immigration from any of the other communities.' After this declaration a depressed Sinha recorded (11 June 1919) 'To me it is clear that there is no room for Indians anywhere in the British Empire outside India itself. If we were able to retaliate, I would prohibit by legislation all forms of intercourse with South Africa . . . but I am sure H.M.G. will not permit such legislation . . . and perhaps rightly so — for India does not stand to gain much by such legislation.'[12]

The glow of wartime comradeship soon faded, and the white communities throughout the British Empire returned to policies of racial discrimination. The first move came in South Africa. A measure to restrict and prevent the acquisition of property by Indians was passed through the Union parliament early in 1919. Like most restrictive legislation in South Africa, the Asiatics (Land and Trading) Amendments (Transvaal) Act, 1919 went much too far for some, and not nearly far enough for others. The Indians were not well organised to protest against the measure. The Natal Indian Congress had sunk into desuetude after Gandhi's departure, and it was left to the little Cape British Indian Council to take the lead. Efforts were made by the South African Indians and their friends in Britain to persuade the home government to intervene to prevent the royal assent being given to the Land and Trading Act. Lord Buxton, the Liberal Governor-General of South Africa made it quite clear that with the development of Dominion status there could be no question of withholding assent. But if South Africa was free to shape its own destiny, India after the 1917 announcement was able to claim the right to defend itself. On 25 July 1919, the Government of India cabled to the India Office 'Having regard to Union Government's action, no course remains but consideration of serious action directed against South Africa in this country.' As a first move, no mining concession would be awarded to a South African company (as it happened, two such applications were pending for concessions in Burma).

Montagu hastened to take up the question with the Colonial Office. Since January 1919, Lord Milner had presided over the Colonial Office, which was still responsible for relations with the Dominions, as well as colonial affairs. Montagu stated officially (11 August 1919):

He thinks that Lord Milner will agree that a situation in which the possibility of retaliatory measures between two members of the British Commonwealth has to be contemplated, indicates a very regrettable lack of coordination in Imperial policy and that it can only tend to loosen rather than strengthen the principle of cohesion which it is desirable to foster.

Milner cabled South Africa (25 August): 'Indian Government regard present situation as so serious that they may be faced with a demand for prohibiting intercourse with South Africa.'

At this moment, Smuts returned to South Africa, after his long service with the British War Cabinet, to become prime minister on the death of Botha in August 1919. He was required to face up to a multitude of domestic problems, and he tried to buy time on the Indian issue by appointing an Asiatic Inquiry Commission, with Sir John Lange, a Supreme Court judge, as chairman. Sir Benjamin Robertson, a former Indian Governor who had played a part in working out the settlement between Gandhi and Smuts in 1914, was associated with the commission. The Governor-General forwarded the commission's interim report to Milner on 28 May 1920.[13] The legislation already in being was accepted, but no further restrictions were recommended. Voluntary segregation was advocated, as a means of keeping down the temperature of white racism, and voluntary repatriation (a part of the Gandhi-Smuts agreement) was considered to be a valuable means of resolving the Indian problem.

South African extremists now organised, to put more pressure on the Indians. Sir Abe Bailey, the mining magnate and defender of white privilege, described the Lange statement as 'the weakest product of any commission that had ever gone forth'. The Government of India, and friends such as Polak, were concerned to ensure that any repatriation was genuinely voluntary, and not under disguised coercion. The first post-war returnees left Durban in September 1920: they numbered ninety-five. Such a trickle would make no difference either way.

At the bidding of Montagu, an official at the India Office, John Walton, was commissioned to draft a memorandum on 'Possible means of retaliation against countries (foreign or British) which impose disabilities on Indians'. Walton accepted that the evolution of Dominion status had made South Africa its own master internally, and also internationally. Yet this precedent applied also to the evolution of India: 'Everything that has been said above as to the new international status (including the Treaty-power) of the Dominions applies also to India. Anomalously, she may be said to have more independence in her external than in her internal affairs.' If India's assent had been requird to the recent peace treaties, then her government was 'manifestly competent to deal with another British state'. All that Indians in South Africa could expect in the immediate future were 'palliatives'; but what might happen if an 'African peril' emerged? South Africa might need India's permission for the movement of troops, and 'It is possible that the anti-Indian campaign . . . might be checked by a threat of retaliation': South Africa should be made to realise that India 'is at liberty to retaliate'. Concluded Walton: 'His Majesty's Government would not wish to interfere in a way which might have the appearance of setting back her growth towards complete Dominion status.'

Walton's analysis of the openings for retaliation was not drafted merely with South Africa in view. He noted the possibility of 'prohibition of emigration to colonies which desire to introduce free Indian colonists, such as Fiji and British Guiana: such retaliation would be used vicariously as a means of bringing pressure to bear in other colonies, *e.g.* Kenya.' He also suggested direct influence upon Kenya by the prohibition of contract labour; influence upon Canada and the United States by a ban on the entry into India of certain categories of persons (such as missionaries); differential import duties, and export duties and prohibition on the export of certain products. The whole exercise (which was submitted in February 1921) represented a remarkable change in the India Office attitude, under the impact of Montagu's leadership. Here was an official (admittedly singled out by Srinivasa Sastri as a 'straight chap' . . . 'with a liberal outlook') who was prepared to think in dynamic terms, and in the interests of India. This could represent a force for change in the direction of equality for India in the British Empire.[14]

In the Colonial Office, a powerful impetus was at work in the opposite direction, working for the emergence of a white Dominion in East Africa; and with the arrival of Milner as Secretary of State, the impetus was complete. To some extent, the assertion of white supremacy came as a reaction to various Indian initiatives in East Africa. A small group of militant Indians were members of the *Ghadr* movement, but they were discovered, and some were hanged for conspiracy. More generally, Indian political organisation was re-energised by a new leader, Manilal Desai, who arrived in Nairobi in 1915 as a lawyer's clerk, and quickly promoted organisations and journals to agitate for Indian demands. Then, outside East Africa, a demand was voiced for transforming the territory of Tanganyika, as it was captured from the Germans, into an appendage of India: the demand was voiced most loudly by the Imperial Indian Citizenship Association, founded in 1915.

Indian pressures were diffused and scattered; white pressures were concentrated and direct. The Kenya settlers' demand for political control was answered by an Electoral Representation Bill, introduced in the local legislative council, which gave to the Kenya Europeans eleven elected representatives, as compared to one nominated Indian representative. Although the Whites were given full adult franchise, the eleven new constituencies were based upon electorates which numbered only between 300 and 800 voters.

Milner accepted this measure, and in February 1920, the first elections were held. In addition, Milner sanctioned schemes for urban segregation, which reserved the best residential and business sections of Nairobi and other towns exclusively for the Europeans. Milner extended the segregation policy to Uganda, and town-planning in Kampala was based upon separate areas for Indians and Whites.

The protests which arose, from Indians in East Africa and their friends, induced Milner to offer a plan supposed to represent concessions. In a despatch dated 21 May 1920, Milner proposed to introduce two elected Indians into the Kenya legislature but he also proposed to reaffirm existing policy of preserving the White Highlands and the segregation in the towns; in addition, he indicated that immigration would be strictly curtailed: another of the white settlers' requirements.

The Government of India replied to Milner's 'solution' by counterdemands, presented in a despatch of 21 October 1920. This called for a common electoral roll, though it was conceded that many Indians were not yet qualified to vote. As most of the land in the white highlands had already been allocated, restrictions on the remainder ought to be lifted. Segregation must be ended in the towns, and health precautions (the ostensible motive for segregation) enforced by stricter municipal regulations. Finally, it was emphasised that besides the 9,000 Whites, and the (supposed) 30,000 Indians in Kenya there were about 2,800,000 Africans: 'Even in the examination of those grievances it must not be forgotten that it is the Native population which forms the predominant factor in the country.'[15] The hope that the question would be re-considered was increased when, in February 1921, Milner was succeeded by Churchill: for everyone knew of the sentiments expressed in *My African Journey*, and few realised the reservations which had always accompanied the praise for the Indians. The first attempt at a new initiative was made when Governor Northey called a conference of European and Indian representatives in May; it soon emerged that the concessions tentatively proposed would not satisfy Indian opinion.

India was not in a mood to consider small improvements. In the post-war mood, the whole future of India's relations with Britain and the Empire was at issue in the minds of the Congress leaders.[16] C. F. Andrews (who had completely identified himself as an Indian by this time) was specially opposed to any pretence that the formula of citizenship and equality could offer India a place in the British Commonwealth. He told Gandhi (8 September 1920) that there could be no real equality: 'The religion of the "White Race" has made that impossible. We have had experience of the past, and I am afraid the experience of the present and the future will be worse, not better. They go on exploiting us as inferiors and treating us politically as inferiors ... We cannot therefore go on talking in the old way of "within the Empire". We must claim unitedly independence, as Egypt claimed it.' Gandhi was still prepared to be patient; he told Andrews (23 November 1920) 'I am not as yet sure that it must be ended at any cost ... The connection must end on the clearest possible proof that the English have hopelessly failed to realize the first principle of religion, namely brotherhood of men.'

The same year, at a special meeting of the Congress in Calcutta, a resolution was adopted which announced 'That this Congress demands that in all Colonies and Protectorates within the British Commonwealth the principle of equal status of Indians with all other subjects of the King Emperor be recognised by the Colonial Office.... and that in all self-governing dominions the same principle be accepted by the different dominion governments on the understanding that reciprocal action by India may follow its refusal.' In Indian eyes, the idea of equality under the British Crown must now be seen to have some reality.

Indian Communities in the British Commonwealth: 1921

Burma	887,077	Jamaica	18,610
Ceylon	635,761	Zanzibar	13,500
Malaya	470,180	Tanganyika	10,000
Mauritius	265,524	Uganda	3,518
South Africa	161,329	Hong Kong	2,000
British Guiana	124,938	Southern Rhodesia	1,184
Trinidad	122,117	Canada	1,016
Fiji	60,634	Australia	300
Kenya	22,822	United Kingdom	5,000

In 1921, the total population of India was recorded as 318.9 millions. It was then estimated that there were 2.5 million Indians living overseas, and as the Table shows this was probably correct (Burma was then a province of British India, as it remained until 1937).[17] Emigration was not, therefore, an important safety-valve for Indian society and the Indian economy (as it was for Italy and Ireland, or Malta and Barbados). This partly explains why Gandhi and other Indian leaders were prepared to advocate the termination of all emigration overseas, other than that of people with some capital. The price for accepting an end to emigration was the assimilation of the existing Indian communities into the social and economic order in the countries of their adoption.

The actual situation in 1920-1 was that Indians could enter most British colonies with a minimum of difficulty, but that entry to most of the Dominions was closed. Indian entry into the United Kingdom was free of all checks upon entry, other than the requirement to produce a British passport or other evidence of nationality. In this respect, the British Nationality Act, 1914, had extended the scope of British citizenship. Previously, a passport issued in India (or Canada, or Southern Rhodesia, etc.) had merely represented British nationality applicable to that particular territory. Only the resident of the United Kingdom was entitled to a British nationality which was co-extensive with the British Empire. The 1914 Act confirmed the existence of a common citizenship which all subjects of the Crown enjoyed, so far as the law of the United Kingdom was concerned. Yet this acknowledgement of a common status for all British subjects was accompanied by the tacit consideration that the vast majority of the peoples of the British Commonwealth would claim their rights either in the lands of their birth or in other dependencies; they would not flock to Britain to take up their claims. *The Round Table* declared: 'Our climate keeps coloured races away more effectively than the most drastic of immigration restrictions.'[18]

The Dominion of Newfoundland, and the newly born Irish Free State also imposed no formal restrictions on the entry of non-Europeans; perhaps this was linked not so much with the climate as the absence of any economic incentives for immigrants. All the remaining Dominions imposed restrictions designed, absolutely, to exclude Indian immigration. Australia imposed a dictation test upon would-be entrants, and the immigration officer might require the immigrant to write out dictation in any European language. Students and temporary visitors were exempted from the test. New Zealand flatly prohibited the entry of all persons, except those from the United Kingdom, unless they carried a permit previously issued by the New Zealand government. Indians were considered for such permits, provided they applied as temporary visitors or students. Canada continued to prohibit the entry of anyone arriving 'otherwise than by a continuous journey' from the country of origin, and by means of a through-ticket; also, no Asiatic might land unless he could provide a deposit of $200. Asians domiciled in Canada for five years were exempted from these restrictions, though anyone who was absent from Canada for a year forfeited his right to return.

By means of these restrictions, the Indian population was reduced by more than half between 1911 and 1921; the increase in the following decade was under 400.

Most draconian of all was the law of South Africa. An Act of 1913 empowered the Minister of the Interior to declare any person or class of persons 'unsuited to the requirements of the Union'. This measure was used to impose a ban on the entry of all Indians, so that the existence of other requirements (such as an Australian-style dictation test) was not called into use. Indians 'domiciled' in the Union (with three years' residential qualifications) were allowed to return, though the admission of their dependents was severely controlled.

Southern Rhodesia took the whole body of its law from South Africa, and also had a South African type law on immigration (the Immigration Regulation Ordinance, 1914). However, the vestigial power and influence of Britain was enough to dissuade Southern Rhodesia from notifying all Indians as unsuitable in advance; instead, as each Indian applied for entry, he or she was individually, automatically declared to be unsuitable. This was supposed to be more acceptable to Indian amour-propre, and indeed there were few protests at this rule which effectively sealed Southern Rhodesia to further Indian immigration. The wives and children under 16 years of domiciled Indians were allowed free entry. Also, teachers and priests who were Indians were allowed to enter on temporary permits and were then usually permitted to make their stay permanent. From 1920 onwards, the Southern Rhodesian Indians were a closed community. The same regulations applied to Northern Rhodesia, where numbers of Indians were very few.

The white settlers in Kenya also desired to impose a South African type ban on the entry of Indians, but the existing law was non-discriminatory and non-restrictive. Ordinances passed in 1906 and 1910 prohibited the entry of persons who were without means, and required a deposit of Rs. 50 per head from all new arrivals. The remaining colonies and protectorates allowed the free entry of Indians: indeed, Indian labour was still desired by the European employers of Mauritius, Fiji, Ceylon, Malaya, Trinidad and British Guiana. Apart from health checks, there was no restriction on entry into these territories.

Regarding the political and civil rights of Indians overseas, with which Indian national feeling was so much more concerned, in most territories there were no political rights for the great majority of the population, and where a democratic system prevailed the Indians were generally excluded.

The few Indians in Great Britain enjoyed the vote on the same basis as all other British subjects. Two Indians — Dadabhai Naoroji and Sir M. Bhownagree — had been elected to the House of Commons during the previous thirty years, and another Indian, Shapurji Saklatvala, was shortly to be elected as Labour, and then Communist M. P. for North Battersea (1922-3, 1924-9). In Canada, the Indians or 'Hindus' of British Columbia were excluded from the franchise — municipal, provincial, and Dominion — as were all other Asians, as well as the indigenous Canadian Indians. The tiny numbers of Indians in Australia were excluded from the franchise in the two states in which they mainly resided, Queensland and Western Australia. The handful of Indians in New Zealand were all entitled to vote, while in Southern Rhodesia the Indians were under no statutory bar and could obtain the qualifications for the franchise. Thus, in 1910, of the 655 Indians then in the territory, 49 were registered as voters; by 1922 of the total of 1,184 there were 138, or 12 per cent, on the electoral roll. By contrast, 55 per cent of the white population were registered voters, while of the 770,000 Africans only thirty-five received the vote — and these were all immigrants from Cape Colony. However limited the Indian share in the electoral process in Southern Rhodesia, most Indian spokesmen were prepared to accept the principle of a qualified franchise, in the hope that they would obtain their rights in the fullness of time. This was the declared policy of Indian leaders in South Africa and Kenya where, in 1920, the community was totally excluded from the election of the legislators.

Within the colonial empire, the elective system was restricted to a few colonies where a resident white population monopolised the franchise, mainly on a class or economic basis of superiority, rather than on a racial basis. In many territories there was no provision for elections; members of the legislative councils were 'nominated' for office, usually by the governor.

Jamaica had advanced furthest towards the acceptance of working people into the electoral process. All persons earning £50 per annum and paying 10s. in taxes on their property were entitled to vote. However, the small Indian community in Jamaica had not prospered; most were day labourers, or marginal smallholders, so that only a few hundred shopkeepers, clerks and mechanics had the vote, and they had no influence whatever upon the development of Jamaican politics. The other sugar colonies — Trinidad, British Guiana, Mauritius and Fiji — had constitutions which effectively limited the franchise to the planters and their henchmen. Two-thirds of the population of Mauritius were of Indian stock, yet less than 1 per cent of the Indians were voters, allowing the white *Mauriciens* and the Francophone brown middle class to elect legislators to represent them. In Trinidad there were no electors, while in British Guiana the constitution was still much the same as when the Dutch handed over the colony, a century before.

Most of the British colonial territories were still at a stage of political development where all non-official members of the local legislative councils were nominated; this was the situation in Uganda and in Malaya where the various sultans had their own state councils with carefully chosen non-official spokesmen. The selection of Indians in Malaya was virtually unknown.

Finally, in this survey of political rights in the British empire in 1920, both Ceylon and Burma were poised to move forward to a new stage of constitutional devolution, and both were sufficiently within the Indian orbit to ensure that the Indian voice was adequately heard.

Still, in 1920, Indian opinion was mainly concerned with the past. The history of bondage on the sugar plantations had only just ended when, on 2 January 1920, the Indian labourers in Fiji had been set free from their indentures. India was concerned to open up a new era of labour relations in the sugar colonies—in which the penal legislation and the distortion of family life had, in the rhetoric of the day, turned the men into slaves and the women into prostitutes. India was determined to close that chapter and to ensure that in future there was compliance with the Salisbury undertaking that 'Indian settlers ... will be in all respects free men with privileges no whit inferior to those of any other class ... resident in the colonies'. Because it belongs to the past rather than to the future, we ought to consider the Wood report on the West Indies, even though it took place after the events which follow at the beginning of the next chapter.

After the 1918 election in Britain, with its overwhelming vote for Lloyd George and the Coalition government, a small number of Conservative back-benchers decided that they should combine to keep a watch on the government to ensure that its Conservative members were not so overawed by the prime minister that they deserted true Tory principles. They were nicknamed 'the Vigilance Group', or more often, 'the Group'. Though they had no special leader, their most prominent member was the Hon. E. F. L. Wood, later as Lord Irwin, Viceroy of India, and as Lord Halifax, Foreign Secretary. Other members were Lord Winterton, an Irish peer sitting in the House of Commons, and W. H. Ormsby-Gore.

In 1921, Edward Wood was appointed Under Secretary for the

Colonies; Churchill had not asked for him, and there was some incompatibility between them. Towards the end of the year it was announced that Wood was departing on a mission of inquiry to the West Indies; he set out in December, taking with him his friend, Ormsby-Gore, 'Billy' Gore, to be associated with the inquiry. They were concerned both with economic and political conditions; the report which appeared over Wood's name was a very conservative document.[19]

Concerning the Indians or 'East Indians', the Wood report mainly considered their situation in Trinidad, as part of a cautious proposal for the colony's introduction to the elective principle. Wood found that the Indian community in Trinidad was 'largely illiterate . . . living a life of its own'. Wood met two deputations of Indians. One represented the East Indian National Congress, and they asked for a communal system of representation, in which the Indians would vote for their own candidates separately, arguing that otherwise they would not be properly represented. They pointed out that in British Guiana the Court of Policy, the Law-making council, had never included an elected Indian. The Congress asked that there should be a wide franchise, and hoped that there might not be a literacy test; but if this were included then it should not be restricted to one language (English). The rival Indian deputation asked for the nomination system to continue; this group claimed to represent the 'wealthiest and best-educated'; doubtless they surmised that under an elective system the successful candidates were not likely to be men of their class.

In this report, Wood rejected the claim to communal representation: 'The East Indians are an important element in the community and it would be a great misfortune if they were encouraged to stand aside from the main current of political life.' Besides, added the report, if separate electorates were granted to the Indians, the same demand would have to be conceded to the small French and Spanish speaking Creole minorities, and that would be 'impossible'. Wood was accompanied by a civil servant from the Colonial Office, and though the main conclusions were doubtless worked out by Wood, with Ormsby-Gore's advice, it seems probable that in detail the report represented the official, Colonial Office policy. To put it crudely, the Colonial Office view seemed to be that wherever communal electorates would favour a weak, disorganised Indian community they should be discouraged, and wherever the Indians were sufficiently well-organised and numerous to compete effectively for political power they should be disarmed by hiving them off into communal electorates. Wood was shortly to adjudicate upon the situation in Kenya where he (or the permanent officials of the Colonial Office) insisted that Indians could not expect to participate in a common electoral roll.

Concerning British Guiana, Wood observed that its constitution was 'unique in the British Empire', and appeared to conclude that this was a justification for its century-old anachronisms. He was again urged by the local Indian community to consider their case, but he observed in his report that the question could be postponed until conversations with the India Office concerning the future of Indian immigration reached some conclusion. India did have one bargaining-counter, the desire of plantation colonies, short of local labour, to recruit from India. But if, under pressure from Indian nationalist opinion, the flow of recruits was terminated, then this asset ceased to count.

For ninety years, Indian emigration to a dozen countries in the British Empire had developed in response to the demands of British business and industry, under the control of British officials. From time to time, the Government of India had been stirred to safeguard the rights of its Indian subjects, and from time to time humanitarians and public men in Britain had expressed their discomfort as abuses were uncovered. But the Colonial Office acting as the agency for British, imperial interests had almost always had its own way, in the end. Times were changing: the British Empire was becoming the British Commonwealth. The overall control of the United Kingdom, in defence of United Kingdom interests, was no longer accepted or acceptable. Was it true, as C. F. Andrews had alleged, that this was merely a new phase of white control; that Canada might successfully assert a right to full self-government which amounted to independence within the Empire, but that the only way open to India to gain independence — and also to protect overseas Indians — was to quit this same Empire?

The question had been removed from the level of theory to that of practical politics by India's great effort in the war, and by Montagu's championship of India as a Dominion, equal with the white Dominions. In 1921, the question came up for an answer; but no clear answer was to emerge.

2
The Claim for Equality
(1921-23)

Montagu's attempt to create a new political initiative had failed to generate sufficient political impetus in India in the face of concerted pressures from two opposed directions. The Indian national movement, which at first inclined towards exploring the possibilities opened up by Dyarchy, was dismayed by the repressive legislation designed to control sedition (the so-called Rowlatt acts) and was inflamed by the Amritsar massacre, with the enforcement of humiliations in the Punjab unparalleled since the Mutiny. Meanwhile, die-hard British opinion in England and in India was consolidating against the Montagu-Chelmsford reforms. Their forebodings were increased by the violence in the Punjab in 1919.

In England, the 'centrist' position which Lloyd George had hoped to reinforce in his Coalition government was giving way to pressure for a Conservative administration. If Montagu was disheartened, he did not give up. He was convinced that the only way to go forward in India was to support the Moderates, the liberals in Indian politics, against those he believed were determined to wreck the empire. The old Congress had divided into two groups. The main body followed Gandhi in a campaign of civil disobedience, designed to create conditions for swaraj. A minority, small in numbers but rich in talent, banded together to implement the Montford reforms. Most of them agreed to form a new group, the National Liberal Federation. Their leaders included the veteran S. N. Banerjea, Lord Sinha, Dr. R. P. Paranjpye, Tej Bahadur Sapru, and the president of the Servants of India Society, V. S. Srinivasa Sastri, who brought along a small band of dedicated social investigators, like H. N. Kunzru.

Montagu now sought to give these moderates a political platform from which they could exercise their persuasion and influence. He had convinced himself that the alternatives were either the steady — increasingly rapid — progress of a constitutional India towards a place alongside the self-governing white Dominions within the British empire, or a disastrous withdrawal from the empire by a militant revolutionary movement. The example of Russia — the collapse of Kerensky and the social democrats, and the rise to power of the Bolsheviks through violence and bloodshed — was very much in his mind, as in the minds of all liberal politicians at that hour.

Balked in his effort to take India forward along the path of internal self-government, Montagu considered another strategy: in effect, to assume that India *had* taken a great step forward, and was now a different kind of polity, and must be treated as the equal of the white Dominions. The means he fastened upon were to assert that India was ready to take its place among the free nations of the international community. At Versailles, the white Dominions had insisted that they should send their own delegates: they were no longer prepared to allow the British government in the United Kingdom to speak for them. Montagu also demanded that India be represented. He went as India's representative, and Lloyd George told him later: 'Throughout the Conference your attitude has often struck me as being not so much that of a member of the British Cabinet, but of a successor on the throne of Aurangzeb.'[1]

Once again, Lloyd George wrote to his brother premiers in the Dominions to bring them all together in their common cause. His first suggestion for a meeting at Ottawa in 1920 was not accepted by Australia, but a gathering was agreed upon at London in the summer of 1921. It was initially called the Imperial Cabinet, but some of the Dominion premiers — especially Smuts — objected to the implications of collective commitment, and perhaps of subordination to the British premier. Planning by British and overseas officials began in December 1920: the draft agenda featured as a prominent item, 'Common Imperial Policy in Foreign Affairs'. Although India participated through an India Office representative there was no indication that an Indian item would appear on the programme.

On 12 January 1921 Lord Chelmsford, soon to end his term as Viceroy, sent a telegram to Montagu: 'Maintenance of the Imperial connection has become living issue here, and the case of the separationists is based largely on the treatment of British Indians in other parts of the Empire. On the other hand, anti-Asiatic movement in White Dominions and Colonies appears to be growing stronger. . . . The time has come when the whole question of future relations of India and the Empire must be fully and frankly discussed.' Two weeks later (28 January 1921) Montagu wrote to the Cabinet Office to ask that the subject of Indian emigration be placed on the conference agenda.[2]

In April 1921, a new Viceroy landed in India: Rufus Isaacs, Marquess of Reading. He was a close friend of the Secretary of State. Both were members of the Jewish *haute bourgeoisie;* both had followed Lloyd George after the schism within the Liberal Party.

They corresponded on terms of intimacy and understanding. The new Viceroy despatched a private telegram on 5 June 1921 which summarised his view of the tactics to be followed at the conference:

If South Africa is left to itself there is no prospect of a satisfactory solution of the Indian problem. Our only hope lies, therefore, in pressure from outside. HMG, of course, is not in a position to exercise effective pressure and immediate efforts should be concentrated on endeavours to induce the Imperial Cabinet to face squarely the issues raised in our memorandum on the position of Indians in the Empire. It would make a great advance if the [Imperial] Cabinet could be induced to record... that the aim should be to make Indians resident in the dominions good citizens of that dominion by merging them in the general body of citizens and treating them on a footing of equality with white men in the matter of political and municipal franchise, ownership of land and trading rights. . . .

Prominence given to the question of renewal of the Japanese Treaty in the agenda indicates recognition, at any rate on the part of Australia and New Zealand, that the centre of gravity in regard to the possibility of future war has now shifted to the Pacific, and representatives of these two Dominions will no doubt recognise the vital importance to them of India as a base in the event of war in the Pacific, and the danger of driving India out of the Empire.[3]

The case was presented by the Government of India in a conference document headed 'The position of British Indians in the Empire'.[4] This began by setting out the conclusions of the imperial conferences of 1917 and 1918. The objective should be to end the disabilities imposed on Indians overseas. Smuts was quoted for his declaration in 1917 that 'Once the white community in South Africa were rid of the fear that they were going to be flooded by unlimited immigration from India, all the other questions . . . would become easily and perfectly soluble'. But the South African government had not responded sympathetically to India's acceptance of the right to stop immigration. The legislation of 1919 had confirmed the much condemned segregationist Transvaal act of 1885. Anti-Indian propaganda had increased with the efforts of the South Africa League, formed to fight Indian settlement. Indian opinion had also strengthened with 'the advance to complete self-government' (i.e. the Montford reforms) and India now claimed equality of status with the white members of the empire: 'full rights of British citizenship'. A resolution was to be tabled acknowledging 'an incongruity between the position of India as an equal member of the British Empire and the existence of disabilities upon British Indians lawfully domiciled in some other parts of the Empire'. The Imperial Conference was asked to endorse a policy of making Indians 'good citizens. . .by merging them in the general body of citizens'.

On the eve of the conference, Montagu was able to inform Reading that the discussions concerning Kenya which were taking place between the India Office and the Colonial Office had been satisfactory: Winston Churchill, the Secretary of State for the Colonies, agreed that all the projected Kenya voters—British, Indian, and the handful of qualified Arabs and Africans — should be combined on a common electoral roll. On the same day (21 June) Montagu telegraphed that though he would be prepared to modify the draft Indian resolution, Srinivasa Sastri, representing India, would not 'dilute' it. Sastri was making his first appearance at a big international gathering; he was accompanied by the Maharao of Cutch (the attendance of an Indian prince was considered obligatory), but of greater significance was the presence of a young I.C.S. officer, Girja Shankar Bajpai, acting as Sastri's secretary. The official report of the conference was preserved, but Bajpai, possessing an almost photographic memory, prepared to set down his own record of the proceedings (providing the source for the quotations which follow). He noted: 'The tradition of white supremacy (in the Dominions) had hardened into a dogma which could not be overthrown in a day.'[5]

Lloyd George's opening speech indicated sympathy for Indian aspirations. India, he said, had 'proved her right to a new status in our counsels; that status she gained during the war, and she has maintained it during the peace'. In more general tones, he pleaded for reconciliation between white and brown: 'No greater calamity could overtake the world than any further accentuation of its divisions on the lines of race. The British Empire has done signal service to humanity in bridging these divisions in the past. . . . To depart from that policy...would divide the British Empire against itself.' Sastri chose to emphasise the continuing inequality of India within the empire by contrasting his own position at the conference with that of the Dominion representatives: 'They are called here by virtue of their being Prime Ministers. We come here by nomination from our Government.' Smuts opened by enunciating his vision of a new international community, expressing his 'fervent wish to see established a real society of nations, away from the old ideas and prejudices of national or imperial domination'.

The early days of the conference passed in surveying the world scene ('generalities' and 'ramblings', as Montagu told Reading). Away from the Cabinet room in Downing Street, where all the meetings were held, Sastri endeavoured to gain the interest and support of the Dominion premiers. Smuts could not be budged, but Massey of New Zealand offered 'loyal and unstinted support' because of India's war record, while Billy Hughes of Australia professed sympathy and Meighen of Canada pleaded lack of knowledge and said that changes in the status of British Indians in Canada must be left to the provincial legislatures. Sastri was heartened by a meeting with Lord Haldane at London University: 'He poured balm on my heart when he declared his faith in a British Commonwealth citizenship and agreed it was a deduction from it to allow Dominions to pass retributive laws. He ... was sure that Smuts could not accept our resolution and keep his position in South Africa for a week. I should be unwise to bring about his fall.... "Try the PM", he advised me finally. "He is the only man in England who could get Smuts to do anything." '[6]

A disturbing factor was the attitude of Winston Churchill. Sastri told his son that Churchill showed 'sparks which come from real genius'. In the British Cabinet 'he is indispensable, though erratic and unstable.' Throughout his life, Churchill was a fascinated admirer of Smuts as a superhuman leader and thinker, and he was now greatly influenced in his approach to the question of Indians overseas by the arguments of Smuts. He believed that the self-government achieved by the Union of South Africa offered an example for the smaller white communities of Southern Rhodesia and Kenya. He began to waver over the Kenya decision: he told Sastri that the reservation of the white highlands against Indian infiltration had been confirmed, though Montagu insisted that the question was still under Cabinet review.

The draft Indian resolution was not put on to the main conference agenda: Smuts said 'it could wait'. The first two weeks of discussion passed by, and Meighen indicated that he must return to Canada. Despite Smuts' demurral, Sastri succeeded in arranging for a discussion of the Indian motion on 8 July, just before Meighen's departure. On 7 July Smuts suggested that the question had better be referred to a special committee, and he received support from Churchill. The Indians did not have Montagu to speak for them on this occasion, so they addressed a letter of protest to Lloyd George at the end of that day. He conceded that Sastri could make a statement next day and then the question would be transferred to a committee under Churchill as chairman.

Sastri opened the proceedings on the 8th, declaring: 'To us, the Empire stands for equality, for absolute justice.' He asked that all peoples 'be entitled to move about freely in any part of the Empire'. He recalled his recent meeting with Haldane, quoting his belief that allegiance to the same sovereign involved community, and equality of rights for all his subjects'. Sastri was often called 'a silver tongued orator', and he struck the right note with Lloyd George, that wizard of words, and the orotund spokesmen of the Dominions.

When they adjourned for the weekend, Sastri was the guest of the British prime minister at Chequers, his new official country house: 'The Prime Minister said [to Sastri] that my speech gladdened the hearts of the British Cabinet Ministers for I arraigned General Smuts who used on every occasion to preach the Sermon on the Mount with a sanctimonious air. They were very sore about it, and told each other: "Serve him right. Where is his justice now, and equality and tenderness to oppressed nationalities?" Hughes remarked that he was very angry with Lloyd George for postponing the discussion for he was eager to declare on my side.'

Lloyd George may have made his New Testament comparison to Montagu also, for on July 14 the latter was writing to Reading: 'General Smuts gives us the Sermon on the Mount, and runs away from its application.' He went on to provide his own impression of the participants:

Hughes spends his time in endless speeches, mainly devoted to causing embarrassment to Smuts and Meighen. Meighen is inaudible, but sometimes very great. Massey is perhaps the most amiable of them all, an Empire-walla if ever there was one, endless in his speeches. . . . Little is done. The talk is endless. . . . But, on the other hand, one cannot help feeling that it is all worthwhile because you see a greater solidarity of Empire and a better understanding growing. I am a little perturbed about our Indian affairs. We have got to ask for something that Smuts cannot give and that none of the dominions like. But I watch these conversations, and at each one the reception of India is more sympathetic, more frank.

The committee on the Indian resolution met on 18 July at the Colonial Office. Smuts opened by declaring that acceptance of the Indian resolution 'would reduce Natal to the position of an Indian colony'. Hughes bluntly pointed to the difference between statements by Smuts on Commonwealth partnership and his attitude to the Indians: 'to send Mr. Sastri back to India, said Mr. Hughes, without a ray of hope as to the future would only be to strengthen the hands of those who, like Mr. Gandhi, wished to wreck the Empire.' Hughes suggested as an alternative to the Indian conclusion a formula which read: 'The Imperial Conference is, therefore, of the opinion that in the interests of the solidarity of the British Commonwealth it is desirable that as a matter of principle the rights of citizenship of such Indians should be recognised.'

The Australian premier was supported by New Zealand and Canada, but the debate was wound up by Churchill with a vigorous defence of Smuts. This brought about what G. S. Bajpai described as 'the defection of Mr. Hughes': he declared that he 'could not afford to place his colleague from the Union in a position of invidious isolation'. He would not vote for his own amendment unless it was accepted unanimously! This left the meeting deadlocked, and it was decided that Churchill, as chairman, should confer with Smuts and Sastri in an effort to reach agreement on words acceptable to all. On 19 July, the private secretary of General Smuts gave Winston Churchill a draft statement in which the Hughes amendment was further amended to read as follows:

In the interest of the solidarity of the British Commonwealth it is desirable that the rights of such Indians in the dominions to citizenship should be recognised. While the application of this principle throughout most of the Empire would present no difficulty, they [the Conference] recognise that in some parts such as South and East Africa there are exceptional circumstances in the way of its adoption.

Churchill sent this draft round to Montagu, and precipitated a correspondence of gathering irritability: for Edwin Montagu was never one to adopt a low posture in any controversy.[7] First, he dismissed the reference to East Africa; they were not now dealing with affairs for which London was responsible. The new resolution, Montagu observed, 'while of incalculable sentimental good, leaves us in profound despair as to South Africa'. He would ask Smuts to promise that no new disabilities would be imposed on Indians in former German South-West Africa (now under Union mandate), that the civic status of Indians in South Africa should not deteriorate, and that their economic disadvantages might be lessened. Montagu added that he was 'fighting a fight ... to preserve the loyalty of India': he could win, if the South African obstacle was overcome. Churchill consulted with Smuts, and informed Montagu (20 July) that Smuts was prepared to amend his draft, omitting any reference to East Africa, and, in deference to the objections, making minor alterations. He absolutely refused to give guarantees as to future policies in South Africa.

These suggestions produced a long and bitter reply from Montagu (21 July). He was 'awfully depressed': Smuts was 'unreasonable' and 'to a man of his political principles it must be due to *force majeure*'. Once again he listed the ways in which the conditions of the Indians were worsening; the real remedy was to give the South African Indians the vote: 'We claim that Indians should rank with Europeans and not with the natives to whom no promise of Dominion or equal status has ever been given.' Montagu admitted that prevailing white South African opinion ruled out the immediate offer of votes to Indians, but he asked that 'the door shall not be closed for all time'. It seemed that Smuts was saying 'I have absolutely nothing to promise': 'it could not be regarded as an attitude which makes for the solidarity of the Empire.' Montagu asked Winston Churchill to use his influence with Smuts to obtain an assurance that things would not be made worse: he accepted that Smuts 'is more with us than any other South African statesman': but this, he concluded, 'is one of the reasons of our dismay'.

This letter provoked Churchill to annoyance; he replied (26 July) that Montagu was splitting hairs: Smuts would resent being pressed. Everybody was getting tired; the summer was one of the hottest on record, and in late July the heatwave was at its peak; also, Montagu was sickening for tonsilitis. He wrote back angrily to Churchill (26 July): 'It was felt [at the committee] that you were going to confer with Mr. Sastri and General Smuts. I have no complaints in the least that you have found it impossible to do more than confer frequently with General Smuts.' It had been hoped to reach a 'concordat': now the only remedy was to inform the full conference of the difference between India and South Africa. He expressed his resentment: the contribution made by Smuts 'to the solidarity of the Empire [is] pathetically inadequate: and I am told by one of my colleagues that I am splitting hairs'; Montagu would press his charge at the full conference: 'The repudiation of his attitude is to my mind infinitely more important to the Empire than any wounding of his susceptibilities.' This concluded their correspondence, and in reporting the breach to Reading, Montagu wrote (26 July): 'Our only resort now is to have our differences with Smuts out in full conference.... When he comes to principles he is unimpeachable, but when he comes to practice he will not move a finger.' As to what would emerge, Montagu hoped the Dominion premiers would recognise that India had tried to compromise: 'But it is not a very brilliant hope.'

The question was considered by the conference on August 2 as the last item on the agenda. Montagu, writing to Reading the next day, reported 'a curious change' at the end: 'While Smuts was actually beginning to show himself more conciliatory, Hughes, who up till now had shown himself not only friendly but helpful to the Indian cause turned against us ... and used all his well-known methods against our case.... There was even a point at which Smuts of all people tried to intervene to tone Hughes down!' The detailed report which Bajpai completed on 9 August was less impressionistic. He recorded that Churchill began with an account of the unacceptable compromise; Montagu stated that he had asked Smuts for an assurance that the position would not worsen; Smuts indicated his acceptance of the Hughes amendment, subject to his own reservations; and Hughes reaffirmed that he must withdraw from his own amendment, adding now that it would be politically embarrassing in Australia if Indians were given equality of status, which was denied to Chinese and Japanese.

When it appeared that complete deadlock was inevitable, Lloyd George intervened with a long appeal, which seems to have sprung spontaneously from his lips and which rekindled the empire unity which had faded away during the latter stage of the conference.

We are trying to build up a democratic Empire on the basis of the consent of all the races that are inside it . . . [If the experiment succeeds] It really transfigures, I think, the human story . . . . The British Empire will be a Mount of Transfiguration, if it succeeds. If it fails, poor old humanity will fall back again . . . after all its Calvaries it goes back and it says "We can do no better" and it throws up its arms in despair . . . . Well, do not let Mr Sastri go back . . . and say "The British Empire has refused us justice". It will be an appalling thing to say to the people who sent a million and a quarter volunteers to aid us . . . . Why should we deny it? Not because we do not believe in it. Here [in Britain] the Indians have the same rights . . . . Then comes Natal. General Smuts cannot see his way to throw over Natal . . . . There you have got one hundred and eighty thousand Indians to one hundred and twenty thousand whites. These are the people who carved that place out of the wilderness . . . and they say "We have certain rights that no other race has" . . . . That is their view. I am not saying that I am for it. I am not saying that I am against it. But I understand their point of view.

I do ask all my colleagues at this table: "Let us go as far as we can" . . . . I appeal to him [the Australian premier] in the name of the British Empire (which means as much to him as it does to me) not to send our two distinguished Indian representatives back to their countrymen to report that the British Empire, sitting in solemn conference, refuses to do justice. I do not know what the result will be . . . . You might have a condition of things in India which would make India simply flow with the blood of men who only a few years ago were willing to give that blood for the Empire and for the flag under which they live. Now, I earnestly appeal to Mr Hughes to take what we can get. It is not as much as Mr Sastri pleaded so eloquently for, here . . . but it is something that will enable them to go back and say . . . "The British Empire has got ears for your wrongs" . . . not to go back and say . . . "They may still be under the British Empire but they will be unwilling subjects, and that is not the sort of Empire we want".[8]

This astonishing speech moved all the delegates, except General Smuts, whose analytical Calvinism was impervious to the Welsh variety. Bajpai reported: 'Even Mr. Hughes melted.' He offered to place the resolution before his Parliament and let Mr. Sastri plead his case there. The Canadian representative hesitated: he thought that the resolution would commit his country to action, but when it was explained that this represented 'the opinion of the conference' only, he signified assent. Massey of New Zealand 'gave it his blessing', and, with the Hughes amendment, the Indian resolution was adopted by the conference. However, Smuts indicated that South Africa must record disagreement (previously, all imperial conference resolutions had secured unanimous consent), while Montagu insisted that India must place on record its 'profound concern' at the South African situation.

Sastri seized the opportunity provided by the euphoria of the apparent attainment of goodwill to press Australia, Canada and New Zealand to agree to receive an Indian delegation 'in order to urge the translation into practice' of their resolution. Bajpai noted that such visits ought not to be delayed; though the prime ministers had been impressed, 'These personal memories have their value, but they are not everlasting'.

In his private correspondence with Reading, Montagu admitted 'what we have achieved does not amount to the fulfilment of these earlier hopes', but in public statements he claimed tangible gains. In an interview, published by the *Daily Telegraph* (16 August 1921), headed 'India a Dominion/New Imperial Status', Montagu insisted there was 'Every reason for . . . the early termination of the transitional stage and the acquisition by India of full Dominion status'. At the imperial conference, India 'was granted full Dominion status — Dominion status in its imperial relations, anticipating its domestic Dominion status'. At the conference, Montagu had spoken not for the British government but for India: 'on behalf of our Indian constituents'. South Africa had declined to recognise its own Indians as equals, but in future the relationship between India and South Africa would be settled by direct negotiation. Edwin Montagu never made a more explicit statement of his hopes for India than in this *Daily Telegraph* assessment.

Montagu's official despatch to the Government of India reviewing the conference (dated 6 October 1921) also placed emphasis on the gains.[9] The Secretary of State advised that Canada, Australia and New Zealand were prepared to accept the Agents of the Government of India with 'quasi-consular functions'. These Dominions had recognised Indian claims to citizenship for those resident in the dominions: 'The idea of citizenship may be one to which it would be difficult to fit an accurate definition . . . . It was first and foremost the exercise of the franchise and of other political functions.' South Africa had 'declined' to accept Indians as citizens; but this conference was but the first of a 'new series of Empire gatherings': there would be 'recurrent opportunities' to raise the issue, and 'the prejudices that animate a certain section of the white community in South Africa' which had prevailed with Smuts might not be so strong in future.

The imperial conference had not fundamentally changed anything. The controversies which had troubled the empire before June 1921 continued to cause trouble after August 1921: there was no appreciable change of policy regarding South Africa, Kenya or Fiji.

Montagu and Sastri made strenuous efforts to obtain private appointments with Smuts, while he was in London, to discuss the implications of the report of the Lange commission, but he was never available (Smuts was closely involved with the attempt to reach agreement between the British government and the Irish leaders). Sir Benjamin Robertson, associated with the Lange commission, gave a cautious assent to its main conclusion: that more emphasis should be put on voluntary repatriation to India. This was not at all acceptable, even to the India Office. How should negotiations be handled? The advice given to Montagu was to allow the Government of India to take the main initiative, and the Secretary of State agreed to this innovation (5 October 1921). Accordingly, the Viceroy addressed a formal despatch to the Governor-General of South Africa (dated, rather oddly, 19 and 27 December 1921). The despatch began by declaring that so long as the South African Indians were unable to express their needs and aspirations through their votes, the Government of India had a responsibility to speak for them. Robertson had reported that two-thirds of the Indians in South Africa were 'comparatively westernised'; yet only in Cape Province did they possess the franchise and legal equality in the holding of property. Their total numbers were small: they represented no danger to the white community. Their standards should be raised, with government help; their educational facilities were poor. The despatch concentrated upon the segregation practised in the Transvaal; the Lange commission had observed of the Indian: 'compulsion makes him a martyr'. Remedial legislation would remove the prospect of martyrdom. Finally, the Government of India rejected 'voluntary' segregation, as advocated by Lange.

The despatch did not find a receptive audience. Smuts addressed his South African Party stalwarts at a convention on 20 December, when he told them that the British Empire was now 'a great Commonwealth of equal nations'; Ireland was no longer its Achilles heel; nevertheless, the problem of the Indians in Natal had far-reaching consequences 'which might even shake the foundations of the Empire'. The only solution was their return to India: this was 'fundamentally sound'.[10]

While India awaited a reply to the December despatch, Lord Reading received a carefully marshalled delegation sponsored by the Imperial Citizenship Association. The leader was Sir Jamsetjee

Jeejibhoy, and it included C. F. Andrews, as well as five delegates from South Africa, with A. I. Kajee, now emerging as a leader among them. The delegation's memorial surveyed the status of Indians in the different provinces; it was by now a familiar story, culminating in the situation in the Orange River Colony where the Indians were denied all rights, including the right of admission, though two hundred Indians were resident as domestic servants. The Viceroy's reply (dated 22 March 1922) was in a low key. He assured the delegation that there was no fear that existing rights in Natal would be 'curtailed or withdrawn', but his chief message was that a South African Dominion was autonomous, and neither London nor Delhi could do more than make representations. The South African Indians were urged to turn to the Union government for redress.

Yet the position was not so simple; South African Whites did not recognise their Indian community as fellow South Africans. Hence, when the reply came from Smuts it was divided in its emphasis. The reply was conveyed by the rather cumbersome mechanism of a Minute, submitted by the Smuts Cabinet to the royal Governor-General, Prince Arthur of Connaught, for transmission to the Viceroy. The Minute (297 of 21 April 1922) began by recognising the right of the Government of India to make representations on behalf of those deemed to be Indians temporarily resident in South Africa: 'Ministers recognise that the position of British Indians in the Union of South Africa is a matter of special interest to the Government of India, and they realise that any grievances which the British Indians residing here may feel are reflected in India and are used there to embarrass the Government.' Having identified the demand for equality as 'agitation' (the standard approach since the days of Gandhian satyagraha), the Smuts Cabinet went on to reject any attempt by the Indian government to modify South African attitudes to the non-white inhabitants. On behalf of the Cabinet, Smuts at the imperial conference 'did no more than state what has been and is the policy of the Government, and that that policy is the only one which the present government of the Union or any other Government which is likely to be in office here . . . could possibly adopt.' The Indian claim for full political rights 'has never been recognised by the Government of the Union'; the assertion of such a claim only added to the problem of 'arriving at a reasonable and fair solution of outstanding difficulties'.

An illustration of the South African syndrome — that what was reactionary according to British-Indian standards was dangerously liberal according to South African standards — was provided by a debate in the South African parliament on 9 May 1922. In reply to the lack of response by the Smuts government to pressures for more effective control over the Indians, a government supporter, H. G. Mackeurtan (representing a Durban suburb) moved a resolution calling for the compulsory segregation of Asiatics. He raised the old bogey: that the Indian population in Natal was outstripping the Whites. A ministerial reply — that the white rate of increase was higher than that of the Indians — gave no satisfaction. Abe Bailey, mining magnate and representative of Krugersdorp, moved an amendment 'to tighten up the operation of the immigration laws as regards Asiatics', and in a speech characterised by another MP as containing 'wild and whirling words' he castigated the South African Indians:

Were they [the Indians] a source of weakness and danger in South Africa? His reply was, they were. Every Indian in South Africa took the place of a white man. He took the livelihood away from the white man and forced the latter to leave the country ... [or] Were they to be the salaried clerks of Asiatics? ... Asiatics were the white ants of this country, destroying the foundations of our institutions.... The sooner they left to enjoy the climate of India the sooner we should be at ease.... His policy was to reserve the whole of the Union for the white people.[11]

Even Bailey's fulminations were not enough for General J. J. Byron, who wanted the Indians sent back to India *'en masse* and *en bloc'*, and only one speaker, the aged J. X. Merriman (who had strongly opposed Indian immigration) spoke in a different voice: 'Now having got all they could out of the Asiatic they said they would kick him out: "Perish the Empire, but save Natal" now seemed to be their cry.' Patrick Duncan, Minister of Justice, accepted the right of the Government of India to speak for the South African Indians; but they were not ready to concede political rights 'anyhow, for a very long time to come'. Duncan said it was an illusion to call for compulsory segregation; a measure of urban separation was desirable, but not 'compulsory expulsion'. This was the answer of 'moderation' to 'extremism'.

Once again, the Viceroy addressed the Governor-General of South Africa (6 September 1922). He expressed his 'disappointment'. Concerning the future policy of the Union government, 'we are in the dark'; if no action was taken to mitigate the grievances, it would prove 'a source of grave embarrassment to both our Governments'. A few days later, at Geneva, Gilbert Murray—acting as a South African, not as an Oxford philosopher — moved the resolution setting forth the League of Nations approach to minorities. On behalf of India, a prince, the Jam Saheb, asked for sympathetic treatment of the Indians in South Africa. Rather lamely (Could he have believed his own argument?) Gilbert Murray replied that this was not a question of minorities but of 'different races at very varying stages of civilisation and development'.[12] The Assembly of the League adopted five resolutions on the treatment of minorities, but these were expressions of aspirations, not legal covenants. Still, Indians hoped that if the British empire failed to provide a forum for their demands the League of Nations might intervene. Smuts had other views.

Before he left London, after the Imperial Conference, Sastri wrote to his friend A. V. Patwardhan (21 August 1921): 'Winston Churchill is still hesitating over Kenya Colony. The European representatives have frightened him out of his wits. But though he will try to please them he must conform his decision to the equality principle.... Still, we shall have got four-fifths of what we want.... The future is safe; that is to say, in the hands of our own people.'[13] Sastri's estimate of Churchill's frame of mind was shrewd enough, though his forecast for the future was hopelessly wrong.

At the Imperial Conference, Churchill had made a statement on 'the status of Indian settlers'. He declared:

There is only one ideal that the British Empire can set before itself in this regard and that is there should be no barriers of race, colour or creed which should prevent any man of merit from reaching any station if he is fitted for it.... But such a principle has to be very carefully and gradually applied because intense local feelings are excited. The question reaches its most acute form in Kenya.[14]

Churchill's thinking was balanced in two differing directions. He was preparing to discuss a new extension of colonial self-government — on the path trodden by Canada, Australia, New Zealand, and South Africa — with the white settlers of Southern Rhodesia. They numbered only 33,000 among a black population of 770,000; but they were to be offered the prize of self-government, through an elected parliament and a responsible ministry. Urged on by Smuts, Churchill was very ready to offer the Rhodesian Whites the alternative of union with South Africa: and if 33,000 whites were to be allowed to decide their future — and that of the black majority — on the lines of separate Dominionhood or a new united, white-controlled Southern Africa, why should not the 9,000 white settlers of Kenya be given the same option?[15] Yet, Churchill could not have entirely forgotten his own discovery of East Africa in 1907-8, when he had saluted the Indians as the pioneers and developers of the country. The recent exchanges with Edwin Montagu may have had their effect upon Churchill: at any rate, while still looking to British (or European) leadership in Kenya, he now prepared to admit the Indians to a much greater partnership in the government of the country.

The Governor of Kenya, Sir Edward Northey (the far from successful commander of military operations against Tanganyika during wartime), was on leave in England for medical treatment after an accident at polo. On 26 August (within a few days of Sastri's speculations) Churchill addressed a 'strictly confidential' despatch to the visiting Governor, enclosing his constitutional proposals. Northey was warned that 'the suggested compromise goes considerably further in the way of meeting the wishes of the Indian community than your Government would advise': this was because of broader imperial interests. Northey was to communicate the terms on his return to Kenya to leaders of the communities in secret; publicly, he was to state that there would be no radical changes for three years. As an interim measure he must add four more Indian nominated members to the legislature (making the non-official representation eleven Europeans and five Indians) and also take an Indian into his Executive Council.

The actual memorandum was given the heading: 'Equal Rights for Civilised Men'. This had been the slogan which Cecil Rhodes had produced to counter the Boer doctrine of undiluted white *baaskap*. Rhodes never bothered to expound his doctrine, but it seems to have been based upon Portuguese *assimilado* theory. Presumably, it was now intended to initiate a process of westernisation, whereby the Indians could look forward to becoming brown Englishmen. The details followed the agreement reached between Edward Wood, Under Secretary at the Colonial Office, with Lord Lytton, his counterpart at the India Office. There would be a common electoral roll for all — Europeans and Indians (and eventually, Arabs and Africans). But whereas all the white adults had been admitted to the franchise, the Indians would have to qualify by attaining a recognised economic status (£1,000 capital or an income of £150 per annum) and a 'reasonable knowledge' of written and spoken English. It was intended to admit between 1,000 and 1,500 Indians out of the Indian population of about 22,000 to the franchise: no Europeans would be disfranchised, thus they would remain the clear majority of the electorate. The memorandum included other nicely balanced concessions to Indians and white settlers. There was to be no segregation in the towns as regards commercial properties, and Indians on the electoral roll were to be free of residential segregation. The white highlands were to continue the exclusive preserve of the Europeans, but a lowland area suitable for farming was to be reserved for Indian settlement. Immigration was to be subject to a set of regulations applicable to Whites and Indians alike; there would be an educational test, similar to that required for the electoral roll.

Montagu was not entirely satisfied with this award. He sent a memorandum to Churchill, dated 5 September, urging: 'It is of supreme importance that there shall be an acceptance by the Colonial Office of the resolution of the Imperial Conference to which Mr. Churchill was a party.' He wanted a franchise on broader lines, so that 10 per cent of the Indian population (2,200, instead of 1,000 as proposed by Churchill) should be enfranchised.

For several months, the issue remained suspended. Northey was reluctant to make any move, in the face of white settler suspicion and resentment. The Indians feared a sell-out, and the British government, preoccupied with a multitude of problems, postponed consideration of Kenya. On 27 January 1922 Winston Churchill was the principal guest at the annual East African Dinner in London, an occasion for announcing important developments. Churchill's speech began by repeating the sentiments expressed to the Imperial conference: 'So far as is practicable, throughout the whole range of the British Empire colour is not by itself to be a bar.' Churchill appealed to the Kenya white settlers to 'help us as much as you can' in honouring this pledge: India was now a partner in the British Empire. Then, an undertaking was given on the white highlands, matched by another reference to 'equal rights for all civilised men' and modulated by an undertaking that immigration would be 'strictly regulated'. The speech closed with a Churchillian peroration: 'We do not contemplate any settlement or system which will prevent British East Africa or Kenya... becoming a characteristically and distinctively British colony, looking forward in full fruition of time to complete responsible self-government.'

This pronouncement encouraged the white settlers to believe that power would soon be put into their hands, while the Indians were outraged. Montagu at once telegraphed Reading (3 February 1922) repudiating the statement: 'Cabinet decision on these matters has not yet been reached.' Resolutions were, nevertheless, passed in both houses of the Indian legislature condemning Churchill's speech as a 'serious violation' of the rights of Indians, recognised at the Imperial conference.[16] A somewhat subdued Churchill met a deputation on behalf of the East African Indians, organised by Henry Polak, on 23 February. He regretted the interpretations which had been placed upon his speech: it was not intended as the 'final decision on the general question of policy'.

Soon after these happenings, Edwin Montagu was compelled to resign, having stepped right out of line from his chief, Lloyd George, over the latter's confrontation with the newly resurgent Turkey.[17] In his place, a Conservative was appointed: Lord Peel, whose principal recommendation was that he was the grandson of a Tory prime minister. Bland, not over-devoted to the cares of office, Peel's main asset was his acceptability to Cabinet colleagues. A Tory patrician characterised him as 'Safe, if rather weak.'[18] There was also a change of Parliamentary Under Secretary: Lytton was replaced by Lord Winterton, a landowner in Northern Rhodesia. In April 1920, he had put a question to the prime minister suggesting that Africans in Kenya were 'strongly opposed' to further concessions to the Indians.

Governor Northey, on his return to Kenya, had dithered interminably over his instructions for a new policy. Indian resentment reached new heights of protest. The settlers were noisily belligerent, and many British officials openly sided with them. On a new public health ordinance F. W. Major, Commissioner of Customs, declared in the legislature: 'Hygienically, the Indian is not a wholesome influence because of his incurable repugnance to hygiene...Plague...has certainly been introduced from Bombay, and Indian quarters are almost invariably the foci of each successive outbreak...The Indian is a menace, not only to himself but especially to the natives of the country.' Winston Churchill issued an official rebuke for this attack. Then, on 29 June 1922, it was announced that Churchill had recalled Governor Northey: the ostensible reason was that a military governor was no longer appropriate, but his vacillation was an obvious factor.

As his successor, Churchill selected Sir Robert Coryndon, born in South Africa, one-time private secretary to Cecil Rhodes, whose previous administrative experience had all been in central and southern Africa. It could not be expected from this appointment that greater favours would be shown to the Indians. Renewed discussions between the Colonial Office and the India Office led to an agreement at Under Secretary level. The Wood-Winterton report, as it was called, was signed on 14 July 1922. While preserving the notion of a common roll, the agreement shifted a little further from the principle laid down at the imperial conference. The qualifications for admission to the franchise were to be defined on the basis of a test census of the Indian population so as to admit 10 per cent of male adults, as Montagu had stipulated, but the constituencies were to be so regulated as to ensure that the number of Indian representatives was only half the number of European members.

Far-off Fiji was not usually to the fore in the political calculations of the Colonial Office or the Government of India, but in the early 1920s the situation in the islands still reflected the enormous interest felt by Indian public opinion in the final abolition of the indenture system. In addition, the major sugar producer, the Colonial Sugar Refining Company, was calling urgently for supplies of labour. While the imperial conference was still sitting, the Viceroy telegraphed the Secretary of State (14 July 1921) to insist that the expansion of the legislature and of the electorate should be based upon a common roll: 'We are now in favour of the principle of a common electoral roll, and this principle we have advocated in Kenya and elsewhere.' A move was at once made to inform the Colonial Office, which replied (18 July) that they could not delay the plans they had already formulated. The Government of India had previously accepted communal representation for Fiji: at any rate a letter addressed to the Bishop of Polynesia (19 March 1920) was quoted as evidence.

However, India still had some influence because of the demand for labour, and the requirement was made that an Indian deputation should first visit Fiji to report on current conditions. Sastri was prepared to lead the delegation, and Pandit H. N. Kunzru was invited to go with him. However, after his return to India from the imperial conference, Sastri's health was poor, and he withdrew from the Fiji commitment. Three members of the central legislature, headed by Venkatapilraju Gani, formed the delegation, and G. L. Corbett of the Government of India accompanied them. On 16 February 1922, Venkatapilraju cabled the Viceroy that the C.S.R. Company intended to lower wages from $2s$ $6d$ per day to $1s$ $6d$ per day; he recommended a repatriation programme for the Indian labourers and, as the local government professed inability to meet the costs, he asked that the Government of India provide a loan for the purpose. With greater foresight, the Viceroy cabled back (3 March 1922) that mass repatriation was 'strongly opposed' by the Government of India. The returned labourers were unlikely to find opportunities in the prevailing economic situation: those who had returned were in Calcutta, 'demanding to go back'. Those Indians who insisted on returning to India must be allowed to do so but 'it is most important that we should not play into the hands of the party that desire the exclusion of Asiatics from the Pacific'.

As the Indian deputation toured round Fiji, the manager of the C.S.R. Company, Knox, began to despatch telegrams of complaint to the Government of India concerning their activities. He said they were telling the labourers that further emigration would not be permitted; one delegate, Sharma, was said to have urged a public meeting to burn the company in effigy. Knox asked to be allowed to negotiate direct with the Government of India, but this was rejected, whereupon he set out for London for talks at the Colonial Office. Although Knox's trip was repudiated from India, the Secretary of State cabled the Viceroy (20 April 1922) to ask that the report of the deputation should not be published before Knox arrived in London for discussions. The interim report of the deputation was signed at Auckland, New Zealand, on April 7.[19] Most of their recommendations concerned better facilities for repatriation; they also called for a minimum wage of 3s per day (as paid to government employees in Fiji), with opportunities for obtaining agricultural land for Indians and the provision of work on public projects for the unemployed. However, Corbett, their adviser, told the Fiji government to proceed slowly with repatriation: 'Sheer pressure of starvation would force Indians to work on reduced wages.' As the deputation also recommended that communal representation would best suit the Fiji Indians, the Government of India abandoned its claim for a common roll and accepted the Fiji government's offer of three seats for Indians on the legislative council. With this conclusion, and with a somewhat improved pay offer from the C.S.R. Co., the problems of Fiji faded from the view of Delhi and London. The report by the deputation was considered so damaging that it was not printed, in the usual way. Emigration to Fiji on a massive scale now came to an end and was not resumed. Despite complaints from the Governor of Fiji that he had 'offered one concession after another', only to be asked for more, the sugar producers had to adapt to methods which were geared to petty incentives for tenant farmers.

If little remained of the gesture towards recognising Indians within the empire as the equals of the Whites, at least the Dominions remembered their invitation to an Indian delegate to discuss policies and problems. Sastri was the obvious choice as India's representative, and in June 1922 he was ready to begin his travels. He was given an impressive send-off, with a viceregal banquet at Simla[20].

Sastri must have realised that his mission was doomed to disappoint any who expected immediate material advantages to follow.[21] Between June and October, he journeyed between Australia, New Zealand and Canada. While at sea, writing to his daughter (8 July 1922), Sastri noted that the weather was rough and Bajpai (his secretary again) was laid low; he wrote: 'I am tired of these frequent journeys... Yet they treated me very well indeed in Australia. Everywhere the best hotel, special carriages on the railways... ministers to escort and look after me... crowded meetings, giddy applause... heaps of little presents.' Sastri's speeches tended to veer between expressions of goodwill and hope, and lamentations at the woes inflicted upon the Indians, especially by South Africa, which he liked to call 'the Boer Empire': before he departed, Sastri had been specifically informed that he would not be welcome if he visited South Africa. On his return, Sastri issued a report, itemising a number of problems requiring solution, but his performance was not applauded by Indian opinion, and he felt compelled to publish an apologia, 'In defence of my tour', in *Servant of India*, 21 December 1922. If he had praised the British Empire it was because he really was convinced it would 'carry its people ever upward'.

The last chance that any concession might be made to Indian sentiment vanished when, in October 1922, the Conservatives withdrew their support from Lloyd George. When the Coalition gave way to a purely Conservative administration, Churchill, as a Liberal, departed from the Colonial Office, though Peel and Winterton continued at the India Office. Churchill's place was taken by the Duke of Devonshire, a cautious patrician, though the more dynamic Ormsby-Gore became his Parliamentary Under Secretary. The real pressure towards policy-making at the Colonial Office came from the officials, especially from Sir James Masterton Smith, the Permanent Under Secretary. Masterton Smith was closely associated with the *Round Table* group, and he rated the importance of white colonisation in the empire as highly as he deprecated Indian colonisation. It was to be India's misfortune that, after Montagu, no Secretary for India was a political heavyweight: though Wedgwood Benn, the Labour Secretary of State (1929-31), attempted to regain the initiative. The officials at the India Office, though they included shrewd and intelligent men, also had no sense of mission. They seemed to assume that they were holding the fort, hanging on, delaying the onset of Indian self-government. By contrast, the Colonial Office was staffed by men with a strong commitment to the British Empire: this maintained a sense of purpose, even when the political chief of the day failed to provide leadership.

One issue now took precedence over all others: the future of Kenya. Devonshire's first initiative was a despatch to Coryndon, sent on 14 December 1922, containing a restatement of the Wood-Winterton proposals. Peel approved its contents, telling Devonshire (13 December) 'I hope it will have the effect of bringing the people of Kenya to reason'. However, the effect was quite the opposite.

The white settlers judged that, with a truly Conservative government in office (after sixteen years), they could exert effective pressure; and they were right. Coryndon attempted to parley with Delamere and other leaders of the white Convention of Associations, but soon he was sending back a despairing stream of telegrams: some of the most abject and alarmist communications ever addressed to Whitehall by a British proconsul. On 3 February he sent a personal and secret telegram to Devonshire: 'Complete machinery has long been prepared and stiffened recently to paralyse the functions of the government.' The Whites would refuse to pay taxes; there would be a boycott of the Indians, and probably the forcible expulsion of all Indians from Nairobi to Mombasa. The troops, the King's African Rifles, 'would refuse to come out' against Europeans; the police would be 'as usual quite ineffective'. Coryndon's conclusion was that 'there is no possibility of triumph of Government if force becomes ultimate issue'. Ten days later (13 February) his cable revealed that not only will but also wish was lacking:

Colony is absolutely solid that ... ultimate responsibility of government must remain in European hands and must not be diluted by being shared with Eastern race, alien in spirit, and recognised as being lacking in the genius of government of backward subject races. The Indian controversy is believed here to be not the end but the beginning of the problem, since any real victory for the Indian race in Africa ... will mean similar, very probably, or larger claims in British Guiana, Fiji, and possibly elsewhere, not excepting Natal or even India itself. If Kenya is successful in preventing the influx of new Indians, political trouble may follow in India, but it should mean the satisfactory end of the whole question of Indian domination in Crown Colonies and Protectorates. On the other hand, if India wins in this fight it will be the signal for years to come for many such political troubles. This is freely stated by Indian leaders here who quote Sastri as having made the same statement. . . . I recommend 'strongly your permission to pass at once in Legislative Council here the Immigration Bill . . . with definite assurance that the main principles will not be emasculated.[22]

The Bill to which Coryndon referred was drafted to meet the white settler demand for a ban on new Indian immigration. It would follow South African and Southern Rhodesian practice, enabling the Governor to exclude any individual as a prohibited immigrant, to require all entrants to deposit 1,000s, as surety, and to pass a reading and writing test in English.

The Duke of Devonshire caused a memorandum to be circulated to members of the Cabinet (CP 99 [23] dated 14 February 1923). The Duke quoted the text of Coryndon's telegrams, and declared that the introduction of British military forces into Kenya to subdue the European community of 9,000 'is in my opinion out of the question'. He agreed that 'strict control' over Indian immigration was needed: he also suggested that the 'maximum' to be conceded to the Kenya Indians regarding political rights might have to be modified. Despite the urgency the Cabinet did not deliberate on the matter until 28 February, when they 'took note' of the memorandum and decided to ask Devonshire to invite the governor to come to London for consultations, 'in connection with the difficulties which have arisen'. Coryndon was therefore asked to come to London, bringing with him spokesmen for the settlers. This invitation was accepted by Delamere and his colleagues: although military force had been ruled out, the Royal Navy had sent three cruisers to Zanzibar, where they remained on silent watch. This was taken into account by the settlers, but in any case they looked like getting their way, with the connivance of the British Cabinet. Indignation among the Kenya Indians, and in India, now reached crescendo. Sastri abandoned his usual moderate stance to launch a protest campaign under the slogan 'Kenya lost, everything lost'. The Government of India pressed for a hearing for Indian representatives, as well as the whites, and a deputation was got up, with Indian leaders from Kenya and a strong delegation from India, headed by Sastri and including M. A. Jinnah and C. F. Andrews. They did not have official status, but they were given strong support by the Government of India. The India Office were not very enthusiastic: perhaps they saw their rightful task being pre-empted.

Sastri and his colleagues reached London in May, and began talks with the Colonial Office. Sastri detected that Indian claims might be undermined by an insistence upon trusteeship — the British responsibility to develop East Africa for future generations (as yet unborn) of Africans. To his brother he wrote (10 May 1923): 'The Wood-Winterton agreement Peel swears by, so does the Duke... I see many minds at work here in this direction. "Natives' interests" is the present cry. I am fighting the idea as hard as I can. I question the *bona fides* of the suggestion openly.' Sastri was also worried by dissent among his own colleagues: Jinnah, the Aga Khan, and Sir Dinshaw Petit thought that communal representation would suit Kenya better than a common roll. This would play into the hands of the settlers.

Reading attempted to arouse Peel to action by a series of letters and telegrams. On 2 May he wrote regretting that under the Wood-Winterton agreement they had given away 'much of India's original claim to equal treatment'. He tried to make the Secretary of State aware that all parties were looking to Kenya as the test case: 'It is regarded as the testing ground of the imperial policy to be pursued relative to Indians outside India, and especially in Africa.'

He hoped 'nothing will be done or said' to exclude Indians from 'equal treatment in one of His Majesty's colonies'. Unless this was obtained, 'what use is it to invite India to take her place within the Empire.... if she is always to be outside the magic circle?' Three weeks later (25 May) he wrote that 'the latest excitement is the answer of General Smuts to the Kenya white community': Indian opinion assumed that 'Smuts intends to throw his weight into the scale against India'. Letters were followed by telegrams, and on 21 June Reading was deploring the atmosphere of secrecy which made India suspect that a bargain was being made behind the scenes: 'there are two parliamentary atmospheres to consider', he reminded Peel, and Westminster should not forget New Delhi.

The suspicion that Smuts was using his unique prestige to influence the issue was not unfounded. On 10 July, the Governor-General of South Africa cabled to the Duke of Devonshire on behalf of the Smuts Cabinet; he reported that 'The persistent campaign carried on by the Indian leadership in regard to the Kenya constitutional settlement is having a very bad effect in South Africa. Sastri's speeches and attacks on the policy of the Union have exasperated public opinion. If,' he went on, 'claim for full civic equality between whites and Indians and unrestricted Indian immigration into East Africa is conceded, it will become impossible for the Union Government to control the situation in South Africa where Indians also agitate for full franchise rights.... Concession of the Indian demands will create a very dangerous situation in the Union. Indian claims for penetration into other parts of the Empire and franchise rights under the guise of the principle of equality which does not even apply among the Indians in India will lead to an intolerable situation in the Empire, and some other formula than that of civic equality will have to be explored.... From the point of view of the Union, I can only counsel extreme caution in dealing with Indian demands outside of India.' The telegram was signed by Prince Arthur of Connaught, but the author was quite clearly J. C. Smuts.

Smuts liked to portray the Kenya settlers as a valiant little band standing up to 'the overwhelming forces' of 'the mighty Empire of India', but the reality was that Sastri and the Indian delegates were groping in the dark, while Delamere was operating, as of right, within what Reading termed 'the magic circle'. A private letter from Lord Chelmsford, standing on the sidelines, to Sir Benjamin Robertson, makes this clear. Chelmsford recorded (15 July): 'Polak is quite stubborn over the question of communal representation. If he is so, I imagine that Sastri will be worse. His line with regard to the African native, and the necessity for communal representation for him, is that it is pure camouflage. I talked to Devonshire and Ormsby-Gore yesterday at Lords [the cricket ground] suggesting reserved seats in a general register, but they both said that Delamere would have none of it.'

On behalf of the Kenya Indians, their leader, A. M. Jeevanjee, addressed an appeal to Baldwin, the prime minister, on 18 July: 'unless the imperial government fulfilled its pledge on equal treatment for the Indians overseas, India's interest in the imperial connection ceases to exist'. At a more personal level, Sastri and Dwarkadas pleaded with Peel on July 20: they realised it was the 'eleventh hour', but they begged that the Wood-Winterton terms would not be whittled away. A communal electorate was 'demanded on the obvious ground of racial superiority', and the combination of a white official majority and white non-officials 'must inevitably reduce the Indian community to a position of chronic impotence and unredeemed humiliation'. Inevitably, the Kenya formula would be extended to other colonies: 'Two, if not more classes of citizenship will then become the distinguishing character of the British constitution — classes based on colour — a distinction inimical to the destiny of the Commonwealth, the ideal of democracy and the hope of humanity.'

However, Peel received advice of a very different kind from his own right hand. In a confidential note, Winterton offered his belief that if his own proposals—the Wood-Winterton report—were implemented there would be 'armed revolt' in Kenya, 'which would have meant probably the disruption of the Empire, at any rate in Africa'. If Peel should take up a position at variance from that of the Colonial Office then he must expect trouble in parliament: 'It would make your position difficult with a good many of our supporters.'

Peel, whatever his shortcomings, was a man of honour, and when he went into the Cabinet room that same day (20 July) he did not desert his comrade, the Viceroy. He communicated the last of Reading's telegrams protesting against a white-dominated communal system, and he added: 'We cannot in any way derogate from the claim that we have always made that Indians in a Crown Colony must be accorded equal status with Europeans.'

The case presented by Devonshire was based upon the discovery that Kenya was a part of Africa: His Majesty's Government was 'exercising a trust on behalf of the African population'. Political development, therefore, was to be postponed: Devonshire insisted that H. M. Government 'cannot but regard the grant of responsible government as out of the question within any period of time which need now be taken into consideration'. The Conservative Cabinet welcomed the proposition that no change was needed in their time. For the present, they were invited to endorse a communal system, under which the Whites would continue to elect eleven legislators, the Indians would elect four, and one Arab would be elected. Representation of the Africans would be deputed to a missionary, chosen by the Governor. This scheme would provide a 'far wider franchise' for the Indians than the talked-about ten per cent of population. There were other proposals: there would be an end of segregation in the townships, but the white highlands would remain a European preserve. Immigration controls were adequate for the present, but might be tightened in future — in the interests of the Africans.

Peel cabled the news to Reading in a private and personal telegram (20 July) which attempted to pretend that the decision was acceptable; the betrayal of the imperial conference commitment and of Indian aspirations was totally ignored. The guiding principle had been trusteeship for the Africans, and a common roll would 'inevitably conflict' with this: because of their 'very backward state' they would require a separate, special franchise which would be 'adaptive'.

The Cabinet decision was published as *Indians in Kenya: Memorandum* on 25 July.[23] It was laid down that 'Primarily, Kenya is an African territory, and ... the interests of the African natives must be paramount'. This principle, it seemed, was consistent with another detailed defence of the reservation of the Highlands for Europeans only: in addition, an area in the lowlands might be set aside for Indian cultivation 'without infringing on native reserves and without conflicting with native requirements'. The white paper ended with the disingenuous claim that 'Their constant endeavour throughout their deliberations has been to relate the principles which must govern the administration of a British Colony in Tropical Africa to the wider considerations of general Imperial policy as enunciated in the Resolution of the Imperial Conference of 1921.

The main parliamentary debate upon the White Paper took place in the House of Lords on 26 July. Davonshire's bald announcement was supported by Randall Davidson, Archbishop of Canterbury, for its promise for the future of the Africans. The most dramatic moments in the debate came when Hardinge and Chelmsford rose successively to protest against the treatment meted out to the Indians in Kenya. Hardinge condemned their exclusion from the white highlands, and Chelmsford complained about the absence of consultation with the Government of India. He called upon the British Government to eliminate racial discrimination from East Africa. Lord Selborne, former High Commissioner in South Africa followed, emphasising that white self-government was out of the question in Kenya, while he expressed doubts about Southern Rhodesia. Peel closed the debate with one of his temporising speeches. The peers thought little of the Devonshire declaration.

On 28 July, Reading was to review events in a speech to the legislative assembly. He was not a popular Viceroy, even with the moderate politicians, for his regime had seen the fading away of any hopes remaining that the Montford reforms could transform Indian politics; indeed, the repression of popular protest seemed the characteristic feature of the Reading regime. Yet, as the correspondence shows, Reading still remained a Liberal in his commitment to civil equality between men of different races.[24] Now he decided to make it quite clear that the Cabinet decision was at variance with his own standpoint. On 28 July he sent a telegram to Peel in which he condemned the '*subservience*' of H. M. Government 'to the threats of the settlers'. He went on: 'Indignation and disappointment is shared by all classes and parties [in India] including those who have usually been our strong supporters. I doubt whether you or H.M.G. realise the national humiliation which . . . is implied in the decision . . . . *I trust that you and H.M.G. understand the difficulty in future of impressing upon the Indians the benefits they derive from associating with the Empire.*' On the same day, Reading told the legislative assembly: 'They [H.M.G] have announced their decision, and the Government of India must consider it, and arrive at its conclusions. If submission [by the Government of India] to Whitehall must be made, then with all due respect to His Majesty's Government it can only be under protest.'

This speech, which so categorically dissociated the Indian government from the Secretary of State and the Cabinet, attracted little attention at the time, and has been overlooked by historians subsequently reconstructing these events.[25] However, the *Daily Telegraph* (30 July 1923) did not fail to grasp the significance of Reading's 'dramatic gesture', as it was termed. A comparison was aptly made with Hardinge's speech at Madras, where he had identified with Indian national feeling in the face of hostility from South Africa and the Cabinet at home. 'Identifying himself wholeheartedly with Indian sentiment, Lord Reading described the Cabinet decision as a great and severe disappointment to him and the Indian Government.' The *Daily Telegraph* added that the Viceroy deprecated the possibility of a plan for retaliation by India against the decision.

Winterton read the *Daily Telegraph* article, and also Reading's telegram of 28 July, on Monday morning (30th). He underlined two sections of the telegram (those given emphasis in the text above) and immediately addressed a confidential note to his chief: 'I feel that it would be impossible to allow these two sentences in question [in the telegram] to pass without a severe rebuke to their author. Their constitutional impropriety can hardly be questioned.' Winterton recognised that the consequence might be to provoke Reading's resignation; but though this might produce 'inconvenience' they must not overlook the offence. Peel took a more relaxed view of the situation. The session was coming to an end, and he looked forward to escaping to the country and to shooting the grouse. When he was required to answer a question in the House of Lords by old Lord Stanmore about the significance of the *Daily Telegraph* report, he replied reassuringly that the Viceroy had 'no idea ... of challenging a decision communicated to them by His Majesty's Government'.[26] In London, excitement over the Devonshire declaration died away, though not before Colonel Josiah Wedgwood, as Labour's spokesman on India, had stated spontaneously in the House of Commons that the Labour Party did not accept the communal provisions of the white paper and would reverse these if it came into office, though he admitted 'It is not easy when a step like this has once been taken ever to put it right'.

Sadly, Srinivasa Sastri prepared to depart. He was bitterly aware of the gulf between the outward appearance of consultation and consideration shown to India and her representatives and the inward reality of British, white solidarity on questions of racial privilege. One last personal humiliation had to be swallowed. Before his departure, Sastri called at the India Office to pay his respects to Lord Peel but the Secretary of State had slipped away to the country. Sastri learned that Lord Winterton was in the office, and sent up his card: only to be told that Winteron would not see him. In writing a farewell note to Peel, Sastri told him (6 August 1923): 'A message from Lord Winterton left me in doubt whether you would have seen me if you had been in.' Edwin Montagu and others protested strongly against this slight to the man who was generally regarded as India's ambassador. The unpleasant incident was not explained away by the issue of an India Office communique.[27] As he returned home, Sastri wrote from the ship to the writer and editor, Benarsi Das Chaturvedi (17 August 1923): 'The Kenya news ... is a terrible blow to me. My outlook is changed. I am not able yet to place myself in the future politics of India.'

The sequel was described by Reading in a personal telegram to Peel (2 September 1923): 'Indian opinion is becoming more consolidated in determination to hit out against the Dominions and England, even though India itself may suffer. Policy of withdrawing from participation in the British Empire Exhibition [planned for 1924] ... is gaining strength ...the boycott of British goods is also proposed! ... The wave of anti-Empire sentiment is gaining strength. Sastri is practically leader of the movement and is now highly praised, particularly by that part of the Press that hitherto has persistently attacked him.'

Sastri issued articles under titles such as 'The Kenya Betrayal', and made speeches reiterating his slogan 'Kenya lost, everything lost': no longer was it a challenge, but now a requiem. There was no trace of his former hope and faith in statements such as 'You could do things, if only your skin were white, which you cannot think of doing, being what you are'. Once again, the Congress took up the cause. In September, a special session of the All-India Congress was convened at Delhi to debate the Kenya issue. A resolution urging separation from the British Empire was moved; but it was rejected. Gandhi, Motilal Nehru and other elder statesmen were still not prepared to commit Congress to a final break.

Another imperial conference was to be held in London in October 1923. India's prospects appeared bleak; especially to G. S. Bajpai who wrote to Sastri: 'I have news that Smuts will probably raise the question of segregation at the imperial conference ... he will ask for a general declaration that segregation on racial and economic grounds is desirable, and the present Cabinet in England will support him ... Mackenzie King [of Canada] may well bless the principle.' Bajpai was doubtful about the man selected to be India's main spokesman: Tej Bahadur Sapru, formerly Law Member of the Viceroy's Council. Sapru had long concerned himself with the grievances of the Indian overseas communities, but Bajpai was evidently not impressed. He commented: 'I am sadly disappointed in him. I expected him to take a firmer stand; but then everyone isn't a Sastri.'[28] Bajpai concluded that Indians overseas must learn to stand up for themselves: 'Our strength must be sought within ourselves ... we must rely exclusively on our own efforts.'

Sapru arrived in London in time to witness the Kenya *debacle*. Sastri at once urged him to return to India, but Sapru decided to stay on.

During the weeks before the conference, he endeavoured to awaken the enthusiasm of Lord Peel, which was at a distinctly low ebb after the Kenya crisis. Peel later wrote of Delamere and the settlers:

I have never negotiated with a more stiff-necked and unreasonable set of people. I could only conclude that the high altitude had had some effect upon their tempers. I was not impressed by the deputation of five or six members that came to represent the Indians in Kenya; if these were the pick of the basket, I could not help feeling that the white settlers had some reason for their dislike.[29]

Despite Peel's desire not to make the position of Indians overseas an issue at the conference, Sapru was working to ensure that the question was given a considered hearing. As the delegates from the Dominions arrived, he was able to interview them privately, and secure their interest and conditional support. This was important, because, unlike the 1921 conference where the British premier and his Dominion colleagues were all old wartime comrades — except Meighen — in 1923 only Massey and Smuts were survivors from the previous conference. Baldwin, Mackenzie King of Canada, and Bruce of Australia were representing their countries for the first time, while Cosgrave and Warren were included as the first representatives of the Irish Free State and Newfoundland at an imperial conference.

The conference opened on 1 October with formal speeches from seven of the delegates. Then followed sessions on the colonies (3 October), Turkey and post-war reparations (5 October), and the League of Nations (11 October). The conference did not meet again in open session until 24 October, when the position of Indians in the Empire was the subject of discussion, as it was on two subsequent occasions (29 and 31 October). Thus the Indian question took up nearly half the time of the formal conference, and filled nearly half the published report of the speeches.[30]

Sapru intended to obtain some commitment from the Dominion premiers to re-examine their domestic policies towards their own domiciled Indians, but his main intent was to involve them in setting up machinery to put pressure on the United Kingdom government to modify the terms of the Kenya settlement. This intent was likely to be resisted by the Secretary of State for the Colonies and by the South African premier; it was also unlikely to be favoured by the Secretary for India, who knew that this was a contest his department could not win. Peel's recollection of the situation, as he set it down later, was as follows: "Sapru was very troublesome on the subject [of Kenya] and threatened more than once to leave the conference if more could not be done for the Indians [in Kenya]. Fortunately, my task was made easier by the fact that he and Alwar [the maharaja who was the other Indian delegate] were on such bad terms that they would hardly communicate with each other.'

Whereas Sastri had fought his battles in 1921 with the unstinted support of Montagu, Sapru had to stand alone; Peel assumed the role of umpire or linesman, while the Maharaja of Alwar pursued his own whimsical, unpredictable way.[31]

Before the Indian question was debated, Smuts attempted to pre-empt the issue, as Bajpai had predicted. From his London hotel, he issued a memorandum on 18 October to all the delegates, in which he urged them to reverse the 1921 resolution. He opened with a fierce attack upon Sastri's mission to the Dominions, which, he suggested, had exacerbated feeling everywhere. For the campaign was based upon a misconception! The Indian claim to equality rested on the argument that the Empire was a monolithic structure with a common citizenship everywhere. But, in practice, 'there is every imaginable difference', and 'The newer conception of the British Empire as a smaller League of Nations . . . involves an even further departure from the single conception of a unitary citizenship'. And so 'Each constituent part of the Empire will settle for itself the nature and incidents of its citizenship'. (This was a shrewd line of argument, designed to appeal particularly to Mackenzie King and Cosgrave, determined to shake off the last shackles of 'the Mother Country'.) Thus, the 1921 resolution 'was a profound mistake', and Smuts asked for a new resolution 'affirming the right of each portion of the Empire to regulate citizenship as well as immigration [covered by the 1918 resolution] as domestic questions'. No 'State of the Empire' should resent 'special treatment' of any persons, originally its own people, by another State where they had settled.

When the Indian debate opened on 24 October, Peel began by emphasising that Indian disabilities overseas were resented by all shades of opinion in India, not merely by the intelligentsia. They resented the 'brand of social inferiority' inflicted on them 'in other parts of the world'. Added Peel 'I am not necessarily, of course, associating myself entirely with that view.' Eventually, he gave way to Sapru, who plunged into a fighting speech which went on for one and three-quarter hours. He began with an appeal to the spirit of empire which was still obligatory, though he managed to give the theme a subtle twist: 'Do not forget that my country, India, is the one country which makes the British Empire truly Imperial. I take pride in that.' Then he got down to the realities. He made it clear that India could not regard the recent Kenya settlement as final: he emphasized that all India, from the Viceroy to the militant nationalists, were united in calling for justice in Kenya. After a survey of the situation in all parts of the empire, he arrived at his 'constructive proposal', which he intended as a resolution. He asked each of the Dominions to set up a committee 'to confer with a committee which the Government of India will send from India in exploring the avenues how best and how soonest the principle of equality implicit in the 1921 resolution may be implemented'.

In the discussion which followed there were no special surprises. In a statement notable for its brevity amid the prevailing verbosity, Devonshire accepted the idea of consultation between a committee representing India and the Colonial Office. He made it clear that this consultation did not include a reconsideration of the recent Kenya decisions. The prime ministers of Canada, Australia and New Zealand repeated their recognition of the principle that Indians domiciled overseas ought to be treated as equal fellow citizens. Massey went further in recognising India as already equal to the White Dominions in Empire or Commonwealth terms, saying he was 'anxious that the representatives of India sitting round this historic table should enjoy all the privileges that we enjoy, and should have exactly the same position'. All the premiers alluded gracefully to Sastri's tour, but when Smuts came to speak he bluntly denounced Sastri's mission and his 'somewhat outrageous statements'. Smuts was equally blunt about the relationship between White, Black and Brown in South Africa; if Indians received the vote, there was no reason why Africans should not be voters also: 'You would be impelled by the inevitable force of logic to go the whole hog, and the result would be that not only would the whites be swamped in Natal by the Indians but the whites would be swamped all over South Africa by the blacks and the whole position for which we have striven, for 200 years or more now, would be given up.'

A very different note was sounded by Desmond Fitzgerald, the Minister of External Affairs in the Irish Free State. He acknowledged that there was little that Ireland could do: the Dominions were separate and autonomous, and Great Britain ruled the colonies: 'but if we had responsibility we should have to protest very strongly against any racial distinctions being made.' He swept away the pretence that India was already virtually a Dominion: 'they cannot really be regarded as equal with the rest of us.' The only valid solution was to bring forward India's full self-government 'with all speed'. He added: 'We in our country must necessarily sympathise whole-heartedly with the Indians both in their protests against their inferior race treatment and in their feelings as to the freedom of their country.' This was a new voice at an imperial conference: the voice of suppressed nationalism, by contrast to the expressions of kinship which had hitherto prevailed—even from Smuts. The others responded by pouring emollient upon the wound. It was agreed that there should be no further resolution on the subject: Peel was as definite as the Dominion premiers that it was not advisable. Baldwin gave the conference the text of a statement which foreshadowed some Commonwealth communiques yet to come by including two opposed viewpoints while implying that they were in harmony: thus, Devonshire was recorded as stating that 'he saw no prospect of these decisions [on Kenya] being modified', and Sapru was recorded as stating that 'the Kenya decisions could not be accepted as final by the people of India'. Yet it was also recorded that 'The Secretary of State for the Colonies ... cordially accepted the proposal of Sir Tej Bahadur Sapru'. Presumably, in conference language, 'the door was left open'.

Before the delegates left the subject, they were treated to a statement by the Home Secretary, W. C. Bridgeman, upon the meaning of imperial nationality. This statement aroused no comment at the time, but it emphasised the inconsistent elements in the dialogue between the self-governing colonies of white settlement and the empire at large, which had been present even before the Diamond Jubilee. The Home Secretary observed: 'At the core [of the British Empire] lies the vital principle of common British nationality'; yet, 'It is not inconsistent with this principle to recognise, as it always has been recognised, that every part of the Empire is free to settle ... the rights to be enjoyed by any person, or classes of persons within its territory'. 'It is important not to confuse the issue by any ambiguous use of words such as "citizen" or "citizenship". If those words are used, as they rightly may be, as ... connoting a status or right which it is within the power of any self-governing Dominion to confer ... they should not at the same time be used as though they were almost synonymous with the Imperial conception of nationality.' 'Imperial nationality is one and indivisible; local citizenship ... may be diverse. If we keep these two conceptions clearly in our minds it ought to be possible ... to maintain ... Imperial unity and local autonomy.' But the coming years were to emphasise that whenever the 'common British nationality' seemed to offer a threat to local autonomy, then it was the local citizenship which would prevail.

What had Sapru achieved? His sole tangible gain was the appointment of his Indian committee to confer with a Colonial Office which was quite adamant upon the main issue of the day.[32] Sapru, like Sastri before him, knew he would be returning to an India which would be sceptical, probably cynical, about the capacity of Indian Liberals to make any progress through reasoned argument. Placed in this frustrating dilemma, the moderate has two possible courses open: he can attempt to claim that he has gained more than he has in reality; or he can make more noise, and pretend that he is being more militant. Sapru adopted both courses. Before leaving London, he launched a violent attack upon Smuts. On the morning of 14 November 1923, there were reports of Sapru's attack in the *Daily News*, the *Morning Post*, *Westminster Gazette*, *Manchester Guardian* and *Daily Express*. Though he stood forth as champion of the unity of the British Commonwealth, 'Smuts has done more harm to the British Empire than anyone else by his attitude of obstinacy towards India'.

On his return to India, Sapru told the National Liberal Federation's conference at Poona that India's position was 'distinctly stronger'. The Kenya door had been 'reopened', machinery for the proper investigation and remedy of Indian grievances had been established. Because Smuts refused to ameliorate conditions in South Africa, the Government of India should consider retaliatory action: it could raise the tariff against South African coal imports, and reduce the railway freight charges on Indian coal. However, he concluded, until India was self-governing, the 'position of her nationals overseas must always be more or less unsatisfactory'.

The reply by Smuts to the attempt to induce him to adopt more liberal policies was swift and grim: in January 1924, Patrick Duncan, Minister of the Interior, introduced the Class Areas Bill in the Union parliament. This measure made compulsory the exclusion and segregation of the Indians into separate urban areas, both for commercial and residential purposes. The measure was one that the South African League and other white racist groups had demanded for years. We need not assume that Smuts introduced it at this moment in order to obtain revenge against Sapru and India: he was much more preoccupied with his domestic political position, which was increasingly insecure. Whenever Smuts had to face his white electorate, he tried to propitiate the racists among his supporters by a gesture towards their prejudices. The Class Areas Bill was a desperate measure to meet a desperate situation.

At the India Office, the news was received with resignation. Sir Arthur Hirtzel, Permanent Under Secretary, argued that any protest must come from Delhi: 'If the Government of India are ever to be able to stand on their own feet in the Empire they must learn diplomatic methods, and they will only do so by making their own mistakes.' He added: 'So far as South Africa is concerned, it is immaterial who makes the representations since the Union Government are not likely to listen to either' [the Secretary of State or the Government of India].[33] An Indian deputation, drawn from the local leaders, waited upon Patrick Duncan, who urged them to accept the measure as inevitable: there was in South Africa 'a predominating majority of the European people who are not willing to share their political privileges with the people of Asiatic race or even the civilised members of some races of South Africa'. Because of these views, some measure of segregation was inevitable, and the best hope was to carry this out fairly, providing adequate facilities for non-Europeans.[34]

The Class Areas Bill did not become law: this was not because parliament declined to make it into law but because the Smuts government went out of office. A general election was held in June 1924, and the white electorate chose General Hertzog and his Nationalist Party, aligned with the Labour Party, as the next government. Smuts was in opposition for the next nine years (1924-33), when he joined Hertzog in an emergency coalition government. The destiny of the South African Indians was now subject to ministers who offered no pretensions of Commonwealth solidarity but whose political philosophy was rooted in the old Afrikaner tradition.

Before this upset occurred, a political upheaval that seemed to promise greater possibilities of change had occurred in Britain. Baldwin judged that in the interests of internal adjustment in the Conservative Party he ought to ask for a general election. The election, held in January 1924, produced no decisive change in the public choice, but it did advance the Labour Party to the position where it commanded more seats in the House of Commons than either of the other parties. Led by Asquith, the Liberals undertook to support a Labour government, and as a result the noble lords presiding over the India and Colonial Offices gave way to an eccentric former colonial administrator, Sydney Olivier (now Lord Olivier), and a former railwayman, J. H. Thomas, who, as Colonial Secretary, rapidly established a genial relationship with the white Dominion leaders (though he was less at ease with black and brown people).

Politics in India also entered a period of uncertainty. Gandhi's effort to obtain swaraj by a mass campaign of satyagraha, non-violent action, had not achieved its end, and his own supporters were divided on the next stage of their programme. The Liberals were disappointed and disillusioned after their first experience of partial ministerial responsibility under Dyarchy. Sastri responded to this situation of uncertainty by reasserting the Liberal values which were as much the bedrock of his political philosophy as for his master, Gokhale. Speaking at St Stephen's College, Delhi, on 24 February 1924, he chose the subject of 'Africa or India'.[35]

> The ideal which the South Africans have is injurious, and diametrically opposed to the ideals of the British Empire . . . . justice all round, equality for all, and brotherhood between all peoples composing the Commonwealth . . . . The Boer is there, every moment thinking of the ideal of the white man's natural and inherent superiority over the coloured person . . . . The white man in East and South Africa will not tolerate another people . . . except they be serfs or slaves or helots: it is he that is the danger to the Empire. He is the wrecker; we, if anything, are the preservers of the Empire.

Smuts had shown the illogicality of blaming white racism exclusively upon the Afrikaners when the attack upon the Indians was concentrated in Natal, the one province in South Africa where the importance of people of English origin was infinitely greater than that of the Boers. Sastri, however, could not abandon his faith in the Britain of John Stuart Mill, John Bright, Gladstone, Campbell Bannerman, Asquith, Lloyd George and Edwin Montagu. Bravely, he distinguished between the influence of a Liberal England in a liberal empire and the racialism of white settlers in Africa. Now, with a Labour government backed by Liberal support, surely the tide would be turned.

3

The Separation of White, Black and Brown (1924-29)

When the Labour Government took office in January 1924, probably most of its members saw themselves as night-watchmen, looking after the establishment, until the confused and contradictory situation should be resolved in favour of a party with a mandate to govern. Certainly Beatrice Webb recorded (16 June 1924) that 'This Cabinet is an abnormal episode—probably a quick-ending one'.[1]

The new Secretary of State for India, Lord Olivier, proved erratic and unreliable. Sastri was struck by his external oddity: 'A man of uncouth appearance, shaggy and awkward, in clothes that had not been pressed for a long time.'[2] In the continuing dialogue with the Colonial Office, he played no major part. J. H. Thomas, in the first of many sojourns at the Colonial Office, was ready to conform to the rules already laid down. When a motion was moved by a Conservative, Sir Sydney Henn, in the House of Commons on 8 April affirming 'unity of policy, both in administration and development' in East Africa, Thomas immediately agreed; and his speech to the annual East Africa dinner, in May, provided him with the occasion for advocating lifting colonial policy, like foreign policy, above party politics in order to maintain continuity.[3]

The new Labour Government was not bothered by Wedgwood's pledge to undo the communal franchise in Kenya (MacDonald had kept him out of the India Office, though he had been Labour's spokesman on India). But the commitment given at the Imperial Conference for the home government to talk to a Colonies Committee nominated by India still remained. Reading put his view to Olivier in a private letter (24 February 1924). The role of the Colonies Committee was, he averred, 'confused in its constitutional aspects': Who exactly was going to make the representations? 'India has been led to believe that ... as a result of the [imperial] conference she would have a free hand to make representations independently of the Secretary of State.' Reading hoped that they could put aside this question as 'of academic interest' and agree to start talking to the Colonial Office. The team chosen to represent India was led by John Hope-Simpson, Liberal M.P. for Taunton and a former member of the I.C.S. There were three Indian members: Dewan

Bahadur T. Rangachariar, K. C. Roy (founder of *Roy's Weekly*) and the Aga Khan, though the last was only an occasional attender. Sir Benjamin Robertson was the other member. Between 3 April and 11 July 1924, the Committee met on twenty-eight occasions, providing almost a full-time occupation for the members. They were dissuaded from taking up the South African problem, and concentrated mainly upon a review of East African questions, though some attention was given to Fiji.

Their object in East Africa was to reopen two subjects—the common franchise and the admission of Indian settlers to the white highlands—and also to prevent the introduction of a severely restrictive immigration law, to which the British government had tentatively agreed. The committee was to attain only the third object.

The Kenya Immigrants Registration and Employment Ordinance would set up a board with power to schedule any trade or business as prohibited in the interests of the natives of the country. The board would also have general powers to scrutinise the credentials of all would-be entrants. Although the measure was supposedly non-racial, it could be operated exclusively against the Indians. In the House of Lords, Olivier described the measure as 'quite unnecessarily drastic'. Thomas was at first reluctant to meet the committee, but eventually he had to agree to a conference. When they met on 24 June, the Committee were able to demonstrate that the evidence upon which the Kenya Government based its case for immigration restriction was quite unreliable; the figures for Indian immigration compiled in Kenya were based upon arrivals and departures at the port of Mombasa, and these included the movements of all the Indians travelling up and down the coast on trade and business between different parts of Kenya, Zanzibar and Tanganyika. Thomas and his officials were nonplussed by the exposure of the falsity of their case (which the committee contravened by citing the real numbers embarking from Indian ports). Three days later, Bottomley of the Colonial Office told Robertson that the immigration bill was 'dead'. Thomas submitted a paper to the Cabinet[4] conceding that the Kenya Government's case 'could not be substantiated'; there were 'serious discrepancies'. While still arguing that immigration controls might be necessary in future, Thomas was content to set up a statistical department ('by consultation with the Union Government') to provide a more accurate assessment of the manpower and employment situation. The Cabinet accepted this conclusion (9 July).

The committee had no success in trying to reopen the franchise and white highlands issues. Nor did they make progress when, at the instance of the Government of India (*vide* telegram of 4 July

1924), they raised the question of appointing representatives of the Indian government in East Africa, Fiji and British Guiana to watch over the interests of the local Indians. The Government of India had insisted, as a condition of further labour emigration, that Agents be admitted into Ceylon and Malaya to supervise the proper working of labour legislation, and to negotiate regarding pay and conditions with estate employers. The first Agent in Ceylon was Subramanya Ranganathan (I.C.S.), and, in Malaya, Rao Sahib Subbaya Naidu; the convention was established that the representatives of India overseas should be Indians, familiar with the problems of the Indian emigrants. In reply to the telegram, the India Office advised (12 July) that it would be best to confine the request, at first, to the case of Fiji, where a demand for Indian labour still persisted.

The representations of the Colonies Committee concerning Fiji were referred to the Governor of Fiji, and many months were to pass before any answer was received. However, the East Africa situation was clarified by a letter from the Colonial Office to Hope-Simpson (6 August) which conceded that the immigration legislation would be deferred, but otherwise conceded nothing. Mr Thomas was said to consider that communal representation suited Kenya better, and there could be no prospect of a common roll being introduced 'at any definite time'. Similarly, there was no change on the white highlands, though the possibility of reserving land for Indian agriculture in the lowlands would be considered. The previous month, J. H. Thomas had announced the appointment of a commission of inquiry to report on development in East Africa. Pursuing his policy of keeping colonial affairs above party controversy, Thomas had selected Ormsby-Gore as the chairman, with one Liberal, F. C. Linfield, and one Labour member—A. G. Church. The India Office asked that an Indian be associated with the commission but Ormsby-Gore personally deplored the proposal (13 August). Altogether, there was not much to show for all the hard work completed by the Committee, though Robertson suggested that the success over the immigration issue 'will be something for the Indian members of the committee to take back'.

In East Africa, the local Congress organisation launched a mass movement to overcome white dominance by Gandhian non-violence. There was a 'no-tax' campaign, and in the general election held in March Indian candidates did not come forward for election. However, the movement failed to maintain its momentum, and divisions appeared among the leaders. Shams-ud-Deen told Benarsi Das Chaturvedi (20 November 1924) that 'Any agitation on our part to force the declaration of the future intentions of the

Government is the surest way of awakening the white settlers of Kenya.... In my humble opinion our tactics should be changed entirely. We must hold no more meetings in Nairobi, should write no more articles in the press.... We must do quiet work until such time as we can, on the strength of our vested interests and established facts, make a demand that cannot be denied.' Following the announcement that immigration control was postponed, the leaders of the Congress cabled Hope-Simpson for his advice on future action. He recommended that they take up the offer by Governor Corydon to accept their nominees as members of the legislative council (29 September), and a few days later they cabled back (3 October): 'Acting on your advice we agreed to accept representation on nominated basis under protest.'

Then, somewhat unexpectedly, the Labour Government ran out of time. Parliament was dissolved on 10 October, and a general election followed, in which the Conservatives secured a substantial majority. This Conservative government was to run for its full five years. Baldwin was not unsympathetic to India's political aspirations but his appointment of Lord Birkenhead as Secretary for India meant that nothing would be done at the India Office: the brilliant lawyer was at the end of his career, and concerned only to live a life of luxury. The editor of *The Times* later informed the Viceroy:

For some time past I have had in my possession a confidential memorandum dealing with the bitter complaints of all sorts of officials, colleagues, and eminent visitors about Birkenhead's utter neglect of his work as Secretary of State. Careful inquiries ... suggest that the number of hours which he devotes to India per week is about three. He ... spends the time there in making money by other means — dictating books, giving interviews, and generally pot-boiling.... The whole thing is a public scandal and can hardly be bottled up for ever.[5]

However, Birkenhead's indifference and absence on holiday had to be endured until he decided to resign in October 1928; Baldwin then brought Peel back to the India Office. Throughout this period Winterton was again Under Secretary, and was often required to function as the parliamentary and political head of the India Office.

Baldwin's choice as Secretary for the Colonies was very different: a Secretary of State with a dynamic policy and philosophy—L. S. Amery. For Leo Amery, this moment was the climax of his life. As a trustee of Cecil Rhodes' imperial and academic legacy, an ardent apostle of *The Round Table* and a fluent writer upon the Empire, he intended to transform the plodding, pragmatic imperialism of the

Colonial Office into something visionary and splendid. To the new Secretary of State Smuts wrote on 25 November 1924:

> You will have to watch the whole East African situation very carefully.... The present tendencies seem all in favour of the Native and the Indian, and the danger is that one of the greatest chances in our history will be missed. The cry should be "the highlands for the whites" and a resolute white policy should be pursued. The fruits of such a policy will be a white state, in time more important than Australia.... A great White Africa along the Eastern backbone, with railway and road communications connecting North and South, will be a first-class addition to the Empire.... It is an expansion of the Rhodes policy. Why should it not become *your* policy?[6]

Why not indeed? But, to keep his feet attached to the ground, Amery had as his Under Secretary W. H. Ormsby-Gore, whose undoubted enthusiasm for white settlement in East Africa was tempered by a sceptical awareness of the limits of the possible.

One of Amery's first important appointments was that of a Governor of Kenya to replace Coryndon, who died suddenly in February 1925. The new man was Sir Edward Grigg: like Amery a former member of *The Times* editorial staff and a member of the *Round Table*, one-time military secretary to the Prince of Wales, private secretary to Lloyd George, and a Liberal M.P. at the time of his appointment. The selection of this distinguished rising statesman indicated that Amery had far-reaching plans for East Africa.

Of less general interest, but of some significance, was the parallel appointment of Sir Muhammad Habibullah as the Member of the Viceroy's Council in charge of the Department of Education, Health and Lands, which included responsibility for Indians overseas. Under the Dyarchy reforms, most of the activities supervised by the department were now handled by elected ministers in the provincial governments; the Overseas Section was the part of the department most exposed to the attention of members of the central legislature. From January 1925 onward, this department was in the charge of an Indian member—right down to independence. Amid the portfolios of the Viceroy's Council predominantly held by British bureaucrats, the department administered by Habibullah and his successors came to be regarded as distinct and different: as Indian and 'national'. Sir Muhammad Habibullah was born in the same year as Gandhi; he came from South India, and was on intimate terms with Srinivasa Sastri. Dignified and courteous, he was nevertheless known to his European colleagues as 'Old Hubble-Bubble'.

The five years, 1924-9, were dominated by two major crises or controversies concerning Indian communities overseas: those in South Africa and in East Africa. The two controversies were going on at the same time, but that in South Africa appeared to be settled by the Cape Town Agreement, announced on 21 February 1927, whereas the debate on East Africa continued into the years of the second Labour Government, 1929-31, and the finale was reached only when that government in turn had been replaced by a National Government. It is convenient, therefore, to examine the phase in South Africa which culminated in the Cape Town Agreement, and then turn aside to consider other areas, before moving on to the controversy over East Africa.

The first warning of ominous events to come was the move by the Natal Provincial Council to abolish the remaining political rights of Indians: the right to vote in municipal and other local elections. The Natal Indian Congress sent a deputation to ask the new Prime Minister, General J. B. M. Hertzog, to disallow the provincial ordinances. The Congress leaders were received by the prime minister, his deputy, Dr. Malan, and several members of the Cabinet, but it was made clear that the government would not advise the Governor-General, the Earl of Athlone, to disallow the ordinances.

Public opinion in India immediately reacted to the news. Since 1923, there had been proposals in the central legislature for the introduction of forms of retaliation against countries which discriminated against the local Indians. There was also talk of taking the question to the League of Nations as a cause of international tension. Birkenhead was moved to write to Amery, who, as Secretary for the Colonies, was still responsible for relations between the United Kingdom and the Dominions. Birkenhead asked Amery (5 February 1925) to 'sound the Union Ministers privately' on the possibility of a conference between India and South Africa; he went on: 'The position is really serious. One part of the Empire is acting in a manner certain to raise violent hostility in another part and to lead to a demand for retaliation which it will be very difficult to resist.' However, Amery was reluctant to intervene, so the Government of India was told to make a direct approach to South Africa.

On 8 April 1925, the Viceroy, Lord Reading, sent a carefully modulated telegram to Lord Athlone: they were 'anxious not to aggravate a delicate situation by indulging in generalizations about aims and motives. The problems of South Africa, we believe, are probably racial only on the surface. They rest on differences in history, outlook and civilisation. To solve these problems can be no easy task'. As a beginning, India asked for a conference with South Africa's representatives.

The reply from Athlone was in equally decorous terms (telegram, 16 June 1925). While South Africa acknowledged the interest of the Indian government in the question, there could be no advantage in a conference. All political parties in South Africa were agreed on 'the broad principles that by strict prohibition of Indian immigration and by means of active repatriation the Indian population in South Africa should be reduced as nearly as possible to the irreducible minimum'. 'The feeling in South Africa in connection with political, economic and racial status of Indians bears a direct relation to . . . effectiveness or otherwise of repatriation.' If the flow of Indians returning home increased, then 'public opinion will come to look much more favourably upon existing and future rights of Indians than . . . hitherto'.

The Government of India responded to this message: they were willing to 'explore' repatriation schemes, they said (14 July 1925) but as 63 per cent of the Indians had been born in South Africa they were 'hardly likely to return to India unless compelled to'. This seemed to close the possibility of any discussion, and in July Dr Malan introduced the Area Reservation Bill in parliament; this provided for the segregation of Indians from Whites in the urban areas. Dr Malan announced that the move was based upon the 'general supposition that the Indian as a race in this country is an alien element in the population'.

The Government of India resisted the desire of members of the central legislature to hit back by a declaration of intent to retaliate. Hard work in the lobbies induced the mover of a retaliatory resolution, Sir D. P. Sarvadhikary, to modify his motion. But this merely gained a breathing space. Once again, Reading appealed to the Secretary of State in frank and urgent terms. In a private letter dated 3 September, Reading lamented the fruitless attempts to appeal to the South African government, 'All to no purpose'. 'At fitful intervals we exchange communications, couched in courteous terms befitting one government in addressing another in which we on our side have urged a conference of some kind and they on their side finding a variety of reasons for refusing to assent to our suggestions'. The absence of support from Britain was having a bad effect: Indians suspected that the Government of India's acquiescence in delay and denial was 'due to lukewarmness to espouse Indian interests as against a Government of Whites'. Reading would be compelled to initiate a course of retaliation; conciliation had achieved nothing: 'Whenever we have held our hand, which has been the course pursued now for some time upon my advice, the result has been that South Africa has come forward with a more oppressive measure.'

The response at the India Office was negative. Winterton noted: 'I think the Viceroy is unduly hard upon the Imperial Government.... The Union of South Africa is a none too secure portion of the British Empire today. Any suggestion of *force majeure*... would mean secession pure and simple. The one issue on which Boers and British Unionists are united is "No surrender to Indian claims". I think successive Viceroys and their Councils are very slow to realise the naked facts of the situation in South Africa.'[7]

Failing any move in London, the Government of India looked around for some other agency, and fell upon the offer of C. F. Andrews to go to South Africa as representative of the National Christian Council of India. Then, with no sign of encouragement from the Union Government, it was decided to send an official deputation, headed by G.F. Paddison, I.C.S., who was Commissioner of Labour for Madras. He was supported by Syed Raza Ali and Sir D. P. Sarvadhikary, both members of the central legislature, and the delegation's secretary was G. S. Bajpai, who since September 1923 had been Under Secretary at the Department of Education, Health and Lands, with actual oversight of the problems of Indians overseas. Paddison recorded that they were at first received 'with suspicion' and even contempt; it was not possible to hire accommodation in Johannesburg for the Indian members of the team.

The initial thaw came about entirely on the initiative of Lord Athlone, who was a much more active and politically sensitive Governor-General than his royal relation the Prince Arthur. Protocol required that high-level correspondence with India must be conducted over his signature. On 1 January 1926, the Government of India again cabled to ask for a conference, and Hertzog's cabinet decided to send back a negative reply. Athlone was on tour, and his private secretary delayed sending off the reply until his chief's return, when he asked him to make a personal appeal to Hertzog. According to Paddison, 'His Excellency needed no special incentive to accept the advice. He had already realised that the passage of the Bill into law would seriously affect the solidarity of the Empire, and was most anxious . . . to prevent such a catastrophe'. Athlone made no attempt to appeal to Hertzog on imperial grounds, but knowing his prime minister to be punctilious and polite, in an old fashioned way, he urged 'that considerations of international courtesy required that they [the Government of India] should at least be given an opportunity to argue their case against the Bill before Parliament was committed to its acceptance'. Hertzog undertook to consult his colleagues, and on 2 February 1926 the Nationalist caucus agreed that the Bill should be referred to a Select Committee before its second reading, so as to allow representatives of India to speak before it was considered in parliament.[8]

In London, the Cabinet considered a paper brought forward by Birkenhead. The South African bill was designed to 'bring about a considerable reduction of Indians in South Africa', he reported; and although the disallowance of Dominion legislation was a thing of the past, the demand would be made in the strongest terms for the United Kingdom to stop this measure. Either they must be prepared to intervene in the internal affairs of a Dominion, or face 'the diversion against Great Britain of the flaming resentment now felt by all classes of Indians, including even the native Princes, against South Africa'.[9] It was fortunate that the efforts of Athlone, Reading and others saved the Baldwin government from this dilemma.

Paddison and his colleagues gave evidence to the Select Committee, but they were conscious that, despite a certain shift of opinion, the committee had not been moved. Only the mining magnate, Sir Ernest Oppenheimer, and Morris Alexander came out in opposition to the Bill. When the Bill was returned to parliament, Alexander moved that it be rejected, but his motion was negatived, 81 to 10 votes. Nevertheless, the Hertzog government was uneasy about pressing on with the measure, and cast around for face-saving devices to enable a pause to be taken for further consideration. Athlone wrote privately to Amery (11 March 1926): 'I have had a talk with my Prime Minister on the matter and though I could not obtain any definite assurances from him, I gained the impression that some move on your part would not be unwelcome. I therefore enquired whether . . . he in company with Malan would be willing to have informal conversations with Bajpai and Paddison in order to ascertain if some formula could be arrived at which would open the road to a solution of the problem.' Athlone then contemplated informal discussions while the Imperial Conference of 1926 was sitting but, before then, an opening move was made on the spot. In a telegram of 2 April, Paddison was able to tell the Government of India that he had talked to Hertzog and Malan, along with Bajpai. Repatriation was again emphasised, though it was stated that 'compulsory repatriation was not contemplated by anyone'. South Africa wanted a settlement 'safeguarding the maintenance of western standards of life'. Paddison committed India to help by 'exploring all possible methods of settling the Asiatic question'. The ministers thereupon agreed to participate in a conference and to withdraw the Bill from parliament. Oppenheimer was able to persuade the opposition leaders, Smuts and Duncan, to welcome this development.

Paddison emphasised in his report to the Viceroy that all this was only a beginning. He knew that 'marked hostility' remained in Natal, and unwillingness to agree to even the present 'meagre facilities' for the Indians, who lacked any opportunities for higher education and were forced into ghettoes because of the absence of public machinery for town planning or social services.

Paddison's confidential memorandum was read by a new Viceroy: in April 1926 Reading was succeeded by Edward Wood, now Lord Irwin. The new Viceroy told Birkenhead that the 'highest credit' was due to Reading for the situation of hope (13 April 1926). If the conference could be held in London, Reading might lead the Indian delegation: Reading was disinclined either to travel to South Africa or to return to India and, after much hesitation, in July he refused the invitation to be leader. Eventually, it was decided to make Sir Muhammad Habibullah the chairman. Irwin told Birkenhead (28 August 1926): 'He is a straightforward gentleman and would do his best. Unfortunately he is not endowed with many brains . . . [But] he is a Muhammadan, and suitable Muhammadans do not grow on every mulberry bush.'

A strong negotiating team left India for South Africa on 14 October. G. L. Corbett, I.C.S., accompanied Habibullah as deputy leader, and the other members were Sir George Paddison (as he now was), Sir d'Arcy Lindsay, Sir Pheroze Sethna (both members of the central legislature) and Sastri. Once again, Bajpai was the secretary. Andrews went ahead of the delegation. His mission (which was warmly supported by Irwin) was to act as an unofficial link-man and mediator between the delegation, the Union government, and the Indian community of South Africa.

The conference at Cape Town opened on 17 December with the Prime Minister and most leading members of the Nationalist Party present, together with F. H. P. Creswell, leader of the Labour Party. Dr Malan acted as chairman of the conference, which closed on 12 January. Malan observed: 'I think that the reason why we have come to such a satisfactory solution is . . . because at the very outset we determined to be good friends and to remain good friends throughout.' A more important reason might have been the narrow area of negotiation. The two main subjects were the examination of the working of repatriation, so as to make the scheme more attractive by action from South Africa and India, with the amelioration of the mechanism of migration, both external and internal, and, secondly, the examination of ways to enable Indians living in the Union to conform to western standards of life by improvements in public health and education. India was quite prepared to welcome back former emigrants (though Andrews was worried, knowing the poor conditions facing those who had returned from Fiji), and this was the nub of the conference for the South Africans; it was far from clear what the commitment towards the 'upliftment' of the Indians who remained implied, but, in any case, this was a problem mainly for British, Unionist Natal. The conference deliberately excluded the whole question of the franchise, and related questions such as Indian participation in the public services (railways, etc.). Andrews wrote to Irwin (29 December 1926) that he was worried that the South African Indians would expect more, including the restoration of all former rights, lost over the years: they would do well to get the Asiatic Bill stopped, and a larger measure of education. When the agreement was announced — and the Area Reservation Bill withdrawn, as a gesture of goodwill — Andrews was delighted. He informed the Viceroy (14 January) that Sastri had experienced a spiritual 'conversion from deep fear to ardent trust': a 'great settlement', Andrews concluded, and mostly due to Sastri; his 'moral personality carried all before it'.

The impact of Sastri on the Nationalist leaders, and on white South Africa, was undeniable. Athlone told Irwin (20 January) that Sastri had shown 'moderation and restraint . . . Hertzog feels the greatest admiration for him'. Athlone concluded: 'With the exercise of patience and goodwill on both sides, the Indians may cease to be one of South Africa's problems and in time be accepted as having a legitimate place in the community.' The delegation returned, rejoicing in the changed atmosphere in South Africa, as Irwin told Birkenhead (10 February 1927), adding that Sastri 'was particularly useful. His eloquence was, I believe, once or twice dangerous, but on the whole he was a great strength to the delegation'.

As a feature of the agreement, it was proposed that the Government of India appoint an Agent to reside in South Africa, with the dual responsibility of watching over the voluntary repatriation scheme and fostering the 'upliftment' of the remaining Indians. Under Gandhi's influence, Andrews had previously opposed the appointment; but now he was convinced that the Agent was necessary, though he urged that South Africa should reciprocate and be represented in India: 'South Africa and India are two nations facing one another in a friendly alliance or league called the British Commonwealth of Nations' (31 December 1926). This was indeed a more mellow C. F. Andrews than the man who had dismissed the British Empire as racialist just a few years before.

Andrews stayed behind after the delegation returned. He set

himself the more difficult task of reconciling the local Indian factions to acceptance of the agreement. He told Irwin (14 January): 'The Indian community's nerves are on edge and resentment is always just below the surface....The long years of oppression and humiliation are bound to have their reaction in a contentious and hypercritical spirit.' He had to convince them that their cause had not been betrayed by the delegation, and the issue of repatriation was 'likely to divide the parties again'. The main rift was between the 'Colonial-born', who accepted South Africa as their home and knew they must come to terms with it, and the trading community who frequently returned to India, sometimes taking their business with them. Andrews thought that the Colonial-born would accept the agreement (12 February). When the details of the agreement were published, the Europeans expressed alarm and the Indians 'complete disappointment', according to Andrews (28 February). His solution to their problems was to link their condition with that of the Africans: 'Whatever rights are conceded to the Indians... must *a fortiori* be granted to the African natives', he said — a somewhat long term solution. However, writing from Johannesburg on March 14, Andrews was able to assure Irwin that the meeting of the South African Indian Congress was a great success; A. I. Kajee was elected secretary, the 'one really good man', in the estimation of Andrews.

Meanwhile, Sastri was being pressed to return to South Africa as the first Agent. Gandhi told him (6 April): 'You will break the hearts of Indians in South Africa if you do not go.... You alone can set the tone.' Although his health was uncertain, Sastri agreed to go for twelve months only. He was instructed by the Viceroy to be a mediator — between the South African Indians and the Union Government, and between South Africa and India — and inevitably he was to be a mediator between the Indian factions also.[10]

The role of Sastri was crucial: the white South Africans, in their little world, were pleased about the arrival of one who was in effect the first ambassador to their country, and 'everyone regards Sastri as one of the world's great men'. When he visited Durban in mid-July, Sastri delivered a carefully prepared speech at the Town Hall, with different appeals to the Europeans and the Indians. He called for 'patient effort', and he asked the rich Indians to help their poorer fellows by endowing schools and entering social work.

Many of the Indians thought that Sastri was being too cautious and conciliatory. He was aware that his speeches in praise of the Empire were more welcome to the Natal Whites than to the Indians. He told his brother (6 October 1927): 'People must make allowance for the differencein latitude and longitude. The public speaker whose conscience is not dead must be content very often to be guilty of *suppressio veri.*' Manilal Gandhi, editor of the Durban paper *Indian Opinion*, complained to his father, but Gandhi hastened to reassure Sastri: 'We are like blood brothers, even though we do not hold the same views about the Empire.' He urged Sastri not to worry about news reports, and concluded: 'Do not hesitate to tell me when you want me to act.'[11] So, for the time being, the spirit of the Cape Town agreement lingered on.

In South Africa, a breathing space had been arranged by the reconciliation of white and brown demands through face-to-face negotiations. The fate of Indians in the colonial empire continued to be subject to the will of the Whites, whether in London or at the headquarters of the colony. The sugar colonies, in the years after indenture was abolished, attracted little attention either from London or Delhi; but a few ripples floated across the mid-1920s to demonstrate that white control could be challenged only by the denial of Indian labour to the colonies.

Fiji still wanted Indian labour, but was not prepared to pay the price demanded by the Government of India. Whereas the debate over the future of the Indians in South Africa was conducted by direct negotiation between the governments of South Africa and India, with the local Indian community able to give vent to its comments, the negotiations over Fiji focussed upon London and the rival bureaucracies of India and Colonial Offices. In this muffled war of attrition, the Colonial Office held the initiative throughout.

The reply to the representations of the Colonies Committee of the Government of India — made in July 1924 — was not delivered for eight months. Finally, on 20 March 1926, the Colonial Office told the India Office that the demand for a common electoral roll could not be granted because of the terms of the original Deed of Cession under which the Fijian chiefs accepted allegiance to Queen Victoria: it was 'impossible, in Mr Amery's opinion, to arrange for the representation of the three sections of the population on the Legislative Council by means of a general franchise'. So there would be three seats for the Indians, and three for the Fijians, separately. The request for the posting of an Agent of the Government of India in Fiji was rejected just as completely: 'The Secretary of State cannot agree that such an appointment is desirable, even in the interests of the Indians themselves . . . . It is to their own representatives [in the legislature] and not to the agent of another government that they should look to express their point of view.' However, the

Governor of Fiji was prepared to agree to appoint a retired British officer from India to advise him, as one of his own officials.

The Government of India was not pleased when this letter was forwarded to them. Cabling the India Office (11 July 1925), they denounced the concessions as 'inadequate': Indians in Fiji should have as many representatives as the Europeans on a communal basis; the argument that representation nullified the need for an Agent was unconvincing; there was no suggestion that the Agent in Ceylon should be withdrawn because the Ceylon Indians had a representative in the local legislature. These objections were sent to the Colonial Office without further comment.

The Governor of Fiji, Eyre Hutson, was no more encouraging when the local Indian community gave him an address (11 January 1926), except to assure them that he would 'encourage by all lawful and proper means the settlement of Indians in the colony'. The eventual reply of the Colonial Office to the India Office was unchanged (5 March 1926); they were not prepared to modify their decision. Birkenhead accepted the position; he told India (31 March 1926) that there was 'a welcome opportunity of improving the position of Indians in Fiji' and he thought any further attempt to gain concessions 'undesirable'. To the Indian government's observation that public opinion in India would only accept a communal system if the Fiji Indians received parity with the Europeans, the answer came: 'Lord Birkenhead would deprecate attaching undue weight to the hypothetical effect which the adoption of the Colonial Office policy . . . might have on public opinion in India.' There was not much left for India to do but acquiesce; as their acceptance was not communicated to Fiji until late in 1926, the Indians could not participate in the election of that year, and they were left with one nominated representative on the legislative council — the complaisant Indian planter, Badri Maharaj. In 1929, when three Indian representatives had been elected to the council, they presented another demand for a common franchise; their resolution was rejected, so they quit the council and their seats remained vacant. The Colonial Office responded to this gesture by reaffirming that there must be a communal franchise in the mixed society of Fiji.[12]

There was even less astir in Mauritius and the Caribbean. The worst labour dispute for many years occurred in British Guiana in 1924, and thirteen persons were killed on the Ruimveldt Estate. Proposals for further Indian migration were opposed by Gandhi and C. F. Andrews (who had favoured a similar proposal in 1920). The Government of India decided to send out their own investigator. A temporary renewal of emigration to Mauritius had been permitted on the explicit condition that an Indian official would be given facilities to report on the experiment. The official selected was an aristocratic Indian Christian, Kunwar Maharaj Singh, son of Raja Sir Harnam Singh, and his first report on Mauritius advised against any further Indian emigration. He was better pleased with the condition of the Indians in British Guiana, but he recommended that emigration should be resumed only if the emigrants went as colonists, receiving grants of land after they had completed a stint of labour.[13] The colonial government was disinclined to embark upon expensive schemes for reclaiming new agricultural land, and dropped the plan. In Mauritius and in Guiana and Trinidad, there was no political change, even of the limited, Fiji variety. The planters continued to monopolise the local legislatures, as they had done ever since the colonies were captured in the Napoleonic wars.

An important Empire conference took place in London in October and November 1926; it was perhaps the most important of the series between the two world wars, but India played virtually no part in the proceedings. At first it was intended to invite Reading to speak for India, but he chose not to attend, and India's representatives alongside the Dominion premiers and cabinet ministers were Birkenhead, the Maharaja of Burdwan, a politically mute landowner, and a discreet second-rank official, D. T. Chadwick. The conference was mainly devoted to defining the new status of the Dominions, and setting them free from the last leading-strings of the Mother Country: as Birkenhead was determined to restrain India from any further move towards self-government, he made no move to associate India with any of the new measures of Dominion independence. Mackenzie King of Canada, Kevin O'Higgins and Desmond Fitzgerald of Ireland, and Hertzog of South Africa were the pace-makers of the conference, and there seems reason to suppose that Hertzog's discovery that Britain was not attempting to exercise authority over South Africa was a factor in his magnanimity to India, immediately after his return to the Cape Town conference.[14] India's progression towards self-government was, if anything, harmed by the 1926 conference: the realisation by the Conservatives that the Irish Free State was moving steadily towards the dissolution of all ties with Britain invited the conclusion that an Indian Dominion would follow the same course. Among its more routine functions, the conference set up a Nationality Committee to consider necessary amendments to the law affecting all parts of the Empire under the British Nationality Act 1914. The question of British women who married foreigners proved vexatious; South Africa differed from the other Dominions on their claim to the rights of British subjects: the conference noted that 'They attached great importance to the maintenance of uniformity throughout the various parts of the Empire in the law relating to British Nationality', and in order to preserve the 'Common Code' they agreed to carry on joint consultations 'to regulate the problem of dual nationality and no nationality'.[15] In 1926, this question may not have seemed vital to Indians: their British nationality could not give them entry into most of the Dominions, and in any case those Indians in East Africa who had been born in an Indian princely state (the majority of the trading community from Western India) and those born in Zanzibar, Tanganyika — and in Kenya before it became a British colony — were none of them British subjects. They possessed the ambiguous status of British Protected Persons, entitled to the status of a British subject when in a foreign country but regarded as a non-subject when on British territory.

Apart from sporadic resolutions, emerging from specific events, the Congress in the 1920s had not often discussed issues outside those of domestic policy. The appointment of Jawaharlal Nehru as secretary of the All-India Congress Committee brought in a man who was intensely concerned about international issues and in 1927 he prepared a paper for the AICC, "A Foreign Policy for India", which included references to the relations of India and the Indians to the British Commonwealth. 'What is the position of the Indian in foreign countries today?' asked Nehru: 'He has gone either as a coolie or as a mercenary soldier on behalf of England.' The Indian overseas was 'a hireling of the exploiter', and Nehru wanted this changed: 'We thus see that there is no possible place for our country in the British group of nations, and it is idle to talk of India becoming a member of this group.' In arguing like this, Nehru was following the C. F. Andrews of a few years before, and he followed Andrews in identifying a new role for Indians in Africa and other lands of settlement: 'An Indian who goes to other countries must cooperate with the people of that country and win for himself a position by friendship and service.... The Indians should cooperate with the Africans and help them, as far as possible and not claim a special position for themselves.'[16] This was a new voice; an unfamiliar voice to most of the Indians overseas.

When the Congress set up a foreign or overseas department in 1929, most of the correspondence was with Indians in Britain and the United States. However, slender contacts were established with the local Congress organisations in South and East Africa. The South African Indian Congress informed the AICC (15 March 1929) that they were worried about the condition of those who had accepted repatriation to India, and Benarsi Das Chaturvedi was asked to inquire into the fate of those who had returned: 'Selling their birthright for £20', as the AICC put it.[17]

The local Congress organisation in East Africa had virtually collapsed. The delegation from India to the Cape Town conference spent some days at Mombasa, and Sastri recorded 'demoralisation' among the Indian leaders; 'Affairs were mad', he told S. G. Vaze (7 December 1926) and he was glad to leave. A similar story was given by a Kenya journalist, S. Achariar, editor of the *Democrat*, to Andrews. The paper was about to close down; since the death of Manilal Desai 'All political activity has come to a standstill — the Congress office is locked up. The community is divided into mutually antagonistic groups and we are all indulging in the unprofitable pastime of mutual abuse and vilification' (7 April 1927).

Nevertheless, as Irwin told Hilton Young — soon to lead a commission to East Africa — 'Indian political opinion is more sensitive about that part of the world than almost any other.'[18] This opinion was soon to be aroused by the ambiguities of the colonial policy of Leo Amery.

The first important statement was the report of the Ormsby-Gore commission, issued in May 1925.[19] By identifying the respective political allegiances of the three members, the report emphasised the all-party character of the statement. The scope of the enquiry was mainly that of economic development, and in broad measure the report was the first of a long series, stretching into the 1950s, which attempted to envisage the somewhat cloudy conception of trusteeship in sharper terms as a coordinated empire development plan. In terms of this philosophy, economic expansion took priority over political advance. The report paid a loud tribute to the contribution of the white settler to East Africa. In Kenya, there was an influx of ex-soldier settlers. Since 1918, 1031 new farms had been started on crown land in the white highlands: 'They are living "rough", often in mud shanties', the report announced; they did not have much capital, many were deep in debt to the bank, and some (about 200) had been compelled to give up. Nevertheless, the report declared, 'Kenya has been fortunate in the type of settlers she has attracted'. The report devoted eight pages to the contribution of the Europeans, and made no specific reference to the role of the Indians. The main conclusion was the necessity for massive capital investment in railways and other public undertakings; the inference was clearly that neither Kenya nor the other territories could finance this expansion from local resources. Despite this conclusion, in one of their rare political judgments, the commission opposed any form of union of the East African territories. They declared: 'We found little if any support in East Africa for the idea of immediate federation and in some quarters we found definite hostility.... We came definitely to the conclusion that any attempt at federation would be premature.'

The report did not appear to cause alarm in India. During 1925, the Indian Legislative Assembly was more concerned about Tanganyika, and passed a resolution asking the Government of India to instruct its representatives at the League of Nations to ventilate the grievances of Indians in Tanganyika and other mandated territories: however, the government took no action. After nearly two years in office, Amery was still giving the impression that he intended to maintain the status quo in East Africa. He told Birkenhead (5 August 1926): 'When Delamere came to see me the other day he broached the subject [of white self-government] but I gave him no encouragement.... I can assure you, and you can assure Irwin, that no change would be considered without the matter being referred to the Cabinet here. As far as I am personally concerned, I am not disposed to favour any further changes in the Kenya constitution in the near future, nor do I wish in any way to depart from the White Paper of 1923.'

Grigg, in Kenya, was also concerned to lower the political temperature. He wrote a private letter to Irwin (28 January 1927) which sought to show that the problem originated in India: 'It has become manifest to me during the last sixteen months that there would be no Indian question in Kenya if it were not stoked up from India . . . to exploit grievances against the British Empire.' With a good deal of shrewdness, Grigg contrasted the political activism of some professional Indians with the multitude of small traders and mechanics who did not want to disturb things because they were so vulnerable to African competition. 'In the course of a generation or two the little Indian will have a hard time to keep his head above water'; the African could not be held back, and there was 'no great future for the Indian in this country', he considered. Grigg's analysis was in striking contrast to the usual screams from the Europeans that the Indians were going to take over Kenya.[20] Grigg ended by hoping that the effect of the Cape Town agreement might be reflected in Kenya, and that inter-racial politics 'may pass into a new phase'. Irwin replied to this letter in conciliatory terms (24 March 1927), though he did point out that the best way 'to keep Indian sentiment in the proper channel' was to agree to the appointment of an Agent, as South Africa had done, to act as mediator. Grigg did not respond. The governors of the East African territories were invited to discuss future policy with Amery in London during the Spring of 1927, when Sir Louis Kershaw, Assistant Under

Secretary, wrote a note for Birkenhead (31 March) to tell him about a meeting in which he and Winterton had discussed future policy with Grigg: 'He is proposing to the Colonial Office a number of important constitutional changes which, I think, will give trouble.' Grigg urged acceptance of federation (often called 'Closer Union') as the goal in East Africa, with a transfer of political control to an electorate in which the Whites would be dominant.

Governor Cameron of Tanganyika led the opposition to this policy, and though Amery was an ardent champion of federation, with support from leading officials, he first had to dispose of the opposition declared by Ormsby-Gore just two years previously. Because of doubts in the Cabinet, an announcement was delayed, and when eventually Amery's White Paper appeared, in July, there was no definite commitment to federation, even as a distant goal.[21] There would have to be an investigation into the question, and Closer Union would only 'proceed... by successive stages'; meanwhile, there would be yet another East African commission to make proposals concerning federation, changes in legislative councils, and the financial implications of any changes. The object of British policy was again stated to be trusteeship, until such time as the Africans could 'take part more fully in their own government and in the common affairs of all races'. What seemed to emerge was the concept of a 'dual policy', giving as much weight to European interests as to African interests.

The East African inquiry was briefly debated on a House of Commons Supply Day.[22] J. H. Thomas, as the opposition spokesman on colonial affairs, reaffirmed his belief in a bi-partisan colonial policy, though other Labour speakers were more critical, and asked why federation should be reviewed after being dismissed two years earlier, why the Devonshire declaration was being diluted to meet the demands of the white settlers, and whether an African would be a member of the commission. To the last question, Amery replied that 'it could hardly lead to good results', but altogether he tried to steer a middle way: 'East Africa is neither West Africa nor South Africa, and it has characteristics entirely of its own. It can never remain a purely black man's country and it is not going to become a white man's country, even in the sense that South Africa is a white man's country.' But, he added that the white settlers should be involved in the task of trusteeship; it would be wrong if they came to regard the United Kingdom government as the trustee, and made claims only on behalf of white interests. Philosophically, it was a convincing argument; politically, it bore no relation to the facts.

The new commission was to be led by Sir Edward Hilton Young, a Conservative with special knowledge of public finance. Amery departed on a long tour of the Dominions and left the question of the commission's membership for the chairman and the Colonial Office to decide. Grigg was anxious to get Patrick Duncan from South Africa appointed a member, but Hilton Young responded unfavourably. Amery had informed the House of Commons that one member would be selected by the Secretary for India. When the Indians on the Council of the Secretary of State, led by Dr. R. P. Paranjpye, asked for Sastri to become 'their' member, the request was refused — on the grounds that, if Sastri were appointed, it would then be impossible to object to a white settler member. The India Office nomination went to Sir Reginald Mant, formerly of the I.C.S.[23] The other two members were Sir George Schuster, recently financial adviser to Amery (shortly to join the Government of India as Finance Member of the Viceroy's Council) and Dr. J. H. Oldham, Secretary of the International Missionary Council, a renowned champion of the Africans.

Hoping to repeat the success of the Paddison mission to South Africa, the Government of India deputed Maharaj Singh and R. B. Ewbank to go to Kenya and prepare the ground for the arrival of Hilton Young and his colleagues. Meanwhile, the Viceroy made personal contact with the principal actors. Irwin warned Young (24 August 1927) that the Indians 'have an ineradicable suspicion that Amery means ... to wangle himself and Kenya out of the White Paper of 1923'. Grigg attempted to overcome Irwin's doubts by a broad-fronted argument (22 September 1927). The local Indian community was 'beginning to recognise — what you in India have never recognised — that they are getting much better treatment in Keyna than in any other part of Africa'. He went on to insist that they could develop a political system which reflected the interests of all the races. This excluded a common roll: it was 'impossible ... madness', but instead there would be communal representation, not based upon numbers but upon each community's 'character, its education, its enterprise, its civilisation, and the contribution it makes in all ways to the development of the country'. It was pretty clear which community would emerge as the leaders, and Grigg made this quite explicit in his conclusion:

The Indian question is a small thing in East Africa compared with the vast problem of the future of white settlement in the midst of this huge mass of primitive African barbarism .... The white race knows in its heart that what it concedes to the Indian it must in the long run concede to the African .... Attempts from India to get more for Indians in East Africa than they in reality deserve or can justify will end in reducing them to something below their real deserts and ultimately, I feel, to something like the desperate position in South Africa. When once white feeling in this matter is definitely challenged it is, believe me, invincible and inexorable.

Grigg, then, had not abandoned the vision of a white, self-governing East Africa; and in 1927 it was still possible to see this as the logical extension of the process of Empire into Commonwealth in which South Africa and Southern Rhodesia formed the latest part. If this thinking was also popular in the Colonial Office, it had little attraction for the Tory Under Secretary, Ormsby-Gore, who wrote to his old friend the Viceroy (24 October 1927) that he was 'thankful the new white paper was no worse. Ned Grigg has become thoroughly infected with Kenyitis, and wanted H.M.G. to go much further than it has. He, of course, is a Liberal and believes in unofficial majorities, etc.' Ormsby-Gore conceded that even Grigg wanted the development towards self-government 'to be by gradual stages rather than by sudden change, as happened in the case of Southern Rhodesia'. All that Ormsby-Gore was prepared to see as advantageous in the Hilton Young commission was that 'we shall gain time'.

When the commission arrived in East Africa in January 1928, it was soon evident that the white settlers would not repeat their success in 1925 in charming their visitors into seeing only their view of East Africa. Certainly the chairman was inclined to favour concessions to the Europeans, but his three colleagues combined to resist. The Indian point of view was presented convincingly and without dissentient voices, thanks partly to the careful tutelage of Ewbank and Maharaj Singh. The white settlers saw that things were not going their way, and Delamere offered the Indians a measure of political participation to gain their support; but the offer was still designed to maintain white dominance and was therefore declined.

This, at any rate, was the version which C. F. Andrews passed on to Irwin after meeting Maharaj Singh on his return.[24] Delamere was prepared to consider a franchise based upon educational attainments, but insisted that there must be a ratio of Whites to Indians of four to one in the legislature. This was merely another kind of communal system, and Andrews advised Irwin that this must be rejected, for 'it means stratification later on. The African race is developing with amazing rapidity and by means of the communal franchise we are putting the constitution into a straight waistcoat. It may fit at present but it will be intolerable later on'. An educational franchise would give an opportunity to bring Africans into the political system; Andrews concluded: 'The essence of trusteeship consists in handing over the property intact when the ward comes of age.'

While Andrews was giving advice which seemed revolutionary in the 1920s, though it was an accurate forecast of the dilemma of the 1950s, the commission was slowly drafting its lengthy report. The statement which the majority wished to make was also forward-looking. However, the chairman was more concerned with the political realities of 1928, as he viewed them. Hilton Young wrote to Irwin from Nyasaland (20 March 1928): 'The native races must be given a government capable of protecting their interests, and that cannot be done without a central authority for the three colonies. The white population in Kenya must be given some satisfaction for their legitimate desire for political self-expression, and that cannot be done without somewhat affecting the position of the Indian community.' In order to achieve what he called 'stabilisation of the institutions of government in East Africa' by strengthening overall controls, Young planned to offer the Kenya Europeans concessions as the price of their acceptance. The Indians, as the political under-dogs, would be expected to pay the bill.

However, Schuster, Mant and Oldham were not prepared to buy off the Kenya settlers at the Indians' expense, and they looked ahead to the day when Africans would demand a share in the control of their own continent. The report which they presented began by restating the demographic facts: whereas in South Africa there was one White to every four Blacks, in East and Central Africa there was one White to every 400 Blacks. In a section headed 'The Political Problem', they turned their gaze upon Kenya. It was 'idle to expect that the present Crown Colony system... can be continued indefinitely'. Within recent years 'local opinion [by which they meant white opinion] has successfully resisted measures which the Secretary of State would have liked to enforce' (a reference to Churchill's abortive instructions to Coryndon), but though the Whites had demonstrated their capacity to be obstructive there had been 'no corresponding advantage in real responsibility': the essence of any advance to self-government. The political demands of Africans could not be 'permanently resisted' and then 'Numbers would come into play'.

The commission therefore recommended a strengthening of the central executive by the introduction of a High Commissioner or Governor-General to 'represent the Secretary of State on the spot'. This would be accompanied by an increase in non-official representation in the colonial legislatures, and in Kenya the expanded legislative council would include a proportionate increase of Indian and African representatives. On the franchise, the majority reported that a 'Civilisation test is best suited to conditions in East Africa': communal systems prevented the 'growth of a healthy political life'. The commission found a convenient support for their argument in the appearance of the *Report of the Special Commission on the Ceylon Constitution*, published in July 1928, which categorically condemned communal representation as encouraging the spirit of racial exclusivism. 'The ideal to be aimed at is a common roll on an equal franchise with no discrimination between the races', but this ideal, the majority concluded, could not be immediately realised.

Hilton Young rejected the majority view and argued in favour of a reduction in the official element on the Kenya legislative council and an increase in the non-officials, providing a 'stable repository of power' in the block of European elected members.[25] Young signed his dissenting note on 17 October 1928, and the report went to the Cabinet, who showed no desire to take early action on its divergent conclusions. Young privately acquainted Irwin with the contents of the report (24 October 1928). He was angry with Mant and Schuster and their 'mischievous' partiality for the Indians: 'With this as the only recommendation the report would have been as dead as mutton.' He made it clear that the killers would be the Kenya white settlers.

When Irwin read Young's letter he was able to check his version of the case by talking to Sir George Schuster, who had taken up his post on the Viceroy's Council. Schuster correctly surmised that Indian opinion in East Africa, far from welcoming the report as a pro-Indian document, would react against the proposals for federation and would be sorely disappointed at the failure to implement the 'promise' (as they saw it) of a common roll, made in 1921 and '22. On Schuster's advice, Irwin cabled Peel, who was again Secretary of State, in a private and personal telegram (20 November 1928), asking for the appointment of a 'representative of the Government of India whom the Indians in East Africa would trust; who would carry weight with them, and who could moderate the feeling when the report became public'.[26] Lord Peel addressed a secret letter to Amery (23 November 1928) asking for the appointment of an Agent in East Africa: he would have a 'restraining effect upon public opinion in India', Peel said, instancing the success of Sastri in South Africa. Amery returned an irritable reply (30 November): an Agent in East Africa was not 'either desirable or necessary'. Grigg was opposed to the idea, and though Amery would mention the matter again to Grigg and Cameron, 'the proposition is not one which I can adopt'. Peel wrote again, urging that if there was an 'uncontrollable outburst' by the East African Indians against the report, the Statutory Commission, then touring India under the leadership of Sir John Simon, would be affected: the antagonism would 'hamper very considerably the already delicate task'.[27] Reporting to Irwin, Peel told him that Amery proposed to follow up the Hilton Young report by another inquiry: clearly, Amery was not at all happy about the majority's recommendations. Peel added that Ormsby-Gore was against any inquiry; he maintained that East Africa should 'move comfortably along' for another ten years under present arrangements. With views 'so contradictory', the Cabinet were reluctant to take any action, though Amery continued to press for unification. On 23 January, Amery informed Peel that he had talked to Grigg (once more in London to discuss the future of Kenya). Grigg declared that an Indian Agent 'could only do harm'. With total insensitivity, Amery commented: 'He feels — and of course he is right — that the Indians ought to look to him and nobody else as their protector.' As 'a gesture of goodwill', Grigg was prepared to appoint an official from the Indian service to his own staff to act as adviser. Amery then informed Peel that he was proposing to send his Permanent Under Secretary, Sir Samuel Wilson, to tour East Africa for discussions. If he obtained agreement, a new set-up would be introduced before the end of the year.[28]

However, the Cabinet were reluctant to agree to the Wilson visit; only in March was assent given. Peel told Irwin about the decision the same day (7 March 1929). He insisted that he had pressed the Cabinet to give Wilson precise instructions as to whether he was to negotiate on the basis of the majority or minority proposal. The Cabinet agreed to refer the question to a committee, presided over by old Lord Salisbury. The information was sent to Irwin by a private and personal telegram, and he replied in the same form (10 March) to acquaint Peel with the Indian reaction. The central legislature was 'deeply distrustful' of the whole report, though the Standing Emigration Committee of both houses of the legislature agreed to accept the majority proposals, if they included the provision of a franchise based upon a 'civilisation test'. Grigg's proposal for an I.C.S. adviser was unacceptable. Irwin reiterated that India wanted a representative in Kenya to 'assist Wilson', and Sastri was the man the legislature wanted.

To return to Sastri in South Africa: despite ill-health, he continued to give a new image to the Indian community and was pressed by Habibullah to extend his time as Agent, but he only consented to remain an extra six months. He advised the Viceroy (and Athlone wrote in the same terms) that his successor ought to be from public life rather than an official: he recommended Dr R. P. Paranjpye, the Liberal statesman, who was now a member of the Secretary of State's Council. Irwin replied to both Sastri and Athlone (20 August 1928) that he had been considering Maharaj Singh as Sastri's successor, but in view of their plea for a non-official he would ask for Paranjpye. Sastri explained his decision to return to Gandhi, who had pressed him to go on in South Africa. His reasons seemed quixotic (7 September 1928): he was 'used these many years to be in the minority, to be misunderstood and abused. I feel like a fish out of water in this atmosphere of adulation and popularity. Something must be wrong.... I am impelled to betake myself to my usual occupation (ploughing the sands of the ocean)'. And with this wry portrayal of the condition of the 20th Century Liberal, Sastri prepared to depart.

The Secretary for India would not release Paranjpye from what he regarded as his important work on the Council of India, so Irwin offered the post to another eminent Liberal from the Bombay side — M. R. Jayakar. Jayakar professed his inability to go: he was the sole support and comfort of his aged, widowed mother. So Irwin passed on to another public man from Madras, Sir V. Kurma Reddi, who had served as India's representative at the League of Nations. Sastri was lukewarm about Reddi (and so was C. F. Andrews) but the appointment was made.

Soon after Reddi arrived, the new Agent questioned Habibullah about whether he should launch into a campaign to extend the franchise to Indians. He felt his hands were tied, because Sastri had declared unequivocally that he would never raise an issue not covered by the Cape Town agreement. Added Reddi: 'part of his success is undoubtedly due to adherence to this policy.' Reddi pinpointed the calculated element in Sastri's tactics; but that was not the sum of his work. Athlone told Irwin that, though Reddi was 'sound', 'He is not a Sastri, who was a far greater success than I could possibly have imagined'.[29]

Sastri came home; but not for long. Irwin was convinced he was the only one to take up the task of acting as the spokesman for the Indians when Wilson visited East Africa. He told Peel that Sastri must be given official status: he would not go as a private person because then he could not 'apply brakes' to Indian indignation. When Peel asked that he be given an 'official cachet', Amery erupted into fury: 'Is the suggestion that he is in some sense an Indian counterpart of Wilson?', he demanded (27 March). 'If anything of that sort is in view the sooner it is dropped the better. There is only one Government that is investigating or deciding this business.' Sastri's mission would 'create considerable alarm among the settlers.... Is [there] any real advantage in sending Sastri at all?'.[30]

References to East Africa produced quite different responses: the Governor of Tanganyika agreed to his coming; the Governor of

Uganda had no objection whatsoever; the acting Governor of Kenya (J. W. Barth) said that 'In view of Sastri's reputation I would welcome any assistance he can give'.[31] Despite these cordialities, Grigg fulminated to Wilson (2 April): 'Sending Sastri will only make things worse than they are already.' He tried to insist: 'If he goes at all he must go with precise instructions on the franchise question: i.e. he must abide by the White Paper.... Let the Secretary of State for India remember that there are many people in Kenya in high positions, officials as well as unofficials, who ... would like to see the Indian question brought to a head in Kenya again, even if that means another 1923 ... [this] is likely to precipitate the crisis they desire.'

While Amery and Grigg thundered away, Ormsby-Gore brought Irwin up to date with the latest instalment of the East Africa saga: 'Leo ... under his *Round Table* inspiration is all for any form of federation. I'm afraid I have been consistently against him. I want Tanganyika and Uganda left alone.... In Kenya it's high time everyone gave up politics for business [he meant development] ... I've been fighting to resist any move in the direction of a High Commissioner or Governor-General.' Ormsby-Gore thought it impossible to have a consistent, overall 'native policy' in Africa: 'Fortunately there was a Cabinet Committee, all very suspicious of Leo, of the Hilton Young report, and determined that His Majesty's Government shall be committed to no decision of policy whatsoever till after the General Election.' The election to which Ormsby-Gore was looking was to come in May 1929; meanwhile, Sir Samuel Wilson was brought before the Cabinet Committee and Lord Salisbury 'rubbed it in that he was only to go to East Africa on the understanding that he would commit the Government to nothing, and that he would merely collect local opinion'. Ormsby-Gore hoped (optimistically) that when 'Sammy' Wilson returned 'he will use his influence to consign the whole Hilton Young report to the limbo from which in my opinion it should never have emerged'. This letter was written on 4 April, and the controversy over an Indian representative to follow up Wilson now reached its *denouement*.

Peel and his senior officials reacted to the opposition of Amery and Grigg in a manner unusual for the India Office in dealings with the Colonial Office: their attitude stiffened. On 8 April, Sir Louis Kershaw had an interview with Amery, Ormsby-Gore and Wilson. Commenting on the 'unusual' aspect of an official representative of India visiting East Africa, Amery read out a draft statement to Kershaw in which the visit was to be announced, with the additional declaration that the question of a common roll would not be reopened. Kershaw objected: no such declaration had been accepted by the Cabinet, and the issue was actually still open. To highlight the question in a statement would have a deplorable effect. Rather hastily, Amery withdrew his suggestion; 'He insisted however that some inspired comment should be made in *The Times* which would make it clear that the common roll would not be discussed.' Kershaw acquiesced in this arrangement, though he asked that Peel should be consulted 'before *The Times* was told what to say'.[32]

Peel now cabled Irwin to tell him that Amery agreed to Sastri's visit (11 April), though he asked that Sastri should get 'explicit instructions to discourage any agitation' for the common roll (the India Office revolt against Colonial Office intransigence was, after all, short-lived). Irwin was not prepared to give up so easily: Sastri could not be expected to accept a mission with such preconditions. A conference of the East African Indian Congress was held at Mombasa, 14 to 17 April, with Sastri's old lieutenant, Kunzru, in the chair. The conference rejected settler government, and called on the British Government to accept responsibility for 'native interests'. In this situation, Sastri insisted that he must be free to stress the common roll as the objective, or else his mission would be disowned. Once again, Amery backed down. Whitehall echoed to praise of Sastri's 'judgment' and 'discretion', and Printing House Square sounded the same note: *The Times* editorial of 24 April praised Sastri almost to extravagance as a man of compromise, who 'knows that ultimate ideals must be postponed if local feeling is quite unready for them'.

As he prepared to set out from his Bangalore home, Sastri wrote to acknowledge the good wishes of the Viceroy (23 April). It was hard upon his wife, from whom he had been separated during his time in South Africa; added Sastri: 'poor creature, she has not heard of Amery'.

Sir Samuel Wilson was already thrusting his way through East Africa — he 'put people's backs up', as Peel told Irwin (9 May 1929): 'he seems to be covering the ground like an American tourist'. On arrival at Mombasa, Sastri at once declared the common roll to be the objective; but he found himself forestalled by Wilson. The Under Secretary first met the white settlers and told them that the common roll had been abandoned. Then he met representatives of the Indian community at Nairobi, before Sastri's arrival, and informed them that Amery had decided not to open up the question of the common roll as there was no possibility of European consent. Irwin's comment was that it was 'impossible to avoid the impression that Sastri and the local Indian leaders were deprived of all chance of working for agreement with success'.[33] European intransigence had been stiffened by the knowledge of Amery's support. The ground was cut from under Sastri's feet; he found himself suspected and his mission denounced as a failure. His attempts to recover some initiative by negotiating with Delamere and the acting governor were useless; and he quit East Africa in mid-June, at the same time as Wilson departed. Publication of his report to the Government of India was postponed because of its capacity to cause 'embarrassment'. Sastri wrote to Gandhi in bitterness and humiliation: 'If Colonel Amery had already instructed his agent, Sir Samuel Wilson, to announce his decision against it [the common roll] he should have cancelled the instructions [for Sastri's visit].' Sastri told Gandhi that he had understood (somewhat naively perhaps) that the underlying purpose of his visit was to persuade the Europeans to accept a common roll, which was stultified at the outset: 'As if to make a difficult task impossible, the Indian community from the beginning suspected me.... My success in South Africa was the result of my giving away the rights of Indians.... These suspicions were confirmed when I spoke of a "give and take" policy and advised entry into the legislature and local bodies. Give and take! They asked what was there to give?'[34]

If Sastri was sore and sad, Sir Samuel Wilson was to have little more to show for his relentless, steam-roller progress across East Africa. On 30 May the electorate gave their verdict on five years of Baldwin and 'Safety First': Labour won 288 seats, the Conservatives 260 and the Liberals 59. On 4 June, Baldwin resigned, and Amery and Peel departed. MacDonald again headed a Labour government, which was to spend over two years in office before going down in the financial crisis of August 1931. This time in 1929, Indians looked towards the new Labour leaders with lower expectations than in 1924. And Sir Samuel Wilson drafted his report for his new masters.

4
Separation Questioned and Affirmed
(1929-35)

The second Labour Government was to be merely an interlude in the long Conservative ascendancy between the two world wars. The Labour interlude was not remarkable for political innovation, and the economic storm which burst across the world soon after the election absorbed its main energies. Within the limitations which circumstances imposed on him, the new Secretary for India, Wedgwood Benn, did manage to energise his department, after its somnolence under Birkenhead and Peel. The world economic crisis coincided with the crisis in Indian political demands. Benn first attempted to break the deadlock by discussion at the Round Table Conference in London; but this attempt did not really succeed, and the focus of demand shifted to Gandhi's satyagraha campaign of 1931 which aroused India to the highest level of political intensity ever experienced.

The campaign had its effects upon neighbouring countries. Ceylon and Burma also stirred into political activity, and the new national feeling produced important side-effects for the Indians domiciled in those countries. In Africa, the Indians struggled on with the familiar situation in which their demands for equality with the Whites were resisted because it was feared that concessions would lead directly to an irresistible demand from the Blacks; but in Southern Asia they found themselves in the unfamiliar situation of being regarded as an impediment to the growth of national consciousness in Ceylon and Burma.

The years 1929-35 were marked by less dramatic events than those of the previous decade. Economic survival took precedence over political demand. Between 1929 and 1931, the Kenya controversy was pursued, until it ground to a standstill. The white settlers preserved their exclusive position; but they had to abandon their dream of creating another Southern Rhodesia in Kenya. In South Africa, the dubious settlement achieved at Cape Town in 1927 was kept from falling apart; but there was no significant change in the relationships between Whites, Browns and Blacks, and the situation was liable to deteriorate whenever political expediency saw an opening. In Ceylon and Burma, nationalism moved several paces ahead, but the influence of the Government of India was powerful enough to allow the local Indian communities some share in the process of emancipation. The tropical colonies — the producers of raw materials — the sugar islands and Malaya, continued to remain firmly under the control of British business interests and their local agents and allies. The 1930s saw the tide of Empire on the turn; and as the tide began to fall it could be seen that counter-currents were running in the 1930s which exerted their pull for a long time afterwards.

Between the new Secretary for India and the new Secretary for the Colonies, it might appear that everything favoured the latter. Wedgwood Benn at the India Office had only joined the Labour Party in 1927, having previously been a Liberal; because of his slight stature, some marked him down as a political lightweight — including the formidable wife of the Secretary for the Colonies. Beatrice Webb recorded in her diary: 'If it were not for an unusual alertness of manner — an almost brilliant rapidity of response ... the Secretary of State for India would appear an insignificant little person — a city clerk perhaps?'[1] By contrast, Sidney Webb — now translated to the House of Lords as Lord Passfield — was one of Labour's intellectual giants, as well as intensely industrious and knowledgeable in the ways of committees. Yet Benn was to use his two years in office to attempt great changes, whereas Sidney Webb became yet another political figurehead of a bureaucracy. If in his time Ceylon made a significant advance in self-government, this was probably due more to the personal interest of the new parliamentary Under Secretary, Dr Drummond Shiels. On East Africa, Webb had only a negative influence; and if the white settler pressures were held in check, this owed more to adverse economic circumstances than to political will.

Contemporary verdicts on Passfield's East African policy were severe among the Labour Party's colonial experts. Norman Leys, a former administrator in Kenya, recorded in a 'Memorandum on Labour's Colonial Policy' that 'the Labour Government of 1929-31 left no mark on colonial policy', and Leonard Woolf wrote to Leys: 'The real difficulty, as we found with Passfield, you know, was how to get the Labour Government when it is sitting there in power to implement its promises.'[2] Webb has found one scholarly champion[3], but the weight of Labour opinion was adverse: according to Woolf, Drummond Shiels was 'dismayed by Webb's conservatism and masterly inactivity'.

When Wilson's report appeared, it sounded a last blast on the *Round Table* trumpet. He called for definite assurances to the Kenya Europeans that 'His Majesty's Government did not regard white settlement as prejudicial to native interests', and he recommended a non-official white majority in the Kenya legislature; but he also argued that the powers of the new High Commissioner should be limited to coordinating economic services.[4] The report was published in September 1929, and predictably was rejected *in toto* by Indian opinion. The Standing Emigration Committee (which included Motilal Nehru and Kunzru) demanded a common roll, an enlarged legislature, and the appointment of more Indians to East African public services. Habibullah came to London to confer with Passfield, and found him unwilling to make any concessions to the Indian point of view. A meeting on 15 October, when Passfield received Habibullah, Bajpai, Mant and Kershaw ended in stalemate. Concerning the new High Commissioner, Passfield accepted Wilson's proposal for a minimum list of functions. Benn told Irwin this was 'quite unsatisfactory', and Irwin told Benn that the proposals 'involve complete defeat for Indian claims'.[5] When the Colonial Office proposals were put to the Cabinet on 18 December, they were referred to a Cabinet committee presided over by the Lord Chancellor, Lord Sankey[6]: this offered a glimmer of hope. For the first time, East African policy would be debated in a neutral context, instead of becoming — as was usual — a dog-fight between the India Office and the Colonial Office.

Sankey's first memorandum (16 January 1930) was a notable departure from all the documents of the previous ten years. In the Kenya legislature, he observed, nobody — except perhaps the Indians — would support the Governor in the event of a disagreement with the settler element; the supposed safeguard of an official majority was 'worthless': 'Experience has thus far shown that with one exception each Governor tends to fall into the hands of the elected settlers.' Referring to the memorandum submitted by the Secretary for the Colonies, Sankey said: 'The argument adduced by Lord Passfield in favour of communal instead of common electorates omits to point out that the phrase "[This has the] support of public opinion" means the opinion of the dominant white settlers. All other opinion appears to favour the common electoral roll.' Webb countered the Lord Chancellor by proposing a formula which would provide for eleven European representatives, five Indians and one Arab.

In his memorandum (13 March) Benn challenged this scheme: he called for a return to the Wood-Winterton formula, and also 'the principle of equality of political status of all British subjects'. It was important that this be accepted by the Labour Government 'without ambiguity'. Once introduced, this could lead to 'a new grouping of parties on economic as distinct from racial lines'.

Thus far, the contest appeared to have left all the parties evenly matched, but now Colonial Office pressure began to be reasserted. When Sankey put together the final paper for the Cabinet[7], Part I recommended a scheme for closer union of the three territories: there would be a High Commissioner and an Advisory Council of twenty-four members (seven from each territory, with three chosen by the High Commissioner), Part II was a note on the Kenya legislature, and it recommended a continuation of the communal system, though the common roll was to be regarded as the 'ideal' ('however distant may be its attainment').

At the Cabinet meeting on 9 April, Passfield accepted Part I, and the main proposal in Part II; but he objected to aspects of the proposal which might, perhaps, prepare the ground for a common roll in Kenya. He announced that 'his advisers took a serious view of the situation which would arise were the common roll to be adopted ... there would follow, in the view of his Department, a situation comparable in its gravity to that of 1923'. Passfield's attitude gave Benn the opportunity to reopen the question of the common roll, which was regarded in India 'as second only to that of the constitutional issue itself' (i.e. Indian self-government). Said Wedgwood Benn: the common roll had been accepted in 1921, it was supported by the majority Hilton Young report, and, he added triumphantly, it was supported by the Labour Party. Passfield had made a serious error in objecting to an eventuality which his Department had all but managed to dispose of; now the Cabinet decided to refer the whole question of Kenya back to their committee.

Wedgwood Benn wrote bitterly to Irwin the next day (10 April) giving a history of the whole situation since Webb had tried to get the Wilson scheme through the Cabinet before Christmas. The committee, he said, had accepted the common roll but 'the Colonial Office, heavily led by Webb, are determined to stop it'. The great difficulty was that the decisions of the committee were interpreted by the draftsmen of the Colonial Office: 'and whenever these drafts are made, we find that they do not carry out the principle decided on. This has been my difficulty, again and again, and the final example of it occurred in the Cabinet on the report of this Committee when a draft was put up which in fact defeated what we were after.' Benn related how he had managed to get the whole question referred back to the Committee, adding that the Cabinet were 'sick and tired of the Kenya question'. Benn concluded: 'What has infuriated me about the whole business is that, owing to the obduracy of the Colonial Office, things that the whole of the Labour Party, and the Liberal Party, and a great part of the Conservative Party want done, are being stopped.' Perhaps he was suffering a little from persecution mania, but Benn's indictment exposed the role of the Colonial Office in terms that all previous Ministers had hesitated to express.

When it met, the committee moved a long way towards meeting Benn's aspirations. Once again, the Duke of Devonshire's pious asseverations on trusteeship were to be reproduced and emphasised. The goal for the franchise was definitely to be a common roll, 'with an equal franchise of a civilisation or educational character, open to all races'. This was to be a matter for inquiry by the new High Commissioner 'in the near future'. The revised draft was considered by the full Cabinet on 30 April, and was given approval. In addition, the Secretary for the Colonies was instructed to move for a Joint Committee of both Houses of Parliament to take the final decision. The Viceroy should be given facilities to make representations to the Joint Committee.

This outcome seemed to be a compromise between the divided positions of the Colonial Office and the rest of the Ministers. Sidney Webb had undoubtedly lost a battle, and his star was slowly sinking. However, if Webb and the Colonial Office had lost some ground, it was by no means probable that Wedgwood Benn's belief that political opinion in the different parties would endorse a common franchise was going to be vindicated.

Government policy was announced in two White Papers, published in June 1930.[8] One outlined the plan for a High Commissioner and closer union; this document also announced the future of the Kenya legislature and declared that a common roll was the objective, with a franchise based upon education and civilisation attainments common to all races. The other paper dwelt upon the nature of trusteeship in Africa. It was not entirely clear that in any conflict of interests between Africans and non-Africans the former would be paramount; indeed, the White Paper dwelt again upon the 'Dual Policy' as 'in no way inconsistent' with trusteeship.

The reception given to these statements of Labour policy by the Conservative opposition was not cordial. Ormsby-Gore told Irwin that Webb was in trouble over his White Papers (for, paradoxically, the opposition had the impression that the Colonial Secretary was the father of these proposals). There was a 'frenzy of indignation' among the white settlers, said Billy Gore (3 July 1930), and he observed rather callously: 'I am not sorry to see it [closer union] wrecked, as it will be now.' Lord Winterton, visiting his estates in Northern Rhodesia, recorded indignation in central and southern Africa in his Diary[9]:

September 26th, 1930
The whole country is up in arms about the White Paper... [which] says native rights must be paramount, and where emigrant and native rights

are in conflict the latter must prevail. Whatever the intention of the framers of the document it is both injudicious and offensive, and the people here are as indignant and apprehensive as they are in Kenya.... Northern Rhodesia is being supported openly by Southern Rhodesia and at least one South African Minister — Groller [Grobler] — has expressed his sympathy with them.

As Winterton recorded, Piet Grobler reacted to the statement on Closer Union by asserting that the white man in Africa 'refused to consider the equality of Europeans and natives ... salvation must be found in the segregation of Whites and Blacks'. Hertzog also expressed his doubts about the East Africa policy and its effect on South Africa. The warning was not lost upon those watching in India. In April 1930, Habibullah was succeeded as Member in charge of the Department of Education, Health and Lands by Fazl-i-Husain, a Punjabi Mussalman, founder of the Unionist Party. Now, responsibility for Indians overseas was given to a party politician even more sensitive to the exposed position of his department. Fazl-i-Husain wrote to Bajpai about the South African intervention (13 October 1930): 'It appears that the Union Government ministers are going out of their way to embark upon racial warfare. I am told that Mr O. Pirow, Minister of Justice, and Mr Grobler, Minister of Lands, have recently made speeches raising the question that His Majesty's Government's policy relating to Kenya is wrong and that they must fight it out to the bitter end. Whether they are prepared to make a distinction between Indians and the natives I do not know; but if they are not, then obviously the principles they enunciate are such that India cannot but contest.'[10]

In general the Indian response to the changes which the White Papers seemed to portend was somewhat muffled by the march of events in India. The year opened with Gandhi's greatest satyagraha campaign, and there was no peace before the year's end. The publication of the Simon report on constitutional development in May, and the announcement of a Round Table Conference in London to draft a plan for India's future had a lesser impact; but they were important to the Indian Liberals. Sastri, that all-purpose Liberal, set out again for London, despite the shattering of his hopes the previous year; and Bajpai, that all-purpose official negotiator, went with him. When the conference opened, Ramsay MacDonald surveyed the theme of equality — the theme which challenged and baffled Indians and British throughout the years between the two world wars. Said MacDonald: 'I hope, I trust, and I pray that by our labours together India will come to possess the only thing which she now lacks to give her the status of a

Dominion — the responsibilities and the cares, the burdens and the difficulties, but the pride and the honour of representative self-government.'

Interest in India and Africa was high in British political circles; as one index, during the parliamentary session 1929-30, 471 questions were put down in the House of Commons for the Colonial Secretary to answer, and 493 were addressed to the Secretary for India.[11] The government intended to introduce a motion to set up a Joint Committee on the future of East Africa in both houses of parliament before the session ended, but there was not enough time to move the resolution in the House of Commons, so (under the rules of parliamentary procedure) in July Passfield had the ignominious duty of moving and then withdrawing his resolution in the House of Lords. He announced the intention to appoint a High Commissioner in East Africa, and then he mentioned the subject of the common roll as inconspicuously as possible. The High Commissioner would look into the question: 'Less than that we could not do. More than that perhaps it would have been rash to do.'[12]

The choice of the members of the Joint Committee assumed critical importance; Passfield leaned very far to make the committee an all-party body, when he got the names together in November. From the House of Commons he chose five Labour members (including Drummond Shiels, his Under Secretary, and Roden Buxton, chairman of the party's Imperial Committee), four Conservatives (including Amery and Ormsby-Gore), and one Liberal; from the Lords he selected two Labour peers besides himself, two Liberals, and five Conservatives (including Lugard). Besides weighting the committee with potential critics (the Labour total was only eight out of twenty), he offered the chairmanship to Lord Stanley of Alderley, a somewhat eccentric Conservative peer, thus depriving himself of the initiative and of the casting vote. It appears as though Sidney Webb felt he had made his contribution to solving the problems of Kenya, and would now leave it to others to decide.[13] The composition of the Joint Committee made inevitable the extinction of Indian hopes, based upon the recent White Papers; but it also ensured that Amery's hopes for Closer Union and white settler advancement were unlikely to succeed.

The committee met on fifty-three occasions and examined fifty-one witnesses, the great majority being Europeans, including Grigg, and the white settlers. Delamere was not among them; his robust frame had at last crumbled, and he died in 1931.[14] The new settler leader was Lord Francis Scott, who accepted that their policy had to be 'rule of thumb'.[15] The Indian witnesses were seen together, on one day, with Sastri as their principal spokesman. His message was the same: the East African Indian community 'wish, in one word, that their status in the Empire should not be inferior to that of any other community; that they should be recognised, as they are sometimes described, as partners in the Commonwealth, not merely as subject nations to be governed'.[16] The African witnesses were led by Chief Koinange: they all opposed Closer Union forcibly.

The Secretary for the Colonies submitted a report on progress to the Cabinet (30 May 1931) in which he anticipated that the Joint Committee would not recommend in favour of Closer Union. The witnesses from East Africa objected to finding the budget of £50,000 for the High Commissioner and his staff amid the deepening economic depression; the native witnesses showed 'unanimity' in opposing union, and the German government insisted that it went against the League mandate for Tanganyika. The Cabinet accepted these findings, but 'took no decision to alter their policy'.

After Sastri had given evidence, he told Benn (2 July 1930) that he had the impression that Webb was again going soft on the common roll, which was now only a 'distant goal'. Sastri was worried about possible effects upon the prospects for the Round Table Conference, which was due to gather for a second session in September 1931, with Gandhi as a participant. If the common roll was to be postponed to an undefined future, this would appear as 'proof that Indians are to be consigned to a position of permanent inferiority at the very moment when they are hoping to get dominion status'. Wedgwood Benn hastened to pass on Sastri's prognosis to Sidney Webb (8 July), and in return received a long handwritten letter which, with its many erasures and insertions, seemed to indicate the mental confusion of a man at the end of his tether. Webb declared (14 July) that all the evidence coming from East Africa was 'decidedly against change'. The Cabinet had never agreed to institute a common roll: they had only agreed to refer the question to the new High Commissioner, and now there would probably be no High Commissioner! Among the Labour minority of eight on the committee, not all were keen on the change, and the Liberals and Tories were 'dead against it'. Altogether, the committee was against the extension of parliamentary government in East Africa: 'Their strong inclination is towards "segregation" and "communal development" . . . each racial community advancing in its own way.'

Benn told Webb (21 July) that Labour members of the committee should go on record in favour of the common roll, even though they were out-voted by the others; then they would not be guilty of 'bad faith'. He also pressed for machinery to keep the common roll alive, in case the High Commissioner faded out. But Webb was not prepared to make such a gesture. When the committee was considering its proposals, Roden Buxton moved that there should be a common roll, based on a civilisation test: there were six Labour votes in favour and none from the other parties. By a majority of six, the proposal was negatived: Passfield, being present, abstained from voting. At the end of it all, Sidney wrote to Beatrice: 'It has been really a triumphant success for the "pro-natives" as against the settlers . . . This is a very satisfactory outcome for the past two years' trouble.'[17] By then, he was no longer Secretary of State for the Colonies, and Labour was no longer in power. The Joint Committee's report left everything more or less as it was. It affirmed the continuance of a dual policy: 'the complementary development of the native and non-native communities'; Closer Union disappeared, with only periodical conferences of the governors as a tenuous link; and the Kenya legislative process remained unchanged except for the contemplated addition of African representation.[18]

As we have seen, the Indians in East Africa were not well organised to respond to these political decisions. Some of the Indian leaders were inclined to accept appeals issued by the Government of India — and, of course, by the local government — to participate in the political process, and thus earn for themselves a larger share in decision-making. The more favourable prospects opened up by the 1930 White Paper encouraged the 'moderates', mainly based upon Mombasa, to contest the policy of non-cooperation laid down by the more radical Nairobi group. The Nairobi leaders in turn fell out, with Shams-ud-Deen advocating entry into the legislature and Isher Dass standing out for a campaign of non-cooperation until the common roll was granted. The acting governor of Kenya informed the Secretary of State (telegram of 5 February 1931) that the Congress desired to participate in the legislature and the municipalities, but three weeks later (11 March) the Governor was cabling that Isher Dass disputed the right of Shams-ud-Deen to speak for the Congress, while other protests flowed in. There was a trial of strength in May 1931, in elections for the legislature, when all five Indian seats were won by non-cooperators. The Indians continued to boycott the institutions of government until 1933, when the moderates, mainly business leaders, again came to the front.

The world slump seriously affected the East African Indians. Immigration had been running high in the 1920s; at the 1931 census it was found that the Kenya Indians had increased by 60 per cent since 1921 (1931: 43,623 Indians), while the white population was up by 75 per cent (1931: 16,182). The effect of the slump was to reverse the flow.

Arrivals and Departures of Indians in Kenya, 1931-1935

	Arrivals	Departures	Surplus	Deficit
1931	9,629	13,153		—3,524
1932	7,799	10,654		—2,855
1933	7,776	9,644		—1,868
1934	10,364	8,857	1,507	
1935	10,745	9,479	1,266	

The Indians were numerous on the railways and in the early 1920s there were 1,698 Indians and only 167 Europeans on the railway staff in Kenya. When the slump came, and staff had to be retrenched, there was discrimination between the two races. Some jobs were regraded and Indians were dismissed to make way for Europeans who did the Indians' old jobs under a new classification. Also, Indians were told that as an economy measure they were to be employed on a temporary basis (thus forfeiting their claim to pension leave and other benefits), while the Europeans were rapidly restored to permanent employment. The Indians learned the lesson that discrimination could be applied by means other than putting up notices labelled 'Whites Only'. After the efforts of the 1920s to force their way into the circle of white supremacy, in the 1930s they were reduced to a struggle to preserve their separate status as the intermediate community in between Whites and Blacks in East Africa.

When Beatrice Webb communed with her diary on the difficulties of applying 'the principles of self government to mixed populations', she was concerned about the difficulties in East Africa, Cyprus and— in particular — Palestine, which gave so much trouble to Sidney. By contrast there was 'the new constitution which is to be granted to Ceylon (said to be the work of Drummond Shiels) . . . on the model of a County Council. But then the population of Ceylon is more homogeneous than that of Kenya, Cyprus or Palestine'.[19]

Everything is relative, and relatively speaking this statement was accurate; but the attempt to make Ceylon a democracy — that is, to introduce a universal franchise — was to bring into emphasis the differences between the majority community and the minorities. The Indians, as immigrants, were the first to feel the force of Sinhalese nationalism.

The cosmopolitan *haute bourgeoisie* who formed the political class in Ceylon looked upon India as a kind of political barometer. Whenever India obtained an instalment towards self-government, the Ceylon elite began to press for a similar instalment of power for their island. The Montagu-Chelmsford reforms in India led to concessions for Ceylon. In 1921, and again in 1924, the legislature was made more representative of the educated elite. From 1924, the legislative council was composed of only twelve officials and thirty-seven non-officials. Of the latter, twenty-three were elected by territorial constituencies where, apart from the Tamils in the north, the representatives were Sinhalese. The remaining eleven seats were distributed on a communal basis and, among them, two were allocated to the Indians. The total electorate numbered only 200,000 out of a total population of five millions, being about four per cent of the population. The Indians voted on a register which covered the whole island, though they were also entitled to vote in the territorial seats. Because their two representatives were not very important in the legislature, the Indian vote was not an issue in Ceylon politics in the mid-1920s.

The working of the Ceylon system in the mid-1920s was said to have resulted in 'the divorce of power from responsibility'.[20] Although a brilliant administrator, Sir Hugh Clifford, was sent to put things right, there was general frustration. Irwin described the situation as 'the almost complete abandonment by Government of its constitutional powers'.[21] In August 1927, Amery appointed a special commission to advise on constitutional reform. The chairman was Lord Donoughmore and the other members were a Conservative historian, Sir Geoffrey Butler, a retired Governor, Sir Matthew Nathan, and Dr Drummond Shiels, the humanitarian Labour M.P. They visited Ceylon for two months, November 1927 to January 1928, and when they came to prepare the report it would seem that Drummond Shiels was able to persuade them to recommend an extension of the franchise on a scale never contemplated within the colonial empire before, and not seen again for another twenty years.

The commission was impressed both by the absence of any organised political parties in Ceylon and by the absence of any 'filtration' of the benefits of government to the mass of the ordinary people. In order to make authority responsive to the needs of the ordinary people, they recommended throwing open the vote to almost the entire adult population.[22] This reform was all the more unexpected because the Ceylon politicians had not included a more democratic franchise among their demands. They were specifically interested in acquiring a substantial instalment of self-government for themselves and their class. The Sinhalese politicians did suggest the abolition of communal representation, but the spokesmen from the minorities (the Tamils, the Ceylon Muslims or 'Moors' and the Eurasians or 'Burghers') all emphasised that without communal representation they would be swamped by the Sinhalese majority.

The Commission wholeheartedly recommended the liquidation of communal electorates. They were impressed with the view that communal institutions were a cause of communal attitudes, and they believed that under a territorial system there was a better hope for the emergence of a new politics based upon principles and parties instead of upon an identification with a traditional community or group. Under the changes they proposed, the island would be divided into fifty constituencies (instead of the previous 23 seats) and this would permit the voters to select representatives from their own local communities. The Commission was not unaware that the Indians on the estates constituted a special case. The report pronounced 'The problem of the Indian immigrant labourers is a serious and difficult one' (p. 95), thus deciding — as so many commentators have done, before and since — that the Indians constituted the problem: *not* those who viewed them as an intrusion. Whereas the Tamils, who were indigenous to Ceylon, were to some extent a separate community in the north, the Indians were located on estates in the heart of the island, around the historical upland capital Kandy. The Kandyans, though belonging to the same ethnic, linguistic and cultural group or society as the Sinhalese of the lowlands, resented their decline in importance since the days of the Kandyan kingdom. Now, they found that their new constituencies would be infiltrated by outsiders — the coolies on the tea estates. The Donoughmore Commissioners were only dimly conscious of these feelings. They recommended that the franchise should be given after five years' residence in Ceylon, so as to exclude those who were transients. With that qualification, they were content to conclude that through their territorial representatives the Indians would achieve 'a more effective expression of their grievances and difficulties' (p. 97).

As soon as the Donoughmore Report was published (1928), a storm broke over the issue of the franchise and the admission of the Indian coolies to the vote. In the debate in the legislature, speaker after speaker opposed the extension of the vote to the Indians and demanded that the franchise be restricted by literacy and income or property qualifications in their case. A resolution was moved on these lines, and the mover stated: 'It has been said that this resolution of mine is brought in with the object of keeping out a large number of Indian voters. There is no use of any camouflage in this matter: I will boldly admit that that is so.' Another speaker declared: 'What I fear most is the cooly on the estate.' D. S. Senanayake, already emerging as a formidable politician, made a different point: 'We were told that if anyone of us went to England it would not be difficult for him to get the vote. But I wonder what the people of England will say if every year hundreds of thousands of people were recruited from abroad into England.'[23] He ended on a more generous note: 'We do not consider the Indians as aliens. We tell them "Become part of ourselves, become Ceylonese, and then share in the government of the country."'

When Sir Herbert Stanley, the Governor, came to address the Secretary of State on the Donoughmore proposals and Ceylon's response to them, he followed up Senanayake's argument: 'Exception is taken to the [estate labourers'] wholesale territorial enfranchisement not because they are Indians but because they are not regarded as Ceylonese.' They were a 'potential menace to the local predominance of the Ceylonese voter' in some constituencies. Fear was expressed that the Indian vote would be 'manipulated' by opinion-leaders in India. Stanley accepted the demand by the Ceylonese politicians that the Indians must provide greater evidence of their 'abiding interest' in the land of their adoption. This could be obtained by their acquring a Ceylon domicile; but this might be difficult to define for electoral purposes, so the Governor recommended that either they qualify for the vote on the old literacy or property qualifications, or else they must obtain 'certificates of permanent residence'.

By the time the despatch arrived in London, Amery had given way to Sidney Webb, but, advised by Drummond Shiels, he accepted the Governor's proposals. In terminating the separate communal seats, the Secretary of State piously expressed his 'sincere hope' that minorities would not be barred from election.[24] On the basis of the modified Indian franchise, the Ceylon legislature voted to accept the new constitution by nineteen votes to seventeen; the Sinhalese members formed the assenting vote, with the minorities recording their dissent.

The decisive vote was taken on 12 December 1929, and the proceedings were noted with resentment and anger in India, where the Central Legislative Assembly debated the 'anti-Indian character of the proposals' on 11 February 1930. The Government of India was moved to send a strong telegram to the India Office on 21 February; it was expected that in order to obtain a certificate of permanent residence the Indian labourers would have to renounce the protection previously afforded by the Agent of the Government of India in Ceylon, and perhaps lose the guaranteed rights which Indian estate labour enjoyed by agreement between the two governments. The Indian Government's Agent estimated that at most five or six Indians would succeed in winning seats: and surely there was 'nothing wrong' in the Indians holding the balance in some constituencies? Objections were made against the device of special qualifications being required from Indian voters only: 'We are sure His Majesty's Government do not expect us to be satisfied with lower status in neighbouring Asiatic colony, a result which would seem to follow from application to Ceylon of the principle which holds the field in South Africa.' The telegram ended by announcing that, unless the franchise terms were reviewed, Indian opinion would demand the termination of emigration to Ceylon. The combination of rhetoric and threat was not perhaps the best opening to a negotiation. When the telegram was passed on to the Colonial Office, it produced a retort in similar polemical vein (26 March 1930). Lord Passfield would discuss the Indian franchise with Stanley before taking a final decision, but Indians in Ceylon were not 'under special disabilities', and Stanley's intention was to 'prevent an outburst in Ceylon of that racial ill feeling'. Subsequently, the Colonial Office told the India Office (30 May) that a threat to stop Indian emigration 'would stiffen rather than relax the existing opposition': sanctions imposed by the Government of India would affect British-owned plantations and would not worry Ceylonese politicians.

Time was now getting short; Stanley pleaded for a decision so that he could return to Ceylon, and Passfield told Wedgwood Benn that he would ask the next meeting of the Cabinet to endorse his proposals. Benn replied (27 May) that the question should be taken off the Cabinet's agenda, so that he might first try to reach an agreement with Stanley and Passfield. He added: 'There are obvious advantages in securing a settlement which the Government of India can defend. Otherwise the position might easily drift into one of open hostility between the two governments.'

The Colonial Office was not prepared to wait any longer, and the Cabinet meeting on 28 May was invited to consider a memorandum on the new constitution.[25] In calling for a decision, Passfield observed: 'The continued impression that His Majesty's Government are considering under pressure from the Government of India proposals for the abandonment of safeguards to which the Ceylonese attach vital importance is creating an unfavourable atmosphere.' He had 'gone to the limit'. Now he asked for approval of his draft Order in Council. However, the Cabinet declined to put aside India's objections, and in giving their assent to the Order in Council insisted that there must be a further consultation between Passfield and Benn on 'any outstanding points of detail'.

Once again Sir Louis Kershaw acted as go-between. He met Webb and Shiels on 30 May and asked for certain amendments. Somehow, Sastri (in London for the Round Table Conference) came to know about the meeting and wrote to Benn the next day that he had heard 'last night their fate was sealed', though he hoped that 'the dark deed has not been wrought after all'. The Colonial Office certainly wanted to seal the affair, and wanted to give as little as possible. When the final draft of the despatch intended for the Governor of Ceylon was shown to Kershaw, he found that certain assurances were missing. He told Wedgood Benn (5 June): 'My conversations ... made it clear that the Colonial Office were endeavouring to wriggle out of the bargain made by Lord Passfield.' Kershaw told the Colonial Office that, unless their requirements were met, the Secretary for India would insist on the question being taken back to the Cabinet. In the end, it was agreed that the despatch would include a directive to the Governor that he must deal with any legislation which would threaten the conditions of the Indian labourers, by 'reserving' the bill for His Majesty's pleasure (that is, referring it to London before giving it the royal assent). On 10 June 1930, Passfield cabled to Governor Stanley that there was 'no intention of repealing or amending to the detriment of the Indians any of the laws of Ceylon affecting their position or privileges'.

The whole long-drawn-out episode left both sides with a sense of grievance. The Ceylon politicians felt that their advance towards self-government was liable to be checked by the interested meddling of the Indian government, while Indians believed that the Colonial Office was (as in so many other colonial territories) conniving at pushing them into an inferior position. The Indians in Ceylon were not always well served by their leaders whose ambitions were bound to upset the Ceylonese politicians. In December 1932, V. Kathrithamby, a prominent Jaffna Indian, sent a manifesto to Sir Samuel Wilson headed 'Constitutional Reforms, Ceylon: Federation with India is the Cure'. Sastri read this document and commented: 'Some day this must happen. Maybe in thirty or forty years. I spoke twice or three times about it in London. There is no chance now. All the tendency is the other way. The Britisher is bent on crippling India.' Sastri did not have Nehru's capacity to see other countries through the eyes of their own leaders.

At the first election under the new constitution, the Indian vote proved less important than expected. Two Indians were elected from territorial constituencies, but two of the 'planting' constituencies returned European members. The authority of the European planters was powerful enough to induce many of their labourers to vote for them. The Sinhalese won 38 of the 50 seats, but this success only made them impatient to move ahead faster. Three years later, D. S. Senanayake, now identified as the contender for political leadership in Ceylon, came to London to talk with the Secretary for the Colonies. In a letter to Sir Philip Cunliffe-Lister (19 June 1933) he put on record the view that the Donoughmore constitution 'was to transfer to the elected representatives complete control over the internal affairs of the island'. Donoughmore and his colleagues had recognised that their reforms were only transitional and temporary: 'a vantage ground from which it would be possible to advance towards full self-government'. In passing, Senanayake noted that the domicile provisions for Indian voters were 'increasingly difficult' to accept. He ended by criticising the habit of travelling British statesmen giving their views of Ceylon's progress: 'Criticism of this nature, if taken seriously, can well make another "India" -of Ceylon.' What he meant, of course, was that if any attempt were made to check Ceylon's further political advance the leaders would switch from cooperation to non-cooperation: it was the gentlest possible hint.

In Ceylon, the discovery that in the advance towards self-government the Indian community could be seen as a barrier, or at least a digression, was translated into a constitutional response: an argument about Indian participation in the electoral process. In Burma the same discovery took place in the 1920s, but the first response was direct and violent: the anti-Indian riots of 1930. As a province of the British Indian Empire, Burma was brought into the Montagu-Chelmsford scheme of reforms; though somewhat belatedly. Beatrice Webb's observations about Ceylon could have been applied to Burma with equal relevance. Burma was more homogeneous than India, with its intractable Muslim minority; yet, beside the majority community — Burmese-speaking, Buddhist, conscious of a long history — there were other peoples cast in the role of minorities in a situation of political competition. Some were indigenous peoples — the Shans, Karens, Mons, and others, to whom Burma was their motherland; but there were also immigrants — Europeans, Chinese, and about 900,000 Indians. Under the new 'Dyarchy', whereby many functions of government were transferred to ministers responsible to the provincial legislature, the Burmese found themselves dependent on the minorities when invited to form ministries and govern their country. The legislature was composed of a total of 103 members, of whom three-quarters (79) were now elected. Of the seventy-nine elected members, only fifty-eight represented 'general' (i.e. Burmese) constituencies. Unless almost all the Burmese seats were won by a single party (an impossibility in the 1920s, for parties were as amorphous in Burma as in Ceylon) then the Burmese ministers had to rely upon the support of the officials, the nominated members, and the minorities—who filled 21 seats, or a fifth of the total. The minorities soon realised their own value, and traded their support for all it was worth.

The Indians formed the largest group among the minorities. There were eight Indian members, of whom four represented Rangoon, which in the 1920s seemed more like an Indian city than the capital of Burma. Perhaps it was not surprising that the Burmese politicians, especially U Ba Pe, began to demand the separation of Burma from the Indian Empire as the necessary starting-point for any advance to self-government. The resentment of a proud people against their subjugation by British, and also Indian troops as recently as 1885-6 had never died down; now it found a focus in the Indians living in Burma: 'Besides taking our country and our property, they take our sisters', said U Pu in the legislature. He referred to the many marriages between Indians and Burmese girls, some being life-long unions but others liable to end when the transient returned to India. 'What use will Home Rule be to us if it is given by the English when the Burmese nation has become half-caste by gradual extinction?'[26]

Frustration increased after the third general elections (1928), when the Burmese ministers relied upon the Indian members to keep them in office. U Ba Pe, the Nationalist leader, proposed a motion on 18 February 1929 for immediate separation from India: 'If we are to get Dominion Home Rule we must first separate from India and ask for Dominion status ourselves.' Among the Indian members, there was S. A. S. Tyabji, a member of a distinguished political family, originally from Bombay, but long identified with Burma. He replied: 'It was a question which Burma itself ought to decide, and Indians would loyally abide by that decision.' But there were other Indian voices insisting that any Burmese calling for separation were lackeys of the British, and when the Mayor of Calcutta, J. M. Sen Gupta, visited Rangoon he made speeches strongly denouncing separation.

The atmosphere was stormy: the world slump had badly hit Burma's export prices, while in India Gandhi's challenge to British authority was about to be answered by Irwin. He was arrested on 4 May 1930 on a day marked by an earthquake in Burma. In

Rangoon, a great part of the Indian labour force went on strike in protest against the arrest: they included the workers in rice and timber mills, railway workers, and the city scavengers. In the docks, almost all the labour was Indian — many from the east coast province of Orissa. When they also went on strike, the port authorities engaged Burmese to unload the ships. Previously, the Burmese had looked down on coolie work, but now times were difficult. 'Burman labour is admittedly more inefficient than Indian labour', the Governor, Sir Charles Innes, told the Viceroy (30 May 1930), and as soon as the Indians indicated they would return to work the new Burmese dockers were discharged. Resentment at being cast aside led to retaliation against the Indians, and within a few hours the centre of Rangoon was a battlefield.

The Indian rickshaw pullers were an obvious target, and about 2,000 of their vehicles were destroyed. The centre of the city was occupied by about 6,000 Burmese bully boys, 'rushed up by motor buses', according to the Governor (9 June), and some 7,000 Indians were temporarily refugees. Many were frightened into leaving Burma, Innes told Irwin (23 June); there were 33,000 departures from Rangoon during June, and very few arrivals. 'The Burman is thoroughly pleased with himself at what he regards as his victory in the disturbances', reported Innes. One response to the riots by Innes was to address the Legislative Council (5 August) with assurances that Burma could choose separation and expect a constitution no less advanced than would come to India after the Round Table Conference. Burma was given its own Round Table Conference; then came a general election contested between separationists and anti-separationists: the latter were Burmese politicians who just did not believe that the British government intended to make the same concessions to a separated Burma as to India. The issue was not clearly decided, and without any strong impulse from the Burmese leaders the country moved towards separation.

Though Ceylon and Burma were beginning to stir to the demands of indigenous nationalism, Malaya remained a country where administration, not politics, provided the framework. The only politics which mattered was the pressure of the European rubber industry upon the government. The United Planting Association of Malaya (U.P.A.M.) addressed the High Commissioner of the Federated Malay States upon equal terms. Apart from some Dutch firms, the industry was almost wholly controlled from the United Kingdom, and a Rubber Growers' Association in London, made up of the big firms (such as Guthries) was always able to put over its views effectively to the Colonial Office. The Indians were almost entirely excluded from politics and power, which—formally Malay in character—was preserved by the British from external intrusion. A few Indians, as individuals, received recognition. P. K. Nambyar, a Penang barrister, was nominated to the legislature of the Straits Settlements in 1923. When Sir Hugh Clifford moved on from Ceylon to become Governor of the Straits Settlements and High Commissioner for Malaya, Lord Irwin wrote to ask him to appoint an Indian to the Federal Council of the Malay States, in conformity with the practice in other colonies with an Indian population (21 September 1927). Clifford replied sympathetically (18 November 1927): 'I realise to the full ... how embarrassing [is] the *non possumus* attitude which the Government of the Federated Malay States has hitherto been inclined to take up.' However, Clifford saw no hope of persuading Ormsby-Gore (in charge at the Colonial Office while Amery was on his world tour) to make the change. In 1928, S.N. Veerasamy, another barrister, was appointed to the Federal Council, while a handful of Indians were brought onto the councils of the Malay rulers, the first being Louis Thivy, the Indian owner of a rubber plantation, nominated to the Perak State Council in 1929.[27]

In the absence of trades unions and political representation, the Indian labourers had to depend upon the activities of the Agent of the Government of India on their behalf. During the 1920s, steady pressure by the Agent had the effect of inducing most of the rubber estates to conform to a standard wages structure. Prices in the 1920s were volatile, but in general the times were prosperous, and thanks to the efforts of the Agent wages were raised until in February 1929 they were 50 cents a day for men and 40 cents for women. These rates were considerably lower than those paid to comparable Chinese workers, but the pace of the work was not so hard.

This era of relative prosperity came abruptly to an end in 1930, and with immediate effect the wages were reduced to 40 cents a day for men and 32 cents for women. The rubber planters saw their hope of survival in a system of reduced production, and the Indian government's Agent also believed that a reduction in the labour force would benefit the Indian community. He informed the Indian Immigration Committee at Kuala Lumpur (which controlled wage-rates): 'It is better that superfluous numbers whom the industry cannot maintain and who cannot find satisfactory work in this country are repatriated home than that they are made to continue on reduced wages under precarious conditions; their numbers being multiplied every week by thousands of fresh arrivals' (16 July 1930). The Agent also wrote to the Government of India (2 August) urging them to assume control over the situation: in Malaya, 'the authorities left the matter to the wishes of the planters, and planters desire nothing but an unlimited supply of cheap Indian labour'. Following these representations, assisted emigration from India was stopped, and the estate workers were given the option of a free return passage to India. Assisted emigration was not resumed to Malaya until 1934, and during three years 330,000 Indians left Malaya, compared to less than 150,000 arrivals.

Arrivals and Departures in Burma, Ceylon and Malaya, 1927-35

BURMA

	Arrivals	Departures	Surplus	Deficit
1927	361,086	280,739	80,347	
1928	360,129	263,345	96,784	
1929	345,906	294,574	51,332	
1930	301,917	314,429		—10,512
1931	266,105	288,696		—22,591
1932	274,193	224,098	50,095	
1933	216,658	194,925	21,733	
1934	228,357	179,773	48,584	
1935	246,059	176,470	69,589	

CEYLON

	Arrivals	Departures	Surplus	Deficit
1927	159,398	89,783	69,217	
1928	133,712	97,088	36,624	
1929	105,095	104,411	684	
1930	91,422	106,190		—14,768
1931	68,337	91,573		—23,176
1932	50,869	72,495		—21,626
1933	32,898	88,969		—56,071
1934	140,607	54,785	85,822	
1935	43,078	49,288		— 6,210

MALAYA

	Arrivals	Departures	Surplus	Deficit
1927	167,624	93,022	74,602	
1928	72,790	91,430		—18,740
1929	133,609	76,854	56,755	
1930	86,152	152,231		—66,079
1931	32,429	102,090		—69,079
1932	27,516	85,051		—57,535
1933	41,177	33,291	7,886	
1934	104,827	24,467	76,360	
1935	81,350	38,869	42,481	

The reverse of the normal outward emigration flow to the nearby lands of Burma and Ceylon was also dramatic. Although emigration eventually started up again, the break in the pattern had lasting results. The planters began to think in terms of economising their use of labour; the indigenous people began to consider estate work as a possible source of employment; and India thought again about the whole system of exporting cheap Indian labour which was expendable and returnable when not required.

The return of the Indians in their hour of distress to the motherland served to demonstrate how much they still regarded India as 'home', and also how far they were treated as transients by the colonies which lived upon their labour. In 1932, Sir Samuel Wilson undertook another busy voyage of inquiry to Malaya. His remit was more general than in East Africa (he was looking at the policy of decentralisation) and his remarks about the Indians of Malaya reflected the vague Colonial Office policy of designating them as an integral element within the colonial population though in no specific way giving them a recognised place in the colonial system. Wilson's report did little to change things. He declared: 'Non-Malays domiciled in Malaya are loyal. So it has been the policy of the Government to accord full recognition to their status as British subjects...and British protected persons.' But this was an empty form of recognition when most of the Indians had no means of obtaining advancement through education—even primary education was lacking—while, for the few who were educated, there were no openings in the higher civil services or in the rubber industry, which was the staple of the Malayan economy. Hence, Wilson's declaration rang hollow, as he partially recognised himself when he went on: 'Subject to the policy of preferential employment of qualified Malays in Government services and the reservation of sufficient lands for Malay needs, I take the view that persons born in the Malay states of non-Malay parents should be treated in those states in exactly the same way as persons born in the colony [the Straits Settlements] of non-Malay parents and should have the same professional and business opportunities as European British subjects.'[28] But equality without any opportunity was equality denied, as the Agent of the Government of India and others were not slow to point out.

In 1930, the relations between the United Kingdom and the self-governing Dominions were adjusted so as to recognise the formal equality of the partner-nations of the Commonwealth. The Governor-General in each Dominion ceased to be the agency for correspondence with Britain; in future he was the representative, the Viceroy of the Crown, seen as the King of Canada, Australia, or South Africa. To mark the new relationship, Great Britain appointed High Commissioners in each of the British Dominions to act as the agents of the United Kingdom. The white self-governing colonies had begun to keep their own representatives in London in the 1880s, but they did not now follow the logic of the new form of association by appointing High Commissioners to each other: Canada to Australia, or South Africa to Eire. India's Agent in South Africa remained the sole quasi-diplomatic representative from one Commonwealth partner to another.

The 1930 conference went a little further towards introducing separate forms of Dominion citizenship in parallel with the common bond of British nationality. The Dominions Office noted: 'As regards Nationality there is the question of the general adoption of a system of citizenship (or nationality) of the component parts of the Empire in addition to "British nationality" in its present sense. If this system is adopted there will be "Australian Citizens", "South African Citizens", etc. . . . If the Dominions act on these lines there will presumably come into existence a recognised category of "Indian nationals".'[29] When the conference came to consider changes in nationality law it was agreed that this should be put into effect only after 'consultation and agreement' among all the members of the British Commonwealth. The effect of this decision was to postpone change indefinitely, for some states — South Africa in particular — were invariably unable to agree to changes proposed.

Meanwhile, India tried to employ the occasion of the conference, with its warm, shared atmosphere, to obtain something nearer to equality for Indians already domiciled in the Dominions. The Government of India had selected a very 'safe' representative at the conference: Sir Muhammad Shafi, one of the few Muslim leaders to cooperate with the Simon commission in its inquiries in India. Shafi was able to report some progress with the Australian prime minister, J. H. Scullin. He told Benn (16 November 1930) that it was Scullin's own view 'now that the Dominions had attained full nationhood they were under an obligation to maintain the unity of the Empire by removing all causes of friction between one another'. Queensland did admit its few Indians to the franchise in 1930, and only Western Australia continued to discriminate against them. Shafi was less successful with Mackenzie King, who told him that 'the penetration of Orientals' was still a 'live issue' in British Columbia.

While the Imperial Conference was sitting, the situation in South Africa was again becoming dark for the Indians. Another bill was introduced into parliament at Cape Town to restrict the activities of Indians: the Transvaal Asiatic Land Tenure Bill. Lord Athlone told Irwin (21 August 1930) that the Bill was not a government measure, and was designed to deal with 'admitted contraventions and evasions of existing laws'.[30] Because the Bill did not touch the field covered by the Cape Town agreement, it was difficult to oppose it, Athlone declared. Reddi, India's Agent, took a different view: Indians were certainly breaking the law by trading without licences; but this was because no new licences had been granted to Indians since 1929 (Reddi to Irwin, 23 August 1930). In September, Bajpai met Hertzog at the session of the League of Nations in Geneva, and found him ready to discuss these 'hard cases'. C. F. Andrews decided to go to South Africa to try to mediate; he found that the South African Indian Congress was getting ready for a bitter struggle, and planned non-cooperation on Gandhian lines. However, the Indian community was disunited, and a total commitment seemed uncertain. Congress set up a committee — C. F. Andrews, and two local leaders, S. B. Medh and P. K. Desai — to try to obtain another round table conference, with the South African Indians included. Meanwhile, Lord Irwin was in touch with the new Governor-General of South Africa, the Earl of Clarendon, who was also worried by Malan's growing hostility. But on 2 February 1931 he was able to assure Irwin that if the Government of India would ask for the postponement of the Bill this might be accepted. Four days later, Reddi informed Irwin that Malan intended to advise parliament to adjourn the Bill. The official notification of the postponement came in a telegram to Irwin on 31 March: the South African government was ready to enter another round table conference.

At this point, Irwin departed from India. He was succeeded by Lord Willingdon. Geoffrey Dawson told Irwin that he was a 'thoroughly bad choice' (21 January 1931), 'he never had much stuff in him'. Subsequent events did not nullify Dawson's verdict. There was also a new Secretary of State, Sir Samuel Hoare, who was to hold office until 1935. His attention was first absorbed by the Round Table Conference in London, which concluded its second session (with Gandhi at the conference table) at the end of November.[31] The sympathy for Indian aspirations which had marked Irwin's regime now gave way to an emphasis upon good government and imperial control.[32] However, the subject of Indians overseas still generated a certain awareness that Indian interests were not always synonymous with those of Whitehall in this area.

Once again, an impressive delegation was assembled to represent India at the second Cape Town conference. Fazl-i-Husain, the Member in charge, led the party, which again included Sastri, d'Arcy Lindsay and Corbett. Sarojini Naidoo, the poet and close friend of Gandhi, was a notable addition, while Reddi and Bajpai made up the official element.

Before departing Fazl-i-Husain told the Viceroy's Council that 'the position of the Indian delegation in the conference was a most unpleasant one — suppliants begging for alms and not negotiators. We had no sanction behind us and the Union Government had the whip hand. I asked for authority to break off in case we found we were to agree to intolerable things'.[33] Fazl-i-Husain was a realist: if they could obtain small concessions, he was ready to agree, knowing that their bargaining power was non-existent; but he was not prepared to capitulate and settle for nothing. The dilemma was to torment Indian negotiators in South Africa thereafter: Should they accept the little that was offered, submitting themselves to gross inequalities? Or should they spurn the offering and enjoy the satisfaction of a moral victory? Either course would end in frustration.

The South Africans also assembled a strong negotiating team. Dr. Malan was leader, with two ministerial colleagues, Oswald Pirow and E. G. Jansen. There were also two representatives of the opposition, Patrick Duncan and G. Heaton Nicholls, a bluff ex-private of the British Army who was to play a lengthy part in the fortunes of the Indians of Natal. Unfortunately, Fazl-i-Husain became seriously ill on his arrival and Sir Geoffrey Corbett had to lead the Indian delegation. It soon became clear that the events of 1927 would not be repeated. The Nationalist leaders were disillusioned over the poor Indian response to the repatriation offer, which to them was the main advantage of the Cape Town agreement. The conference opened on 12 January, and at once confronted deadlock. Sastri managed to attract some South African interest by suggesting that if return to India was an inadequate solution perhaps the South African Indians might be interested in emigrating to new lands where no colour bar existed. However, the local Congress leaders refused to endorse this suggestion, and on 21 January the Union government replied that the time had come to return to a tough policy, pushing on with the Transvaal Asiatic Land Tenure Bill and other measures to squeeze the Indians. Mrs Naidoo went back to the local Congress leadership, and on 26 January was able to report that they were prepared to cooperate in exploring outlets for colonisation; though they still insisted that they disliked the proposal. The conference ended on 4 February with agreement that a committee would examine the possibilities of emigration to Brazil, British Guiana, Tanganyika, and other places; a representative of the South African Indian Congress would be associated with the committee. However, this conclusion still left the future of the restrictive legislation undecided. The Union government was only prepared to offer one more year's extension of the 1927 agreement, pending the new inquiry. Fazl-i-Husain, who had somewhat recovered, regarded this as inadequate, and informed the Government of India that he proposed to break off negotiations. But when he asked Malan whether he was prepared to offer any new terms, he produced new suggestion which kept the door of negotiation ajar. The delegation embarked for India, with the future of the Land Tenure Bill still in the balance, but with the possibility of an agreement.

On their return to Delhi, the delegates reported their problems to Lord Willingdon. Fazl-i-Husain was embarrassed to find that the Viceroy knew very little about the South African question: 'It was a great relief when it was one o'clock and we went to lunch.'[34] Not until 5 April was it possible to issue a joint announcement by South Africa and India concerning the future. Emphasis was laid upon the new project of exploring suitable openings for Indian emigration from South Africa, but to India the most important gain was the elimination from the Land Tenure Bill of penalties against the Indians. South African Indian leaders were beginning to divide into two groups. The moderates, led by A. I. Kajee, realised that in the prevailing atmosphere the most they could achieve was to prevent the situation from deteriorating further. Recognition of the Indians as full South African citizens would have to wait for better days. The more radical Indian leaders were not prepared to wait; if negotiation yielded no results, then they must resort to direct action. It was the unenviable task of the Indian government's Agent to try to hold the radicals in check and, at the same time, to coax the Union government into giving some appearance of credibility to a policy of patience by not making things worse. Reddi had not been a great success; he had been ill, and he had faltered at the crisis of the Land Tenure Bill. 'He has not got a clear grasp of our views', reported the Viceroy.[35] As his successor, Maharaj Singh was sent to South Africa. An old Harrovian, an aristocrat, he brought dignity and experience to the task, while his wife contributed a notable grace and charm. These qualifications were more likely to impress the South African Whites than the Indians, however.

Maharaj Singh was not encouraged by what he found. He told Sastri that there was 'little else that one can do besides creating future opinion in our favour'; he added 'It is our own people that disappoint me most, it seems; and that is the hardest to bear. I know that you have suffered great things at the hands of some of our great Indian leaders out here.'³⁶ A few months later (6 June 1933) he was writing to G. A. Natesan, the veteran publicist, 'Those loyal to Mr. Sastri and the vision of a true Liberal policy out here consider the general atmosphere is better than it was five, ten, or twenty years ago. But there are likely to be setbacks and in any case there are serious difficulties ahead. Probably a self-governing India *will* help us here. Here again, excessive optimism is undesirable, for an existing self-governing China is more helpless with her nationals here than the Government of India.'

In 1933, South African politics entered another chapter of the same story, with the setting up of a coalition government, headed by Hertzog, with Smuts as his deputy and with Malan leading a faction of 'pure', unreconstructed Nationalists against this deal. The new government appointed an Indian Colonisation Enquiry Committee. The chairman was James Young, a former Johannesburg magistrate, and the members were P. F. Kincaid, Commissioner for Immigration and Asiatic Affairs, and Heaton Nicholls. In addition to his participation in the second Cape Town conference, Nicholls had initiated an important change in relations between the races in South Africa when, in 1930, he proposed that Africans should be removed from the common electoral roll of the Cape Province in exchange for separate representation in the Senate.³⁷

It was now necessary to find an Indian member of the committee. The Executive of the South African Indian Congress agreed that they should join the committee and nominated S. R. Naidoo as their representative. The radical minority opposed cooperation, and endeavoured to reverse the Executive's decision by calling an emergency conference at Durban in August 1933, where militants would be able to exert pressure on the moderates. Sir Maharaj Singh (as he now was) opened the conference: he urged cooperation, saying 'Sink your differences. You are not strong enough to be divided'. Kajee served notice that if they were opposed they would fight, with their backs to the wall.³⁸ The appointment of Naidoo as the Congress representative was approved by 63 votes to 8. The radicals, led by Manilal Gandhi, P.R. Pather and Albert Christopher, tried to reverse the decision at a series of public meetings in Durban. At one of these, Lady Maharaj Singh faced the unruly audience with the unpopular message: 'You talk of non-cooperation, but two can play that game. You can refuse to cooperate with the government and it can refuse to cooperate with you.' Unfortunately, this was all too obvious.

When the committee met, probably the only participant who believed that it might yield positive results was Heaton Nicholls. As a younger man he had been a pioneer district officer in Australian

New Guinea, and he was enthusiastic about the possibilities for Indian settlement in the Pacific. S. R. Naidoo was soon disenchanted; he complained to Sastri 'I am sick and tired of the whole thing ... There is a real split in the community'. He wrote again that the Indians 'charge me with treachery and with having been heavily bribed by the Union Government'. Later, he told Sastri that 'A country annexed to and ruled by India primarily for colonisation by people from India was to be searched for and its possibilities examined'.[39] Swaziland was mentioned: but this came to nothing.[40] The committee amassed detailed information about British Guiana, North Borneo and New Guinea, which was issued as the *Report of the Indian Colonization Committee, 1933-34*, but this was received almost in silence. C. F. Andrews declared that the inquiry had shown that no colonisation scheme was possible, and Maharaj Singh noted that there was 'surprisingly little interest' in the report.[41]

The report led to a debate in the Council of State, the upper house of the Indian legislature, on 9 August 1934. Fazl-i-Husain moved a resolution calling upon the South African government to implement the promise of the 'upliftment' of the Indian community, asseverating: 'there is hope that civilised world opinion will one day be moved to overcome these racial prejudices.' A surprising feature of the debate was a move by a private member, Hossain Imam, inviting the Government of India to urge the United Kingdom Government to set apart a colony for Indian emigration. Speaking before his departure to South Africa, Syed Raza Ali was scornful of Indian emigration: 'The kind of stuff that India sent out to various colonies is not one of which we as a nation could be very proud.... These men do not add to the good name or reputation of India, and do not produce an impression that India is one of the civilised countries of the world.' This was not in itself an impressive reply to Hossain Imam, but Fazl-i-Husain, in winding up the debate, did better by rejecting the idea of a separate, unequal colonial haven for the Indians: it was a 'defeatist policy', he said, and must 'create a *Harijan* [Untouchable] quarter amongst the colonies of the British Empire'. If the Government of India had gained only 'indifferent success, does that justify our abandoning the position of equality in the civilised world?' Despite Fazl-i-Husain's spirited reply, when a vote was taken nine members voted to ask for a separate colony (including Sir Jagdish Prasad, who was to succeed Fazl-i-Husain in the Viceroy's Council), while twenty-seven—including the official bloc—voted to reject the motion.

As time passed, and it became obvious that the Heaton Nicholls inquiry would never be followed up by the Government of India, the South African leaders again became restless. When the imperial leaders gathered in London in March 1935 for the Silver Jubilee, the Indian representative, Sir Joseph Bhore, was asked to assure Hertzog that the Government of India had not backed down from the 1932 undertakings. When Bhore talked to Hertzog he found him ready to be mollified: the fraternal atmosphere of imperial conferences appeared to have a striking effect upon recalcitrant Dominion premiers. Hertzog even observed that 'The more he came into contact with the best type of Indians . . . the more he regretted the attitude of his people. . . . Time, however, was required to educate them'. And so another awkward corner was turned.

When Fazl-i-Husain and the other delegates to the 1932 Cape Town conference were returning to India, their ship put into the port of Dar-es-Salaam. The local Indian community presented a petition (15 February 1932) in which they complained that, despite a theoretical policy of racial equality in Tanganyika, there were no Indians in the judiciary or the administration. They suggested that this contravened the mandate and should be reported to the League of Nations. When the question was referred to the India Office it was explained that India, as a member of the League, was entitled to refer a breach of the mandate to the Permanent Court of the League of Nations: except that all the Dominions had agreed that internal differences within the British Commonwealth would not be taken to the League. Only the Irish Free State had not accepted this agreement; so India could hardly appeal to international opinion : not in 1932.

There were other voices from East Africa, and one of the most impressive was that of the Aga Khan, speaking on behalf of the Ismaili community, who were powerful in trade and industry, especially in Tanganyika. The Aga Khan told the Secretary for India, Sir Samuel Hoare (27 September 1932): 'I am proud to say . . . that my followers have during the past eighty years been absolutely loyal, and, in East Africa especially, have prevented a kind of Gandhi influence that permeated South Africa from getting hold of the imagination of the Indians'. The Aga Khan was anxious that this loyalty should be recognised by generous treatment of the Ismaili community and support for the schools they had founded. He did not feel that they were adequately treated. The Colonial Office 'makes no difference between my people and Gandhi's' he told Hoare (8 December 1932), though the Ismailis were the 'real and important pivot in the East for the British Empire' (30 May 1934).

The base from which the Ismailis had spread out in East Africa was Zanzibar, and it was in Zanzibar that the Indians — domiciled on the island for centuries — suddenly had cause to feel that their whole future was threatened. During 1934 a series of decrees was issued in the name of the Sultan by the British Resident which undermined Indian interests in every way.⁴² The Government of India and the India Office made protests. Hoare told the Secretary for the Colonies, Cunliffe-Lister (25 July 1934): 'Indian opinion is intensely sensitive about the treatment which Indians have received in the past in some of the colonies.' Nationalist India might seek to retaliate against British trade and industry if this was intensified. Cunliffe-Lister tried to justify the decrees by reference to the 'extortionate rates of interest' of Indian moneylenders and by the new colonial policy of establishing government marketing organisations (31 July). The Government of India was not appeased, and despatched K. P. S. Menon (formerly Indian Agent in Ceylon) to make an on-the-spot investigation. Menon reported that he had found the Indian community 'in a state of panic'.⁴³ He examined the decrees and their application in quite a detached way, and concluded that some were justified but that the measures directed against the marketing and export of cloves were 'calculated to cause irretrievable damage to Indian interests and will practically oust the Indian traders from Zanzibar'. Despite mounting Indian concern, the Colonial Office adhered to its policy of dismantling the Indian commercial network in Zanzibar.

The next attack upon Indian interests (in the somewhat overwrought estimation of the East African Indians) was the report of the Kenya Land Commission, usually called the Carter Report. Sir Morris Carter and his colleagues were given the task of working out a policy of land tenure in Kenya. Like Ormsby-Gore in 1925, Carter does not seem to have been bothered by any view of East Africa other than that of the white settlers. He and his two colleagues (R. W. Hemsted and Captain F. O'B. Wilson) took it for granted that 'the higher and cooler areas [should be reserved] for the Europeans while allowing the Indians and Arabs to take up land in the lower and warmer climates'.⁴⁴ Their plan was to reserve all the farming land above the 5,000 foot contour for the Europeans. It was unfortunate that portions of the White Highlands were actually at a lower altitude; in the area of Muhoroni, several English soldier-settlers had tired of this lower farmland and sold out to Indians, while to the east of Muhoroni there was a block of land which had been alienated to Indian farmers in 1906, even though it was above the 5,000 foot line. Carter's overall recommendation was that the Highlands be reserved for European occupation and that other areas be scheduled as Native Reserves and kept for

African use. All the remaining land in Kenya would be available to any race, except for the Indian farms east of Muhoroni. These would be excluded from the Highlands, and the owners were free to sell to Indians or Europeans; any farm sold to a European would thereafter become part of the highlands and therefore reserved for the Whites. Carter suggested that to give finality to the existing arrangements the boundaries of the European highlands and the native reserves be defined by an Order in Council from London. The detailed maps which accompanied the report designated an area of 16,700 square miles as the White Highlands portion; this enlarged the area from an existing total of 11,850 square miles under white ownership. When the Carter report was released, it was accompanied by a white paper stating the policy of the United Kingdom government: which agreed in every particular with the report and announced that an Order in Council would be issued to give effect to the Carter proposals.[45]

Not surprisingly, the Indian response to this development was shocked and surprised. In the Legislative Assembly, Satyamurti moved an adjournment motion in protest. Fazl-i-Husain was at the end of his time as Member in charge of Indians overseas, and in reply to the motion he looked back upon the five years he had devoted to his unpromising task:

I was able in a few cases to achieve very minor successes. These successes really are very minor and dwindle into insignificance when one thinks of the numerous failures that one has come up against. There is nothing to be proud of in the line of achievement. The utmost one could say is that I have not lost very much ground.... We must remember that the struggle is more or less a hopeless struggle. We must not run away with the idea that we are united and there is no difficulty in the way of achieving our desire. Nothing of the kind.... The struggle cannot be given up. It has to be fought. It has to be continued. It will never do to lose heart. We believe that there is a future...

This abject presentation was not to the liking of his listeners; Satyamurti interjected: 'We must go to war on that.' But Fazl-i-Husain tried to suggest that there was an alternative: 'What is really wanted is a certain amount of honourable propaganda enlisting the sympathies of people in Britain and elsewhere to take up the case for a sympathetic hearing.' The assembly was not reassured, but Satyamurti withdrew his adjournment motion, acknowledging that from his uncomfortable position Fazl-i-Husain had done his best.[46]

5
A Pattern of Inequality
(1935-39)

There is no special reason for pausing in 1935, except for the coincidence that important changes occurred in 1935-6 among the leading actors in Britain, India and South Africa; and, perhaps more compelling, during the last two or three years before war again engulfed the world, there was a current of unrest which rippled across the tropical territories of the British Empire. In the sugar colonies, where time had stood still since the ending of slavery, there was a new mood amongst the plantation workers. For the first time they questioned the right of the bosses to dictate to them the entire circumstances of their lives. The Indian workers caught something of this mood. They were quite unsuccessful in challenging their conditions of inequality; but at last they became aware of the nature of the inequality.

The changes which came within the British political leadership resulted from nothing more remarkable than the general election of 1935 at which Stanley Baldwin obtained his last vote of confidence from the British electorate. Baldwin succeeded Ramsay MacDonald as prime minister just before the election. He moved Sir Samuel Hoare from the India Office and brought in the Marquess of Zetland, an aristocrat whose interests tended towards literature and horse racing. The term of Lord Willingdon as viceroy came to an end, and he was replaced by Lord Linlithgow, a staunch conservative, whose approach to Indian problems may be understood from a remark he passed to Irwin: ' I am still steady in my view that we are fighting a rearguard action in the East, and I am for giving as little ground as possible.'[1]

Then there were changes at the Colonial Office: for a brief while (June to November 1935) Malcolm MacDonald was Colonial Secretary, and he showed himself prepared to be more sympathetic to Indian feelings — as in the case of the white highlands in Kenya — though he declared that his hands were tied by all the precedents. He was succeeded by the egregious Jimmy Thomas, but a real change occurred when, in May 1936, Ormsby-Gore was given the post for which he had prepared himself so long; he was a vigorous, powerful Secretary of State, and Zetland told Linlithgow that 'his iron hand is very lightly covered by a velvet glove' (5 April

1937).² The 1935 general election brought a number of new men into the House of Commons, including Arthur Creech Jones, who rapidly made a reputation on the Labour side as a zealous campaigner for colonial peoples.

There were changes among the Indian administrators who watched over Indians overseas. Fazl-i-Husain was succeeded by Sir Jagdish Prasad, after an interregnum in which Bajpai officiated as Member in charge of the Department of Education, Health and Lands. Having served with the department continuously since 1923, Bajpai's influence was pre-eminent. K. P. S. Menon joined the department at this time and found 'the atmosphere somewhat suffocating'. He conceded that his superior had a 'handsome face and shining intelligence', but he also possessed 'vaulting ambition . . . which spurred him on to outwit and outshine all other officers, Indian and British alike'.³ When Sir Maharaj Singh was replaced in South Africa by Syed Raza Ali, Bajpai found him to be 'a great menace'.⁴ After the arrival of Raza Ali the South African government agreed to raising his title to that of Agent-General.

The melancholy which had haunted the Indians in South Africa in the past, and which was so soon to return, was briefly replaced by an atmosphere of farce. Soon after his arrival in South Africa, the new Agent-General announced his intention of marrying Miss Sammy of Kimberley. Miss Sammy's parents had arrived as indentured labourers, and she was said to be the proprietor of a sweet shop. It might have been supposed that this was a gesture towards Hindu-Muslim harmony, but the South African Hindu community was unanimous in condemning the marriage. When the matter was reported to Delhi, Bajpai who was acting as Member in charge of the department disapproved severely of the *mésalliance*. He put up a minute to the viceroy, advising that if Raza Ali persisted with his intentions he should be recalled. Lord Willingdon approved the proposal. At this point Sir Jagdish Prasad assumed his duties as Member; he regarded the affair as the private concern of the Agent-General; in any case, the marriage might do good. His Excellency approved this advice; the reverse of his previous decision, and Raza Ali was told to go ahead. The consequence was that the Hindu members of the South African Indian Congress resigned en bloc as did the hot-headed Parsi Sorabjee Rustomjee. Kajee remained, the lonely leader of the rump organisation, which never completely recovered from the split.⁵

Kajee's technique was demonstrated in the next manifestation of South African white racism. A private member's bill was introduced to ban the employment of white women in shops or offices run by

Asiatics. Led by Kajee, the South African Indian Congress gave an undertaking that if the bill was withdrawn his community would set up the necessary organisation to ensure that all Indian employers voluntarily accepted the prohibition. This approach was suggested to Kajee by J. F. H. Hofmeyr, and had the backing of Smuts. After a protracted sitting, the Cabinet accepted the proposal, and Hertzog announced that no time would be granted in parliament for discussion of the bill.[6] The Indians kept something of their dignity, in that they were not put under legal constraint; but the price was another surrender of a portion of the ground they had won.

Despite their differences over the colonization scheme, the governments of South Africa and India remained on good terms. The viceroy sent a despatch to the South African Governor-General (30 January 1937) to underline the assurances that India had not resiled from the 1932 agreement: it was intended to maintain the 'friendly relations that now happily exist between the two governments'. The despatch pointed out that, under the 1935 Government of India Act, it was expected that the present wholly official central government would give way to a federal structure with Indian political participation; nothing much could be done until the transfer was carried out. The Union Government agreed to wait (21 April 1937).

Although relations were cordial at the inter-government level, Indian national feeling remained dissatisfied, and looked for means to exert pressure upon South Africa. During the mid 1930s the Congress entered the Legislative Assembly and Pandit Govind Ballabh Pant, deputy leader of the Congress group, introduced a private member's bill to ensure that 'Wherever British subjects are subjected...to any disability, restriction, condition or liability... to which the subjects of, or European subjects in that state are not actually subjected, the Government of India shall... publish a notification in the Gazette of India specifying the name of the state...' If six months elapsed after such notification without relief being afforded, the possibility of applying penalties to the subjects of that state resident in India would be initiated. This mild proposal was not resisted by the Government of India, and the India Office were told (3 May 1936) that sanction to introduce the bill would not be withheld. The India Office noted this 'rather regrettable' development, but as the new Government of India Act and Government of Burma Act specified that discrimination against Indians in Britain would be met by 'eye for eye' retaliation against United Kingdom subjects in India, the proposal had a solid precedent.[7] However, Pandit Pant's bill lapsed, being squeezed out by other assembly business. At the beginning of 1938, twelve members of the assembly gave notice that they would introduce bills identical with Pant's abortive measure, and on 18 February G. V. Deshmukh introduced such a bill; this also failed to receive attention. But Indian nationalists were determined not to forget the need for a legal sanction against South Africa.

It could not be said that relations with East Africa were particularly happy. The Carter report displeased all the communities. The Africans protested against the permanent alienation of the best farmland. The Indians in Kenya were divided over whether to continue to press for parity with the Whites or to renounce any special treatment in recognition of the Africans' prior claims. The Europeans were not satisfied with the Carter concessions, and wanted their privileges to be given the protection of the British parliament: several M.P.s, led by Sir Edward Grigg and Captain Freddy Guest, were ready to intervene on their behalf.

Most colonial issues were decided by the Secretary for the Colonies on the advice of his own officials, but the Kenya question was sufficiently important, in British political terms, to be taken to the Cabinet. The first move was a statement from J. H. Thomas, which he circulated in draft to the India Office. He gave notice that 'The perennial antipathy between Government and settlers in Kenya shows every sign of becoming acute in the near future': there was 'the possibility of serious trouble'. Unless they agreed to the white demand for statutory recognition of the white highlands there might be settler resistance; for example, a no tax campaign. Zetland did not come back with the standard Indian protest against racial discrimination; instead, he raised the ingenious argument that discrimination against the Kenya Indians in land-holding was a violation of international law. The St. Germaine Convention was one of the postwar series of treaties, and regulated colonial practices throughout central, east, and west Africa. It was negotiated during Edwin Montagu's tenure of the India Office, and he had insisted that India should be an independent signatory.[8] Consequently, Great Britain and India had mutually resolved that there should be no racial discrimination in the ownership of land in Africa. Predictably, the Colonial Office rejected Zetland's argument on the grounds that the highlands policy antedated the convention: which in any event did not cover relations between different parts of the British Empire. However, they were somewhat on the defensive, and when the Cabinet came to deliberate upon the problem they had to digest two papers: one each from the Colonial and India Offices.[9] The Cabinet meeting on 19 February 1936 made as little as possible of the controversy. Zetland was told to inform Willingdon about the legal position in the strictest confidence and

Thomas was told to go ahead with an Order in Council which would define the highlands as a 'geographical delimitation' without notifying the area as reserved for European settlement.

Zetland described this subtle sidestepping of the issue as a 'reasonable compromise' (24 February 1936) which he expected the settlers would 'bitterly resent' as they were denied statutory recognition of their preserve. Thomas obligingly put off publication of the Order in Council until the Indian legislature had finished its Spring session. At this point the Colonial Office merry-go-round came up with Ormsby-Gore as Secretary of State (29 May 1936). Billy Gore made his first pronouncement on the Carter report in the House of Commons on 9 July 1936. He assured the House that 'This will not finally divide up anything like the whole of the territory [of Kenya] or even the whole of that part which is called the Highlands', and he followed his customary policy of moderate conservatism, making no new commitments and offering no new concessions. When a Labour member, Morgan Jones, asked why no land had been reserved for the Indians, Ormsby-Gore replied that 'the practice will continue in the future as in the past', adding: 'There will be no legal colour bar'.

Another measure of exclusion which worried the Kenya Indians was the Native Marketing Bill which would regulate their trading activities in the African reserves. The Indian elected members of the Kenya legislature addressed a telegram to the Government of India; and from Delhi a message was passed on to the India Office signifying that they wished to reply to the Kenya Indians directly, without communicating via London. It is not clear why the Indian government should have raised the issue, as they had been accustomed to correspond direct with Indian organisations in South and East Africa for many years. Now, the matter was brought directly to the attention of the Colonial Office, and the practice of direct communication was strongly deprecated. The Colonial Office told the India Office (12 July 1935) that India ought to use 'the recognised official channel'. It was deplorable that the Indian government had told the Kenya Indians that they could 'rely on the support of the Government of India': 'For the Government of India to promise its support to any section of the community of a colony can only be described as a regrettable interference in matters of colonial government'.

The India Office continued to make excuses for the practice of direct communication: it had produced beneficial results in East Africa in persuading the local leaders to cooperate with the local government. The Colonial Office was not assuaged, and on 30 April

1936 formally asked the India Office to insist that India corresponded through the 'normal channels': after all, they pointed out, the Colonial Office did not deal directly with individuals or organisation in the colonies, but only through the Governors as intermediaries. This brought a direct request from the Government of India for Colonial Office agreement to the posting of a Trade Agent to Mombasa. The departmental letter to the India Office (10 September 1936) enclosed a draft of the instructions to be given to the Agent. This might have been more carefully phrased, as it was bound to be shown to the Colonial Office. The instructions included the following:

The lack of an agent or other diplomatic representative of the Government of India in East Africa, which is due to financial considerations, has on various occasions handicapped the Government of India in making representations on behalf of Indians resident there.... Pending the appointment of a separate agent, the Government of India would expect the Indian Trade Commissioner at Mombasa to watch local developments... that appear to concern the Indian community and to report such of them to the Government of India... as are in his opinion likely to justify their intervention at some stage to safeguard their interests.

The proposal for an agent in East Africa was supported by the Viceroy in his weekly personal letter to the Secretary of State. Linlithgow was aware that the Government of India must stand up for Indians overseas, for if they were seen to sacrifice the interests of their own people to those of the imperial power then this would unite Indian feelings solidly against British rule in a way that nothing else could do. So Linlithgow told Zetland (17 September 1936) that they must either correspond directly with Indians in the colonies or have the right to appoint agents: 'The real trouble is that our people overseas... seem entirely unable adequately to safeguard their own interests.'

It was some time before a reply was sent to the request for an agent at Mombasa. When it was delivered to the India Office (26 January 1937) it was a formal communication, signed by a civil servant at the Colonial Office, J. E. W. Flood, and referring to the Secretary of State in the third person: yet it is apparent that the letter emanated directly from Ormsby-Gore, for it was a thunder-clap. The letter examined the Indian government's proposal and found it 'open to serious and insuperable objection'. In effect, the trade agent would be discharging the functions of a political agent: and the Secretary of State for the Colonies had never accepted the idea of a political agent.

Mr Ormsby-Gore is fully satisfied that the appointment of such an Agent would be most undesirable either now or in the future, and he is unable to agree to the issue of instructions which purport to contemplate such an appointment.

It was explained to the India Office that there were two kinds of Indian in the colonies; one was a person actually from India, visiting, or on business, and the others were 'persons of Indian race... [who] have no connection with India'. The majority of 'Indians' in East Africa belonged to the second category.

It is very doubtful how far the Government of India ought properly to concern itself in their affairs. They may justly be regarded as citizens of the colony in which they reside.... While Mr Ormsby-Gore is fully prepared to admit that the Government of India has an interest in the Indians in East Africa who have not established a domicile there, he is unable to agree that the Government of India has a similar interest in the domiciled or long-established Indian communities either in East Africa or elsewhere in the Colonial Empire.

Relenting a little, the Colonial Secretary examined how a Trade Commissioner might be allowed to function. He must give no encouragement to the East African Indians to make political demands. The local Europeans were 'very sensitive' to pressure from Indian political sources: the trade commissioner must not stimulate 'political aspirations in Kenya which in present circumstances it is impossible to satisfy'. Any acceptable trade commissioner must be a civil servant and must 'receive the most categorical instructions restricting his functions to those normally employed [sic] by such officials'. As a last warning, the letter ended: 'It must be emphatically re-asserted that the position of Indians in a Colony is in no wise different from that of any other sections of the community.'

There was dismay at the India Office when this letter arrived. Sir Findlater Stewart told Zetland (10 February 1937) that he was reluctant to forward the letter to India: 'It seems certain to provoke a first class dispute'. Perhaps Lord Zetland could help by writing privately to Ormsby-Gore?

Just at this moment, an official letter arrived from the Government of India (16 March 1937) couched in terms even more likely to arouse the ire of Ormsby-Gore. Bajpai now extended the demand: to an application to appoint agents in East Africa and also Fiji, with an intention to send an Agent to the West Indies later. The letter was courteously phrased; the intention was not to encourage Indians overseas to turn to the Government of India but rather to inculcate the idea that they should look to the local government 'for ultimate relief': 'Agents have played an effective role in educating Indian opinion in this direction in countries where they have already been appointed. Despite tactful observations like these, the India Office was nervous of the effect the letter would have. F. F. Turnbull was of the opinion that if it was forwarded to the Colonial Office it would meet a 'flat refusal'. Perhaps it would be better to keep the letter pending until it was possible to obtain an interview with the Secretary for the Colonies? And so the India Office was left holding on to two key letters, which it was not prepared to forward because it wanted to avoid trouble: while both its correspondents assumed that the letters had been delivered.

In the summer of 1937 there was to be another Imperial Conference to which India would be sending Sir Muhammad Zafrullah Khan as principal representative. Zafrullah Khan, a member of the Viceroy's Council, was a formidable advocate and negotiator and it seemed a good idea to arrange for him to meet the Colonial Secretary. Bajpai was coming to London also, and Zetland asked Ormsby-Gore if he would meet the two men; this was accepted, and an agenda was drawn up which included the subject of Agents and the situation in colonies where tension had been felt, such as Zanzibar, Kenya, Ceylon, Fiji and Malaya. Optimistically, W. D. Croft of the India Office noted: 'Possibly Mr Ormsby-Gore will be less sticky'. More apprehensively, Zetland wrote to Linlithgow (5 April 1937) 'I shall not be surprised if sparks fly when he and Zafrullah and Bajpai get together'.

Others were hoping that something would come of the meeting. Creech Jones was in touch with the Zanzibar Indian leaders and had asked questions in parliament about the impasse. He worked closely with Polak, also a member of the Labour Party. Henry Polak told him (20 May 1937) that the 'obvious remedy' for the grievances of Indians in the colonies lay in the appointment of Agents: 'The difficulty is that the Colonial Office, without in fact ensuring equal and considerate treatment of the Indian populations, is jealous of its own prestige and does not at all like the idea of action or representation by the Government of India or its Agents'. Perhaps the visit by Zafrullah Khan and Bajpai would help to 'break down this hostile attitude'.

The first meeting between Sir Zafrullah and Bajpai with Ormsby-Gore took place on 5 June. The Secretary of State was flanked by Sir Cecil Bottomly, G. L. M. Clauson, and J. E. W. Flood. The first topic discussed was the situation in Zanzibar. Since 1934, there had been several inquiries, but the Colonial Office had not modified the original decrees as they affected the Indian merchants. Indian opinion was increasingly hostile, and confidence in the ability of the

Government of India's handling of the issue had waned. There was a growing campaign to counter the actions of the Zanzibar government by a clove boycott. The Congress set up a boycott committee at Bombay, with Gandhi's toughest lieutenant, Vallabhbhai Patel, as chairman and S. K. Patil as secretary. As India was the largest buyer of cloves in the world, the threat had a serious ring.

Sir Zafrullah asked for certain concessions to bring back the Indian merchants into the Zanzibar trade, and Ormsby-Gore undertook to follow this up (as he did, quickly and effectively). Then Ormsby-Gore raised the question of how an Indian Agent would operate in East Africa: he insisted that such an appointment would conflict with his own responsibility to parliament. Zafrullah argued that an Agent would help the colonial authorities to 'establish better relations' with their Indians. Bottomly suggested that this was the responsibility of Indian members of the legislative councils, but Zafrullah replied that this 'was not sufficient to be effective'.

There was another meeting on 19 June, and this time Sir John Shuckburgh, the Deputy Under Secretary, was present while the conversation was mainly about the functions of an Agent. Bajpai insisted that there would be no interference in domestic politics: the Agent would not stir up demands for a common roll, for example. Ormsby-Gore 'promised to look into the matter': or at any rate that was what Bajpai recorded he had said in the meticulous note of the proceedings which he supplied to the Secretary for India. But soon after a Colonial Office record of the meeting was received at the India Office, and no-one seems to have noticed that this made no mention of Ormsby-Gore committing himself to consider the question further.

There was no improvement concerning the Zanzibar controversy. Creech Jones followed up his previous inquiries by asking a parliamentary question on 24 June concerning the legislation which was pending. Ormsby-Gore wrote to Creech Jones (14 July 1937) inviting him to come to the Colonial Office to talk about Zanzibar, providing that he came alone, and not with 'self-styled Indian representatives'.[10] 'I have to look to the interests of the African and Arab native population of Zanzibar', wrote Ormsby-Gore, and government action was 'designed to protect them from exploitation by the middle-men and speculators (mainly Indian) . . . . A subject regarding which I feel sure that you and I are in complete agreement'. This plea for acceptance of the bi-partisan approach to colonial problems fell flat: Creech Jones declined the invitation (17 July) as there was nothing to discuss if the legislation went ahead. Winterton, still Under Secretary for India, tried to suggest to Creech

Jones that the Colonial Office had made 'substantial concessions' (16 July) but the Labour M. P. was steadily resistant to overtures from the Establishment. By now, the clove boycott was firmly applied, and the loss to the Zanzibar revenues amounted to £30,000 by the end of the year. Ormsby-Gore remained obstinate: he passed on a message via Zetland for Linlithgow to give to the Indian politicians: 'The Government of Zanzibar has no intention of giving way . . . and I have certainly no intention of advising Zanzibar to yield to clamour'. The Aga Khan bewailed the 'irony' that those who were suffering were loyal Muslims: he was 'proud to say that their loyalty to England has not been less than that of any section of the English'.[11]

As public opinion hardened in India, Linlithgow had to face the situation which he had foreseen, when the Government of India was universally criticised as subordinate to British interests. With an adverse debate looming up in the central legislature, Linlithgow was anxious to demonstrate some tangible gain from the Colonial Office which might make a more favourable impression. Could he make a reference to the appointment of an Agent? The most that the Colonial Office would offer was that the appointment of a Trade Commissioner was 'under consideration'. Linlithgow did not think that this card was worth playing. By now, Ormsby-Gore had examined the India Office version of his meetings with Sir Zafrullah and Bajpai: he drew attention to the discrepancy over the Agent and denied that he had made any promise. He reminded Zetland in a private letter (21 August) that the India Office had not responded to the departmental statement made on 26 January, when 'serious and insuperable objections' were recorded, and he ended: 'Frankly I do not see my way clear to the appointment of an Indian Agent in East Africa'.

The India Office was in a dilemma: it had not told the Indian government about the letter of 26 January, and it had pigeon-holed the application from India for Agents in East Africa and Fiji. It was decided to send a formal explanation of why it was essential either to continue direct correspondence between the Indian government and Indians overseas or else establish Agents in the colonies, (21 September 1937). Heavy emphasis was placed upon the strength of Indian nationalism: 'The status of Indians in other parts of the British Empire has always been a principal concern of the Indian National movement and on the question of Indians overseas all sections of Indian opinion, whether extreme or moderate are united in demanding that the Government of India should exert its influence'. If their claims were ignored, it would provide a 'powerful appeal' to all those wanting India to leave the Empire. In his covering note, when he placed this letter before Zetland, F. F. Turnbull observed: 'It would not perhaps be unfair, though no doubt undesirable, to say that the Indian communities are entitled to look to the Government of India in much the same way as Europeans [Britishers] in the Colonies look to His Majesty's Government for the protection of their interests.' It was an extreme situation which compelled Mr. Turnbull to speak some of the truth: that the British colonial empire was managed in the interests of the British, and Indian interests automatically came second every time.

When the Colonial Office reply was drafted, Ormsby-Gore was a little more forthcoming (26 October 1937). He recognised the 'political difficulties' of the Government of India and he would agree to a Trade Commissioner, subject to very strict conditions: he must not attempt to make representations to the local colonial government, and he must not act as a go-between for the local Indians, and he must be a regular official. However, the Indian government had really wanted a *trade* commissioner, and they had selected and trained a member of the western Indian commercial community; they could not now discard him because he was not a proper official. So they inquired if they could send their (commercial) trade commissioner to Mombasa and appoint an (official) trade commissioner at Zanzibar. Somewhat wearily Ormsby-Gore told Zetland in another private letter (19 January 1938) that this had 'explosive political possibilities'. Even one trade commissioner would be regarded by the settlers as a 'thinly disguised harbinger of political trouble'; but two would never be accepted: they must 'acclimatize' one Indian agent first.

Then, unexpectedly, the demand was dropped by the East African Indians. Bajpai fumed at this ineptitude. He wrote to Sastri: 'As for the Congress, I am in despair . . . in regard to questions dealing with Indians overseas. . . . Now the Mahatma wants us to uplift the African native, and Isher Dass and Co. want us to appoint no Agent in East Africa. What a hopeless attitude' (20 February 1938). Officially, he told the India Office that the proposal was 'in abeyance' (10 December 1938). But this was to be only a pause in the long battle with the Colonial Office for recognition of India's right to send official representatives to the countries where there were settled Indian communities. The battle went on until Indian independence — and after.

Meanwhile, Zanzibar continued to be the focal point in the battle in East Africa. The concessions obtained by Sir Zafrullah Khan left the Indian community dissatisfied, and the drive to ban the import of cloves into India intensified. The moderate Imperial

Indian Citizenship Association issued a statement (January 1938) deploring the 'unfortunate break' in the policy of the Government of India, laid down by Hardinge in 1912 and continued by Reading and Irwin, but now discarded by Willingdon and Linlithgow. The Government of India was now 'antagonistic' to Indian interests in Zanzibar.

It was time for a compromise. In India, the price of cloves had doubled, while Bombay had lost almost all its trade to Calcutta and Madras. The Indian merchants in Zanzibar were in a perilous condition, and Arabs and Africans were becoming increasingly hostile to their sectional attitude. The Zanzibar revenues were badly depleted. Negotiations were re-opened, and in March 1938 the Zanzibar government agreed to give up the monopolistic powers of the government clove growers' association. A conference was held in May 1938, and India was represented by G. S. Bozman, Assistant Secretary for Indians Overseas. As a result the Congress-sponsored boycott was terminated.[12] A year later an official report declared that 'Indians have recovered their full share in the trade which they had in 1934'.[13]

Measures to put Indian trade and industry under government control — ostensibly in the interests of the Africans — were also introduced in Uganda. It was of Uganda that Sastri had written, somewhat over-exuberantly, in his 1929 report: 'We [the Indians] dominate the situation by numbers, wealth, capacity and magnitude of interests'.[14] This dominance was resented by the African farmers and by the Protectorate government. A committee of inquiry was appointed to investigate the marketing and processing of cotton, 1935-6, and came forward with a critical account of the dominance by Indian middle-men of the market. The Uganda government encouraged the formation of growers' co-operative societies, and most of the Indian middle-men were put out of business. The factories in which the cotton was ginned were almost all Indian-owned (187 out of 194) and these proprietors, the big men, survived and flourished though the petty Indian brokers went out of business. The latter protested to the Government of India through their Middlemen and Cotton Growers' Association, but when the India Office was asked to address a complaint to the Colonial Office, Lord Zetland was advised to be cautious: 'This is a new situation: one set of Indians in Uganda is appealing to the Government of India against another set of Indians. I think that we had perhaps better not send the enclosed [memorandum] to the Colonial Office'.

The non-official members of the Uganda Legislative Council were all nominated by the Governor, and in 1933 he intimated that an additional Indian member would be added to give parity with the Europeans (two and two). This occasioned another demonstration of the disunity endemic among the leaders of the overseas Indians. P. V. Mehd told Sastri (27 July 1933) 'There became a scramble between two candidates, one Mr Shah and the other Mr Patel, with the result that the Central Council [of Uganda Indians] has been split. The Governor has made his own choice... to nominate Mr Shah. This reflects very much on our mentality.' In Tanganyika, also, the legislature was a nominated body, and the non-officials comprised five Europeans and three Indians. There was little protest against the European advantage, though Indian financial holdings in Tanganyika were greater than those of Europeans. This acceptance was largely due to the predominance of the Ismailis among the Tanganyika Indians, for the Aga Khan continued to advise his followers to be politically co-operative and to demonstrate their loyalty to the Empire.

Doubts only arose about the position of the Indians when, during the late 1930s, Neville Chamberlain attempted to appease Hitler and made tentative overtures concerning the return of Germany's former colonies — in particular Tanganyika. The Aga Khan wrote anxiously to the Marquess of Zetland (11 November 1938), 'Under the mandate, we Indians were on terms of absolute equality with everyone else — I may say that it is the one country outside India where we are treated as equals... Indians in commerce, enterprise and ability have shown themselves to be the equals of white people.' Zetland replied courteously but without offering any real assurances, so the Aga Khan wrote again (14 March 1939) to underline the importance of preserving the status quo in Tanganyika: 'In South Africa, and now in Kenya, Indians are humbled and harassed and so many humiliating restrictions are placed on them... that Tanganyika was a sort of haven of rest.'

The last tremor to agitate the Indians of Kenya, in these years in the shadow of world war, also originated in Nazi Germany. Some Jewish refugees in their search for safety began to move to Kenya. The movement was welcomed in Britain by Sir Edward Grigg and others, as bringing desirable skills and energy toward the development of East Africa. There was talk about *kibbutzim* in the white highlands, and the Government of India decided to protest. However, the Kenya Government was more worried about the possibility of having to cater for a stream of penniless refugees, and hastily drafted new regulations to make entry more difficult.[15] The existing rules provided that the immigration officers might require a new arrival to deposit £50 as surety; the new regulation raised the limit to £500. The Indians suspected that this might be the excuse for imposing similar restrictions upon Indian immigrants, and the Government of India asked the India Office to insist (24 February 1939) that a published statement be issued declaring that the new ordinance would not apply to British subjects or British protected persons. In the end, the Indians were reassured by the addition of an Indian (Eboo Pirbhai) to the Board set up to advise on immigration, which hitherto had consisted only of three European non-officials.

The East African Indians watched suspiciously throughout the 1930s for any sign that the campaign for closer union in East Africa was being revived. Even an agreement on a common postal system was criticised. It was therefore with relief that the findings of a Royal Commission on closer union in Central Africa were received, when proposals for a form of political association were rejected by Lord Bledisloe and his colleagues.

The Indian community in Southern Rhodesia was perhaps the most isolated and introverted of all the overseas communities. Total numbers were small — 2180 were registered in 1936, and only wives and children were allowed in, to augment the community. Most were traders, with some market-gardeners, and the majority originated in Gujarat. Because Southern Rhodesia did not have a 'Poor White' problem, like South Africa, there was no pressure to eject the Indians from semi-skilled occupations to give places to Whites. The Indians were very sensitive about their status as a group. When Indians first penetrated the country they came as single men, and took Africans and Coloured women as their wives; now, the 'pure' Indians resented the inclusion of the children of these unions within their community, and demanded separate schools — 'Indian purity schools' as they were called. There was also resentment at the classification of Indians with the Coloureds as a single category; for example, the Old Age Pensions Act of 1936 listed the Indians as Coloureds. The Southern Rhodesian British Indian Association addressed a letter of protest to the Government of India (24 July 1937) asserting that 'this is an insulting term, used for Indians'. They were also worried about the Town Planning Act, 1937, which reserved land for non-Europeans. However, Sir Godfrey Huggins, the prime minister, assured the Governor (25 January 1938) that the reverse was not implied: fears that the Indians would be required to move out of European areas were 'groundless'. During the 1930s Southern Rhodesia contemplated the neighbouring regime of Hertzog and Malan with reserve; they insisted that they were different; and the Indian community was content with a form of discrimination which avoided an overt colour bar. When Sir Maharaj Singh visited the country in 1934, he reported that the Indians were 'prosperous, contented, and generally free from the disabilities' which afflicted their brethren in South Africa. About 200 were registered as voters, and sixty enjoyed the municipal franchise in Salisbury.

Indian opinion remained most sensitive concerning conditions in Africa; yet it was in the neighbouring countries of Southern Asia that there were the most urgent difficulties for Indian Immigrants in the mid-1930s. The previous pattern was repeated: in Ceylon, pressure against the Indians was exerted in constitutional and administrative terms, whereas in Burma the pressure was physical and violent. In Malaya, the first stirrings of protest were felt by the government and the planters who had hitherto regarded the Indians as anonymous units of production.

The separation of Burma from India in 1937 intensified the pressures upon the Burma Indians. As in Ceylon, they were seen by nationalist politicians as another obstacle to the attainment of nationhood. If it was not yet possible to pull down the fabric of British overlordship, it was at any rate within the power of the Burmese to dissolve the Indian ties which formed part of the imperial edifice.

During the debates in the British parliament upon the separation of Burma, the position of the Indian community was referred to and assurances were given by those in charge of the legislation. Sir Thomas Inskip told the House of Commons (10 April 1935) that the instruments of instruction to the Governor would direct him to 'reserve' any bill which contained discriminatory measures for the consideration of the Secretary of State.[16] Later, when Lord Winterton asked for a statement on Indian immigration into Burma, the Under Secretary, R. A. Butler, replied that 'There can be no discrimination against Indian immigrants into Burma without prior consultation with the Governor-General of India who himself will take care of the interests of Indians who may wish to enter Burma'. Butler conceded that there might be 'possible restrictions in certain cases of unskilled Indian labour . . . while at the same time we do not wish to stop the free entry of Indians in general'.[17]

The new legislature of Burma, which took on much wider powers than the provincial legislatures in India, included 36 representatives of the various minorities among the 132 elected members: this reduced the minority element to a level at which it was important, but not dominant, as in the previous 'Dyarchy' assembly. The Indians claimed thirteen of these minority seats. In the various ministries which came and went during the following five years, no Indian ever participated as a minister. Chauvinistic gestures by Burmese premiers became increasingly popular. In May 1937,

Jawaharlal Nehru attended the second All-Burma Students Conference at Mandalay (accompanied by his daughter, Indira) at the invitation of the student leaders. A new group of political activists calling themselves *Thakins* ('masters') had taken over, and Nehru was welcomed at Mandalay by Thakin Aung San, the future prime minister. Said Aung San: 'That a leader of millions... should be standing amidst us and instructing us makes us feel depressed for Burma, that is denuded of leaders'.[18] Dr. Ba Maw, the premier, resented this thrust and went out of his way to insult Nehru, warning him to keep out of Burma.

The worst exploitation of chauvinism was fomented by his rival U Saw, in his determination to topple over Ba Maw and seize the premiership for himself. U Saw wanted a big public demonstration to discredit his rival. He seized upon the appearance of a book by a Burmese Muslim, which criticised the Buddhist religion, for his outburst. Gangs of militant young monks, not under the discipline of the great monasteries, were brought into the centre of Rangoon, and along with the local toughs marched towards the Surati Bazaar where the Ismaili merchants had their stores. The Indians had no connection with the Burmese author of the offending book, but that was immaterial. Rioting started on 26 July 1938 and continued in the centre of Rangoon till the end of the month; news of the outbreak spread to Mandalay and other towns, and the violence was repeated against the local Indian Muslims. The officially recorded casualties totalled 164 killed and 711 wounded. The damage to Indian property was estimated at a total of Rs. 6,79,059 for Rangoon and Rs. 10,96,093 for other riot centres (about £140,000) while 11,000 Indians were repatriated to India as destitutes.

As an immediate response to the outbreak, the Government of India appointed an Agent in Burma, C. A. Henderson, I.C.S., from the Madras service. The Governor of Burma set up a Riot Enquiry Committee, with a High Court Judge, H. B. L. Braund as chairman, two Burmese lawyers (U Po Han and U Khin Maung Dwe) and two Indian Muslim lawyers (Dr. M. A. Rauf and A. Rahim) as members. The committee spent several months collecting evidence, and its report was a solemn indictment of the Burmese press and the political fringe of the monastic order. Only Khin Maung Dwe dissented from the unanimous verdict. The committee went on to analyse the deeper causes of Indo-Burmese disharmony, and pointed to the problem of Indian landlords and moneylenders and the competition of cheap Indian labour. It was recommended that a further inquiry be instituted into these causes. The question was urgent, for despite Mr Butler's reassuring statement in parliament, the interim standstill agreement covering trade and migration between India and Burma only covered the two years until March 1940. When the report was debated in the legislature, the question of the victimisation of the Indians was forgotten in a verbal vendetta between Ba Maw's ministry who were accused by U Saw of negligence and loss of public confidence, and who returned the same kind of abuse with accusations directed at U Saw and his newspaper the *Sun*. When the vote was taken on the issue of confidence, the Ba Maw ministry survived by 66 votes to 61, thanks to the support of the European members. The Indians had no cause to thank any of the Burmese politicians: in the intervals of attacking each other they had united to attack the report and Justice Braund and his colleagues. There was further sporadic violence against Indians during the next year and into 1940.

It was characteristic of the ambiguities of Burmese attitudes to Indians that a leading member of the Thakin group which had welcomed Nehru, Thakin Ba Swe (who was to be prime minister of Burma, 1956-7), also formed a secret society, *Kala Htoon Thin*, which organised what would now be called 'Indian-bashing' incidents in which Indian labourers were beaten up, usually at night.[19]

As recommended by the Riot Enquiry Committee, a wider investigation into Indian immigration was entrusted to James Baxter, a senior Burma civil servant, with a shrewd knowledge of the economic reality. The Baxter report did not appear until 1941 when it demonstrated that Indian labour had made a contribution to the country which could not have been supplied from indigenous sources.[20] It was brushed aside, as the Jackson report on Indian labour in Ceylon (1938) had been brushed aside.

In September 1939, a new Agent from the Government of India arrived in Burma; R. H. Hutchings, I.C.S., who had previously worked in Bengal. He found the local Indian community 'nervous and touchy . . . guilty of the dismal folly of having their own Hindu-Muslim riots after the main riots'. He argued that 'The Burmese appear to think that they can get rid of or retain as many Indians as they like to suit their own purposes and that it does not matter how they are treated when they are here'. Hutchings questioned whether unrestricted migration was really an advantage to India: 'Restriction might be used here, as elsewhere, not only to make the true economic position clear but to maintain [Indian] prestige'.[21]

A policy of restricting or prohibiting Indian emigration to the neighbouring lands of Southern Asia was now increasingly accepted by the Government of India, just as the same policy had been accepted for South Africa and the sugar colonies. Malaya was indeed the first territory to be accorded that treatment.

The first real move towards generating a sense of common

purpose among the Indians of Malaya came with the setting up of the Central Indian Association. The inaugural meeting took place on 20 September 1936. Most of the preliminary organisation was undertaken by K. A. Neelakandha Aiyer, who was elected secretary. The new association had an incentive to be active, because of the announcement that Srinivasa Sastri was coming to Malaya to conduct an official inquiry into conditions among the Indian estate workers. Sastri arrived in December 1936, accompanied by G. S. Bozman. He visited about thirty rubber estates, and also the immigration depots and other installations. The planters and British officials (including Sir Shenton Thomas, the Governor) were very attentive throughout his visit, which lasted for a month.

Sastri drafted his report quickly, and dated it 6th February 1937. His overall impression of the Malayan rubber industry was favourable: the Indian workers enjoyed 'a healthy respectable life and aspire to a standard distinctly higher than they could obtain in their own villages'. Sastri could find 'no justification for preventing Indian labour from emigrating there', though he listed a number of changes which ought to be made. Education and medical care were not adequate: there was 'great room for improvement' in the estate schools. The depots where the Indians first lodged had 'a prison camp appearance'. The system of enlistment by *kanganis*—gang bosses—ought to be brought to an end. Indian participation in the management of labour was insufficient: the Indian Immigration Committee which was empowered by the Malayan government to supervise recruitment, wages, and conditions generally, was 'heavily weighted in favour of the employers'; there should be at least two more Indian members of the committee. Sastri pointed to the paucity of Indians in the public services and in deliberative institutions, such as the legislatures and municipalities. It was time that the Agent, as the representative of India, should be an official of higher status. These and other recommendations were made, but Sastri laid most stress upon the urgent need to restore the wage cuts made in the depression years and return to the statutory rates of 1929 with 50 cents a day as the standard wage. Sastri stressed that the continuance of Indian emigration should depend upon an immediate return to the 1929 wage-levels.

Sastri was certainly over-optimistic in some of his assessments; in particular, his judgment that the control by the government's Labour Department over the employers was 'real and effective' was to be badly disproved before many years had passed. But those who dismissed his report as an exercise in whitewash did not take his warnings—particularly upon wages—sufficiently into account. The Malayan Indians disliked the report because, while it accepted the continuance of labour emigration, it did not protest against restrictions upon the employment of educated and professional people from India. Others condemned the report for its approval of the British rubber firms, and wanted a complete ban upon Indian emigration to Malaya. By this time, Sastri had few illusions about his own role as an intermediary, pulled between the Indian communities overseas, the Government of India, and Indian political and public opinion, and he thought that Bajpai might have to bow to political pressure. He therefore wrote, somewhat wryly (20 March 1937): 'The Government has acquired a certain amount of popularity in recent years for identifying itself with Indian sentiment' over the woes of Indians overseas; if his report took the unfashionable line of commending Indian emigration, and this embarrassed the department, then he did not mind if his advice was rejected. However, he insisted that 'The right to emigration is an attribute of high grade citizenship, and I would not sacrifice it lightly. . . . If we are to use it only when we become independent or acquire Dominionhood we may have to wait for years'. Sastri left Bajpai to decide: 'If you decide to compromise . . . I shall not feel hurt . . . My business is over.'

However, Bajpai had not deserted his old chief: he hastened to assure him 'I would not alter a comma in your report. . . . Nor will I . . . sacrifice . . . the best interests of our people merely for the sake of easy, cheap popularity.' Bajpai ended by telling Sastri that his recommendation for restoring wage cuts made during the slump had been acted upon within two days of receiving his report.[22] Soon after, Kangani recruitment was terminated, while the status of the Agent in Malaya was enhanced when the next representative was appointed—C. S. Venkatachar, I.C.S., was an experienced administrator, originally from south India. The last of Sastri's many interventions on behalf of the Indian communities overseas was certainly not a failure.[23]

Another important visit to Malaya followed when Nehru arrived after his trip to Burma. He encouraged the new Central Indian Association to work for better standards of living and a better voice for Indians in the institutions of government. 'Indians are entitled to equal privileges with the Malays, the natives of the soil, and their political and other rights have to be protected', said Nehru. Communications were established between the Malayan Indians and the special department for Indians overseas set up early in 1936 by the AICC. The secretary was Rammanohar Lohia, the future Socialist leader. He wrote to the Central Indian Association:

'I want the Indians of Malaya to take an increasing share in the political and economic management of their country. . . We are very keenly aware of the all-round humiliations of our overseas countrymen, and not only those [of] labourers.' Lohia urged the professional Indians to get in touch with the workers more closely, and to speak to them in Hindustani and Tamil.[24] The All-India Congress Committee sent another emissary to Malaya in 1939; A. K. Gopalan, later a Communist, and president of the All-India Kisan Sabha.

The future of emigration to Malaya was now determined by an unexpected fall in the price of rubber. Though the wage-cuts were restored to the former levels on 1 April 1937, because of fluctuations in rubber prices the planters again lowered wage-rates to 42 or 45 cents per day for men and 35 cents for women. Protest by the Government of India was waved aside, so from 15 June 1938, all assisted emigration from India to Malaya was stopped; the emigration depot at Negapatam was closed, and no fares could be paid for labourers wishing to travel to Malaya. Even estate workers who had returned from Malaya for a holiday in India could not go back if they had remained in India for two years or more. Whereas 104,977 labourers entered Malaya in 1937, only 20,912 came in during 1938 and the total was reduced to 2,166 for 1939.

The members of the United Planting Association of Malaya and their London principals were alarmed at the cutting off of their labour supply, and urged the Malayan authorities to have the flow restored. A delegation of four, led by the Federal Secretary (the Governor's principal aide) came to Delhi to meet the Standing Emigration Committee of the central legislature and to talk to Bajpai and Venkatachar. After their departure, Bajpai addressed a long confidential letter to the Colonial Secretary, Singapore (28 March 1939) for the consideration of Sir Shenton Thomas. In most respects, the letter went over ground which Sastri had covered in his report. Bajpai did not try to bargain over wages; rather he attempted to propose a charter for the Indian community of Malaya. Having suggested a new mechanism for fixing wages under government supervision, he went on to outline a scheme whereby future emigration would be directly related to the demand for labour in Malaya. The rest of the proposals related to social and political questions. He asked for stricter controls over alcoholic liquor, better facilities for primary education, fuller representation on local municipal boards, and the legalising of trade unions. He wanted a more meaningful form of citizenship in Malaya: 'The retention of British citizenship does not help the Indian to overcome disabilities'. When a reply came to this important letter, the Colonial Secretary chose to ignore most of Bajpai's points. He confined himself (15 May 1939) to quibbling over wages and allowances for dependents; more than a year was to pass before the other questions received a reply. Meanwhile, Indian emigration to Malaya virtually came to an end.

Relations between India and Ceylon also developed, cumulatively, to a point where Indian emigration was terminated as a deliberate act of policy. The situation was mainly affected by two forces: the world depression, which hit the island with severe effect, and the steady growth of nationalist feeling under the leadership of the Sinhalese politicians. Often, the effect of the two forces coincided in new pressures exerted upon the Indians. The year 1934 was specially trying in Ceylon, when the failure of the monsoon led to food shortages and near-famine, to add to the general economic depression. The politicians saw a remedy for their difficulties in the exclusion of the Indians, who were filling jobs wanted by the Ceylonese. On 23 March 1934 the Ceylon State Council (the legislature) resolved to implement a policy of Ceylonisation in all branches of the public services, including the manual workers employed by the Public Works Department known as daily-paid workers. This was followed by another resolution in December 1934 in which the State Council declared that in view of the serious and increasing unemployment, a general policy of Ceylonisation should be introduced 'with a view to the restriction and effective control of immigration into Ceylon of workers from other countries'.

Perhaps such a policy was justifiable if the definition of 'Ceylonisation' included all the Indians permanently settled in the country: but this was not the intention of the new political leaders or of the administrators whom they were bringing into their camp. The Land Development Ordinance of 1934, which defined those who might receive grants of Crown land, restricted the grant to a 'Ceylonese' who was to be 'a person domiciled in this island and possessing a Ceylon domicile of origin'. This excluded persons of Indian origin born in Ceylon. When the Government of India protested, the Colonial Office came back to the India Office with a ruling (24 April 1935) that it was the accepted practice in the British Empire, when disposing of Crown land, to give preference to the 'permanent population': hence the Colonial Secretary would not refuse assent to the bill as it was drafted. The Eastern Department of the Colonial Office which made this ruling blithely ignored the practices of the East Africa Department which consistently favoured the white immigrants in Kenya at the expense of the African 'permanent population'. The Colonial Office followed this up by advising the India Office (10 January 1936) that the Attorney General of Ceylon had ruled that the category of 'Ceylonese' 'does not include persons born in Ceylon whose parents at the time of their birth had not actually acquired a Ceylon domicile'. The drive to make the Indians in Ceylon a community of transients had begun in earnest.

The chauvinistic character of Ceylon politics was given a boost by the results of the 1936 general election which served to polarise the situation further. The low-country Sinhalese increased their standing in the State Council from 28 to 31, and succeeded in acquiring all the posts of chairmen of the executive committees which made them members of the Board of Ministers and for the first time, all the ministers were Sinhalese. The leader of the Council was Sir Baron Jayatilaka, though the political pace-maker was Don Senanayake; however, a rival now entered the council—S. W. R. D. Bandaranaike, who became Minister of Local Government and who at once began to outbid Senanayake in his nationalistic demands. The election left the Indians with two representatives in the council; these two had to struggle for their seats, for they were opposed in the planting constituencies by European planters who were actually able to exclude the Indian candidates from the estates: one Indian was unable to rent a campaign headquarters within his constituency, and had to try to lobby the voters in a nearby market.[25]

In an attempt to acquire a firmer understanding of the role of Indian workers in Ceylon, in October 1936, the government deputed a former Attorney General, Sir Edward Jackson, to investigate; his report did not appear until 1938. Meanwhile, the Board of Ministers, known as the Pan-Sinhalese Board, pressed ahead with demands for the liquidation of the Donoughmore constitution in favour of full internal parliamentary government. The minorities, aroused to the probability of Sinhalese dominance, called for further safeguards, and many asked for a return to a communal system of representation. Henry Polak introduced Creech Jones to G. G. Ponnambalam, one of the Indian members of the State Council. Creech Jones asked the Colonial Secretary whether he was consulting the Government of India on the Indian workers' franchise in Ceylon (House of Commons, 22 December 1937), but Ormsby-Gore gave one of his stone-walling replies. Creech Jones also forwarded a memorandum on behalf of the Ceylon Indian Association to the Colonial Office. This averred that the Sinhalese had only accepted the Donoughmore constitution to 'emasculate' the Indians: 'The majority community now feels that every weakening of the position of the Indians is an accession of strength to itself'. As the Indian community formed one-fifth of the total population, the Association asked that Indians should be awarded eight of the fifty elected seats in the Council.

During 1937 the Ceylon tea planters announced that they required 20,000 extra workers, but the Ceylon Government gave sanction only for the recruitment of 5,000 from India. The Government of India replied that a new recruiting campaign must be related to an improvement in wages on the Ceylon estates and the grant of the vote to the Indians at the local, village elections, from which they were excluded. The Ceylon government could not agree to the latter condition, so the recruiting campaign was refused. Indian labourers were still allowed to proceed to Ceylon under schemes of assisted emigration, whereby all travelling arrangements were made for them, but the Madras government issued instructions that all intending emigrants must be questioned before departure to ensure that they had not been 'induced' to go. The Government of India also equipped itself with the legal authority to prohibit all emigration of unskilled labour to a designated country.

In an attempt to improve the political climate a new Governor, Sir Andrew Caldecott, was brought over from Malaya, and was instructed by Ormsby-Gore (5 November 1937) to report on the constitution and the political demands. Caldecott reported in a despatch dated 13 June 1938.[26] He rejected the demands made by the minorities for a fixed ratio of seats between the Sinhalese and the others: 'Fifty-Fifty Demand', and 'Sixty-Forty Demand', as they were termed. He wanted 'to interfere with the Donoughmore scheme as little as possible', but he was impelled to move towards a Cabinet system: 'the present State Council is a political debating society rather than a Government'. He argued that reforms designed to lead to Cabinet government would reduce communalism in politics: 'we shall have seen the first and last pan-Sinhalese ministry'. Malcolm MacDonald was again at the head of the Colonial Office, and he responded to Caldecott's despatch (10 November 1938) by calling for further 'public discussion'. In addition, the matter was reported to the Cabinet, with the recommendation from MacDonald that they support the Governor's proposals. There should be no return to a communal system, though the constituencies should be readjusted to give greater representation to the minorities. If opinion in Ceylon agreed to the Governor's proposals an Order in Council would be drafted: 'In this task I should hope to avail myself of the experience of the India Office' observed this unusually accommodating Secretary for the Colonies.[27]

There was little sign of accommodation in Ceylon. *The Report of the Immigration Commissioner*, by Sir Edward Jackson, appeared in

April 1938 and attempted to show that Indian labour immigration had benefited Ceylon: the Indians had contributed to 'an economic and general advance which could not have taken place without them'. There was no evidence that they were a factor in lowering wages in the island, and controls over immigration were stated to be adequate. The Jackson Report was given a hostile reception by the Sinhalese nationalists, and in reply the Board of Ministers announced that they would consider a scheme for the restriction of immigration. More to their taste was a circular issued by the Legal Secretary, J. C. Howard, (30 June 1938) which drew attention to irregularities in the registration of Indians as voters. Many had been registered on the basis of five years' residence in Ceylon, but the law required the Indians to prove that they intended to make Ceylon their permanent abode: 'Domicile...could not be construed as residence'.

The climax of the Ceylonese-Indian confrontation came in 1939. The 1934 resolution on the Ceylonisation of the public services had not been systematically adhered to; Indians had been engaged in the menial grades, as before. At the beginning of 1939 the ministers decided that a strict Ceylonisation policy would be enforced; the Indians would be weeded out, and no more enlisted. A scheme for the phased retrenchment of the Indian employees was communicated to the State Council, and a vote was taken on the scheme on 23 May 1939. It was accepted by 34 votes to 10, and a European motion to refer the question back for further consideration only obtained seven supporting votes. The Agent of the Government of India, A. V. Pai (a Madras I.C.S. officer), saw the Governor and was assured that 'Ceylon-born persons of Indian race will be treated as Ceylonese'. The Indian legislative Assembly were incensed at the news and urged that in retaliation a prohibitive duty should be imposed upon the import of coconuts from Ceylon.[28] At this time, discussions were pending on the future terms of Indo-Ceylonese trade, and this was an obvious bargaining counter; on 3 July, the Government of India announced that the scope of the trade discussions would be enlarged to include all economic questions then under consideration.

At the same time, the Indian National Congress decided to intervene to resolve the question of the Indians employed in the Ceylon public services. Following his visits to Burma and Malaya, Nehru was asked to go to Ceylon as an 'ambassador of peace'. He arrived in July 1939 to a very mixed reception. The local Indian community wished to turn the visit into an Indian demonstration, but Jayatilika warned Nehru (11 July) that this would be a mistake. He was welcomed as an honoured guest by the Sinhalese ministers, and assumed, a little naively that as brother-Asians and subjects of

British colonial rule they would soon compose their differences. He wrote to J. L. Kotelawala (29 June 1939) that with a 'friendly appraisal from both sides there is no reason why an honourable settlement should not be arrived at'. A few Sinhalese leaders opposed his coming: A. E. Goonesinha, the Colombo labour leader, urged a boycott of the visit. But there were public meetings and speeches extolling the ancient ties between the two countries: though there were no changes in Ceylon government policy. On his return, Nehru reported to the AICC who eventually passed a resolution (10 August 1939) heralding Nehru's 'success ... in bringing the people of India and Ceylon nearer to each other' but regretting the intention to remove the Indians from their employment; this action was 'not in conformity with justice and international practice'.

The Government of India anticipated that Congress would come out with a demand for retaliation against Ceylon. It was desirable therefore, to take immediate action, and not to appear 'forced to it by Congress pressure': as Linlithgow was to tell Zetland, 'The Zanzibar affair... colours all our Ceylon doings' (17 August 1939). Congress action in organising the boycott of the Zanzibar cloves had left the government isolated and condemned by all groups of Indian opinion: Bajpai did not intend to let this happen again. So, before the AICC resolution was published, India informed Ceylon on 28 July 1939 that with effect from 1 August all unskilled emigration from India was prohibited, except for dependents joining men already working in Ceylon.

This action brought an immediate response from Malcolm MacDonald. He cabled to Caldecott on 28 July: 'I cannot be satisfied with the apparent failure of efforts to reach understanding with the Government of India.' It was necessary to re-examine the directive on the retrenchment of Indian workers and to meet with the Indian government 'to consider suitable adjustment'. If the ministers would not co-operate in this effort, Caldecott ought to consider whether he could make an announcement, stating how far he was prepared to go in sanctioning the ministerial policy; if this was difficult, then a statement should come from the Secretary for the Colonies. The ministers had to be reminded of the limitations on their powers: 'It would be essential that the constitutional powers of the Governor and the Secretary of State should first be fully appreciated in relation to any eventualities.'

Caldecott returned a sober, steady answer (31 July) to MacDonald's rather hasty telegram. He would make a speech, stating the facts, and he would insist that there would be no compulsory repatriation of Indians. He was seeing the ministers to tell them he would not approve any legislation 'which did not secure for immigrants already in the island treatment on a par with the Ceylonese'. There followed an exchange of telegrams between Ceylon and India, in which the Government of India tried to get a promise that the retrenchment scheme would be postponed, while the Ceylon government evaded this question and tried to get the emigration ban lifted. On 7 September, Ceylon asked if they could come together in a conference to resolve their differences; the Indian government welcomed the proposal, but stated it was 'assumed' that the retrenchment scheme would be postponed. In a further telegram (3 November) the Ceylon government offered minor concessions: a scheme for voluntary return to India by retrenched employees would be shelved, and Indian employees with more than ten years' service would be treated equally with the Ceylonese employees. This failed to satisfy Bajpai who told Linlithgow (13 November) that Ceylon was 'seeking to establish in advance a principle to which we object, and which we wish to discuss'. He concluded: 'If the Ceylon government insist on discriminating against their Indian employees, I fear that a conference would be wholly unfructuous.' Linlithgow agreed with Bajpai, and on 13 December 1939 the Government of India issued a communique announcing the cancellation of the India-Ceylon conference.

The whole episode was an illustration of the dilemmas of an imperial system approaching dissolution. The metropolitan government in London was the ultimate authority; but it was reluctant to impose its will upon the dependencies, because instalments of power had been devolved upon these dependencies, and could not be easily withdrawn. The authorities in India and Ceylon possessed a considerable formal power of decision-making; but they hesitated to act, for fear that they might provoke a nationalist outcry. The nationalist leaders were able to talk to each other, but they were already constrained by the hopes and fears of their own nationalism. And so, in the end, a new form of diplomacy by head-on collision was attempted; and notably failed to solve anything.

While Indian opinion was stirred by events in Africa and worried by the evidence of emergent nationalism in Southern Asia, the sugar colonies failed to arouse much interest or support. Mauritius, the nearest in geographical distance, was perhaps the most remote in the thoughts of politicians and administrators in Delhi. Even Fiji—where the wrongs done to the Indians had been the keen concern of Delhi and Whitehall during the years before indenture was abolished in 1920—was almost forgotten. Only those who had devoted their whole lives to the cause of Indians overseas, like Sastri and Kunzru, Polak and Andrews, remained in touch with the Indian community of Fiji. So remote was it all, that in 1935 the Governor of Fiji could come forward with the proposal that elections for the legislative council should be abolished, and the members chosen by nomination in future; and in making this proposal he could obtain a considerable degree of support from some community leaders. Thus, the two Indian representatives in the legislative council applauded the idea though the Indian Association (the somewhat ineffective community organisation) came out in opposition. When the issue was put to the Fiji legislature, only two Europeans voted against. In consequence, the Colonial Office sent a despatch to the governor (20 July 1936) observing that (though there was general agreement that the different racial groups should each have equal representation) as the Indian community was 'sharply divided', the Secretary of State would make a compromise award. The Indians, it was alleged, had never been unanimous about wanting a common roll, so Ormsby-Gore continued the policy of Amery (enunciated in 1925) of maintaining the communal system. In future, the legislature would consist of sixteen officials and fifteen non-officials: the five Europeans would include three who were elected and two chosen by the Governor; the Indians would get exactly similar representation, and the Fijians would be represented by five appointed chiefs. Under this system three north-Indian Hindus were elected—Chattur Singh, Visnu Deo and Tulsi Ram, while a Sikh (K. B. Singh) and a Muslim (Said Hassan) were nominated by the Governor.

When C. F. Andrews paid a last visit to Fiji in 1936 he felt able to record a 'story of encouragement', which demonstrated the 'latent powers of recovery' of the Indians originally shipped out as indentured labourers.[29] It seems probable that Andrews' judgment no longer had the old incisive power, for the labouring Indian population was still strictly held in the grip of the Colonial Sugar Refining Company which dominated the Fiji economy. Attempts were made to organise the Indians in the sugar industry by the founding of what were, in effect, trade unions: the *Kisan Sangh* for the tenant farmers (1937) and the *Mazdur Sangh* for the labourers. A faint realisation that things might be better penetrated to the Government of India, and in the same letter in which Bajpai postponed the request for an Agent in East Africa (10 December 1938) he put up a proposal for an Agent in Fiji, with particular reference to the land policy of the government which continued to favour the Fijians. The appointment of an Agent would have a 'stabilising effect' on the Fijian Indians, declared Bajpai, but though the India Office passed on his proposal to the Colonial Office without demur, it was treated with the same stone-walling tactics as before. There was a new Governor of Fiji, so he must have time to assess the situation; his assessment did not arrive at the Colonial Office until early 1940.

In Fiji the tensions remained just below the surface; in the West Indies they emerged, boiling and bitter, to signify that the Caribbean was at last shaking free from the grip of the plantocracy, perpetuated when slavery was formally abolished. During the 1930s, the price of sugar fell to the lowest level ever recorded.[30] The wages of the sugar-workers, which had crept up a fraction, slipped down again. An Indian field-hand in Trinidad would be paid 1s 6d per 'task' in the mid-1930s; this compared with 1s per task paid to the Indians when they first arrived in the 1840s. Such a worker could expect to earn up to 30s a month to keep his family. By contrast the prices of foodgrains and other necessities had increased, so the sugar workers were reduced to a condition of poverty and even starvation. In this atmosphere, discontent erupted into strikes, demonstrations, and riots. The first disturbances occurred in Dutch Surinam, and were triggered off by the arrival of De Kom, a fighter against colonialism, regarded by the local Indian and Javanese workers as a Messiah. In the disturbances caused by De Kom's visit, the police fired upon crowds and an Indian was killed; sixteen Creoles, Indians and Javanese were wounded. Then followed strikes and riots in Trinidad in 1934, while in 1935 the tidal wave of unrest spread to St Kitts, St Vincent, Jamaica, and British Guiana.

As in Fiji, the British Guiana sugar industry was dominated by one giant combine: Booker Brothers, who controlled almost 70 per cent of the industry; and inevitably this giant firm's methods were reflected in the triangular relationship between the workers, the management and the government. Since 1919 a nominal trade union had existed—the British Guiana Labour Union, whose secretary was Hubert Critchlow, a Guiana Black, who visited the USSR in 1931, and therefore was regarded by employers and government as a Communist. Critchlow's union still had less than five hundred members in the mid-1930s and was disregarded by the sugar producers. In 1935 the sugar crop was a record in quantity, and Critchlow tried to claim higher wages at crop time, when long hours had to be worked. During the indenture period the hours of work were supposed to be fixed by statute, and conditions were supposedly watched by a 'Protector' of the Indian workers; when indenture was abolished, these safeguards disappeared and the field hands were expected to labour from 6 a.m. to 8 p.m.

The bumper crop of 1935 only gave the workers harder work for the same rates of pay, and discontent began to smoulder and burst into flames. At first, the protest came mainly from black workers, who were angered by Italy's invasion of Abyssinia which symbolised a western assault upon the stronghold of their people. Then the example of black revolt was imitated by the Indians, who began to threaten and strike their overseers, and even to hit back at the police. The first strike came in August on *Plantation Leonora*, which had a long history of bad labour relations. The main demand was for better wages, though an important grievance was the practice of fixing the rate for a particular job or task after a gang had already begun work upon the task. Another strike followed on the *Wales* estate, while violence erupted at *Rose Hall*, scene of one of the worst disputes of the past, when in 1913, fifteen Indians were killed and forty wounded by police firing. Once again the workers defied the police; red flags were hoisted, drums beaten, and cutlasses drawn.[31]

The Governor appointed a Commission of Inquiry, consisting of the local Attorney-General, A. H. Hill, and the Manager of the Bauxite Company mining in Guiana, F. B. Henderson. A request by the East Indian Association to be represented on the Commission was rejected by the Governor, and in consequence the members of the association refused to give evidence. They were compelled to testify by means of subpoena, but the British executives of the sugar companies were not required to offer their evidence. The commissioners asked some pertinent questions: for example, they said to Dr J. B. Singh: 'The only difference between the indentured labourer and the labourer of today is that the indentured labourer could have been prosecuted for not turning out to work: but the free labourer of today is entirely dependent on the estate?' Dr Singh agreed that the worker was virtually at the mercy of his manager; if he gave trouble, he could not expect to be employed on any other estate. The commissioners' report was a stern document.[32] They stated that labour in 1935 was 'without the assistance, safeguards, and means of ventilating grievances' given to the former indentured people (meagre though their supports had been) and they found that the labourers, especially the Indians, were afraid to protest for fear of victimisation. No estate worker had given evidence to the commission voluntarily: 'We believe the cause of this to be fear.' Altogether, wages were lower, and conditions worse, in 1935 than they had been in 1925. The report contrasted the employers, with their 'highly organised Sugar Producers Association', and labour which was 'entirely unorganised'. In the near future unemployment was likely to become 'acute'; it was necessary to set up a government body to regulate the whole field of work and wages.

The despatch which Governor Northcote sent to Ormsby-Gore, enclosing the report (4 March 1937) was a singularly tepid response to the review. A number of small suggestions were made for remedies, but the despatch made no proposal for what Northcote himself diagnosed as the 'root' of the trouble—the wretched wages—and ended by suggesting a wholly inadequate inspectorate.

Ormsby-Gore dealt with the general situation by issuing a circular despatch to all the sugar colonies (24 August 1937). He recalled that encouragement to the formation of trade unions was first given by Lord Passfield in September 1930. Unless unions were explicitly recognised, secret societies might take their place. There was now a Labour Adviser at the Colonial Office, Major G. St J. Orde Browne, and there were laws in most colonies permitting the registration of trade unions. However, there were noticeable gaps: Mauritius had no labour union law, and Malaya had only legislated for 'societies', which might include unions.[33]

Once again, discontent flared up in Trinidad, and there were serious disorders in June 1937; again, a commission was appointed—this time with the direct authority of the Secretary of State—and their report deplored the absence of negotiating machinery in the sugar industry and stressed the need for a Labour Director. In Guiana, something more like a genuine trade union now appeared: the Man-Power Citizens' Association (MPCA). The organisers were both Black and Brown, African and Indian, and the President was Ayube M. Edun.[34] But Bookers and the other big firms (Sandbach Parker and Co, S. Dayson and Co) ignored the MPCA. The friends of the Indians had some difficulty in deciding whether to continue to look back to India for support, or to encourage the 'East Indians' to merge themselves into their adopted country. Henry Polak, with his contacts in East Africa and the Indian Ocean area, still saw India as the main support. He wrote to the India Office on 11 October 1937 to draw attention to a conference of the East Indian Association at Georgetown which demanded an Agent-General in British Guiana on the model of South Africa. Would the India Office press this upon the Colonial Office? He was told that all this had been considered when Sir Zafrullah and Bajpai met Ormsby-Gore (which, of course, was incorrect). But Polak did not give up; he persuaded Creech Jones to put down a question in parliament on the subject. On 14 January 1938 Creech Jones asked Ormsby-Gore whether he was 'aware that the Indian community in British Guiana are anxious that an Indian Agent-General should be appointed in that Colony, primarily to assist them in their social and industrial difficulties, and whether he will accede to that request?' Ormsby-Gore was, no doubt, somewhat fatigued by the flow of questions from Arthur Creech Jones and he replied blankly that he had received 'no representations on this subject from the Indian community in British Guiana' and therefore the question 'does not arise'. On 16 May 1938, Wilfred Paling, another Labour M.P. deeply interested in the colonies, asked Malcolm MacDonald to state his attitude to the Government of India's desire to appoint an Agent in British Guiana. He received a reply similar to that given before: there had been no formal proposal for the appointment of an Agent.

The next question to provide a puzzle was that of repatriation. Seemongat Maraj, of Triumph Village, Demerara, presented a petition, supposedly on behalf of 6,000 Indians, asking that their rights to passages back to India should be honoured. The Guiana administration responded with unwonted alacrity: the Immigration Fund, set up in the mid-nineteenth century to provide return passages, was £93,569 in credit: why not send back some of the Indians who seemed likely merely to face unemployment in Guiana? The Government of India was nervous about this unexpected return home: and so were those Indians who had seriously studied the conditions of emigrants sent back from the colonies. Pandit Kunzru initiated a debate on the question in the Council of State (the upper house of the central legislature) on 21 February 1938. He called for a scheme of land grants in British Guiana 'to discourage their repatriation to India'. Experience showed that the returned labourers could not adapt to Indian conditions and 'lapse into a state of destitution'. Those who had returned found that their villages 'knew them no longer'; their caste brotherhood rejected them, and their traditional occupation was closed to them. C. F. Andrews had discovered the 'depths of destitution to which they have been reduced'. They drifted to Calcutta, and formed miserable colonies around the old emigration depot at Matiabruz, near the docks, where they hopelessly interceded for passages back to the colonies. Kunzru hoped that, instead, the time-expired Indians of Guiana might be given grants of land as had been done in Dutch Surinam where 6,000 time-expired Indian emigrants were cultivating land from the government. Kunzru's motion was seconded by Hossain Imam, who paid a tribute to the department responsible for Indians overseas: they looked upon it 'more as a popular ministry than as a bureaucratic department', he said. It was left to another member, Syed Mohammad Padshah, to suggest that the British Guiana Indians were no longer their affair: 'Most of them have adopted...a hybrid, half-baked Afro-American culture. They are neither Indians nor are they Americans'. They must go their own way.

However, the British Guiana administration insisted that they had a legal obligation to provide return passages if they were claimed, and it was announced that the S.S. *Ganges* would be taking back returned emigrants to India in September 1938. The Government of India tried to stem the return flow: the Colonial Office should be obliged to refuse passages to applicants 'without means of support or assurances of assistance', but the colonial authorities professed themselves unable to get local Indian cooperation in dissuading unsuitable people from returning. And so the *Ganges* departed from Georgetown on 12 September carrying 867 Indians, of whom 261 were destitute and 317 had to be put on the invalid list. After more than twenty years in the colony, the emigrants brought back an average of less than £10 per adult passenger.[35] Those who were destitute received Rs. 25 (or £2) on arrival to start another life.

But these were not typical of the Guiana East Indians, who mostly wanted to put the indentured system, with its emphasis upon impermanence and return, behind them. When the Man-Power Citizens' Association came to address the Government in August 1938 upon the shortcomings of the new Labour Commissioner, they emphasised their rights and their standing as Guiana citizens: 'It appears that the Labour Commissioner harbours the delusion that the working people on the sugar estates are immigrants still.'

The MPCA told the Governor that the Labour Commissioner did not have their confidence. At first he had tried to be a mediator between managers and men, but increasingly he was acting as an apologist for the estate authorities. A savage demonstration of the actualities of labour relations in British Guiana followed soon after at the notorious *Leonora* estate. The complaints were the same as always—long hours and no additional wages to make up for the overtime. In February 1939 the factory firemen walked off the job, followed by the No. 2 shovel gang (some of the strongest workers) when the manager refused to raise their wages to the former level. The men asked for a meeting with Ayube Edun of the MPCA, but the manager replied that they could only hold their meeting off the estate on the main road. Next day there were pickets on the entrance to the estate and none reported for work. The workers decided to march off to Georgetown, but at Vreedenhoop they were stopped by the police. An Indian leader arrived—Charles Ramkissen Jacob, a member of the legislature and Vice-President of the East Indian Association. He advised the labourers to return home, and they dispersed without violence. Next day, District Superintendent Weber arrived at the estate with armed police to arrest the leading demonstrators on a charge of disorderly conduct; the traditional method of breaking a Guiana strike by arresting the leaders was to be employed. Gradually tension mounted and disorder increased; the crowd pelted the police with bricks and the police fired at the crowd, and four were killed. Late in the day, at 5.30 p.m. the magistrate appeared, accompanied by Edun. The strikers were addressed in the local temple, and agreed to go home. Next day they returned to work.

Another commission of inquiry was appointed, with A. H. Hill again a member and with J. A. Luckhoo, an Indian barrister, also a member. Their report established that the cause of the strike was general discontent over poor wages; the discontent had become active because of the emergence of the MPCA as a trade union.[36] The commission was critical of the new Labour Department, which had not won the confidence of the workers by effective action: there were 'No organised means whereby a dispute arising between employers and labourers might be settled by peaceful negotiations'. Subsequently, the Sugar Producers' Association agreed to recognise the MPCA. The commission said that the workers' grievances did not justify their use of violence; they declared that the persons who were shot had not been 'criminally liable', but they congratulated Superintendent Weber and his men on doing their duty. All the police except two were African Creoles; all the strikers were Indians. This was inevitable in the British Guiana situation.

The unrest in the West Indies led to the appointment of a Royal Commission (announced in parliament on 14 June 1938) with a strong membership and Lord Moyne as the chairman. The commission spent many months during 1939 in the Caribbean and the Government of India decided to send their own representative to present the Indian case, as they had done in East Africa. J. D. Tyson, formerly Sastri's secretary in South Africa, was despatched and he helped the local Indian organisations to prepare their statements, as well as giving evidence himself. He compiled a report which provided much-needed information on the Indians of the Caribbean and the Spanish Main.[37] The Jamaica community was in the worst straits; they were 'the most backward, depressed and helpless of the Indian communities', numbering only 18,000 in the total population of 1,200,000. Unemployment was general, and at best there was only two days' work per week; they had nobody in the public services or in the legislature. British Guiana was also reported upon adversely; the East Indian Association was divided between activists, and those who favoured 'cotton wool methods'; in consequence, it did very little. The Man-Power Citizens' Association had recruited 10,000 members, 90 per cent being sugar workers, but the MPCA was being victimised by the firms. Tyson condemned conditions on the estates, where many workers still lived in barrack-like 'ranges' dating back to the aftermath of slavery. The Indians had obtained two seats among the fourteen granted to elected members under the 1928 constitution; but though 82 per cent of the Guiana Indians were born in the colony, they were hopelessly under-represented in the public services. Of the 805 members of the police, only forty-two were East Indians, and of the 568 posts in the civil service which were on a pay-scale up to £150 per annum, the East Indians held fifty-three (including seven interpreters). Tyson's account of Trinidad was more promising; Indians were rising into the professional and commercial class, though in doing so they discarded their inherited religions, Islam and Hinduism, for Christianity. Among the seven elected members of the Trinidad legislature (out of twenty-five) three were Indians. Tyson concluded: 'If the Indian [in the West Indies] is now becoming race-conscious the blame is not his; .... [it was] forced on him by a realisation of the very definite prejudices existing against him.' When Tyson appeared before the Royal Commission his main plea was for an Indian Agent-General for the British West Indies, in order to help build better labour relations and to inform India of conditions in general.

The Moyne Commission finished their work in 1939; their approach to the future was enlightened and positive, for they declared:

The discontent that underlies the disturbances of recent years is a phenomenon of a different character, representing no longer a mere blind protest against a worsening of conditions, but a positive demand for the creation of new conditions that will render possible a better or less restricted life.

Their positive proposals were overtaken by the onset of war, and political and economic change had to await the coming of peace. They opposed the specific request for an Indian government agent because they argued that this would perpetuate a sense of alienation among the East Indians: but this lay concealed in the womb of the future, for publication of their report was postponed until after the war.[38]

Far away in the Indian Ocean, Mauritius went through the same cycle of unrest as Guiana during the late 1930s: except that instead of having the usual humdrum colonial governor, the island was ruled by a haughty patrician, Sir Bede Clifford, whose previous experience was not that of a bush district officer but was gained in South Africa, where he had served for many years. His attitude reflected this background, for when considering the development of politics in Mauritius he commented: 'The franchise problem in Mauritius was in fact similar in many respects to that of the Union of South Africa with which C[lifford] was familiar'; there could be no question of extending the franchise, which would thereby remove Mauritius from the hands of the Whites, 'who were the indigenous population'.[39]

For thirty years the Indians of Mauritius had been denied a spokesman, since Manilal Doctor departed in 1910 smarting with humiliation.⁴⁰ The leading progressive politician in the island, Dr Edgar Laurent, was indeed the son of an Indian; but he had assumed a French name and the Protestant creed, and his politics reflected the mild discontent of the urban lower middle class: he was not regarded by the Indians as one of them. During the mid-1930s, another doctor, J. M. Curé, a French Creole, began to try to arouse some feeling for the labouring masses. His first venture was a mass petition to the new king, Edward VIII, who was supposed to care for the ordinary people. The petition, signed by more than 17,600 persons, was despatched on 1 August 1936. The main emphasis was upon the narrowness of the constitution: there were about 8,000 electors in the population of 450,000, and the vote was confined to those with *Rs.* 3,000 capital. Curé's petition asked for the vote for all male adults who were literate, and for the abolition of plural voting; it was pointed out that Ceylon with universal adult franchise was not more advanced, politically, than Mauritius. This petition inevitably went to the Secretary for the Colonies, who replied that he would consider any representations forwarded through the legislature: which effectually closed that question. Dr Curé moved a little further towards action by forming a 'Labour Party' — *Parti Travailliste* — to demand a more democratic system: his party emerged at the beginning of 1937, and then in August the situation exploded with a series of strikes on the plantations, especially at *l'Union Flacq*, one of the few Indian-owned estates, that of R. Gujadhar, a member of the legislature. Gujadhar was an equivocal figure, half capitalist, half populist; in July 1935 he had aroused a mass-meeting in the Champ de Mars above Port Louis to demand higher wages: those in Mauritius were 'the lowest paid in any British colony', he said. At Rs. 10 per month (about 17*s.*) the sugar workers were as badly off as their forbears after slavery. But when his own workers demanded higher wages, with menaces, Gujadhar responded by giving out rifles to his clerks and overseers to overawe the field-hands; in a panic they fired, and four workers dropped down dead (two with wounds in their backs) while six were wounded. The firing led to a wave of violence across the island, and in the south the police opened fire at the village of l'Escalier, killing one and wounding another. The strike extended to the dock-workers who were African Creoles, and the acting-governor declared a state of emergency. The strikes flickered on, to fade out at the end of September. The government urged the employers' organisation, the Chamber of Agriculture, to negotiate; but the Chamber replied that this was impossible because of 'the influence of agitators, backed by small but organised gangs of intimidators'; instead, they proposed a lock-out. The government eventually told the employers that conciliation machinery would be imposed upon them unless they agreed to review their wages.⁴¹ A Commission of Enquiry was appointed in August 1937, with the legal chief, the Procurateur General, C. A. Hooper, as chairman, the Protector of Immigrants, Lionel Collet, two legislators — Dr Laurent and P. Raffray, K.C. — and the President of the Chamber of Agriculture. It was not a promising group, from the workers' viewpoint. However, when the report appeared it conceded that there was a lot wrong with the system.⁴² 'The average day labourer . . . is underpaid, and it may well be that he and his wife and children are underfed', said the report; wages should be raised by at least 10 per cent. The small farmers who brought their cane to the big Europan factories were at their mercy: this was 'an evil part of the system'. The committee concluded that political frustration was a major cause of discontent: 'The unofficial element had representatives of the white population, identifying themselves with the agricultural [sugar] interest principally, and also representatives of the coloured population, but not elected representatives of the Hindu and Mahommedan section of the population'. One witness alleged that this 'acts as an incitement of labour against capital'. When the committee came to make recommendations, they passed over the political aspects and urged only that unions should be recognised and a government department of labour and social welfare constituted; they suggested that an experienced officer might be brought from India.

Creech Jones was now actively in touch with the Mauritius labour leaders.⁴³ In parliament he called for union legislation and an extended franchise (24 November 1937) but received only a nebulous reply. Henry Polak supplemented his information, and assured him (28 March 1938) that 'the really important point' was the admission of an Agent from India into 'the largest Indian colony in the world'. In April 1938, H. T. W. Oswell, formerly of the Labour Department in Malaya, arrived to create a new industrial department; in May, an Industrial Associations Ordinance was approved by the legislature, which permitted the registration of trade unions. Twenty-five unions were registered during 1938, mostly small and local in character; on the other side a powerful Employers' Federation was also registered under the ordinance. Then in August 1938 another wave of strikes occurred; most serious in its effect was the shut-down of the Port Louis wharves, which was timed to coincide with the seasonal arrival of the great sugar steamers. Sir Bede Clifford, the new Governor, struck hard to break the strikes. J. E. Anquetil, identified as the principal leader of the workers, was banished to the remote island of Rodriguez, along-with his son, though no charge was ever laid against him. Dr Curé, Pandit Sahadeo and other leaders were confined to their own immediate neighbourhoods. Anquetil was not allowed back to Mauritius until the end of November.[44] Three hundred dockers were arrested, and loaders were brought in from the sugar factories to fill the holds of the ships; the dockers were African Creoles, the loaders were Indians. Seeing that they were beaten, the dockers went back to work, virtually unconditionally. The estate workers also gave in, and nineteen Indians who were convicted of 'inducing [the strikers] to abstain from working by intimidation' were sentenced to nine months' imprisonment, while three of them received an additional twelve months for assaulting the police.

The Under Secretary for the Colonies, the Earl of Dufferin and Ava, wrote to congratulate Clifford: 'We feel that the firm attitude you adopted on this occasion should have an excellent effect in discouraging the lawless elements in Mauritius who have been giving us all so much anxiety.' Arthur Creech Jones was appalled at the draconian measures taken against what were simply industrial protests. Between October 1938 and April 1939 he addressed six long letters to Malcolm MacDonald and Dufferin on the Mauritius labour troubles; he received eight letters in reply, and in addition had a meeting with Dufferin which was also attended by H. B. Kemmis of the International Department of the T.U.C. on 2 November. According to the note made by Kemmis: 'Mr Creech Jones criticised the drastic repression of labour unrest in the colony where the workers had neither political nor industrial equality and could ventilate their grievances in no other way. He urged that the strikers still imprisoned should be at once released and that immediate action should be taken to provide the working population with the means of industrial and political expression.' These demands for reform did not arouse even the faintest response, and when the imprisoned strikers were released, in November, this resulted from no act of clemency but from the action of the Mauritius Supreme Court in quashing the sentence on technical grounds. Dr Curé was demanding a Royal Commission, similar to the Moyne Commission, but this also was not granted. When Creech Jones took up the story in the House of Commons, declaring that 'there has been a complete outrage in the administration of justice' in Mauritius, MacDonald did not trouble to reply to the accusation. When he was pressed, two weeks later, MacDonald answered that he had 'no reason to believe that the law as it stands has been administered otherwise than with complete impartiality'.[45]

Throughout these troubled months, the Indian authorities remained silent. Whereas the slightest upset in Kenya had Bajpai firing off a telegram, these monstrous events in Mauritius left Indian administrators and politicians apparently unmoved. On 3 February 1939, the Colonial Office wrote to the India Office to dispose of outstanding problems. Blandly they declared that the Indians in Mauritius were prospering: they received Rs. 10 per month in wages, and they now had an industrial relations ordinance. There was no need to take up the question of political representation, and 'no further action' was required on the shooting of estate workers. The India Office noted that this dealt with outstanding questions 'adequately', and — when consulted — the Government of India replied that they 'do not desire to press the matter' (1 June 1939). It appeared that pressure was forthcoming only when pressure was applied by nationalist politicians.[46] However, Mauritius did not just sink gently into the sunset; the strain and stress could not just be ignored.

The position of India in the company of the Dominions did not undergo a dramatic change with the passing of the Government of India Act, 1935. At the Imperial Conference of 1937 India made no new claim to equality, as had been done in 1921 following the 1919 reforms. Overshadowed by the growing menace of Hitler and Mussolini, the 1937 conference considered how far they could go in collective commitment. The nationality question was not revived; though the Irish Nationality and Citizenship Act, 1935, had driven straight through the common code of the empire. The Irish Act specifically provided that Irish citizens were not British subjects, and it was necessary to evoke the conception of the 'external' association of the Irish Free State with the British Commonwealth to provide any explanation for the continuing presence of Irish delegates at Commonwealth conferences. Many British statesmen saw in the Irish development a warning of what would follow if India were granted full Dominion status. Meanwhile, the Indians continued to be British subjects, fellow-citizens in name, though not in reality.[47] In the Dominions, the status of the Indians remained much as before. Following the relaxation of Australian disabilities on votes for the Indians, sporadic efforts were made to induce Canada to enfranchise the Indians or 'Hindus'. However, suspicions of the Chinese in British Columbia (27,000 in 1931) and even more of the Japanese (22,000 in 1931) whose numbers were rising, prevented any move to recognise the Indians. Indeed, in 1934, the Doukhobors, a Russian primitivist sect, were actually removed from the franchise.[48]

As always, the main threat was to be feared in South Africa. For several years Kajee had avoided discriminatory action by persuading his community to bow to white prejudices and white demands: in 1938 he offered the 'Kajee Assurance' of restraint. But in the Transvaal there was a growing antagonism to Indian 'penetration' and a demand for legislation. The device of a judicial commission under Judge Feetham did not appease European demands; and in May 1939, the Transvaal Asiatics (Transvaal Land and Trading) Bill was brought before parliament. Hofmeyr regarded this as provocative, and spoke out in criticism; Prime Minister Hertzog demanded his resignation from the United Party caucus, and Hofmeyr resigned. The Bill continued on its way, and the Indian community had to decide what action to take. Kajee's strategy offered no solution, and the Indians turned to Dr Y. M. Dadoo who urged another satyagraha campaign on Gandhian lines. The moderates and the militants clashed in physical violence in June 1939, and the move towards satyagraha was only halted when Gandhi implored the South African Indians to hold back, in view of the drift of the world into war. The campaign was called off; and over the issue of South Africa joining Britain against Germany, or staying neutral, Hertzog fell from power. Smuts returned as prime minister and at once announced that there would be no legislation directed against the Indians during wartime. Again, it seemed, the Indians had been saved from outright debasement.

As Britain drifted towards war, Henry Polak inscribed yet another letter to the India Office, directed to Lieut. Colonel J. R. Muirhead who had succeeded R. A. Butler as Under Secretary for India. Polak wrote (15 June 1939) 'The question of the treatment of Indians overseas is becoming one of increasing irritation and exasperation in India. It is bad enough with South Africa and Kenya, who set the example of intolerance, but that it should be followed in Ceylon and Burma is alarming. . . . There are surely enough troubles in the international waters without this being added to them by aggressive and provocative policies in British territories.' The permanent officials at the India Office were not impressed: Mr Dibdin commented to Colonel Muirhead: 'Mr Polak's efforts in this country serve no purpose except to encourage those elements amongst Indians in India and elsewhere who wish to deprecate both the will and the power of the Government of India to serve the cause of Indians abroad.' The India Office might thus brush Henry Polak aside, as they had tried to do for twenty years; yet, during the next five years, this issue was to confront viceroys and national leaders with a challenge almost as difficult to meet as the challenge of India's demand for independence.

6
Coercion and Conflict
(1939 - 44)

The onset of the second world war seemed to portend enormous changes. Even the cautious, aloof Marquess of Zetland was aroused by the ominous knocks upon the door. 'When Parliament accepted Dominion Status as the goal [for India] the feeling was that the journey was a long one', he told the War Cabinet, 'but the effect of the outbreak of war has been to bring us hard up against the implications of Dominion Status for India' (23 October 1939), and again he told the prime minister, Neville Chamberlain: 'War on the grand scale seems to be accompanied by the churning of the ocean of thought.... I do not believe that the picture of India moving... by smooth, measured and leisurely stages... is likely to be realised' (1 December 1939). However, the strangely uneventful period which followed the destruction of Poland served to blur over the sense of urgency. Linlithgow, in India, was not to be excited; he made stately, largely empty gestures; and he assured Zetland (6 April 1940): 'For the present, we should continue to mark time.'

The early stages of the war were marked by the evacuation of civilians from certain outposts which might be plunged into the zone of hostilities: Gibraltar, Hong Kong, Aden and Somaliland were all partially evacuated during 1940, and small Indian communities were moved away. This movement stimulated one of those expansive gestures which Winston Churchill sometimes liked to make; he directed that the colonial authorities should be told: 'Mr Churchill is strongly averse from there being any discrimination on grounds of destitution or for other reasons, in the matter of evacuation, against any class of loyal British subjects abroad.'[1]

When Churchill formed his government in May 1940, Leopold Amery took over at the India Office, where he remained until the Labour government came to power in August 1945. He was not high up in Churchill's regard, and he hankered after a bigger part in the war effort; however, he applied his imperial expertise to the problems of India and Burma with the competence of experience, though not with much imagination or sympathy. Churchill seems to have regarded the Colonial Office as a staging post for peers; ministers came and went rapidly. Lord Lloyd, Lord Moyne and Viscount Cranborne passed in succession, and then Colonel Oliver

Stanley — another aristocrat — stayed for the remainder of the Churchill administration.² While the Colonial Secretary was in the House of Lords, the department was represented in the Commons by George Hall, a Labour M.P. and former miner who was Under Secretary. He soon adapted himself to the style of the Colonial Office, and especially that of the permanent Under Secretary, Sir Cosmo Parkinson.

The former Secretary for the Colonies, Malcolm MacDonald, went off as the United Kingdom High Commissioner in Canada, to begin a second career in many parts of the Commonwealth; Ormsby-Gore had also come to the end of his parliamentary life, and as Lord Harlech went to South Africa as the U.K. High Commissioner. Things went on much as before in the Government of India, with Lord Linlithgow very conscious of the siege situation of India at war, and Bajpai presiding as the Member for the Department of Health, Education and Lands and the incontrovertible authority on Indians overseas.

The year 1940, so momentous for Europe, was relatively quiet for the Indians of the British Empire. The quarrel between India and Ceylon was patched up, and a joint 'exploratory' conference was held in November 1940 at Delhi. In Burma there were desultory riotous attacks upon Indians, but no significant political developments affecting the Indians followed. South Africa was quiet, and the crisis for the Indians was delayed until 1943, and will be discussed in the following chapter. The year 1941 was ominous in the wider context of the war, and there were dramatic happenings for the Indian communities of Malaya, Burma and Ceylon, in which the Government of India and Indian political opinion were closely involved. The following year was chiefly remarkable for the mass exodus of Indians from Burma, caused by the Japanese invasion. Then, 1943 — the hinge year of the Second World War — saw the recrudescence of action at the ground level among the forgotten sugar workers of Mauritius and Fiji; as well as the beginning of the last attempt to resist white racism in South Africa. In October 1943, Linlithgow handed over the viceroyalty to Field Marshal Wavell, who had to confront the full fury of Indian nationalist feeling on South Africa. During the war years up to 1943, Indian demands for equality for their folk overseas became insistent and assertive; after 1943 those demands could not be held in check by officials in Delhi or in Whitehall. What Linlithgow had long before described as 'the rearguard action' of the British Empire in the East ended at last.

All this was unsuspected in 1940, as India and the British Empire, East of Suez, looked on as spectators as the Nazis conquered Europe; though it was clear there would be changes. Reflecting upon the position of inferiority of Indians in the Colonies and Dominions, Gilbert Laithwaite, the private secretary to the Viceroy, suggested to his counterpart, the private secretary to the Secretary of State, in a note written in October 1940: 'If the new post-war order is to depend for its stability on the solidarity of the constituent parts of the Commonwealth, then this particular sore must be healed.'

During 1940 the interminable correspondence between the India Office and the Colonial Office on the subject of Agents overseas was carried on, without making any headway. The Trade Commissioner had taken up his duties in East Africa in January 1938, but after the volte-face by the East Africa Indian Congress there was no further discussion of Indian representation at a quasi-political level. Concerning Fiji, the Colonial Office informed the India Office on 5 April 1940 that the Secretary of State had decided that an Agent 'would not be in the best interests of the Indians in Fiji or of the Colony as a whole'. The Indians were permanent settlers: 'and it is the duty and policy of the Government of the Colony . . . to promote the welfare of the Indians as of the rest of the community.' They possessed adequate means of pressing their grievances already, and the Secretary for the Colonies decided that they were 'sufficiently and impartially safeguarded'; if an Agent arrived from India this might impair 'the harmonious relations which at present exist between the Indians and other sections of the population'. This outright refusal dissuaded the India Office from trying to argue the case for an Agent in the West Indies, or elsewhere.

In South Africa, Raza Ali had been succeeded as Agent-General by Sir Benegal Rama Rau, an I.C.S. officer who had previously been India's Deputy High Commissioner in London. In the line of Indian representatives in South Africa, he adopted the most official or 'correct' approach to the office; consequently, when in 1940 Canada decided to appoint a High Commissioner in South Africa, Rama Rau sounded out Smuts on designating his post as that of High Commissioner also. This entailed certain modification of his duties: it was 'not appropriate to act as spokesman of the Indian community in the Union, as the Indian Agent-General has done'; he would therefore approach the Union government only on behalf of the Government of India, not on behalf of the South African Indians, and he would not correspond with the provincial authorities as in the past. The Government of India approved of the change, and asked the Secretary of State to give his approval (20 September 1940). 'In view of the growing disunity among Indians in South Africa, it would relieve our representative of the embarrassment of identifying himself with any particular group'; it would thereby raise India's political status. Amery asked whether South Africa would reciprocate by appointing a High Commissioner at Delhi (29 October 1940), but of course this was not planned; nevertheless, the alteration in status was approved.

Another minor event of 1940 was the visit by the Secretary to the Indian Agent-General in South Africa to Mauritius. Although Mauritius was, so to speak, just over the horizon from India's shores, there were no regular direct passenger services between the two places. It was therefore easier to send over S. Ridley from South Africa. Ridley spent most of his short time in Mauritius (from 29 May to 3 July 1940) with the British officials, and his account was largely a view of the scene through their eyes.³ This was his portrait of the Indian sugar worker: 'He is a regular visitor to the cinema, the races and football matches, and spends more on clothes and rum. He also seems to be taking to inferior types of food. On every hand there were complaints that his physique was deteriorating.' It was good to be able to ascribe the semi-starvation of the Indian labourer to his own bad habits. Mr Ridley with his blinkered view was not able to find much that was encouraging. The Industrial Associations Ordinance and the new Labour Department had accomplished little for the workers; where the Indians tried to set up unions, the employers retaliated by dismissing the officials of the new unions: 'The Department has prosecuted in a few cases of victimisation,' wrote Ridley, 'none has been successful.'⁴ In consequence, most of the unions collapsed. He also found that the Indian children, an increasing percentage of the population, were a decreasing percentage of the school population. Indians were badly under-represented in the public services, especially in the police; of 570 constables, only 105 were Indians, and only one of the eight Assistant Superintendents was an Indian.⁵ In the choice of representatives for the island legislature, the Council of Government, only two Indians had ever been elected; 'when an Indian stands for election other parties combine against him. An Indian will vote for a candidate of another race, but the other races will never vote for an Indian.' It was the same in the municipal elections in Port Louis; Indians owned two-thirds of the property in the town, but there were only two Indians among the twelve municipal councillors; only three of the others actually lived in Port Louis; the remainder owed their election to the business vote. This depressing account was sent to the Government of India who forwarded it to London (31 January 1941) with no demands for remedial action.

The recurrent controversy with Ceylon was interlarded by industrial conflict during 1939. Nehru had advised the estate workers to organise trade unions, and when these started the employers reacted as they had in Mauritius: by dismissing the leaders. The sackings provoked a wave of strikes, beginning in August and rising in their intensity to the end of the year; the victimised leaders were thrown out of their estate dwellings with their families, and this practice was specially resented. Early in 1940 there was considerable violence on Mooloya estate, and the police were called in to arrest the leaders. One Indian worker was shot, and this precipitated a constitutional crisis when the Inspector General of Police tried to get a prosecution of the police postponed. The Ministers objected; the Governor backed the Inspector General and the Colonial Office backed the Governor. The Board of Ministers resigned; but agreed to return when the Governor offered to have the procedural question examined by a Select Committee.[6]

Against this background, attempts were made to reach agreement on the future of the Indians in Ceylon; at first the negotiations were conducted in the old and laborious way — through the India Office and Colonial Office in London — but the urgency and political sensitivity of the subject led to direct negotiation between Colombo and Delhi. Unfortunately, this did not make agreement any easier; rather, the reverse.

At the beginning of 1940, Malcolm MacDonald received a deputation from the Ceylon Association, representing the tea and rubber planters; they pressed for the removal of the Indian ban on the emigration of unskilled labour. MacDonald told Zetland (23 January 1940) 'The Ministers in Ceylon, heavyfooted and tactless as they were in the early stages of this controversy have gone some way ... in modifying the original scheme' for reducing Indian employment. MacDonald regretted that an impasse now existed; perhaps a conference in London between the two responsible departments might ease the deadlock? However, the quarrel was resumed when, in March, S. W. R. D. Bandaranaike made a speech to the State Council which called attention to the number of Indians registered as voters. He alleged that the electoral officials 'had absolutely flouted the spirit and the letter of the law' and he demanded that the provisions on domicile and permanent residence be strictly enforced. Observed Bajpai (21 March 1940) 'Statements of this nature ... cause both resentment and alarm.' The comment of Governor Caldecott to Lloyd was that this motion was 'primarily a nationalist vote-catching stratagem of Bandaranaike and Senanayake.' Under the Donoughmore constitution another general election was due before the beginning of 1941, and the Sinhalese leaders were determined to reinforce their hold on the government. 'So long as the State Council is the chief executive authority, Ministers will never act responsibly,' Caldecott telegraphed (11 May 1940). Clearly, a conference in London would not provide the answer, and this was called off.

The position which Bandaranaike had taken up on the franchise was underlined when on 14 May he moved a resolution in the Council of State to define the Indian franchise more severely. Any Indian claiming domicile must 'prove positively' that he had acquired domicile (though Bandaranaike did not indicate how this might be done) and any Indian attempting to obtain the vote on the basis of permanent residence must be required to renounce any claim to the protection of another government (India) and forego any rights not enjoyed by all Ceylonese: this was a thrust at the estates' labour code. The motion was debated for four days, and then was carried by 30 votes to 17. But the Governor declined to accept these proposals, as he told the Secretary of State in a long despatch dated 14 June 1940.[7]

It will be recalled that in June 1930, under pressure from Wedgwood Benn and Sir Louis Kershaw, Passfield had agreed (as India's price for accepting the Donoughmore constitution) to announce (10 June 1930) that there was 'no intention of repealing or amending to the detriment of Indians any of the laws of Ceylon affecting their position or privileges' (see p. 120 above). Caldecott told Lloyd: 'Any idea of now going back on Lord Passfield's telegram after the passage of ten years appears to me quite outside practical politics, inconsistent with Ceylon's obligations under international conventions, and incompatible with such a development of a representative democratic tradition as alone could form the basis of any future constitutional advancement.' Lloyd concurred; he cabled to Caldecott (3 July 1940) that it was 'Imperative that the Ministers should clearly understand the threat to Ceylon which is likely to result from their intransigence *vis-à-vis* India.' They must modify their policies.

At this point, an Order in Council was issued, postponing the Ceylon elections for a two year period. The announcement took some of the heat out of the Indian question, as it was no longer of immediate political urgency to neutralise the Indian vote. The ministers told the Governor that they wanted to deal directly with the Government of India, not via London (5 July 1940). They also advised that the Indian ban on emigration was 'salutary' as estate labour was in surplus supply, but Caldecott foresaw this situation changing, which 'will present an increasingly serious racial and economic problem.' The first move made by the ministers under the new direct arrangement was to cable Delhi (23 July) asking for a conference at which Ceylon would be represented by three ministers. It took the Government of India a little while to ponder over this proposal, but on 8 August they signified that they would ·'cordially welcome' a conference.

Conveying to the Colonial Secretary the ministers' message to Delhi, Caldecott commented that there was 'generally a more realistic attitude' on their part, since the announcement of the postponed elections; he urged them to go without 'pre-conditions', for these might make them vulnerable to opposition attack, if they had to accept modifications. Lord Lloyd telegraphed a personal reply to Caldecott (17 September 1940): he hoped that the ministers would discard their State Council resolution, which could fatally prejudice the talks: 'I hope the Board [of Ministers] will on further reflection agree that those who genuinely choose to adopt the status of Ceylonese should not suffer special disabilities.... Such discrimination would appear to me difficult to contemplate.' Caldecott was worried by the selection of the ministers to represent Ceylon: these were Don Senanayake, Claude Corea (president of the Ceylon National Congress) and George de Silva, all 'notoriously irresponsible', according to Caldecott (22 October 1940).

The talks ran from 4 to 11 November, and despite expressions of goodwill, there was no basis for agreement.[8] On their side, the Ceylon ministers declared: 'We cannot absorb the full number of Indians in Ceylon ... the absorption of what corresponds to one-sixth of the total population ... would undoubtedly lead ... to the extermination of our own people ... it is really becoming now a stark question of survival.' The Ceylon proposals were to accept Indians of the third generation born in Ceylon as Ceylonese; to grant the franchise to those Indians 'with a domicile of choice', but to impose certain restrictions; and to allow Indians with less than five years' residence the right to work, but to deny them for all time the possibility of acquiring political rights; the same to apply to their children. All this would be accompanied by a drive to reduce numbers and a repatriation scheme 'on the South African model'. India replied by asking for political rights after five years' residence, though suggesting that Indians should accept that Ceylonese would receive priority in government service. As both sides were so far apart, the talks were adjourned, and the trade talks which should have followed never took place. In his personal account of the conference, Linlithgow told Amery (19/20 November 1940) that the Ceylon ministers' purpose was not to reach agreement but to strike attitudes which would satisfy their nationalist supporters; they had no authority to agree to terms, and had to report everything back to their colleagues. If India had given way, this would have weakened 'the stand for equality of status for Indians resident in other parts of the British Commonwealth'.

When Caldecott discussed the stalemate with his ministers, the talk was 'not without heat' (according to his account to Lloyd, 20 December 1940) and there were murmurings of resignation from both Senanayake and Bandaranaike when the Governor reminded them of 'still current undertakings given by Ceylon in respect of immigrants since 1923'. Senanayake followed this up with an attack on the Indians at a rally of the Ceylon National Congress on 21 December. He spoke of 'the treacherous variety [of allegiance] which gives its entire devotion to the country of origin and bestows on the country of residence mere lip-service, vilification, and misrepresentation'. The speech was applauded by the major newspaper syndicate, the Lake House Press, in its English-language and Sinhalese papers which all adopted a strong anti-Indian line.

In an attempt to salvage something from the fiasco, Bajpai accepted an invitation from Caldecott to pay a private visit to Ceylon. In their conversations, the Governor complained that under the Donoughmore constitution he had no 'positive power of initiative'; only a power of veto. Caldecott wanted to remind the Ceylon politicians of the various commitments accepted by the Ceylon government in the past, but there was some difficulty in finding the relevant papers; the Secretariat records were 'little short of chaotic'. However, he was determined to make the State Council understand that they must honour undertakings made on behalf of Ceylon. Both Senanayake and Bandaranaike were bent on making political capital out of the Indian question: 'These two ministers are rivals in the race for political leadership of the Sinhalese and think that he who displays the greater degree of xenophobia will be the winner.' Caldecott regarded Jayatilaka as 'the one statesman', adding that therefore he was 'distrusted by the rest who were working for his downfall' (a prophecy which soon came true).[9]

An indication of how far the administration was beginning to respond to nationalist criticism was given when the revision of the electoral rolls was published in January 1941. There were 141,899 Indians eligible for the vote; of these 66,200 were placed upon the preliminary lists of voters, 43,900 of these were orally examined on their qualifications, and it was established that at least 80 per cent of these people had lived in Ceylon for ten years or more. However, their claim to have made Ceylon their permanent home was in most cases rejected; 19,234 Indians were registered as 'domiciled' and only 532 were given certificates of permanent residence: though previously the majority of Indian voters had qualified by this means. The names of 161,676 former voters were struck out of the registers.[10]

The Governor was not prepared to bow to the nationalist pressure: on 13 February, he caused the Speaker to read to the Council of State a message listing the undertakings which Ceylon had given to India under five main heads. Sir Baron Jayatilaka moved the adjournment of the legislature to express 'dissatisfaction with the action taken by the Governor'. The ministers instructed the Legal Secretary to prepare a Bill to deal with 'the Indian question'. When the Council of State reconvened on 4 March, two Bills were brought forward covering registration and immigration. These measures had actually been drafted the previous year, but had been kept back, pending the Delhi conference.[11] In future, all Indians entering Ceylon must produce passports and apply for residence permits, which would be issued for three months, only if the applicant could prove that he was not taking the job of a Ceylonese. All non-Ceylonese already in the island must obtain residence certificates; if they were without, then they were liable to deportation. The Chief Secretary introduced these measures with the observation that he did so under orders; they were 'inopportune and unnecessary'. Senanayake replied with an attack upon the British bureaucracy: 'Whilst being in a position of trust they are doing what damage they can'. The Bills obtained 30 votes in support, with 13 against, but it was all rather a charade as it was known that the Bills would not become law.

For a few months there was a lull in the long drawn out Indo-Ceylon tussle, and the spotlight turned upon the Indians in Malaya. The initiative taken by Bajpai in March 1939 to try to obtain a charter of rights for the Malayan Indians received a belated acknowledgement in June 1940, when the Malayan government approached India once more to try to reopen the flow of emigration. To sugar the pill, the letter from the Federal Secretary (18 June 1940) took a glance back at the questions raised by Bajpai. Although the superior posts were reserved for Malays or Europeans, Malayan Indians were offered the empty promise of equality of opportunity, while the adequacy of Indian representation in the legislatures was also touched upon. This meaningless appraisal was received with the indifference it deserved.

Since the outbreak of war, rubber prices had risen steeply and production was booming; but the prosperity had not been shared with the estate workers. Chinese labour had shown a capacity for militancy in the strikes of 1937, and once again resorted to strike action in Negri Sembilan in December 1940.[12] The Indians had always been regarded as 'docile' by the employers, but in certain areas they were beginning to be organised for action. The Klang District Union had a specially vigorous Indian secretary, R. H. Nathan, formerly a journalist. The employers began to restore the wages to the level of the old standard wage of 50 cents per day, but there was no general levelling up of wages and on some estates where the managers resisted pay rises the Indians went on strike, as at Ebor Estate in Klang district. C. S. Venkatachar was almost at the end of his tour as Agent for India, and on his farewell visit to the Ebor workers on 30 March 1941 he gave them some advice: 'I am not of the opinion that you labourers are doing anything wrong, but I strongly advise you not to accept any outsiders to help you. You must save your self-respect, and the Union.' Nathan also addressed the Ebor strikers, urging them to follow Gandhi's example of non-violent resistance. The strikes spread; then N. Raghavan, a Penang lawyer who was president of the Central Indian Association offered his services as mediator, and most were quickly settled. From 1 April, the standard wage was raised to 60 cents a day, but upon some estates the increase was delayed, so that the concession did not stop the trend to strike action (especially as Chinese workers on the Dunlop estates were striking for a daily wage of $1.30). Between mid-April and early May there were twenty-eight strikes on estates around Klang.

The response of the government was to hit at the leaders: the standard response. The police urged that three men be arrested: Nathan, U. K. Menon and Thangiah, all officials of the Klang union. On 18 March, the High Commissioner, Sir Shenton Thomas, gave his approval to their arrest, and warrants were subsequently issued. But the arrests were postponed on the advice of the Labour Commissioner, C. Wilson. As the situation seemed easier, thanks to Raghavan's mediation, this policy was accepted by Major Kidd, the Resident of Selangor, within whose state the main industrial action occurred.

However, by 3 May, Wilson had changed his mind: he advised Major Kidd that Nathan was 'intriguing to introduce Indian politics. This justified his removal'. Wilson's observation seems to refer to the new style adopted by the Indian labourers of wearing the 'Gandhi cap' (as Indian Congress workers do to this day), flying the Congress tri-colour flag in their lines, and not pausing to dismount from bicycles when passing Europeans. Shenton Thomas later called Mr Wilson 'short sighted, unsound and ineffective', but on his advice the arrests were now made.

At once the character of the strikes changed, and violence replaced non-violence. The numbers involved were still relatively limited—

between seven and eight thousand workers—but things passed out of the control of Major Kidd and the local administration. The arrival of five hundred additional police did not restore order, and the Selangor police chief asked for military reinforcements. The nearest army units were those of the Australian Imperial Forces, but when the Australians were contacted their commander replied that they were not 'empowered' to aid the civil authorities. Shenton Thomas then made an approach to Major-General Barstow, commanding a Division of Indian troops. The nearest Indian unit was at Ipoh, distant 125 miles, but they were put on alert for riot duty. Thus it was by a weird combination of circumstances that an Indian battalion, despatched to Malaya to keep India safe from possible Japanese attack, fired its first shots against Indians, brought across the seas to produce rubber for British industry.

The 1st Battalion, Frontier Force Rifles, was deployed in the area of Port Swettenham, and was ordered to send out patrols. On 11 May there was a fracas in which Indian strikers tried to attack a British plantation assistant; the troops intervened to arrest the attackers, and an Indian labourer was killed from a head wound. Four days later, the Frontier Force Rifles were involved again, two hundred strikers tried to rush a detachment, and in fighting them off the troops had to fire; three labourers were shot and two were bayonetted (one died of his wounds).

The Malayan Indians were frightened by this tough action, and Raghavan went round the estates appealing to the labourers to return to work unconditionally. Shenton Thomas emphasised the tough policy to any Resident who might hesitate; on 17 May he addressed a circular to all the Residents, deploring 'the growing strength of Indian political organisation in this country. The strikes have been mainly political' he insisted, and he concluded: 'Malaya is not India, and I will not have labour and politics mixed up if I can help it.' Thomas followed this up by deporting Nathan to India on the next boat. U. K. Menon, the president of the Klang Union prudently withdrew to Penang, and under the peculiar laws governing the Malay states and the Straits Settlements he was immune from arrest. However, five of the union officials were arrested, while four absconded; after a short interval, Raghavan was also deported to India.[13] The strikes were over, and the military were withdrawn on 26 May.

Even in wartime, Malaya was not insulated from the outside world, and these events became the subject of comment. Questions were put down in the House of Commons by worried Labour M.P.s. George Hall was primed to give the Colonial Office reply. There was 'considerable intimidation...by bands of strikers', he said; Sir

Shenton Thomas had assured them that there was no economic justification for the strikes, which had been brought about by the propaganda activities of the Central Indian Association: there was 'clear evidence of subversive propaganda' by Nathan, especially; and if there were still any doubts the Secretary for the Colonies (who was now Lord Moyne) would consider 'a full and sympathetic examination of any grievances'. A somewhat astonished Reginald Sorensen retorted that Hall's statement 'sounds very similar to a report that might have been given on industrial unrest in South Wales'; trying to arouse the former miner to some sense of identification with the strikers. 'There must have been some other cause than subversive activity', Sorensen insisted, but Hall doggedly repeated that there would be a full investigation, and when Creech Jones pressed for more satisfactory industrial machinery the Speaker cut the debate short.[14]

The Colonial Office was anxious lest the evidence of police repression in Ceylon the previous year, combined with the present military repression might move parliament to press for a commission of enquiry. This, Sir Cosmo Parkinson wanted to avoid; and it was gratifying that Hall hastened to inform the Permanent Under Secretary that he did not dissent from this viewpoint.[15] As the evidence accumulated, Hall was to get a little further than the 'agitator' explanation; but for the present all was well at the Colonial Office. A general letter of guidance was sent to Shenton Thomas from the Colonial Secretary (4 June 1941): 'From our experiences in Ceylon we must expect that the principal ingredients of Indian labour problems will increasingly be social and political in origin'. The planters should not be left to deal with the problem; the Labour Department must take the initiative, and the Agent of the Government of India must be kept informed.

If the Colonial Office was slowly beginning to recognise the right of labour to press for change, the employers firmly resisted any such development. Guthrie and Co., the major rubber producers, wrote to their London associates (5 May 1941) ascribing the strikes to 'agitators' and 'ringleaders'; when complaints were made to the Colonial Office, Clifford Figg replied 'Political and Trade Union activity in this country and in the Empire is not a crime'; it was accepted government policy to encourage trade unions, and Malaya must cooperate in this process. He replied in the same vein to the Chairman of the Malaya Committee in London (J. L. Milne, of Shaw, Daly and Co.): 'Labour both in Ceylon and Malaya is now becoming politically conscious... they wish to have some say in their mode of life and conditions of work'; it was dangerous to drive the unions 'underground', said Clifford Figg (20 June 1941). In

Malaya, the planters' organisation, U.P.A.M., was telling Shenton Thomas that he had been dilatory and weak: why were Nathan and Menon not arrested in March when the warrants were signed? For U.P.A.M. knew everything that went on in the government departments.

However, in India there was resentment and anger at the crass and callous way in which the Indian expeditionary force had been expected to suppress Indian workers on behalf of the Malayan government. The evidence supplied by the newly-arrived Agent, Subimal Dutt, was very different from that given by Governor Thomas and the planters. The Central Indian Association was 'a body seeking improvement in the political status of Indians by constitutional means'; workers who 'sought to voice comparatively minor demands for improvement' had been summarily dismissed, and the planters resorted to the law to eject them from their estate dwellings. The use of force by the authorities 'might intensify labour troubles'. The use of the Banishment Ordinance against labour leaders was objectionable: the Government of India demanded the immediate appointment of a conciliation officer and the setting up of a judicial inquiry into the shootings: as was 'the usual practice in the British Empire' (4 June 1941). Urged on by Linlithgow, Amery wrote personally to Lord Moyne (26 June) to remind him of the rather fruitless exchanges between the Indian and Malayan governments regarding 'the position of inferiority' of the Malayan Indians in public life; Amery asked for some indication that they would now obtain 'equality of status'.

After this approach, a telegram was despatched from the Colonial Office to Shenton Thomas (9 July 1941) conveying a general assessment of the situation. The new 'assertive' attitude of the Indian workers must be accepted; there must be an overall policy of cooperation, and 'mishandling' by individual planters must be checked. The 'important influence of the Government of India must necessarily be recognised. Questions of prestige of the Malayan Labour Department should not have such effect as to interfere with this purpose', and it seemed advisable to bring in experienced labour officers from India to help set up conciliation machinery. The Agent of the Government of India must be associated with the 'new phase in relations with Indian labour'. Moyne wrote in equally conciliatory terms to Amery (12 July): 'Every encouragement should be given to the responsible elements in the Indian community' of Malaya, and the Government of India would be asked to provide a memorandum on 'removing any apparent discrimination against Indians in Malaya'.

Events in Malaya reflected this conciliatory approach not at all;

Mr Dutt reported that 326 Indians were in detention under emergency regulations; all but six or seven were labourers. Their cases were reviewed by a government advisory committee, and deportation orders were being passed upon some Indians, few of whom had secured legal aid. Indian opinion regarded the whole proceeding as one of victimisation: 'Having regard to the traditional docility of Indian labour, no one will believe that all these persons have been guilty of subversive activities' observed the Government of India (14 July) and there would be a massive demand for retaliation against Malaya; perhaps for the withdrawal of Indian troops. The Colonial Office must press for a normal process of trial, or at least for proper legal aid: also, there must be the 'earliest possible' inquiry into the shootings. Amery rushed this telegram round to Moyne (15 July); the 'difficulties are pretty serious and urgent' he noted.

One reason why Linlithgow was anxious to demonstrate that the situation in Malaya was being fully investigated was that he was just about to enlarge his government, so as to associate the Indian public more fully with the Indian war effort. Linlithgow's attempts to bring in leaders of the Congress and the Muslim League to form a widely-based administration had failed; both Congress and League demanded long-term political concessions which the Viceroy was not prepared to give. Linlithgow had therefore to produce some kind of substitute for genuine cooperation from the big political movements. He planned to create a National Defence Council, an advisory body of distinguished Indians, and also to expand his own executive council so as to create an Indian majority. The members of the Viceroy's Council had always individually supervised departments of government; it was decided to sub-divide some of the departments to provide executive functions for the new councillors. An obvious opening existed with the Department of Education, Health and Lands—already regarded as in some sense a 'nationalist' department. A new Department of Indians Overseas was now created, and as its head Linlithgow selected a former leader of the Congress, Madhao Shrihari Aney. Aney was from Maharashtra; a politician held in high respect. Linlithgow looked down from his great height on most of his associates, British and Indian with a certain condescension; but he came to feel real affection and regard for Aney. This was to come; just now he was aware that he was departing from his habitual caution in putting Aney's name forward; as he told Amery (1 July), 'We are running a little close to the wind in getting Aney in, though I do not feel any doubt... that *politically* as distinct from *administratively* he is the desirable choice'. The new appointments were to be announced on 21 July, though the actual handover was to be delayed till later. Clearly, Linlithgow could not happily contemplate Aney taking over such a mess as the current unresolved crisis in Malaya: nor was Amery any happier about the situation. Deliberately, Linlithgow was converting his Council from an official body of seven, of whom only three were Indians, into a committee of twelve, in which there were to be eight Indians, mainly from political and public life. In theory—and perhaps in practice—they could outvote the Viceroy, the Commander-in-Chief, and the two other English members. Beyond the Malayan imbroglio, there were difficult questions in Ceylon and Burma to be tackled; no wonder that Linlithgow and Amery were worried.

Linlithgow supplemented the 'official' telegram of 14 July with a 'private and personal' telegram on the 26th. The political or 'subversive' aspect of the strikes had been exaggerated by the authorities in Malaya; even the existence of trade unions was seen as 'a danger to the state', and the estate workers had 'lost all confidence' in the Labour Department, according to Dutt. Feeling in India against the involvement of Indian troops was 'very strong'; Linlithgow concluded: 'This is an issue which one could wish put into better shape before Aney, who is a strong Nationalist, assumes charge for Indians Overseas.' Amery hastened to pass on these views to Moyne (30 July) and he received his answer on 2 August: Moyne wanted to try to establish 'a common meeting ground' between India and Malaya. One improvement would be to enhance the status of the Agent of the Government of India 'beyond the very limited purposes for which the office was instituted'.

Moyne, like MacDonald, was able to see the limitations of the traditional Colonial Office attitude to the overseas Indians; but the Office was ultimately more powerful than the Secretary of State. When Cosmo Parkinson read the Government of India telegram of 14 July, he noted: 'The Government of India—and Indians overseas—can be, and I fear not infrequently have been, very tiresome and *difficile*... The Government of India must be forthcoming, and not expect Malaya (or Ceylon) to do all the giving.' It was the Parkinsonian view which prevailed in the long term; but meanwhile Moyne sent a 'secret and personal' telegram to Shenton Thomas (5 August) which sought to give satisfaction to India. Moyne proposed a 'full public inquiry' into the shootings, which should include a High Court judge from India in the tribunal; he asked that the proceedings against the detainees should be held in public, and he asked for 'no large-scale deportations' to India. Unless these proposals were accepted it was likely that all emigration from India would be halted and India would require assurances that Indian forces in Malaya would not be used against the working population. Moyne believed it was 'politically advantageous on the widest imperial grounds to satisfy the Government of India's feelings as far as possible'. It was essential to convince India that the Malayan Government was 'not dominated by the planting interest'. He hoped that Thomas would now release all the detainees except those 'principally responsible for agitation against the war effort'.

Shenton Thomas was in a predicament; after all, the Malayan Government was openly influenced by the rubber industry. Even before Moyne's telegram arrived, the planters had received rumours of an inquiry, and had begun to bombard the High Commissioner with protests against any inquiry. On 11 August, Ward Jackson sent a cable on behalf of U.P.A.M. to the chairman of Guthries' in London: they were totally opposed to any inquiry which would 'unsettle' the labour force.

Then, the strikers had not been acting against the war effort: the only political motive which could be ascribed to them was a vague identification with the Indian National Congress; they had simply agitated for higher wages. For the moment, Shenton Thomas sat tight. He sent a cable to the Colonial Office on 6 August, but it was not a reply to the previous day's communication. He listed the results of the proceedings of the so-called Advisory Committee (which actually had quasi-legal powers). Of the 363 detainees, twelve had been released unconditionally; 185 were released but not allowed to return to the district where they had been employed (and were thus deprived of home and job), forty-nine—mostly local-born Indians—were kept in detention, twenty-one had been deported, and ninety-five 'accepted repatriation' (as an alternative to some other form of sanction). This was supposed to dispose of the arrests of the strikers.

One of the next moves by Shenton Thomas was to send for the Indian Agent, Dutt, and grill him upon his reports to India: Dutt feared that pressure was being exerted by 'the planter type'.[16] Next, Thomas talked to Major Orde Browne, the Labour Adviser at the Colonial Office, who was on a short visit to Malaya with instructions to examine the situation after the riots. Orde Browne's own experiences of labour conditions had been with Africans in Tanganyika; he was committed to a paternalist, welfare approach. He obligingly cabled the Colonial Office to advise against an inquiry; it would be a 'triumph' for the local Indian politicians, he said, and later he suggested that any concessions would be 'exploited by the Chinese Communist element' (without explaining how this would arise).[17]

The High Commissioner now felt ready to reply to the Secretary of State, and he cabled on 28 August. He referred to his official despatch concerning the Klang disturbances, which had not yet reached the Colonial Office.[18] This had shown that Nathan and Raghavan were behind the strikes, but Thomas opposed any inquiry because this 'would expose the subversive activities of Nathan and others which might be regarded as reflecting upon the Indian community as a whole, which would have been unjust'. He revealed that Wilson, the Labour Controller, would leave his post on retirement (he had actually left) while Major Kidd, the Resident of Selangor, had been transferred elsewhere. He justified the use of the so-called Advisory Committee, and he ended by deploring the intervention of the Government of India: it was 'an unwarranted attempt to interfere with the administration of another country'. An inquiry commission 'would be disastrous locally'; in short, he rejected every one of Moyne's proposals.

There was anxious consultation at the Colonial Office. Edward Gent (who was to be Governor of the shortlived Malayan Union after the war) disapproved of the prevailing attitude in Malaya; 'There are strong "conservative" influences both in the central and state governments in Malaya and amongst the employers, where sighing for the good old easy conditions will discourage any imaginative policy towards Indian labourers', he noted, adding: 'It has always been a difficulty with Malaya that India must be kept at arm's length'; the appointment of the commission was seen as a question of 'face', though it could be set up without being a surrender: but Gent ended by advising that they postpone any action until Orde Browne's return. W. B. L. Monson would concede less: 'Our object in accepting the representations of the Governor [sic] of India is not to exaggerate the importance of local Indian politicians, but only to do something to show the Government of India that these politicians are not right, and the Malayan Government wrong, every time'.

When the file had circulated, and everyone had done, there was a meeting between Lord Moyne, George Hall and Edward Gent. Hall had now revised his former assessment; the strikes had been 'mishandled' and Sir Shenton Thomas 'cannot avoid responsibility' he said. But Moyne had also shifted his ground; now he was against any post-mortem on the shootings, and he was against a visit by Aney to Malaya, which had been suggested by Amery. He proposed that there should be a new kind of inquiry which would examine the work of the Labour Department, the role of the Agent of the Government of India and the representation of Indians on public bodies. This was suggested to Thomas, who accepted the proposal in a telegram dated 24 October, adding that the commission should review the question of Indian emigration to Malaya.

All this had moved far away from the original situation. The Government of India attempted to recall the issue of the shootings.

Somewhat late in the day, information was passed to the India Office (10 October) that the Agent had attended the hearings of the Advisory Committee. There were no proper rules; of thirty-three witnesses to the shootings, only two were labourers, one of whom was himself in custody. The Agent said the Indians 'dared not state what they knew' and accused the tribunal of 'removing or muzzling witnesses'. Perhaps this might have been acted upon earlier, but now the affair was going stale. Linlithgow still adhered to his former position. He told Amery (12 October) that Orde Browne's views had been 'largely influenced by the Planters' Association'. He was astonished that the Malayan administration had not instituted a public inquiry: this was 'the rule rather than the exception'.

Moyne put his new proposition for a general inquiry to Amery (21 October) who passed it on to Linlithgow, who was appalled: any commission must begin with the strikes, or else it would appear to be 'an ingenious method of eluding responsibility'. India was not interested in the new proposition, and if asked officially he would give 'neither consent nor approval'. Meanwhile, after a long wait for an aeroplane in West Africa, Orde Browne had returned to London. His report showed that the Malayan Labour Department kept no statistics on wages and prices and did not know whether the trade union's demands were justified or not. It was all very disquieting, as George Hall observed; but no-one seemed to know what to do. On 27 November Moyne told Amery that he had decided to put the proposal 'into cold storage'.[19]

Indian public opinion remained dissatisfied but impotent. The banished Raghavan had behaved with restraint on his arrival in India; Bajpai had demonstrated the official response by giving a party in his honour at his Simla home. There was a debate in the Council of State (20 November 1941) initiated by Pandit Kunzru. He condemned the 'unexampled arrogance' of the Malayan authorities in using Indian troops against Indians, and another member, P. N. Sapru burst out: 'If India were an independent state it would know how to deal with this most rotten of all governments imaginable, this Malayan government'. The official reply was given by Mr Bozman, who rendered a full account of the proceedings against the Indian workers. The Government of India had made 'repeated requests' for a judicial inquiry; they expressed 'extreme resentment' against the use of Indian troops. The only gain had been that the Agent had ensured that 195 of the Indian detainees received legal representation. It was a sad story; but there was not much that Kunzru could say in reply; there was so much general agreement between the government and the politicians.

Long before the Malayan controversy had wandered to its unsatisfactory end, attention in India had been concentrated upon other neighbouring lands; first upon Burma, and then again upon Ceylon. The situation of the Indian community in Burma had remained insecure; there were riots in Rangoon in April 1940, in which 26 Indians were killed and 170 wounded. These riots re-echoed the anti-Muslim theme, but were partly within the Indian community, so that 162 Indians were deported.

Robert Hutchings, the Agent of the Government of India, was specially worried by the Land Purchase Bill, directed against the Indian landholders who were mainly Chettyars of the banking caste. He told Gilbert Laithwaite, the Viceroy's private secretary (20 April 1941) 'To all outward appearances the Government of India and the Secretary of State have been unwilling to bring Burma to book by a demand for compensation'. This was a reaction against the politics of Dyarchy in which the minorities had meddled on behalf of their own interests: but now, 'If a Ministry has no major riot or breach of the peace to its discredit, payslip service to the principles of democracy and is not too blatantly corrupt it can rely on their support'. Hutchings concluded 'Burmans intend to get Burma for the Burmans with a vengeance'.

As in Ceylon, a general election was due to be held in Burma before the end of 1941. U Saw's majority was by no means secure, and the Indian question had explosive possibilities. In this situation, Bajpai went to Burma to negotiate an agreement to replace the interim arrangements which had followed Burma's separation from India. He arrived in Rangoon in June 1941, and with Hutchings and Bozman as his advisers, he met the Burmese ministers. Their team was led by U Saw, with Htoon Aung Gyaw, the shrewd Minister of Finance, two other ministers, and Tin Tut, the senior Burmese I.C.S. administrator as adviser. Negotiations lasted from 20 to 28 June, when an agreement was concluded.

At first Bajpai doubted whether Saw was genuinely interested in agreement; there was much talk of the Burmese fear of being 'swamped' and forebodings about the forthcoming election giving rise to 'racial passion'.[20] In the background there was the Baxter report on Indian immigration, which was still unpublished, but which proposed a system of regulations for the future. The ministers wanted to go further than Baxter. Bajpai was prepared to agree to restrictions upon unskilled labour; he found it 'degrading' that Indians did all the menial work in Rangoon. Gradually, Bajpai made some headway: Hutchings reported that his 'unfailing courtesy and patience made a tremendous impression', and he established 'most cordial relations' with U Saw and Tin Tut.[21] A draft began to take shape, though Bajpai still had to face critical questions, as when the Burmese brought up the sensitive subject of 'cohabitation' between Indian men and Burmese women: they were determined to end the recurring situation where Indians went home, leaving their temporary wives in the lurch. While the discussions were in progress, Bajpai 'took unlimited pains' to carry the leaders of the local Indian community with him in his dealings, according to Hutchings. Bajpai did not put the agreement before them for formal discussion, but he did consult them fully, and he recorded that they accepted unwelcome details, like the cohabitation clause, rather than face a breakdown; S. A. S. Tyabji was specially helpful. So Bajpai returned, confident that they had obtained the best terms.[22]

Hutchings believed that 'the so-called "immigration problem" . . . has been brought to the front primarily by racial, sectional, and political considerations, and not by economic factors'. He thought that there were 'certain risks' in the agreement, but that it would 'secure the safety and interests of Indians domiciled or settled in Burma'.

At first it seemed as though Hutchings' assessment would be endorsed by Indian opinion. The Standing Emigration Committee of the central legislature met at Simla in mid-July and accepted the agreement.[23] Aney was amongst those present. Bajpai telegraphed to U Saw to 'formally confirm acceptance by the Government of India' on 20 July; he raised two points of interpretation, but he hoped that the agreement would be worked in 'a spirit of mutual confidence and cooperation'; it represented a 'reasonable compromise', he said. Maybe Bajpai was over-confident; he had been appointed the first Agent-General for India at Washington, and naturally he wished to leave his old department with a glow of success. The terms of the agreement were released in India and Burma simultaneously, on 22 July: and then the trouble began.

A public meeting was organised at Madras on 28 July. It was called an 'All Party Protest', though it was mainly representative of the Chettyars with some fringe support (as by the Madras Muslim League). The meeting protested that what should have been exploratory talks the previous month had presented a *fait accompli*. The viceroy became a little worried, because an immigration treaty was being negotiated with China, and it seemed possible that the terms might be somewhat more favourable: then the Bajpai agreement would be 'impossible to defend', he told Amery (7 August). A few days later, Tyabji and other Indian leaders flew to India; their object was not simply to condemn the Bajpai terms but to work for a settlement. Bajpai was becoming very unhappy: his 'personal honour [had been] persistently and publicly impugned' he told Hutchings (10 August). But the bombshell was to burst with a pronouncement by Gandhi on 24 August. The agreement was 'panicky and penal' declared Gandhi; 'a brutal reminder that they are under the British heel', 'an undeserved slur on India and Burma'. Gandhi tried to blur over the pressure from the Burmese politicians to exclude the Indians: he said that U Saw 'has played himself into the hands of those who would want to exploit Burma to the exclusion of any rivals', and he appealed to the Burmese premier to postpone negotiations on immigration 'till both of us are free'. But Gandhi was not engaging in polemic only; he cited the assurances given by Inskip and R. A. Butler just five years before: these were 'promissory notes', he said, and it was difficult to deny the charge.

Linlithgow told Amery that Gandhi's intervention was designed 'to have a weapon against Aney' (26 August) but in reality Aney was deeply impressed by Gandhi's statement, and he informed Bajpai 'I have read Mahatma Gandhi's trenchant criticism of it [the agreement] ... I think you should press the Secretary of State to withhold his consent ... during the period of the war. Indian feeling is strong, and H.M.G. may be inclined to respect it at a time when they want India to make the supreme effort to help the war'. There were further protests; the All-India Muslim League condemned the agreement on 26 August and the Deputy Mayor of Calcutta, M. A. H. Ispahani, presided over a clamorous public meeting on 12 September.[24] Linlithgow decided that it was expedient to accept the criticisms, and on 23 September he cabled Dorman-Smith to ask him to persuade the Burmese ministers to re-open conversations for the 'adjusting of a limited number of points'.

Meanwhile, Bajpai had led a delegation to talks with Ceylon, and was ready to set out for Washington. Amery wondered whether perhaps a safer custodian for Indians overseas should be found (29 September); Firoz Khan Noon, another new member of the Council, perhaps? But Linlithgow was not going to try to de-emphasise the crisis. He told Amery that Aney was 'deeply and closely associated with this issue, and any effort to transfer it back to a "tamer" member would be seen through at once' (9 October). On 12 October, Aney took over the department, with its new name.

There was an enforced lull in the telegraphic exchanges between India and Burma (which Dorman-Smith described as 'long distance bombing')[25] because U Saw, the chief protagonist had departed for London, where, with Tin Tut at his elbow, he attempted to pressurise the British Government into making major concessions to Burma. (Walton, head of the Burma Office, later called it a 'process of squeeze'). There were three meetings—14 and 22 October, and 1 November — at which the officials tried to get U Saw to drop the cohabitation clause. They argued that any discrimination was contrary to Part V of the Government of Burma Act. U Saw was adamant, but when it was hinted that unless this concession was given Amery might not introduce the Order in Council to give effect to the agreement, he at last consented to revise the bill for the Burma assembly.

There was no tendency for the mood of anger to abate in India. Linlithgow warned Amery (25 October) 'There is the strongest disposition to hold both Burma and Malaya to ransom by refusing supplies of labour, and these are not matters (for they cut too deep into the Indian political field) in which either you or I are in as strong a position as we would like to be'. An angry debate took place in the Legislative Assembly on 4 November, when Sir A. H. Ghaznavi moved that the agreement should not be implemented unless 'such provisions as are discriminatory and humiliating' were removed. Typical of the speeches was that of Jamnadas Mehta (president of the All-India Nationalist League) who said 'The British imperialist and the British industrialist does not care one brass button for the destiny of the Empire or the Commonwealth. . . . This country of four hundred millions who can conquer the whole world if necessary, with a national government, is to be insulted.' Aney promised to try to obtain 'the necessary modifications to meet the requests of the Indian people'. Linlithgow's comment the same day was that 'no government could possibly hope to get away with this agreement in its present form'.

Amery completely under-estimated the strength of Indian feeling. On 9 November he cabled to ask that Aney should 'promote accommodation of this tiresome matter', as if it were some procedural detail. On receipt of this telegram, Linlithgow sent one of his most blunt replies to L. S. Amery (10 November):

Matters of Indians Overseas are now no longer matters on which, with a political Council and a non-official majority I can hope to take a rigid line. They fall essentially into what I may call the 'nationalist' area of my Council and its work, and His Majesty's Government must, I fear, be prepared to find that in future the Government of India . . . will be inclined to take its stand on the nationalist platform. Indeed, were it to fail to do so, criticism from public opinion here would, I am certain, be so strong that we could not stand it.

All that he could do, said Linlithgow, was 'to try to keep things within reasonable limits', and at once it became plain that even this was now beyond the Viceroy. On 12 November, the Viceroy's Council met to consider the Burma agreement. The Commander-in-Chief (Wavell) supported the Viceroy in pleading for the agreement; if it was repudiated there might be disorder in Burma which would have to be quashed by Indian troops which 'would still further aggravate relations'. Maxwell, Raisman, and Clow — the other English members of the Council also gave support, as did Sir Akbar Hydari; but all the other Indian members were 'unanimous' for repudiation; and so the agreement was rejected 'by a narrow majority'.[26]

Linlithgow informed Dorman-Smith how matters stood; unless modifications were accepted by Burma, India 'would have no option but to repudiate the agreement'. Dorman-Smith professed to be 'amazed'; he told Amery 'I fail to see how my Ministers can meekly surrender to this threat', especially as U Saw had agreed to drop the cohabitation clause (13 November). There was now an impasse; Linlithgow could not persuade his Council to think again: 'we are up against something that will not easily be moved,' he reported (24 November). Dorman-Smith reluctantly brought pressure to bear upon his ministers; Hutchings — whose personal relations with them were cordial — was employed as an intermediary; Dorman-Smith was worried that repudiation of the agreement could bring down the ministry.

Then, without warning, a greater event drove the controversy out of the political arena. On 9 December, Dorman-Smith reported that military operations had begun against an invading Japanese army, and three days later he informed Amery: 'Recent events have deflected interest from this parochial question.' The agreement became part of the waste-paper of history.

Japanese expansion in South East Asia had been half expected for some time. In February 1941 an Indian Committee for Evacuation had been formed, with Tyabji as its secretary. A scheme to evacuate Rangoon was worked out, but U Saw was reluctant to sanction the expenditure for a scheme likely to benefit Indians, not Burmans. In the autumn of 1941, the civil defence philosophy was altered, and 'stay put' became the motto. On 23 and 25 December there were heavy Japanese air raids on Rangoon, and most of the Indian labourers left the city, heading up the Prome road in the direction of Arakan and India: it was an 'orderly, quiet and determined march', said Hutchings who was there. The Government sent an urgent message to Hutchings to persuade the Indians to return; otherwise the port, with its cargoes of war material, would shut down completely. Hutchings departed with a loudspeaker van, and succeeded in persuading four-fifths of the exodus to turn back. To encourage the Burma Indians, M. S. Aney spoke to them over the radio: 'Each man who continues his daily work is helping to defend India as well as Burma. . . . Now is the time for the utmost cooperation and the utmost selflessness . . . in carrying out your gallant duty you have the love and prayers of Mother India.' Hutchings commented: 'Indian labour and Indian traders kept Rangoon Port a going concern up to the time that they were told to leave.'[27]

While the controversy over Indian emigration to Burma built up to its dramatic crescendo, the argument between India and Ceylon was almost—but not quite—settled. Bajpai arrived in Ceylon at the beginning of September 1941 accompanied by Mirza Ismail, Dewan of Mysore, a leading statesman, and Venkataravu Sastri, with Mr Rutherford of the Madras Government. The representatives of Ceylon were, once again, Don Senanayake, and G. C. S. Corea, with R. Drayton, the Legal Secretary. The starting-point was the Immigration Bill, introduced back in February. The talks began on 5 September, and the focus was upon the franchise question; the Ceylon ministers proposed to restrict the franchise to those Indians who had been five years in Ceylon before August 1939; Bajpai asked for a simple five years' residence qualification; on 10 September he cabled to Delhi that the outlook was 'not very hopeful', although the atmosphere was better than at the previous Delhi conference. Eventually, the Ministers offered to give the vote to all Indians with seven years' residence, with no further admissions to the franchise after 1941; they also wanted quotas for Indian employment. Slowly, Bajpai managed to broaden this offer: he aimed at getting full rights for those already in Ceylon, and it was agreed that all Indians with seven years' residence would be exempt from quota regulations; children of Indians with certificates of permanent residence would also be eligible for certificates. The terms would 'secure the franchise to all those who can reasonably be said to have identified themselves permanently with Ceylon', recorded Bajpai; all Indians with both parents born in Ceylon received the vote; certificates of permanent settlement would be issued as of right to all after seven years' residence. Absence from Ceylon for a year would lead to forfeiture of rights, except in certain cases (such as absence for educational purposes). All Indians admitted in future would come for limited periods and would not qualify for privileges. The agreement was to be subject to ratification by the State Council of Ceylon. Bajpai was about to depart for Washington: he was to be absent from Delhi for five years. Now, he recommended that the Ceylon agreement be submitted to the Indian Legislative Assembly.[28]

A debate duly followed on 17 November; Aney moved that the

joint Indo-Ceylonese report 'be taken into consideration'. Objections were raised to certain features — such as the extension of the qualifying period from five to seven years — but the demands lacked the acrimony of the debate on the Burma agreement, just two weeks earlier, and Aney's motion was adopted by 37 votes to 14. It appeared that the way was now clear towards a full agreement, but this was overtaken by outside events.

First, a statement was issued by the United Kingdom government on the question of Ceylon's constitutional advancement on 28 October. This stated that there was 'so little unanimity' between the different groups in Ceylon that another commission or conference must review the situation before any further change was made. This announcement diverted the attention of the Sinhalese politicians from their relations with India.

Then came the outbreak of the war with Japan; Ceylon was not under fire, yet there were massive Indian departures: 6,870 *more* Indians left the island than arrived during December, and over 7,000 more in January: withdrawals from the savings banks exceeded deposits by over Rs. 10,00,000. Governor Caldecott became worried, and asked the Colonial Office to get India to lift the ban on the movement of Indian labour, so far as it affected work for the army and R.A.F. Lord Moyne wrote personally about this to Amery on 16 February, but it was not until 25 February that Amery cabled Delhi. At once the Government of India notified the Ceylon Government (26 February 1942) that there would be 'the fullest measure of cooperation', and the ban on emigration would be lifted 'for war purposes'. However, India also suggested that because of the crisis their negotiations should be suspended and 'the problem re-examined in the light of post-war conditions'. For the remainder of the war, the *status quo* should continue, and Ceylon was asked to hold back any further legislation until after the war. Presumably it was believed that by postponing the signing of an agreement India might obtain better terms later. It was a grievous misjudgement.

A few days later, Bills were introduced into the Ceylon State Council (4 March) to implement the joint report: entry would be controlled, all without Ceylon domicile must register for stay permits; it seems as though this move was intended as a bargaining counter with India. There followed a visit to India by Senanayake. This was partly to discuss the siege situation in which Ceylon was placed, necessitating food supplies from India to replace food from sources now cut off, and partly to make an assessment of the political climate, in which the Indian Congress was oscillating between identifying with the war against Fascism (Nehru's choice) and a Gandhian withdrawal from any association with violence.

Senanayake returned on 13 March to tell the Governor that the Government of India accepted Ceylon as within its 'orbit' for food rationing purposes. A few days later, the Ceylon Government told India (18 March) that they agreed to a standstill arrangement, if this included 'the maintenance of your ban on the emigration of unskilled labour': a major reason for keeping a tight ban was that the Indian labourers in Ceylon would know that they could not leave the island except on pain of forfeiting their right to return. The need for additional labour for military work was now less urgent: Ceylon told India that this might be needed later.

During the first months of 1942 the tide of war crashed ever closer to India. It had been possible to treat the war as above and beyond Indian politics when the conflict was mainly in North and East Africa. Now, India's neighbours, Malaya and Burma, were visibly falling apart under Japanese attack; the Raj itself seemed threatened. Yet no recognition of the dramatic change was vouchsafed from the stonewalling Viceroy. In despair, Tej Bahadur Sapru wrote to Aney (1 February 1942):

> You should tell the Viceroy plainly and bluntly that the situation in the country is not so happy or satisfactory as English people in India believe . . . and that anti-British feeling has grown enormously during the last few weeks. The mishaps in Malaya and Burma have come as a rude shock. . . . The essential fact of the situation is that even in this hour of crisis English and Indian people are living in two different spheres in India and there is no frank talk between them. The Englishman will not talk frankly about the situation because it hurts his pride to admit before an Indian that he has been outwitted . . . . The Indian will not speak to him frankly partly because of his bitterness against him . . . . This is the state of demoralised feeling in the country.

While India's outer bastions were falling, the Churchill Cabinet at last made a gesture towards bringing the nationalist leaders into the direction of the war effort. It was announced that Sir Stafford Cripps was to visit India to discuss immediate and also long term objectives with the Indian political leaders. Senanayake and the Ceylon nationalists were very interested; their own hopes had been disappointed by the announcement of 28 October; perhaps they might cash in on the Cripps visit. They invited Stafford Cripps to visit Ceylon after his discussions in Delhi. Also, the Governor reported in a telegram of 31 March that if the negotiations secured for India the definite prospect of an advance to full self-government, the Ministers were prepared for the alternative that 'Ceylon might seek admission to the Indian Union'. But everything went wrong;

Cripps was unable to reach agreement with the Congress, and his plans collapsed; frustrated and weary he cancelled his visit to Ceylon. The Ministers sent a message to the Secretary for the Colonies registering their 'disappointment and dissatisfaction'. The episode was a reminder of the opportunistic approach of the Sinhalese elite towards independence: the means were always justified by the end.

A Ceylon government press communique was issued on 12 March, advising all non-Ceylonese not engaged upon essential services to leave the island; there was a 'considerable exodus' of Indians of the trading community, though not of labourers, and the Governor reported that 40,000 had left by mid-March. Then came a Japanese air attack on Easter Sunday which hit Colombo and Trincomalee. Many of the Indian port workers got out; those remaining wanted higher wages to work under dangerous conditions. The ultimate authority in Ceylon was now a duumvirate: Admiral Layton, the Commander-in-Chief, shared the responsibility with the Governor. He appealed to the Indians to support the war effort, but Linlithgow commented, a little tartly, 'Appeals to national honour will be the more effective if backed by solid assurances' (23 April 1942).

Perhaps Linlithgow was thinking of the Indians of Malaya and Burma when he made this comment. In Malaya, their fate was settled over their heads. The Indians on the plantations watched, bewildered, as the British fell back and the Japanese swiftly took over control. The first important town to be captured was Penang, and here the hastily improvised evacuation scheme was confined to Europeans only: all but three were saved. Neither the Indians nor the Chinese — some of whom were identified with anti-Japanese activities — were given any chance of leaving. There was an outcry against this blatant racial discrimination, and on 23 December Sir Shenton Thomas went on the radio to deplore the discrimination and to promise that any evacuation scheme from Singapore would be implemented on non-racial grounds. On 24 December 1941, the Government of India asked the Malayan government what assistance was required from India in the evacuation of the local Indian population; they were told that none was required. Then, too late, on 14 January 1942 the Colonial Secretary, Singapore asked India for ships. Only about 5,000 Indians were able to return to India on military transport vessels; all the rest of Malaya's 625,000 Indians passed under Japanese rule.[29] So did almost all the 70,000 Indian troops who had been sent to defend the colony and who were overwhelmed, though the 13th Frontier Force Rifles — those required to shoot their countrymen in April 1941 — fought their way down the peninsula, and some managed to escape. T. G. N. Pillai, who was acting as Agent of the Government of India, was captured.

The Indians in Burma did have some sort of choice; whether to stay and face the Japanese, or struggle back to their homeland. More than half of them stayed; these included people with property or other assets which they could not transfer to India, and people who through long residence had dropped their ties with home or who had married Burmese women and regarded Burma as home. There were also thousands who, in the end, had no choice but to stay. The actual evacuation fell into three major parts. There were those who left by sea, before the fall of Rangoon; those who trekked out immediately after, by the Taungup pass through the hills to Arakan; and those who first moved up to central or northern Burma and then wended their way through the difficult and widely-separated valley routes into Assam. The actual numbers who went are in doubt. Amery told the House of Commons on 16 June 1942 that 400,000 had arrived in India as refugees; other accounts by British officials involved in the evacuation give higher estimates amounting to about 475,000. Eventually, a Census of British Asiatic refugees was taken and 393,735 were enumerated, though the census officials estimated that the refugee total was as high as 450,000 to 500,000.[30] The numbers of those who did not reach journey's end are similarly difficult to estimate; the number of fatalities might have been as low as 10,000 or as high as 50,000. The trek out of Burma was an epic of patient endurance, in which the great majority of the refugees were saved by their own heroic tenacity rather than by any official efforts on their behalf.[31]

The departure of Indians from Rangoon by sea increased rapidly in January. The (Indian-owned) Scindia Steam Navigation Co. stopped its services to Burma, while the (British-owned) British India Steam Navigation Co. was said to be giving priority to Europeans. The evacuation had to be improvised in requisitioned ships. Hutchings tried to organise the issue of tickets through his office, but 'for three days the office was besieged by a disorderly mob', and it was decided to get all intending evacuees together on the race course, when an Indian committee directed departures: altogether 67,000 were evacuated by sea. It had been announced that Rangoon would definitely be held. Hutchings wrote later: 'I made the mistake of thinking that the Governor and the Government in Maymyo would have the necessary information . . . but I am now of the opinion that even the Governor knew very little, about the probable course of events.' On 19 February, General Hutton, then commanding in Burma, said there was still a fifty-fifty chance of holding the city; Dorman-Smith left on 1 March, and the army pulled out on 7 March.

As a result of this hasty change of plan, there was no real preparation for the next phase of evacuation—via Prome and the Taungup pass. About 100,000 refugees tramped over the pass, with no medical or feeding arrangements provided; at least 4,000 died en route, but the main body struggled out via Arakan to Chittagong. Many Indians were too late to attempt the Taungup route, and they made their way to Upper Burma, as it still seemed probable that the British-Indian forces could establish a line across middle Burma. Some began to make their way up the Chindwin river to Kalewa, and thence walked along the dirt track to Tamu on the Burma-India border, and up over an old mule track to Manipur, next to Assam.

By the end of February, the Burma Government was 'suffering from a degree of disintegration', according to Hutchings; there was no attempt to organise escape routes. As General Wood observed, looking at the problem from the India-Burma border, it was 'difficult of comprehension why, when the advance of the enemy progressively released so many [Burma] Government officers, so few were spared for service' in assisting the refugees. General Wood was given the assignment of building a motor road between India and Burma: he received his posting on 10 March. Within eight weeks, a road had been driven through hill and jungle for 54 miles to the border at Tamu. Between 25,000 and 30,000 Indians crossed into India by the Tamu route in March. Hutchings moved to Monywa, a junction on the route, while the number of refugees built up to 2,000 per day. Many, however, had gone further north to Mandalay and the uncertain life of the refugee camps was made more horrible by Japanese air raids in which many died. All but 2,000 of the 75,000 Indians around Mandalay were shifted further north to Shwebo and other towns. It was hoped to organise an airlift, mainly by American transport planes, but not enough were available.

Finally, on the night of 25/26 April, General Alexander, now in command in Burma, ordered a complete withdrawal of the British-Indian military forces up the Chindwin, via Tamu, into India. This meant that the civilian refugees had to give priority to the movement of troops, many of whom had lost formation and were in a poor state of morale. General Wood forwarded a plan to the Burma Government to re-route the refugees via more northerly routes; but, he recorded 'It had been clear for some time that the Government of Burma had ceased to exercise any effective control over the Upper Chindwin District' through which the northern routes passed.

The retreating army pulled back from Kalewa, and even from

Tamu, and the hastily scraped-up camp organisation was pulled back also. But the Indian refugees were still arriving, and in May the dusty track became a morass as the heavy monsoon rains poured down. There was a need to set up reception camps in the Manipur area, but supervisory staff were lacking. The British officials coming through from Burma might have been asked to take over, but Sir Andrew Clow, the Governor of Assam, reported to Linlithgow (11 June 1942) that when he put the request to one administrator, 'He made so much bother about it that I dropped the proposal. . . . Local officers complain that several Burma officers have done little to help . . . [and] have contented themselves with ill-informed complaints.' The main assistance came from the tea planters, organised by the Indian Tea Association, who brought up labour to clear the roads, and lorries to bring up food. Judge Braund was one Burma official who rose to the occasion; he took over the central organisation at Imphal in Manipur. A difficult test came on 16 May when Imphal came under air attack, and many working with the refugees fled themselves. At the end of May, Braund reported that there were still 25,000 Indians, virtually cut off by the monsoon, between Kalewa and Manipur. Those who arrived now were in acute distress; a senior medical officer, Brigadier Short, reported 'Complete exhaustion, physical and mental, with a disease superimposed is the usual picture. . . . They suffer from bad nightmares and their delirium is a babble of rivers and crossings, of mud and corpses. . . . Emaciation and loss of weight are universal; 4 stone is the usual weight for a well-built man.'

Only a fraction of the truth was known in Delhi, and Linlithgow told London (9 June 1942) that the flow had slackened though there was 'much dysentery, smallpox and malaria'; just over a week later (18 June) he had to report 'cholera in epidemic form' along the escape route. Gradually, communications were improved, and the refugees were moved on to camps in Assam and Bengal, and then sent on to their home places in Madras. Those who had been marooned in north Burma were less fortunate; they straggled along the Hukawng valley, making for Ledo in north Assam, but most were stranded by the monsoon rains. Air supplies were dropped to them, and some were brought out by elephant.

When it was all over, the inquest on this tragedy was heard, but in a strangely muted and mangled form. The first important charge of discrimination between Europeans and Indians appeared in the *News Chronicle* of 9 April. When questioned in the House of Commons on 3 May, Amery spoke of a 'misleading report'. Indeed, some of the accusations were disgracefully irresponsible. On 18 March a member of the Council of State, Syed Muhammad Husain, accused Hutchings of having 'whipped' thirty or forty Indians off a ship at Rangoon to give places to Anglo-Indians (Eurasians). When Aney asked Muhammad Husain to give his evidence for the charge, it emerged that it was a piece of hearsay from somebody the Syed could not identify. But some charges were more substantial, as Linlithgow admitted to Amery in a telegram of 6 May 1942. One series of charges related to the priority given to Europeans and Eurasians in allotting places upon air flights.[32] Hutchings agreed he had given priority to Anglo-Indians; he felt that the Japanese would treat them with special severity, and he argued that their patriotic contribution (which he assessed as greater than that of the Europeans) merited special treatment. Then there was a charge that on the last stage of the road between Burma and India—on the section from Tamu to Palel, on the Manipur border—the mass of Indian refugees had been diverted along the old, circuitous route, while the Europeans were allowed to proceed along the new, direct road. General Wood did not deny that this was true, though he argued that the two routes were about the same distance, and he added that 'superior Indian types' (he meant senior civil servants) were allowed along the new road. The third major complaint was that British (European) refugees were receiving a higher rate of maintenance grant in the relief camps than the Indian refugees. This also was happening, though it was explained that the Europeans were being supported by the United Kingdom Government, while the Government of India paid for the Indians. Eventually, there was substituted a system under which the evacuees received grants linked to their former salaries: which, in effect, created a distinction between the Europeans and all the Indians except 'superior types'.[33] Churchill's directive that there should be no discrimination 'against any class of loyal British subjects' was evidently overlooked or forgotten.

When Linlithgow was pressed by Amery, following the exchanges in the House of Commons, to repudiate suggestions of racial discrimination, he declined. He told Amery (25 June 1942) that he had discussed the question with Aney, who was 'not satisfied that unreasonable or avoidable discrimination has not taken place': there were 'Numerous and consistent reports ... [which] indicate at least a lack of understanding of Indian sentiment and Indian requirements.'

There were widespread repercussions from the unequal treatment of the refugees from Burma. When Krishna Menon in London asked Jawaharlal Nehru why Congress was not giving support to the war, when the Soviet Union was under attack from Fascist forces, Nehru replied (a little disingenuously, perhaps) that Congress noncooperation was justified 'especially [by] exceedingly bad differential treatment of the Indian evacuees from Burma' (telegram, 5 June 1942).

After it was all over, Dorman-Smith was installed at Simla with a collection of officials from Burma who soon became known as 'the typewriter government'. On arrival, he asked that Tin Tut as the senior Burmese official should be accredited as 'Agent of the Government of Burma' in India; Linlithgow referred the question to his Council, but had to inform Dorman-Smith (14 April 1942) that Tin Tut would be *persona non grata*. He had functioned briefly as Immigration Commissioner, after the initialling of the immigration agreement, and he 'made it quite clear from his attitude that he was animated by no desire to assist the Indian community in Burma but rather intended to extract from the restrictive provisions of the agreement their fullest measure of severity'. However, that was not to be the last of U Tin Tut in regard to Indian settlement in Burma.

For the Indians left behind in Burma and Malaya, the next three years formed a strange, unreal interlude in their long experience as the unequal and under-privileged subjects of the British Empire. For some, their status was suddenly and unexpectedly enhanced; for others, the interlude brought forced labour like slavery—and frequently death. The overall political situation in the two countries was rather different. In Burma, there were political leaders who had been trained by the Japanese, notably the 'Thirty Comrades', while Dr Ba Maw, the pre-war prime minister, was very ready to take up the reins of government under Japanese patronage. Ba Maw took over on 1 August 1942, and subsequently Burma was recognised as independent by the Axis powers.[34] In this situation, the local Indian community was excluded from the levels of power, as before. However, in Malaya there were no national leaders who the Japanese could mobilise to do their work. The Sultans and the Malay officials retained their old positions; but were clearly subordinate to the Japanese military regime. Chinese collaborators were found, as in all the areas of Japanese occupation: but the real Chinese leadership —recognised by friends and enemies alike—was with the jungle resistance forces. Under these circumstances, the lowly, excluded Indian community might have a definite part to play in the Japanese Co-Prosperity sphere.

An Indian organisation had long been fostered by the Japanese, the Indian Independence League, whose head was Rash Behari Bose, an old revolutionary from the *Ghadr* movement. The League had been functioning in Thailand, and was therefore ready to move into Malaya and Burma and incorporate the local leaders into its organisation. Branches were formed in Rangoon, Akyab, and the main urban centres of Malaya. The main objective was to overthrow British power in India. For this purpose, a military army was important, and out of a prisoner of war camp in Malaya stepped Captain Mohan Singh to create the *Azad Hind Fauj* or 'Free India Army', always known as the Indian National Army or I.N.A. A nucleus of Indian officers was persuaded to join hands with Mohan Singh, and strenuous attempts were made to persuade the Indian soldiers held as prisoners to enlist. Despite the appalling way they had been led in the Malayan retreat, the great majority of the Indian prisoners refused to join, even when they were put under extreme pressure, while obdurate Indian officers were suspended in cages to starve as a warning against refusal. The I.N.A. had better luck with the local Malayan police forces, and Sikhs were prominent among the recruits. However, it was necessary to draw the bulk of the recruits from the Tamil estate labourers. Indian women were also encouraged to join, and a special 'Rani of Jhansi' regiment was formed in memory of the heroine of the Great Revolt of 1857.

Ba Maw recognised the Indian Independence League, and all Burma Indians were ordered to join, from January 1943. The League acted as a welfare organisation, representing the local Indians in their requests to the Ba Maw government. To some extent the League acted as custodian of Indian property, including the lands left behind by the Chettyars. Unlike Malaya, the Indian— mainly Chettyar—investment in Burma was the most important foreign holding; estimated at Rs. 750 million in value, as well as at least one-quarter of the best cultivated land. Most of this property was taken over by Burmese tenants and managers, though some of the Chettyar land went out of production.[35] In return for its position of prestige, the Indian Independence League was required to raise gifts and loans on behalf of the Indian community for the Japanese war effort. Enthusiasm for the League waned, while the role of the I.N.A. seemed far from clear.

The moment for the invasion of India passed, before either the Japanese or the I.N.A. could seize the opportunity. After the failure of the Cripps mission, Gandhi called for the British to quit India. The Quit India movement attained its climax at the beginning of August, when the Congress High Command issued a call to patriots to Do or Die (*Karenge ya Marenge*). The British arrested Gandhi, Nehru and all the High Command, but the direction of the movement had anyway passed into the hands of young militants who attempted to launch a guerrilla war. However, the campaign was really successful only in Bihar and the eastern districts of the United Provinces where for three weeks or more the British entirely lost control. The British-Indian forces on the Burma-Assam border were completely cut off from their bases, and even their local communications were sabotaged. During August and September 1942, India lay open to the invader, and invasion was fully expected as in south India, where plans were hastily concocted for a withdrawal from Madras city and the coast. But the Japanese were stretched to their limits, and the moment passed, never to return.

As disillusionment took hold of the Indians of South East Asia, a new leader appeared: Subhas Chandra Bose, who had been the guest of the Nazis and now appeared after an adventurous voyage in a German submarine. Bose—*Netaji*— 'great leader' as he was always called—arrived in July 1943, and put new life into the Indians.[36]

Netaji impressed the Japanese: he seemed a man in their own martial tradition—strong, ruthless, determined. He also greatly impressed Ba Maw, whom he resembled in external characteristics— a love of jackboots and uniforms, and a talent for ferocious rhetoric. Netaji persuaded the Japanese to recognise the authority of his government over the Andaman and Nicobar islands—the only Indian soil under Japanese occupation—and he required all the overseas Indians to take an oath of loyalty to the Provisional Government of Azad Hind. Doubtless, this enhanced their morale, but it served to underline their separateness from the lands of their adoption, Burma and Malaya. Netaji transported the main fighting formations of the I.N.A. to the front line in Burma; in 1944 the Japanese planned an offensive on the central front to break through Manipur and into Assam and Bengal in a 'March on Delhi'. Subhas Bose was determined that the I.N.A. would lead the march. The reality was tragically different. The Japanese did not trust the I.N.A. for serious fighting, so they were used as decoys: but even in this role they were unreliable, and most surrendered with relief to the British-Indian forces, to be taken away for confinement in Attock Fort on the river Indus.

Netaji somehow managed to disguise the extent of the debacle. He also managed to conceal a less heroic enterprise which the League and the I.N.A. arranged for the Japanese. A railway was designed to link Burma with Thailand, and thus eliminate the long and hazardous communications by sea. British, Australian and Dutch prisoners of war were put to work on the 'Death Railway', but their numbers were insufficient and the Japanese turned to their South East Asian allies, or stooges. In Burma, thousands of Burmese were forcibly conscripted in what was blandly called the 'Sweat Army' (*Let Yon Tat*) but in Malaya the burden fell almost solely upon the Indians. Some military prisoners were drafted, but the great majority were labourers from the rubber estates. The number of those Indians who died to build this useless monument to militarism and imperialism cannot be known, but an estimate puts the figure at over 60,000.[37]

The seismic shocks of 1942 were followed by tremors and disturbances throughout 1943 in the Indian Ocean and Pacific areas, as though they were still shuddering in the wake of the Japanese earthquake. The most obvious consequence was that Ceylon was now 'in the front line', especially to those warriors consulting their maps in Whitehall, to whom the island assumed a new, and perhaps undue importance in strategic thinking; there was the immediate problem of keeping its plantation industries going at full stretch, to compensate for lost production in Malaya and elsewhere, and the longer-term problem of assuring the cooperation of the Ministers and their supporters by giving a fully sympathetic hearing to their political demands.

In order to replace some of Malaya's lost rubber output, the Ceylon rubber estates deliberately adopted a programme of 'slaughter tapping' of their trees.[38] This required a larger labour force, but neither the Indian nor the Ceylon governments were prepared to adopt the obvious solution—new recruitment from India. The Ceylon ministers would only sanction the import of labour from India under the strict conditions that all labourers would be sent back to India after the war. While India was prepared to negotiate on this basis, it was expected that this arrangement would be balanced by concessions to the existing Indian population of Ceylon. In addition, the Government of India was concerned about the effects of the ban on those Indian labourers who wanted to revisit their homes, but could not return because they would forfeit the right to re-enter the island. On 28 August 1942, a press statement was issued notifying the lifting of the ban from 1 September 1942, so that labourers could return on holiday to India. All this produced a voluminous exchange of letters and telegrams, restating the two countries' viewpoints.[39] Governor Caldecott assured the Secretary for the Colonies in a despatch of 7 September 1942 that what was regarded as India's unilateral action would not induce a 'further precipitation' of the situation; but he went on 'The India-Ceylon problem however remains unsolved and the promise of settlement afforded by the conversations of September 1941 has, I fear, been dissipated in the subsequent correspondence.' The failure of the 1941 conference, wrote Caldecott, was 'the greatest disappointment I have suffered during my governorship of this island'. In an effort to improve communications Sir Baron Jayatilaka was appointed Ceylon's representative at Delhi; it was, of course, a convenient way of removing him from the formal leadership of the State Council which in practice he could no longer command.

Meanwhile, the long-term question of Ceylon's constitutional advance was considered by the War Cabinet on 9 December 1942; the ministers were pressing for some commitment from Britain. The Cabinet were prepared only to send a message to the Ceylon ministers promising 'the fullest possible development of self-governing institutions in the island'. Aware that the minorities might object, the Cabinet gave them a message also: it was curt: they could give no undertakings 'to any particular section'. Without doubt, the Cabinet had in mind the safeguards which Cripps had conceded to the Muslims of India.[40] Altogether, the Cripps Mission and the Congress response leading on to the Quit India movement, had soured the attitude of British ministers—and Churchill in particular—to the future of India in the British Commonwealth. Churchill seems to have decided that India should now be written off. These sentiments were now much to the fore in discussions on Ceylon.

The message conveyed to the Ministers by the Governor elicited from them a demand for 'full responsible government' or Dominion status, and the demand was elaborated in a telegram which the Governor sent (in conjunction with Admiral Layton) to the Secretary or the Colonies on 17 February 1943. Caldecott was specially concerned that the Government of India should not become involved in the discussions: 'Our joint opinion, moreover, is that in view of the definite secessionist tendency in India, the security of Commonwealth communications and defence imperatively demand that Ceylon should not (repeat not) be subordinated to India and that any possible future movement towards fusion should not (repeat not) be encouraged': apparently Caldecott still suspected a possible deal between Senanayake and his colleagues and the Indian national leaders. Caldecott went on to deprecate any attempt to hold back political progress because of the minorities: 'The minority communities are just as keen to be released from Whitehall apron strings as the majority....' The Governor ended this rather direct statement by rejecting in advance any suggestion that he might come to London for discussions: there was nothing further to discuss.

Oliver Stanley, Secretary for the Colonies, accepted Caldecott's *démarche*. In the paper he circulated to the Cabinet, he proposed an immediate announcement that Ceylon was entitled after the war to claim 'full responsible government... in all matters of internal civil administration'.[41] Stanley declared that this did not mean Dominion status, but was the equivalent of the status of Southern

Rhodesia. Stanley justified this proposal by reason of Ceylon's war effort: they had 'deserved extremely well of the Empire' he said, adding: 'It would be a natural thing for them to compare the definite promise made to India when, with all respect to India's war effort, the political element at least has been largely non-cooperative, with the indefinite hopes held out to Ceylon where the elected Ministers have thrown themselves heart and soul into war production. This comparison may lead to the argument that more can be obtained from His Majesty's Government by making trouble than by methods of cooperation'.

Stanley excluded any reference to minority safeguards, except to observe that any constitution must be endorsed by three-quarters of the State Council, in which there were currently thirty-nine Sinhalese, six Ceylon Tamils, four Indian Tamils, five Europeans, three Muslims and one Burgher: a total of sixty-one members. It would be necessary for the Sinhalese to carry with them seven minority members.

The Cabinet memorandum was seen by a select number at the India Office; they did not object, and Sir William Croft, Deputy Under Secretary, commented that Ceylon was offered less than India under the Cripps plan: for India, 'the obstacle arising on account of minority interests has been relieved by the option of partition'. The shadow of Pakistan was beginning to lengthen.[42]

In the Cabinet discussion on 1 April, there was agreement that they should not be side-tracked by the minorities problem, for India provided a 'dangerous precedent'. The whole question was referred to a Cabinet committee, presided over by Sir John Anderson; this committee worked out in detail how far Ceylon would stop short of complete self-government, and then the proposition was cabled to the Governor to discover whether the Ministers were likely to accept these terms. Caldecott found it impossible to be certain how they would react; but 'moderate opinion' saw that independence was impracticable, and 'apart from absorption by India the only other possibility... is internal home rule'. Unless the United Kingdom government made a commitment: 'the trend of all Ceylonese opinion will be towards throwing in their lot wholeheartedly with the Indian Nationalists and of making the best terms possible with them'. Confronted with this alternative, the Cabinet agreed to the Colonial Secretary's proposals at their meeting of 18 June: possibly the absence of Winston Churchill on a foreign mission made agreement easier.[43]

A planted question in the House of Commons on 26 June gave Stanley the opportunity to make his declaration, which was soon subject to critical examination by the Ceylon Ministers. They disliked the reservation of external relations to the control of the United Kingdom Government: this might mean that India could refer all questions affecting Indians in Ceylon to London.[44] However, Stanley was not going to be drawn further, and on 17 July Caldecott was able to tell the Secretary for the Colonies that they were now satisfied and were going ahead to draft a constitution, without waiting for the arrival of peace.

The Government of India also wanted to know more about the conduct of Ceylon's external relations. A. V. Pai drew attention to the unhappy precedent of the Donoughmore constitution when India had been 'hustled into an unwilling acceptance' (15 April 1943). The Colonial Office gave the lofty answer (18 December 1943) that it would not be 'wise or necessary' to define these things too exactly, and India had to be content with this cryptic reply. The initiative was now with Don Senanayake and his colleagues, aided by the ingenious Principal of the new University of Ceylon, the constitutional lawyer, Ivor Jennings. Senanayake did not disguise his intentions from the Indians of Ceylon. He told I. X. Perera that 'I, for one, am convinced that no useful purpose will be served by our trying to meet the Indians in Ceylon, and that the only thing to do is to look after our own interests' (12 January 1944).

Negotiations between India and the refugee government of Burma were almost at a standstill. At the beginning of 1943 Aney asked to discuss the future with Linlithgow, who by now entertained a high regard for the former Congressman; he was 'quite astonishingly stout-hearted', the viceroy told Amery in his account of their discussion.[45] Aney said that his own private and personal opinion was that India could not allow any [Indians] to go back to Burma until a settlement had been reached with Burma as to the future. He had been appalled at the collapse of Burmese morale, and could not contemplate a weak Burma as India's neighbour: 'he, for one, could no longer contemplate complete separation', and independent India would insist upon the whole relationship being re-examined. Linlithgow commented that Aney's 'honesty and straightforwardness is one of his many attractive qualities', and when the Viceroy attempted to answer Aney he was told 'India must have, and certainly will insist on having a major say in the future position of Burma'.

The furthest ripple of the Japanese onslaught in South East Asia was felt in faraway Fiji, almost entirely isolated from India in terms of human movement, though not beyond the movement of ideas.[46] The two Indian trade unions were recognised by the government in 1941, though the employers, led by the Colonial Sugar Refining Co resisted negotiating with them. Then Japanese expansion reached out across the Pacific, and Fiji, at the end of the world before, became a forward base. The response of the Polynesian Fijians to the challenge of war was in their noble warrior tradition; thousands offered their services, and went across the seas to fight; one Fijian man out of three, between 18 and 60 years, became a soldier.

The response of the Fiji Indians was very different. In September 1939 the Indian platoon of the Fiji Defence Force had demanded the same rates of pay as the white soldiers; this was refused, and the Indian platoon was disbanded. When the Pacific war exploded, the Indians were asked to provide a thousand recruits to work as labour with the military forces. Nearly six hundred came forward, but less than two hundred were considered suitable to be retained with the forces.[47]

The Indians argued that they were agriculturalists, contributing to the war effort by growing sugar. The purchase price was fixed at 30s. per ton, and there were no increases, despite the steep rise in the cost of living (calculated at 60 per cent between September 1939 and June 1942). In March 1943 the farmers claimed an increase. Commenting on the situation from Delhi, A. V. Pai recorded that the current price in India was Rs. 20.4 (or 34s. 6d.) per ton, for cane with a lower sugar content. The Fiji demand was 'rather modest', he observed.

In June 1943 the labourers of the Colonial Sugar Refining Co went on strike for higher pay; the Director of Labour negotiated new terms for the workers, but the C.S.R.Co rejected his suggested rates. The Government appointed a tribunal which made an award similar to the rates approved by the Director of Labour; the company accepted this award and the labourers returned to work.[48] All this seemed to provide a pattern which might be applied to the farmers.

The leader of the farmers' protest movement was Swami Rudranand of the Ramakrishna Mission, dedicated to social and religious upliftment. He urged the farmers not to cut their cane at the prevailing price. Rudranand was disciplined by the Fiji Government; he was ordered to stay within five miles of the mission and report regularly to the police; he defied this order, and was sentenced to three months' imprisonment. On appeal, the sentence was quashed; the Supreme Court ruled that it was no offence to withhold the cane harvest. New regulations were introduced to enforce the restrictions on Rudranand and on Ambalal Patel, his helper. The censor intercepted a letter from them to *The Times of India* in which they complained that, though the protest was peaceful, units of the Fiji Defence Force had been posted in the sugar districts 'to frighten and terrorise them into harvesting'.

The Fiji Government set up a Commission, composed of the

Attorney-General and the Director of Agriculture, to review the price question. Their report, released on 8 November 1943, stated that 'no further increase in the price of sugar-cane is justified'.

The Indians appealed to the Governor, Sir Philip Mitchell. Unfortunately for them he had passed all his years of service in central and east Africa, where Indians were regarded as interlopers. They told the Governor that they were prepared to bring their cane to the factory, leaving it to him to determine a fair price. Mitchell replied on 29 December that 'The question of the price to be paid is one not of conscience but of contract. The agreement between the Company and the growers must be regarded as remaining in force'. The Government of India urged the India Office to intervene (telegram, 17 December 1943) but nothing happened; the Colonial Office was at its most stubborn. Most of the 1943 sugar crop was left to rot, or else was ploughed back into the soil.

'The Fiji Government is more concerned with bringing the Indian growers to their knees than to help in arriving at a settlement' wrote Mr Pai. When Mitchell sent off a demand for the recall of Rudranand to India, the Government of India retorted that it would be 'undesirable' to ask for the return of the swami (5 May 1944). There was deadlock; but the Indian farmers could not afford to prolong the fight. The 1944 crop was harvested normally, though the Fiji economy did not recover, fully, for several years. The only concession made by the Colonial Office was to institute an inquiry by an expert, Dr C. Y. Shephard of Trinidad; but as his report was not received until June 1945 it was too late to remedy the wartime grievance.

The long-drawn-out affair left relations between the Indians and the other communities in Fiji in a state of mutual disgust. The Indians were labelled as 'disloyal', and their status as citizens of Fiji was further diminished.[49]

The industrial conflict in Fiji ended in bitterness but not in bloodshed; in Mauritius, in 1943, the sickening old pattern of violence and repression was repeated. As the commission of inquiry later commented, Mauritius was an ailing society and the violence of 1943 represented 'a sudden rise of temperature in a patient who is permanently unwell'; it was also, as they observed, 'the end product of an historical process which should be reckoned in generations.'[50]

Between 1938 and 1943, the cost of living in Mauritius had increased by about 150 per cent; however, this was not officially recognised, as the Labour Department made no attempt to collect statistics. In the early months of the year, labourers from the congested northern districts, where wages were specially low, several times banded together to go on hunger marches to Port Louis;

however, their protests were ignored by the authorities, while the employers ascribed all the trouble to 'agitators'. During the months of July and August 1943 as the crop time approached, the workers began to make demands upon the planters. On several estates, the wages were actually less than those fixed by the Minimum Wage Board in 1941 with Rs. 20 per month as the minimum. On *Labourdonnais* Estate (scene of a violent dispute in 1909) the stronger workers of the *Grande Bande* received Rs. 18 per month, while the weaker people of the *Petite Bande* were paid Rs. 16.50. Strikes began, spasmodically and with no coordination, on several estates, including *Beau Séjour* where an official of the Labour Department dealt with the situation by singling out the leaders to be conscripted for National Service. The employers rejected any attempts to negotiate; they had successfully eliminated all but two of the trade unions established in 1938 after the troubles the preceding year. The most important remaining association was the 'North and Central Riviere du Rampart Labourers' Industrial Association', and this owed its continuance in the face of the planters' pressure mainly to the efforts of Harryparsad Ramnarain, formerly secretary of the Labour Party. Although the employers and the Labour Department disliked and distrusted Ramnarain, they found themselves compelled to deal with him, quite simply because he was the only leader whom the estate workers trusted, and who could therefore hope to 'deliver' an agreement.

The most intractable dispute was on *Belle Vue Harel*, where the workers were not members of Ramnarain's union, though when a conciliation board was set up by the Labour Department they asked Ramnarain to act as their spokesman. After discussion, the employers offered, in effect, to come up to the level of the government's minimum wage; Ramnarain did not want to accept this offer without first consulting the work-people but under pressure from the Director of Labour he agreed to sign. It seems to have been hinted that he must sign because he was now also employed as an Information Officer to boost the war effort for the government. The labourers refused to ratify the agreement and struck work on 23 September 1943. On 27 September, a senior police officer, the Deputy Commissioner, was casually asked to go to *Belle Vue Harel*. The labourers were assembled in their *baitka* or prayer place, but they seemed truculent, and Deputy Commissioner A. M. Bell quickly summed things up: 'There had been a lot of trouble going on for months, and it occurred to him that something should be done to put an end to it'.

His solution was the usual one: to arrest the troublemakers. The crowd retaliated by throwing stones, and Bell gave an order to fire.

His intention was unclear, but fifteen rounds were fired, and three people fell dead, with sixteen badly wounded. One of the estate supervisors was present, carrying a shot-gun, and he also seems to have fired: later, doctors reported that people had been peppered with lead pellets. The episode seems to have shattered Ramnarain, who retired to a temple to fast for eight days. The dispute dragged on, but the labourers finally returned to work on 2 November.

On 27 October, Creech Jones asked the Colonial Secretary in the House of Commons to make a statement on Mauritius; he was informed that a commission of inquiry would investigate the occurrences, and that a Conciliation Board would be set up. Creech Jones was not satisfied; 'So long as we treat Mauritius as a "plantation" island, dominated by the old conception of "colonial economics", the acute problems will remain', he told C. W. W. Greenidge, Secretary of the Anti-Slavery Society (4 December 1943). Greenidge, replied (10 December) that 'crude poverty, malnutrition and disease, and fierce conflict between employer and employed' told the story of Mauritius.

The commission was composed of local people; the Colonial Secretary of Mauritius, Sydney Moody was the chairman, and for the first time two of the members were Indians. Within its report, the commission encapsulated the whole record of Mauritius since the days of slavery. The employers thought of themselves as benefactors, while refusing to give their workers more than the bare necessities to preserve life; the commission found that improvements in the workers' conditions had been 'negligible'; on the evidence, they might well have stated that conditions had deteriorated. Any attempt by the workers to press for betterment was rejected by the employers, the 1943 strikes did not stem from any real grievance they said, but merely from the mischievous intervention of strangers 'and particularly the caprice of one man', Ramnarain.

The power of the government was exercised on behalf of the employers and against the employed. The Labour Department was mainly occupied in administering the Poor Law, which absorbed the bulk of its resources, but also it was involved in the prosecution of any workers said to be involved in illegal strikes, and the commission concluded: 'We formed the impression...that many officers of the Department made the assumption, largely unconsciously, that the main object of their activities is to keep labour quiet at any price'. Even more directly, the function of the police was to keep the masses quiet; but as a force largely composed of non-Indians they were ill-equipped to do this. At *Belle Vue Harel* 'The police officers could not speak directly to the people...Interpreters were necessary. The senior police officers hardly knew what a *baitka* was. They could not understand whether the people assembled...were praying or not. In short, they were unfamiliar with the language, religion and customs of the people whom they wished to persuade and perhaps to coerce'. Finally, the commission, including its official chairman, condemned a system of administration in which there were no responsible officers in the field. The government was out of touch with the people; concerning the strike area they observed: 'The district Magistrates of Pamplemousses and Riviere du Rampart do not reside at those places. They reside at Curepipe [a hill resort]. They visit their Courts twice a week, on Mondays and Fridays....' Amid this gloomy scene, the Commission pinned most of its hopes upon the Colonial Development and Welfare Act, 1940, which might achieve what had so signally not been done during a hundred and thirty years of British rule: raise living standards above those of the plantation slaves.

This report was so damning that, even under the precarious conditions of wartime, it was deemed wise to print it in England. When the report appeared, the Secretary of State observed that there was 'no simple answer' to the problems it had high-lighted; certain nostrums were to be applied, but no fundamental change was made in the feudal society of Mauritius.

The year 1943 saw the departure of Lord Linlithgow, after the longest viceroyalty since Curzon. His departure marked the end of the pomp and circumstance of his office; his successor, Lord Wavell, arrived as a wartime viceroy, in bush-shirt instead of grey top hat and morning suit. Before Linlithgow departed in October he was preceded in February by his friend, M. S. Aney. When Gandhi decided to fast in his confinement at Poona, all the Hindu members of the Viceroy's Council submitted their resignations in protest at his not being released. Linlithgow greatly missed his Member for Indians Overseas, and believed that Aney had resigned against his own better judgment, only to show solidarity with the others. With some misgiving, Linlithgow invited Dr N. B. Khare to succeed Aney; he was also from Maharashtra, and had formerly been Congress premier of the Central Provinces, but he had broken with Gandhi, whom he detested. Khare was a more coarse-grained politician than Aney, more fond of the limelight and more hungry for applause. It seems as though Aney quickly regretted his resignation, for when Khare asked him to go to Ceylon, to become India's representative—a position superior to that of Agent—Aney accepted, and arrived in Colombo on 23 August 1943.[51]

Linlithgow was the last of the viceroys to define his task as that of upholding British power and British interests. Events in South

East Asia led the Cabinet to embark upon the exercise of planning a new, post-war international system; one that would be acceptable to the United States. A number of ministers joined in the game, submitting their paper proposals, and the Viceroy also made his contribution.[52] He wrote:

Great Britain is going to be pretty tightly squeezed after the war . . . and the importance to our trade of the colonial empire is clear . . . my very strong disposition therefore would be to give nothing to any foreign power . . . that we can possibly hold on to.
I am quite conscious that South Africa has always had ambitions to absorb as much of the pre-1900 British Empire in that continent as she can.

According to Amery the Cabinet discussion of post-war colonial policy was 'hopelessly muddled', though Stanley's main recollection of what must have been a confused meeting was that Linlithgow's comment (quoted above) on South Africa 'sent Winston off the deep end.'[53] It would appear that Linlithgow's conception of maintaining the United Kingdom's post-war position went further even than that of the man who had announced that 'he had not become His Majesty's First Minister in order to preside over the liquidation of the British Empire'.[54] It was his gruelling experience of attempting to defend the position of Indians overseas which finally led Linlithgow to conclude that Britain must maintain its hold in Asia: he told Amery in a private letter, near the end of his time in India, (8 March 1943) 'I do not believe myself that there is the least chance of the Cabinet or His Majesty's Government washing their hands of responsibility for India . . . so long as . . . in disputes with other parts of the Empire about the position of Indians overseas, etc. the Government of India remain in the last resort as wholly dependent as they are on the support and goodwill of His Majesty's Government'.

Linlithgow appeared to believe that the British connection provided an effective protection for the overseas Indians. Perhaps he was entitled to claim that during his period of office their position had nowhere noticeably deteriorated. But now the overseas Indians were about to be attacked in their most sensitive place: in South Africa. And the great majority of politically active Indians were to deduce that the only hope for their countrymen overseas was to be identified with an independent India. The claim to equality was now to be asserted in real earnest.

7

Equality: The Claim Asserted
(1943-45)

Just one month after he became Viceroy Lord Wavell addressed a personal and secret letter to Field-Marshal Smuts (23 November 1943). Relations between India and South Africa were again at a critical point. Indians were united in condemning 'inequality or indignity' inflicted on their countrymen in different parts of the British Empire, Wavell wrote: there was a 'belief that negotiation is useless and a demand that all possible means of retaliation against South African nationals and South African interests shall be put into force at once by the Government of India'. He was determined to avoid a clash, but only action by Smuts could save the situation: 'you can help me by agreeing to begin negotiations': they must have another conference. Wavell felt confident that Smuts would make this his personal responsibility because: 'You and I know better than almost anyone what we owe to India in the defence of the Middle East bastion'.

At almost the same moment, Amery was putting his thoughts down for the benefit of the new Viceroy (25 November 1943): 'I have never felt that the South African [Indian] case was really a very strong one, except in so far as India has a chip on her shoulder with regard to discrimination against persons of Indian descent.' In any quarrel between South Africa and India, the British Cabinet — representing the British people — saw the South African side of the case.

From 1939 to 1943, the condition of the South African Indians suffered no serious deterioration. On becoming prime minister at the outbreak of war, Smuts gave the Indians an assurance that there would be no legislation for the segregation of the Indians during wartime, and that a commission of inquiry would be appointed to examine their conditions of living. This assurance depended upon continuance of the Kajee policy of voluntary Indian restraint and especially no change in the housing field.

The Indian response to the assurances by Smuts depended upon who was speaking for the Indians. There were two rival organisations — the Colonial-Born and Settlers' Indian Association (founded in 1932) and the Natal Indian Congress, headed by Kajee. Sir Benegal Rama Rau, Agent General, induced the two bodies to amalgamate as the Natal Indian Association late in 1939, but within a few weeks Kajee and his associates had seceded and refounded the Natal Indian Congress. The Government of India ignored Kajee and supported the N.I.A. Paradoxically, when the Kajee policy of restraint was to be tested, he was not involved. A committee was formed under H. G. Lawrence, Minister of the Interior, to control the sale of property in the Durban area by voluntary agreement; it was composed of representatives of the Durban City Council and of the N.I.A. At first, all went well.

To fulfil the second part of his assurance to the Indians, Smuts set up a body called the Indian Penetration Commission, with Mr Justice Broome as chairman. The N.I.A. worked with the Penetration Commission, but Kajee and the Congress imposed a boycott. Rama Rau urged cooperation, and he was denounced by Kajee, who said he had 'bartered away legitimate rights hitherto enjoyed by Indians', while Manilal Gandhi's *Indian Opinion* declared that the Agent-General was not intended 'to play the role of an importunate beggar but to uphold the honour of India. It is not his function to lead Indians to adopt a defeatist policy'.[1]

Meanwhile, the Broome Commission inquired diligently, and reported towards the end of 1941. Regarding the Transvaal, they found that 'the extent of penetration since 1927 [the year of the Cape Town Agreement] does not appear to us to be alarming or even surprising'. They found that the expansion of Indian settlement into European areas was actually a movement into areas which had ceased to be attractive to Europeans: 'The European exodus preceded, and did not follow (and was obviously not caused by) the Indian entry'. The phenomenon in Natal was similar: 'Whenever the invasion and exodus have occurred it will, we think, be found that the area concerned had already become less desirable to its former residents for other reasons. In Durban, the opening up of suburbs... rendered possible by improved transport facilities has made much of the 'A' and 'B' areas less attractive to one class and has brought them within the reach of another.' The Broome report noted that many of the purchases were for investment, not occupation; 70 per cent of the properties acquired in the 'old' (central) borough were not actually occupied by Indians. The report commented — rather boldly for South Africa — 'This is nothing but a manifestation of the ordinary instinct to make money which is said to be a feature of Western civilisation'; this represented an Indian acceptance of the Western way of life, supposedly a part of the Cape Town Agreement.[2]

In the spirit of the Broome Report, Smuts persuaded the United Party caucus to accept recommendations by another judge, Richard

Feetham (one of the original *Round Table* group) that areas near Johannesburg should be assigned to the Indians for residence; this was accepted by the Union parliament by 61 votes to 40. However, when things seemed to be going smoothly, the Lawrence Committee split into its two halves; its last joint meeting took place in June 1941. At this critical time, India was without a High Commissioner in South Africa; Rama Rau departed in April 1941, and it proved difficult to replace him. The post was offered in July to Sir Mirza Ismail who refused, and because it was desired to appoint a Muslim, there followed the rather surprising choice of a former professor of history at the University of Allahabad: Sir Shafa'at Ahmad Khan. He arrived in South Africa in November 1941.[3]

Almost at the same time, a significant debate took place in the Indian Legislative Assembly, where on 4 November Dr G. V. Deshmukh introduced a bill on the lines of Pandit Pant's abortive measure of 1936: to provide for reciprocal measures against countries which discriminated against Indians overseas. M. S. Aney resisted the bill: he agreed 'there may be a time when retaliatory measures may have to be moved', but he added: 'Is it wise for us to proceed with legislation which is likely to be a source of bitterness between the people of India and the people of the Colonies and the Dominions?' Several members, including Raza Ali, deplored the treatment of Indians overseas, but the Assembly agreed to defer consideration of the bill.

During 1942, so momentous in South-East Asia, the South African Indians marked time. At the beginning of the war, a recruiting drive opened for the ancillary military services: motor transport and ambulance units, in particular. Only five hundred Indians enlisted. Then efforts were made to persuade them to join the Indian Malay Corps, which became an engineer unit; this too was not successful, so finally in 1942 an all-Indian unit was constituted. In the South African forces, arms were only put into the hands of Whites; it was therefore not surprising that the Indians hung back. But in Natal, 'British to the core', this was taken as another sign of the 'disloyalty' of the Indians.

The Broome Commission had condemned the negative attitude of the Durban City Council to Indian housing. A scheme was now announced for the removal of hundreds of Indian families from an area which had once provided marginal cultivation and was now an Indian township, Riverside. The Indians would be moved farther out to low-lying areas, and £2 million would be allocated for a housing scheme. Riverside (an attractive location near the sea) would be re-zoned for Europeans. The Indians protested vigorously, and in October 1942 the Riverside scheme was shelved. Next month, the Lawrence Committee, long dormant, was wound up. Among the thousands of Natal Indians, a few hundred made a spectacular profit out of the many convoys of troops that put into Durban through providing supplies for the ships. These businessmen had money to invest: and they put it into property. The Durban Whites demanded tough measures against the Indians, and Judge Broome was asked to make another investigation. This time he worked alone and he worked fast. His second report was signed on 25 March 1943. He found that since the terminal date for the first inquiry (30 September 1940) 326 sites had changed hands from Whites to Indians, to the value of £601,385, while sixteen sites had been transferred from Indians to Whites, value £25,525. In 1942 alone, the Indians bought 195 sites in what Broome called 'good class European residential areas', though the building societies suspended giving loans for Indian purchases in white areas. Broome suggested that some Indians concluded that because the first report was in a low key, they could go ahead without opposition, while others — the shrewd ones — decided 'to pass through the door while it is still open'.[4]

By a curious coincidence, the day before Broome signed his second report the Indian Legislative Assembly produced a counter-blast: Act IX of 1943 was passed: the Reciprocity Act, which empowered the Government of India to retaliate against discrimination. This, however, was not headline news in South Africa where the Broome Report seemed likely to become a leading issue in the general election which Smuts had just announced. Lord Harlech told the Dominions Office (1 April 1943) that the opposition were 'delighted' at the Broome revelations: they 'intend to exploit racial prejudice for all they are worth at the forthcoming election', he cabled. Smuts was always ready to reply to a racial campaign in similar terms. On 7 April the Union Government announced the introduction of the Trading and Occupation of Land (Transvaal and Natal) Restriction Bill; this renewed the 1939 Transvaal Act, passed by Hertzog (see p. 174) for another three years and extended the 'pegging' provisions to Durban, with power to apply to all Natal if needed. Within two weeks the Bill had become law.

The response in Britain to the 'Pegging Act' (as it was immediately called) was to close ranks with Smuts. Clement Attlee told Leopold Amery (8 April 1943) that it would be 'inadvisable for the United Kingdom Government to rush into this matter with representations to the Union authorities . . . . Harlech's telegram shows that the political circumstances which have led to this legislation being decided upon are acute'. But Amery was being bombarded with protests from Delhi, and he had to do something: he reminded

Attlee that Smuts had promised not to introduce legislation for segregation during wartime: could he be asked to make a declaration that this Bill was intended to meet 'a special case' only? Harlech was asked to inquire, and he reported to Attlee on 14 April that Lawrence had assured him that it would be explicitly stated that the new legislation was an 'interim and temporary measure and is not intended to lay down any policy of discrimination or segregation'. Lawrence emphasised that the Union Government was quite prepared to receive representations from the Government of India, though any suggestion of recalling the Indian High Commissioner would 'greatly aggravate' the situation. Next day Harlech attended the debate in the Union Parliament: it was a 'crowded house', he said; Hofmeyr offered to resign, but this was refused. Lawrence justified the Bill as providing a 'breathing space' and Smuts was generally conciliatory, though he condemned those Indians who had bought property instead of investing in war loans. Harlech concluded: 'The two extremes of Right and Left [the Republican and Dominion parties] met on the common ground of racial prejudice'.[5]

On 28 April, Harlech sent a long personal letter to Clement Attlee, expanding on the Broome disclosures. Many Indians had made 'enormous profits' from the war, he said, but they hoarded their wealth and lived in 'appalling squalor, and their social and domestic habits make them most unpleasant neighbours': for the Whites, it was like living 'on the edge of Negro Harlem'. Harlech embarked upon some sociological conclusions:

Hindus are apparently content with, and make "slum" conditions even when they have not the excuse of poverty. This phenomenon is not peculiar to South Africa, but obtains in Indian cities in India with the banya caste as you know from your own Indian experiences.... There is no solution of this problem, particularly in South Africa, other than some form of residential segregation.

If you talk to the average (not the exceptional) European... he — and again, still more she — will tell you that all Indians should be compulsorily repatriated to India. The mere fact that Indians as "British subjects" claim equal rights with the European... and openly claim "superiority" to the negro makes the social and emotional clash worse.

In parliament, the only champions of the Indians have been the "Native Representatives" and at some risk to themselves. They have espoused this cause because they are "Liberals" not because their native constituents want them to do so. Probably the only natives who in some measure support the Indians are the avowed native Communists.

Harlech concluded that the valiant deeds of the Indian Army in North Africa had not helped the standing of the local Indians: the soldiers belonged to the 'martial races' and were different! Harlech added: 'I feel very sorry for Sir Shafa'at Ahmad Khan ... he is a misfit, both vis-à-vis the Indians here and vis-à-vis the Union Government.... He is a lonely and rather pathetic though most conscientious figure.... He has inevitably lost 'face' with all, though [sic.] no fault of his own.'

With this advice coming in, it was not surprising that the Churchill government did nothing. Amery cabled Linlithgow (15 April 1943): 'Take a firm stand against any action which might lead to deterioration of relations between India and the Union, such as recalling the High Commissioner or accepting his resignation if offered.' Linlithgow agreed that it was 'an extremely tiresome business' (15 April). At his most sardonic, he added: 'We might well kill two birds with one stone by threatening to send Gandhi to South Africa if the South African Government do not mend their ways.'

The Government of India did deliver three official protests to South Africa and issued a communique denouncing the 'Pegging Act' as 'repugnant, unnecessary and inopportune'. Public opinion was even more severe. Srinivasa Sastri, Maharaj Singh and Raza Ali combined to send a telegram of protest to Smuts: the Bill 'would shatter the faith of those Indians who still advocate India remaining within the British Commonwealth'. Aney, after his recent resignation said it was 'an abject surrender to the pernicious doctrine of racial prejudice'. This was the voice of moderate opinion; the more militant leaders were, of course, in detention or in hiding.

In Britain there was little comment on the Pegging Act. Sorensen, and other Labour M.P.s asked questions in the House of Commons (22 April) and attempted to get an adjournment debate in the Commons on 1 June. They did not succeed. Henry Polak arrived back from a lecture tour of North America in the autumn, and he attempted to enlist the dubious support of the Canadian prime minister, Mackenzie King. However, King still resisted all attempts to induce him to change the law denying the vote to Indians in Canada: it was 'an extremely complex problem', he told Polak.[6]

In South Africa, there was a strong movement towards civil disobedience, satyagraha. P. R. Pather took up occupation of his partly-finished house in a European Durban suburb. He was prosecuted under the Pegging Act and received a suspended jail sentence.[7] The High Commissioner called together a conference of the two rival associations, the N.I.A. and the Natal Congress. The N.I.A. boycotted the occasion, but the Congress decided to come, though S. R. Naidoo resigned over the issue. They met on 23 June, and Sir Shafa'at Ahmad sponsored a proposal for a round table conference between the governments of India and South Africa with the South African Indians. This was rejected by 49 votes to 13, and a motion calling on the Indian government to sever diplomatic relations with South Africa and recall the High Commissioner was adopted instead by 49 to 15. The currents of Indian opinion were flowing in strongly opposite directions. Kajee was able to consolidate the moderates, and the resolution of 23 June was modified: the High Commissioner should be recalled only in the last resort, but meanwhile India should apply the Reciprocity Act. Once again, the two rival Natal organisations agreed to merge as the Natal Indian Congress (July). Shafa'at Ahmad attributed the success of the merger to the departure of the militant Sorabjee Rustomjee from Natal to the Transvaal.[8] J. W. Godfrey became president of the new organisation, while Kajee was chairman of its managing committee.

Amery had decided that he could not direct this controversy from London. 'India's relations with South Africa are now India's responsibility and under the Government of India's control', he told Linlithgow (16 July 1943) — 'Do what you can to mitigate any tendency to retaliatory action'. Linlithgow, waiting to hand over to his successor, replied that the argument that the United Kingdom had 'washed their hands of this business' would merely expose the Government of India to greater demands for action (18 July), but Amery retorted 'There are admittedly spheres of Government activity in which India has by convention acquired practical independence of United Kingdom control. Fiscal autonomy is the obvious instance [Amery could never resist giving a lecture on the constitution] and to all intents and purposes another is the protection of Indian interests in a Dominion.... As for retaliation... had H.M.G. openly intervened and failed, as I think they inevitably would ... your Government would in that event have been in no stronger position than at present'. This was a considerable departure from Amery's stand in April: and it would leave the new Viceroy, Wavell, very much on his own.

Meanwhile, Dr Khare had assumed charge of the Department of Indians Overseas. The pressures upon him were powerful, and he sought to ease the situation by convening an all-parties conference in July. He invited Sastri, Maharaj Singh, Raza Ali, and leading moderate politicians, including Pandit Kunzru, M. R. Jayakar, and Sir Jagdish Prasad. Jinnah was asked to come, but declined, as did Bhulabhai Desai, a moderate Congress leader. The conference called for action against South Africa, and the issue was discussed further in a long debate in the Legislative Assembly which commenced on 30 July. Khare moved a non-committal resolution: 'That the position arising out of the present pegging legislation in South Africa be taken into consideration'. He gave a long account of the history of exchanges between the two countries from March onwards.⁹ Khare concluded:

> Some means must be found for maintaining the dignity and prestige of Indians and the Government of India, even in wartime. . . . Had India been independent, she would have considered this a *casus belli* against South Africa. But we may not think lightly of breaking away from the British Commonwealth of Nations because the ideal of cooperative interdependence on a footing of absolute equality is better than the ideal of isolated independence.

This spirited tone was not enough for some members, including Sir Raza Ali:

Raza Ali: Use your knife against South Africa.
Khare: I know when to use a knife and when to stop using a knife . . .
Raza Ali: This is a case of gangrene.
Khare: That should be left to the Government.

In this heated atmosphere, Linlithgow summoned his Council to consider the position in South Africa. He found that 'opinion was unanimous' on the need for action: even the new Commander-in-Chief, General Auchinleck, agreed while Sir Ramaswamy Mudaliar, the Member for Industry and Civil Supplies, announced that if a force was raised to attack South Africa, he would enlist. It was agreed that the trade agreement between the two countries should be abrogated. Linlithgow was too clever openly to oppose a trade boycott, but he asked for a study of the consequential effect upon the war-effort, and the memorandum submitted showed that this would be significant; thereupon, Auchinleck and some other members changed their views. Eventually, 'The Council were divided at least fifty-fifty as to the wisdom of going ahead in these circumstances'; it was decided to defer the decision; at least for two weeks.¹⁰

No decision had been taken when Wavell took over. Sir Shafa'at Ahmad Khan was recalled to Delhi for consultations; Wavell assessed his attitude as one of 'wounded pride'; he asked the High Commissioner to return with the personal letter for Smuts quoted at the beginning of this chapter. Some kind of opening now appeared in South Africa with a speech by Senator C. F. Clarkson, Minister of the Interior, and a man much respected in Natal, who urged that Indians should be given representation at all levels — municipal, provincial, and parliamentary — by means of a communal franchise. He declared that 'The Indian is here and entitled to be here' (3 December). The *Rand Daily Mail* commented: 'If democracy in

South Africa is not to become a farce, the different groups at present voiceless must be given some representation' (6 December 1943).

On his return to South Africa, Shafa'at Ahmad had an interview with Smuts. He asked for an electoral system which placed the Indians on a common roll with the Whites, but accepted that in no constituency would they form more than one-fifth of the electorate. He told Khare that Smuts was 'attentive, and more conciliatory than I have known him' (18 December 1943). He added that 'The Viceroy's letter seems to have made a considerable impression'. In this mood of euphoria he saw Lord Harlech, and confided to him his hopes. Harlech replied that no South African Government could get acceptance for a common roll; then (according to Harlech's account) the Indian High Commissioner said he was 'not interested' in any settlement which relegated Indians to a position similar to that of the Africans (who had token representatives in parliament) because the Indians were a superior race. Harlech concluded:

> It is difficult to discuss any question with him on any realistic or practicable basis. He only sees his own racial point of view.... I am convinced that he is essentially one of those "clever fools" who are so dangerous in international or inter-racial relations.[11]

On 6 February 1944, Wavell cabled anxiously to Smuts: 'Can you give me any news of conciliatory action by your Government?'; up till then he had received no answer to his letter of 23 November 1943. Smuts telegraphed back (7 February); 'I would much deprecate precipitate action by your government... accept my assurances that I am busy about a possible solution.' Wavell's anxiety was sharpened when he was given notice of an adjournment debate on South Africa in the Legislative Assembly. In order to induce the mover to withdraw his motion, Khare was authorised to tell him about Wavell's letter to Smuts. This had the desired effect, though the information was subsequently leaked out to the press and published in the *Statesman* newspaper. However, the news item did not reach South Africa.[12]

As Wavell waited for news from Smuts, Khare's patience ebbed, and he insisted on bringing the matter up again at the Viceroy's Council meeting of 31 March. Two somewhat wild telegrams from the High Commissioner in South Africa were read to the Members, but before any other proposal could be put forward Wavell suggested that they should defer considering economic sanctions and first ask Shafa'at Ahmad to call for the repeal of the Pegging Act or an equivalent concession. Wavell informed Amery (8 April 1944) that his Council 'fatigued by a long controversy on railway affairs agreed without discussion'. Wavell added that he was worried by Shafa'at Ahmad's conduct: he was 'egging the Indian community on', and 'It would be very awkward if it could be represented that negotiations between the [South African] Indian community and the Union Government had broken down owing to his intervention.'[13]

At this time, the Department of Indians Overseas was renamed the Department of Commonwealth Relations (30 March 1944). Khare's responsibilities were expanded to include relations between India and the Dominions and the supervision of all Indian High Commissioners. This ended a departmental squabble in which the Foreign and Political Department and the Department of Commerce had claimed that the new High Commissioners should be under their charge. Besides the Indian High Commission in London, there was now an exchange of High Commissioners between India and Australia. Sir Iven Mackay of Australia arrived in Delhi in March 1944, though the appointment of Sir R. P. Paranjpye to Canberra was not made until December 1944. There was the promise of an exchange with Canada, though Wavell told Amery that this appointment was held up by Mackenzie King 'mainly for fear of the votes of a handful of Sikhs in British Columbia' (16 March 1944).

In South Africa, the first sign of Smuts' intentions was the appointment of a commission, with the indefatigable Judge Broome as chairman, to 'inquire into matters affecting the Indian population of Natal'. The other two white members were Senator D. G. Shepstone, a very liberal United Party member, and W. M. Power, a Natal provincial legislator. There were two Indian members — A. I. Kajee and S. R. Naidoo; once again the moderates of the Natal Indian Congress were in the ascendant. These appointments were announced on 7 March 1944, but before the commission had really started work an important development occurred at a higher level. Kajee evolved a plan which might be acceptable and which might overcome the indignities of the Pegging Act. There would be no restrictions on the transfer of land between Europeans and Indians in the rural areas of Natal; outside Durban, the urban areas would only be subject to voluntary restraint by the Indians; within Durban a joint European-Indian Board would control all transfers of property, with power to reject inter-racial transfers. On 29 March the plan was presented to the prime minister.

Smuts had to watch his opponents — and his allies: a Dominion Party speaker, Ascutt, declared 'The history of the Indian question in South Africa had been one long history of concessions to the Indians. ... It would only be a question of time before the Indians swallowed up the whole of South Africa'; Swart, a Nationalist, attacked the Indian High Commissioner for calling for a common franchise.[14] But since the election Smuts' own United Party had an impregnable majority. He could afford to conclude a deal with Kajee's Natal Congress: especially as he was shortly going to a conference of Commonwealth Prime Ministers in London, and did not want to be bothered there by the Indian question.

And so, on 18 April there was a meeting at Pretoria. Smuts brought in Lawrence, Shepstone, Heaton Nicholls (now Administrator of Natal) and Douglas Mitchell, leader of the Natal United Party caucus. Kajee attended with S. R. Naidoo, P. R. Pather, and four other colleagues. Agreement was soon attained; a joint European-Indian Board would be set up under a Natal ordinance, and thereupon the Pegging Act would be withdrawn. Smuts immediately cabled the news to Wavell: it was a 'fair solution' he said. The biographer of A. I. Kajee describes this Pretoria Agreement as 'Munich' for Kajee; 'as well as for the Indian community'.[15] At the time, the Natal Whites regarded it very much as a Munich for Smuts.

The India Office had been bracing up for a difficult time at the Prime Ministers' Conference. R. N. Gilchrist, an official specially detailed to watch the affairs of Indians overseas noted (18 April) that they must prevent the South African Indian question 'becoming a topic of controversy'; they must take care 'not to embarrass Field-Marshal Smuts ... in particular by ensuring some restraint in the public discussions in India of the South African problem while the conference is in session'. In a private letter to Lord Cranborne, Amery suggested they must 'consider how best we can assist Smuts' (24 April). So Smuts arrived to a warm welcome. India's representative at the conference, Sir Firoz Khan Noon, was very much the poor relation; he was not admitted to confidential discussions on inter-Commonwealth cooperation. As Mackenzie King effectively torpedoed a proposal for an imperial secretariat, Noon's exclusion was not vital.[16]

Because Smuts departed for London immediately after the Pretoria Agreement (which was not committed to writing, beyond a press announcement) its implementation was left to others; mainly to Heaton Nicholls, the Natal Administrator. The first draft which was produced under Nicholls' instructions was criticised in detail by the Natal Indian Congress, and several weeks elapsed before a second draft ordinance was completed which met with the approval of the Indian leaders. According to Nicholls, this 'offered opportunities to the extremists on the European side to work up feeling'.[17] Smuts had given a message to Durban, commending the Pretoria

Agreement, and when this was read out in the City Hall on 17 June 1944 by Douglas Mitchell it was 'loudly booed'. The Nationalists dryly observed that Natal — "Little England" as they called it — was at last 'showing a healthy Nationalist and South African attitude'.[18]

The United Party in the Natal legislature began to be undermined. First, three Labour members withdrew their support; then four members of the United Party indicated that they would abstain when the issue came to a vote: this meant that there was no majority for the ordinance, as agreed at Pretoria. In an effort to strengthen the position of Nicholls and Mitchell, Smuts paid a visit to Durban soon after his return to South Africa, on 29 July. Yet this personal intervention by the Field-Marshal, with all his international prestige, only gave the Durban Whites the opportunity to demonstrate their antagonism to his policy: 'The Government of India should not be surprised if the Prime Minister is compelled to let the ordinance go', Shafa'at Ahmad told Khare (1 August 1944).

The United Party caucus had adopted the expedient of referring the Bill to a Select Committee; only when the Committee reported on 17 October did it become clear that an entirely different series of measures had been substituted for the former Bill.[19] The Residential Property Regulation Ordinance was designed to provide a 'permanent solution . . . to the dangers inherent in the residential intermingling of Europeans and Indians in Natal': this would be achieved by 'bringing about a separation of the races'. Three complementary ordinances were also brought forward to close every loophole in the housing field.

The Government of India now realised that any retaliation against South Africans in India which involved taking them off the voting registers would require an amendment of the Government of India Act, 1935: and only the British parliament could make the amendment. Wavell first raised the subject privately with Amery (20 July 1944): Khare was committed to enforcing the Reciprocity Act, 'and as Head of the Indian Government I feel bound to support him', said Wavell. Amery was adamant; acquainting Cranborne (now Secretary for the Dominions) with the situation, he declared: 'I do not propose to trouble the Cabinet with a proposal which I cannot support' (17 August), and this refusal was officially conveyed to Wavell.

Events reached a climax at the end of October when the debate was resumed in the Natal Council. Kajee applied to speak on behalf of the Indians at the Bar of the House; he made his speech on 30 October; the ordinance deviated from the Pretoria Agreement, he said. Nicholls produced the reply that the ordinance was 'an admission that henceforth the Indian population is a permanent part of Natal'. Not surprisingly, the Natal Indian Congress publicly rejected the ordinance. The effect of the new legislation was to apply segregation to all boroughs and townships throughout Natal. There was to be a residential Licencing Board in each town, composed of three Whites and two Indians. Any transfer of *occupation* (including letting) must be approved by these boards. The bills were finally passed by the Natal Council on 3 November: but the Governor-General, Patrick Duncan, had to give assent before they became law. On 3 November, Sir Shafa'at Ahmad Khan sent a cable to Dr Khare: 'This morning, the Indians in Natal have been enslaved. . . . It is now clear that Smuts instigated these ordinances and it is certain that he will carry them out ruthlessly. You have to deal with pure Nazis whose archpriest is Smuts.' The strain was becoming too much for a man who had served for almost three years as High Commissioner in South Africa.

Just before the ordinances were passed, Wavell tried another direct approach to Smuts; the official notes of protest had gained no relief. On 27 October, Wavell cabled privately to Smuts: 'The belief here is that the Union Government has repudiated the Pretoria Agreement.' Smuts replied next day that there was 'no intention to repudiate' the agreement: but he went on: 'If it [the ordinance] fails to pass there [the provincial council] I see no hope of passing the Pretoria Agreement through parliament which could not wish to override Natal . . . in a matter which she has rejected.' This confusing message seemed to indicate, first that Smuts still imagined that the ordinances fulfilled the agreement, and second that they might be rejected. It seemed that he had lost his accustomed firm grip on the situation. From this moment, South Africa and India were on collision course.

A peremptory telegram from Wavell warned Amery what to expect (31 October 1944): 'I have stonewalled on this for over a year but it has always been clear that the issue might come to a head at any time.' It was now obvious that Khare would wish to give notice of the termination of the trade agreement between the two countries; Wavell could only try to delay things by emphasising the difficulties. Next day, Wavell enlarged upon his telegram in his weekly letter to Amery: 'Linlithgow delayed action with his customary skill, and I have stonewalled myself for over a year,' he began. This was the one issue on which all Indians of all classes and faiths were 'solidly united': 'The feeling is so strong that the Council will almost certainly feel compelled to justify themselves by drastic action.' At this point, Wavell broke off his letter to go to the Council meeting; he resumed next day (2 November).

Before the formal meeting he had invited along Khare, Mudaliar, Azizul Haque and Sultan Ahmed — the most politically-minded of the Indian Members — for a preliminary discussion. Wavell stated the case for caution ('on the lines agreed between us') but Mudaliar replied on behalf of his colleagues to tell the Viceroy he could not realise the 'intensity of Indian feeling' on this issue; however, he agreed that it would be futile to try to terminate the trade agreement without obtaining the support of the United Kingdom government. The Council accepted this argument, but there was still pressure for immediate action and the issue was raised again at a Council meeting on 3 November. At this meeting, Mudaliar came up with a new suggestion; 'He favoured a high level delegation to London' to discuss South Africa with the Cabinet; other members were not in favour. Wavell commented: 'I have great sympathy with my Indian colleagues. They behaved in Council with dignity and moderation. . . . But their feelings are deeply hurt and they are under great pressure'; he added that there was no personal animosity against Smuts. It was decided to apply the Reciprocity Act to South Africa forthwith. Wavell was not too happy about the decision; lapsing into criticism, he observed that his present Council were sensitive because they 'have neither the stolidity of an official body nor the fighting power of a political Cabinet'.[20]

The Gazette of India published on 4 November announced that South Africans in India would be subject to the same disabilities as Indians in South Africa, and India's premier hotel, the Taj Mahal at Bombay, promptly put up a notice barring South African visitors. But the gesture was little more than token retaliation, and was recognised as such by everybody. Shafa'at Ahmad sent an effusive telegram to Dr Khare (6 November) 'The whole Indian community in the Union salutes you as the greatest champion of their racial rights and honour.' Dr Khare was in an almost equally ebullient mood. The same day (6 November) he went down to the Legislative Assembly to repeat the news of India's retaliation; the Viceroy's Council were unanimous on the issue, he said:

I wish India was in a position to declare war on South Africa. Some day or other — and we are all hoping it will be sooner rather than later — India will come into her own and will be in a position to take more effective action against those who persist in assailing her national honour and self respect.

The other speakers were equally belligerent; G. V. Deshmukh, initiator of an earlier bid for retaliation, said 'I wish very much Indian regiments could be sent to drive some sense into the South African Whites': an interesting observation from a Congress member who had opposed Indian participation in the war. Others brought up the position of the Indians in East Africa also; Hooseinbhoy Lalljee demanded the repatriation of all Indians from South and East Africa: 'Another 200,000 of our own countrymen will not make much difference'. Amendments were annexed to the government motion, demanding the recall of the High Commissioner from South Africa, and also, on the motion of Bhulabhai Desai, a moderate Congress member, the application of the reciprocity rule to Kenya, Tanganyika and Uganda.

It was all very distasteful to Amery, with his old South African loyalties. He confided his own views to Wavell in the course of three of the weekly letters. 'Any system of completely equal treatment is impossible in South Africa with a small white minority and a vast majority of Africans barely emerging from primitive barbarism' (26 October). 'If this [Natal] Ordinance does not go through, you may be quite sure that no successor of Smuts is likely to produce a more favourable one' (2 November); if the ordinance passed, 'Denounce the Trade Treaty if you must, and then go on playing for time afterwards as long as you can.' 'There is racial discrimination in many parts of the world ... not to speak of the far more rigid discrimination against the Scheduled Castes [Untouchables] in India' (9 November); 'I am truly sorry that Khare spoke so intemperately in the Assembly about South Africa.'

And in South Africa, events moved on inexorably: on 3 November Judge Broome announced that his commission would hold no more public hearings until the atmosphere was calmer. On 7 November Senator Clarkson gave Shafa'at Ahmad the Union Government's official response to the reciprocity notification; its general tone was dismissive: 'As the Government of India have now applied the same treatment to South Africans which the Union applies to Indians they can no longer be heard to make a complaint of the treatment of Indians in South Africa.' More particularly, the South African note complained of 'unhelpful' interference by the Indian High Commissioner in the affairs of the South African Indians: 'Once they begin to regard themselves as South Africans and cease to look outside for remedy of their grievances the way will be clear for happier relations in the future.'

There was a new High Commissioner for the United Kingdom in South Africa — Sir Evelyn Baring, till recently Governor of Southern Rhodesia — who as a young I.C.S. officer had been secretary to the Indian Agent in South Africa in 1929. He possessed a much deeper understanding of the South African Indian community than Harlech, and although he was determined not to get personally involved in the imbroglio he was able to interpret both sides to each other very helpfully. On 8 November he had an interview with Smuts: 'He said that he had always disliked the Pegging Act', and he would instruct the Natal Administrator to delay the formal approval of the new ordinances 'which he admitted to be a breach of the Pretoria Agreement. In the meantime, he would try to come to some arrangement with the Indians'. Smuts added that Judge Feetham would be president of all the licencing boards under the new (still to be approved) ordinance; he also ndicated that instead of throwing the Indians out of Riverside, Durban City Council would be asked to provide a new housing estate for the Riverside Indians.[21] It was a mixed, and not very coherent programme.

Unheeding of the Union Government's references to his interference, Shafa'at Ahmad now plunged into his most risky gambit. He seemed to fear that Kajee was planning to sell out the Indians, somehow.[22] On 8 November he cabled Dr Khare: 'Kajee has been following a dubious policy since passage of the Ordinance and is playing a part which he played in March and April 1943 [the time of the Pretoria Agreement] when he acted as Basson's spy,'[23] 'I fear Smuts may use Kajee against the Government of India and may induce him to agree to some compromise which is bound to be repudiated by the community.' Next day, Shafa'at Ahmad sent Kajee a form of ultimatum: 'The Government of India would like to inform you and the Union Government that they will not be bound in future by an agreement or undertaking arrived at between the Natal Indian Congress and the Union Government ... unless the High Commissioner approves of such an agreement or undertaking.' Shafa'at Ahmad announced that the Government of India 'will exercise in future the right to deal directly with the Union Government on basic questions concerning the Indian community without the intervention of any Indian organisation in South Africa.' Obligingly, the High Commissioner also despatched a copy of his letter to Kajee to Senator Clarkson.

Shafa'at Ahmad appears to have entertained no qualms about this move which, without any reference to Delhi, reversed Indian policy since the Cape Town agreement. On 10 November he informed Khare: 'Kajee has agreed with the contents of this letter, hence Smuts in future must deal with me'. Perhaps one of his motives was resentment that Smuts had given him no private interview since March. Shafa'at Ahmad dismissed Kajee as a leader — 'his head has been turned by his interviews with Smuts and membership of the Broome Commission'; 'Kajee will be eliminated soon from Congress as he is following a defeatist policy and wishes to serve his economic enterprises through his political contacts.' In conclusion, he alleged that Smuts was going round saying that the Government of India was making a stir in South Africa so as to induce the world to forget about Hindu-Muslim differences: 'Smuts' Machiavellian move is to make the international world overlook his treachery and ruthless Nazism.'

In case all this seemed too sombre, Shafa'at Ahmad followed next day with another cable in praise of Dr Khare: 'Never in the history of our race in South Africa has the morale of all, young and old, rich and poor, been so greatly improved. Dutchmen in Pretoria are astonished at your power, and have told Indian shopkeepers that they are not displeased, as our quarrel is only with Britishers in Natal.'

The reaction of the South African Government to the High Commissioner's rodomontade swiftly arrived in a Note of 13 November: 'They can but understand this declaration as a warning to the [South African] Indian community to make no agreement or understanding with the Union Government... It would therefore have the effect of preventing any attempt in South Africa to arrive at a settlement between those principally interested.' The Note ended: 'The Union Government can only view this declaration of policy as an open attempt at interference in the domestic affairs of the Union, and as a result, violation of clearly established rules of international behaviour.'

The response of the Commonwealth Relations Department of the Government of India was also prompt and forceful. On 14 November, Shafa'at Ahmad was told that he had departed from his instructions, which explicitly stated that he was not to try to act as spokesman for the South African Indians.[24] He was to inform the South African Government that the Government of India made no claim to stand between them and the local Indian community. Shafa'at Ahmad was annoyed: 'The tone of your cable is unprecedented and inconsistent with the dignity of my office' he retorted (14 November). He insisted that 'Both Smuts and Hofmeyr are trying to drive a wedge between the Indian community and the High Commissioner', and he dilated on the 'habit of dialectical subterfuge' of Smuts; but in the end he went to Senator Clarkson and said that on explicit instructions from his government he would not stand in the way of direct negotiations between the Natal Congress and the Union Government. Clarkson curtly replied that no intervention by the High Commissioner would be accepted by the Union Government.

All this was very relevant, because an early meeting between Smuts' ministers and Kajee was already planned; Shafa'at Ahmad made a last attempt to persuade Dr Khare to step in. If a deal was negotiated on the basis of dropping the Natal ordinances, this would be 'an exceedingly bad bargain, as the Government of India's power and influence throughout East, Central and South Africa would thereby disappear' (21 November). But Khare did not reply; the great diplomatic offensive was over.

At this moment, a voice from the past was heard; the voice of Srinivasa Sastri, making his last appearance in the Council of State on 17 November. Sastri was now a sick man; he was also a very sad man, as he looked back on a life spent in bringing together the English and the Indians in a British Commonwealth which should have nothing of a 'Boer Empire' about it. Yet, at the end, it was the South African view which had won. Why had India not recalled her High Commissioner from South Africa? Why had she not introduced economic sanctions?

Are we to understand that Whitehall raised some eleventh hour objection? ... If this is going to be our position, even at the end of this war, in the British Commonwealth — if all that we are allowed to do for them is to die for them in war, and when the war is over to be despised, exploited and squeezed by them — if there is no room for us there, then we have to seek our destiny outside the British Commonwealth.

It might appear as though the ageing Sastri had some special vision, for there was indeed a move afoot in Whitehall to favour South Africa and demean India. India's invocation of the Reciprocity Act, and the pressure to denounce the trade agreement were reported to the Cabinet by Amery.[25] The question was deliberated in Cabinet on 16 November, and it was decided to send off two messages; one to Smuts, and one to the Viceroy. The message for Smuts was reassuring: the United Kingdom Government 'could not acquiesce in the application of a trade embargo ... on essential war supplies'. Smuts was notified that he need not take this threat into his calculations, and the message ended 'We can only add how fully we appreciate your difficulties and how grateful we are for your efforts'.

This was a salute to a comrade; the telegram despatched to India on 21 November was a reproof for an underling: 'His Majesty's Government have noted with great regret that the Government of India have felt compelled to resort to retaliation against South Africa'. The United Kingdom Government 'Could not and would not approve the enforcement after the expiry of the Trade Agreement of prohibitions on the import for South Africa' of war supplies.

Wavell replied by cable: 'I am afraid His Majesty's Government's telegram will be interpreted as most unsympathetic to India's case'

(22 November). 'My Indian colleagues respond readily to friendliness', he went on, and the stiff opening of the Cabinet telegram was a poor reward for the contribution they, and the Indian armed forces had made to the allied cause. Wavell did not try to alter the 'meat' of the telegram, but he did offer an entirely different opening which would suggest that the British Government recognised India's part in the common effort. Wavell ended: 'I wish the Cabinet would realise that politeness and some show of sympathy count for a lot in this country . . . I do wish His Majesty's Government would do something to help me.'

Next day Wavell indicated his concern — and his anger — in a personal letter to Amery: 'I do wish I could get into H.M.G.'s mind how much more difficult they make my already difficult task with Council, and how much they damage the situation in India by their failure to conciliate Indian feeling in any way, and the contemptuous attitude they often adopt towards Indian susceptibilities.'[26] As always, Amery was willing to help the Viceroy, and as always he was not very effective about it.[27] It was necessary to get agreement to the substitution of Wavell's opening for that approved by the Cabinet from the Prime Minister himself. Churchill was seldom gracious about admitting an error, and Amery was reluctant to tackle him. On 30 November he had his chance; he found Churchill in the morning 'in happy birthday mood'; he was 'most agreeable' to Leo Amery, and consented to the new form of words; the Cabinet endorsed the change the same evening. Wavell signified his relief to Amery: the changes in the telegram would enable the Council 'without loss of face to stress the war effort and the common interests of the United Nations in deciding, as I trust they will, that further counter-measures will be held in abeyance' (5 December 1944).

In South Africa, Baring called on Smuts to give him the Cabinet's message. Baring found the Prime Minister in a communicative, accommodating mood. He told Baring that the Natal ordinance was drafted while he was in Britain, and it was 'not in accordance' with the Pretoria Agreement: 'The Durban City Council are as much to blame as the Indians', said Smuts; they had sabotaged the agreement. Smuts deplored the gap between the leaders of the Indians and the mass of their people: 'who are on a kaffir level'.[28]

A few days later, Smuts, flanked by Clarkson, Shepstone and Mitchell saw Kajee, Pather and other Congress leaders. Smuts told them at this meeting on 28 November: 'I cannot quarrel with you when you say that it [the ordinance] is in conflict with the Pretoria Agreement. . . The Pretoria Agreement is stillborn and dead. The attempt was made, and has failed.' Smuts asked Douglas Mitchell, now Administrator of Natal, to refuse assent to the Residential Property Ordinance.[29] On 6 December Smuts announced that the Land Purchase Bill passed by the Union Parliament had been 'reserved', while he again saw Baring and gave him a copy of a Note to the Natal Congress. Smuts reiterated that the ordinance was not in the spirit of the Pretoria Agreement, which was now 'of no further effect'. Smuts could not 'undertake to repeal the Pegging Act' (which was anyway due to expire in March 1946), and they must pin their hopes on the third Broome Commission's recommendations on the condition and status of the Indians. Baring took away the impression that Smuts might promote a settlement in the Union Parliament if the Government of India did not proceed with its trade embargo. However, the local Indians were totally dissatisfied with Smuts' Note, and on 7 December Kajee and Naidoo resigned from the Broome Commission. Three days later the Natal Indian Congress met and endorsed the resignations, while condemning what they called the repudiation of the Pretoria Agreement. The Congress demanded restoration of the parliamentary and municipal vote, but did not adopt a more militant policy. On the motion of Kajee and Pather they decided upon a 'campaign of publicity and propaganda' only.

Where did all this leave relations between South Africa and India? Two more Notes were exchanged at the official level. On 4 December, the South African Government again rejected any Indian Government claim to speak for the local Indian community: the High Commissioner was 'the representative solely of his government to the union government; any other claim was 'contrary to all rules of international courtesy and practice'. The Government of India replied that they 'do claim the right to make diplomatic representations on important matters affecting the Indian community': this had been conceded at the second round table conference. The absence of the vote was 'the core of the whole problem. If the Indians in the Union were South African citizens in the ordinary sense, the Government of India would not be under constant pressure from all sections of opinion ... to protect them against discrimination and unfair treatment'. So long as their status was unequal, this was 'a fit matter for diplomatic representations'.

So much for the record: but how could the deadlock be resolved? Optimistic as ever, Amery told Wavell (7 December 1944) that things were simmering down; 'Smuts has been genuinely helpful'; he hoped that 'Shafa'at did not try to spoil a settlement.' Wavell cabled that another conference between South Africa and India 'might perhaps do good', but in the prevailing strained conditions it was more likely to be favourably considered if the proposal was made to Smuts through the United Kingdom High Commissioner (12 December). The Dominions Office obligingly cabled Baring (15 December) — would a high-level conference on the lines suggested by Wavell be acceptable: or was the atmosphere in South Africa 'too supercharged'? Baring soon obtained an interview with Smuts, and got a mixed reception. Smuts was prepared to make a gesture when the new Indian High Commissioner arrived, and he might get his colleagues to agree to a conference, provided it did not take place 'under the threat of punitive action' by India should agreement not be reached.

Smuts thought that the moderate Indians had held on to their position temporarily, and they had quashed a Natal Congress resolution calling for a trade embargo. He understood their dependence on the Government of India when they themselves had no parliamentary votes.[30] So often, when Smuts was talking to a reasonable, civilised, humane person, he himself assumed those values; unhappily there were a majority of unreasonable people among the South African Whites; and Smuts spoke their language fluently, when required.

Sir Shafa'at Ahmad Khan made a dignified exit from South Africa: in his last speech (21 December 1944) he put aside politics, and saluted Hofmeyr as the friend of the Indians.[31] As 1944 ended, Amery suggested to Wavell that they needed 'a period of forbearance in which each side abstains from provocative action of any kind' (2 January 1945). It was perhaps a wise observation; but it implied that the Indians would accept indefinitely their position of inequality. For his part, Wavell was ready to cooperate. Dr Khare had signified that he still wished to give notice of the termination of the trade agreement, but the Viceroy managed to head him off. The subject of the Indians in South Africa was postponed from one Council agenda to the next; and so 1944 came to an end. At Dr Khare's urging, India had rattled the sword at South Africa, but largely due to Wavell's blend of firmness and conciliation it had not been drawn from the sheath.

In South Africa the war years were the crisis years, the crunch years; elsewhere in Africa they formed a kind of interregnum for the various Indian communities. Southern Rhodesia remained the territory most withdrawn from controversy. While Sir Evelyn Baring was Governor, he established closer contacts with the Rhodesian Indians, and on 3 August 1943 he sent a long, personal account of their condition to C. R. Attlee at the Dominions Office. It was a small community, numbering 1,546 males and

1,001 females, and all new immigration was closely restricted (as was the immigration of Africans). There were 238 Asiatics on the voters' register (including two Chinese). In response to demands from among the Indian community for 'Indian purity schools', one purity school had been opened in Salisbury, and one in Bulawayo. The new Town Planning Bill for Salisbury provided for an area to be reserved for the Indians: an 'excellent locality' said Baring. Salisbury was expanding fast, and if the Indians turned this site down, they might not get another so convenient to the business and industrial areas. If they tried to force their way into European suburbs they could 'raise the sort of storm now raging in Durban'. During 1944 the Town and Country Planning Bill tightened up zoning regulations, but there was no compulsory segregation for the Indians. The new Indian housing estate was equipped by the Salisbury City Council with schools and an area for sports; there were the 'usual protests' by some Europeans against giving these facilities to Indians.[32]

The Rhodesian Indians kept out of politics, and Rhodesian politics was altogether somewhat parochial, apart from the perennial question of a link between Southern Rhodesia and neighbouring territories. Smuts had never abandoned the hope of amalgamation with South Africa, and in January 1942 he told his English friends, the Gilletts: 'They may yet be in the net. I am working on some such plan as that of the Pan-American Union.'[33] In May 1943, the parliament of Southern Rhodesia passed a motion urging the government to approach South Africa for a joint conference on closer union. The Colonial Office was apprehensive of this development, and in reply sponsored a Standing Central African Council, which started in October 1944, with representatives from the two Rhodesias and Nyasaland, and a small secretariat.

East Africa was more directly affected by the war. When Kenya and the other colonies began to mobilise their resources, there was an offer from some of the Indian leaders to bring forward their compatriots for military service. However, their enlistment into the infantry and other front-line units raised difficulties; the Indians would not be drafted into the African fighting formations, and they were not acceptable in the white battalions. In consequence, those Indians who enlisted were enrolled as clerks or storemen or fitters; and in due time the Kenya Whites turned round to condemn their war record as combatant soldiers! Indians in Kenya between the ages of 18 and 55 became liable to compulsory service as clerks and artisans in military establishments and firms engaged on war work.[34]

At the outbreak of war, many of the Indian community returned to their old homes, and when Italy entered the war, and a threat from nearby Italian Somaliland seemed probable, Indian families were advised by the Kenya Government to take part in an evacuation scheme back to India. Later, in 1942, when a Japanese incursion into East African waters seemed possible, the Indians in Mombasa were advised to send their families, and also people in non-essential occupations, back to India. These evacuations became the subject of white criticism: the Indians were said to be 'running away'.

Arrivals and Departures at the Port of Mombasa
1939-1945

	Europeans Immigrants	Europeans Emigrants	Indians Immigrants	Indians Emigrants
1939	6,962	5,806	11,185	14,284
1940	3,152	2,320	6,343	11,382
1941	1,574	1,398	11,090	8,872
1942	1,377	478	6,139	4,617
1943	738	356	4,410	2,495
1944	841	821	7,703	5,107
1945	1,626	1,945	7,236	6,304

Source: *Report by the Government of India Delegation to East Africa*... 1946.

India was also asked to restrict the movement of people from Indian ports to East Africa, and this was implemented, though in March 1942 the Government of India asked the East African governments for an assurance that the restrictions were regarded simply as a wartime measure. Then, early in 1944 the East African governments introduced strict controls upon entry into their territories: Tanganyika imposed restrictions from 14 February 1944, and Kenya and Uganda followed suit from 1 March. The only immigrants admitted were those who had been given certificates from the Director of Manpower indicating that their admission was essential for the war effort. The Government of India protested to the East African governments (23 March 1944) complaining that the leaders of the East African Indians had not been consulted, and asked for a declaration that the regulations were to last for the duration of the war only; on 12 April 1944 the Colonial Office assured the India Office that the regulations were not intended to be permanent.

When many of those evacuated in the earlier wartime emergency situations wanted to come back to East Africa they found that the immigration regulations applied to them also; up to 10,000 were affected. The Government of India asked the East African governments to exempt all these people from controls, and also that Indian firms might be allowed to bring in new assistants to replace employees who retired. The Government of India contrasted the ban imposed on Indians with the admission of numbers of Europeans (especially Poles) as refugees, and observed that the economic benefits of the restrictions were 'not commensurate with the racial bitterness which the regulations have produced'.

There was also a debate in the Indian Council of State on 6 April 1944, in the course of which H. N. Kunzru stressed the need for a regular channel of information to the Government of India; he revived the question of the appointment of an Agent, but to this R. N. Banerjee (who had succeeded Bozman as Secretary of the Department) replied that 'The Indian community in Kenya are none too anxious to have an Agent'. It appeared that they felt this would inhibit them in making demands from the Kenya Government.

During the closing months of 1944, a parliamentary delegation proceeded on an official visit to Central and Southern Africa. The party included four Conservative M.P.s, one of whom was the financier, Sir Alfred Beit, and three Labour M.P.s, one being a future Minister, Hector McNeill; the chairman was Sir Geoffrey Shakespeare (National Liberal). The delegation spent the longest part of their tour in South Africa, but they visited Kenya on their way. On their return they put in a secret report which unanimously recommended an immediate ban on Indian immigration into all African territories in the interests of the Africans. There were also 'Numerous signs from censorship intercepts that feeling in the African colonies on the subject of Indian penetration is exceedingly strong': though all the objectors were recorded as Europeans![35] The subject was raised in the South African debate in the Indian Legislative Assembly on 6 November 1944, when Khare stated: 'The [immigration] regulations were also sprung as a surprise on the Indian community in East Africa, and the Government of India was much hustled in the matter'.

The Indian attempts to get the ban lifted were answered by a letter from the Colonial Office dated 13 March 1945, enclosing a memorandum from the East African governments. They intended no general scheme to restrict Indian entry, they wrote; there was a severe food shortage during 1943 and 1944, and there was still food rationing in East Africa; there was a housing shortage, especially in Nairobi, accentuated by wartime building restrictions (paradoxically, there was also unemployment in Kenya: about 3,000 Indian masons and carpenters were out of work). At Dar-es-Salaam, the

Medical Officer reported that of the 14,500 Indians in the Asian quarter, at least 2,500 needed rehousing. However, the East African governments insisted that no returnees had been refused entry, and though the numbers returning were limited, the overall Indian population was rising sharply. Whereas there were 46,026 Asiatics in Kenya in 1938 (overwhelmingly from India) there were 61,127 in 1944; for Uganda the figures were 17,256 and 26,537, and for Tanganyika they were 24,144 and 38,500. Moreover, in answer to a question in the legislature about food rationing, the Kenya Government stated that 86,000 Indians were in receipt of rations: a rise in numbers which the other communities received with consternation. Anyhow, for the present, the immigration controls remained.

The other main wartime measure which aroused the protests of the Indians was the enlargement of restrictions upon the transfer of land to non-indigenous peoples. Tanganyika moved first with the Land (Restriction on Transfer) Ordinance of 1943, which prohibited the alienation of land to any non-African without the permission of the Governor, but this measure caused nothing like the trouble aroused in Kenya by the Land Control Bill, first published in October 1943.

E. R. Edmunds of the Colonial Office noted (31 May 1944) 'Few colonies, perhaps fortunately, can reproduce the influential political atmosphere of Kenya'. The leaders of the Kenya Whites were now Lord Francis Scott and Major F. W. Cavendish-Bentinck; they enjoyed greater power and influence than the Governor (Sir Henry Moore until July 1944), or the Chief Secretary (G. M. Rennie). The Kenya settlers had increased their grip on the country considerably during the war years: the innumerable boards and committees were run by them, and their production of foodstuffs and raw materials was so important that they virtually dictated the regulations. They now altered the Land Control Bill to serve the interests of the white community.

The Kenya Indian Congress attempted to arouse Whitehall to what was happening; cables were sent to the Under Secretary for the Colonies, the Duke of Devonshire, to interested M.P.s, and to Henry Polak. The white highlands policy was being expanded further, the Congress alleged; the sale of land to companies with Indian shareholders would now be forbidden, and land transfers would be controlled by a Board appointed to represent the settlers. The Select Committee drafting the Bill was composed of seven white settlers and no Indian: 'The present steps are preparatory to establishing self-government for Europeans only in the highlands', the Congress declared.

Immediately he received the cable, Polak wrote off in his usual methodical way to the Duke of Devonshire (5 June 1944). Kenya was tending to move in the Southern Rhodesian direction, and the white settlers were encouraged by a statement from Smuts that South Africa should share in deciding policies for Africa: this was a matter which united all Indians in protest, and Polak asked for a halt to the bill. Devonshire replied (14 June) that the Bill had been introduced to prevent speculation in land, in anticipation of a post-war boom. There was no case for asking the Governor to hold up the Bill.

In a letter to G. F. Seel at the Colonial Office the Governor, Sir Henry Moore, revealed that the Bill had doubled in length since it was given to the Select Committee, which had also taken control over land transfers out of the Governor's hands (as it remained in Tanganyika) and committed this all-important function to an Assessment Board to be appointed by the European, non-official members of the Legislative Council. Moore's sense of political realities in Kenya led him to go on: 'It did not seem to me either necessary or politically desirable to challenge the unofficial majority.' He conceded that the Bill had been 'bitterly opposed' by the Indians, but the Kenya Government had taken the line that the changes in the Bill did not amount to a change of policy. Moore concluded that it would not have been 'politically possible' to postpone the second reading of the Bill until it had been vetted by the Colonial Office (12 June 1944). Perhaps it was this masterly demonstration of politics as the art of the possible that determined the Colonial Office to appoint Sir Henry Moore to be Governor of politically explosive Ceylon, in place of Sir Andrew Caldecott. Gilbert Rennie was left to officiate as Governor of Kenya until the arrival of Sir Philip Mitchell.

Meanwhile, the Government of India had informed the India Office that they were 'gravely concerned' (24 June); the Bill would 'place on Indians a statutory disability in place of administrative practice'. This had been the sticking point ever since the so-called Elgin pledge: India had resisted all attempts to give the White Highlands policy the force of law, and the 1923 Devonshire declaration had endorsed this position. The Colonial Office was sufficiently impressed to instruct Rennie as acting governor that the formal Royal assent would be delayed until the views of the Government of India had been considered (27 September 1944).

The Indian government's view was conveyed in a telegram dated 5 October. The Land Control Board would be composed of Europeans only, yet they would have authority over the Muhoroni farms owned by Indians since before 1906; to set up the board was to admit by 'statutory recognition' that the Indians 'have no interest in the Highlands', and to accept 'discrimination against Indians'; there was no justification for introducing such a radical measure during wartime. Conveying these remonstrations to the Colonial Office, the India Office observed (10 October 1944): 'Although the Government of India have perforce acquiesced in the reservation of the Highlands for Europeans, they have always successfully resisted the incorporation of the principle of reservation in a legal enactment.'

G. F. Seel was a little worried because the Kenya legislation had followed so swiftly in the wake of the Pegging Act in South Africa; this 'would add fuel to the flames'. Mr. Edmunds feared that this might 'develop into a first class issue' with India, and he compiled a long memorandum in which, to his own and Colonial Office satisfaction, he refuted the Government of India, point by point: there was nothing in the new ordinance, he observed 'imposing any legal disability against Indians or against any person on the ground of race, colour or creed.'[36] However, the Attorney-General of Kenya was sufficiently bothered by the question of the Muhoroni farms — twenty in number — to point out that whereas at present they could be (and were) transferred from one Indian owner to another, the Bill would allow the Land Control Board to stop such transfers: he recommended that the Governor should issue an assurance that this would not happen (21 October 1944).

Rennie sent this proposal on to Moore, who was in London for consultations with the Colonial Office; it was only reasonable to exempt the Indians from any restriction on the Muhoroni farms, he said, but this 'would cause resentment locally'; the white settlers would object — 'one never knows how they will jump' (27 October). Moore merely commented that 'the fewer assurances anyone gives to anyone, the better', and the Colonial Office adopted the same tone. In the formal reply to the India Office (20 November) it was said that there were no grounds for disallowing the Bill, and 'nothing to be gained by further protracted correspondence with the Government of India'; moreover, 'Mr Secretary Stanley cannot be expected to risk serious political trouble in Kenya by further delay in giving assent.' A *sens du possible* animated Oliver Stanley also, where a question upsetting to the white settlers was concerned.

On 9 December Kenya was informed that the Royal assent had been given, though subsequently a secret despatch (no. 333 dated 30 December 1944) instructed the Kenya governor that the Muhoroni farms would be exempted from the sphere of the Land Control Board.

It was against this background that the leader of the European group in the Kenya legislature, Vincent, moved a resolution calling on His Majesty's Government to ask Field-Marshal Smuts to summon a conference of all the British territories of East, Central, and Southern Africa, to consider their future within a Pan-African context. The resolution was moved on 4 January 1945, and was opposed by all the non-European members of the legislature — that is, five Indians, an Arab, and an African recently added to the legislature — who all voted against the resolution. As the officials abstained, the resolution was adopted by eleven (European) votes to seven.

When the resolution was forwarded to the Colonial Office, there was much masterly inactivity, for they had no wish to transfer British colonial policy from London to Pretoria. The move aroused wide resentment among the Indians, who began to talk about organising their own Pan-African conference in reply. The mood was reflected in India; Shafa'at Ahmad, now returned from South Africa, told Khare 'that the general hostility to Indian immigrants in the East African territories was not an accident, but was part of a plan concerted with the Union Government'.

Wavell reported these allegations to Amery (21 February 1945). He also passed on an even wilder thought from his Member for Commonwealth Relations:

Khare also suggests that Eritrea might be handed over to India as a colony, as Indian troops played so large a part in conquering it. There may have been from time to time discussions about the possibility of finding some country to which Indians could emigrate without being treated as inferiors. I do not know what H.M.G.'s ideas are about the future of Eritrea, but I think India could make quite good use of it, and Khare's suggestion seems to me worth consideration.

Amery in his reply (28 February) disposed fairly briefly of Khare's colonial ambitions: 'I doubt very much whether at a Peace Conference it would be possible to secure Eritrea as an actual colony for India . . . it would be a mistake to try to overload the Indian constitutional problem . . . by adding the responsibilities of colonial administration'. His comments on the white Pan-African movement ranged further, for this idea was close to his own dreams. The Colonial Office was opposed to any federation of Southern Africa which leaned towards the Union, wrote Amery, because that 'would lead to the Southern Rhodesian outlook on native and native labour questions displacing the Colonial Office outlook'. Amery seemed unconvinced; the parliamentary delegation led by Shakespeare had reported that the Africans were better off in Southern Rhodesia and the Union than in the East African territories; the 'direct influence' of the white farmer was better than government instruction; white development by white enterprise meant there was more for the Africans: 'the native makes more progress where white enterprise has scope'. The Whites disliked the Indians because 'the Indian, starting from a higher level, prevents the native rising in the social and industrial scale'. Amery concluded: 'Anything like an attempt by the Colonial Office to enforce a drastic policy overriding their [the Europeans'] point of view might very well incline their minds to look to the Union for moral support'.

The lull in the storm blowing over relations between India and South Africa which had appeared at the end of 1944 persisted through the remaining months of the second world war. The lull was soon over, but while it lasted the South African-Indian relationship appeared to have become more hopeful.

On 12 January 1945, Khare met Gandhi again, after many years and much controversy. Gandhi said that he was ready to go to South Africa as leader of an Indian delegation. Khare's comment later was: 'My only desire was to take revenge upon him by debunking him, because I knew ... that in South Africa he would enter into some patched-up compromise with General Smuts.'[37] Khare's assessment was never tested, as Smuts had set himself against any conference with negotiators from India: he still seemed to think a *quieta non movere* policy would suit best.

If there was an interlude of calm, part of the credit for creating this went to the new Indian High Commissioner, R. V. Deshmukh, an 'intimate friend' of Dr Khare and a man of wide experience as a Minister in Khare's Congress government in the Central Provinces and later as Dewan of a princely state.[38] Deshmukh left India at the beginning of February. He took with him a personal letter from Wavell to Smuts (29 January 1945) in which the Viceroy said of his High Commissioner that he was 'quiet and reserved', but also 'Like all good Indians he is a strong nationalist'. Deshmukh also carried with him a set of instructions, similar to those given to Shafa'at Ahmad four years previously, though certain aspects of the late High Commissioner's activities were to be avoided — thus the warning, 'He must not ... give the impression that he is, or regards himself as the leader or spokesman of the Indian community or wishes to oppose any honourable settlement.' The desired goal for the South African Indians was 'a status equal to that of Union citizens of European origin'.

Deshmukh sailed at a moment when the Natal Indian Congress was again under pressure from the activists, for on 5 February they cabled to Amery that he should not come until their grievances had been eased. A discerning assessment of their predicament was made by Sir Evelyn Baring in whom Kajee frequently confided. First the Indians had been accused of being poor and dirty; now they were in trouble for imitating the Europeans, Kajee said. Anti-Indian feeling in Durban was now worse, and affected working-class Whites. The Durban City Council was dominated by land agencies, who wanted to compel the Indians to buy land on the far fringes of the city. Kajee recognised that they needed the help of the Government of India, though he 'had no use' for Shafa'at Ahmad. He was opposed to the introduction of sanctions, and he was ready — with Naidoo — to rejoin the Broome Commission if the ordinances were shelved. Thus Kajee: still hoping that moderation might pay in the end.[39]

Smuts did not appear to realise the necessity to act, fast, if he was to regain the initiative. On 24 January he sent a soothing message to Wavell, via Heaton Nicholls and Amery, 'You may feel assured that nothing will be said or done to prejudice an eventually satisfactory Indian settlement'; the question of sending a delegation from the Government of India was 'in abeyance' (24 January). Wavell told Amery he was disappointed by this message (30 January) adding: 'It will be very difficult to restrain Khare if I have nothing to offer him except the hope that relations may improve after the Broome Commission report.'

If Khare was impatient, it was partly because even the most moderate and conservative of Indian politicians were impatient. He had to face a Legislative Assembly on 9 February which had lodged a censure motion against the Government of India for failing to enforce sanctions against South Africa. Five members of the opposition spoke — representing the Congress, the Muslim League, and other parties — and the motion was approved without a division. Sanctions must be introduced immediately; the Reciprocity Act was quite inadequate; the High Commissioner should not go to his post until justice was done. The speakers were militant: said G. V. Deshmukh (Congress): 'If the Government of India have any guts, then give a fight! The whole House and the whole country is behind you.' Said Maulana Zafar Ali Khan (Muslim League): 'Cannot you bring South Africa to its knees by invading it? We have got twenty lakhs [two million] of patriotic soldiers.' More practically, Sir Cowasji Jehangir, moderate of moderates, asked whether the new High Commissioner had left? Dr Khare said he did not know, whereupon Jehangir replied: 'Government is irritating public opinion... quite unnecessarily.' Then Khare admitted Deshmukh had sailed, but pleaded that it was really a military secret. It was not an easy moment for the Member for Commonwealth Relations.

Echoes of the debate reached South Africa, and impelled Smuts to write to Wavell, whose letters thus far had been left unanswered. The problem was made more difficult by the tone of the speeches in the Assembly he insisted, but still 'I personally do not take too pessimistic a view of our local Indian situation'; 'patient, resolute action to make progress, step by step, will win through in the end' (6 March 1945).

On 21 March the question of sanctions was raised in the Viceroy's Council by Dr Khare; as Mudaliar was in London, waiting to go to San Francisco for the inauguration of the United Nations, and as Smuts was going with him, it was decided to see whether a direct approach could achieve anything. On 22 March, the Council of State followed the lower house in calling for sanctions and asking for the return of the High Commissioner: this resolution also was accepted unanimously, though the more staid upper house accepted a government amendment that sanctions should be introduced 'as and when expedient'.

Deshmukh quickly made himself familiar with the difficult problems and people he had to cope with. Soon after he arrived, Smuts delivered a speech on 14 March indicating the new approach to the urban housing situation in Natal; there would be a provincial Housing Board, under this proposal, and the local Indians feared that this could mean their expropriation. Deshmukh spoke of these fears to Senator Lawrence, who promised to give him a draft of the new Bill in advance of publication; in itself, a sign of a new relationship of confidence. He saw Hofmeyr on 6 April, and received the assurance that 'it was the government's policy to sort out racial groups without compulsion'. Deshmukh considered that the legislation was acceptable to Indian opinion, provided that it was accompanied by a declaration that the Pegging Act would not be renewed when it expired. Deshmukh also had a conference with Mitchell, the Administrator of Natal, Senator Shepstone, and A. I. Kajee. Kajee 'visualised the racial sorting-out ... process [as] covering possibly several generations'. He was 'particularly anxious to provide housing for poorer Indians'.[40]

All seemed set fair, though once again Smuts had departed from South Africa at a crucial period in order to participate in a summit conference on the foundation of the new international order, the United Nations. He stopped in London, and found time for a conversation with Wavell and with Ramaswamy Mudaliar, who was on the same U.N. mission: Smuts called it a 'preliminary canter'. Once again, Smuts went over the history of the Pretoria Agreement and its demolition; clearly the subject nagged uncomfortably at his conscience. Smuts believed that the key to any progress was an agreement about urban living conditions. His idea was to balance the separation of the urban population on racial lines by the designation of 'free areas' where anybody might reside. When land was acquired on a compulsory basis, Smuts promised that Indians would be treated 'exactly as Europeans': he meant that any proposal for acquisition 'would be judged solely on the basis of need'. He also promised that the Pegging Act would 'lapse' in a year's time. Smuts was ready to give the Indians the franchise on the basis of separate representation in parliament. Khare's response to this information was to reply that the Government of India would accept the new legislation for separate areas if there was no expropriation of Indian property in the areas designated for Indians, and if the 'free zones' provision went through. Khare added that though they were committed to the principle of a common electoral roll they would consider the Smuts proposal for a communal franchise.[41]

On closer examination, Deshmukh decided that the Housing and Slums Bill was objectionable: it was 'little different from the Class Areas Bill which was abandoned in 1927', he told Hofmeyr (3 May). The acting prime minister and his colleagues seemed to agree with this, for on 15 May they met Deshmukh to tell him that the Housing and Slums Bill would be scrapped; there would be a new measure designed to provide regulations for three years only. When Deshmukh saw the Housing (Emergency Powers) Bill he agreed that it was a great improvement on the previous Bill: 'the regulations have been 'placed in a framework more in accord with Indian views'; Kajee, also, was pleased. Deshmukh informed Khare (22 May 1945) that 'Mr. Hofmeyr personally took charge of drafting the Bill ... on the basis of a memorandum outlining our views ... Everything possible has been done ... to ensure that ... it should not be used as a discriminatory measure against Indian interests.' The main danger was that the Natal M.P.s would realise how liberal the proposals were, and therefore lead an attack on the Bill. Deshmukh advised the Natal Indian Congress: 'Comment publicly as little as possible.' Subsequently, at meetings with Hofmeyr, Clarkson, Lawrence and Mitchell, Deshmukh promised 'as little disturbance ... as possible'.[42] All were agreed to observe a low posture and introduce reform by stealth.

The observant Baring reported on these developments to London. He told Sir Eric Machtig that Deshmukh had 'conducted his negotiations with patience and considerable success' (25 May) and he provided a lengthy assessment of the local Indian political leadership (29 May). There were three main groups. The moderates, led by Kajee, were in control of the Congress, and they enjoyed considerable support in the country districts of Natal, but in Durban the Anti-Segregationist Council group were dominant; they could win over a general meeting and elect their own men on a show of hands; for this reason, the moderates had postponed new elections for positions in the Congress. The third group in Natal Indian politics were the Communists, led by Albert Christopher. This group were drawn more from the working class; Manilal Gandhi, editor of *Indian Opinion*, was identified with them, though he was not a Communist.

Baring saw a fundamental division between those who fought only for Indians' rights and those who thought in terms of a broad-based battle against white dominance. Thus, the Anti-Segregationist Council belonged to the Non-European Unity Movement. Baring commented:

European South Africans are apt to assert dogmatically that Natives hate and despise Indians. I have always doubted the truth of this generalisation. It is perhaps true that in the Zulu reserves the Gujarati traders are disliked; but in the working class districts of Durban, conditions are different. There the ... descendents of the indentured labourers mix with Natives at cinemas, at boxing matches, at hot dog stalls in Grey Street, the centre of the Indian trade district.

There was inter-marriage, wrote Baring, which was encouraged by the Communist Party: the C.P. chairman for the Cape Province was H. A. Naidoo, from Durban, whose wife was Jewish.

However, the Natal Congress was cool about non-white or anti-white cooperation; the dictum of Dr Xuma, president of the all-African Congress, powerful on the Rand, was quoted: each section 'should fight its own fight'. Kajee was identified with this approach, and he was therefore losing ground. Partly, this reflected his changed economic status: fifteen years before he had been 'a struggling Indian broker living in a dirty little office' and could appeal directly to the Indian workers; now, he was 'extremely wealthy, and therefore suspect to the working class' said Baring. He was gradually losing his influence, and this had 'led to a weakening of those who counsel moderation'. One sign of this was their silence on the question of the Indian members rejoining the Broome Commission. Although there seemed to be prospects of agreement on the new housing legislation, it was 'difficult to avoid the conclusion that a clash is about to occur'.

Baring was proved right in these assessments though a few months of fair weather still remained. The publication of the Broome Report in June 1945 was an indication of the difficulties.[43] The final months of the Commission's existence had been wholly frustrating. Not only had the Indian members withdrawn, but there was also an almost complete boycott by white opinion; the Durban Council sent no memoranda and gave no evidence.

In this limbo, F. N. Broome and his two colleagues tried to present a 'balanced view'. In their conclusions, they restated the basic philosophy of Natal:

Long before the first Indian ever set foot in the country, the standard of western civilisation had been set up in Natal and that standard must be maintained. This matter is fundamental. It can never be made the subject of negotiation or barter or compromise.

It therefore followed that there could never be a common roll, on which the Indians might form a majority; equally, Indian opinion was dead set against a separate franchise. The Commission proposed to solve the deadlock by creating a 'loaded franchise' in which the Indian electors would be required to meet certain qualifications, while white adults would obtain the vote automatically: this was a revised version of the proposals for Kenya under the Wood-Winterton agreement. There was currently an atmosphere of hostility between Whites and Indians; in fulfilment of the 'balanced view' approach, some of this was blamed upon 'propaganda now emanating from India.' The solution was not compulsory repatriation for Indians — neither was it 'immediate assimilation' with the Europeans: it was a 'middle course': 'to live side by side and to develop with the minimum of friction'. *Apartheid* without tears. Only Senator Shepstone in a dissenting note tried to emphasise that the situation was not really one of live and let live but of Indians being the victims of white racism. The Commission just could not face up to the grim reality: that in an essentially illiberal situation there was no liberal solution. And they were not prepared to make a fresh start by standing up for liberal things.

The third Broome report received a good press initially; the *Rand Daily Mail* called for a new era in South Africa, without preconceived conditions on either side. At the India Office Broome III was hailed as 'one of the most important documents that has ever been issued'. But it was stillborn. Smuts described the 'loaded franchise' as impossible, and Hofmeyr seems to have agreed with him: communal representation was the limit of political possibility. Smuts continued to resist a South Africa-India round table conference, though he was ready for discussions with the local Indians. With meaningless hopefulness he told Amery (4 July 1945) that he was still 'not entirely pessimistic' about a solution.

Outside of Africa, the last two years of the war brought rumblings of great events to come rather than actual changes of significance. In the sugar colonies this was a period when the long political hegemony of the sugar barons was questioned; though their economic hegemony continued unchallenged. In Southern Asia, presentiments that the Japanese Co-Prosperity Sphere was going to be rolled back, raised the political temperature to a critical level. Britain, the most war-weary country in the Commonwealth, looked forward with euphoria to a welfare state future, in which British (United Kingdom) emigration would play a part; but in which the movement of Indians throughout the Commonwealth was only incidental.

In the West Indies, political initiative began in Jamaica and was taken up by Trinidad, which enjoyed a wartime boom, thanks to the build-up of the American base, as well as expansion in the oil industry. A May Day conference of trade unionists demanded independence for India in 1943. When the Colonial Office passed on their resolution to the India Office (16 June 1943) it was noted that the majority of the 1,441 members of the All-Trinidad Sugar Estates and Factory Workers Union were Indians. In 1944, a new constitution based upon universal franchise was brought forward. The debate in the legislative council led to the appointment of a Franchise Committee which recommended full adult franchise, with the qualification that a voter 'can understand the English language when spoken'. Even this minimum language test was resented by the Indians, for it would disqualify many of them. In the end, by a strange Trinidadian compromise, although a resolution in the legislature calling for a universal franchise was rejected by eight votes to six, another resolution *omitting* any English language requirement was passed, by eight votes to five: so all the Indians received the vote. The Secretary for the Colonies accepted this recommendation.

British Guiana, the third West Indian colony in size and importance, also came up for discussion, but a reform of the constitution towards universal suffrage was delayed. The franchise was enlarged in 1945 from its previous oligarchic limitations, but as it was tied firmly to a literacy test, and 44 per cent of the Guiana East Indians were illiterate (as compared to only 3 per cent illiteracy among the Blacks) this did not admit the Indian community to any effective share of political power.

Once again, the Government of India took up the fruitless business of applying for an Agent to be appointed to a territory administered by the Colonial Office. On 5 August 1943, P. N. Sapru moved a resolution in the Council of State calling for an Agent in the West Indies, and this was accepted. On 27 October 1943, the Government of India asked the India Office to pass the request along: wartime experience showed the need for 'greater vigilance' over 'isolated' Indian communities. The request was not welcomed. R. N. Gilchrist minuted: 'If the Colonies are to develop towards self-government then nothing could be more prejudicial to their future integration than encouragement of the fissiparous tendencies which separate Indian representation would inevitably foster.' P. J. Patrick commented that the Government of India had 'a very poor case'; but then the demand 'emanated from a traditionally Indianised department'. Patrick suggested that the Secretary of State write a personal letter to the Secretary for the Colonies as they could not entirely refuse to support the request. Accordingly, Amery wrote to Stanley (22 December 1943) suggesting that they had a talk: 'a bald refusal ...might lead to a delicate situation'. But Oliver Stanley was not specially concerned to make life smooth at the India Office. He replied—three months later—'I cannot accept this proposition'; the Government of India was 'on very weak ground'. A suggestion that an I.C.S. officer might be seconded as an Adviser to the Colonial Office (like Major Orde Browne, the Labour Adviser) was also rejected: 'I could obviously not undertake to be guided by his advice in everything.' In East Africa the 'Indian Question...looks like becoming particularly acute as the end of the war approaches'; there would have to be constitutional changes, and the Colonial Office must appear 'manifestly unbiased'.

The Colonial Office attitude was not affected when the British Guiana East Indian Association at its Silver Jubilee celebrations early in 1944 asked for the appointment of an Agent from India. The Colonial Office merely asked the India Office to signify that they 'agreed that no steps should be taken...for the time being' (9 May 1944). Eventually, after Mr Banerjee had sent several reminders about the case, the India Office told the Government of India that the question should be deferred until the report of the Moyne Commission had been published: at present there was an 'unfavourable climate' at the Colonial Office (14 May 1945). As the Moyne Commission Report advised against the appointment of an Agent of the Government of India in the West Indies it was a little difficult to know when the climate was likely to improve.

Politics in Mauritius followed the familiar pattern of protest and repression. Despite the collapse of the strike movement at the end of 1943, Ramnarain retained his unique importance in the politics of protest: the only other popular leader was B. Bissoondayal, an intellectual. Although Ramnarain had been employed in the Government Information Department he was suspected of leading an 'anti-Allies' campaign. The Governor, Sir Donald Mackenzie Kennedy, reported that he had accused the government of reducing the food ration and encouraging drink to 'keep down' the Indians; for Ramnarain believed that prohibition would strengthen the movement for *swaraj*. He was said to have prophesied that 'the time was not far distant when the Indian flag would fly not only in India but in Mauritius'.

Bissoondayal was also advocating *swaraj*, and Dr Ramgoolam, hitherto a moderate, was said to be 'making political capital out of the situation and to be fishing in troubled waters'. The situation was made more difficult by the 'incredibly stupid' action of the planters in victimising Indian leaders, said Kennedy: he had issued a warning to the planters' organisation, the Chamber of Agriculture.

Because he could obtain no concrete evidence against Ramnarain, the Governor decided to detain him under the Defence Regulations. This produced mass demonstrations in Port Louis; about 1,500 demonstrators were dispersed by baton charges and tear gas, but they re-formed, so were charged again, and 200 were arrested.[44] These events took place when the Report of the Commission of Enquiry into the 1943 disturbances was being issued in the island; nothing had been learnt from the report, as with all its predecessors. The Governor turned from these events to draft recommendations for political reform; the starting-point was a population of 419,185, of whom 11,437 were electors. There was a long way to go.

The sugar colonies remained forgotten in London and Delhi, but Southern Asia was too insistent to be ignored. Malaya still remained out of sight until after Hiroshima, but Burma was again coming into reach. Decisions were needed on the short-term question of bringing back Indian labour to help in the build-up of Rangoon as the jumping-off point for the liberation of Malaya, as well as the long-term question of Indian immigration and settlement. Even from the point of view of the Indians there were divergences between those to whom Burma was a place to make money in, and those for whom it was home. Dorman-Smith, the Governor of Burma, told Amery (16 March 1944) that he had found the Indians with trading interests in Burma clamouring for unlimited emigration, even if this brought unemployment, whereas 'Indians who looked upon Burma as their home were in favour of regulation'.

U Tin Tut had a series of discussions with R. N. Banerjee and others concerned. On some points, there was agreement; on others, the gap had widened. Tin Tut was quite prepared to accept the abrogation of the 1941 agreement, if this would give Dr Khare 'political credit'; he was prepared to 'consider' (no more) the return of all Indian evacuees; but he was not prepared to agree that restrictions upon Indians entering Burma in the future should apply only to unskilled workers. It was fundamental that Burma should be able to regulate the composition of the future population, and to replace Indians of the merchant and professional classes by Burmese: there would have to be annual quotas for immigrants in these categories. On the question of domicile, Burma was prepared to extend 'domicile' to Indians already settled, but for newcomers 'domicile should not accrue, except with the specific permission of the Government of Burma'. These propositions were discussed by the Standing Emigration Committee of the central legislature (H. N. Kunzru and Raza Ali) along with leading Burma Indians, M. A. Rauf and S. A. S. Tyabji. They appeared to envisage—along with a Burma Government version of domicile—a 'right to intervene' in Burma for the Government of India: predictably Tin Tut recorded that it was 'now unlikely that the negotiations will result in a satisfactory new Indian agreement' (2 August 1944).[45]

At this time, the Government of Burma and the Burma Office in London were planning on the assumption that Burma would not return to a system of internal self-government until seven years after the end of hostilities. Amery was questioned upon the subject in the House of Commons on 12 December 1944. The occasion was of significance for the observations of Arthur Creech Jones. He called for a more rapid approach to self-government, in accordance with his championship of the colonial peoples, but he also criticised the role of Indian capital and labour in Burma: there was 'an intense feeling of nationalism', he said. This was contrary to his earlier defence of the Indian capitalists of Zanzibar, and a sign, perhaps, of his conversion to a hostile attitude towards Indians in plural societies. Amery rejected a description of the Indians in Burma as an 'alien element...cleared for good out of the country'; there must be cooperation in future between Burma and India in many spheres, including defence. He declined to commit himself on the period which would elapse before Burma regained self-rule.

Meanwhile, there was the immediate question of providing a labour force for South-East Asia Command, poised to reoccupy vast areas, and equipped with a military administration prepared to take over the occupied territories: in Burma, it was called Civil Affairs Service (Burma) or CAS(B).[46] It was calculated that a labour force of 150,000 to 200,000 men was wanted, but to take this enormous force of Indians into Burma clearly posed problems for the two governments. Not wishing to be pushed into premature conclusions on emigration policy, India was disposed only to sanction recruitment of labour in para-military formations, to be demobilised back in India when their job was done.

Eventually, the Government of India agreed to the recruitment by S.E.A.C. of 161,000 labourers for Burma in quasi-military pioneer units; all to be repatriated to India. CAS(B) was also permitted to recruit 16,000 skilled and unskilled workers for special jobs in the rice and rubber industries. A request to recruit 20,000 Indians as sweepers (removers of excrement) was turned down; India was no longer automatically the provider of the most menial kinds of workers.[47] S.E.A.C. discovered that Indians were unwilling to enrol in the Pioneer units when they found that they would be returned to India; the emigration to Burma was still attractive to the poor people of south India, and in April 1945 the military authorities made a further attempt to get the governments of India and Burma to modify their positions. The Government of India did agree to repatriation being waived in respect of the unskilled men of the Pioneer Corps, providing that Burma allowed them to settle permanently. Still no agreement could be reached, but the question settled itself: CAS(B) found enough Indian labour in the Rangoon area to meet all its needs.

Burma's political demands were expected to wait. Amery and his advisers retreated somewhat from the decision that there would be no politics for seven years, but when an announcement was made on 17 May 1945 there was still to be an interregnum till December 1948, when Burma would return to the 1935 constitution; even then the 'Scheduled Areas' (the Shan States, and other hill areas) would remain under a special regime. The young Burmese leaders who had formed the Thakins and played a major part in Ba Maw's New Order Plan and who now dominated the Anti-Fascist People's Freedom League (A.F.P.F.L.) had very different ideas. However, when Rangoon was re-occupied by the British-Indian forces on 3 May 1945, and CAS(B) arrived a few days later, it appeared as though the British intentions would be followed through: for the military forces of South-East Asia Command amounted to 1,304,126 men at arms. Paradoxically, the Supreme Commander of S.E.A.C., Lord Louis Mountbatten, was to do more than anyone else to upset and overthrow the India and Burma Office time-table.

All this was still to come: but in 1944 it was clear that the Ceylon political leaders were already chafing at the United Kingdom version of their progress to independence, or Dominion Status as it was still called. The Colonial Office intention was very clear: under the 1943 declaration, Senanayake and his colleagues were invited to formulate a constitution, but they were required to obtain the consent of three-quarters of the State Council before it would be accepted by the United Kingdom government. Obviously, it was expected that a long series of consultations would take place within the Ceylon political framework before any proposal was put to London. Senanayake saw it all quite differently, as he frankly stated in a public speech: 'The best way of settling the matter is to settle with the other side [Britain] first.... If we adopt any other view, I am sure the fate of India would be our fate. They will sit there, on the other side, and say: "Compose your differences"...'[48] The Senanayake government at once drafted a constitution, and this was forwarded to the Colonial Office by April 1944. Oliver Stanley informed Oliver Lyttleton (a confidante of Churchill's, and a candidate for the viceroyalty in 1943) that the Ceylon Ministers had 'cut out all local discussion' in submitting their constitution, and were asking the Churchill government to consider it 'at once'. If consideration were delayed, then 'serious political developments would follow', according to the Commander-in-Chief, Admiral Layton. There would be a withdrawal of cooperation which could 'jeopardise' the coming operations against Japan (25 May 1944). This moved Stanley to act quickly.

These developments—which did not remain secret in the indiscreet atmosphere of Ceylon politics—were observed with misgiving in Delhi. Indeed, the Government of India had already responded to the 1943 declaration with some concern and had asked for 'elucidation' in November 1943, only to be brushed aside by the Colonial Office (see p. 212). Aney reported to Wavell that under the proposed arrangements India would be in a worse position to make a bargain. Wavell asked Amery whether the introduction of a new constitution could be conditional upon a settlement of the various disputes between Ceylon and India (25 February 1944). When the Cabinet considered the Colonial Secretary's proposals to announce a visit by a commission from Britain, and to extend the life of the State Council for another two years, Amery merely asked that the announcement should include a reference to the position of the minorities.[49] The Cabinet accepted that the minorities could meet the commission: moreover, it was argued that the appointment of the commission did not commit the British Government in advance to constitutional changes.

Wavell was appalled by the way the Ceylon scheme was being handled; he told Amery (4 July 1944) 'the Cabinet had shown undue regard for the susceptibilities of the Ceylon Ministers, who appear to have gained their point by a kind of political blackmail, and a complete disregard of the request which the Government of India had made.' When the Viceroy's Council were informed, Khare protested at the way in which they had been kept in the dark; the

Council 'obviously sympathised with Khare,' added Wavell, and he cabled to the Secretary of State: 'I agree with Council that we have been badly treated, and if H.M.G. disregard Indian opinion in this way they cannot expect full cooperation from Indian Members [of Council] when they want it' (5 July 1944).

However, the announcement by the Colonial Secretary in the House of Commons on 5 July that a commission would go to Ceylon within the next year to assess public opinion, including that of the minorities, brought an adverse reaction from the Senanayake Cabinet; Don Senanayake told the State Council on 12 July: 'If this attitude were adopted they did not propose to collaborate with the Commission.' Sir Andrew Caldecott, at the end of his seven years of hard labour in Ceylon, tried to ease the Ministers out of the blind alley down which they seemed to be heading. 'It is important to study means of helping Ministers to extricate themselves from their present position, without, of course, yielding any major point in our case,' the Governor cabled (24 August 1944).

He need not have worried; Senanayake and Bandaranaike were both masters of manoeuvre. On 7 September, S. W. R. D. Bandaranaike gave a dinner party for forty-four guests; all were members of the State Council, and five were Ministers, but besides the Sinhalese guests, there were four Ceylon Tamils, three Muslims, two Indian Tamils, a Burgher (Eurasian) and two British non-officials. The idea was to form an all-party committee to present a united reform demand. This ingenious move was partially successful though the minorities stuck to their demands. Having declared in advance a boycott of the commission (whose members were announced on 21 September 1944) Senanayake and his colleagues might have missed their opportunity; the minorities might have gained their objectives in the absence of the Sinhalese leaders. However, Senanayake's interpretation of the meaning of a boycott was very different from the form developed by Gandhi and Nehru.

While still declining to give evidence in formal sessions, Senanayake made himself master of ceremonies for the visit of Lord Soulbury and the commission. On all their tours around the island, the commissioners found themselves talking to people carefully planted in their path by Don Senanayake. The commission stayed in Ceylon from December 1944 to April 1945; their report was submitted to Oliver Stanley as Secretary for the Colonies in July 1945, though its implementation was to fall to his successor.[50]

Regarding the Indian population of Ceylon, the conclusion of the Soulbury report was somewhat facile. It would be for the leaders of Ceylon to determine how they defined their citizenship, but the new constitution ought to recognise the rights of Indians 'who by birth or by long association have so identified themselves with the affairs of this country that their interests are no different from the rest of the population'. Under the new constitution, 'The Government of Ceylon [that is, the Senanayake government] will have the ability, as we feel sure it already has the desire, to assimilate the Indian community and to make it part and parcel of a single nation.' Such a pleasant but totally unreal picture of the place of the Indians in Ceylon could only have come from the bluff and genial Don Senanayake: who, glowing with goodwill at the prospect of early independence, did perhaps half-believe that this transformation could be brought about.

In its proposals, the commission recommended 'that universal suffrage on the present basis shall be retained'; the only safeguard for the Indians was a recommendation that the Governor-General (as he would be, under the new arrangement) should have the power to 'reserve' (refuse assent to) an immigration bill if it prohibited the re-entry of Ceylon residents. It was little enough in the way of protection; as events had already shown. In addition, the commission proposed that Ceylon should adopt a bicameral parliamentary system; this also, they hoped, would give protection to the minorities by somehow sharing out the prize of power.

Ceylon was offered a new form of government, which was yet to prove acceptable; the tropical colonies—the West Indies, Mauritius and Malaya—had no idea what political future awaited them; above all, India, the Jewel of the Empire, peered into a future where the cry *Swaraj* was answered by the cry of *Pakistan*. Amid these uncertainties, the future of the overseas Indians must appear especially uncertain.

To try to answer these questions, a gathering of Commonwealth leaders assembled in London in February 1945. They did not come as politicians, but more as experts, observers rather than actors; they came to attend a conference on the British Commonwealth and World Society at the Royal Institute of International Affairs, Chatham House. The England they came to was accustomed to regard itself as the Mother Country; but this was a mother who sent her (white) children across the seas, rather than offering a home to her (coloured) children. Yet this England in February 1945 was not entirely made up of white Saxons and Celts; there were 7,128 persons from India amongst the population.

Many of them were doctors and professional people and therefore invisible; but in the ports of the United Kingdom there were small sections which were inhabited by 'Coloureds'. There were approximately 700 Coloureds around the London docks in Stepney; about

400 of them had homes, and about half of these were Indians. Most of the Indians in Stepney were sailors, *lascars*, who had jumped ship on arrival in London, having discovered that they could earn more ashore than the £6 to £8 per month they were paid as *lascars*. Most of the Indians were Muslims, and they contracted temporary marriages with local women who were prostitutes, or the daughters of prostitutes; there were 136 children in the dock area whose fathers were Indians: 'Once on the labour market they have to face the prejudices against colour. Normally, great difficulty is experienced in placing them in jobs'; the boys picked up casual work, and most of the girls drifted into prostitution.

In the past there had been 'open hostility' against the Coloureds in Stepney, and there were several race riots during the inter-war years. During wartime they were left alone; there were other things to think about: nevertheless, among the Indians 'most of them have a strong feeling that the British have not treated the Indians fairly.'[51]

Not a breath of this disturbed the delegates to the Third Unofficial Conference on British Commonwealth Relations. They were a very impressive group. There were eighteen United Kingdom delegates, and among them were Lord Hailey, Lionel Curtis, Sir Walter Layton, Sir Frederick Whyte, Viscount Hinchingbrooke, Professor Vincent Harlow and Arthur Creech Jones. The two next largest delegations were from Canada and India, with ten from each country. The Indian delegation rivalled that of Britain in distinction: it was led by Sir Zafrullah Khan, and it included Sir Maharaj Singh, Sir B. P. Singh Roy (former president of the National Liberal Federation) and K. M. Panikkar, philosopher-statesman. New Zealand and South Africa each sent six representatives, Australia sent five, and there were two observers from Burma and one observer from Southern Rhodesia. The last two, not yet Dominions, were denied full status, but India by convention ranked as a Dominion. There was no representative from Ceylon at the conference.

The conference devoted a good deal of its time to Commonwealth migration. When they arrived, the delegates received a number of papers as background information. From India, there were two papers relating to migration: *Population Problems in South-east Asia* by Radhakamal Mukerjee, and *The Status of Indians in the Empire* by 'An Onlooker'.[52] Mukerjee's paper was almost a statement of Indian imperialism; he sought to demonstrate that India had a kind of manifest destiny to send out its peoples: 'In the Pacific area there are extensive empty lands at an easy distance from the vast reservoir of humanity in South and East Asia'; Burma and Malaya were 'major safety-valves of population pressure' for India. But his ambitions did not end there; 400 millions could settle in Australia, and Mukerjee urged Canada, New Zealand and Australia all to imitate the example of the United States as he saw it:

> Instead of rigidly adhering to the myth of racial superiority with its corollary of unalterable racial composition...they should study the U.S.A.'s remarkable success in the task of assimilating her diverse stocks into a wonderful culture, enriched instead of being impoverished by racial contrasts.

The analysis by 'An Onlooker' possessed more durable qualities, though it was infused with pessimism. He deplored the transient character of some Indian emigration, especially that of the traders: 'Indian emigrants have not displayed the quality, or indeed the desire of the Western emigrant to settle and colonise in the ordinary sense of the word'; they must adopt a new approach. In relation to India's neighbours, Burma and Ceylon, in future permanent emigration should constitute the exception rather than the rule; where Indians did become permanent residents, 'the writer firmly believes it is legitimate to expect every Indian settler to reach a clear decision whether he belongs to India or to the country where he has settled; when he makes the latter choice, he should be granted complete identification and not a grudging recognition'.

The Australian papers had a good deal to say on immigration, but almost all concerned immigration from Britain; P. D. Phillips did comment that 'the restricted immigration policy has had its reflection in the public attitude to the whole problem of India'; Phillips deduced that Australians just did not want to get involved in that problem. The United Kingdom paper, prepared by the Information Department of Chatham House was entirely about European emigration to the white Dominions; if there were not enough British candidates, the Dominions should consider 'the admission of a carefully regulated flow of foreign immigrants of assimilable types, preferably from those countries whose inhabitants are sprung from the same stock as ourselves'. Clearly, the old Lionel Curtis conception of a White Commonwealth still dominated Chatham House.

The discussions which followed these papers reproduced the same divisions between the views of the Indian and the white participants.[53] Among the Dominion representatives there was a 'powerful impulse to preserve their identity as white communities and to maintain the high standard of living which they enjoy'. Their discussion of emigration was therefore strictly related to Britain—and marginally to Europe. The Indian delegates tried to make the issue of Indians overseas the main topic of discussion; Sir Zafrullah put forward the demand for votes for Indians in South Africa 'on the same conditions as to Europeans'; Professor S. H. Frankel, leader of the South African delegation, said hopefully that there was 'a strong body of liberally minded opinion' in South Africa, but added immediately that it was 'unable to make much headway'. Frankel insisted that any external pressure 'would aggravate rather than improve the situation'; it was only a slightly less restricted version of the Smuts 'Slowly, slowly' solution.

It all sounded familiar, but there was one forward-looking Indian proposal: that, as 'the rights and obligations of citizenship in the Commonwealth are united by allegiance to the Crown...instead of local citizenship there should be a Commonwealth citizenship, giving all citizens of the Commonwealth the same rights throughout the Commonwealth.' The Indians showed that they were very ready to participate in a new association of the Commonwealth: but it must be an equal association.[54]

How significant was this Chatham House meeting? If one judged by the stature of the participants, it was very significant: and the treatment they were given seemed to suggest that this was the contemporary view. They were entertained by the King and Queen and by the British Cabinet Ministers in turn. It was all very splendid. Yet one cannot discover any trace of the influence of the conference in the subsequent correspondence of British politicians and civil servants. It was just a sounding board: though the sounds that emanated were to be the sounds of the 1940s and 1950s.

In the Viceroy's House at Delhi, having descended from Simla after his first great abortive attempt to get the leaders of the Congress and the Muslim league to work together, Wavell sat down to write a personal letter to Smuts. Just for the moment there was no dramatic crisis between India and South Africa to compel an urgent message. Greeting Smuts upon his return from drafting the U.N. Charter at San Francisco, Wavell hoped that the United Nations would prove 'more effective' than the League of Nations. He was disappointed at the Simla breakdown (this was 19 July 1945), yet 'I cannot believe in Pakistan as a remedy; it would simply be another minority problem'.

Wavell observed that there was a 'temporary lull' in India concerning the dispute with South Africa; but fundamentally, he concluded, there was no subject upon which Indian feeling was stronger.

8
Equality: the Claim Vindicated
(1945-47)

Looking back in time, it seems as though the advent of the Labour Government to office (26 July 1945) and the surrender of Japan, ending the Second World War (14 August), heralded the liquidation of Western colonialism and of the British Empire. This was certainly not obvious then; and it was not part of the programme of Clement Attlee and his colleagues. Of course, they were prepared for India to take the last step towards self-government: this had been accepted even by the caretaker Conservative government, for Amery had told parliament on 16 June 1945 that the Cripps offer of March 1942 'stood in its entirety, without change or qualification'.[1] But the new Labour government had no intention of pushing Ceylon or Burma forward to independence; they must first demonstrate their capacity for responsible parliamentary government in their internal affairs.

By the middle of 1946, the Labour Government was beginning to change its ideas. The reason was not ideological but practical; though Britain still had a vast army on a war footing, the global commitments were stretching its capacity to cope. On 31 May 1946, Wavell sat down with the ministerial delegation who were then in India—Sir Stafford Cripps, Lord Pethick-Lawrence, and A. V. Alexander—to consider a draft telegram to the Cabinet on the situation which would arise if the constitutional discussions broke down. The Viceroy asked why, in the draft, it was stated that 'reinforcements of British troops required for a repressive policy would not be available'. The Secretary for India (Pethick-Lawrence) replied that early in the year he had been told that two British divisions would be needed to restore order, and these were not available: 'General Auchinleck said that he thought that nothing much less than three divisions would be of much use....'

Thus it was becoming recognised, at the end of 1946, that those places where open rebellion threatened—India, Burma, and Palestine—could not be held by force, and must be abandoned, as an act of imperial load-shedding. The case of Ceylon was rather different; the British Government was afraid that the wrong policies might push Ceylon into the same category as India and Burma, but equally it was envisaged that a far-sighted policy of conceding Dominion status would retain the island as a loyal member of the

Commonwealth, with its naval and air installations available as important links in the chain of imperial communications and defence.

This was as far as the Attlee government intended to go: there was no consideration of giving Malaya independence, for example; Malaya was considered an essential part of the Empire, earning more hard dollars than any other unit of the sterling area. Africa was regarded as only just beginning a new imperial phase of education and development, and the Whites were expected to play a key role in this development. Hence, although India's departure from the Commonwealth seemed increasingly probable and the repercussions upon Burma, and perhaps Ceylon, were accepted by the British Cabinet, the whole of the rest of the British Empire remained firmly under the control of Whitehall. Whereas morale at the India Office —in decline ever since the First World War—was now depressingly low, the Colonial Office was beginning what was to be its *belle époque*. The senior officials included men who were progressive, forward-looking, but also firm administrators—like Charles Jeffries, in charge of Ceylon's future, and Andrew Cohen, increasingly the mentor of Africa. Attlee chose as Labour's Colonial Secretary the same George Hall who had graduated from the coalface to the Treasury Bench; but he was already an ailing man, and from the beginning of 1946 he was incapacitated until he finally resigned in October. What was much more intriguing, Attlee appointed as Under Secretary Arthur Creech Jones, whose terrier-like persistence in parliament, and patent devotion to colonial causes outside, made him the ideal choice for a Socialist colonial (or, rather, anti-colonial) minister. But, as we shall discover, Creech Jones, the stern critic of the Colonial Office and colonial governors, was within a few short months transmogrified into Creech Jones, the ardent apologist of the Colonial Office and colonial governors.[2] There need be no danger of hasty, ill-considered change while he was in charge.

All this was in the future. In the first few months after Labour came to power, their friends in England and overseas had great expectations. They did not know that Labour would turn on its head the Palmerstonian doctrine of 'liberal abroad, conservative at home'. Thus, Henry Polak, veteran Labour supporter and campaigner for the rights of colonised peoples, must have thought that after thirty years of knocking upon the doors of indifferent or hostile Conservative Secretaries of State his day had come at last. And so he wrote to Pethick-Lawrence, the new Secretary for India (9 October 1945), urging that they tackle the grievances of the overseas Indians in conjunction with the Dominions and the Government of India, 'facing the dangers squarely'. Poor man, he was to be fobbed off with the same prevarications as always; though this did not make him give up. And in 1945 there were more people alert to hold the new Labour Government to its promises and principles: the best organised being the Fabian Colonial Bureau, founded in 1940, with Creech Jones as chairman. Now, the Fabians wanted to see their ideas put into effect.

In India, the position of Indians in the Colonies and Dominions as a political issue had to take second place to the burning and immediate issue of swaraj. This occupied the minds of everyone all day and every day, though the overseas Indians were not entirely forgotten, thanks mainly to the concern of Jawaharlal Nehru. Nehru was only released from jail on 15 June 1945, and, in accordance with the strange rules of the game of British-Indian relations, he was taking tea with the Viceroy and his wife and son just two weeks later. Nehru and Wavell had another private talk at the Simla Conference, and their third meeting seems to have been that of 3rd November.[3] Then, Nehru asked to be given facilities to go to Indonesia; Wavell said that it was impossible, but he could ask the military authorities in S.E.A.C. if he could visit Burma and Malaya. Thanks to the cooperation of Mountbatten, this was arranged, and the visit (which will be considered in detail later) made a considerable impression upon him and was important in his subsequent thinking on imperialism and the Commonwealth.

The two years 1945-7 have to be viewed as a whole in relation to the goal of independence, but in relation to the overseas Indians they fell into two equal parts. Till July 1946, Dr Khare remained the Member in charge of the Commonwealth Relations Department, and pursued the same policy—though with greater emphasis—as during his previous two years in office. Then, along with all the others who had been Members of the Viceroy's Council, he was asked to resign in order to make way for a new government in which it was hoped the Congress and the Muslim League would combine and cooperate. This 'interim' government was slow to emerge. Wavell had to mark time with a 'caretaker' Council of officials, in which Commonwealth Relations was managed by Sir Gurunath Bewoor, I.C.S.[4] Finally, on 2 September 1946 a nationalist government was formed, led by Nehru. Throughout all the years of British rule, the Viceroy had always kept the portfolio of foreign relations for himself. As vice-chairman of the Viceroy's Council, Nehru took over foreign relations, which were combined (as, logically, they should be) with Commonwealth relations. India was henceforth to adopt a co-ordinated policy towards foreign and Commonwealth relations, as later became the norm. The arrival of Nehru in this key position did not mean a break with the past;

indeed, there was complete continuity, except that the pace was quickened.

The change was most obvious in relation to South Africa, when Nehru appealed beyond the Commonwealth circle to the United Nations. The success of this appeal was the main feature of this transitional phase, in which India was virtually independent in external policy, though still dependent on the British overlord internally. India also made a bid to place relations with the nearest neighbours, Burma and Ceylon, upon a more intimate basis. They, too, were in a transitional phase, with independence just out of reach; India's hopes of taking on the role of elder brother were not to be wholly realised.

Regarding the colonies and Dominions with Indian communities, a note of warning was sounded by the appeal to the U.N. against South Africa, but India's capacity to influence these areas was still small. The Colonial Office maintained its traditional, aloof attitude towards India's claims, and in the post-war changes in the colonies the dominant voice was that of Whitehall—and of the European settlers and capitalists. The Indian communities overseas are still to be perceived as unequal partners in a British, white empire.

India's first task was to discover its own identity as a nation—a task which acquired a greater urgency by the partition of the sub-continent and the pulling away of Pakistan. Hopes and expectations were high, and there was still a confident belief that the reborn Indian nation would be able to do great things for the Indians overseas: an expectation which some people in Whitehall apprehensively shared, so that the reaction to India's desire to establish closer relations with the Indian communities overseas was cautious, and indeed suspicious. We shall begin by examining the working of Colonial Office administration in the territories where British rule was confidently expected to continue for twenty, thirty, or forty years longer; then we turn to India's efforts to obtain improvements for Indians in self-governing countries, or those about to be self-governing—Burma, Ceylon, South Africa—and, finally, we notice India's first attempts to set up a system of liaison with Indian communities overseas, which brings us back to the policies and practices of the Colonial Office.

It was over Kenya that the conversion of Creech Jones to the point of view of the Colonial Office, and—as it appeared to his critics—to undue appreciation of the white settler point of view, was most obvious. From 1945 onwards a series of controversies developed in which the Indians were deeply involved. All were concerned with the central question of white dominance; they were not distinct and separate but closely inter-related, but for clarity we need to list them in separate order. There was the political or constitutional question of government: was Kenya still to be governed by the Whites, with token participation by Indians, Africans and Arabs? Associated with this was the question of the character of the administration: was it to be, for all time, controlled by expatriates from Britain and by the local, white British? Then there was the central economic question of whether the white monopoly over the most fertile farmland in Kenya was to be perpetuated—and perhaps even extended. There was the wider question of the place of Kenya and the place of East Africa in white domination of the Dark Continent: Would there be a revival of the proposals of the late 1920s for closer union in East Africa? And who would be in control—the local white settlers, or the Colonial Office, or a medley of the political forces paramount in East Africa, among whom the Africans could not, for ever, be pushed to the back? This question brought up again the horny subject of providing trusteeship for the Africans, which implied that opportunities would be available to them as they qualified through education and experience. This led on to the subject emphasised by the Kenya Whites ever since the first World War: the need for an immigration policy to keep out the hordes of Indians who would elbow the Africans out of the jobs for which they were becoming qualified.

All these questions were the subject of uninterrupted debate from 1945 onwards, but separate questions were highlighted by the appearance of important government white papers in series: there was the white paper on the reorganisation of the administration, issued in July 1945, the white paper on land policy which appeared in November, and the white paper on inter-territorial organisation, issued in London in December 1945. Immigration was the subject of Bills, published simultaneously in the four East African territories early in 1946. These events provide milestones in the discussion which follows of inter-racial controversies and conflicts. Opinion in India was not fully aroused to the situation in Kenya until early 1946: till then, the position in Ceylon and Burma was more in the consciousness of the public and of the government.

The conversion of Creech Jones, whether willingly or unwillingly, may best be followed by his reactions to a subject which was only marginal to the position of the Indians in Kenya, though central to the whole question of white dominance: this was the question of admitting children of mixed parentage to the European schools.

Education in Kenya was just as stratified as in South Africa; there were separate schools for Africans, Indians and Whites. The African schools were controlled almost entirely by the Christian missionaries, but the schools of the other two communities were managed by committees—more or less self-perpetuating—drawn entirely from that racial bloc. Under the education code, 'Admission to European and Indian Government School Rules, 1932', each school committee had the power to select children for admission; this power was exercised to refuse admission to those whose racial identification was doubtful. Thus, the small community of Syrian traders in Kenya found their children were deemed ineligible for the European schools.

A Britisher married to a Coloured woman was not prepared for his family to be excluded in the same fashion: he appealed to the Director of Education, and the case was passed on for a ruling by higher authority. When Sir Philip Mitchell communicated with the Secretary for the Colonies (16 June 1945), he observed: 'However unreasonable prejudices of this kind may be ... they are real, and cannot be removed in this way' (by order). He added that he had told the Europeans he disagreed with their policy. At the Colonial Office, H. S. Scott, originally responsible for giving power to the school committees, noted: 'It is necessary to be honest about it: I aimed at the exclusion of Indian or African children from European schools.' As if that explained everything, a letter was drafted for the signature of the Secretary of State to the Governor of Kenya, in November 1945, which accepted that it was not possible to go further than 'encouraging a more liberal outlook', in view of white opinion in Kenya.

This draft was shown to Creech Jones (about the end of November) and he saw red: it was 'an intolerable situation which we dare not acquiesce in', he minuted. 'We have a naked colour bar which we are asked to tolerate in the public schools of Kenya.' He was sure that parliament would not accept such a situation, and he concluded: 'There ought to be no encouragement of white settlement if such outrages against children are going to continue.' No less would have been expected from the man who had condemned racial discrimination in Mauritius, East Africa and the West Indies. He told the officials that he wanted to discuss this question more thoroughly.

Then followed a pause of more than four months. On 30 March 1946, A. B. Cohen told Rennie, Acting Governor of Kenya, that they were not yet in a position to comment on Mitchell's letter of 16 June 1945; Creech Jones wanted to have a talk with Archdeacon L. J. Beecher, a Kenya missionary nominated to represent the Africans in the Kenya legislature. Rather tentatively, K. G. Lindsay, Director of Education in Kenya, suggested to Cohen (12 April 1946) that the primary schools, anyway, ought to be prepared to take 'very near white' children, providing, he added hastily, it was not 'the thin end of the wedge'. Still nothing happened, and in July and August 1946 Creech Jones paid a long visit to East Africa, a visit which was to make a lasting impression upon him.

After his departure, Sir Philip Mitchell wrote to George, Lord Hall (still nominally Secretary for the Colonies), on 2 October 1946. He had discussed the vexed question of the children of mixed blood and the European schools with Creech Jones: it was 'impolitic at the present time to alter the existing legislation so as to enable these children to be admitted to European schools'. Creech Jones confirmed this judgment in a letter to Mitchell, written soon after he had taken over the seals of office as Secretary for the Colonies: in view of the attitude of the schools committees, they must make alternative arrangements for the 'mixed' children (24 October 1946). As these children numbered in all Kenya only twenty-seven, in different urban centres, it seems probable that the alternative arrangements ended with their not going to school at all.

What had happened between November 1945 and October 1946 which had so altered the circumstances of the case as to make the unacceptable solution acceptable? Clearly, nothing had happened; but in the meantime Creech Jones had certainly altered.

Meanwhile, planning for the post-war Kenya proceeded at the Colonial Office with no awareness that a new era was opening. The draft proposals of Sir Philip Mitchell were received in London in June 1945; these covered reorganisation of the administration, together with new schemes for settling demobilised soldiers upon the land. The reorganisation was geared exclusively to the resettlement scheme: the Chief Secretary was to assume overall responsibility for development, now expected to move ahead fast under the greatly expanded resources of Colonial Development, while actual management of the Department of Agriculture, Animal Husbandry and Natural Resources was to be assumed by Major Cavendish-Bentick. The resettlement schemes were, of course, organised on racial lines and there was a remarkable disparity between the allocation of resources to the three races. For the five hundred new white settlers who were to move into the White Highlands, a budget of £1.6 million had been prepared, worked out in detail: £950,000 was to be advanced to the new settlers to enable them to equip and stock up their farms, while £650,000 was to be invested by the Kenya Government in 'infrastructure' for the white farmlands. For the Indians, there were plans for a joint training centre with Tanganyika at Morogono; for the Africans—thirty thousand of whom were to be demobilised as agriculturalists—there was only a vague promise of land in the Native Reserves: no financial proposals were included at this stage.[5]

In a letter to Gerald Creasey of the Colonial Office (5 June 1945), Mitchell insisted that there must be no compromise over the white highlands policy: they must be clear about the impossibility of giving agricultural land to the Indians, and the even greater 'impossibility of throwing this already congested country open to agricultural settlement from India'. Mitchell had talked to Pandit Kunzru, currently visiting Kenya: 'He knows as well as I do that none of the people here in fact wish to farm at all'; there were no restrictions on Indians farming in Uganda or Tanganyika, Mitchell wrote (though in fact there were restrictions), and in those territories the Indian demand was 'negligible'. At the Colonial Office, Cohen contented himself with noting that the African squatters in the highlands constituted an 'insoluble problem', and they would need to have another land commission like the Carter commission (6 June 1945).

On 10th July 1945, *The Times* reviewed the White Paper on the Reorganisation of the Administration under the neutral heading 'Change in Kenya'. There was nothing neutral about the reception of the plan in Kenya where the Indian community was indignant, and at once fired off telegrams to its friends in England and India. The appointment of Cavendish-Bentinck to the key position of Minister for Agriculture and Natural Resources was particularly resented. He was clearly identified as the leader of the Kenya Whites, and had many times led the Europeans in pressurising the government to accept their terms. Moreover, he had served for ten years upon the Governor's Executive Council as a non-official Member, when the constitutional limit was eight years.[6] This appeared to be a device for perpetuating his membership of the Executive Council, and adding yet another European member, bringing their total to eleven compared to one Indian member, and no African or Arab member.

When the Legislative Council met to debate the White Paper on 18th July, there was strong criticism from the Indian members and from Eliud Mathu, the sole African member. A. B. Patel, leader of the Indian group, condemned the device for adding another white settler to the Executive Council; he also criticised the inadequate plans for giving land to the Indians. There was 'much intemperate racialism', said Mitchell, who, as chairman of the legislature, was observing the debate. Patel moved the adjournment as a protest: the five Indian members and Mathu voted in favour; the elected Europeans, the European officials and Archdeacon Beecher (nominally for the Africans) voted against, so the debate was resumed the next day. But Mitchell now moved an adjournment in order that he could talk to representatives of the Africans and the Indians.

When he saw Mathu and other Africans, they asked for additional representatives in the legislature and an African member of the Executive Council; Mitchell reported that they made their demands moderately, and Mathu presented the case reasonably in the legislature. Mitchell then saw five Indian representatives; they discussed the Indian settlement scheme, and Mitchell admitted that it had given insufficient consideration to the Kenya-born Indians, who might wish to farm. Then, the Indians put up a proposal for an Indian Member of the Executive Council in charge of Indian affairs; if this were accepted, they undertook to vote for the White Paper. The Indians considered Cavendish-Bentinck as the watchdog for white settler interests, installed in a key position, and wanted a similar watchdog on their own behalf. Mitchell told them that he could not give an immediate reply, but he promised to 'give it a run', and he recorded that the Indians were 'pleased'; they assured the Governor that they would not press the debate to a division.

When the legislative council reconvened, Mitchell announced from the chair that he would welcome an Indian land settlement scheme under an Indian chairman. Relating all this to the Colonial Office, Mitchell commented upon the proposal for an 'Indian affairs' member: 'Although I opposed an analogous proposal for Fiji, I am much attracted by the proposal and impressed with the possibility that it may do good, even in India.' The Indians accepted that their Member would speak from the official benches and must support the government: 'My first reaction is that it is a useful suggestion.' Mitchell summed up thus: the debate had 'greatly increased the realisation amongst all races of the futility of racial conflicts'.[7]

A week later, Mitchell cabled that the White Paper had been adopted without a division: the Indians had not raised any difficulties (25 July). Mitchell informed Creasey (27 July) that the debate had done 'good in race relations here'; he now intended to add another African to the legislative council, though the obstacles to African elections were 'insuperable'. When the Labour Secretary for the Colonies, George Hall, moved into his new office, the Fabian Colonial Bureau hastened to send him a memorandum on the reorganisation proposals (7 August 1945), pointing out that the white settlers were becoming 'increasingly powerful'. Hall was to listen more carefully to the advice of his officials, and Mitchell was now having second thoughts.

His doubts were accentuated by the factional disputes which once again ravaged the East African Indian National Congress. A. B. Patel, a moderate leader, had managed to preserve a coalition among the different groups, but now—after the Simla Conference, when the split between Congress and the League was sharpening—Hindu-Muslim conflicts rent the East African Congress. Mitchell told the Colonial Office it was 'in a state of schism' (25 August); on instructions from the Aga Khan, the Ismaili Muslim K. R. Paroo, resigned from the legislative council, while Shams-ud-Deen, the doyen of Kenya politics, resigned from the presidency of the Congress. The split deepened, and on 9 October Mitchell was cabling news of an 'acute crisis' in the Congress: the annual meeting was due to be held at Mombasa, and the Hindu leaders intended to move a non-cooperation resolution and resign from the legislative council, while the Muslims had announced that they would not resign.

All this made it easier for Mitchell to back away from his first enthusiastic response to the request for an Indian Affairs Member. On 29 August 1945 he wrote at length to Gerald Creasey, with his considered assessment of the place of the Indian community in the political and social life of Kenya: 'Political life is organised on a communal and racial basis', he began. 'At this stage it is wise and wholesome that it should be so.' There were insufficient inter-racial institutions to allow anything else, though there ought to be 'collaboration to the fullest extent'.

How to integrate the Indians? There was 'not only a basic cleavage between Hindu and Muslim... but innumerable factions, personal intrigues, and so on'. By comparison, the Arabs intermarried with the Africans (in passing, Mitchell noted that 'the expression "African" does not really mean anything': they were just so many tribes). Mitchell was 'not too worried' about the future of the Africans (he meant that they had not yet reached a stage of political consciousness). The Europeans provided 'the steel framework of the building'; and, in maintaining their trusteeship, they must 'Resist the temptation of giving to an immature ward an excessive degree of freedom from control before he is ready'.

So Mitchell returned to the Indians: 'The hard core of the [political] problem is the Asiatic, and especially the Hindu'; their position was similar to that of the Jews in Europe. Indian politicians suffered from 'persecution mania'; their political technique was limited to delivering 'a series of ultimata'. They convened mass meetings of ignorant, poor people, and passed resolutions: they would pass anything the man on the platform told them to pass.

As a result, the East African Indians 'have forced themselves further away from all other communities than they were thirty years ago'. It would be helpful to appoint Indians to public bodies, but there was the problem of corruption: there had been 'unpleasant examples on the Nairobi Municipal Council'. So, at last, Mitchell came to the question of a Member for Indian Affairs: he would get a salary of £2,000 per annum 'for doing very little work', and 'He would no doubt double his salary by what he would receive from members of his community, who would suppose that he was able to do things for them if it were made worth his while'. Would such an appointment help, 'from the Delhi point of view'?

It would be difficult to make this concession without also doing the same for the Arabs; but Mitchell had just turned down a similar Arab request. So either he would have to 'put the Arab nose out of joint' or make another concession. But this would begin to alter the character of the Executive Council, and it was 'too soon to contemplate any real change in the nature and structure of the Executive Council'. Mitchell's last word was that he was 'in a state of indecision'; but it must have been plain to Creasey that he really wanted a negative reply.

Mitchell's problem was considered to be sufficiently important for all the regional departments to be asked to submit memoranda on the position of their local Indian communities and the possibility of repercussions from appointing an Indian Affairs Member in Kenya. Would the Government of India make this a pretext for demanding such appointments elsewhere? Outside Africa, there were no objections. Concerning Malaya, Leslie Monson stated that they would not be embarrassed: 'We are in fact attempting to create in Malaya a community of interests, culture, etc. between the various communities, such as Sir Philip Mitchell implies would be impossible at present in Kenya.' Appointments to the Executive Council in the reconstituted post-war set-up would not be on a racial basis, though an Indian would be a Member. Monson doubted whether the Government of India would 'demand' a place for an Indian; anyway, in Malaya there was an alternative means of hearing the Indian case: 'Our machinery for protecting the interests of Indians in the shape of the Government of India Agent'.

John Hayward intimated that Mauritius would not be affected; P. Rogers said the West Indies would be caused no 'embarrassment'; and Trafford Smith stated that in Fiji an Indian and a Fijian had been appointed to the Executive Council specifically to safeguard the interests of their communities, though 'This is contrary to what Sir Philip Mitchell advised when he was Governor [of Fiji]'.

African experts were not to be reassured: Cohen minuted (17 September) that he doubted whether there was enough work to justify the new Member, he doubted whether there was a suitable candidate, and 'I fear his loyalty would be divided between the

Kenya Government and the Government of India'. The only advantage would be that a Member would 'canalise' Indian grievances.

Just at this moment the India Office sent along a communication from India relating to the question (29 October 1945). The Government of India had chafed at the continuing uncertainty about restrictions on immigration into East Africa. On 4 September a telegram was sent to the India Office with a reminder that the war had ended; When would restrictions be lifted? There was no reply, and on 23 October the Government of India cabled again to state that Aden had lifted restrictions on entry: Why not East Africa? The delay was causing public apprehensions to 'harden'. At the same time, India asked for an additional Indian Member on the expanded Kenya Executive Council. There was a 'lack of information' about what was going on, so it was intimated that India would shortly apply for the appointment of an East Africa Agent: this was necessary if India's relations with East Africa were to be placed on a better footing in the post-war era.

The Colonial Office returned a temporising answer on the immigration issue to the India Office (1 November 1945). The East African governments could not yet relax the immigration restrictions. The employment situation was uncertain, while the African ex-soldiers were being demobilised; it was hoped to end the wartime restrictions in twelve months' time. Meanwhile, the East African governments were making a long-term assessment of immigration and control, and the Government of India would be informed in due course. The Government of India sought to exert influence by despatching A. V. Pai to London to act as liaison officer with the Colonial Office. Pai's main task was to try to improve upon the recommendations of the Soulbury Commission for Ceylon, published on October 31 (Pai had been Agent in Ceylon), but in addition he took up the Kenya question. He had no success. On 19 November, Creasey wrote officially to Mitchell. The question of the Member for Indian Affairs was discussed by Creech Jones on 13 November, and it was decided that there was 'no logical case for meeting the Indian request'. Africans had a Commissioner for Native Affairs because they were still 'wards'; but Indians had elected representatives in the legislature. On 28 November, Mitchell met the Indian leaders and told them that the Secretary of State had turned down their proposal. Did Mitchell feel that he had led them to expect more? At any rate, 'The Governor informed the deputation that he regretted this [refusal] because he was very anxious to improve relations with the Indian community'.[8] The extent of Mitchell's regret is a little difficult to estimate because he was also putting down his thoughts on the influence of Indian politics upon the Africans in very different terms:

> At this juncture in our affairs, Indian politicians, especially those who support the Congress, seem to be attempting to stir up race hatred and bitterness, and to induce Africans to embark on the same dangerous course. The small number of Africans ... who are inclined to political association and activity are undoubtedly at present being prompted and advised in evil ways by the irresponsible and malicious element in local Indian politics; and there are not wanting signs that they may develop the same objectionable technique and phraseology.[9]

Cohen had talks with Pai concerning immigration into East Africa, and also about administrative reorganisation. A special 'Note on Additions to Kenya Legislative Council' was compiled as an aide-memoire for Pai (forwarded to the India Office, 31 December 1945). The Cavendish-Bentinck appointment was justified on the grounds that he was the most suitable candidate; it was disingenuously suggested that, as he was now an official, he would cease to behave like a settler. Cohen also told Pai that the Indians might be encouraged by a new proposal for inter-territorial association, in which they would participate; the same bait was dangled by Mitchell before the Kenya Indians at their November meeting.

As the white papers appeared, they were to disappoint Indian hopes. Before the next public controversy is considered, however, mention should be made of the perpetuation of racial divisions in the Kenya civil service during 1945. A general survey of the civil service was made by L. C. Hill, a senior civil servant specially sent out from England. He reported to the Governor that there were three separate civil service cadres on racial lines, all recruited locally: the Kenya European Civil Service, the Asian Civil Service, and the African Civil Service.[10] This, however, was only part of the structural separations: there were also the officials recruited through the Colonial Office. Thus, there were in Kenya 710 European civil servants on overseas (United Kingdom) terms of service, 512 Europeans on local terms, 586 Indians on overseas terms, 1,014 Indians on local terms, and 504 Africans on local terms.

Hill recommended a unified service, with recruitment on merit and qualification, and with promotion open to all. The Hill Report was not well received by the Kenya Government, or even by the Colonial Office: Cohen observed that it was 'a very radical recommendation'. The only important support for the Hill Report came from Sir Charles Jeffries, then in charge of personnel questions at the Colonial Office. When he first read the report, Jeffries commented: 'It is noticeable, not only in Kenya, that although our proclaimed policy is to raise the standard of living of Colonial peoples, any proposal which means doing it arouses acute controversy' (28 June 1945). Thereafter, the Colonial Office *sens du possible* began to make itself felt; on 28 August, Jeffries was writing: 'It is one thing to say what ought to be done to provide Kenya with a properly organised civil service and quite another thing to decide what can be done in the political and racial atmosphere which prevails.'

The Asian officials remained on a separate and lower rate of pay, denied promotion even to what in India were called 'gazetted' posts (virtually all executive positions). An inquiry led by Sir Maharaj Singh, a few months later, discovered that throughout the whole of East Africa only one Indian was holding a responsible administrative post: that of Auditor General in Tanganyika.

The heaviest storm was to burst over the publication of the Statement on Land Policy, in November.[11] As a result of the row in the legislature there was some improvement for the Indians; an Indian and Arab Settlement Board would be established, with an Indian chairman to replace the unserviceable Indian Land Settlement Board, formed in 1941. There would be land for 'locally-born' Indians possessing their own capital. The report also referred to Indian needs for urban housing and employment to create 'a reasonable standard of living for a rapidly increasing population'. There was nothing concrete at all for the Africans; and, beside the five hundred farms to be given to white ex-service men, there was provision for 200-300 European assistants to come onto existing farms: they would be trained in farming and eventually would require their own land.

As soon as this document reached London, protests started. On behalf of the East African Indians, Henry Polak asked Creech Jones to appoint a Royal Commission to investigate the Kenya situation (22 December 1945), while the Fabian Colonial Bureau sent in a stern memorandum (19 December). On 29 January 1946, a deputation from the Bureau, led by Frank Horrabin, M.P., met Creech Jones. Professor Arthur Lewis told him that the proposals were 'absolutely wrong and indefensible': he wanted the liquidation of white agricultural settlement in Kenya. Creech Jones replied that it was 'necessary to accept the situation as it had developed in the past and existed at present'. This somewhat sterile exchange was to continue for the remainder of the time Creech Jones was in office.[12] Meanwhile, he was already on public record, in a speech delivered to the Fabian Colonial Bureau on 9 January 1946. It was an uneasy occasion:

Creech Jones admitted feeling that he was 'on trial'; but, after all, he believed that he was still the man he had always been, and he asserted defiantly that 'the problems of East Africa . . . are really touchstones in British Labour policy.'

He defended white settlement, going back to the Carter Commission and urging that Labour must continue the policy of the previous twenty years. Somewhat tangentially, he observed: 'It would be folly to discuss the liquidation of European settlement without liquidating Indian settlement as well', and he was even more aggressive when he discussed immigration:

It is a thorny problem, but we will have to face up to it. . . . It should be remembered that there is much opposition from Africans themselves to Indian penetration. They argue that their position is prejudiced in commerce and trade by the initiative shown by the Indians, and they rather hope that somehow or other these activities can be curbed for their advantage. The problem creates feelings in India, though there may be some good from the criticism that the Indians in Kenya should pay less heed to Indian politics and more to the common necessities of East Africa itself.

Creech Jones ended with the claim that 'on the whole the Labour Government is doing very well'. When Indians read these criticisms of their people in East Africa they were appalled. It was the first time that a British Minister at the Colonial Office had publicly rebuked the Indians, whatever past Ministers might have said or written in private. It was one of the first shocks of disillusionment which Indians, and especially Congress Socialists, experienced from the Labour Government.

Pressures from the reformers — particularly pressure from the Anti-Slavery Society — had enough effect to induce Sir George Gater, the permanent Under Secretary, to write to Rennie to urge the Kenya Government to give more urgent attention to African agriculture and land occupation. Gater referred to criticism that the White Paper gave no indication that racial discrimination in the white highlands might be modified; it was difficult to deal with this criticism, Gater admitted; they were still implementing the Morris Carter report: 'Criticism tends to ignore the fact that any attempt now to modify that policy would put the white community against the Government.' Gater did not feel able to face that spectre, so contented himself with arguing that 'increased white settlement must be looked at not as a thing in itself but as an integral part of the Kenya development programme'. He ended by calling for 'rapid progress' in African development, and also 'progress in dealing with the squatter problem' (14 February 1946). In all the six-page letter there was no reference to the Indians: as Whitehall became more conscious of the need to accommodate the Africans, so they spared ever less thought for the Indians of Kenya.

When the third White Paper — that on inter-territorial organisation — appeared, it was the white settlers who protested.[13] It appears as though this plan was drafted in haste by Mitchell on a visit to London. The dream in the 1920s of political union leading to an East African Dominion was discarded; but there was to be an East African High Commission, with a secretariat, responsible for common services throughout the three mainland territories, including road and rail transport, posts and telegraphs, research, and conservation of resources. The Governor of Kenya would be chairman of the High Commission, and there would be a legislative assembly. It was the composition of this assembly which now put the Kenya Whites into one of their periodical states of excitement. The assembly would consist of twelve official members and twenty-four non-officials. The latter comprised six Europeans, elected from the three territories by the European members of the legislatures, six Indian members, similarly elected by the Indians on these legislatures, six Africans nominated by the High Commission, two Arabs similarly nominated, and four others nominated by the High Commission. If it was assumed that all the official members were Europeans — a certainty — then the non-Europeans could not out-vote the combined European officials and non-officials. Nevertheless, the proposal infuriated the settlers. The Colonial Office paper explained that the representation ratio had been adopted 'because of the impossibility of devising any generally accepted formula by which to decide the relative importance of the respective claims of the communities concerned'; the paper made it clear that the proposal was only for discussion.

The chairman of the Electors Union, the organisation of the Kenya Whites, Humphrey Slade, addressed an appeal to Smuts (19 February 1946) asking him to intervene to help them re-establish white control. The Africans were 'just emerging from barbarism' and had no claim to equality of representation. As for the Indians:

We absolutely refuse to accept the principle that the Indian community has any right to equal representation with the European community in the control of the British or the native African inhabitants, or in fact that they have any right to participate other than to protect their own interests, in the legislation of the Colony at all.

Lord Francis Scott also wrote to Smuts: Was it any use appealing to the Prime Ministers of the Dominions? They had reached the parting of the ways: 'Except for you, we have no friends.'

Smuts replied to Scott (7 March 1946): it was useless to approach the other Dominions; the Kenya settlers must rely on their own resources; Smuts would contact the Colonial Office, but 'Europeans in East Africa must make their own strong case clear'.

Sure enough, the Colonial Office listened to the white settlers, and fourteen months later emerged with a different formula. The legislative assembly was called the East African Central Assembly, having had its legislative powers severely reduced. It was now to comprise twenty-three members in all, seven being officials of the High Commission. The remainder consisted of fifteen 'territorial' members and one nominated Arab, and the territorial members — five from each territory — comprised one official, one member elected by the legislature, a European, an Indian, and an African. The European and Indian member from Kenya were to be elected by their groups in the legislature. As a consequence of the revision, the non-European component was reduced from nearly 39 per cent of the total to just over 30 per cent (for the territorial members elected by the three legislatures, sitting as a whole, seemed certain to be white). This scaling down of the importance of the joint legislature and cutting down of African and Indian participation made the scheme palatable to the white settlers.

Because the East African Indians had been unenthusiastic about a joint legislature, they were not greatly concerned when this formula was announced in February 1947; long before then they had become agitated about the innovation which most affected their community — the restriction of immigration.

There was a sharp response to the publication of the Immigration Bills from India. In the normally staid Council of State there was a heated debate on 3 April 1946. H. N. Kunzru moved a resolution on Kenya calling for free entry for Indians. He regretted that they had no Agent in East Africa; he read quotations from Creech Jones's speech to the Fabian Colonial Bureau and called upon the Council of State to condemn the Under Secretary for the Colonies for making such a speech. Finally, he protested against placing a white settler in charge of Kenya's agricultural policy: it was a 'danger signal', he said. 'Do they expect a free India to take [such] a step... lying down?'

V. V. Kalkar moved an amendment to Kunzru's resolution, providing 'that Indians should occupy a position of equality with the non-official Europeans', both in the legislative council and on other public bodies. Five hundred Europeans were being settled on the land: would Indians be allowed to settle? If the Colonial Office would not offer them equality, they should call for the administration of Kenya to be transferred to the Government of India:

President of the Council: That will never happen.
Kalkar: If we get independence, and if we are ready to fight, then it will happen.

Dr. Khare's response was muted: the East African Indians were 'not very keen' to have a Government of India representative there; he accepted the resolution, as amended, and observed that the British Government's 'attitude has not been very helpful to India'. Subsequently, it was decided to send an official mission to East Africa to inquire into the proposed immigration legislation. The leader was Sir Maharaj Singh, the counsellor of the overseas Indians; the other members were K. Sarwar Hasan, Secretary of the Indian Institute of International Affairs, who along with Maharaj Singh had attended the Commonwealth conference at Chatham House, and C. S. Jha, since 1944 Controller-General of Emigration for India.

The Indian delegation reached Nairobi on 27 August; Creech Jones had departed after his five-week East African tour, on 18 August. They stayed for only twenty-two days in East Africa, and yet compiled one of the most valuable accounts of the situation of the Indian community in the area.[14] The heart of the report was Chapter IV: 'The Immigration Bills — their necessity and justification'. The delegation were told that the Bills were designed to check an inflow of displaced persons from central Europe, to protect the existing population — especially the Africans — from unemployment, to calm growing hostility between Africans and Indians, and to control 'the large increase in the Indian population and the high birth rate amongst them'.

Maharaj Singh dismissed the bogey of the displaced persons: there was no sign of their arrival in large numbers, and, anyway, the Kenya Government had permitted 2,500 persons from central Europe, who had arrived as refugees, to remain. In the employment field, it was emphasised that Indians did not directly compete with Africans for the most part, while Indian firms gave work opportunities to Africans. Concerning relations between Africans and Indians, Maharaj Singh reported that Africans stressed the contribution of the Indians to the fight for freedom (otherwise, 'the Africans might have been relegated to the position of their brethren in South Africa'), though it was admitted that Africans opposed unrestricted immigration and 'would welcome any measure that would have the effect of reducing the number of immigrants into East Africa'. The Indians, of course, condemned the proposed controls, except for some of the long-domiciled Muslim community, especially the Ismailis. Maharaj Singh found there was an atmosphere of panic, and a boom in applications for entry in order to anticipate the new controls. On immigration figures, the report displayed a tendency to play what is called 'the Numbers Game' and to oppose the argument for control by questioning inflated figures; also, the extent to which Indians were being illegally smuggled in by dhow was questioned.

The delegation reported that the problem was really one of white discrimination, and they singled out discriminatory features in the new Bills (which were identical for all four territories). They particularly deplored the speeches by Creech Jones, who had gone on record during his very recent visit with the statement: 'It has become significant to me as I have gone round the country that the Africans are beginning to appreciate that the Indians are becoming a menace to them.'[15]

Maharaj Singh urged the East African Indians to make a greater contribution towards African education and development: 'It is definitely recognised by Indians that they have not done as much as they might for Africans in the past.' He was distressed to discover that the Indians were divided, and there was 'considerable ill feeling' between Muslims and Hindus and Sikhs. In Nairobi, tension had been heightened as a result of the recent municipal elections in which, although Muslims formed a majority in some wards, no Muslim had been elected among the seven Indian representatives. An attempt was made to resolve this question by convening a conference presided over by Sir Maharaj Singh, but 'unfortunately no agreement could be reached'. Perhaps because their own voice was now so ineffectual, the East African Asians announced that they would like to have an Agent of the Government of India appointed to East Africa.

The delegation were received with courtesy by the governors, especially by Sir John Hathorne Hall, Governor of Uganda, and they were promised that 'full weight' would be given to their observations. However, in the usual way, though the objections of the Government of India had the effect of slowing things down, they did not really affect the result. In October 1946 Creech Jones again went on record concerning the East African Indians: 'There has been considerable criticism from the Europeans regarding their lack of public spirit, and sometimes of their commercial morality. Among Africans there is a feeling of uneasiness lest Indian trading hampers their own efforts in that field.' Concerning the immigration legislation, he observed: 'It is the duty of the Government to secure the welfare of the people in their control . . . the situation in the world today is such that the Government would be shirking in its duty if it refused to regulate immigration.' Creech Jones added, somewhat inconsequentially, that white settlement was 'essential'.[16]

So East Africa, and especially Kenya, moved into the era of planned colonial development under firm white control. In an official despatch, Mitchell dismissed African politics as a debating society: 'high-sounding phrases which have largely taken the place of hard thinking'. The reality, he wrote, was tribalism and communalism: 'Issues are continuously complicated, and often obscured, by communal questions'. As an economic base, the African, the man with the hoe, was 'totally inadequate' for development; for that, the Europeans were required. As he declared later, 'We do not assert an exclusive right [of control] but rather a joint one. . . . Our task is to civilise.'[17]

In most of the Colonial Office territories, the years 1945-6 were a period of recovery or adjustment from wartime abnormalities. Trinidad held its first general election in July 1946 against a background of industrial unrest, centred upon Uriah Butler and the workers in the oil-field. Four out of the nine elected members of the legislature were East Indians, though two of them owed their election to Black support. Mauritius stumbled towards a less oligarchic system, though it had to wait for the stimulus of the approach to the transfer of power in India before there were tangible results.

Governor Kennedy sent a long despatch to George Hall (23 February 1946) listing the practical efforts made since the 1943 report on Mauritius. There were the Minimum Wages Board, a Trade Union adviser from Britain, Works Committees, an Industrial Court and an anti-malaria campaign. It all sounded promising, though actual change was slow to come. In response to a Government of India suggestion that more Indians should be taken into the police, the Governor retorted that as 90 per cent of the Mauritian Indians spoke Creole there was no language barrier (this was the opposite of the 1943 Committee's findings), while 'promotions are made not on racial considerations but on merit'. In consequence, Indians continued to be found only in the lowest ranks of the police.

Not until 29 October 1946 was the new draft constitution presented to the Council of Government.[18] It was an uneasy compromise between autocracy and democracy, designed, it seemed, to meet the feelings of the white *Mauriciens*, from one of whom the Governor quoted approvingly: 'If the Asiatic element is allowed to obtain the upper hand over the Mauritian Christian element the effect on the populations in Ceylon and Kenya will be disastrous.' Doubtless the writer was referring to the white planters of Ceylon and the white settlers of Kenya, but preferred to rely upon the religious rather than the racial argument. The legislature was to be broadened to admit nineteen elected members; there would be twelve nominated members, of whom one would be nominated by the Chamber of Agriculture and three by cooperative and industrial associations (unions), while the Governor and eight officials would also be members. The result would be to place the Governor and his known supporters in a slight minority, but presumably it was calculated that the elected members and the representatives of the unions would never *all* agree on any issue.

The franchise would be given to all British subjects resident in the colony for two years, who fulfilled the qualifications; in marked contrast to Ceylon, this favoured the newcomer — who was, however, more likely to be a British or French businessman than an Indian labourer. The qualifications were either payment of Rs. 240 rent per annum (£18), a salary of Rs. 600 per annum (£46), education up to the Standard IV examination (entry into secondary school), or service in the armed forces. The requirements appeared modest by European standards, but they would exclude all the Indian labourers, except those enlisted into the Labour Battalions, of whom hundreds had served in the Middle East.

The proposal had a poor reception; it pleased neither the *Mauricien* bourgeois nor the workers. Bissoondayal—now known as Professor — began to organise a popular protest movement. His first demonstration was little more than a gesture. During a visit to the island by a party of South African tourists, Bissoondayal took a little procession through Port Louis, carrying pictures of Gandhi and slogans. According to the official account, his party consisted of seventy-three marchers and three carts. On 6 February 1947 he was found guilty of organising an illegal procession. The magistrate called on him to give surety of Rs. 1000 for good behaviour for two years. He refused to pay, and was sentenced to sixty-five days' imprisonment. However, the surety was later paid and he was released from jail on 14 March 1947. The freedom movement had a long way to go in Mauritius.

During 1945-6, the Colonial Office was treating Ceylon as the constitutional priority. The response of the Labour Government to the Soulbury Report appeared in a White Paper on 31 October 1945.[19] It was very much in line with previous policy. The demands of Senanayake's ministry were not conceded, Ceylon was not advanced to Dominion status, and the request that its affairs should be transferred from the Colonial Office to the Dominions Office was refused. The Soulbury proposals for an expanded legislature were accepted, but the Governor did not become Governor-General. The control of the United Kingdom Government over external relations, defence, and the final veto on legislation remained, yet the promise of Dominion status 'within a comparatively short space of time' was reiterated.

The war was over; the trump card — non-cooperation in the offensive against Japan — could no longer count. Senanayake decided to play along with the British offer, and he asked the State Council to agree, while expressing their disappointment. The move succeeded very well: the motion was accepted by 51 votes to 3, and Senanayake had secured the requisite three-quarters majority. Two Indians and one Sinhalese opposed the motion.

Constitutional rules had to be drafted to give effect to the Soulbury proposals, and the work was done by the Legal Secretary of the Ceylon Government, who took his draft to London, being accompanied by Sir Oliver Goonetilleke, a shrewd senior civil servant who had established himself as broker between the Senanayake group and the Governor, Sir Henry Moore, and who now assumed the same role with the Colonial Office. It was propitious that at this moment the affairs of Ceylon passed into the hands of Sir Charles Jeffries, to whom proclaimed policy meant also actual implementation. He conceived the new constitution as a bridge to independence.[20]

The Government of India received the White Paper on Ceylon's future without enthusiasm. There was no mention of a solution for the Indian minority (or any minority) and the Viceroy's Council was asked to approve the secondment of A. V. Pai to join Mudaliar in London in pressing for concessions to the Indians before the draft constitution was approved. Wavell told Pethick-Lawrence that the political atmosphere in Ceylon was deteriorating: there were attacks upon Aney as the Indian representative by certain Ministers, and suggestions that India was trying to interfere (5 November 1945). However, it was really too late to get across the Indian view; the Colonial Office was not prepared to accept the additional trouble this would involve. Pethick-Lawrence followed tradition, as Secretary for India, in being a weak member of the Cabinet whose views were brushed aside in any inter-departmental dispute. He had to inform Wavell (2 November 1945) that the Colonial Office declined to take up the question of the Indian franchise in Ceylon; this must be settled by direct negotiation between Ceylon and India.

Ceylon's constitution was brought into operation by the device of an Order in Council in May 1946. The Ceylon Indians responded in militant vein. S. Thoundaman, President of the Ceylon Indian Congress, denounced the Sinhalese leaders for joining in 'a conspiracy with Whitehall' in order 'to oppress the Ceylon Indians'. He declared that they were 'determined to put an end to that condition of servitude and humiliation' imposed since 1930. A *hartal* or boycott was introduced on 8 June as a prelude to 'continuous struggle'. The labourers on the estates were urged to strike. It was they who were to suffer most from the angry Sinhalese reaction. The Ceylon ministers were ready to make the most of their opportunities. The next event to afford the possibility of pushing the British Government into giving them what they wanted came in December 1946, when Attlee and his colleagues made a considerable concession to the nationalist forces in Burma.

The British programme for Burma remained that announced in May — a three-year interim period before ministerial government was restored — and meanwhile the military administration, CAS(B), was running Burma under the direction of Major-General H. E. Rance, while the civil government (still headed by Dorman-Smith) waited impatiently at Simla. The greatest impatience of all was being shown by the Thakins, whose acknowledged leader was Aung San, now *Bogyoke*, Great General. The Anti-Fascist Organisation was expanded into the Anti-Fascist People's Freedom League (A.F.P.F.L.), and in August 1945 Aung San presented his demand for independence.[21]

Discussions continued with Dorman-Smith's government for a long-term agreement upon Indian emigration to Burma. The Burmese insisted that all immigration into their country must be limited to quotas for the different categories. At a meeting of the Viceroy's Council on 6 September, it was 'reluctantly agreed' that they must accept the quota system, and a draft agreement was finalised between Tin Tut and Banerjee.[22]

During the summer of 1945 there was strong pressure both from Dorman-Smith and the Burmese politicians for a return to civil government. Mountbatten agreed, and the whole of Burma west of the Salween River was handed over, though CAS(B) was not finally wound up until 31 March 1946. The Indian question was taken up soon after Dorman-Smith returned on 16 October: he told Pethick-Lawrence (18 November 1945): 'The more I consider this subject, the less I like it.' Plans had been prepared for the return of 400,000 Indians and their temporary accommodation in camps, but 'Conditions in Rangoon are such [as] to make it positively dangerous to increase the population to any large degree'. It would be wrong to encourage the return of thousands of refugees: 'I doubt whether Burma will ever again be a happy hunting ground for the Indian.'

Dorman-Smith was still working with a government headed by the faithful few Burmese politicians who had accompanied him to Simla. They were very nervous about the agreement so recently concluded with Banerjee and the Commonwealth Relations Department. The agreement was delegated to a sub-committee, which included the signatory of the abortive 1941 agreement, Sir Htoon Aung Gyaw. Dorman-Smith was positive that his Council 'will decline to touch the matter which is political dynamite'.

On 30 December 1945, Dorman-Smith informed Pethick-Lawrence that he had seen Jamnadas Mehta, the Indian representative, the previous day. Mehta undertook to discourage Indians from returning to Burma if the Burma Government would issue a statement that they would have the right to return when conditions had improved; this would be 'difficult', replied the governor. The Rangoon Press was urging the evacuation of the existing Indian population, on account of food shortages, and the Indians displayed a pathetic desire to return to India, Dorman-Smith said.

Six weeks later, Dorman-Smith was lamenting to Pethick-Lawrence that he had 'failed so signally to persuade my colleagues to deal with immigration in a realistic way' (10 February 1946). He repeated that it was political dynamite, though under pressure from India the repatriation of Indians to Burma was about to begin: it would 'lead to friction between India and Burma', he expected, and he was still not prepared to allow the Chettyars to return to claim their lands — despite representations from their head, the Raja of Chettinad — because they were 'not prepared to supply credit at low rates'. Indian labour was needed for agricultural work in Arakan, but not elsewhere.[23]

Dorman-Smith had matters of still greater urgency and difficulty to resolve: Aung San was building up a para-military force, the *Pyithu Yebaw Ahphwe*, called in English the People's Volunteer Organisation (P.V.O.), in an open bid for power. Dorman-Smith could not decide whether to recognise Aung San as the popular leader or to strike him down before he became all-powerful. In April, he resolved upon the latter course. During the British retreat in 1942, Aung San had bayonetted an Indian headman; it was now decided to put him on trial.

The Government of India was informed of the impending arrest of Aung San just at a moment when the Cabinet Mission were attempting to devise a constitutional scheme to put before the Congress and the Muslim League. They did not want to be disturbed.

On 18 April 1946, the Viceroy and the ministers sent a cable to the Prime Minister: there were 'great risks . . . at this juncture'. 'We are approaching the crucial stage of our work and nothing would be more disastrous than a situation of this sort just at the time when we are trying to form an interim government. We trust, therefore, that if it is inevitable from Burma's standpoint that allegations against Aung San should be investigated, the question of his arrest can be postponed at any rate for two or three months.' The telegram added that Indian troops could not be made available to put down unrest in Burma if the interim Congress-League government were formed: British troops would have to be made available. This, the Viceroy and the ministers already knew, was a near impossibility.

On 29 April, Pethick-Lawrence cabled Attlee that Aung San was reported to have arrived in Delhi to consult with Nehru and the Congress: 'If it were not for the impending charge of murder I should be disposed to see him', he said.[24] On the same day, the Viceroy and the Cabinet Mission sent another combined telegram urging that the arrest of Aung San be postponed until the circumstances of the 1942 killing were fully investigated and a prosecution established to be 'feasible'. Mr Attlee was equally dubious about Dorman-Smith's prospects (though, in fact, the Chief Secretary, F. S. V. Donnison, had a mass of evidence relating to the murder), and the strained relations between the Governor and the British Government contributed to his decision to tender his resignation in June 1946. After some weeks of marking time, the late military Governor, Sir Hubert Rance, was brought back as civil head of the Burma Government. Soon after his arrival, on 5 September, *Bogyoke* called a general strike, demonstrating his ability to paralyse the country. The moment was well chosen: there was only one British battalion stationed in Burma, and Nehru had just become the head of the interim government in India, so Indian troops were confined to their lines. On 26 September, Rance reformed his Executive Council with Aung San as its leader, and six A.F.P.F.L. men among the nine members. The general strike was called off on 2 October, and Aung San prepared to bid for independence.

It was so obvious that this was the next step that it is somewhat surprising to find Rance writing to Pethick-Lawrence on 16 October deprecating a congratulatory telegram from Nehru to Aung San, in which the Indian leader greeted his former student admirer 'as a sort of Prime Minister'. Attlee rapidly adjusted to the changed situation; on 20 December he announced in the House of Commons that there was a new policy for Burma: a delegation would be invited to London to negotiate the transfer of power to an independent government which would have complete freedom to decide whether or not to remain within the Commonwealth. This was a momentous step in the world of 1946.

On 21 December, Creech Jones informed Attlee that the announcement on Burma would inevitably trigger off a new demand from Ceylon. Up till then, Ceylon had been comfortably ahead of Burma in the constitutional race-game; but all at once the concessions they had obtained would seem to be devalued to the Ceylonese ministers.

While Burma and Ceylon moved towards independence, Malaya was still slowly shaking off the effects of the wartime occupation. Military government was the first step as in Burma, but whereas there was a Burma Government, with governor, ministers, senior administrators, all waiting in nearby Simla, there was no Malayan government: the officials were all physical wrecks after $3\frac{1}{2}$ years in Japanese prison camps, and the Governor-designate, Sir Edward Gent, was sitting in the Colonial Office in London. There had been a long drawn out inquest on 'What went wrong in Malaya' — for clearly things had gone wrong — and in particular the traditional policy of favouring the Malays had evoked no answering response when the moment of truth had arrived.

The Malayan military administration functioned under the immediate surveillance of the Supreme Allied Commander, Admiral Mountbatten, whose headquarters were at Singapore. Soon after British control was reimposed, Sir Harold MacMichael arrived — on 11 October 1945 — on a mission from the Colonial Office designed to launch new constitutional and administrative arrangements. MacMichael visited the Malay Sultans in turn, and obtained their signatures of acceptance to a new constitution. In January 1946 it was announced that the Malay States would be amalgamated with Penang and Malacca to form a Malayan Union, administered by a British Governor; Singapore became a separate colony, also under a Governor; the anachronistic units of British Borneo were brought under Crown Colony government: all were to be placed under a Governor-General, who was to be Malcolm MacDonald.[25] There was to be a new British empire in South-East Asia to replace the Indian Empire. The Malayan Union would create a single citizenship for all its peoples, and this could be acquired by Malays, Chinese and Indians upon equal terms. The citizenship proposals were perhaps the most obnoxious to the ruling Malays: 'Malays will become slaves of the Chinese and Indians', the Sultan of Johore told George Hall (5 June 1946).

Before the civil government arrived, the Government of India moved to secure Indian interests. S. K. Chettur, I.C.S., was appointed to the vacant position of Agent, though he was to have the more elevated title of 'representative', as in Ceylon, and he was to reside at Singapore, the seat of the Governor-General. There would be a separate agent at Kuala Lumpur concerned with labour problems. It was hoped that this would promote 'better and more harmonious relations between the two countries'.[26]

Chettur arrived to find the Indian community in a poor way. The collapse of the Japanese Co-Prosperity Sphere, the mysterious death of Subhas Bose in an aircraft crash, the end of Azad Hind, left them leaderless and bewildered. After the British return, seventy-three Indians were arrested for war crimes. Because the trials of the Indian National Army leaders staged at the Red Fort in Delhi (beginning November 1945) were such a fiasco, many I.N.A. accused were retained in Malaya and Burma for trial. At Madras, the Bar Association formed a Defence Committee, and Dr. Khare asked the Viceroy's Council to accept responsibility for the legal defence of Indians in Malaya; after some opposition, it was agreed that India would finance the defence of civilian accused. In addition, H. N. Kunzru and Kodananda Rao proceeded to Malaya on behalf of the Servants of India Society in January 1946: they reported that there were 25,000 Indians in Malaya who wished to return home.

This was the background to Nehru's visit, which was probably most significant for his own political development, rather than for its effects upon the Malayan Indians. Nehru applied to visit Burma also, but was refused clearance by the Dorman-Smith government. His visit to Malaya was conditional upon his undertaking not to 'indulge in political agitation or [make] speeches against the existing administration'.[27] What might have been a difficult and frustrating trip was transformed by the imagination of Lord Louis Mountbatten.

Nehru was to be assisted on his travels by F. V. Duckworth, Commissioner of Labour, and before he arrived Mountbatten told Duckworth that, as Nehru had not long left jail, he was facing a strange world and the Malayan visit was 'a magnificent opportunity to begin the cure'. The British Military Administration refused to release a car for Nehru's use: thereupon, Mountbatten announced that he was 'quite prepared to let Nehru have his own car and walk if need be'. On arrival, Nehru was received by a guard of honour of 2,000 former I.N.A. members: they hoped that the visit would rehabilitate their fallen fortunes. But Nehru was driven straight to the Singapore Y.M.C.A. to meet the Mountbattens, and at once responded to their friendly reception. At Mountbatten's request, he cancelled the first ceremony, a public laying of wreaths at the site of the demolished I.N.A. memorial. Next day he crossed to Johore, and was received by Indian women of the former Rani of Jhansi Regiment and members of the *Balaksena* youth organisation; the ex-I.N.A. men set up their cry 'Blood . . . blood', but Nehru emphatically dissociated himself from any cry for revenge.

Throughout the tour, his speeches referred almost exclusively to the new era of peace dawning in Asia, when India and China would come together as brothers. This exalted tone was not much to his listeners' liking: at one evening meeting where three thousand Indian soldiers of the occupation forces came to hear him, they walked out because he would not speak about the current situation in India.

During his trip, Nehru was presented with a gift of $100,662 (Malayan) which he directed should be handed to an Indian Relief Committee for the welfare of distressed Malayan Indians.[28] Nehru advised against large-scale repatriation; only those who were destitute should return to India. When he was questioned about the future of the Malayan Indians under the new constitution, he replied: 'When India attained independence she would immediately define who her nationals were, and Indians overseas would be Indian nationals unless they chose to be otherwise.'[29] Nehru left Penang airport on 26 March: he had made twenty speeches in eight days and met about 60,000 people; he was said to be 'extremely weary'.

During his Malayan visit the Burma authorities had second thoughts, and Nehru was invited to break his journey at Rangoon. His reception was on a much smaller scale. He conferred at the Strand Hotel with Zora Singh, S. M. Bashir and M. G. Kapachi, while about two hundred Tamils, formerly in the I.N.A., paraded outside: 'Nehru advised them to work hand in hand with the Burmese people for the welfare of the country. He also stressed the undesirability of demanding or agitating for any safeguards or special rights or privileges for Burma Indians.'

Mr Duckworth observed that Nehru's visit had provided a 'safety valve' for the Malayan Indians; they needed some relief. Because of the privations of the Japanese occupation, the population had fallen from the previous recorded total of 620,000 (1931) to under 590,000. Indian children at school in 1946 numbered only 16,000 compared to 26,000 in 1941, itself a poor figure.[30] A medical team sent by the Government of India treated 36,000 patients; passages were secured for 8,000 to return to India, while another 20,000 also applied for passages.[31] On the rubber estates, the British planters, released from Japanese camps, tried to put the clock back to 1941. There were strikes, especially in Kedah, where the Kedah General Labour Union organised a Youth Corps, *Thondar Padai*, on the pattern encouraged by the Japanese. In August 1946 the Malayan Indian Congress was founded as an avowedly activist political organisation. The first president was John Thivy, son of Louis Thivy, a former legislator. John Thivy had been active in the Indian Independence League and was a member of Netaji's Azad Hind government. The Malayan Indians were determined that the image of the docile Indian coolie should be obliterated.

All these changes were overshadowed by the great event of 1946: the confrontation between India and South Africa at the United Nations. The deceptive lull in their long controversy ended abruptly in January 1946. Smuts did not fully realise what a storm was about to break, for on 14 December 1945 he sent two letters to Wavell which were the least anxious or contentious in their long correspondence. The sudden break came because the South African Indian leadership had irrevocably passed into the hands of the militants; there could be no compromise. At the same time, the mood of the white Natalians became inflamed and they demanded even more severe measures to force the Indians into segregated areas. Smuts, the old trimmer, could not find a way out of this confrontation.

As early as August 1945, Sir Evelyn Baring was reporting to his new chief at the Dominions Office, Lord Addison, that white Durban was 'obsessed' with the Indian problem, and angry at what they regarded as neglect by the Union Government of their demands. Durban Council was 'a deplorable organisation', wrote Baring, and their handling of Indian housing 'a squalid story' (27 August 1945). On 12 November 1945, Baring addressed a personal letter to Sir Eric Machtig: the situation was polarising. Natal had passed a new Housing Ordinance which destroyed the spirit of Hofmeyr's proposals: it was 'more severe' than the Pegging Act — which prevented Indians from acquiring new property — whilst the new measure threatened even their existing property. For the moment, the measure hung fire because assent had not been given and the Ordinance went into the 'reserved' category.

At the same time, Baring reported the collapse of the Indian moderate position. The Anti-Segregation Council obtained an injunction from the Natal High Court requiring elections to be held for the Natal Congress before the end of October. Faced with a packed mass meeting, Kajee and his friends did not even fight. The new president was Dr. G. M. Naicker, and the Joint Secretaries M. D. Naidoo and A. B. Maharaj. These were new men, working-class and young, the descendants of the indentured coolies, workers not merchants, Tamils not Gujaratis. Though they still spoke in moderate tones, they demanded the common roll franchise, and no compromise.

Baring reported that the Indian High Commissioner was still trying to find a middle way; he was prepared to recommend a communal franchise as a first step, pointing out that this would give the vote to the working-class whereas the 'loaded' franchise would confine the vote to the merchants. Baring recorded his own distress at these developments: for the first time since Gandhi, Kajee 'had established a strong personal position with a strong Union Prime Minister'; Kajee 'might, through General Smuts, have obtained much for his community'; now nothing remained.

Ten days later, Baring gave Machtig an account received from Smuts of his meeting with the new Indian leaders: they were 'uncompromising and ill-informed', observed the Prime Minister there could be 'no progress' with them, and their demands would create even stronger anti-Indian feeling. Smuts announced that the new Natal Housing Ordinance 'must receive assent'. Clearly, a fight was imminent.

Yet all this was muted in the letters Smuts wrote to Wavell just before Christmas. Though both were sent on the same day, the first was more personal, devoted to Smuts' reflections and convictions on the future of India. He was far from happy about the political situation after the elections for the central assembly, which had just finished: 'There is a grave risk that the removal of the British control — the steel framework of the Indian structure — may mean the collapse of the whole vast system.' The whole of Asia, in consequence, 'may wander in the dark into dangerous paths'.

'Nobody will envy you the job of liquidating the old system' Smuts told Wavell; though he, if anyone, could succeed in 'this new adventure, greater than any of your previous career'. Finally, he reminded Wavell of advice he had given him in London when he was chosen to be Viceroy; and it was good advice:

Keep your eyes not only on India but also on London. Your difficulties may be as much in the one as in the other. And you will be in the position of an honest impartial broker between these two vast interests.[32]

The second letter analysed the South African situation: it was difficult 'to see a way through this welter of difficulties and prejudices'. The position was much worse than at the time of the Pretoria Agreement: the Indians had moved to the Left, the Whites were 'panicky', the coalition government was breaking up, leaving the Dominion and Labour parties 'inclined to exploit the Indian question'. The third Broome Report had been 'singularly unfruitful' and Smuts would not accept the conference recommendation because 'this time a failure would be more serious'.

Smuts planned to introduce legislation to give the Indians representation, in the Union parliament, in the provincial councils, and in municipalities, as well as 'better opportunities in the public and railway services and in educational and economic directions'. The Land Tenure Bill would create 'open or free areas in Natal' but in the remainder of the province property would be controlled by a Board, with equal representation for Indians and Europeans. The Representation Bill would give the Indians three elected members in the Natal Assembly and one in the Transvaal Assembly. Natal and the Transvaal would have one elected and one nominated senator to represent the Indians in parliament. The franchise would be on a separate, communal basis, and there would be qualifications 'so as to exclude the lower classes of illiterates'. Whether the representatives would be Indians or Whites 'still remains open for further examination'.

Smuts announced the new measures in the Union parliament on 16 January 1946.[33] It was clear that the new restrictions on housing went further than the Pegging Act, and even Wavell, with his understanding of Smuts' difficulties, could not swallow these terms: They were 'entirely unacceptable', he told Pethick-Lawrence on 29 January, and he asked Smuts to hold them back until Deshmukh, on leave in India, could return; a round table conference was now more important than ever.

The last chances of compromise fell away, one by one. Kajee was still in control of the moribund South African Indian Congress, and he mobilised this defunct body for a meeting with Smuts; it was a failure, and Smuts did not hide his anger. Deshmukh hastened back to South Africa and publicly appealed for another solution; he was ignored. The Bill was introduced into the lower house of parliament on 15 March. Even the meagre benefits promised by Smuts to Wavell on 14 December 1945 had been eroded: there was to be no representative of the Indians in the Transvaal Assembly in deference to Afrikaner obduracy, and in Natal there were only two, while the representatives in the Natal Assembly and the Union Parliament were all required to be of European descent. But, of course, it was the segregation provisions which bit deepest; the 1939 interim provisions in the Transvaal were made permanent, while the Pegging Act was extended throughout the whole of Natal on a permanent basis.

A warning of the grave mood of the Indian government was given just before the Bill was introduced. On 6 March the Viceroy's

Council 'decided practically unanimously to give notice to South Africa of the termination of the trade agreement in retaliation for their Bill against the acquisition of land by Indians,' wrote Wavell. 'I have managed to keep this in abeyance for about two years, but with the war over, it is essential to make this concession to Indian feelings. It is not likely to do any good at all . . . but it has become a matter of national prestige.'[34]

Khare announced in the Council of State on 12 March that three months' notice of cancellation of the agreement had been given; he added that, in addition, South Africa had been told that his Government 'consider themselves free to take counter measures'. This could only mean an appeal to the United Nations.

Smuts received another message, which may have disturbed him more than the Note from the Government of India. On 18 March a telegram arrived from Gandhi. It was private and not for publication, and it read: 'Your Asiatic policy requires overhauling (.) It ill becomes you (.) Least you should do is to withdraw threatened Land and Franchise measures and call Round Table Conference.' It was signed 'Your and South Africa's sincere friend'.

Smuts sat down to write the reply in his own awkward, angular handwriting. He expressed appreciation for the message, but stated that the situation in Natal had deteriorated, and conferences with the local Indian leaders had proved useless; an international conference was 'not politically feasible'. He tried to emphasise the benefits of the new measure: 'Conferment of political status on Indians has become highly expedient and is a great step forward even though the representation is by Europeans under South Africa Act.' Smuts concluded: 'I assure you of the friendly spirit in which I am acting in a situation which has been forced on me by circumstances beyond my control.' Smuts looked over his message and thought again; he crossed out all the words after 'situation' and substituted 'which may easily get out of control'. But the first, candid statement was the true one. Smuts and Gandhi were, as always, so near and yet so far from each other.

On 24 March, Wavell recorded: 'The three Magi have arrived' — as he greeted the Cabinet Mission. From this time forward the Viceroy was involved, hour by hour, in the constitutional issue; but the South African problem could not be pushed aside. Two days later, there was an adjournment motion in the Legislative Assembly to discuss Dr Khare's 'appeal that the Government of India should raise the South African question before the Security Council'. Sri Prakasa, a leading Congress member, said slyly of the Viceroy's Council: 'Usually they are a happy family. One Member does not say very much against what the whole Cabinet does.' But now, it seemed, Dr Khare was leading an opposition group. Mr Banerjee promised the Legislative Assembly that there would be a decision soon; he indicated that it was not clear whether the complaint should be sent to the Security Council or the Assembly of the U.N. thus putting the differences on a technical plane.

There was another adjournment debate in the Legislative Assembly on 2 April, when Sir Ramaswamy Mudaliar intervened with assurances that the question of the reference to the U.N. was being actively considered, though attempts were still being made to induce Smuts to agree to a conference. Then, on 16 April 1946, the Legislative Assembly was told by Mudaliar that if the Land and Franchise Bill became law in South Africa, then the Government of India would complain to the U.N. Meanwhile, Deshmukh was being asked to return to India 'very shortly'. The announcement appeared to satisfy the critics.

The Asiatic Land Tenure and Indian Representation Bill had a very rough passage through the Union Parliament. Only those Europeans representing 'Native' interests said that it was unfair to the Indians: Hofmeyr and Shepstone accepted the Bill because of its enfranchisement of the Indians, bringing them into the South African family, while the Dominion Party, the Labour Party and the Nationalists loudly condemned the franchise provisions as a sell-out. The Bill became law on 3 June 1946, and in accordance with his announcement of 16 April Mudaliar sent notice to the Secretary-General of the United Nations on 22 June that India wished to place the issue upon the agenda of the first session of the General Assembly, due to begin on 3 September. Mudaliar's letter began with a reference to the claim made in 1875 in Lord Salisbury's despatch, that the Indians shoud be 'in all respects free men with privileges no whit inferior to those of any other class of Her Majesty's subjects' (see p. 22), a somewhat fragile foundation; it then referred to the Cape Town Agreement as another legal prop. India's case was better founded in equity than in law.

Immediately after the Land and Franchise Bill became law, the South African Indians launched a satyagraha campaign against the Ghetto Act, as it was called. According to figures issued by the government, 733 Indians were sentenced for defying the Ghetto Act down to the end of September 1946; according to the Passive Resistance Council, total convictions numbered 1,286, although some satyagrahis were sentenced more than once.[35] Because the South African Government still wished to enjoy international goodwill, sentences were relatively lenient; for the first offence a fine of £3 or thirty days was usually imposed, though second offenders received sentences of three months' imprisonment.[36]

Certain efforts were made to induce Smuts to agree to a round table conference. While South Africa still maintained a Trade Commissioner at Bombay, Grant-Smith, the Commissioner, urged the Department of External Affairs to 'modify its decision' (8 August 1946). A round table conference would spread 'healing balm over injured Indian national pride'; Grant-Smith warned his department that otherwise the dispute with India would cause long-term damage to their trade. At the Department of External Affairs, D. D. Forsyth, a close associate of Smuts, forwarded Grant-Smith's letter to the Prime Minister, recommending that they take his advice (23 August 1946). A round table conference would 'enable India to retire with some show of grace from the position she has taken up'. He added that the Aga Khan strongly urged the same course for the same reason. But now it was the turn of Smuts to be obdurate. He had to show the world, publicly, that South Africa was in the right.

The debate at the U.N. on the Indians in South Africa provided one of the first Cold War encounters in which the Soviet-controlled bloc voted as one, with most of the North Atlantic countries lining up on the other side, and the majority of the still small number of Third World countries inclining towards an anti-colonialist attitude, though American influence was strong enough to win over some of the central and south American states.

Before the U.N. convened, the Congress had entered an interim government in India and Jawaharlal Nehru was Member for External Affairs and Commonwealth Relations. He sent his sister, Mrs Vijaya Lakshmi Pandit, as India's principal delegate to the U.N., supported by M. C. Chagla, a Muslim Nationalist lawyer, and K. P. S. Menon of the Department of External Affairs. J. C. Smuts was present at the opening of the Assembly, supported by Heaton Nicholls, now High Commissioner in London.[37]

Smuts began by calling for the removal of the Indian complaint from the agenda on the ground that it was purely an internal South African question. This happened in the General Committee on the opening day, 24 October 1946, but though he was well supported in this committee Smuts could not expect such an easy victory: it was resolved to refer the question to the Legal Committee and the Political Committee, meeting jointly. This meant that each member nation would send along two representatives, making a forum of over one hundred participants. The joint committee deliberated between 21 and 30 November, holding six long sessions. Smuts must have been fortified by a personal letter from Lord Addison, Dominions Secretary, despatched on 20 November. Addison deplored the 'confused' debate at the U.N. in which Britain 'has backed up her friend': South Africa 'can confidently rely upon us', said Addison. Attlee, no less than Churchill, was a staunch supporter of J. C. Smuts.

At the second meeting, Chagla presented the Indian case at length, beginning once again with the Salisbury despatch: he tabled a resolution from India which condemned South Africa's 'discriminatory treatment of Asiatics in general' as a denial of human rights, and the Ghetto Act which 'impaired friendly relations' between India and South Africa; the Union Government was called upon to revise their policies and report back to the Assembly next year. At the same meeting, the French delegate moved an alternative resolution which stated that 'the treatment of Indians in South Africa should be in conformity with international obligations', and asked the two governments concerned to consult, and report back.

At the fifth meeting the United States, Britain and Sweden moved another alternative resolution to refer the whole issue to the International Court at the Hague, to obtain an advisory opinion as to whether the Indian complaint was 'essentially within the domestic jurisdiction of the Union'. This was devised in consultations between Smuts, Hartley Shawcross of Britain and Warren Austin of the United States.

The debate was repetitious and rhetorical and eventually the Chairman decided first to ask the Joint Committee to vote upon the resolution drafted by France, as amended by Mexico, and this was passed by 24 votes in favour, with 19 against and 6 abstentions.

When the resolution was brought back to the General Assembly, Smuts pointed out that it was backed by less than half the votes of the members (for five states had been absent from the roll call). The next substantive question to be settled was whether this should be accounted 'an important issue', in which case a resolution would require a two-thirds majority in order to pass, or whether it was an ordinary issue to be passed by a simple majority. It was not difficult for those who wanted the issue side-tracked to argue that from the mouths of the Indians and their sympathisers came the message that this *was* an important issue; Sir Hartley Shawcross developed this argument with persuasive skill; his speech brought from Mrs Pandit the sad reflection: 'I expressed a hope that the Commonwealth would at least remain neutral in this controversy, which vitally concerns one of its important members. But Sir Hartley Shawcross's speech has shattered my hopes. He has spoken in a manner which I consider to be entirely partisan'.

When the vote on the two-thirds majority was called, there were 29 votes in favour and 24 against; one delegate abstained. It must have seemed to South Africa that the attack had been beaten off. If this vote was a demonstration of strength, then India could not possibly summon up a two-thirds majority.

Smuts, at any rate, must have been thinking on these lines. On 4 December he cabled to Hofmeyr; 'the position is very difficult', but he hoped that they might still get the question referred to the International Court. Feeling reasonably confident, he hastily left New York and flew off to Greece. What was awaiting him there was not a political crisis but a young Queen whom Smuts found very attractive.

It was a fatal decision; Heaton Nicholls was left in charge, and although he persevered manfully he was hardly a world figure. He moved an amendment to the Franco-Mexican resolution, referring the legal question of whether this was a domestic or an international matter to the International Court; this was rejected by 31 votes to 21, with two abstentions. When the roll-call vote came on the Franco-Mexican resolution, the first to vote was Afghanistan. Afghanistan had voted with the North Atlantic group on the two-thirds majority question, being with Lebanon the only Afro-Asian state to vote against India; on the South African amendment they had abstained; yet now they cast their vote for India. That was bad, but next came Argentina, a firm supporter of South Africa, and still voting true to form. Now it was the turn of Australia.

The White Commonwealth had steadily supported South Africa, thus contributing to Mrs Pandit's bitterness: but on this crucial vote Paul Hasluck of Australia announced they would abstain. Heaton Nicholls' heart sank. Six other nations abstained; three West European countries voted for India and there emerged a bare two-thirds majority — 32 votes in favour with 15 against. The President of the Assembly declared the Franco-Mexican resolution— calling for the treatment of Indians in South Africa to be in conformity with international obligations and the Charter of the U.N. — to be carried.[38]

The voting on the successive occasions falls into a clear pattern, and may be assessed as follows:

For India   *For South Africa*

First Vote: Joint Committee, 30 November: Franco-Mexican Resolution

For India		For South Africa	
Communist bloc	6	White Commonwealth	4
Afro-Asians	9	West Europeans	7
Latin Americans	8	U.S.A. and Latin American allies	8
West Europeans (France)	1		
Totals:	24		19

Abstained: 5 (New Zealand, Denmark, Ecuador, Honduras, Turkey)
Absent: 5

For India		For South Africa	
Second Vote: General Assembly, 8 December: two-thirds majority			
Communist bloc	6	White Commonwealth	5
Afro-Asians	10	West Europeans	9
Latin Americans	8	U.S.A. and Latin American allies	13
		Afro-Asians	2
Totals:	24		29

Abstained: 1 (France)

Third Vote: General Assembly, 8 December: South African amendment (two-thirds majority now required)

Communist bloc	6	White Commonwealth	5
Afro-Asians	11	West Europeans	7
Latin Americans	11	U.S.A. and Latin American allies	9
West Europeans	3		
Totals:	31		21

Abstained: 2 (Afghanistan, Bolivia)

Fourth Vote: General Assembly, 8 December: Franco-Mexican Resolution

Communist bloc	6	White Commonwealth	4
Afro-Asians	12	West Europeans	4
Latin Americans	11	U.S.A. and Latin American allies	7
West Europeans	3		
Totals:	32		15

Abstained: 7 (Australia, Bolivia, Brazil, Denmark, Ecuador, Sweden, Turkey)

Total Membership of U.N. 54.
Communist Bloc (above) includes Yugoslavia and Czechoslovakia.
West Europeans include Turkey and Greece.
Afro-Asians include Liberia, Lebanon and Philippines.

In the aftermath of the U.N. resolution, the situation in South Africa deteriorated further. South African Whites were especially angry about the South African Indians who had gone to New York to advise the Indian delegation. In the prevailing temper of South

African Indian politics they had gone as separate, rival factions Sorabjee Rustomjee, leader of the Passive Resistance Council now carried most weight with the Government of India; A. I. Kajee also went, reluctantly, but he was relegated to the background. On their return, all these leaders were attacked as disloyal to South Africa, and all — even Kajee — answered in the language of militancy.

In the same way, when Smuts returned from Greece he spoke with a new bitterness, condemning the United Nations. But he was quickly reminded that in the game of white racism others could always do better. On 21 January 1947, Dr Malan introduced a motion in parliament calling on South Africa to turn its back on the U.N. and withdraw the recent measures for the representation of Indians in institutions of government; instead parliament should 'devise a comprehensive policy . . . to be based upon the principle of separation of Europeans and non-Europeans politically, residentially, and as far as practicable also, industrially'. Smuts realised that he was falling into a trap; he was to open the way for *apartheid* on the Nationalist pattern. He refused to touch the Malan motion and instead asked parliament to approve his own policy — defined as 'a conciliatory but firm policy'.[39] A few days later he wrote to his English friends, the Gilletts.

We bump up against the claim for equality which is most difficult to satisfy except in very small doses which will not satisfy the leaders. I have so far done my best to follow the other line (of improvements) as less open to white prejudice and opposition. I must try again.[40]

He was checked on every side. The Transvaal and Natal Whites replied to the satyagraha campaign by a boycott of Indian shops and firms. In Natal, proposals to bring Indians into municipal government were frustrated by white opposition; in Durban a referendum was held among the white voters who rejected a separate Indian franchise by 15,066 votes to 1,639 votes. Meanwhile, the satyagraha movement continued, though on a reduced scale.

There was only a limited reaction to the South African turmoil in India, where the statement by Attlee, delivered on 20 February, that the British would leave India in 1948, and that Wavell would be replaced as viceroy, was being hastily digested. The main development in India's international activities was the convening of an Asian Relations Conference at Delhi in March 1947. Nehru was president, and Sarojini Naidoo chairman, with Kunzru and B. Shiva Rao among the committee. The subjects considered included racial problems, inter-Asian emigration, industrialisation, and labour. The atmosphere was not, overtly, political. There was a resemblance to the Chatham House conference of two years before, but instead of bringing in the established, the dignified, the men of yesterday it brought together the men of tomorrow. The largest numbers came from the neighbouring South-East Asian countries, including representatives of Ho Chi Minh's Viet Minh republic. Two of the South African Indian leaders attended: Y. M. Dadoo and G. M. Naicker, leaders of the satyagraha campaign (there were no Africans). Among those from Malaya was S. A. Ganapathy, formerly an instructor in the Indian National Army and now President of the Pan-Malayan Federation of Trade Unions, a Communist organisation. Nehru proposed the creation of a permanent pan-Asian organisation, with a secretariat at Delhi, but there was a lukewarm response from the Asian neighbours, some of whom suspected a bid for the Indian leadership of Asia.

Nehru turned from the conference to take up the question of the U.N. resolution with Smuts; his first letter (dated 24 April 1947) was conciliatory and urged 'the speedy restoration of normal and friendly relations between our two countries'. Smuts' reply (dated 28 April) was also friendly in tone; but he stipulated that the first step must be the return of the Indian High Commissioner to Pretoria before conversations could begin. Nehru replied at considerable length (6 May) stating that Deshmukh could not return while their mutual relations were at such a low ebb; Smuts took over a month to answer this letter, and then replied in a much colder tone (18 June) reiterating the demand for Deshmukh's return. He felt in a stronger position now, because he was able to cite the support of Indian opinion in South Africa for the return of the High Commissioner.

A. I. Kajee had made yet another come-back; this time at the head of a new body called the Natal Indian Organisation. They had a meeting with Smuts, but it was clear that the Prime Minister had nothing fresh to offer; the Ghetto Act was not up for negotiation. Indeed, Smuts' whole attitude had hardened. The *laager* mentality of the Afrikaners, against which he had fought all his life, seemed to be affecting him in certain ways. His attitude to India, which he had always insisted was friendly, was now definitely hostile.[41] On 12 May 1947 he gave Clement Attlee his appreciation of the meaning of the current trend:

For India an entirely new situation has been created by the latest development, and minorities may well ask for an opportunity to reconsider their position. Britain, on her part, may well pause before voluntarily quitting India with a prospect before it of partition, chaos, and possibly civil war ... Britain still has a duty to India's dumb millions who look to her for justice, as well as to the minorities who may be driven to despair.

All I can suggest under these circumstances is that the dissenting communities should have a chance not only of independence and partition but also of remaining, if they wish, under the British raj.

It was a strange apotheosis for the freedom fighter who had defied Chamberlain and Milner and the British Army; but old men forget. The correspondence with Nehru petered out in August 1947. Smuts had convinced himself that the Indian government was acting in a manner contrary to the wishes of the South African Indians; a manner which was hostile to the Union Government. There was no scope for negotiation.

Smuts also appeared to discard his liberal, moderate supporters in South Africa, both White and Indian. D. G. Shepstone wrote anxiously to Smuts on 19 July 1947: he had not managed to see the Prime Minister, and he was concerned that they should not abandon the attempt to induce the Indian High Commissioner to return: 'to disabuse U.N.O. of any intent on our part of merely adopting delaying tactics'. Shepstone added that Kajee was disheartened: he 'talks of going to see Jinnah in India'. Kajee himself tried to get in touch with the Prime Minister: 'The internal situation in the Indian community is disturbed,' he wrote to Smuts' secretary, 'I fear that the moderate policy, which I and those with me have pursued, is being undermined by an extremist group openly backed by the Communist Party; in fact the movement is led by some members of this party'. Kajee had plans to recapture the Natal Indian Congress, but he wanted some kind of backing from Smuts: it 'would help me considerably'. Smuts did not send any reply.[42]

As the date for the termination of British rule in India — 15 August — came nearer, Smuts was no nearer to being reconciled to the break; on 5 July he telegraphed, objecting to the term 'independence' in the draft Bill; he suggested that 'autonomous' should be substituted. Mackenzie King also objected. But Attlee and his colleagues had travelled too far to turn back: and they did not intend to turn back.

The U.N. debate had certain repercussions upon Commonwealth attitudes to the Indians. Southern Rhodesia proposed to introduce legislation on South African lines to prohibit Indians from buying property in certain European areas. The United Kingdom government still exercised residual powers over law-making in Southern Rhodesia, and it had to consider whether to block such a measure. In September 1946, Sir Arthur Guest, the Rhodesian Minister of Finance came to London for discussions, and saw Machtig about the proposed restrictions on Indians. The justification advanced was that South African Indians, prohibited from acquiring property under the Ghetto Act, were transferring their operations to Southern Rhodesia, where Europeans were becoming restive. Arthur Bottomly, Under Secretary for the Dominions, informed Guest (16 September) that the United Kingdom view was that to proceed with the legislation would provoke agitation in India and another reference to the U.N. Because Britain was 'internationally responsible' for Southern Rhodesia, this would be 'very embarrassing'; Rhodesia was therefore asked not to go any further until after the U.N. debate on South Africa. This was sufficiently ominous to Southern Rhodesian susceptibilities to cause them to suspend their restrictive proposals. On 24 April 1947, the Dominions Office told the India Office that no more had been heard of pegging legislation in Southern Rhodesia.

Even more striking was the impact of the debate upon Canada. Louis St. Laurent, the Canadian Foreign Minister was present in New York, and like the head of the External Affairs Ministry, Lester Pearson, he was disturbed. It appeared as though Mackenzie King's combination of isolationism and chauvinism was not going to serve Canada any longer. On 6 December 1946, A. V. Pai wrote on behalf of the Government of India directly to the Canadian Ministry of External Affairs to ask that the Canadian Government should use its influence with the franchise committee then at work in British Columbia. Pai received the standard Canadian answer from St. Laurent on 6 January 1947: 'the problem is very complex'. However, the spectacle of South Africa's indictment at the U.N. had not been lost on Canada. The British Columbia committee recommended by a majority that the vote should be given to Indian and Chinese Canadians (a minority also recommended giving the vote to Japanese Canadians). Assent was given to the recommendation in April, and St. Laurent asked the United Kingdom High Commissioner to offer his congratulations to India. The U.N. High Commissioner told the Dominions Office (15 May 1947) that Indians were now eligible to stand as candidates in the elections, and also to serve as jurymen. They had to possess an 'adequate knowledge' of English or French to claim the vote: and they were still excluded from the municipal franchise in British Columbia.

The official British, United Kingdom view remained distinctly cool about the success of India's U.N. appeal. On 10 May 1947, R. H. S. Allen of the Foreign Office wrote to A. Campbell at the Colonial Office about Indian diplomatic activity. The South African defence — that the issue was a domestic matter — was legally correct, observed Mr Allen: but 'Politics and emotionalism defeated this legally correct view'.

Meanwhile, Burma had reached the ultimate stage before independence. At the beginning of January Aung San arrived in London, with Tin Tut at his elbow, to negotiate terms; on 27 January agreement was reached between Attlee and Aung San, summarised by the latter as 'full independence within one year'; in the interval, Burma would have the status of a Dominion Government. Nehru recognised the changed circumstances by withdrawing Mehta as India's representative, appointing in his place Dr M. A. Rauf, who was born in Burma and had played an important part in Indo-Burmese politics. Governor Rance received a visit from a High Court Judge, Ba U (later President of Burma) to complain about the appointment. Rauf had been suspected of taking bribes when he was Second Judge of the Rangoon Court, Ba U alleged, and when 'caustic comments' were made by the High Court he 'found it prudent to leave Burma'. Rance related this story to Pethick-Lawrence (8 January 1947) adding that Rauf's brother, M. A. Raschid had played a key role in trade union politics in Burma and was a close associate of Aung San; Rance suggested Nehru was hoping that his new appointment 'will pay good dividends'. It was the first of a number of 'political' appointments to diplomatic posts which Nehru proceeded to make.

The announcement of 'full independence' and Dominion status for Burma, followed closely by Attlee's statement that Britain would quit India in 1948 had the effect of bringing Ceylon politics up to the boil again.

Senanayake presented the Governor with a *démarche*, as Sir Henry Moore described it.[43] He also wrote to Creech Jones, stating bluntly 'We cannot accept a lower status than they [India and Burma] or be told patronisingly that we may possibly be fit for self-government if we behave well under the new constitution.' In Ceylon they were saying that 'Dominion status by evolution' was only required from those who did not take part in a rebellion against the British. Senanayake said quite frankly that a considerable number of his colleagues in the State Council wanted an immediate agitation, and it was necessary for him to provide evidence that moderation also paid dividends, or else 'the pressure upon us to agitate for complete independence will become overwhelming'.

Senanayake repeated the demands he had made on his visit to London in 1945; he wanted the 'very early' grant of full Dominion status and, immediately, the excision from the new constitution of Britain's overall control over defence and external affairs.

Creech Jones immediately acquainted Attlee with the purport of Senanayake's demands (22 March 1947). He endorsed them completely:

> Mr Senanayake confidently claims that, if early action is taken to meet his request, he will be able to keep Ceylon within the Commonwealth, which he is most sincerely anxious to do.
>
> The Governor of Ceylon has also written to me endorsing Mr Senanayake's view as to the dangers of the political situation, and supporting Mr Senanayake's request for further concessions, which, he urges, should have serious and urgent consideration.
>
> Mr Senanayake has sent Sir Oliver Goonetilleke, the Financial Secretary of Ceylon, who is a close personal friend of his, over here to conduct discussions with me on his behalf. I propose to see him and hear what he has to say.

In his own personal account of the next critical phase in Ceylon's drive for independence, Sir Charles Jeffries observes 'It fell to Sir Oliver to do a good deal of the batting in private and informal discussions with the Ministers and senior officials with whom he was *persona grata*'.[44]

Just how skilfully Goonetilleke batted may be gathered from the record of a lunch-time discussion with John Strachey, then Minister of Food. Sir Oliver aroused Strachey by emphasising 'the intense fears which he and his government entertained of an independent India'. They feared armed aggression by India, and did not believe that Britain would move to protest. Strachey was reassuring: the transfer of power was 'a purely voluntary act', and the present British government—or any future government—'would regard it as an inescapable obligation to protect any state which remained within the Commonwealth' (though Strachey did discount an Indian invasion as 'a very unlikely event'). Great Britain could be relied upon to bring its 'ample armed forces' into action to protect Ceylon against India; Strachey recorded that Goonetilleke was 'much comforted' by his assurances. The gullible future author of *The End of Empire* reported his conversation to his colleague, Creech Jones, (9 May 1947). The intention of the Sinhalese in power was to create the impression of a dangerous and threatening India and of a loyal, willing Ceylon: whose future could be assured by the immediate grant of dominion status, but who in default might run wild and fall into the clutches of India.

In Ceylon the Governor and his lady observed events with their shrewd *sens du possible*. Lady Moore had become an intimate friend of

Smuts while they were in Kenya, and now she passed on her impressions of the Ceylon bid for independence. When she wrote to Smuts on 2 April, S. W. R. D. Bandaranaike had just returned from the Asian Relations Conference at Delhi: 'He is the most brilliant and the most anti-British' of the Ministers, she wrote; he wanted an end to the British ascendancy, 'but Ceylon's fear of Indian domination is the life-belt that may keep us afloat here for some years to come'. Sir Henry Moore was supporting the 'reasonable request' of the Ministers for Dominion status—as he had done in 1945—Lady Moore hoped that the Colonial Office would 'swallow the gnat this time'. 'Senanayake is prepared to withstand Left Wing pressures and the blandishments of India and to keep Ceylon within the Commonwealth provided his hand is strengthened by the Cabinet decision to grant Dominion status immediately': it was partly a question of national prestige, and getting a seat at the U.N. 'If Dominion status allows us an opportunity of playing for time, it is worth trying and at least it can do no harm': Senanayake wanted this status 'For their own sake, and not for love of us, to keep out of India's clutches'.[45]

The finale to Goonetilleke's lobbying operation in London and to the persuasive influences upon Sir Henry Moore was very satisfactory to the Sinhalese Ministers. On 18 June, Creech Jones told the House of Commons that as soon as the next elections were held and a new government assembled in Ceylon: 'Immediate steps will be taken to amend the constitution so as to confer upon Ceylon fully responsible status within the British Commonwealth of Nations.'

Concerning Bandaranaike's visit to the Asian Relations Conference, the *Ceylon Daily News* (7 April 1947) reported the Minister as declaring that he hoped that India and Ceylon could now settle their differences. Among his reasons were the success of the Delhi conference which, said Bandaranaike, had spread 'a new conception of unity among the Asian countries'; the next negotiations between India and Ceylon would be free of 'old suspicions'. India now appeared to recognise the impossibility of dual citizenship; Nehru was appealing to Indians overseas to identify with their adopted countries, as Bandaranaike observed. However, he had told Nehru that talks would only be possible when both countries had emerged from the transitional phase.

It appeared that the Burma Government was not prepared to wait for independence before settling the immigration issue. The Emergency Immigration Act was promulgated on 14 June 1947 to control all immigration, foreign and Commonwealth. Mahn Ba Khaing, the Minister for Labour and Industries, announced that this was an emergency measure, and long term arrangements between Burma and India would be 'based on friendly relations... between the two countries'. Nehru sent a telegram to Aung San on 16 June protesting against the move, and professing 'surprise and disappointment': 'I consider the present time most inopportune for passing an Emergency Act in such a hurried manner', he concluded. The Government of India announced that the new act would prevent 150,000 Indians, mostly labourers and their dependents, from returning to their old homes in Burma.[46] There was an official Indian protest, which Burma rejected: 245,773 Indians had entered Burma during the sixteen months ending April 1947, against 141,728 Indians who had left. No obstacle would be erected to stop returning evacuees, the Burma Government declared.[47]

In Malaya, the year 1947 was largely one of marking time so far as the Indians were concerned, though a fierce political debate was in progress over the future of the Malayan Union. This was largely a Malay and British controversy; there was little to be gained for the Indians by intervening in this debate about the rights of sultans. Industrial conflict became acute during the early months of 1947; Indian workers were no longer prepared to accept pay-scales markedly lower than those gained by the Chinese. Disputes were specially fierce in Kedah, and on one estate on 3 March, fifty-seven labourers were arrested and given six months' imprisonment. Chettur, the Agent, was active in trying to bring about conciliation, but he only earned the enmity of the British planters. Early in May he informed the Government of India that there was a danger of simultaneous strikes on 250 estates. The Government of India addressed a request to Sir Edward Gent for a commission of inquiry into the conditions of the Indians: 'Failure to hold an inquiry will very seriously prejudice the prospects of the supply of Indian labour to Malaya in the future', the Malayan Government was told.[48] The Governor of the Malayan Union replied to the Indian Government that 'no useful purpose' would be served by the inquiry: the grievances of the Indians had been 'fully ventilated' (26 May 1947). Creech Jones concurred; he told the India Office (2 July 1947) that he was satisfied that labour problems were getting proper attention.

S. K. Chettur had not managed to satisfy the Indian community, though he had been bold enough in his speeches. The Indian Regional Congress in Singapore (a branch of the Malayan Indian Congress) cabled Nehru to ask for another Indian representative, who should not be a civil servant. Nehru selected John Thivy; an appointment very similar to that of M. A. Rauf in Burma.

The question of India's representation in Colonial Office territories where there were sizeable Indian communities—so much considered in the 1920s and 1930s—had become important again when Nehru took charge of external relations. On 27 November 1946 the Commonwealth Relations Department of the Government of India addressed the India Office on the subject once more: 'With the present change in the Government of India the need for the appointment of its representatives in different parts of the Commonwealth has received additional importance.' It was desired 'to foster closer and more cordial relations between the people of India and of those Colonies [East Africa, the British West Indies, and Mauritius] as well as to establish closer relations with the Governments of those Colonies'. As a first step, India would like to send a delegation to Mauritius.

There was no written response to this request; perhaps because C. S. Jha and R. N. Banerjee came to London in December 1946 to discuss a number of questions, including that of the Agents. A reminder was sent to London from Delhi in January, and on 18 March 1947, Sir Terence Shone, the new U. K. High Commissioner to India, cabled to Whitehall to ask whether a reply was coming.[49] The Colonial Office was consulting with the Foreign Office, and R. H. S. Allen told Campbell (10 May) that 'Indians both want to have their cake and eat it: i.e., to be members of the British Commonwealth with full civic rights, including the franchise, and to retain a right of appeal to India for support.' Minority groups could be dangerous, said Allen, citing the case of the Sudeten Germans. Would the Indians in the colonies be compelled to opt either for British or Indian nationality, 'and whether, in the latter case, they will be liable to be sent back to India?' he asked. There could be no objection to the appointment of Agents, but their functions 'should be clearly limited and defined' and Indians 'should be obliged to decide whether they wish to be regarded as Indians or settlers in the territories concerned'.

Creech Jones was not ready even to go as far as the Foreign Office suggested, and he caused one of his officials (J. S. Bennett) to write thus (22 May) 'Until the national status of Indian populations in the Colonies has been defined and until the transfer of power in India has taken place, Mr Creech Jones does not consider that it would be practicable to determine on the appointment of Agents, or with the definition of their functions'. Nor did he see 'what useful purpose' a delegation to Mauritius would serve; it would be 'premature'. The letter ended: 'Mr Creech Jones trusts that the Secretary of State for India will share these views and will be prepared to send a suitable reply to the Government of India opposing the Government of India's proposal.'

This was too much even for the expiring India Office. P. J. Patrick ruefully noted that even if India remained in the Commonwealth, the Colonial Office 'would no doubt find reasons to avoid accepting official Agents' (27 May 1947). Another reminder from Delhi indicated that something ought to be done. Pethick-Lawrence had left the India Office in April, and Lord Listowel was Secretary of State for the brief period remaining until the transfer of power. He told Creech Jones (6 June) that 'it would hardly be good policy to support them [the Colonial Office views] at this present delicate juncture': could they discuss a compromise?

This did not elicit any response, but Listowel was goaded into activity by a personal letter from Nehru, dated 20 June and received on 26 June. The letter was courteously and tactfully phrased:

Our proposals were inspired not by any desire to promote any separatist tendencies amongst the Indian populations of these Colonies or to alienate them from the Governments under which they live but to help them and their Governments to understand each other better and also to establish closer relations.

The long delay in replying to the letter of 27 November 1946 was creating 'impatience'; could the Indian Acting High Commissioner see Creech Jones, and could Listowel discuss the matter personally?

When Creech Jones was supplied with a copy of this letter he at last responded. His letter (dated 30 June) was in the ponderous Colonial Office style, four pages in length. He was 'prepared to agree in principle to the appointment of Indian representatives in the Colonies with effect from the enactment of the legislation in August which will confer Dominion status on India or on Hindustan and Pakistan'. Paragraph 4 explained why the Colonial Office had hesitated so long:

The danger of Indian representatives or agents is, of course, that their appointment in colonies where there is a substantial Indian population would be liable to encourage the local Indians to think of themselves as a self-contained national community and to discourage the process of assimilation which we have been trying to foster in the Colonies. In the past, many Indians have treated their life in a colony as a sojourn for making money and have returned to India, or at least remitted their profits to India . . . Even in those territories [where Indians are permanently settled] however, the problem of discouraging Indian segregation or separation from the general life of the community is a real one. In territories nearer to India, such as East Africa and Mauritius, the difficulty is even more acute. Since Indians in all our colonies share in the common life and all political or social rights of other inhabitants of the territory, such protection by an outside authority is not called for, and indeed is something which in my view we ought to discourage as being against the best interests of the local Indians themselves.

If there were to be Indian representatives, the Colonial Office would insist on 'severe limits on the intervention of the Indian Governments [sic] in colonial affairs...They would be there not as 'protectors' of persons of Indian race...but to represent the legitimate interests of the Government of India'. Creech Jones expected difficulties in defining the boundaries of these 'legitimate interests' because of the common code of nationality throughout the British Commonwealth:

So long as India remains part of the British Commonwealth there is no short way on nationality grounds of distinguishing those Indians in a colony who are genuine local residents and part of the local community, and those Indians who may just be, so to speak, visiting the territory ... All Indians are British subjects, and I fear it will be very difficult to draw an effective line.

Clearly, Creech Jones had forgotten the time, not so long before, when he had stood up in the House of Commons to ask for the appointment of Indian Agents in the West Indies, etc. The suspicions which had engrossed Ormsby-Gore, Cranborne, and almost every politician translated to the Colonial Office had enveloped Creech Jones. He had at least conceded the appointments 'in principle', but there was a further delay in replying to Nehru because it was considered necessary to convey the information first of all to Sir Terence Shone. Meanwhile, Mountbatten joined in the dialogue: he wrote to Listowel on 4 July 1947. An assurance to Nehru would be welcome, declared Mountbatten, 'in view of his peculiar frame of mind and the difficult negotiations I have on hand'.

At last it was done. On 18 July, Listowel informed Nehru that H.M.G. 'are agreeable in principle to the appointment of such representatives in East Africa, Fiji, Mauritius, and the British West Indies'. Instructions were being sent to Sir Terence Shone, said Listowel, and a telegram went off to him next day.[50] The Colonial Office indicated that 'We would like to see instructions...so framed as to ensure that they refrain from encouraging separatist tendencies among Indians settled in Colonies: before appointments were made, H.M.G. would like to discuss with the Government of India the text of the instructions to be given to its representatives.' The India Office noted (31 July 1947) that the Colonial Office telegram was an 'irritating and turgid document...not calculated to achieve the desired ends'.

By now, the officials of the India Office and the Dominions Office were preparing to make a reluctant marriage under the new name of Commonwealth Relations Office. India was about to be free. On 15 August, 'At the stroke of midnight, India will awake' said Jawaharlal Nehru. And all across the world, in Mauritius, in Kenya, even in South Africa, in Trinidad, in Guiana, in Fiji, Indians awakened to the same feeling that the slave Blacks had awakened to in 1834: they were free—they were the equals of their British masters at last.

9
The Test of Independence
(1947-49)

At the moment when the new India and Pakistan became independent there were about four million people originally from undivided India within the Commonwealth. The largest communities were those in Ceylon and Burma, each numbering over 750,000, but proportionally the Indians in Ceylon were more important, forming 12 per cent of the total island population, whereas in Burma they were less than 4 per cent of the total. As noted previously, the Indians in Malaya had suffered a serious decline because of the Japanese occupation; the 1947 Census enumerated 520,000 (11 per cent of the total) in the Malayan Union, while in Singapore Indians numbered 69,000 (7.5 per cent). The South African Indians formed the next largest community: 285,260 (1946) with the Indians of Mauritius almost as many, 265,247 (1944), though in South Africa they were only 3 per cent of the total population while in Mauritius they were more than two-thirds of the whole.

Then came a group of sugar colonies in which the Indians were substantial minorities, on the way to becoming in time the majority of the population. In Trinidad, at the 1946 Census, the Indians (or East Indians) numbered 195,747 in a total population of 557,970, and thus formed 35 per cent of the total; in British Guiana they were already the largest racial group, and 163,434 Indians (1946)—compared to 143,385 Africans and 37,685 persons of mixed origin—formed 42 per cent of the total. The situation was very similar in Fiji where there were 125,000 Indians enumerated at the 1948 Census (47 per cent of the total population), compared to 121,000 Fijians.

There were other Indian communities in the West Indies: 26,000 in Jamaica, 4,000 in Grenada and 3,000 in St Lucia, but these were fragmented and separated groups; their other stronghold, beside Trinidad and Guiana, was Dutch Surinam, where they numbered about 65,000 or 30 per cent of the colony's population.[1]

In East Africa the Indians were a minute fraction of the total population, but their numbers had increased markedly since before the Second World War; immigration had certainly been a factor in this rise. At the 1948 Census there were 90,528 Indians in Kenya (as well as 7,159 Goans) 44,248 in Tanganyika and 33,767 in Uganda with 15,812 in Zanzibar. Nearby Aden had an Indian population of 9,456 (1946).

Most of these Indian communities were preponderantly Hindu in origin, though the Muslims in East Africa were important and well established in trade and industry. Of the Kenya Indians (90,528) 45,000 were Hindus and 28,000 Muslims, with 11,000 Sikhs; many of the latter were concentrated in Nairobi. Tanganyika's 44,248 Indians included 26,000 Muslims and 15,000 Hindus, with 2,000 Sikhs; Uganda contained 20,000 Hindus, 11,000 Muslims and 1,550 Sikhs. A large majority of the Zanzibar Indians were Muslims, and in Aden 7,500 were Muslims and Parsis with only 1,957 Hindus.

In the West Indies the Hindus formed the majority of the Indians, descendants of indentured labourers; the Trinidad Indians—195,747 —included 126,300 Hindus, 32,600 Muslims, and an important minority of Christian converts. The Fiji Indians consisted of 103,000 Hindus, only 18,000 Muslims, 2,200 Christians and 1,000 Sikhs. The Indian population in Malaya and Singapore in 1947 totalled 599,616; of these 545,385 came originally from South India, 460,985 being Tamils. The great majority of them were Hindus, mostly from the lower castes and Untouchables. There were 10,132 Sikhs also, and 20,460 classified as Punjabis, of whom most were Muslims. The Indians in Ceylon and Malaya were overwhelmingly Hindus, though in Burma there were Muslim communities of importance in Arakan, and a group formerly called *Zerbadis*, Muslims of mixed Indian and Burmese parentage, numbering 122,705 in 1931.

Perhaps because of the small proportion of Muslims in these overseas communities—perhaps because of the traditional preoccupation with the Muslims of the Near and Middle East—the new Pakistan was slow to take an interest in those whom it seems natural to continue to call overseas Indians, though in East Africa they were increasingly referred to as Asians.

The new Government of India was anxious to see Indian representatives installed in those colonial territories which Creech Jones had agreed 'in principle' should receive the Indian Agents—or Commissioners as he preferred to designate them—on the analogy of High Commissioners.

On 2 August 1947, just before independence, Subimal Dutt of the Department of External Affairs and Commonwealth Relations wrote to the United Kingdom High Commissioner (called the British High Commissioner hereafter) to enclose a draft of the instructions it was intended to hand to the Government of India's Agent in East Africa, which would form a model for the others. The draft began reassuringly: 'You will be the representative of the Government of India in the East African territories and not a spokesman of the resident

Indian community'. But some of the additional instructions were likely to cause raised eyebrows at the Colonial Office. The Agent was told to 'use your good offices with the Governments of the territories in order to explain to them whenever necessary the point of view of the resident Indian community'; he was also 'to foster and promote good relations between the various sections of the Indian population and between the resident Indian communities on the one hand and other races inhabiting East Africa, and the Governments of these territories on the other'. He was told that the Government of India 'will continue to communicate direct with His Majesty's Government' on questions of policy though the Agent might 'discuss routine administrative problems affecting Indians' with the local governments.

India had been quick off the mark; the Colonial Office also had its own formula for the new 'Commissioners', but took its time in bringing it forward because in its usual circumambulatory way the office desired to clear the formula with its own departments and with the Foreign Office and the Commonwealth Relations Office. It was not until 23 August that a telegram went off to the British High Commissioner at Delhi with a proposed draft instruction, which it was expected the Government of India would adopt for its representatives. The draft read exactly as though India was still subordinate to Whitehall.

The Commissioner would be informed that he was to promote good relations between India and the Colony and to discharge consular functions: 'He will be guided in his contacts with the local Indian community by the principle that all inhabitants of the territory owe their first duty to the duly constituted Colonial Government, which in turn is responsible to His Majesty's Government in the United Kingdom... He will not therefore intervene in local political matters. These fall to be dealt with under the normal constitutional machinery of the Colonial Government.' The Commissioner 'will have as his concern Indians who are in the territory otherwise than for the purpose of permanent residence... The interests of Indians born in, or permanently resident in the territory will not (repeat not) come within his sphere. This dictum will apply *inter alia* to the issue and renewal of passports.'

The whole question had become complicated before discussions had even started. H. A. F. Rumbold of the Commonwealth Relations Office told J. S. Bennett of the Colonial Office quite bluntly (9 September 1947) that they had lost the initiative; they must now act upon the Indian draft: 'The instructions are, after all, their instructions to their own men.' The Colonial Office with its tradition of overriding the India Office was certainly not going to accept that argument. When the Governors of the East African and West Indian territories, Mauritius, and Fiji were informed on 20 September that Indian Commissioners would shortly be appointed, they were informed of the Colonial Office version of the instructions (including, 'They will not meddle in local political matters'). There might be 'certain difficulties', the Colonial Office advised.

The Government of India did not tamely accept the Colonial Office formula, as the British High Commissioner reported to the Commonwealth Relations Office (C.R.O.) on 11 October: they did 'not feel able to disinterest themselves in the fate of Indians established in the colonies'. Indeed, Sir Terence Shone enquired: why should not the Indian Commissioners 'take an unofficial interest in the well-being of all Indian communities there? My own position *vis-à-vis* the domiciled European community here is after all likely to become *mutatis mutandis* somewhat similar.' Surely if Indian propaganda was cultural, not political, this was acceptable? 'If this assumption is not correct and if fundamentally your policy is one of de-Indianisation of these communities' then it would be necessary to introduce further restrictions on the Commissioners: though 'there would be little prospect of the Government of India agreeing to them'.

Shone was puzzled by the 'vexed question of nationality': Indians who had renounced British citizenship 'will, I imagine, be entitled to look to the Indian representative for protection'. But citizenship laws were in the melting pot, and all that Galsworthy of the Colonial Office could suggest to Gilchrist at the C.R.O. was that 'when both sides have concluded the citizenship arrangements...it should be possible to determine by reference to citizenship the categories of Indians in Colonial territories for whom Indian representatives can legitimately exercise functions analagous to those of consular representatives' (20 October 1947). This did not get over the immediate difficulties. Rumbold told his chief, the Secretary for Commonwealth Relations, Philip Noel-Baker, that though India was unlikely to accept the Colonial Office formula they must pursue this line. Noel-Baker noted: 'I confess to grave and continuing doubts about the wisdom and utility of the agreed [Colonial Office] instructions'; reluctantly, he wrote to the British High Commissioner at Delhi to urge the Colonial Office line: the overseas Indians 'should identify themselves with the territory in which they have chosen to reside'.

A. C. B. Symon, now British High Commissioner, had an interview with Sir Girja Shanker Bajpai, now permanent head of the Ministry of External Affairs and Commonwealth Relations. Symon told Patrick (25 October 1947) 'Bajpai said that he did not think that we need worry unduly about the so-called instructions since the Indian

Agents or Commissioners would not do anything to affect H.M.G.'s interests... It would create suspicion and perhaps further criticism of our intentions if the matter was not settled soon.' Bajpai said in conclusion that he was 'One of perhaps a small group of people who wished to see India remain in the Empire and that he was doing everything he could to bring this about'; British attitudes to the new Indian representatives could affect this question.

Perhaps in response to Bajpai's shrewdly aimed thrust, Whitehall came up with a proposal for instructions based upon the Indian Government's first draft, though considerably modified to suit the Colonial Office. It included the proviso that the Commissioners should not intervene in questions relating to Indians 'permanently identified with the territories'. Bajpai saw Symon about this; the proviso was 'entirely unobjectionable' he said, but where the laws did not permit them to acquire the status of 'permanent residents' (as in Malaya) the distinction would be difficult to follow. Altogether, Bajpai felt that the instructions were 'too narrow...[they] smacked of former days and might...argue a lack of trust'.

However, the Government of India eventually agreed to the draft in February 1948, for time was passing. L. A. C. Fry of the British High Commission observed to Gilchrist (12 February 1948): 'The Government of India, anxious as they are to appoint these representatives...have decided to stop arguing about the instructions their men are to be given officially; official instructions can always be varied unofficially.'

In order to prepare the colonies for the new situation supposedly created by the arrival of the Indian Commissioners, Creech Jones circulated a despatch to all the governors on 7 April 1948 laying down a general policy towards Indian intervention: the new Commissioners must be dissuaded from taking up the cause of Indians who 'belonged' to the colonies. But there was no indication of any positive Colonial Office initiative to induce the colonial Indians to feel more of a sense of belonging.

Probably Nehru's most talked about 'political' diplomatic appointment was to bring V. K. Krishna Menon, former secretary of the India League, St Pancras borough councillor, and expelled member of the Labour Party, into India House in London as independent India's first High Commissioner. He now took over some of the functions on India's behalf that the old India Office had discharged: he became the Government of India's go-between in dealings with Whitehall departments. Thus, he now approached the Commonwealth Relations Office to obtain clearance for India's first Commissioners.

Four names were submitted in May 1948. Satya Charan was

nominated as Commissioner to the British West Indies; he was from the United Provinces, and was a protégé of Pandit Pant, the Congress leader of the U. P. Charan had been Secretary of the Indians Overseas Department of the All-India Congress Committee. S. A. Waiz was nominated to go to Fiji; he was a Christian, and at one time secretary to C. F. Andrews; he was now secretary of the Imperial Indian Citizenship Association of Bombay. For Mauritius, the name of Dharam Yash Dev was submitted, he was Director of Publicity for the Constituent Assembly and had also been Secretary of the Indians Overseas Department, AICC. As Commissioner in East Africa, Nehru wished to send Apa B. Pant, son of the Raja of Aundh, and a disciple of Gandhi. Krishna Menon put his name up to the Commonwealth Relations Office on 25 May 1948.

The agreement of the Governors of these colonies was sought, and by the third week of June the names of Satya Charan, Waiz, and Yash Dev had all been approved. Replies had been received from the Governors of Uganda and Tanganyika accepting the nomination of Apa B. Pant. Kenya, however, responded in a style reminiscent of every other suggestion that an eminent Indian should be received as an Indian Government emissary, from the time of Sastri and Grigg onward. Sir Philip Mitchell cabled the Colonial Office on 11 June that he had been informed by a retired I.C.S. officer now resident in Kenya that Pant was 'far from being desirable. He is said to be extremely Left in sympathies, known to have been involved in sabotage in India during the war, and is most likely to cause trouble if he comes to East Africa. Indeed, I am told that it is not beyond the realms of possibility that he is being sent here for that purpose'.

The Colonial Office reacted solemnly to this revelation, but the response at the C.R.O. was almost flippant. F. H. Cleobury wrote to J. O. Moreton at the Colonial Office (18 June 1948):

It seems agreed that he is quite a pleasant person to deal with and is intellectually sound. He was at Balliol. So far as his extreme views are concerned, the simple truth is that they are no more extreme than those of the leaders of the Government of India. We can find no support for the suggestion that he has engaged in sabotage. Incidentally, if he had so engaged after the entry of Russia into the war it would at least show that he is not a communist. We can in any case feel confident that he is not a communist and he has the confidence of the present Government of India. The worst that can be said about him . . . is that he was regarded as an enthusiast.

A Colonial Office version of this testimonial was cabled to Mitchell (29 June): 'No one whom we or C.R.O. have been able to contact is of the view that there are sufficient grounds for refusing him. He will of course be a keen champion of Indian causes but so would any representative nominated by the present Indian government.'

Mitchell briefly acknowledged the message (2 July 1948), 'Pant: I agree'. And so, on 8 July, 44 days after Apa B. Pant's name was first put up, the C.R.O. told Krishna Menon that they accepted his nomination. It was not a hopeful start, on the British side, and it was clear that Apa B. Pant would be watched, and his every pronouncement scrutinised, for evidence of the Left Wing, revolutionary, subversive tendencies of which he had been accused.

The Colonial Office still wanted to make sure that its conditions were going to be observed. An official announcement about the Indian Commissioners was issued in July stating that their 'duties are similar to those of consular representatives. They will be concerned *only* with Indians visiting their territories otherwise than for the purpose of permanent residence'. This was not the final, agreed formula at all, and Krishna Menon protested to Noel-Baker (10 August 1948); the garbled version 'has naturally created some misunderstanding in India'.

Nehru was obliged to try to reassure the Constituent Assembly on the position. There was, indeed, considerable ambiguity in the minds of Indian politicians about the Indian communities overseas, which Nehru tried to dispel. In an interview given to the *Statesman* newspaper (24 November 1947) Pandit Kunzru hoped that the new representatives would foster cultural relations between India and the overseas Indians, who had been 'cut off from their mother country for decades. There is no culture in the colonies... which can take the place of their ancient culture, and the absence of a vivifying contact between them and India has stunted their growth'. But this did not help to define the future political relationship between Indians overseas and the Indian Union. The difficulty was explored by Nehru in a speech to the Constituent Assembly on 8 March 1948:

Now these Indians abroad, what are they? Are they Indian citizens — are they going to be citizens of India or not? If they are not, then our interest in them becomes cultural, humanitarian, and not political. That interest, of course, remains. For instance, take the Indians in Fiji or Mauritius; are they going to retain their nationality, or will they become Fijian nationals or Mauritians? The same question arises in regard to Burma and Ceylon. It is a difficult question. This House gets mixed up. It wants to treat them as Indians, and with the same breath it wants a complete franchise for them in the countries where they are living. Of course, the two things do not go together. Either they get the franchise as nationals of the other country, or, treat them as Indians minus the franchise and ask for them the most favourable treatment given to an alien.

In the context of the Colonial Office announcement, Nehru rose on 9 August to answer a question put to him in the Constituent Assembly by B. Shiva Rao: could the Indian Commissioners deal with the problems of permanent residents? Nehru responded with an answer which was more gratifying to the British High Commissioner than to Indian nationalists of the 'forward' school: 'The Indian Commissioners will not be entitled to discharge consular functions in respect of Indians who may not be considered to be nationals, that is permanent residents in these territories or to act as the spokesmen of such Indians'. Supplementary questions followed after Shiva Rao's first question: where Indians were denied the rights of citizenship would the Commissioners protect them? Nehru replied: 'It is a question of constitutional nationality. Either they are nationals of India or they are not. We are intensely interested in them, but legally, can we help them? This is a doubtful matter which will have to be decided as developments take place'. The draft Indian constitution was already being evolved, and overseas Indians could claim citizenship by ancestry, if registered with the consular or diplomatic representative of India in that particular country. But Nehru did not examine the question of dual citizenship, which was to play a major part in the future.

And so the new commissioners took up their posts, along with the representatives already installed in Burma, Ceylon, Malaya and other Commonwealth countries. There was one notable absentee: the post of High Commissioner in South Africa remained unfilled.[2]

The dispute between India and South Africa simmered on, though at the beginning of 1948 it appeared that some kind of bargain might be arranged; then came the shock of Smuts' defeat at the polls (May 1948). There was a final, vain attempt at a meeting between India Pakistan and South Africa in February 1950. With its failure began the long descent of the South African Indians into political oblivion.

For the second session of the United Nations, due to begin in September 1947, both India and South Africa prepared reports to be submitted to the General Assembly.[3] The Indian statement was a factual, although perhaps partisan, account of events since the previous December, ending with the Smuts-Nehru correspondence; it was claimed that South Africa had 'completely ignored the resolution of the U.N.G.A.' The South African document was much more like an address by Counsel for the defence in a legal action; it suggested that the interpretation of the U. N. Charter accepted the previous December was erroneous, while India was said to be attempting to go beyond the terms of the Franco-Mexican resolution.

The first committee of the U. N. reached the South African Indian question on 12 November 1947. Senator Lawrence was now the spokesman for South Africa, while Mrs Pandit again appeared for India and Sir Zafrullah Khan and M. A. H. Ispahani represented Pakistan. The debate wound its way through six sessions of the first committee. It was noticeable that (by contrast to the previous year) the White Commonwealth members remained almost silent throughout the debate, though Berendsen of New Zealand made another plea to refer the question of jurisdiction to the International Court, and Hector McNeill, now Minister at the Foreign Office and a conspicuous anti-Communist, made a number of Cold War comparisons.

The draft resolution which India put to the first committee was considerably diluted as a result of the discussions, and in the form presented to the General Assembly expressed no criticism of South Africa. The resolution of the previous year was reaffirmed, and in addition the U.N. would request 'the two governments to enter into discussions at a round table conference without any further delay and to invite the Government of Pakistan to take part'.

When the question was debated again in the Assembly, Lawrence made as effective a case as he might, stressing the repatriation provisions of the Cape Town agreements, which India had made no effort to implement, and also emphasising that as the South African Indians were now represented in parliament there was no longer an argument for the Government of India to intervene as their advocate. Mrs Pandit rejected the representation argument: 'We look upon it as a sham franchise and we are perfectly willing that that franchise should be repealed now and at once'. She appealed once again to the Commonwealth, asking them 'to reflect very seriously over the certain consequences all over Asia and Africa of voting down a resolution of this character'. No other Commonwealth spokesman participated in the Assembly debate; not even Pakistan.

When the roll-call vote was taken, India received virtually the same support as the previous year:

General Assembly, 20 November 1947: Indian-Mexican Resolution

For India		For South Africa	
Communist Bloc	6	White Commonwealth	5
Afro-Asians	14	West Europeans	7
Latin Americans	8	U.S.A. and Latin American allies	7
West Europeans	3		
Totals:	31		19

Abstained: 6 (Bolivia, Cuba, Dominica, Ecuador, Peru, Uruguay)

Yet the resolution failed to obtain a two-thirds majority, and was rejected. India maintained the previous support of the Communist bloc, and also received three West European votes (France, Iceland

—and Turkey in place of Norway). The Afro-Asian vote remained absolutely firm, and was augmented by the new votes of Pakistan and Yemen. However, the Latin American vote fell away, and three previous Indian supporters abstained this time. For South Africa there was solid White Commonwealth support, with the return of Australia to the fold, and a welcome rise in West European support, with the adherence of all the Scandinavians except Iceland. The support of the United States and its Latin American followers remained constant. There was a subsequent attempt to secure a compromise with a resolution sponsored by Belgium, Brazil, Cuba, Denmark and Norway which also called for a round table conference, but stipulated that if it did not succeed the question should be referred to the International Court. This muddled motion—which clearly gave South Africa the trump card—attracted most of the countries which had voted against the Indian resolution, and was opposed by India's supporters. The result—29 in favour, 24 against —was nugatory.

The Soviet diplomat Gromyko was serving as President of the Assembly on this day, and he endeavoured to assist Mrs Pandit to salvage something from the wreckage by bringing forward a milder resolution. The same evening, Gromyko announced that he had received a new resolution and proposed that it be discussed at a future meeting. There was a legalistic argument, led by Hector McNeill, and the question was postponed, not to be raised again at the 1947 session of the U.N. India had suffered a significant defeat. The South African question had sunk into the same international swamp as Palestine and Kashmir, as a U.N. perennial which could never be resolved.

Lord Mountbatten made a personal effort to create an initiative. Towards the end of November 1947 he announced that he would visit South Africa as soon as the internal situation in the Punjab and Delhi had quietened down sufficiently for him to be away from India. 'He will go, he said, in the hope of bringing about an effective reconciliation between the Indians and South Africans...and a firm understanding between the two governments. After the royal wedding [between Princess Elizabeth and Prince Philip on 20 November 1947] he had several talks with General Smuts [in London] regarding the position of Indians in South Africa and India's retaliatory measures against Smuts' Indian policy.' Mountbatten's genius for bouncing people into decision-making did not work on this occasion, however.[4]

The U.N. debate had important repercussions in South Africa. Mrs Pandit's rejection of the franchise provisions gave Malan an opening to move the repeal of that part of the Asiatic Land Tenure and Indian Representation Act which had provided for Indian representation. Smuts' hold over parliament was strong enough to ensure Malan's defeat. The failure of India to obtain a passage for the 1947 resolution seemed, paradoxically, to smooth the way towards a round table conference, which Smuts would never have accepted under pressure from his adversaries in the U.N. Independently, he had changed his mind during the previous year, as Wavell discovered on a visit to the Union. His diary for *3 February* included this note: 'I motored into Cape Town this morning and saw Smuts and Hofmeyr... We talked of the state of Europe and then he went on to speak of the problems of Indians in S. Africa and his hopes of arranging a round table conference...' *15 February*: 'Everyone in S. Africa talks with apprehension about the Indian problem and the Native problem...and Smuts is now anxious for a round table conference to which I tried to get him to agree before the sanctions when I was Viceroy.'[5]

On 7 February 1948, Smuts' private secretary wrote to A. S. Kajee (brother of the late A. I. Kajee), President of the Natal Indian Organisation, appealing to the South African Indians to assist in bringing about a conference between the Union Government, India and Pakistan. The N.I.O. prepared to send a delegation to India to explore the prospects for a conference, though there was considerable opposition, even in the moderate N.I.O. to the Indians acting as Smuts' messengers.

The possibility of progress—a meagre possibility—was overthrown by the outcome of the general election held in South Africa at the end of May 1948. The United Party fought the election in alliance with the Labour Party. There was no disposition to move towards a more accommodating policy in the United Party's statements on race.[6] 'The Indian's prosperity is due to the inventive genius of the white man', the electors were told; while the demands of the South African Indians were ascribed to 'the situation in India'. The election brought the downfall of Smuts and the start of the apparently never-to-be-ended hegemony of the Nationalists.

Dr Malan did not immediately slam the door upon negotiation. He indicated that he was prepared to receive the leaders of the N.I.O., because they were not Communists; he was even prepared to consider a round table conference, provided that its agenda excluded domestic questions, and that it considered 'the objectives of the prior conferences of 1927 and 1932'. There could be little doubt that Malan intended to raise the almost defunct question of repatriation to India.

The other, and more fundamental side of the Nationalist programme was quickly revealed; in August 1948 Malan announced his intention to remove the Indians from the franchise, and also to abolish African representation in parliament while placing the Cape Coloured population upon a separate roll with their own representatives. These measures were partly tactical—to consolidate the Nationalist position in parliament against any possibility of a United Party come-back—but also they began the long process of Apartheid or Separate Development which would exclude the non-whites from any place within the white system for all time.

The policy of the Nationalist Government to the more militant Indians was almost openly punitive; they were forbidden to leave South Africa, and their U.N. activities were prohibited. The 1948 session of the U.N. passed without the South African Indian question being reached. Already, South African white leaders were questioning the further participation of their country in an organisation which held them up to open criticism.

Then came the most grievous incident in the history of the Indians in South Africa: the Durban riots of January 1949 in which Africans assaulted Indian shops, homes, and individuals. The rioters were severely repressed, and the final toll of the violence amounted to 142 deaths (including 50 Indians and 87 Africans) and 1,087 wounded, while a factory, 58 shops and 247 houses were destroyed, with severe damage to another thousand buildings. An official inquiry, headed by Judge van der Heever, attributed the riots to African resentment at Indian dominance in the labour market and in trade and industry.[7] The leaders of the two inflamed communities discovered the causes of the riots in the slum conditions into which their people were driven, and the growing atmosphere of repression. They replied to white condemnation by forming a joint council of the African National Congress and the South African Indian Congress (now under activist control) to promote understanding and cooperation between Africans and Indians.

Once again in 1949 the South African Indian issue came up for U.N. review. Eric Louw, South African Foreign Minister, attempted to forestall the usual criticism by submitting a resolution declaring that the issue was a domestic matter, not within the jurisdiction of the U.N. When the first committee voted on this proposition there was a noticeable change in the entrenched positions previously assumed by most states. South Africa obtained support from only four other states: Argentina, Brazil, Greece, and the Netherlands; the usual supporters of India united in voting down the resolution, but they were also joined by the United States, while all the White

Commonwealth countries abstained on the question. The South African proposal was therefore defeated by 33 votes to 5, with 12 abstentions; the worst result for South Africa to date. Subsequently, a Franco-Mexican resolution calling for a round table conference was adopted by 47 votes to the solitary negative vote of South Africa, with ten states (including the White Commonwealth) abstaining. It was a bitter moment for Eric Louw and his government.

In view of the usual Nationalist *laager* response to attack, it was surprising that in July 1949 South Africa should have renewed the proposal for a conference to India and Pakistan. A suggestion that trade sanctions should be suspended was met with a firm refusal by India and a more equivocal response from Pakistan, which was itself suffering badly from India's trade boycott over the Kashmir issue, so that South Africa's cheap coal was an attractive prospect, in place of the interrupted supply from India.

Preliminary discussions took place, in which India was represented by H. N. Kunzru, Pakistan by Sayyid Mahommad Hussain, and South Africa by Dr Dönges. A decision to go ahead with the conference was announced—and then in April 1950 the terms of the new Group Areas Bill were released, and in consequence the Government of India announced on 6 June 1950 that they could not participate in the agreed conference. Although the South African Indian question continued to be paraded periodically at the United Nations, the last chance of compromise on any terms had gone by. Jawaharlal Nehru sadly recognised the bitter reality; that they had reached the limits of their capacity to persuade and pressurise the Government of South Africa. The bellicose speeches about military pressure, so often heard in the Indian central assembly, echoed mockingly still. Indeed, there were many Indians—inside South Africa and outside —who did not understand that the long night had set in.

The ambiguities of the contemporary situation were illustrated when Nehru visited Canada in 1949, staying in Vancouver on 2 and 3 November. He received an enthusiastic reception from the so-called 'Hindus' of British Columbia, about 1,800 in number, and mainly Sikhs. In their address to Nehru, the Sikhs said 'We have watched the struggle of your government to consolidate and establish the new nation of India' and welcomed Nehru's efforts to 'extend a helping hand to our brothers in South Africa'. The Sikhs complained that there was widespread discrimination in employment opportunities in British Columbia. Reporting this occurrence, the British High Commissioner confirmed that there was 'still a good deal of anti-Asiatic feeling in British Columbia', and that the Sikhs' greeting to Nehru had caused 'some misgiving' to the Canadian Government which was 'only too well aware of the difficulties which have arisen in South Africa'.[8]

The late 1940s in Kenya were the last years in which the Europeans could still look to South Africa as the exemplar for their own pattern of development. Then came the shock of Mau Mau to compel them to realise how fragile was their grasp upon this African land. The Mau Mau rebellion might be suppressed, but it remained necessary to provide African leaders with evidence that they had a future in their own country. The 1950s were the transition period between a white-dominated system and an African, national, political system. The late 1940s were a kind of Golden Age for the Kenya Europeans; but for the Indians these years were the time when it began to be obvious that in the struggle between European and African interests, they were hopelessly vulnerable to pressure from both sides.

Political change was slight, but perceptible. The first shift came in Uganda, when in November 1947 the non-official membership of the Legislative Council was adjusted to provide for four African members, three Whites and three Indians. Because there was still an official majority, the African trend was symbolic rather than actual. The non-official side of the Kenya legislature was expanded in April 1948, while simultaneously the official side was reduced. The European and Indian membership remained unchanged (11 and 5) but there were now two Arab members and four Africans, chosen by the Governor from a panel submitted by African local authorities and selected by them. There was now parity between the White and non-White unofficial members (11, 11) but as the Whites could always find allies among the officials the change was not fundamental.

The political philosophy which this represented was well expressed by Sir Philip Mitchell in a speech to the Nairobi Rotary, 24 November 1947. He talked about the migration into Kenya of the Africans, and then of the Whites: 'Although there was in the past ... a time during which it would have been possible for an exclusively negro African state or states to be established, that time has vanished for ever. ... But there is a corollary to all that, and that is that the establishment of an exclusively British, or an exclusively Indian state or society is equally impossible. Whether we like it or not we are committed to a joint enterprise.' This would be a society 'which places no insurmountable obstacle in front of anybody of any race, but demands only that if he wants to join others on the hilltops he should be capable of the climb involved, instead of deluding himself and others that the road is flat.' And so, Mitchell concluded, the goal for Kenya was 'the establishment of a civilised state in which the values and standards are to be the values and standards of Britain in which everyone, whatever his origin has an interest and a part . . . the planter, the farmer, the lawyer, the little Indian shopkeeper in the countryside and the wealthy Indian merchant in Mombasa all have a stake in it.'

The rhetoric of 'Equal Rights for all Civilised Men'—the slogan of Cecil Rhodes which still seemed absurdly liberal to most Kenya Whites in 1948—can best be compared to the reality in relation to immigration and land settlement, the two subjects which had concerned the Europeans most ever since the 1920s.

The Immigration (Control) Bill, to which the Government of India had objected through the Maharaj Singh mission, received its second reading in November 1947. The Kenya Bill was identical with the legislation introduced in Tanganyika and Uganda at the same time. Moving the Kenya Bill, Foster Sutton, the Attorney General, said its objects were to control the entry of displaced persons from Europe and to protect the economic interests of the existing Kenya population. He emphasised the effect of the increased numbers of school-leavers, both African and Asian, who would be candidates for the jobs for which Indians had been imported in the past. The Ordinance came into effect on 1 August 1948.

Various classes of entrants were defined. Class A consisted of permanent residents, and Classes B to G of various categories of persons arriving to take up employment. Class H consisted of persons settling in East Africa with their own incomes (essentially retired people). The decision on admission was taken by the Immigration Officers, with an appeal to the Minister, or Member, for Labour. The introduction of controls had a markedly greater effect upon the entry of Asians than upon that of Europeans.

Temporary Employment Passes: Issued/Refused

		Europeans			Asians		
		Issued	Refused	Total	Issued	Refused	Total
1949	..	2,239	20	2,259	2,389	904	3,293
1950	..	2,246	41	2,287	751	474	1,225
1951	..	2,202	37	2,239	611	463	1,074
1952	..	2,414	33	2,447	403	633	1,036
1953	..	2,792	23	2,815	283	224	507

The applicants from India and Pakistan were mainly artisans (masons, carpenters, mechanics, etc.), shop assistants and bookkeepers. As a strict policy of controlling Asian entry made itself felt, the number of applicants declined, though Kenya was still in need of technical workers in the categories in which the Asians applied. In their place, a number of Italians were imported as craftsmen and technicians.

Entry Permits for Classes B to G, 1949-55

	Granted	Refused
British	2,504	28
Italians	489	8
Other Europeans	458	35
Total Europeans	3,451	71
Asians	1,461	772

Source: *Kenya Government, Sessional Paper No. 78 of 1956, Immigration Policy* (1956).

Clearly, a much tougher policy was followed in screening Asians than Europeans; the Government of India protested against the situation, but was told that the policy was not discriminatory.[9] So far as the Kenya Europeans were concerned, the immigration policy was not tough enough; in 1949 the Electors Union, the organisation of the Whites, issued a 'Kenya Plan' calling for a sharp reduction in Indian immigration. The press reflected a tone which at times neared the hysterical in the alarmist reports of Indians 'swamping' the native population.[10] The policy of admitting technicians, artisans and foremen from Britain was justified by Creech Jones; he praised the 'valuable contribution of British settlement and technical skills to the development of these [East African] territories'.[11]

The official justification offered for the immigration controls—the increase in numbers of school leavers—was certainly a factor, but not in comparison to the total numbers involved.

Leaving Secondary Schools, Kenya, 1948-53

	European boys	African boys	Asian boys
1948	135	186	760
1949	145	219	1,150
1950	160	220	1,520
1951	170	228	1,380
1952	205	299	1,670
1953	220	434	2,000

The policy of white settlement in the Highlands continued, and was extended during this period. Provision for loans to new settlers was augmented from £1 million to £1.5 million, and the five hundred settlers introduced after the Second World War were supplemented by an additional two hundred tenant farmers. By contrast, the promise made by Mitchell to the Indians, to foster Indian settlement on the land, came to very little. The Indian and Arab Settlement Board was constituted early in 1946, and after three years was given the administration of fifty square miles of land near Mackinnon Road, a station on the railway line from Mombasa. The original terms of settlement were rejected by the Indian members of the Board, headed by the Indian chairman. The Indians wished to lease the land to landlords who would then let out farms to tenants. The Government opposed this kind of absentee system. An official report stated 'It has been virtually impossible to get information about bona fide Indian and Arab settlers who genuinely wish to settle on this land and to carry on stock raising'.

Because the Indian demand for farms appeared to be 'very small', Cavendish-Bentinck, the Minister responsible, decided that the policy of the Board was ineffective; he replaced the Indian chairman by a European, Major-General Edwards; but the scheme still did not prosper. The official view was that the Indians merely wanted to include the demand for agricultural land among their political grievances, though they would like to buy land as an investment, as land values were rising.[12]

The controversy about land might be a small-scale issue for the Indians; for the Africans it was of vital urgency, and the arrival of more white settlers in the Highlands made the situation of the African farmers, the 'squatters', more precarious. It was not until 1950 that the Annual Report on Kenya mentioned the emergence of an unlawful religious sect known as *Dini ya Msambwa* and an even more obscure 'anti-European secret society'—*Mau Mau*.[13] It was not until 21 October 1952 that the new Governor of Kenya, Sir Evelyn Baring, proclaimed a State of Emergency.

The Mau Mau rebellion caught the Indians in the middle of the cross-fire. They were expected to take sides: and because very few openly sided with the British government, they were accused of siding with the Mau Mau. A principal victim of the polarised situation was the Indian Commissioner, Apa B. Pant, who attempted to fulfil his mission by making a wide number of friends among the Africans and by encouraging the East African Indians to identify with the new Africa. Inevitably, this brought him into the crossfire.[14]

An episode in 1950 illustrated both the contribution to a new Africa—and the limits of this contribution—by Indians in East Africa: this was the attempt to call a general strike. The issue concerned Makhan Singh (or Machan Singh), a veteran of East African trade union politics who had been previously banished to India in 1939 after the first major strike, among the dock workers of Mombasa.[15] In 1950, Makhan Singh formed the first overall East African Trade Union Congress, but the government refused to recognise and register the Congress on the grounds that it was really a political association. Makhan Singh was placed in detention, and an attempt was made to launch a general strike to secure his release. According to the official account, the strike was confined to the Nairobi neighbourhood and lasted only ten days, affecting about 3,000 workers, many of whom were Africans. The government alleged that intimidation was employed to bring the workers out, and there were violent clashes with the police. Makhan Singh was again deported, and the movement collapsed.[16] With this failure, the moderate leaders such as A.B. Patel reasserted control over the Kenya Indian Congress, though they soon found their leadership contested by activists who demanded closer cooperation between Indian and African politicians.

As in South Africa, Indian politics in East Africa were partly a reflection of the competing interests of big business men; concerned to protect their own interests, and therefore ready to cooperate with the government, and acquiesce in its policies to perpetuate white dominance; and the lawyers and journalists who wanted to attempt a mass appeal to an urban audience of Indians and Africans. The preoccupation of the economically important Indians with their own interests was even more a feature of the politics of Uganda, Tanganyika and Zanzibar. The Indians were having to accept government control and public ownership in enterprises they had formerly dominated, such as cotton ginning in Uganda and the clove market in Zanzibar; however, there were new industrial fields into which they could move, if this were acceptable to the British officials and the rising African politicians. The smalltime Indian traders, builders and brokers were much more vulnerable to African demands that they should take over their rightful share of these types of business.

An attempt was made by Krishna Menon in London to raise general issues of policy with the Colonial Office. In March 1948, he had an interview with Creech Jones to discuss various problems of the Indians in colonial territories. Krishna Menon sensed that the Secretary for the Colonies was not prepared to modify Colonial Office policies. Writing to Patrick Gordon-Walker, Minister at the C.R.O., Krishna Menon observed (18 March 1948): 'Though the

Secretary of State [for the Colonies] agreed with me at length, I got little satisfaction and I expressed this sentiment to him. Both time, and as far as I was concerned, energy, was well-nigh exhausted by that time, as [so] it was said that officials might discuss certain matters. The Government of India is much perturbed by the lack of response at the Colonial Office on issues relating to their nationals, and Indian public opinion is much exercised over them.'

Where the Indians were mainly estate workers, at the base of the economic pyramid, their political status remained very backward. It was becoming noticeable that, as the Colonial Office proceeded to revise the constitutions of the sugar colonies, dismantling the oligarchic structure of control by the white planters which had survived from the eighteenth century, and widening the franchise to bring in the mass of the workers, there was a marked reluctance to extend the process to those colonies where the descendants of Indian indentured labourers were in the majority—or were becoming the majority. Jamaica, Barbados and even Trinidad, followed in the steps of Ceylon; but Mauritius, Guiana and Fiji trailed a long way behind.

In the Caribbean, Trinidad was well ahead of British Guiana in the advance towards self government, and the Trinidad East Indians appeared to be capable of holding their own in this development. At the Colonial Office it was noted that the arrival of the Indian Commissioner in Trinidad 'was greeted with jubilation, and has undoubtedly strengthened the tendency of the East Indian community to preserve its association with India, thus helping to maintain their sense of separateness from the rest of the population'. At this time, the Indians were mainly organised on a religious basis. The *Sanatan Dharma Maha Sabha* was the temple organisation of the orthodox Hindus, firmly under upper caste control, while the *Arya Samaj*, the reformist, fundamentalist, missionary organisation was also anxious to attract low-caste membership. However, the professional elite among the Indians, while not discarding their traditional caste ties, were mostly members of the (Canadian) Presbyterian church.

The Governor of Trinidad, Sir John Shaw, reported that the new Indian Commissioner was 'scrupulously correct and circumspect' (24 August 1948). However, a few months later (19 April 1949) the Governor was reporting that Satya Charan was being egged on by the local Indian politicians to greater activity; he made enquiries about the teaching of Hindi in the schools and also about facilities for the traditional Hindu form of cremation. Sir John Shaw observed a little tartly that if the Commissioner 'rigidly restricted his activities to the letter and spirit of his terms of reference there would not be much for him to do'. He reported that the East Indians were 'increasingly communalistically minded', and in August 1949 an Indo-Caribbean Cultural Institute was inaugurated at Port of Spain. These Indian activities brought comment and questions in the Legislative Council (August 1949).

The 1946 constitutional reforms did not satisfy Trinidad political aspirations for long. The legislature appointed a committee to recommend further changes, and the majority of its members asked for an elected majority in the Legislative Council, suggesting that two-thirds be elected. This was accepted, and elections were held in September 1950 in the eighteen constituencies which were to form the elected Bloc (with three official members, and six nominated non-officials making up the total: 27).

There were fifty-one candidates from five political factions, and ninety independent candidates. The two factions which approximated most closely to political parties were the Trinidad Labour Party, founded by Captain A. A. Cipriani, a white Trinidadian, with some Indian participants, such as Arien Cola Rienzi (born Krishna Deonarine) and the British Empire Workers and Citizens Home Rule Party, founded by Uriah 'Buzz' Butler. Most of the East Indian groups linked up with Butler for electoral purposes. The election did not result in a racial alignment. The members of the new legislature consisted of seven Indians, five Blacks, two white Trinidadians, a Chinese, a Syrian, and two *mestizo* members. The Indians formed the largest group, and with 39 per cent of the seats were well represented in communal terms, though they lacked any coherent approach to future policy.

British Guiana lagged behind. The Indian leaders were 'at sixes and sevens' according to the Governor, Sir Charles Woolley.[17] The leadership of the East Indian Association was disputed between Dr Lachman Singh and Jenarine Singh, a labour leader. Edun was still leader of the Man Power Citizens' Association, flanked by Dr J. B. Singh, who had been ejected from the East Indian Association. The Muslims were led by G. A. McDoom and, since the partition of the sub-continent, they seemed to be drawing apart. As in Trinidad, the most important Indian organisations were the religious societies—the Sanatan Dharma Maha Sabha, and the Sadr Anjuman-e-Islam for the Muslims. Satya Charan found that the different factions tried to acquire legitimacy by getting his patronage. He strove to keep aloof, and even cancelled a visit to Guiana early in 1949, telling Woolley (1 April 1949) 'I can ill afford to give an impression that I have partial leanings towards any party or individual'.

The Governors of Trinidad and Guiana reported on Satya Charan's difficulties to the Colonial Office, and although they still described him as discreet the Colonial Office decided that he must be given a warning of the danger of straying beyond the limits of his office. A despatch was sent to the two Governors, signed by H. Beckett (5 July 1949). 'We had no illusions as to the potential embarrassment and danger in this course', the despatch began, for even though the Government of India agreed to written instructions being given to their representatives they were not always easy to observe: 'even supposing that they set out genuinely to do so'. The Colonial Office felt that Satya Charan had 'certainly gone considerably further' than Apa B. Pant or the others in trying to stir up local politics. The Governors were asked to issue warnings: he must be discouraged 'from stepping outside his crease'; they should issue 'a friendly verbal hint to him that he is getting too far offside'. One might have supposed that the games-conscious Colonial Office would not have mixed up cricket and football quite so heedlessly! The despatch ended: 'Relations with India, especially where colonial matters are concerned, are always rather tricky.'

Behind this curious exchange there was a growing feeling that the 'Indianness' of Guiana was going to create friction with the other West Indian colonies. One Royal Commission had the idea of transforming the racial situation by a new programme of immigration from the overcrowded Caribbean islands and perhaps from the refugee camps of Europe, but this recommendation (known as the 'Evans Report') was not taken up as part of the new Colonial Development and Welfare programme.[18] Meanwhile, Guiana had to wait until in 1951 a constitutional commission was appointed to report on future progress. The members were an ex-Governor, Sir John Waddington, the Director of the Fabian Colonial Bureau, Rita Hinden, and an Oxford historian, Vincent Harlow. They reported in 1951 that British Guiana should move forward to universal suffrage and ministerial government; their report included admonition: 'If Indians seek free and equal participation in the life of British Guiana it is manifestly wrong that they should look continuously over their shoulders towards a mother country with which the present life and polity has little contact.'

It must have seemed that the Indians listened to these words, for they now turned away from all the old, discredited figures from the East Indian Association and the Man-Power Citizens' Association, and listened instead to one who had been a member of the legislature since 1947 but had played little part in communal politics. This was the son of an Indian 'Driver' or foreman, trained as a dentist in Chicago, married to a Jewish nurse, a student of Marxism: Cheddi Jagan.

Fiji was even more of a constitutional backwater than Guiana.

There was a widespread consciousness—articulated by the Governor, the Fijian chiefs, and the Whites—that the expansion of the Indian population must be checked. There was little sign of voluntary restriction by birth control, and the enactment of an Immigration Ordinance in 1947 made little difference to the rising population. Indian immigration had long been reduced to a trickle of commercial and professional immigrants. A committee of inquiry reported that the chief effect of the restrictions was to reduce the numbers of white vagrants—beachcombers—entering the islands.[19] Even if this was so, Indian immigration during the 1950s declined even further.

Entrants into Fiji by race 1953-56.

	1953	1954	1955	1956
Europeans	350	451	406	443
Indians	522	613	378	156
Pacific Islanders	64	118	89	163
Chinese	38	46	96	73
Total	974	1,228	973	837

The European members of the Fiji legislature asked for a non-official majority in 1948. This was supported by the Indians, but when the question was referred to a Select Committee this body recommended retaining the official majority. In the debates which followed, in 1949, the majority of the Indians asked for a non-official majority, but the Muslims joined with all other groups in asking for no change. Endorsing this view, the Secretary for the Colonies stated that there would be no new move until 'a majority of the accredited representatives of public opinion' wanted this. In this somnolent situation, it might have been supposed that the new Indian Commissioner would not make much impression. To the contrary, the arrival of Mr. Waiz was invested with foreboding. When this worthy gentleman, who had spent his life in social service, announced that he would receive any Indian 'at any time of the day or night' this was given a sinister significance, and when he said his task was to see that 'Indians remain Indians' this was considered 'provocative'.[20] However, S.A. Waiz did not stay long, and by 1951 he had departed.

Mauritius was now to move forward from the Pope Henessey constitution of 1885, the most ancient in all the British Empire. In April 1947, the Governor wrote to Creech Jones to announce that he wished to go beyond the 1945 proposals, which he admitted 'will certainly not be acceptable in 1948'. He still insisted that 'we must for a considerable period base our elective system on a franchise short of universal suffrage and retain the power of nomination'. He pointed out that the existing constitution gave the vote to 9 per cent of the non-Indian communities (White, Chinese, and African Creole) but to only 3 per cent of the Indians.

It was now proposed to extend the vote to everyone 'able to read and write simple sentences' in different languages (which included the main Indian languages), as well as to all who had served in the armed forces. The business vote was retained (though it had just been abolished in Britain). The legislature was expanded to include nineteen elected members, with twelve nominated non-officials and three official members under the Governor as president. Accepting this formula, Creech Jones observed (16 August 1947): 'These changes go as far as is practicable in the direction of developing democratic institutions at the present stage.'[21]

When a general election was held under the new constitution in August 1948, the electorate had increased from 11,437 to 71,230 — about two-fifths of the adult population. Eleven Indians were elected, and eight Creoles; no Muslim candidate was elected. Port Louis returned three Creoles and one Indian, with Guy Rozemont, who had emerged as leader of the Labour Party, at the top of the poll. But there was no real party alignment in the legislature; the Colonial Office noted: 'Indian divides against Indian, Coloured against Coloured.'

Following the complaints about Satya Charan's activities in Trinidad and Guiana the Colonial Office wanted to know how Yash Dev in Mauritius was interpreting his duties. When the inquiry arrived, the island was under the administration of the wise and kindly James Harford, and he sent back a sympathetic account of the pressures under which the Indian Commissioner had to function.[22] Harford declared that when Dev arrived his behaviour was absolutely correct, and he avoided identification with the Bissoondayal faction. He announced publicly that the Indo-Mauritians should give their loyalty to Mauritius. However, he did associate with Dr. Ramgoolam and J. N. Roy, moderate leaders of the Labour Party, and also with Coloured Labour leaders. He was criticised by the politicians of the Right, who said that he wanted Indians who had become Christians to return to Hinduism. Aunath Beejadhur, the Gallicised editor of *Advance* complained that Dev had tried to get him to 'Indianise' his newspaper. Dev was also criticised by the Left Wing: *Zamana*, a radical journal complained that when the Indian cruiser *Delhi* visited the island, Dev ensured that they did not go to visit any of the poorer places.

Harford considered that Dev had stretched his authority on

certain occasions. He had promoted a protest cable to the Secretary for the Colonies, calling for a ban on KLM planes landing at Mauritius at a time when India was organising an Asian boycott of KLM in reply to the Dutch 'police action' in Indonesia. And he had persuaded the island radio to broadcast 'News from India'; 'Mr. Dev is an experienced and highly skilled publicist' observed James Harford.

The acting governor decided to ascertain Dev's own view of his situation, and he invited the Commissioner to dine at *Le Réduit*, the Governor's mansion, on 18 July 1949. He made a favourable impression, reported Harford, though he spoke with bitterness 'at the master and servant relationship of the two races', the Whites and the Indians, in Mauritius. Dev said he was 'under fire' from two sides. Bissoondayal sent critical reports about him to his political contacts in the Government of India, alleging that he was 'a tool of the local government', while the French *Mauriciens* had 'adopted a suspicious or hostile attitude to him'. The conservative newspaper, *Le Cernéen* was specially antagonistic. Harford enclosed an example of its general attitude: 'The first settlers [of Mauritius] were undoubtedly French . . . Under the Treaty of Paris, Britain guaranteed to safeguard the interests of the French settlers and it could not, with justice, cede its authority or its duties to another power.' The newspaper continually suggested that an Indian takeover was being planned.

Harford's own comment was: 'I have never felt any particular conviction about the sinister designs of the Government of India;' the possibility of a takeover was 'fantastic', he wrote, and 'completely alien to Pandit Nehru's policy'. Harford added: 'I consider that the French Mauritian community by its attitude of aloofness and suspicion has unnecessarily alienated Mr Dev and driven him unnecessarily deep into the other camp.'

Having received this cool, sober assessment from a senior administrator, the Indophobia of the Colonial Office was soon aroused again by a report from Royal Navy intelligence in Mauritius.[23] This alleged that Dev was fomenting trouble and that Rozemont ('a Communist') was 'in his pocket'. The visit of the cruiser *Delhi* had been exploited to create Indian nationalism; youth organisations wearing Gandhi caps were drilling with shields and truncheons. 'Things must come to a head very soon' observed the Major of Marines responsible for this analysis: there would be strikes in the next month when the sugar was to be cut: 'This is a political trial of strength so that Mr Dev can see what forces he has at his call when the time comes to take over Mauritius as an Indian colony.' The Colonial Office may not have taken this naval review at its face value; but certainly in the following years the attempt was made to dam up or divert Indian political consciousness in Mauritius, by getting the leaders interested in local government, community development and other alternatives to a transfer of genuine political power.

While India experienced frustration in attempting to establish greater influence in territories under Colonial Office control, an even greater disappointment was awaiting in the response of the national leaders of newly independent Ceylon and Burma. It was not that these countries lacked anything in respect for India, as the acknowledged leader of Southern Asia, while Jawaharlal Nehru was admiringly hailed as Asia's spokesman in the counsels of the world. But their feelings towards India and Nehru were not extended to the Indians in their midst; these were regarded as part of the now-departed imperial system, which they were determined to sweep away in the forward march of nationhood.

In Burma, the break with the past could be made swiftly and suddenly, because of the break in continuity caused by the Japanese occupation; moreover, the clear wish of the Government of India to forget the abortive 1941 agreement and start again, meant that the Burmese leaders could make their decisions without bothering over continuing arrangements. India's ties with Ceylon had not been snapped in the same way. As Ceylon moved forward into independence, there remained many features of the 'special relationship' which were still functioning. Nevertheless, Ceylon, like Burma, moved swiftly to erase the past, as soon as the formal transfer of power had been completed. The first general election to be held under the Soulbury constitution was also the last one to take place in the manner that Lord Soulbury and his colleagues had recommended: with the Indian electors playing their part as future citizens of Ceylon. Despite the de-registration of thousands of Indians by the severe interpretation of the 'permanent residence' provision, there were six constituencies under the Soulbury arrangement in which the Indian vote was decisive. These were all planting districts in the Central Province. These seats were won by the Ceylon-Indian Congress, and with 12 per cent of the population, the Indians obtained 6.5 per cent of the representation.

Perhaps the Indians might have been permitted to retain this modest share of power if only Senanayake's position after the election had not been so indefinite. He went into the election with a newly-organised party machine, under the banner of the United National Party.[24] Only 49 per cent of the voters went to the poll, so that

Senanayake must have been conscious of the unknown half of the electorate who did not vote. The U.N.P. won forty-two seats out of the total of ninety-five. Most of the twenty-six independents supported him, and he was able to choose the six nominated members from known friends. He was in firm control, for the time being. But the Left had presented a strong challenge, and won eighteen seats, and the attitude of the Tamil Congress (seven seats) was watchful and wary.

Senanayake put together a Cabinet in which there were eleven U.N.P. members, two Tamil independents and a member of the Labour Party. To consolidate his position he needed the six Central Province constituencies in which the Indians formed the bulk of the voters: but where, if they were eliminated, the rural Kandyans were likely to give these seats to the U.N.P.

Senanayake was not going to stir things up before independence was fully accomplished. He was therefore uneasy when he was told about proposals from Britain designed to bring about an overall Commonwealth agreement on nationality and citizenship, on a reciprocal basis. In November 1947 he gave Sir Henry Moore a message to be transmitted to Creech Jones. Negotiations with India regarding the future of the 600,000 Indians living in Ceylon were about to begin: 'A considerable section of these Indians will fall outside the pale of Ceylonese citizenship if domicile is adopted as the basis for citizenship. If, on the other hand, India accepts birth as the basis, it is likely that some of these Indians will also fail to obtain citizenship of India.... The passing at this juncture of the United Kingdom Nationality Bill, recognising birth as the basis of citizenship will enable India to urge that Ceylon should adopt the same basis for citizenship.' Here was a clear indication that Ceylon did not intend to make any concessions on this extremely important issue, but intended to press India for concessions. P. J. Patrick at the Commonwealth Relations Office noted that unless agreement were reached between India and Ceylon, 600,000 Indians would remain 'British subjects of the United Kingdom and Colonies ... which will have disadvantages' (11 November 1947). Despite this warning, no effort was made at the Colonial Office to influence the matter; presumably it was believed that the day had passed for Britain to exert influence when Ceylon's independence was already fixed for 4 February 1948.

At this moment, Aney was replaced as India's representative by V. V. Giri, a former Minister in Madras and a future President of India. In reply to a letter of congratulation from G. A. Natesan (an old friend of the Indians overseas) Giri wrote from Colombo that he was 'trying to get the Indo-Ceylon problem solved at the earliest opportunity' (12 December 1947). Nehru and Senanayake would meet to work out a solution almost immediately: 27-30 December. The starting-point for their discussions was the almost-agreed formula of 1941. However, Senanayake was now in a stronger position: there was nothing that Ceylon needed from India, while Nehru was torn between a concern for the Ceylon Indians and a desire to promote better relations between the new India and her neighbours.

The two prime ministers jointly signed a six-point formula which seemed to embody a form of agreement: but all the hard questions were left to be answered later. Thus, Senanayake insisted upon Indian applicants for citizenship having completed nine years' residence in Ceylon if they were married and had their families with them, with a longer qualifying period for single men. Nehru was only prepared to discuss an eight-year residence test, applicable to married and single people alike. Both alternatives were, of course, less favourable than the terms negotiated by Bajpai in September 1941 (see p. 198).

Nehru refused to haggle over bargaining points; he believed that such questions should be resolved by reference to principles. He did not see that delay could only further weaken the position of the Ceylon Indians. The Correspondence between the prime ministers continued until after independence arrived for Ceylon.[25] Then the question was decided, unilaterally, by three draconian measures. The Citizenship Act (No. 18 of 1948) limited the status of Ceylon citizen to persons who could claim it by descent or by registration. The conditions applying to the Indians were defined in the Indian and Pakistani Residents (Citizenship) Act — No. 3 of 1949 — which required continuous residence since 1946, and before that residence of seven years for married people, and ten years for the unmarried. The applicant had to produce documents establishing his antecedents, which most of the estate labourers did not have and could not acquire. Finally, the Ceylon (Parliamentary Elections) Amendment Act (No. 48 of 1949) removed the voters of Indian origin from the register. This measure produced the required effect: five of the six former 'Indian' constituencies elected U.N.P. members at the following election. The effect of these changes was to make the great majority of Indians in Ceylon stateless persons.

The Government of India protested against these Bills, especially the Citizenship Act, and Nehru made a personal appeal to Senanayake not to proceed with the provisions which would render the Indians stateless. He was informed that Ceylon was only prepared to discuss details: the principle of the Bill was not negotiable. As before, Ceylon was willing to make concessions only if India was prepared to offer advantages in return: and Ceylon wanted India to take back a sizeable proportion of her people from Ceylon. As Nehru rejected in advance any such agreement based upon a bargain, the whole question was suspended in limbo. And the Indian tea estate workers remained in a political limbo also.

The fate of the Indians in Burma was strikingly similar. Burma's political format was decided not by Royal Commission and Colonial Office draughtsmanship but by the deliberations of a Constituent Assembly meeting in Rangoon in June 1947. The assembly was elected, mainly on a territorial basis, though there was separate representation for the indigenous minorities — the hill peoples (Shans, Kachins, Chins, etc.), the Karen community, and the Anglo-Burman community. A few individuals of Indian descent were elected — notably Abdul Razak, the political mentor of the Thakins — and two Indian Muslims were among the representatives of the Akyab constituency. From the Constituent Assembly of over 250 members, a Constitution Committee was chosen, and this committee (which numbered seventy-five) co-opted certain outsiders, mainly legal experts, but also including M. A. Raschid and Zora Singh. Finally, M. A. Raschid participated in the twenty-five man Drafting Committee, which brought forward the completed constitution early in September. If the Indians received little consideration in the final terms of citizenship, they had not been altogether excluded from the constitutional process.

Some Indians could claim citizenship under the provision admitting persons born in Burma 'at least one of whose grandparents belong or belonged to any of the indigenous races of Burma'; but most qualified as a person 'born within His Britannic Majesty's dominions and who has resided [in Burma] . . . for a period of not less than eight years in the ten years immediately preceding . . . this constitution or immediately preceding 1 January 1942 and who intends to reside permanently therein'. As in Ceylon this was a 'once for all' admission of those who had qualified by residence *before* independence.[26] When a treaty was signed between Britain and Burma on 17 October 1947, there was provision for residents of Burma who were British subjects (which still included most Indians) to retain their British status and renounce Burma citizenship: but there was no explicit reference to the situation of Indians in Burma, so fully treated in the previous legislation of 1935. In April 1948, talks began at Delhi concerning future Indian immigration into Burma led by U Win, Burma's ambassador (himself of Indian ancestry) but these made no progress.

With immigration at a standstill—the Immigration (Emergency Provisions) Act was further extended in 1949—the resident Indian community was bewildered about its status and its future. It was estimated that 35,000 to 40,000 Indians actually applied for citizenship, and because of the delays and obstacles experienced less than 10,000 became citizens. As foreigners, not Commonwealth citizens, they became aliens so far as India was concerned.[27] All the remaining Indians had to register under the Foreigners' Registration Act; many failed to obtain certificates, and became liable to deportation.

The uncertainties of the Indians in Burma were reflected in disputes between their leaders, in which those who fled to India in 1942 frequently found themselves opposed by those who had remained. Thus, S. A. S. Tyabji was pushed out of the leadership of the Muslim community by Abdul Latif, who had been an official of the Indian Independence League under the Japanese, and in 1945 helped to organise the Burma Muslim Congress. After his defeat, Tyabji returned to India. Latif assumed the Burmese name of Khin Maung Lat, was elected to the Constituent Assembly, and became a Minister in 1950. Other Indians born in Burma who identified themselves completely with the land of their birth, in language and culture, were accepted into the political system: the deputy prime minister at the time of independence, Kyaw Nyein, the leading Marxist intellectual of the A.F.P.F.L. was said to be an Indian, though wholly assimilated to Burma.[28] One of the main leaders of the underground resistance in the White Flag Communists was an Indian, H. N. Ghoshal, known as Thakin Ba Tin: it was he who gave the underground Communists their ideology.

These were the exceptions — the Indians accepted as Burmese — but the great majority, even of those born in Burma, were rapidly eliminated from public life. In 1947 they were still an important element at all levels of the public services; almost all were then prematurely retired, and most returned to India. For those who were less in the public view — doctors, teachers, traders — there were still to be a few more years in which they were permitted to earn their livelihood in Burma.

Despite the discrimination against the Indians in Burma, the Government of India did not attempt to bring pressure to bear upon the Government of Burma, which almost immediately after independence day (4 January 1948) was beset by threats of rebellion. In June 1948, Bajpai confided his fears about Burma to the British High Commissioner; U Nu was on a 'slippery slope' he said, and his efforts to conciliate the Communists would make him slide further. As a reply to the Communists, the Burma Government had announced a Leftist Unity Plan, with a programme of expropriation of capitalist interests, including the landlords. Bajpai wanted to try to protect the Indian landlords, but Nehru thought otherwise.[29] Early in 1949 the situation deteriorated to the point where the control of the government barely included the whole of Rangoon. At this critical moment, Nu hurried to Delhi to consult with Nehru; he was promised assistance in military arms and supplies. With other help from Britain, Nu's government pulled through and slowly pushed back the insurgents.[30] As a symbol of their close association, India and Burma concluded a Treaty of Friendship in July 1951; in September 1951 they concluded a Trade Agreement. But these negotiations did nothing to assist the Indians remaining in Burma.

Though independence did not create a new and better situation for Indians overseas, either in the Colonial Office territories or in the newly independent countries of Southern Asia, there was some gain in Malaya and Singapore. Almost before Malaya recovered from the Japanese occupation, there was a new period of troubles — the Communist Emergency. Once again, Indians found themselves in the crossfire: this time, between the Chinese guerrillas and the British security forces. The Indians tried to keep their heads down and avoid being caught up: inevitably they were expected to decide which side they were on. A historian of this period considers that in the dilemmas of the late 1940s 'The Indian community had reached the nadir of its political influence.'[31] Things could have been worse for the Indians, however, but for the pressure exercised by the Government of India: and it was in Malaya that the difference between the capacity of India to exercise effective influence, before and after independence, was most sharply demonstrated.

The first important political event was the announcement that the Malayan Union would be dissolved and the Malay rulers would be restored to their former position within an overall Federation of Malaya.[32] As a result, the traditional Malay political dominance was reasserted, and the admission of Chinese and Indians into the political process, and into the privileges of citizenship and nationality was made more restricted. A new federal legislative council was to be constituted, with fifty non-official members. Malays received nearly half the seats (twenty-two) while seven were allotted to the Europeans, fourteen to the Chinese and only five to the Indian community. It was a bitter disappointment, and the Malayan Indian Congress joined with Chinese groups in a protest movement, the All-Malaya Council of Joint Action. The M.I.C. managed to launch a boycott movement, mainly in the form of a *hartal*, a compulsory closure of shops, but the British government was not impressed and the new federation was inaugurated on 1 January 1948. The M.I.C. struggled on, until in July 1948 it issued an announcement that the Committee of Joint Action had ceased to exist, and therefore the M.I.C. would observe a 'political truce' towards the government. By this time, Malaya was plunged into the Emergency, and the M.I.C. entered a period of internal controversy from which it more or less emerged in May 1950 with an announcement that it would cooperate with the government.

On the estates, industrial conditions remained unsettled. The labour population in the federation consisted of 205,723 Indian workers and 141,486 Chinese (Total—456,636). In Singapore the Indians formed only 24,257 out of a total of 124,244, but among the government, port, and municipal employees of Singapore the Indians numbered 17,620 out of a total of 24,257.[33] In September 1945 John Brazier arrived from Britain to organise industiral trade unions as a recognised part of the negotiating process. His job was not easy; the employers were not all ready to deal with trade unions, while industrial leadership was in the hands of Communists or those who had been brought forward during the Japanese occupation. A Pan-Malayan Federation of Trade Unions was founded in February 1946 under Communist control; most of its officials were Chinese, though the president was Ganapathy.

The government did not recognise the PMFTU, and John Brazier tried to encourage alternative leadership. Meanwhile, the estate workers were alternately under pressure from the Communist labour leaders and the management. According to Sir Edward Gent (30 September 1947), as a legacy of the Japanese period there were 'a substantial number of Indians... who engage in such activities as intimidation, extortion, blackmail, and other serious forms of crime including murder'. According to John Thivy (who passed the information on to Krishna Menon in London) 'Workers are dismissed without being accorded proper reasons or sufficient time, and [this is] followed up by trespass proceedings'.[34] This was the old, pre-war practice of dismissing anyone making demands from among the workers, and then ejecting him from the estate lines by bringing an action for trespass and getting the police to do the manager's job by eliminating a nuisance. When these allegations were put to the Federation Government they were denied: like Shenton Thomas in 1941, Gent insisted that the grievances were artificial.[35]

Krishna Menon also made representations on behalf of the Chettyars who alleged that the British were discriminating in favour of their own business people in the restoration of commercial activities in Malaya. Particular exception was taken to a new measure called the 'Titles to Land Ordinance'. In the style of the old India Office, Krishna Menon asked the C.R.O. that before the measure became law the view of the Government of India should be considered (14 February 1948). In its accomplished way, the Colonial Office replied that they could not act while the bill was before a Select Committee in Kuala Lumpur. Correspondence passed back and forth, and on 16 December 1948 Menon told Gordon-Walker 'I very much wish to avoid being confronted with the now familiar formula that representations were made either too early or too late'. His sarcasm achieved no more than the old India Office carefulness; Creech Jones answered (17 December 1948): 'I regret that there seems now little room for further discussion here in London.' The Chettyars, like the labouring Indians, were pawns in a much bigger game.

The unrest in Malaya was not diminishing; this was no mere aftermath of wartime guerrilla activity; this was the next phase in a Communist attempt to bring the revolution to Malaya. The first strategy was to bring about the collapse of British authority by strikes and violence in the urban centres, especially Singapore. This effort had been defeated while the military administration was still functioning under Mountbatten. The civil officials, waiting to take over, pressed that the pre-war policy of banishing all suspected agitators should be applied again. Mountbatten rejected this policy. But on the resumption of civil administration in April 1946 banishment was re-introduced. At first Creech Jones directed that this penalty should apply only to criminals and not to political agitators; he also insisted that only aliens should be banished, and not British subjects as before. In October 1946 ten members of Chinese secret societies were deported to China.

On 30 September 1947, Gent wrote to Creech Jones asking that power of deportation be revived in respect of Indians in the Malay states. Gent recalled that Indians who were British subjects had never been deported from the Straits Settlements but up to 1941 had been liable to banishment from the Malay States. Gent accepted that it might be difficult to deport Indians born in Malaya; the Government of India and its representative, Thivy, might refuse to agree to this. But if there was evidence that an agitator was born in India, or what was now Pakistan, Gent recommended that banishment should be applicable. However, on 18 October 1947 Creech Jones replied by cable that he would not accept the proposal.

In June 1948, the Malayan Communist Party opened up its second strategy: a campaign designed to destroy British economic power in the rubber plantations and to bring the rural areas under revolutionary control. The British reply came swiftly; in June 1948 a State of Emergency was declared, and in July the M.C.P. was banned.

As one of his emergency measures, the High Commissioner of Malaya asked the Secretary for the Colonies for 'limited and temporary' powers to deport British subjects: he admitted that 'in practice Indian British subjects only would be likely to be concerned' (4 June 1948). Malcolm MacDonald (who since the dissolution of the Malayan Union had become Commissioner-General, South East Asia) added his support (6 June). He suggested that the Communists might deliberately recruit British subjects, knowing that they were immune from banishment. He added: 'The principle ... of the new British Nationality Bill seems to admit that members of the Commonwealth must in present day circumstances be allowed to regulate residence within their own territories of British subjects who are not their own citizens .... I see every reason why the Federation of Malaya should be permitted to oust the comparatively small number of British nationals ... who have proved themselves a grave menace.' MacDonald observed that the Governor of Singapore had objected to this change because agitators would move to Singapore where they had immunity; but as Penang and Malacca would also remain 'refuges', MacDonald regarded this fear as exaggerated.

Creech Jones cabled his reply to MacDonald on 16 June 1948. He agreed that the High Commissioner of Malaya might banish British subjects, provided that they were 'implicated in acts of violence or in organising or inciting persons to take part in strikes, disturbances or demonstrations in which violence or the threat of violence is used'. He would consider 'additional categories of malefactors', Creech Jones added, but he then went on to recall his despatch of 7 April 1948 regarding the Indian commissioners: 'We could not with consistency expel Indians who "belong" to Malaya and still resist the interference of the Government of India in matters concerning similarly situated Indians on the ground that they belong to Malaya' Creech Jones found himself face to face with his own insistence that the colonial Indians were not really Indians. He was given a way out by the fact that so many of the Indians in Malaya were first-generation immigrants. The new banishment edict applied to the whole of the Federation (including Penang and Malacca) but not to Singapore, whose Governor declined 'to seek powers to deport a British subject'.[36]

The delicate matter of telling India and Pakistan that they might expect shortly to receive unwanted guests, ejected for acts of violence, was entrusted to the High Commissioners at Karachi and

Delhi. Bajpai told the British High Commissioner that they accepted
that it was essential to restore law and order in Malaya therefore
'He did not complain of any action taken by the Malayan authorities
against Indians, but he did say that the Government of India would
have to protect their nationals'.[37] The House of Commons also
wanted to know what was intended by the new instructions. D. N.
Pritt was told that banishment proceedings 'may be taken against
British subjects who do not belong to Malaya'.[38] The principle of
'belongers' and 'non-belongers' was already being enunciated
by a British Government to distinguish between different types of
British subjects.

At the Commonwealth Relations Office, Horace Rumbold tried
to see the new policy in a more positive way: 'Our general policy
ought to be to give as much information as we can to the Governments of India and Pakistan about Communist activities in South
East Asia,' he minuted; 'I know that this may go further than past
practice,' he admitted, but it would prepare the way for a concerted
plan to fight Communism throughout Southern Asia. Some members
of the Government of India were ready to join in actions against
Communists, especially in the Ministry of Home Affairs, under the
stern control of Sardar Vallabhbhai Patel. The intelligence bureau
of the Home Ministry supplied the British with details of Indian
Communists going abroad, and the British responded with full
reports on persons banished to India. In December 1948, banishment
orders were passed on Kharter Singh and Puran Singh, Punjabi
Sikhs, and on Sockalingham from Madras. Other Indians were
deported on a 'voluntary' basis: as an alternative to being kept in
detention. Of the first group of 31 Indians deported or repatriated
to Madras, 24 were arrested on arrival and when a further group of
thirty arrived on 27 December 1948 the whole group were arrested.
Some of the deportees were not admitted into India, but were sent
back to Malaya because they did not fulfil immigration requirements
in India. These were arrested on disembarking in Malaya.[39] In
September 1949, the President of the Indian Estate Owners Association, R. N. Annamalai Chettiar, returned to Madras after a period in a
detention camp, after he had been passing money to the terrorists as
'protection'.[40] Even Singapore deported Indians on a 'voluntary'
basis: in November 1948, thirty-one Indians were thus deported.

The Colonial Office took care to keep the Government of India
informed: 'Since in our dealings with the Government of India in
regard to Indians in United Kingdom Colonies we have been at
pains to emphasise that we regard them, unless they are merely
temporary visitors, as residents of the Colonies and as owing their
first allegiance thereto', the compulsory return of colonial Indians

to India might be resented. This, however, did not affect 'voluntary' repatriation: India could not refuse to accept 'persons of Indian race', returning of their own accord, the Colonial Office argued.[41] The Government of India acquiesced in this proceeding; though Nehru informed the Indian parliament (erroneously) that no Indian detainees were being compulsorily returned to India.[42]

Compared to the Malayan Chinese, the Indians were not deeply involved in the guerrilla campaign. Dr B. V. Keskar, Deputy Foreign Minister, told the Indian Parliament on 15 December 1949 that, down to mid-November 1949, 295 Indians had been repatriated to India, after arrest; 270 were detained in Malaya for some alleged part in the campaign, and 40 Chettyars were arrested for paying protection money. The number of Indians being held declined thereafter, and early in 1950, only 187 Indians were under detention, compared to 5,621 Chinese, 1,005 Malays and 25 others; 6,105 aliens (almost all Chinese) and 121 British subjects (all Indians) had been deported. During the first two years of the Emergency, ninety-four Indians were killed, twenty-seven being Indian police constables while twelve were insurgents; the remainder were rubber tappers, caught in the crossfire. This compared with over a thousand civilians of all races killed during the same period, and also about 990 armed guerrillas shot by the security forces.[43]

Most of the Indians involved in the underground guerrilla movement were small people, more or less conscripted to serve and follow the terrorists. One of those who was shot was a leader: P. Veerasenam, formerly President of the Singapore Federation of Trade Unions (later proscribed). He went underground in May 1948 and was killed when a military patrol surprised his jungle camp. His death did not cause much of a sensation, but the capture of two other Indians of some political standing—Ganapathy and Sambasivam—created a considerable sensation among Indians in Malaya and brought repercussions in the relations between Britain and India.

Ganapathy went underground in June 1948. In March 1949, he was surprised on a rubber estate in Selangor, where he was trying to get supplies from estate workers. The estate manager and some auxiliary police surrounded him; he grabbed for his gun, but he was overpowered and arrested. Under the Emergency regulations, the unlawful carrying of arms automatically imposed the death penalty upon anyone caught and sentenced. Ganapathy was sentenced to death.

Thivy, the Indian representative, appealed for commutation, and in London, Krishna Menon wrote at once to Creech Jones to ask him to intervene (28 March 1949). 'The Government of India understand that he was charged of [sic] unlawfully carrying a revolver and a few rounds of ammunition,' wrote Krishna Menon, appealing for clemency; the 'overwhelming majority' of Indians in Malaya were law-abiding people, and leniency would make a good impression upon them, he suggested. Listowel replied, as Creech Jones was in Africa. Ganapathy had been tried before a High Court Judge, sitting with two Assessors; he had appealed against his sentence to the High Commissioner of the Federation (now Sir Henry Gurney) but the appeal was dismissed on the grounds that in exercising clemency the prerogative rested with the Sultan of Selangor in Council. Listowel's letter was dated 21 April; on 3 May, Krishna Menon went to see Listowel in the afternoon to ask for a stay of execution to enable the Government of India to make a 'formal submission'. A telegram was despatched, which reached Gurney on the morning of Ganapathy's execution; he refused to intervene, in consideration of the 'constitutional position', and also of 'the merits of the case'.[44] The execution was carried out.

In India, there was 'a storm of protest', according to the British High Commissioner (now Sir Archibald Nye). In parliament, Dr Keskar spoke with moderation; he acquitted the United Kingdom Government of responsibility for the decision, which was made in Malaya. He described conditions in Malaya: the insurgents shot at anyone moving down a road; John Thivy had twice been shot at. But his attempt to calm the atmosphere was ignored: Dr Sitaramayya, the Congress President said: 'Comradeship in the Commonwealth on the one hand, and utter want of consideration on the other, stand as poles opposed.'[45]

The situation acquired greater urgency and difficulty because Nehru had just returned from the critical conference of Commonwealth Prime Ministers at which agreement was reached on the continuing membership of the Republic of India in the Commonwealth. An announcement was issued in London in April, but Nehru had still to render his account of the proceedings to the Indian parliament. He was to address the Constituent Assembly on 16 May, and the death of Ganapathy might adversely affect his reception; what would make things impossible would be a further execution of an Indian insurgent; and this seemed very probable, for Sambasivam lay under sentence of death. Nye cabled London urgently to say that after consulting with Bajpai he considered it was essential to postpone the execution (9 May 1949).

Creech Jones acted at once; he cabled Gurney the same day to ask him to approach the Sultan of Johore with a view to a reprieve or a postponement of the sentence. The case of Sambasivam had proceeded more slowly and less surely than that of Ganapathy.

Sambasivam had been a Tamil school-teacher before the Japanese occupation when he lost his job, and worked as a clerk, translating pamphlets into Tamil. He joined a trade union as a clerk, but his union was declared illegal, so he again lost his job. His former Chinese associates in the union who were now with the underground, persuaded him to come into the jungle, where he was again given the task of translating pamphlets. One day he was told to go with his Chinese companions on a journey and was given a pistol, wrapped in a cloth, which he was told to use if they were attacked. The guerrillas were challenged by Malay estate police; Sambasivam pulled out his revolver, but was shot and overpowered. He spent some months in hospital recovering from his wound; thus, although he was arrested in September 1948 he was not tried until March 1949. On 2 March, the Assessors at this trial found him not guilty, and the judge ordered another trial. At the second trial on 22 March the Assessors (an Indian and a Malay) found him guilty, and he was sentenced to death.

Thivy interviewed Sambasivam several times, and was given the story of a poor clerk, pressurised into acting against his will: while he was wounded he had made a statement which implicated him; and at his trial this confession was the main proof of his guilt; consequently, the first two Assessors declined to find him guilty. Thivy reported that these were extenuating circumstances, and Krishna Menon took up the case with vigour; he interviewed Creech Jones, and also Attlee, and as a result a stream of telegrams began to flow from London to Kuala Lumpur.

Gurney was not impressed by this high-level intervention. He cabled Creech Jones on 11 May to inform him that Sambasivam had aimed his revolver to fire at the Malay policemen. His case had been considered by the Sultan of Johore in Council on 9 May, and the sentence was confirmed. Gurney pointed out that for the offence of carrying arms, up to that date fifty-six Chinese, five Malays and one Indian had suffered execution. Local opinion bitterly resented 'one law for Malays and Chinese and another for Indians', he said; feeling in Malaya would be 'inflamed' against the Indian community 'if there are suggestions that the administration of the law in this country can be influenced by the Government of India'.

For the moment, the stern words of Sir Henry Gurney were accepted. A telegram was drafted which was to form a message from Clement Attlee to Jawaharlal Nehru, stating that the United Kingdom Government was 'constitutionally unable to intervene with the discretion of the local authorities' in Malaya. This was despatched to Nye (11 May) with the request that he use his discretion as to whether to show the message to Nehru, or to Bajpai, or to hold it back; he was told to avoid 'a major issue' if that were possible.

Nye talked to Bajpai, who from his years of experience of the realities of empire was not impressed by Attlee's 'legalistic' explanation. Bajpai was most concerned because the Indian representative in Malaya had been ignored and because the Malayan Government had offered no information to the Government of India about what was happening: 'Had the Indian Government been informed before the execution of Ganapathy as to the decision which had been taken they would have had less cause for complaint' said Bajpai. Dr Keskar also complained to a member of the British High Commission that his government had been 'treated in a very offhand manner'. Nye insisted that whatever happened India must be informed in advance, with a full explanation of the reasons for the action. The decision to hang Sambasivam was 'universally condemned' in India he concluded, and it would be 'most unfortunate' if the execution was fixed for the day on which Nehru had to address the Assembly. India's relationship with the Commonwealth might thereby be damaged.[46]

All this counted for more than Gurney's local difficulties. He was told to find a way to lower the temperature immediately. Gurney saw Thivy and told him that there was no intention to execute Sambasivam on 16 May; in fact there was no immediate plan for an execution. The High Commissioner asked Thivy if he had considered taking an appeal to the Privy Council if it became necessary? Thivy replied that he did not think such an appeal would be allowed in a criminal case.

The Sultan of Johore reviewed the sentence on Sambasivam, and with a bland disregard for the wider implications, confirmed the death penalty. Execution was provisionally fixed for 4 June, and as if to make sure he was not bothered again, the Sultan departed for Europe on 29 May. However, the hint which Gurney dropped to Thivy had been taken. On his advice, Sambasivam petitioned the Sultan for leave to appeal to the Privy Council, and the Johore Government gave its sanction, on 3 June. Thivy and Krishna Menon put the legal process into motion and on 27 July the Privy Council in London granted Sambasivam leave to appeal. He was now effectively reprieved.

In India, the critical debate on India's future relationship with the Commonwealth passed off without embarrassment. One M.P., S. L. Saksena, moved an amendment to Nehru's motion endorsing the decision to remain in the Commonwealth. Saksena wished to defer the vote, on the ground that there was no advantage to India when Britain 'cannot give up imperial and racial policies'. Nehru turned aside the amendment, and informed the Assembly that the Government of India was interceding for Sambasivam; but they 'could not tell the Malayan Government that if Indians were arrested under the same regulations they should not be punished'. It was a helpful speech, reported Nye. India remained a valuable member of the Commonwealth, and Sambasivam remained alive.

His case was not reviewed by the Privy Council until 30 March 1950, when Lord Simonds announced that his appeal had been allowed; the conviction and sentence were set aside. The reasons for the judgment were not given until 10 May when it was announced that the main defect in the second trial in Malaya was that the judge omitted to advise the Assessors that Sambasivam had been found not guilty at his first trial.[47]

However, he was not yet a free man. He was kept in detention under the Emergency Regulations and then offered 'voluntary' repatriation to India. He arrived by ship at Madras on 8 June 1950. He informed the press that he was not a Communist and that he had not been a member of the I.N.A. He departed for Arcot, to join his parents.[48] After some time he disappeared; he was supposed to have gone to China.

During the years 1948-9, the Malayan Indians were concerned about their future status under the laws of Malaya and of India. The Federal constitutional solution left many Indians without citizenship rights, and even those eligible for citizenship hesitated to apply for fear that this would deprive them of their rights as Indians. The refusal of India to accept some of the deportees added to these fears.

The attitude of the Government of India was not altogether consistent. The message which Nehru had given to the Indian overseas communities — that they must identify themselves fully with the country of their adoption — had not been communicated so clearly to the Malayan Indians when Nehru paid his visit in 1946. The Indian representative, John Thivy, came down squarely for a Malayan citizenship which would give the Indians full rights and which all could accept with confidence. 'The Dominion Government [India]', Mr Thivy said, 'did not believe in divided loyalty and therefore did not favour the proposal [for federal citizenship] which, it suspects, aims at dividing naturalised Indians and Malayans.'[49] Thivy made this statement after receiving a letter from the Government of India (25 June 1948) which 'admitted that they realised the peculiar situation of Malayan Indians and they were considering measures to safeguard Indians who took up federal citizenship from losing their Indian nationality'. When the Indian Constitution was enacted it gave the option of registering for Indian citizenship to all whose grandparents were born in India: this included virtually all the Malayan Indians. This was welcomed by the President of the Malayan Indian Congress, Budh Singh, as offering protection 'until such time as Malayan citizenship became fully fledged and was internationally recognised'.[50] Most Indians sought Indian citizenship, though at least half of them were eligible for Malayan citizenship. When they realised that the time to register for their local citizenship was running out (after 1 February 1951 the conditions became stiffer) many also became Malayan citizens, and about 217,000 had acquired citizenship by 1951. At the same time, the Malayan Indian Congress changed its policy and advised Indians to register for the vote and in other ways claim their rights as Malayans.

The Federation Government was concerned to implement the Colonial Office policy of getting colonial Indians to look to their local government rather than to India. As part of this policy, the special position of the Indian Agent in relation to wage-fixing and the superintendence of immigration was abolished in 1949. R. G. D. Houghton, the Commissioner for Labour, justified these modifications by the termination of Indian immigration in 1938. He added 'I hope Indian immigration will never be resumed,' by which he meant that the supply of labour within Malaya was already sufficient for industrial purposes.[51] Commenting upon the abolition of the Agent's special powers, Sir Henry Gurney observed that the Indians 'should look to the Malayan administration and not to a government outside Malaya to promote their welfare'.[52]

It appeared as though the Government of India was prepared to cooperate in fostering this development. Subimal Dutt was now the second ranking official in the Ministry of External Affairs.[53] Concerning the Indians in Malaya, Mr Dutt told a member of the British High Commission, 'He had been very glad that there had been an increased tendency on their part to regard themselves as citizens of Malaya, and not as Indians temporarily resident overseas. He said that this tendency was being strongly encouraged by the Government of India, and particularly by the Prime Minister himself, who realised that in the modern world Indians could not expect to have it both ways and to claim the benefits of local citizenship and also of Indian protection. The Prime Minister had been giving this advice to Indian colonies not only in Malaya but throughout the world. It was not always very palatable to the Indians concerned, but the Prime Minister and the Government of India felt that they must encourage a more realistic attitude on the part of Indians overseas and they had been glad to note increased consciousness of this among Indians in Malaya.'⁵⁴

While India was prepared to encourage Indians overseas to make a commitment to the lands of their adoption, this was conditional on their being treated as equal fellow-citizens with others: and this equality did not just have a local significance, now that there was a new conception of Commonwealth citizenship, to which India subscribed. The Colonial Office still thought in terms of adherence to Britain, and, perhaps, of a status of 'British subject' which was superior to other kinds of status. The question was reviewed when India applied to appoint a Commissioner at Aden in October 1949. The British High Commission at Delhi wanted to know where the Aden Indians stood? They formed a community of about 9,500 out of the total population of 80,000 in Aden Colony: but were they 'potential Indian nationals or . . . potentially citizens of Aden, and presumably therefore of the United Kingdom and Colonies?'⁵⁵

Discussing this question, J. B. C. Huisjman of the Colonial Office wrote to F. H. Cleobury at the C. R. O. (4 November 1949) that the distinction they had drawn in 1948 between 'permanent' and 'temporary' residents was now inadequate, in view of the British Nationality Act, 1948. Would the C. R. O. be reviewing the status and functions of the Indian Commissioners in the light of the Act? The Colonial Office was a little out of its depth.

Mr Cleobury wrote back (16 November) that the 'lines of demarcation' should be based on citizenship and not on residence. It was important to make it clear that an Indian Commissioner could not make representations 'on behalf of any Indian citizen who also possesses United Kingdom citizenship. Only by doing so shall we avoid extending greatly the class of Indians whom we at present allow an Indian Commissioner to represent, for a great many permanent residents in the Colonies will be Indian citizens.'

There were difficulties in Malaya because only the Indians of Penang and Malacca were British subjects; therefore the Indian representative was in a position 'to make representations on behalf of a much greater proportion of Indian citizens than would be the case in United Kingdom colonies'. However, acceptance of Malayan citizenship by a sizeable proportion of the Indian community would reduce the number of those for whom the Indian representative could claim to speak.

This attempt to define the Indian commissioners' responsibilities more exactly did not seem to free the Colonial Office from its worries. A. G. Denton-Thompson replied to Cleobury (18 November 1949): 'The question as to whether Indians in the Colony of Aden who are at present citizens of the United Kingdom and Colonies are potential citizens of India must, as you have already pointed out, depend on a number of factors, and I am afraid that we are in no position to express any very definite opinion on the subject.' Indians from the Bombay side would be expected to register as Indian citizens; but then, three-quarters of the 'Indians' in Aden were Muslims. The Governor's opinion on this subject would be 'based on guesswork'.

It seemed that the emergence of India as a sovereign state with its own citizenship, along with the introduction of the British Nationality Act, had produced two divergent trends. There was a trend towards 'Commonwealth citizenship' which was interchangeable, and inevitably pointed towards equal rights and equal status for all at the end of the road. And there was a possible trend towards a comprehensive British and Colonial citizenship, which would be different from the separate citizenship of India — and, of course, different from that of the white Dominions. It was not apparent in 1950 that there might be a third trend: towards a white United Kingdom citizenship, which would leave the overseas Indians high and dry. At that moment the assimilation of different forms of status into a common Commonwealth citizenship seemed most probable. The British Nationality Act, 1948, although designed to confirm the existing rights of British subjects, seemed to have opened a door to a new kind of Commonwealth.

10

The Moment of Equality

Among the events of the early post-independence period, the most important for the overseas, colonial Indians were the passing of the British Nationality Act, 1948, and the acceptance by India of continued membership of the Commonwealth as a republic no longer owing allegiance to the British Crown (for the recognition of the British monarch as Head of the Commonwealth was devoid of any precise constitutional meaning). This decision — to achieve comprehension rather than definition — was at first of great advantage, to the colonial Indians especially. It meant that they got what the Colonial Office had been trying not to give them — the best of two worlds — or rather, three worlds — for they could be three different kinds of people, politically considered, at the same time. They could remain Indians — not merely in their culture and tradition, but also in their political status — they could be citizens, or subjects of the colonial territory in which they resided, with whatever political and civil rights this might offer — and they could also remain British subjects, citizens of the United Kingdom and Colonies, able to claim equal treatment with those born in Britain, should they decide to go to Great Britain for study or settlement.

It was hoped by those who promoted the British Nationality Bill, 1948, and by many others — such as Sir Benegal Narsinga Rau, the jurist and political philosopher — that there would be even wider advantages: a common Commonwealth citizenship, inter-changeable between all the members of the Commonwealth (or almost all, for even then South Africa was obviously never going to participate in that kind of association).

Yet there was another tendency that was strong, even in the 1940s; as it had been ever since the white colonies of the British Empire began to take charge of their own affairs. This was the determination of the different Commonwealth members to keep their own exclusive kinds of society. This determination had been stated by Smuts at the 1923 Imperial Conference, and had been voiced at every successive gathering of Commonwealth leaders. In 1923 the British Home Secretary had tried to reconcile the broad imperial idea with the narrow idea of Dominion exclusiveness by positing two concepts — one of nationality, which would be empire-wide, and one of citizenship, which would be determined by each individual Commonwealth country to suit its own political ideals. But this inevitably meant that there was a dichotomy between the two concepts; and if the individual, Dominion share of the domain of civil and political rights increased, this could only be at the expense of the common, shared, Commonwealth rights.

The 1948 British Nationality Act, and the creation of the concept of Commonwealth citizenship formed the greatest single effort to emphasise the shared rights — without, however, infringing upon the individual rights of each Commonwealth member. The effort succeeded for about ten years. The 1950s were to be the Commonwealth decade. Then came the reassertion of the exclusive nature of the society of the several member states: and in this reassertion, Great Britain took a leading part with the ambiguously-named Commonwealth Immigration Act, 1962. If the Commonwealth survived this shock, it was as a very different organisation than the hopeful band of comrades of the early 1950s.

That it was a Labour Government which launched the new ideas of Commonwealth citizenship was largely coincidental. The approach to imperial and colonial problems in 1945 started upon a bi-partisan basis. The Second World War, like the 1914-18 War, had brought the Commonwealth closer together and had again demonstrated how important Indian manpower was in the imperial war-effort. However, the sense of a shared purpose and identity had not focussed upon the question of Indian participation in Empire migration and settlement. When the Chatham House conference met in 1945 to survey the future of the Commonwealth, the white participants (including Creech Jones for the Labour Party) discussed only British (United Kingdom) settlement in the White Dominions. When a Labour Party committee had last considered the question of migration, they adopted the suggestion that the United Kingdom should confer with Canada, Australia, and the other self-governing Dominions 'with a view to a more liberal immigration policy...'. But the original draft, which continued '... without discrimination between nationals' was amended by the omission of the last four words.[1] The Labour Party, like the Conservatives, thought of the British Empire as a series of territories across the seas to which British people might emigrate, they did not think much about other peoples of the Empire emigrating; they did not think at all about other peoples coming to Great Britain as immigrants.

The starting point for the 1948 Act and the introduction of Commonwealth citizenship was actually a measure which sought to take a lead in the opposite direction: the Canadian Citizenship

Act of 1946.² This measure was the culmination of the long policy of isolationist Canadian nationalism which Mackenzie King had pursued. It represented a unilateral departure from the practice of the inter-war period in which matters of nationality had been reviewed by committees of successive Imperial Conferences on the basis of a common code. The common code had been breached by the Irish Nationality and Citizenship Act, 1935; but it had been possible to pretend that this had not affected the other Dominions because Eire was supposed to have opted for a special form of external relationship with the British Commonwealth. Canada, even more than Australia, was the foundation-stone on which the Commonwealth was built; the Durham doctrine provided the pattern for all subsequent constitutional development, even for the latest development in India. Now, Canada came forward with a new formula. On examination, the new formula was remarkably like the old one; only Canada had introduced the conception of Canadian citizenship as the source of political status for Canadians, rather than accepting this as the outcome of their status as British subjects, subjects of the Crown.

Having made their point, that they were Canadians first and British second, they went on to extend their citizenship to all other British subjects who were full members of the Commonwealth. Clause 27 of the Canadian Act provided that 'A person who has acquired the status of a British subject ... under the laws of any country in the British Commonwealth other than Canada ... shall be recognised in Canada as a British subject.' This was explained in the first schedule of the Act where the countries in the British Commonwealth were listed as: the United Kingdom, Canada, Australia, New Zealand, South Africa, Ireland and Newfoundland.

The rationale of the Canadian Act was clear: Canada recognised all the fully self-governing Dominions as enjoying a special relationship and status which made their peoples British subjects in a special and full sense. Canada was prepared to treat them as honorary Canadians. They could vote after one year's residence in Canada and could apply for a certificate of Canadian citizenship after five years (aliens residing in Canada could not vote, were not eligible to join the public services and were also disqualified from certain occupations).

In 1945 the status of full British subject (in the Canadian context) represented the political realities — Canada did not recognise the Southern Rhodesian as a full British subject, because his country was still subject to vestigial United Kingdom control. But Canada had legislated just before India, Burma and Ceylon acquired full self-government — Dominion status, as it was still called by some. Was

Canada going to change its attitude towards the 'Hindus' because they now came from an independent country? How far had the Canadian capacity to equate Canadian citizen so smoothly with British subject been assisted by the fact that, in 1945, the 'full' British subject was also, invariably, White?

Canadians would have to ask themselves these questions; in the United Kingdom they did not arise as all British subjects enjoyed automatic right of entry (providing they produced their British passports on arrival). The Canadian Act was welcomed as a helpful development. It had broken out of the straitjacket of the common code which had prevented Britain from bringing its nationality law up to date in many vital respects: especially with regard to British women married to aliens — who had, in many cases, found themselves very invidiously placed during the war years.

Therefore, when the Home Office put up a paper to the Cabinet on the implications of the Canadian Act, their conclusions were encouraging: the Act 'affords a convenient opportunity for considering whether the system now proposed by Canada is not, after all, preferable to the existing arrangements'. The Home Office was conscious that in Britain the distinction drawn between 'full' British subjects and other British subjects had never applied. But this was not a difficulty:

No distinction up to now has been drawn in the United Kingdom between different classes of persons who are British subjects, and all British subjects have enjoyed the right of entry into the United Kingdom. Under the Canadian system it would still be possible for the United Kingdom to continue to grant free right of entry into the country of all British subjects, from whatever part of the Empire they come, a privilege which has contributed to the loyalty and solidarity of the Empire.

Before introducing new legislation, the Attlee Government decided to consult with their partners in the Commonwealth. The matter was mentioned at the conference of Dominion Prime Ministers in May 1946, and at the request of Mackenzie King a preliminary meeting of constitutional experts was brought together at short notice to explore the situation. The chairman was Sir Alexander Maxwell, the permanent Under Secretary at the Home Office, who was to play the leading part in promoting the new concept of mutual citizenship. The preliminary conference was held on 30 and 31 May 1946. Maxwell led the discussions; he observed that the Canadian Bill preserved the principle of the common code: 'In the Canadian Bill, the gateway to Canadian nationality was also the gateway to British nationality'.

This phrase 'the gateway' of nationality and citizenship was to be in constant use during the debates of the next year or so. Almost all British politicians and civil servants accepted — and, indeed, rejoiced in — the concept of 'the gateway'. It was a revealing metaphor. A door may be kept shut, or open, or ajar: but a gateway is there to be walked through, and this was clearly how the right of entry of British subjects was viewed in the late 1940s. However, at this preliminary meeting of experts, Sir Alexander Maxwell did make the observation that 'If the United Kingdom introduced citizenship legislation, one of the questions they would have to consider would be the continuance of the unrestricted right of entry to the United Kingdom possessed at present by all British subjects'. On this point, Professor K. H. Bailey of Australia commented: 'The question of national status in respect of immigration was legally irrelevant'. He did not elucidate this delphic utterance.

At a Cabinet meeting on 27 June 1946, a memorandum was considered relating to nationality in which the status of married women was the main topic.[3] It was decided to proceed with a full-scale conference of Commonwealth representatives. It was 'impossible' to say whether India would participate, in view of the critical stage reached in the negotiations with Congress and the League. There was some worry from the Colonial Office point of view that the Canadian legislation would 'encourage a certain disintegrating tendency if applied to the Colonies'. The whole subject was referred to a Cabinet Committee, of which Chuter Ede, the Home Secretary, was Chairman, with the Lord Chancellor and the Secretaries for the Dominions, India and the Colonies as the other members. After two months they reported back to the Cabinet again.[4]

The Committee decided that there was 'no alternative but for the United Kingdom to participate in the new citizenship system'. The creation of a separate citizenship for Britain, and for each of the Colonies, had been considered — and rejected. The Committee recommended 'The creation in the United Kingdom legislation of a combined citizenship of the United Kingdom and the Colonies which would be the gateway through which the status of British subject should be conferred upon the inhabitants of both the United Kingdom and the Colonies'. The Committee conceded that there were 'obvious objections to the omnibus and somewhat unwieldy term' of citizen of the U.K. and Colonies, but these objections were linguistic, not legal; the Secretary of State for the Colonies was asked to produce 'a more convenient term'; therefore it appears to have been his brainchild.

It was recognised that India and Burma would join the White Dominions as countries entitled to enact their own citizenship laws; but as yet Ceylon was not regarded as being within the Dominion group. 'Under the new citizenship plan, United Kingdom legislation would . . . no longer recognise Eire citizens as British subjects, and the present cause of friction with the Eire Government would therefore be removed', though any Eire citizen who wished to remain British would be provided for, while all the Irish in Britain could acquire U.K. citizenship 'without undue formality'.

The final recommendation was that there should be 'A combined citizenship of the United Kingdom and Colonies which would be the gateway through which the common status of British subject should be conferred upon the inhabitants of both the United Kingdom and the Colonies'. The report of the Home Secretary's committee was adopted by the Cabinet at their meeting of 9 September, with very little discussion and no strong objections, though A. V. Alexander, on behalf of the Royal Navy, was worried lest the new law of nationality might exclude recruits who were coloured or who came from Eire.

Invitations were issued to the Dominions and to India and Burma to attend the Commonwealth conference, and the parliamentary lawyers produced a draft Bill just before Christmas 1946. The India Office comment on the Bill was that there were several possible courses which India might take: India *might* remain within the Commonwealth, India *might* agree to all Indian citizens being British subjects, India *might* make no distinction of race in granting citizenship to all who were resident in the country (including Europeans): but unless India was prepared to accept each of these provisions, then the proposed legislation would not cover future developments. M. J. Clauson of the India Office sent R. N. Banerjee an explanation of the new proposal (20 December 1946) with the comment that under the Bill British subjects residing within the territory of another Commonwealth country would enjoy 'a position which may be said to come between that of (*a*) local citizens, on the one hand, and (*b*) aliens on the other'. The explanatory note issued by the Home Office was rather more encouraging, stating that Britain 'will be anxious to preserve as far as possible within the limits of the new Commonwealth Citizenship scheme the privileged position hitherto possessed by all British subjects, whether they are of United Kingdom, Dominion, or Colonial origin and connections'.

It seemed necessary to reassure the Dominions — who were the only part of the British Empire to be put into a somewhat different category under the new legislation — that they would still be part of the family: 'Citizenship of the United Kingdom and Colonies can be acquired as of right, and once acquired cannot be revoked as can a certificate of naturalisation granted to an alien'. Indeed, the purpose of the Commonwealth conference was to encourage the development of reciprocal relationships equivalent to a combined nationality and citizenship for all: 'In order to give practical value to the common status it would be desirable that, as far as practicable, equal treatment under its domestic law should be accorded by each member of the Commonwealth to citizens of other parts when residing in its territory. It is appreciated that this ideal could not in practice be fully realised.' Having stated the argument for a reciprocal Commonwealth, the Home Office Note then went into reverse and stressed the individual, exclusive character of nationality arrangements:

The governments of many countries of the Commonwealth could not for reasons of immigration policy accept a system of unrestricted movement of British subjects inside the Commonwealth, and Clause 25, pages 42-43 of the draft Bill itself (following Section 26 (1) of the 1914 Act) preserves for Colonial Governments their powers *inter alia* to restrict the admission of British subjects to their colonies [this was recorded while Kenya and Fiji were preparing to impose restrictions on entry]. As to the position of the United Kingdom, it will be remembered that at the meeting in May, it was indicated that the adoption of the Commonwealth Citizenship system could involve an examination of the question whether the unrestricted right of entry to the United Kingdom possessed at present by all British subjects could be continued.

This British insistence upon invoking a right to control entry, never exercised in the past, may have arisen from the uncertainties of the hour; nobody knew what was going to happen in Burma, or even in India. A. F. Morley of the Burma Office issued a warning: 'H. M. G. should be careful... not to be landed on the departure of India from the Commonwealth with the protection of such Indians in Burma as the Government of Burma, whether or not Burma remains within the Commonwealth, is unable to accept as citizens of Burma'. If Indians in Burma were denied citizenship, then Clause 4 (1), i, of the draft Bill — which conferred citizenship of the U.K. and Colonies on any person whose father was British, that is a subject of the British Empire — would make these Indians a British (United Kingdom) responsibility. Mr Morley suggested that Clause 4 (1), i, the 'mopping up clause', as it was being termed, should be looked at again.

On the pattern of the Canadian Act, the draft Bill provided a schedule defining the 'Members of the Commonwealth.'[5] Schedule 1 was broader than its Canadian counter-part, but was still curiously selective. The Members of the Commonwealth were given as Canada, Australia, New Zealand, South Africa, Eire, British India, Newfoundland, Southern Rhodesia and British Burma. When the

Ceylon Prime Minister obtained a glimpse of this provision he asked that Ceylon be brought into the schedule. This was recommended to the Cabinet in a paper presented by the Secretary for the Colonies (12 August 1946) which argued: 'If Ceylon were included in the First Schedule...a powerful weapon would be provided which a responsible Ceylon government could use against India.' An impression of loyal little Ceylon needing to be protected against an Indian Juggernaut in settling the question of the Indians living in Ceylon was being sedulously promoted by the Colonial Office. The plea was accepted; Ceylon was invited, and yet another bargaining point in obtaining a solution for the Ceylon Indians was abandoned.[6]

However, India was taking little interest in the question of British or Commonwealth citizenship at this stage. Although Mr. Banerjee had asked for an invitation to the conference, the decision had been taken in the Department of External Affairs and Commonwealth Relations not to send anyone from India. Perhaps somebody might have been sent from the office of the High Commission of India, but the High Commissioner, Sir Samuel Runganadhan, was due to go to Geneva, his deputy, Vellodi, was on leave in India, and Waris Ameer Ali, Legal Adviser, refused to attend the conference 'on political grounds' (presumably he was an adherent of Pakistan). This astonishing state of affairs was accepted; in the disorganisation into which India's interests in London had fallen by the end of 1946.

When the British Commonwealth Conference on Nationality and Citizenship assembled in London on 3 February 1947, ten countries were represented: Britain, with a team of nine, Canada (5), Australia (3), New Zealand (2), South Africa (3), Eire (4), and Newfoundland, Southern Rhodesia and Ceylon with single representatives. Runganadhan was supposed to be present as an 'observer' for India, but he disappeared after the formal, opening session. A representative of Burma joined the conference at its fourth meeting.[7]

The Conference held eleven sessions before agreeing upon the final report on 26 February, while two committees were also set up to compare the British and Canadian legislation and to examine the different classes of citizens of the U. K. and Colonies. The main work of the Conference was to go through the draft British Bill in complete detail, introducing revisions where these were desired to suit the interests of the other participating countries. From time to time Maxwell emphasised that the conference had not been convened to draft or redraft the Bill; but the distinction was rather meaningless because the 'scheme' which the conference finally produced (it was carefully not referred to as a Bill) was substantially different from the 'scheme' which was put forward in the name of the U. K. representatives at the start of the proceedings.[8]

Each participant approached the problem from that of his own country's needs and aspirations. Almost alone, Britain attempted to broaden the conception of citizenship so that the Commonwealth became much more of a mutual, reciprocal association. Canada, Australia, New Zealand and Southern Rhodesia wished to preserve the easy assimilation of people from Britain into their own polities. South Africa and Eire were determined to reassert their own national integrity and independence. Ceylon and Burma were preoccupied with the question of their Indian immigrants.

Although the conference included formidable legal expertise, there was no breakthrough to more exact and efficient definitions of legal status. W. E. Beckett, legal adviser at the Foreign Office, attempted to secure agreement on the basis of the willingness of all to unite: the status of a British subject, he suggested, rested upon 'the sum of citizenships' of all the countries represented there. This definition was immediately repudiated by Eire. Mr Boland indicated that for Ireland cooperation with the Commonwealth represented their 'many interests in common': they were ready to concede privileges not granted to aliens, but there was no question of any common status. Nobody else was so dogmatic, but it emerged that the two Asian participants were equally shy of generalised commitments.

It was impossible to get agreement on a common approach to citizenship. The White Dominions and Southern Rhodesia all demonstrated that British (United Kingdom) immigrants were treated on a separate standing to aliens. Mr Hogan of Australia said British subjects were 'on the same footing as Australians'; Mr Adams of New Zealand said they made 'as little distinction as possible' between Briton and New Zealander: Mr Morton of Southern Rhodesia mentioned that their immigration practice was to admit eight British subjects to every one alien, while farming land was restricted to British subjects. There was nothing new in this: but nobody was announcing that in future these brotherly gestures would be bestowed upon all British subjects, White, Black and Brown.

It was left to E Maung of Burma to state candidly they 'had of necessity to differentiate between two classes of British subjects—Indian nationals, and nationals of other Commonwealth countries'. Whereas the others were given the same privileges as Burmese citizens, the Indians were liable to deportation if 'convicted of certain criminal offences' and were subject to restrictions on the holding of land. Mr de Silva was not so blunt; he did not announce that Ceylon intended to discriminate against the Indians. He did indicate that they rejected the *jus soli* (or qualification by residence and upbringing) and recognised in its place *domicil* [sic]. Hence, in Ceylon there would be two classes of British subjects—Ceylon citizens, and non-citizens who were 'British subjects by reason of birth there: and the latter class might be a permanent one'. In relation to civil and political rights, the latter class would only obtain the vote if they 'could pass certain domiciliary tests'. Sensing, perhaps, that his remarks were out of tune with the proceedings, de Silva made a perfunctory attack upon Wessels of South Africa concerning 'the position of Indian British subjects in that country'. Helpfully, de Silva pointed out that British subjects residing in Ceylon, but excluded from citizenship, would either qualify for the citizenship of another Commonwealth country or else 'would become citizens of the United Kingdom and Colonies'. As his country did not become independent until a year after the conference, it was not too late for the Colonial Office to remonstrate, but no notice was taken by Whitehall of these frank warnings, perhaps because in the final report, although Ceylon went on record as insisting that it was not even desirable to link nationality and citizenship, still, if all the rest were committed to this, Ceylon 'would endeavour to fall in'. In a Commonwealth which included South Africa, this was a safe promise.

The question of dual citizenship was extensively discussed, and a memorandum on the subject was submitted by the United Kingdom. The white Dominions opposed dual citizenship: they argued that if it were made easy for British subjects to acquire full rights in other Dominions, and also easy to reclaim the original citizenship on returning home, then the dual provision was unnecessary. Eire also objected strongly to provisions for enabling Irish citizens to be part of the United Kingdom. The U. K. view was that 'double nationality cannot be avoided unless all countries are prepared to frame their nationality laws on identical lines'. Earlier British attempts to restrain dual nationality had given way to an acceptance of *jus saguinis* as legitimate and even desirable: 'Experience of two world wars has shown that the loyalty of British communities abroad in time of national emergency has justified the course pursued in the United Kingdom of allowing these families to remain British subjects even at the cost of perpetuating double nationality'. In the report it was stated that Britain suggested: 'It would be desirable that a citizen of one Commonwealth country should be in a position to obtain the citizenship of another Commonwealth country as of right.' The conference divided over this proposition, though it was acknowledged that 'a properly qualified person could not be refused citizenship'.

Another issue on which the United Kingdom was in a minority

concerned the liberalisation of the rules concerning British Protected Persons. Mr. Beckett indicated that it was proposed to make it easier for them to acquire British citizenship: they would qualify after one year's residence in Britain or in a British protectorate, and once acquired this citizenship might not be revoked. Morton of Rhodesia opposed making things easier for British Protected Persons. He pointed out that such persons might enter Southern Rhodesia from Nyasaland, and acquire the vote 'if they passed an educational test (which was easy) and a property test (which was small)'. This might be the means of 'swamping' the native vote. The conference left aside the question of British Protected Persons.

Altogether, the conference endorsed the British proposal for a new formula for citizenship and there were indications that most of the Dominions would reciprocate the United Kingdom's recognition of special relationships in their own legislation.

The first half of 1947 was a period when many of the Labour Government's policies were being put onto the statute book. The Cabinet was not able to turn to the nationality question until August: and then pressure of business pushed back their consideration until September. In its dying days, the India Office prepared a brief on the British Nationality Bill: mainly for the benefit of the Home Secretary, it would seem. As the Government of India had failed to send an expert to the February conference, 'the two successor governments will not be in a strong position to raise objections', the India Office observed unkindly. It was hoped that India and Pakistan would take the British Bill as a model when they came to frame their own legislation. Part II of the Bill, defining the various classes of citizens of the U.K. and Colonies 'so defines citizenship... that persons who properly 'belong' to these territories should qualify for citizenship of them while persons who 'belong' to other Commonwealth countries should be catered for by the Governments of those countries'.

It was important to include as many as possible of the Europeans living in India as citizens of the U. K. and Colonies: 'they would resent being regarded as citizens of India or Pakistan and not as citizens of the United Kingdom'. Most would qualify by virtue of their birth, or father's birth, or—if born before 1915—grandfather's birth in Britain; but inevitably there would be some 'heartburning'.

The India Office noted that 'a large proportion of Indians settled in the Colonies will be regarded as citizens of those Colonies'. Any person who before the Bill was a British subject would become a citizen of the U. K. and Colonies. 'The governments of India and Pakistan may not like to be deprived of the opportunity...of intervening on behalf of Indian communities whether in Colonies or in Protectorates, etc.' It was 'inevitable' that some Indians in the Colonies would have dual nationality.[9]

Creech Jones was concerned that this opportunity to wean the colonial Indians away from attachment to their motherland should not be missed. He hoped to get the citizenship provisions extended so as to include British Protected Persons. He wrote personally to Chuter Ede (6 August 1947):

> It is the policy of H. M. G. to encourage such Indians [in Protectorates and Trust Territories] to regard themselves as an integral part of the local population and to look to the Colonial Governments to safeguard their interests and welfare; for the same reason any attempts on the part of the Government of India to interfere on their behalf are resisted. It would not accord with this policy at all that Indians born in these territories, the great majority of whom will belong to families permanently settled there, should under the new citizenship legislation be excluded from citizenship of the United Kingdom and Colonies ... I should therefore prefer that the Bill should be amended so as to include such Indians among those British subjects who, when the Act comes into force, will become automatically citizens of the United Kingdom and Colonies. This procedure would have the additional advantage of avoiding the marked difference which would arise between the treatment of Indians born in Protectorates and Trust Territories and those born in the Colonies ... It does not seem unreasonable that this procedure should be so designed as to confer citizenship of the United Kingdom and Colonies upon persons who as British subjects have their homes in territories administered under the authority of the United Kingdom Government. But there is less reason to depart from the ordinary principle of the *jus soli* in the case of persons born in these territories in the future, whose parents are already the citizens of another country of the Commonwealth.

The draft Bill included certain additional sections designed to improve the position of British Protected Persons, but Chuter Ede and his advisers were not prepared to give them parity with Colonial-born British subjects.[10] And so, Indians born in Uganda, Zanzibar and Tanganyika were not automatically brought within the provisions of the 1948 Act.

During the summer of 1947, Burma drifted out of the Commonwealth (though formally the break came on Independence Day, 4 January 1948). The decision by the Constituent Assembly to proclaim a republic appeared to clinch the matter, though in the last months of his life Aung San wondered whether he had been too hasty in rejecting the Commonwealth idea, and questioned Sir Hubert Rance about the possibility of forming an external association, like Ireland. Sir Benegal Rau acted as constitutional adviser to the Burmese leaders, and he emphasised the significance of Commonwealth membership. In June 1947, Rance wrote to Mountbatten: 'The time seems ripe for a new conception of association within the Commonwealth, not necessarily owing allegiance to the Crown, especially for those countries which have no ties of blood, culture or religion.' However, the assassination of Aung San in July, and the succession of U Nu (who did not want to be premier) meant that the question of continuing Commonwealth membership went by default. On 23 August 1947 A. F. Morley, with what remained of the old Burma Office, informed the Government of Burma that as they were leaving the Commonwealth their citizenship practices were no longer of concern to Britain. They were on their own.

The draft British Nationality Bill was sent directly to the governments of the White Dominions. Relations with India and Pakistan were still rather tentative, so the Bill was sent to the British High Commissioners in those two countries. However, when the contents of the Bill were shown to S. Dutt at the Ministry of External Affairs, he replied that the Government of India did not object to the Bill (5 November 1947). There would be no citizenship legislation in India until after the Constituent Assembly completed its work. Similarly, the Pakistan Government raised no objection to the Bill.

Sir Terence Shone was most concerned about the status of the domiciled European and Eurasian community in India. Many thousands of 'first-generation' Anglo-Indians would become U.K. citizens under the Bill; but what of the remainder? Shone reviewed the question in the light of three developments: at this time, the Commonwealth Relations Office was thinking in terms of 'Situation A', in which India continued to be a Dominion, on the same basis as the White Dominions; 'Situation B', in which India would leave the Commonwealth, but preserve some vestigial links, like Eire; and 'Situation C', in which India would pull out entirely.

H. A. F. Rumbold of the C.R.O. addressed L. S. Brass at the Home Office (6 December 1947) on the plight of Europeans living in India whom the British High Commissioner could not 'protect' if they were not United Kingdom citizens. He asked that U.K. citizenship be granted to Europeans born in India, Pakistan, Ceylon and Burma but 'domiciled in the United Kingdom or in any Colony'. Rumbold acknowledged that this proposal went against the policy of the Foreign Office and the Home Office, which were 'opposed to any mention of domicile' because of the 'inherent difficulty' of proof. It would also give a lever to Ceylon, which the Colonial Office reported was pressing for postponement of the British Nationality Bill and urging 'the principle of domicile rather than the *jus soli* for Commonwealth citizenship'.[11]

In order to meet the point raised by Rumbold, the Home Office eventually extended the provisions of U. K. citizenship considerably. Clause 12(6) provided that U. K. citizenship could be claimed by anyone 'descended in the male line' from a person born in the United Kingdom or the Colonies who intends to 'make his ordinary place of residence within the United Kingdom and Colonies'. This took care of Europeans and Eurasians in India and Pakistan who intended to emigrate to Britain or a British Colony; there also remained the 'mopping up clause'—13(2) which gave citizenship of the U. K. and Colonies to all British subjects 'on the day on which a citizenship law has taken effect' in any of the independent countries of the Commonwealth, unless they opted for the citizenship of that country. This disposed of the problem of British subjects without citizenship; it also enlarged the number of citizens of the United Kingdom and Colonies, which, in 1947 and 1948, appeared to be a desirable consequence.

While these extensions of U. K. citizenship were being negotiated, the Home Secretary was pressing for an early place for his Bill in the business of Parliament; the Legislation Committee of the Cabinet recorded on 18 November 1947 that the Home Secretary 'pressed very hard' for his Bill: the 'whole present position was most untidy' he complained. It was settled that the Bill would be published in two weeks' time, but again there were delays and it was not issued until February 1948, when an explanatory White Paper was also published.[12] This included an outline of the provisions of the Bill, with a brief account of the consultations which had gone into its preparation and an explanation of the philosophy which it expressed.

The underlying principle was that 'the people of each of the self-governing countries within the British Commonwealth of Nations have both a particular status as citizens of their own country and a common status as members of the wide association of peoples comprising the Commonwealth'. The Bill was said to be acceptable to all the member countries: 'The new scheme under which the citizenship of a Commonwealth country becomes the gateway to British nationality results in the creation of a common citizenship for the people of the United Kingdom and of the Colonies... The principle of complete equality of status has been preserved.' Britain and the Colonies were said to be 'one community'.

The White Paper then went through the Bill, clause by clause: thus, under Clause 6(1) 'A citizen of a Commonwealth country... will have an absolute right to become by registration a citizen of the United Kingdom and Colonies' if resident in Britain for twelve months 'or such shorter period as may be allowed by the Secretary of State', or if he were in Crown service he automatically acquired the same right. Of British Protected Persons it was stated that though not British subjects they were 'members of the association of peoples comprised within the Commonwealth' and therefore not aliens and entitled to apply for naturalisation while living in a protectorate. The citizens of Eire, while not British subjects, 'will continue to be treated in the same manner as British subjects' on a basis of reciprocity. It was all very hopeful and forward-looking and in the spirit of comradeship which the Commonwealth had demonstrated in the recent war.

While Britain prepared to consider the new citizenship based upon partnership, there were others in India reflecting upon the way ahead. Sir Benegal Rau, as constitutional adviser to the Constituent Assembly, was specially attracted to the idea of a new Commonwealth, transforming the old Empire, in which India would play a full part. Between October and December 1947, Rau visited the United States, Canada, Eire and Britain for discussions with constitutional experts. In Canada and Ireland he talked to two of the participants in the Commonwealth Conference on Nationality and Citizenship—M. H. Wershof and F. H. Boland. Boland, the Irish Foreign Secretary, explained to Rau how the reciprocal arrangements between Eire and Britain would give both countries mutual benefits of citizenship: 'This indicates a possible mode of evolving a common citizenship,' noted Rau, 'even as between countries that do not acknowledge a common allegiance.'[13] Rau also was advised by those he met that India should settle the question of nationality and citizenship without delay.

When he returned to India, Rau put together his ideas in a paper entitled 'India and the Commonwealth' which was given to Mountbatten (still Governor-General of India), Jawaharlal Nehru, and a few others in January 1948. Rau demonstrated that the English legal and constitutional ideas which had inspired the Commonwealth were in full accord with India's own ancient political philosophy. He urged that there were also practical reasons why India should remain in the Commonwealth 'at least for the present'; it would help to provide stability, while India dealt with the conflicts which had emerged with independence, such as the disputes over Kashmir and Hyderabad.[14] As he wrote, newly-independent Burma—outside the Commonwealth—was confronting the challenge of a Communist rising, and doubtless this example was alarming to Rau.

In his lawyer's way he asked himself a number of questions: Was there room within the Commonwealth for a state with a republican constitution? In view of the treatment of Indians in certain Dominions...would it not be better to sever the British connection?

Was membership of the Commonwealth consistent with, or detrimental to India's membership of the United Nations? If India stayed, what changes would have to be made in the status of the Dominions, as the political units of the Commonwealth?

Rau tackled the last question first: he decided that if the constituent units were called 'Sovereignties' this would describe their status accurately; they were, as he argued, independent already. The U.N. question also was not troublesome. In its brief existence, the U.N. had seen the Commonwealth members voting on different lines (Rau was too tactful to mention South Africa; he cited the case of Palestine when Canada, Australia and South Africa voted for partition, India and Pakistan voted against, and Britain abstained).

Over the question of a republic within the Commonwealth, Rau suggested that a process of evolution was continuing and that a stage had arrived at which the unity of a common allegiance to the Crown might be realised within a common citizenship.[15] The British Nationality Bill appeared to be a sign that this development had already begun. Then what about the overseas Indians? Rau recorded:

This is an issue on which India will have to fight with all her might and main ... It is hardly to be expected that the position of Indians [overseas] would improve by India's severance of the British connection. Indeed, the reverse may well be the case. If India continues in the Commonwealth she would be in a better position to fight for a common citizenship with full civil rights and no racial discrimination. There is a growing consciousness in England and perhaps elsewhere that the British Commonwealth, as at present constituted, consists for the most part of persons who are not of the British or any European race and that any form of racial discrimination should be strongly discouraged as disruptive of the Commonwealth. A sign of the times [was a speech in parliament by a Labour Minister who condemned] ... "The grave injury done to the interests of the British Commonwealth by any form of racial discrimination" ... The idea of human rights is on the march throughout the world and its progress can in no way be impeded by India's continuing to be within the Commonwealth.

This paper brought an immediate comment from one who was a trusted adviser of Earl Mountbatten, Lieut.-Colonel V. F. E. Erskine-Crum, whose official position was that of Conference Secretary to the Governor-General. Erskine-Crum's memorandum (dated 6 February 1948) differed from Rau in that allegiance to the Crown was seen as the main stumbling-block in the way of India's continuing membership. The argument that a common citizenship would provide the bond did not solve that problem: 'Should we not face up to the fact that it is highly improbable that India—and out of the question that Burma—will agree to remain in (or return to) the Commonwealth so long as allegiance to the Crown remains a prerequisite for this?' Erskine-Crum suggested that the solution might be to recognise a common citizenship for all, but to accept two categories of Commonwealth members: those who remained Dominions, offering allegiance to the Crown, and those who accepted the Crown 'as a symbol of unity'. Mountbatten approved of the suggestion. He pointed out that already the Commonwealth had swallowed the existence of one member (Eire) in a different category to all the rest. The only alternative, he believed, was to reduce all the members of the Commonwealth to the second category of states which acknowledged the Crown as a symbol of unity.

Just at this time, the Drafting Committee of the Constituent Assembly finished the first stage of the task of producing a constitution. The committee was headed by Dr B. R. Ambedkar, the Law Minister, and from October 1947 it had been preparing a constitutional draft, with Sir B. N. Rau to provide guidance. The result was a parliamentary constitution, with nothing of the Gandhian ethos; its spirit represented the viewpoint of the anglicised constitutional lawyers: and although the Congress had been committed to proclaiming India as a republic for over a decade, the draft opened with a preamble which made no reference to India as a republic and described the new polity by the neutral term of 'state'. The draft constitution was published on 26 February 1948.

Against this background, Mountbatten discussed Erskine-Crum's ideas with Nehru and other leaders, and the two papers were passed on to the Ministry of External Affairs, where V. P. Menon read them, and gave copies to the British High Commissioner, A. C. B. Symon. Symon transmitted them to Sir Archibald Carter at the Commonwealth Relations Office (4 March 1948); he added that according to V. P. Menon, 'Prior to the Kashmir issue Pandit Nehru's attitude to India remaining in the Commonwealth had been a somewhat wavering one, but that he was veering round to the desirability of India's staying in. The Kashmir issue, however, might have caused him to start wavering again.'

Apparently Rau's attempt to argue the case for Commonwealth membership on realistic grounds—as insurance in dealing with disputes, such as that over Kashmir—made no immediate appeal to Nehru. The appeal of a common ideal was more powerful. Symbols were of vital significance to Nehru and he would not accept the continuance of the terms 'allegiance' and 'subject'. If India was to remain in the Commonwealth, new expressions signifying a new relationship must be found. Sir B. N. Rau approached the British High Commissioner in mid-March to acquaint him with current thinking: it was unlikely that there would be any immediate decision concerning India leaving the Commonwealth. For India the 'nexus' of the new relationship was the evolution of a 'common citizenship'; this was his personal view. This would necessitate the substitution of a new term for that of British subject, 'from its feudal implications of inferiority': Rau wondered whether 'Citizen of the British Commonwealth of Nations' would be an acceptable substitute?[16] At this same time, Gordon-Walker had talks with Rau and Bajpai and was given a similar message: he learnt that an official Indian request for a change of nomenclature would follow shortly.

Gilbert Laithwaite at the C.R.O. read Symon's despatch, and telegraphed back (19 March 1948) that the term 'Commonwealth citizen' would be examined as an alternative to that of British subject—implying 'the same meaning with the same rights and obligations'. But he was worried lest Rau had modified his views since composing his paper in January: 'The proposition [regarding the change of nomenclature] becomes a very different and much more difficult one if the conception of Commonwealth citizenship is disassociated from allegiance.'

In answer to this, Symon could only send back a personal message (26 March) repeating that Rau had told a member of the High Commission that in his view the 'nexus' of the constitutional situation was citizenship of the Commonwealth; Rau agreed, from his point of view, that 'the position is entirely different' if citizenship was disassociated from allegiance.

If the words of Rau were scrutinised carefully it could be seen that he had slightly shifted his position: he was no longer talking about a 'common citizenship' but now of 'citizenship of the Commonwealth'. The first might imply a supra-national arrangement; the second could function on a basis of agreement between states, as the Canadian scheme did. Perhaps Rau realised that his conception of a Commonwealth united by a common citizenship was opposed to the whole trend of Dominion policy: the White Dominions had reserved all questions relating to civil and political rights to be dealt with according to their own philosophies of race and culture. The retention of the status of British subjects was their link with the Mother Country: its main realisation had been the willingness of the Dominions to stand beside Britain in war. Yet this kind of allegiance was being openly questioned by South Africa and Canada; only Australia and New Zealand still honoured the old loyalty. A new commitment to a common, comprehensive citizenship went against the trend of the times. Beside, it was soon to appear that Rau had not sufficiently considered Indian nationalism in his enthusiasm for his ideal Commonwealth.

On 27 March, the British High Commissioner at Delhi was formally handed a request for a change of nomenclature: it was couched in pleasingly informal language: 'It would seem to us to be a good idea if the term "British subject"... be replaced by some such term as..."Commonwealth citizen"...' The same request was made directly by Krishna Menon in London to Clement Attlee on 30 March; it would be 'more acceptable to Indian public opinion', he declared. He added that he was aware that the proposal was being made at a late hour, after the Government of India had already formally indicated that they accepted the British Nationality Bill as it stood.

So, the matter had been put directly to the Prime Minister; but he seemed to be in no hurry to take it up. His private secretary wrote to Laithwaite to ask for advice (31 March). The question was now debated between the Home Office and the C.R.O. The Legal Adviser at the Home Office rejected any thought of substituting the new term for the old one; it would be 'void for remoteness' he stated. However, the Home Office was ready with a compromise. L. S. Brass wrote to J. P. Gibson at the C.R.O. (5 April) indicating that they were prepared to amend the first clause of the Bill by the addition of the words: 'Any person having the status aforesaid [of a British subject] may be known either as a British subject or as a citizen of the British Commonwealth of Nations.'

It was a clumsy solution, but it was something. Gordon-Walker was more enthusiastic than anyone about pressing ahead. On 7 April he wrote to the other Whitehall departments arguing for the introduction of 'interchangeable terms' into the Bill; they should start by getting opinions on the acceptability of 'Citizen of the British Commonwealth of Nations' with 'Commonwealth citizen' as the alternative: it was 'perhaps a question of saving the Commonwealth', he added dramatically. The Home Office, the Foreign Office, and the Cabinet Office all disliked the new terminology, but said that they would not oppose the addition: they were 'prepared to accept that the point is political'. On 8 April, Gordon-Walker was minuting 'We should come clean for Commonwealth citizen, but should clear it with Australia first of all'. In Australia, the term 'Commonwealth citizen' had been in use for nearly fifty years—but to denote the status of citizen of the Commonwealth of Australia, as compared to the status of citizen of the state of Victoria, Queensland, etc.

Next day (9 April) Gordon-Walker addressed a memorandum to the Prime Minister. 'It is clear that we cannot go the whole way to meet India by abandoning the term 'British subject'. [According to Parliamentary Counsel, this was legally impossible anyway.] My own strong inclination would be to go straight for Commonwealth citizen' as an alternative to British subject; but first they ought to 'meet the possible difficulty with Australia in the most tactful and persuasive manner possible'. This memorandum drew no reply from Attlee for over three weeks, but meanwhile the C. R. O. began to sound out the Dominions.

On 13 April, the Commonwealth Relations Office sent a circular telegram to the Governments of Canada, Australia, New Zealand, South Africa, Newfoundland, Southern Rhodesia and Ceylon informing them that India wished for the introduction of the term 'Commonwealth citizen' (there was no mention of the cumbrous alternatives). 'All that would be involved is a change of nomenclature' urged the C. R. O. 'It has been suggested that a favourable decision on this request might have an important bearing on India's future relationship with the British Commonwealth'. Trying to reassure the Anglo-Saxon Dominions, the C. R. O. concluded: 'We should be reluctant to see the complete disappearance of the time-honoured and well-understood phrase "British subject",' but according to individual preference each Commonwealth member could use either term.

Almost at the same moment (on 16 March) Dr Ambedkar, Law Minister and Chairman of the Drafting Committee of the Constituent Assembly of India issued a statement to explain why they had substituted the term 'state' for 'republic' in the preamble to the draft constitution: 'The object of the amendment is to see that nothing brings about an automatic and instantaneous severance between India and the British Commonwealth of Nations'. Ambedkar acknowledged that 'a very large body of Congressmen are opposed to any amendment'. He explained that it was incorrect to assume that Eire and South Africa had taken powers to adopt republican forms of government while still within the Commonwealth. He insisted that in their constitutional documents they were described as 'sovereign independent states': 'It is the existence of these words in the constitutions which have enabled the Courts to hold that South Africa and Ireland are still members of the British Commonwealth... "Republic" is incompatible with the allegiance to a King and has therefore the effect of terminating straight away India's membership of the Commonwealth,' declared Ambedkar.

Here was Rau's answer to Rumbold's doubts about the compatibility of Commonwealth citizenship and allegiance. It was ingenious; but would it satisfy the very different views of the Commonwealth relationship entertained by the different members? Would it satisfy those who had fought for India's freedom?

Replies to the C. R. O.'s cable of 13 April were slow in arriving;

on 22 April Ceylon cabled acceptance of the proposed new term and also requested that 'British subject' should be discontinued, though a compromise would be accepted. As no other reply had arrived by 23 April, the C. R. O. cabled again asking the others to respond. This produced an immediate response from Australia: it was adverse: the proposal had been given careful consideration but there were 'serious objections from Australia's point of view'. Southern Rhodesia also replied immediately and in the negative: they regretted the change very much: 'Very considerable importance is attached in this Colony to the term British subject'. Southern Rhodesia would not alter its own citizenship Bill to accommodate the change. New Zealand replied next day (24 April): 'The proposal is not viewed favourably here and we would be glad if it could be avoided.'[17] Newfoundland and South Africa indicated that they did not object to the proposal. It seems probable that Smuts would not have allowed such a sweeping innovation to pass without a more careful consideration of its implications, except that he was having to devote all his energies to the General Election looming up in one month's time. Despite the reminder from the C. R. O., Canada did not come forward with any response at all.

In view of these developments, Noel-Baker, Secretary for Commonwealth Relations, sent a telegram to the Government of India on 26 April to announce that there were 'no serious objections' on the part of Britain to making a change: a U. K. citizen 'while possessing the status of British subject could be described either as "British subject" or as "Citizen of the Commonwealth of Nations" '.

Noel-Baker also drafted a memorandum to the Prime Minister (1 May 1948) to inform him that the legal experts pressed for 'Citizen of the Commonwealth of Nations'. Noel-Baker appreciated that the alteration might delay the introduction of the Bill until after Whitsun, 'but the political issue is so important that I feel that is a risk we may have to face'. When he received Noel-Baker's note, Attlee commented, somewhat belatedly: 'I don't like the term, but you may try it on the Old Dominions, C. R. A. 2 May 1948.' Perhaps fearing that his chief was rather out of the picture, Noel-Baker went to see Attlee the next day. He was told that Lord Jowitt, the Lord Chancellor was strongly against the term 'Citizen of the Commonwealth of Nations'. 'The Lord Chancellor's view was that the phrase meant nothing, and that everybody would immediately ask "What Nations?" or "What Commonwealth?"...' The Prime Minister therefore suggested that those parts of the Bill which treated of citizenship and nationality should be taken out, and that a short measure dealing with the status of married women (the most prominent item in all previous discussions) should proceed.[18]

For different reasons, Noel-Baker and Chuter Ede were determined to go ahead with the whole Bill. A Cabinet meeting was to be held on 6 May, and they rapidly drafted a Cabinet paper for the purpose of convincing their colleagues of the urgent need to arrive at a decision.[19] Their memorandum began with some general observations: the populations of some Commonwealth countries were 'proud to be described as British subjects'; while to others, the term 'seems to indicate the continued domination of them by the inhabitants of the British Isles'. The older Dominions were reluctant to accept the use of 'Commonwealth citizen'; but its introduction into the United Kingdom Bill 'need not be dependent on the concurrence of each of the self-governing countries'. Those Dominions who wished, could frame their own legislation 'in terms of "British subject" only', and if this were so, Australia could 'no doubt be persuaded' not to object to the new term in the British Nationality Bill.

The Bill was ready to be taken in the House of Lords: its consideration was already fixed for 11 May (one week later). It should be prefaced by an announcement about Commonwealth citizenship. If the Bill were postponed until after Whitsun it could not pass in the present session. Postponement might leave India less willing to accept the present compromise proposal; it would also mean that Britain 'will lose the initiative and leadership in this matter'; different Dominions might then come forward with 'various discordant proposals'.

It should be recognised that the Commonwealth was in a transitional phase; in the future, some 'differentiation' between types of members might become inevitable; 'while some remain full members of the Commonwealth, others will fall into the position of associates rather than members.' The Bill provided a framework for such a possible development.

The conclusion of Chuter Ede and Noel-Baker was that they must face up to the situation at once if they wished to avoid India and Pakistan leaving the Commonwealth. They proposed that on 11 May it should be announced that the term 'Commonwealth citizen' would henceforth be accepted as the alternative of 'British subject'.

The matter was discussed in Cabinet on 6 May. There does not appear to have been any argument; it was stressed that there was 'no time for further consultation with Commonwealth governments if the Bill was to pass this session'; it was therefore agreed to present the new formula of Commonwealth citizen as the alternative to the old term British subject.

At once telegrams were sent off to Australia, New Zealand, Canada and South Africa: 'If the present opportunity is allowed to pass it may never recur,' said the C. R. O. If the formula was accepted by India and Pakistan, then it would be included in the British Bill. Although it was desirable that all Commonwealth countries adopted the same nomenclature, it was 'not inconsistent with our new scheme of nationality legislation' if Britain adopted the alternative forms while others preferred only the usage "British subject". 'It would of course be understood that in any such country, citizens of another country which [used]...only the term Commonwealth citizen... would be treated as if they were British subjects': this was introducing another dimension to the situation. Britain had argued that they were concerned only with nomenclature; now the question of practice seemed to be raised: a move towards the Indian idea of common citizenship.

In their cable to the Government of India, the C. R. O. stated (7 May) that they could not abandon the term British subject, but they were 'advised' that there 'would be no legal objection' to the use of Commonwealth citizen as an alternative. Whatever other Commonwealth countries might do, concerning their own nationals, Britain would treat Commonwealth citizens 'as if they were British subjects'.

'We have done our utmost to meet your wishes in this matter' the C. R. O. cable, drafted by Laithwaite, concluded. India was not disposed to argue: 'We agree with amendments proposed', came the reply on 9 May.

Canada at last awoke to the situation, and on 10 May told the C. R. O. that they would 'take no exception' to the alternative terms; indeed, they would amend the Canadian Citizenship Act to recognise the alternatives. Canada was now in a kind of interregnum between the old 'isolationism' and the 'internationalism' which was to come. Canada was now quite ready to be as Commonwealth-minded as anybody. New Zealand did not move so fast to learn new tricks; when its reply arrived (12 May) it was to say that there would be no objection to the changes in the British legislation provided that the new term 'shall have the same meaning' as the old. New Zealand did not want to oppose change; but equally she did not intend to give up trusted British standards for the unknown.[20]

The Commonwealth had survived its first test, in the transformation of a family into a club. But a great deal of the family atmosphere remained. More changes were needed before Indians could feel that this was the equal partnership to which they desired to belong.

The debate now moved from Delhi and Whitehall to Westminster. On 11 May 1948, the Lord Chancellor, Lord Jowitt introduced the British Nationality Bill with a panegyric on the British Commonwealth: 'Of all the remarkable contributions which our race has made to the art of government, the conception of our Empire and Commonwealth is the greatest' he said. The Bill became necessary because the common code convention had been 'completely shattered' by the Canadian Act. The new Bill reaffirmed the concept of a common nationality, but 'let it be plainly understood that common nationality does not necessarily confer rights in other member states': Australia's immigration policy was Australia's own affair. The conception of a common status was 'not mainly important because of its material advantages. It is, if you like, rather mystical', said Jowitt; he who had pooh-poohed the idea of Commonwealth citizenship because people would ask, what Commonwealth?

The main, solid fact that emerged from Jowitt's presentation was that any British subject (or Commonwealth citizen) 'is entitled to enter or leave the country at any time', and could exercise the franchise, being eligible to become a member of the Privy Council or the House of Commons.

Jowitt was followed by Lord Simon, the eminent lawyer, speaking first for the Conservative opposition. He declared that the self-governing Commonwealth was a 'two-decker arrangement', with its members as citizens of their own countries and also British subjects. Now that citizenship of Britain and the Colonies was unified, while the Dominions were separate, somebody from Jamaica was better off than someone from Australia or Canada: this was 'not a very happy result'. Simon observed that the formula had been evolved by an experts' conference, and asked how much time the Government had devoted to the subject? Jowitt assured Simon that there had been adequate discussion; he had spent 'nearly a morning' with Smuts on the subject, and had also talked to Mackenzie King. But Simon continued to insist that the Bill had not been preceded by a period of discussion.

Then up stood Lord Altrincham, formerly Sir Edward Grigg. He argued that there should have been a purely United Kingdom or British citizenship: to conflate this with Colonial citizenship meant that in the Colonies they would 'assume that it confers a right to political equality, whatever the constitution of the Colony to which they belong'. Why not just have British citizenship, he inquired?

Lord Jowitt professed to find Altrincham's argument difficult to follow; he commented 'Hitherto, we have not had any law discriminating against any British subject. I hope we never shall, but I do not know. If you are minded to discriminate, you can discriminate whether you call them subjects or whether you call them citizens'. When Altrincham pressed the question as to why it was necessary to have a citizenship for the U.K. and Colonies, Jowitt answered: 'If he accepts the principle that citizenship is the only gateway through which one can attain nationality, then if we do not have a citizenship of the United Kingdom and Colonies...we still have to deal with the Colonies.'

Altrincham, followed by Simon, asked for a white paper reproducing the views of the Dominions. Lord Addison replied that this would cause delay, and they intended to pass the Bill during the current session.

During the course of the debate, *The Round Table* appeared with a denunciation of what was called 'A Disintegrating Bill'. Ministers 'have been bamboozled by the notorious plea from "experts" for uniformity', *The Round Table* declared: 'It does not involve a levelling up to the wise and generous practice of the United Kingdom—; it must in practice involve a levelling down to the narrower nationalism of which, in this field, Canada has been the chief exponent.'

The debate wound on until 21 June, when the *Round Table* veteran, Altrincham, moved an amendment to replace the expression 'Citizen of the United Kingdom and Colonies' throughout the Bill by the words 'British subject of the United Kingdom and Colonies'. The purpose was to ensure that there should be no change in the previous status of all those affected. The Labour Government objected to the change, which made nonsense of the careful distinction between the general, Commonwealth or British 'nationality' and the specifics of citizenship, provided by Britain, and devolving upon the member states as they attained independence. Most of the peers thought otherwise, and Altrincham's amendment was carried by 75 votes to 21. The Government announced that the previous form would be restored when the Bill reached the Commons.

While the debate revealed clearly that the Peers disliked the new concept of U.K. citizenship and wished to retain the term British subject, their reasoning appeared to show that they wanted to preserve the traditional role of Britain as the Mother Country, for her brown and black wards as well as for her white children. There was hardly any discussion of the radical new proposal to make the terms Commonwealth citizen and British subject interchangeable. This seems to have been accepted as a sign of the times.[21]

When the Bill was discussed in the Commons, Chuter Ede opened the debate on 7 July by moving the restoration of the term 'Citizen of the U.K. and Colonies'. He claimed that the Bill was the 'natural sequel to the Statute of Westminster'. There were those who regarded a British subject as 'a person belonging to Great Britain' instead of 'a person belonging to any country of the Commonwealth who is a subject of the King'. It would be 'disastrous' if in the succeeding phases of transferring power 'a country should create British subjects without passing them through the gateway of its own citizenship'. The question of separate forms of citizenship had been discussed at the 1937 imperial conference, said Chuter Ede (he might have added that the question had been discussed since 1923) and now Britain was stepping into line with the Dominions. Chuter Ede justified the joint citizenship of Britain and her Colonies: 'By linking the United Kingdom and the Colonies we must give these people a feeling that...we recognise them as fellow citizens', he said. What was unspoken, but lay behind his argument, was the belief that the Colonies would long remain subordinate to Britain and would not need to claim their own separate citizenship.

Maxwell Fyfe, the Conservatives' legal spokesman (later to be Lord Chancellor), made a number of tactical criticisms: he suggested that the Bill had been formulated in mysterious circumstances—the proceedings of the committee of experts had not been published, and a decision should have awaited the declaration by the Dominions of their views. But his structural criticisms related to the supposed narrowing down of the concept of citizenship within the Commonwealth. 'The common basis of personal status' throughout the British Empire was 'not a shadow' he insisted. The new Bill reversed the process of the evolution of British nationality from Britain as the fount; henceforward, Britain would be enclosed within its own local citizenship: it was the end of 'The proud boast of the open door in this country to people from all the Colonies'. 'We were proud in this country', Maxwell Fyfe declared, 'that we imposed no colour bar restrictions, making it difficult for them when they came here.' The Conservatives objected to the U.K. citizenship innovation because 'we deprecate any tendency to differentiate between different types of British subjects in the United Kingdom. We feel that when they come to the United Kingdom there ought to be an open door and a reception for every type ... We must maintain our great metropolitan tradition of hospitality to everyone, from every part of our Empire.'

Some Conservative speakers were worried about the effect of the introduction of U.K. citizenship upon the position of Indians in Ceylon and South Africa. Lord Hinchingbrooke said that under the Bill they would be deprived of existing rights as British subjects and would be handed over to the governments of Ceylon and South Africa: 'We deprive them of equal rights against our own citizens.' Sir John Foster, a Conservative lawyer, saw the problem differently. The Indian in South Africa was a citizen neither of South Africa nor of India; 'Under the Bill he would be a citizen of the United Kingdom,' said Foster, 'he is still a British subject, but this is all an unnecessary complication.' Only one Conservative M.P. applauded the Bill: Sir Ralph Glyn welcomed the provisions bringing British Protected Persons nearer to the status of British subjects.

At the committee stage, Maxwell Fyfe again spoke as though the Bill created a legal barrier against British subjects heretofore partaking fully of British rights: 'It is wrong to invent the machinery of discrimination,' he said, 'when avowedly we do not seek to discriminate'. The Labour Government wanted to 'establish their own gateway, built in a manner which they alone decide, by which the citizen will come into the other stages... Our gateway should be the well-tried gateway of British subjecthood, as it has existed.'

Other Conservative M. P.s were stimulated to rhetorical gestures by the now beloved gateway simile; Ronald Chamberlain exclaimed: 'This old country should have kept the door wide open all the time for British subjects from the whole Commonwealth... I should have liked... the situation that any member of the Commonwealth became a recognised British subject immediately he set foot in this country.'

To one who listens to the echoes of this debate of 1948 in the 1970s, what seems like the sound of another language is the continual emphasis upon the need to treat all other members of the Commonwealth as equals whenever they set foot—as of right—in Britain. Throughout the debate—which continued, intermittently, from 7 to 23 July—there were only two speeches which could be explicitly construed as antagonistic to the free entry of black and brown Commonwealth citizens into Britain—though there were veiled hints that the Conservatives were prejudiced against coloured people, which John Foster found necessary to repudiate: he emphasised that coloured people 'can come to this country—even if it is distasteful to the Ministry of Labour—to get jobs here; they are entirely equal in this country'.

Two Members seem to have doubted this proposition. A Labour M. P.— A. E. Davies of Burslem—said: 'We who have our roots in the soil of Britain are proud of our nationality and are very jealous that it should not be lightly given away'. But he did not suggest any restrictive innovations. Kenneth Pickthorne, the High Tory representative of Cambridge University asked if Indians, disfranchised in South Africa, could come to Britain and acquire U. K. citizenship? When the Attorney General indicated that this was so, Pickthorne went on: 'We are now putting it in the power of a Dominion, by legislating any large class of its inhabitants out of citizenship, to put them... without our consent into our citizenship. That seems a very odd result of an excessive pursuit of equality of status'.

Concluding the Committee stage of the Bill, the Attorney General,

Sir Hartley Shawcross, declared: 'There is no such thing as a British subject who is a British subject only in a local area, and I hope there never will be, although there would be if this Bill were passed into law in the form in which Honourable Members opposite desire.' If any Dominion should discriminate against any group of British subjects, then the United Kingdom would announce: 'Those persons who are British subjects today will continue by our laws to be recognised as British subjects, and if you do not accept them we will pass them through our own gateway'. When the Committee of the whole House of Commons divided, the Government's amendment, restoring the Bill to its original form was carried by 308 votes to 111. Sir Ralph Glyn was the only Conservative to vote with the Government.[22]

The debate in the Commons, as in the Lords, was marked by an overall concern to ensure that British nationality preserved its empire-wide significance, and that all members of the Commonwealth, without distinction, should be free to come and go, so far as Britain was concerned. Again, the concept of Commonwealth citizenship failed to arouse comment, either favourable or adverse. The British Nationality Act came into force on 1 January 1949.

Sir B. N. Rau continued to be one of the most enthusiastic supporters of the idea of Commonwealth citizenship. When he presented the paper, 'India and the Commonwealth' (which had formed the main starting point for the Indian request for the introduction of the term, Commonwealth citizen) to a conference of international lawyers at The Hague in August 1948, they were moved to pass a resolution which stated:

That this Conference would welcome, as an [example of mutual or reciprocal citizenship] any arrangement whereby the incidents [sic] of Commonwealth citizenship under the British Nationality Act could become available, on a reciprocal basis and under agreed conditions to the citizens of countries outside the Commonwealth.[23]

The first (and only) example of this kind of external recognition of citizenship on a reciprocal basis was now to be formulated with the final departure of Ireland—the Republic of Ireland—from the Commonwealth. The process had been very like the disappearance of Alice's Cheshire Cat, but now came the last phase in which not even the smile remained. Attlee told the House of Commons on 25 November 1948: 'The Government regret that Eire will no longer be a member of the Commonwealth .... Accordingly [they] will not regard the enactment of this legislation by Eire as placing Eire in the category of foreign countries.' The declaration was followed by the Ireland Act, 1949, of which Clause 2 states: 'The Republic of Ireland is not a foreign country,' and enacted that the British Nationality Act should still apply to Ireland.[24]

This development might have seemed to suggest a model for India's future relations with Britain and the Commonwealth. The Constituent Assembly was to convene again in November 1948, and there were a great many amendments lying on the desk of the president, Rajendra Prasad. It was plain that the main body of Congressmen would not be prepared to blur over the standing of India as a republic. This was a fundamental doctrine to them. It seemed as though this was the sticking-point. The Republic of Ireland finally ceased to be associated with the Commonwealth when it adopted a republican constitution, though retaining all the benefits of being a Commonwealth member: this seemed the obvious way.

Before the Constituent Assembly met again, Rajendra Prasad asked Rau to meet him at Simla to go over controversial aspects of the draft constitution, 'point by point'. Concerning Commonwealth membership, Prasad noted: 'The question needs to be discussed on a plane higher than that ordinarily allotted to other questions of policy, and you have raised it to that plane. It will, of course, be for the Government and the members of the Assembly to take the decision in the matter, but it is useful as well that people generally give thought to it'.

Rau's mind was now concerned more with function than form. The Commonwealth was increasingly being described as a 'club'; Rau made the comment:

It must, however, be remembered that a club . . . cannot grow or flourish merely by liberal rules of admission; to attract or retain members, it must give them something worth-while and satisfying, not necessarily in material privileges, but at least in companionship in the pursuit of high ideals. Above all, there must be a sense of genuine equality among the members; for only then can each country be expected to give of its best and to contribute to the peace of this weary old world.

This theme closely coincided with the direction of Nehru's thoughts. The years 1948 and 1949 appeared ominous. In Europe, the Iron Curtain seemed to have turned eastern Europe into a prison, and the eye-ball to eye-ball confrontation over Berlin looked as though it must end in violence, war, conflagration. In Asia the stubborn, rear-guard action of Dutch and French colonialism continued in Indonesia and Indo-China, while in China the final crash of the Kuomintang regime and the end of the long march for the Communists presaged, perhaps, a new Communist forward march. An association which might work together for peace in this uncertain world needed to be sympathetically considered.

In October 1948, Nehru came to London to participate in a Commonwealth prime ministers' conference; the first such gathering he had attended. He was agreeably impressed by the atmosphere of mutual understanding: 'We may not agree about everything, but it was surprising what a large measure of unanimity there was,' he recorded. The subjects under discussion were mainly in the international sphere, and Nehru concluded that the objectives of the Commonwealth—as they emerged from the discussions—were 'the establishment of peace, the prevention of conflict, and the establishment of human rights all over the world': 'This meeting has shown me that there is great scope for the Commonwealth to function in this way,' declared Nehru.[25]

The atmosphere of the meetings was still very informal in 1948: eight men sat around the Cabinet table at Ten Downing Street, or strolled casually in the garden. The question of India's relationship with the Commonwealth was not on the agenda of the conference, but as Nehru later told the Indian Constituent Assembly, there were ample opportunities for 'private discussions, because it is a matter of high moment not only for us but also for other countries as to what, if any, relations we should have, what contacts, what links we should bear with these other countries'. Nehru explained that he could not enter into any commitments before the Constituent Assembly had completed the new constitution, but he pointed out that as long ago as 13 December 1946 the Assembly had agreed that India would be an independent sovereign republic, and this was immutable. On this basis Nehru emphasised that 'We desired to be associated in friendly relationship with other countries, with the United Kingdom and the Commonwealth.'

'How in this context it can be done or it should be done is a matter for careful consideration and ultimate decision, naturally, on our part by the Constituent Assembly, on their part by respective Governments or peoples,' so said Nehru, following Dr Ambedkar in the debate on the motion in the Constituent Assembly that the draft constitution 'be taken into consideration' on 8 November 1948.

India's gesture of friendship soon followed. At the annual gathering of the All-India Congress at Jaipur, a resolution was passed on 18 December 1948 which acknowledged that India's 'present association with the United Kingdom and the Commonwealth of Nations will necessarily have to change' on the establishment of a republic, but nevertheless 'Congress would welcome her [India's] free association with independent nations of the Commonwealth for their common weal and the promotion of world peace.'

Nehru communicated informally with Sir Stafford Cripps about the terms whereby a new Commonwealth association might be created: he suggested that acceptance of Commonwealth citizenship on a mutual basis could provide the formal link previously established by the common allegiance to the Crown. When this idea was circulated to the white Dominions there was a negative response, particularly from Canada. Lester Pearson, now Canada's Minister for External Affairs, cabled his country's representative at New Delhi: 'We have some misgivings about having the Commonwealth link with India based primarily on the common status of Commonwealth citizens on a reciprocal basis in view of our immigration policy.'[26]

In London, the whole question was still being examined at the constitutional level, being delegated to Jowitt and the legal advisers. Nehru was irritated by this approach. He told Krishna Menon (12 January 1949): 'I do not understand this discussion of technical and legal issues on a matter which is essentially political, as Stafford recognises it to be.'[27] The British Cabinet got no further forward when the question was reviewed in January 1949; it was argued that the legal solution was for the King to appoint the President of India—a solution which Nehru had already brushed aside. Bajpai informally revived the idea mooted by B. N. Rau, Vernon Erskine-Crum and Mountbatten on different occasions: that the King be recognised as the Head of the Commonwealth. This formula was not then acceptable either to Attlee and his collegues or to Nehru. The deadlock was not allowed to continue, however, and on 3 March the British Cabinet took the crucial decision that India as a republic must be accommodated within the Commonwealth and that the formula for inclusion must be adjusted to this decision. Attlee was fortified by the conclusion reached almost simultaneously by J. B. Chifley, the Australian prime minister, that India's continuing membership was so important as to override other considerations.

Attlee informed the other premiers that a special Commonwealth conference would be convened in April to settle the matter. In advance of the meeting, emissaries from Whitehall were despatched to prepare the ground in the Dominions: Lord Listowel visited Australia and New Zealand, while Gordon-Walker flew successively to Karachi, Colombo and Delhi. He came out strongly in favour of recognising the King as Head of the Commonwealth as the key to the constitutional question.[28] Meanwhile, Attlee addressed an extremely long letter to Nehru (20 March) extolling the advantages of a monarchy over a republic; in some irritation, Nehru enclosed a copy to Sardar Patel, his deputy premier (in some ways the co-premier), commenting: 'I just do not know what we are going to discuss in London if this is the approach of the U.K. Prime Minister' (26 March).

B. N. Rau went ahead to London to assess the situation. He tackled Jowitt with his own interpretation of the 'Head of the Commonwealth' formula; his memorandum read as follows:

> There is no lack of understanding in India of the deep-seated sentiment felt for the Crown in the United Kingdom and certain other countries; but there are genuine political difficulties. There are certain parties in India opposed to membership of the Commonwealth on any terms. Recent events in south Africa, and statements of immigration policy in Australia have made Indian public opinion peculiarly sensitive and even suspicious just now.... Therefore those who desire India to remain in the Commonwealth should make it as easy as possible for her to do so...
>
> Just as the member-states of the United Nations are completely sovereign and yet find it possible to recognise certain organisational authorities for the purpose of working together, so too the members of the Commonwealth can, without impairing their own sovereignty or independence in any way, recognise the Crown as the Head of the Commonwealth association. The Crown will thus be the symbol of association for all members.

Rau was able to inform Bajpai (2 April) that Jowitt accepted much of this argument and in return offered a formula for India's continuing membership on the basis that India 'recognises that position of the King as the (Fountain) Head of the Commonwealth of which she freely elects to become a member'.[29] Nehru, however, was still reluctant to assent to such a formula: he was concerned to demonstrate that the new situation represented change as well as continuity. Before departing for London he agreed with Patel on a draft proposal which would endorse three propositions, namely to recognise the King 'as the *symbol* of this association' of partners, to propose a Commonwealth citizenship on the lines of the British Nationality Act, and suggest that in future the association be named 'The Commonwealth of Free Nations'.

All the Dominion premiers gathered in London, except for St Laurent, the new Prime Minister of Canada (Lester Pearson came in his place). Cripps and Noel-Baker sat alongside Attlee for Britain. A phalanx of advisers stood by, in case the going proved difficult. Max Wershof accompanied the Canadians as specialist on nationality and citizenship; Ivor Jennings arrived from Ceylon in case his constitutional inventiveness was needed; and Bajpai attended for India, as he had so often before. The decision was soon accomplished, however, because all really wanted a decision.

The conference lasted only from April 22 to 27, when the

Declaration of London was issued. The one premier who might have been expected to be difficult—Dr Malan—proved to be the strongest supporter of India's position. There were two main propositions before the conference: that from India, and another from Australia which sought to re-emphasise loyalty to the Crown as well as the common concern of members in matters such as defence. In the end, all made concessions in order to obtain the widest measure of agreement. Nehru agreed to accept the King as Head of the Commonwealth (Patel was urging him in this direction), while Australia and New Zealand agreed to water down the definition of common objectives. The Indian proposal for a common citizenship was excluded from the public statement, though in a separate confidential minute the Dominions all agreed 'that nationals of other member nations are not [to be] treated as foreigners'.[30]

Different claims have been made for the authorship of this declaration which brought the new Commonwealth into being: credit has variously been assigned to Lester Pearson, V. K. Krishna Menon, Stafford Cripps—even to the Cabinet Secretary, Sir Norman Brook, and to Sir G. S. Bajpai.[31] These—and others—may have played significant roles at difficult moments, by assembling forms of words agreeable to all. The key figure was, in fact, Nehru, who throughout was flexible yet firm on essentials. He took pains to keep Patel informed throughout, and was clearly anxious to obtain the reactions of the hardest-headed man in Indian politics. Patel reassured him: cabling his congratulations(27 April), he commented that in future 'our membership would be full and equal'.

Although all the premiers echoed Lester Pearson in acknowledging that among them *as nations* there would be 'full equality of status ... no inner or outer circle of membership', they also followed Canada in considering it prudent not to venture into the more delicate question of how far there would be 'full equality of status' between *peoples* when some happened to be black or brown. The minute on citizenship did not specify how this inter-recognition was to be implemented. India had laid down the challenge—full acceptance of an equal, mutual Commonwealth of peoples—but there was a turning aside from the challenge. There was to be no genuine community of equals in the new era of independence.

Yet the compromise of April 1949 might not have been achieved at all if the attendance of prime ministers had included some who were prime ministers lately—or soon to be. Robert Menzies was to return to power in Australia in December 1949, making no secret of his dislike of the dilution of Commonwealth loyalties to the Crown. Smuts—so recently displaced—voiced his opposition upon the same grounds; he cabled Churchill (21 May 1949): 'It is a most unfortunate development.' Churchill, that equivocal champion of equal rights within the Commonwealth, cabled back (22 May): 'When I asked myself the question "Would I rather have them in, even on these terms, or let them go altogether?" my heart gave the answer "I want them in". Nehru has certainly shown magnanimity.'[32] It was the soft, not the hard, answer; and thus was set the pattern of the Commonwealth of the 1950s.

Nehru felt well satisfied with his mission to London. However, when he returned to India he felt a little uncertain. He knew that there were critics and sceptics who would scrutinise the new situation for any sign of a sell-out, while there were Indian imperialists and loyalists who would hail the move as a return to the fold of the British Empire. His position was difficult and delicate. Thus, in his speech to the Constituent Assembly (16 May) in which he asked for ratification of India's continued membership 'in the Commonwealth of Nations' he trod rather softly. His technique was to insist that India was not really committed to anything by remaining in the Commonwealth. In particular, he felt it necessary to emphasise that the recognition of the King as Head of the Commonwealth did not bind India in any way at all. 'The King has no functions at all', he insisted; and from this he drew important deductions:

Obviously, the Commonwealth countries belong to different nations. They are different nationalities. Normally either you have a common nationality or you are foreign. There is no intermediate stage. Up till now in this Commonwealth ... there was a binding link which was allegiance to the King. With that link, therefore, there was a common nationality in a sense and in a broad way. That snaps and ends when we become a Republic ... [The Constituent Assembly might decide to grant reciprocal citizenship rights to Commonwealth countries]. What they are to be, of course, we shall in each case be the judge ourselves ... Nothing has been decided in secret or otherwise which has not been put before the public.

The House will remember that there was some talk at one stage of a Commonwealth citizenship. Now, it was difficult to understand what the status of a Commonwealth citizenship might be except that it meant that its members were not completely foreign to one another. That un-foreignness remains, but I think it is as well that we left off talking about something vague, which could not surely be defined.

Thus, Nehru acknowledged that the trend towards a common citizenship would not be realised, at any rate in the near future, and perhaps not at all. If the new Commonwealth was not going to evolve reciprocal relationships, then it was important to emphasise that India would take the lead in fighting for the rights of those exposed to racial discrimination, especially the overseas Indians:

I am often asked how we can join a Commonwealth in which there is racial discrimination . . . That, I think, is a fair question . . . Nevertheless, it is a question which does not really arise. That is to say, when we have entered into an alliance with a nation or a group of nations it does not mean that we accept their other policies . . . One of the pillars of our foreign policy, repeatedly stated, is to fight against racial discrimination, to fight for the freedom of suppressed nationalities. Are you compromising on that issue by remaining in the Commonwealth? We have been fighting on the South African Indian issue and on other issues even though we have thus far been a Dominion of the Commonwealth. It was a dangerous thing for us to bring that matter within the purview of the Commonwealth . . . The Commonwealth might have been considered as some kind of a superior body which sometimes acts as a tribunal . . . That certainly would have meant a diminution in our independence and sovereignty if we had once accepted that principle.

Nehru continued to speak—exploring the consequences of his own arguments—for an enormous length of time.[33] Most of his speech was intended to reassure doubters. He ended by telling the Assembly that they must either accept or reject the motion: there could be no question of introducing amendments designed to qualify the commitment which he had accepted on their behalf.

In the debate which followed it was clear that a majority of the members of the Assembly approved of the continuance of India's Commonwealth membership: of the nineteen who spoke, thirteen (including H. N. Kunzru) favoured the terms proposed: many wanted to go further than Nehru in developing this association. In winding up the debate, Nehru again spoke at length. His tone was pragmatic; the exhilaration, even romanticism, with which he often spoke of India's past and future was quite absent. The decision must be weighed, he said, by the extent to which it would contribute to India's development. Did it contribute towards the cause of peace? Nehru seemed to feel that, at any rate, it would help promote a spirit of tolerance:

Goodwill is always precious from any quarter. Therefore, I had a feeling when I was considering this matter in London and later that I had done something that would in a small measure, perhaps, have met with the approval of Gandhiji. I am thinking of the manner of it more than the thing itself. I thought that this in itself would raise a fund of goodwill in the world — goodwill which in a smaller sense is to our advantage, certainly, and to the advantage of England, but also in a larger sense to the advantage of the world in the psychological conflicts which people try to resolve by blaming one another, by cursing one another and saying that the others are to blame.

From this moral or metaphysical plane, Nehru turned to the charge that he was not being true to his own record of opposition to British imperialism. He appealed to his critics to 'come out of the cage of the past'; British imperialism was dying, he said (Suez was seven years away), and he wanted to look to the future: they must 'act in a big way': 'big action which shows generosity of spirit brings generosity from the other side'. In thus evoking the Golden Rule, Nehru was evoking the language of Gautama the Buddha, Sophocles and Jesus Christ. It was an appeal which had always been recognised in the rhetoric, yet also in the basic philosophy of the Congress view of politics, particularly in its moderate and liberal as well as its Gandhian forms. The Constituent Assembly responded to his appeal and wholeheartedly endorsed the London declaration with only one dissenting vote.

Nehru's speech was perhaps more remarkable for what lay behind it, rather than for what was actually in it. As he often observed of himself, Nehru was identified with both the East and the West; he was also identified with the values of liberalism, as well as those of socialism (which he so often expounded) and of nationalism. Fundamentally, his speech was an expression of Afro-Asian nationalism. Whereas the Indian leaders of the first two decades of the twentieth century, like Sastri—and even Gandhi—were primarily concerned to establish their claim to equality and political and civil rights, Nehru saw all this as less important than the rediscovery of India's national identity and her re-emergence as a nation in a world in which the uniqueness of Asia would be fully recognised.

Hence the idea of the Commonwealth, which had drawn Sastri, Sapru, Kunzru, Maharaj Singh and the Indian moderates of the 1920s and 1930s along in a quest for equality with their English or Anglo-Saxon fellow citizens, was not enough when independence came. It was strange that in 1920 the only leader in India to see that a *British* Commonwealth could never be enough for an India which intended to realise its full stature in the world was the Englishman, Charles Freer Andrews. Nehru had never been such an intimate friend as Gandhi had been, but as a young man he had been stirred by his call for full independence, and now it was the message of Andrews that Nehru translated to his countrymen. Nehru was prepared to participate in a multi-racial Commonwealth, but not as an end in itself. The asseveration *Civis Britannicus Sum* was of no interest to him. For India to be India within a group of like-minded nations, Black, Brown and White, was one thing; but to be a step-child in a predominantly British family of nations was to perpetuate the condition of colonialism.

It seems that Sir B. N. Rau understood that India's continuing membership of the Commonwealth represented a more pragmatic, less organic development than he had envisaged. Early in 1949 he went to New York as India's representative at the U.N. and he gave his assessment of the import of the April Declaration on the U.N. radio:

> There are deep-seated affinities between India and the United Kingdom in ideas and institutions, such as the rule of law and the parliamentary system of government; but apart from these there are cogent practical considerations... There were the interests of Indians overseas to consider — mainly Indians settled in various British Colonies and the countries of the Commonwealth. These could be better served if India remained within the Commonwealth herself than if she went out.[34]

Rau made no further mention of his hopes for a common citizenship.

Besides the 'big way' of thinking, Nehru was influenced in his approach by the immediate pressures of the times, particularly by the conflict with Pakistan. When partition was first accepted as a reality, few imagined that the new boundary would be very much different from the provincial boundaries, or the borders of the old princely states: an invisible political line over which people and their transport could move freely. Instead, the frontier between India and Pakistan — especially West Pakistan — became as tightly controlled as any in central Europe. Persons crossing in either direction had to go through laborious checks concerning passports, money and goods.[35] With these restrictions affecting relations with the closest Commonwealth neighbour, it was clear that any discussion of a common citizenship must appear theoretical indeed. The Indian Constitution, when it was promulgated in November 1949 reflected very clearly the realities of the confrontation with Pakistan, and made no reference to the Commonwealth.

Part II of the Constitution begins with the citizenship provisions. These were designed to embrace all who might consider themselves Indians, whether born within the territory of the Indian Union or elsewhere. Article 6 gave citizenship to anyone born in the area now comprising Pakistan, if that person emigrated to the Indian Union; Article 7 deprived a person of Indian citizenship if, though born within the territory of India, they emigrated to Pakistan. Article 8 provided that anyone with a grandparent born within the former, undivided India and 'ordinarily resident outside India' could obtain Indian citizenship by registration at an Indian embassy or consulate. Article 9 provided that 'No person shall be a citizen of India... if he has voluntarily acquired the citizenship of any foreign state.' The 'Declaration as to Foreign States Order' followed in 1950: this declared all Commonwealth countries not to be foreign states. Pakistan was naturally included in the list, but nevertheless, under Article 7, no person could hold the citizenship of both India and Pakistan.

The terms of citizenship were further defined and codified by India under the Citizenship Act of 1955. This Act gave Indian citizenship 'by descent' to anyone whose father was an Indian citizen (including those who acquired that citizenship from the birth of a grandparent in India) if his birth was registered at an Indian consulate within one year of the event, or by permission of the Government of India after the year had elapsed. This provision extended Indian citizenship virtually indefinitely to the overseas Indians resident in Commonwealth countries other than Pakistan. Clause 11 of the Act provides that 'Every person who is a citizen of a Commonwealth country specified in the first schedule, shall have the status of a Commonwealth citizen of India'.[36] This was the Indian equivalent of the status of a British subject which, prior to 1962, gave automatic right of entry into Britain to all members of the Commonwealth. It was notable that when Pakistan adopted a Citizenship Act in 1951 there was no provision for reciprocity of citizenship with other Commonwealth countries: nor under any subsequent legislation, though apart from the citizens of the Indian Union all persons from a Commonwealth country were freely admitted into Pakistan.[37]

The Pakistan Citizenship Act of 1951 laid down that any Pakistani who can also claim an alternative nationality must, on attaining his majority, renounce the other nationality on pain of forfeiting Pakistani citizenship.

We have noticed that dual nationality could not be exercised by the Indians in Burma. Other Commonwealth countries, beside Pakistan, decided to go against the trend towards mutual citizenship and deny their own citizens the possibility of choice. The Ceylon Citizenship Act of 1948 made it a condition for all Ceylon citizens to renounce alternative nationalities, including citizenship of the U.K. and Colonies. When South Africa passed a Citizenship Act in 1949, this was also designed to frustrate the concept of mutual, Commonwealth citizenship. Any South African who became a citizen of the United Kingdom automatically forfeited South African citizenship. Hard choices had to be made by the Indians in these countries.

However, for most of the colonial Indians these dilemmas did not arise. In the Caribbean, Mauritius and Fiji, the Indians mainly accepted their citizenship of the U.K. and Colonies without looking for an alternative. In East Africa and Malaya, the Indian communities registered as Indian citizens in large numbers while also retaining or adopting British or U.K. and Colonies citizenship. In East Africa Apa B. Pant advised the Indians that though they might claim dual citizenship they must recognise where their first loyalty was due: it was their 'duty to be completely loyal and belong without any reservation to the country where they were living permanently', he told an audience at Dar-es-Salaam: it was 'urgent and necessary for Indians to acquire British nationality in order to integrate themselves fully': they could retain dual nationality, but 'the country of residence always took precedence in loyalty'.[38] It was a commitment which not all East African Asians were prepared to accept.

The events of 1948-9 did not radically alter the balance of influences between Britain and India in their different attitudes to the Indians overseas. Despite Nehru's efforts to distinguish between cultural interests and political commitments between India and the overseas Indians, the Government of India continued to behave on the assumption that they had a watching brief on behalf of Indian communities in British Colonies and Dominions (as the British Government recognised).[39] The Colonial Office continued to proclaim a policy of regarding the colonial Indians as full members of the territories in which they lived. And Britain continued to maintain an open door to all Indians, and other Commonwealth peoples coming for periods of residence, short or long. In the late 1940s, Britain still considered it was a country of emigration. The latest wave of emigrants were the so-called wartime brides; the English wives of American and Canadian veterans. While thousands of these young women were leaving Britain to make their homes overseas, nobody noticed the arrival of black and brown people from the Commonwealth in a new kind of immigration.

In the late 1940s, the arrivals of Indians and Pakistanis (other than the accustomed arrival of students, which rose to new peak levels) were few and unobtrusive. One or two Sikhs, restless after wartime service in the Indian Army, and the experience of a Punjab divided and disrupted, made contact with a former British officer to find if there were jobs in Britain. One by one they arrived, to work in factories, at hard jobs for long hours. Personnel officers began to appreciate their toughness and self-discipline. Here and there they purchased houses, which became contact-places for new arrivals. At first the men came singly, leaving wives and families in the Punjab; some of them living with English women, in places like Gravesend and Southall. Then, very gradually, they brought over their families. The strange adventure began to be a normal part of the Sikhs' experience. But nobody in Britain seemed to notice. In 1950, the more far-sighted in Britain were trying to educate public opinion towards the idea of a mutli-racial Commonwealth. Nobody saw what was happening already in London and other cities—the beginning of a multi-racial Britain.

It was therefore not on a full basis of realism and understanding that Britain in 1950 moved into the Commonwealth decade of partnership. Nor were the Indians overseas, and the Indians now moving overseas, alert and prepared for the changes which were to overtake their way of life in years to come.

Yet, in a way which could never be forgotten, India and the Indians in the Commonwealth, had achieved a moment of equality. The imperial relationship of the past had been transformed. India had persuaded Britain to listen and act upon her advice. The nature of British nationality had been redefined and renewed; the British Commonwealth itself had been given a renaissance by the initiative of India's leaders. If the Commonwealth failed to respond to the changes and challenges which punctuated the 1960s and 1970s this was because the Britain which emerged in the post-imperial era was essentially the same society which had condoned and even encouraged the white dominance of the 1920s, 1930s and 1940s.

Yet the moment of equality had happened: it could still happen again, if men wanted it to happen.

Notes

References from the text to these notes have been kept to a minimum and, as far as possible, one main reference to a documentary source covers a number of citations in the text. A discussion of the unpublished materials utilised follows in the Note on Sources; published materials are listed in the Select Bibliography.

CHAPTER 1, THE HELOTS OF THE EMPIRE

1. See the author's 'Colour and Colonization', *The Round Table*, October 1970, for a brief account of the growth of anti-Asiatic discrimination in the British white self-governing colonies.
2. The circumstances behind this important despatch are discussed in detail in the author's *A New System of Slavery* (London, 1974), Chapter 7.
3. R. A. Huttenback, *Gandhi in South Africa: British Imperialism and the Indian Question, 1860-1914* (Ithaca, New York, 1971).
4. Correspondence between the Secretary of State and the Viceroy, Morley Papers, India Office Records.
5. Letters of Lionel Curtis, in the Papers of Lord Meston, India Office Records.
6. The narrative in the two preceding paragraphs draws upon Ronald Hyams, *Elgin and Churchill at the Colonial Office, 1905-08; the watershed of the Empire-Commonwealth* (Oxford, 1968).
7. Johnson's account of the progress of the Sikhs overseas comes from *Report of the Committee on Emigration from India to the Crown Colonies and Protectorates*, 1910, Cmd. 5193, Part II, *Minutes of Evidence*.
8. 'White Canada for Ever' is reproduced in full by Khushwant Singh, *A History of the Sikhs*, Vol. II (Princeton, New Jersey, 1966), pp. 168-9. His chapter 'Xenophobic Nationalism' includes a full account of Sikh emigration.
9. Commenting upon the same phenomenon, John Morley told Lord Minto (9 November 1906) 'To make races "mix" is about the most desperate task that fate can set a statesman. Sir Curzon Wyllie has just been visiting Cambridge where sixty Indians are dispersed through the colleges. The reports of conduct and character are very good. But Wyllie does not think that they make friends outside of their own circle'. Morley Papers.
10. *Report of the Committee on Distressed Colonial and Indian Subjects*, April 1910, Cmd. 5133 and 5134.
11. Viceroy's Correspondence with Persons in India, Vol. I, 1918, Chelmsford Papers, India Office Records.
12. India Office, Industry and Overseas Department, Volume 88/1921, 'Indians in the Union of South Africa'. Quotations which follow are also drawn from this long volume, which contains letters and minutes from 1919 to 1925.

13. *Asiatic Inquiry Commission, Interim Report* . . . , Cape Town, 1920, and *Report*, Cape Town, 1921.
14. Walton's memorandum is filed with India Office, Industry and Overseas Department, Volume 88/1921.
15. Kenya Correspondence, *Emigration Proceedings* (Government of India), 1922.
16. The subject is analysed in detail by S. R. Mehrotra, *India and the Commonwealth, 1885-1929* (London, 1965), Chapter 3 'The Indian National Congress and the Commonwealth' and Chapter 4 'The National Liberal Federation and the Commonwealth'.
17. Vera Anstey, *The Economic Development of India* (London, 1929), esp. pp. 39, 309.
18. *The Round Table*, December 1922, 'The Coloured Question in Politics', an article by a South African, was preceded by a preface by the editor containing the observation quoted.
19. *West Indies: Report by the Hon. E. F. L. Wood . . . on his visit to the West Indies and British Guiana*, December 1921 — February 1922.

CHAPTER 2, THE CLAIM FOR EQUALITY

1. Lloyd George to Montagu, 25 April 1920, quoted by S. D. Waley, *Edwin Montagu: a Memoir* . . . . (London, 1964) p. 246.
2. File: 'Imperial Conference 1921; preparation of agenda and distribution of subjects among delegates', I & O 138/21.
3. Private telegrams from the Governor-General to the Secretary of State, in the Reading Papers, India Office Records.
4. Located in *Emigration Proceedings*, 1922.
5. Bajpai's memorandum, headed 'Imperial Conference' and dated 9 August 1921, was enclosed by Montagu with his private weekly letter to Reading of 15 August 1921. A verbatim record was made for the Cabinet: CAB 32/2 Part 2 (Public Record Office).
6. This narrative comes in Sastri's letter to his son, V. S. Sankaran: see T. N. Jagadisan, ed., *Letters of the Right Honourable V. S. Srinivasa Sastri*, (1944, 2nd edn, London, 1963) p. 74. The assessment of Churchill which follows is on p. 73, and the Chequers letter on p. 75.
7. Montagu enclosed copies of his letters from Churchill, and his own replies, with his weekly letters to Reading of 21 and 26 July 1921 (the Reading Papers).
8. Lloyd George's speech is reproduced in full in Bajpai's momorandum (only about half is given in the text here). The White Paper, Cmd. 1474 of 1921, *Conference of Prime Ministers and Representatives of the United Kingdom, the Dominions and India held in June, July and August 1921*, only includes Lloyd George's opening speech (together with the main speeches of Winston Churchill, Sastri, etc.). A reviewer in the *Round Table* complained that the official summary was a 'document of the consistency of cracknel biscuit': *Round Table*, September 1921, 'The Imperial Conference'.
9. The despatch is included in *Emigration Proceedings*, 1922.

10. Reported in *Rand Daily Mail*, 21 December, and *Westminster Gazette*, 22 December 1921.
11. The reports of Abe Bailey's speech reproduced in the *Cape Times* and *Natal Mercury*, both of 10 May 1922, differ somewhat. The former quotes Bailey as saying: 'My policy is to reserve the whole of South Africa for white people and the natives.' But the whole of the speech is devoted to the case for the Whites.
12. *Daily Telegraph*, 22 September 1922. An extended account of the incident is given by Bridglal Pachai, *The International Aspects of the South African Indian Question, 1860-1971*, (Cape Town, 1971), pp. 97-99.
13. *Letters*, op. cit., p. 83.
14. Cmd. 1474, *Conference of Prime Ministers* . . .
15. The Southern Rhodesian referendum, with its fateful consequences for southern Africa, was held in October 1922. There were 5,989 vote for union with South Africa and 8,774 votes for separate, self-governing status. Of the 14,826 voters who thus decided the future of Rhodesia, 35 were said to be Africans and about 130 Indians.
16. The Legislative Assembly passed a resolution on 9 February 1922, and this was accepted by the government; the Council of State passed a similar resolution on 23 February.
17. The events leading to Montagu's resignation are described in detail by S. D. Waley, op. cit., pp. 269-77. It has been suggested that there was a connection between Churchill's after dinner speech and the resignation. C. F. Andrews told an official in the Government of India, following the speech, 'either the Viceroy or Montagu or both should resign', and he later publicly alleged that Montagu 'had threatened resignation in connection with the discussion of the Indian problem in Africa', as Reading informed Peel (2 September 1923). Peel caused inquiries to be made, but was unable to discover any evidence of 'threatened resignation'; he noted: 'The best answer is that he did not resign. He therefore acquiesced in whatever decision was taken.' (Private Office Papers, Secretary of State for India.)
18. Linlithgow to Irwin, 5 November 1928, when Peel was again appointed Secretary for India.
19. The 'Interim Report of the India [sic] deputation to Fiji' is included in *Emigration Proceedings*, 1922.
20. Lady Reading noted in her diary that the Viceroy 'Gave a death-blow to murmurs and fault-findings against him in the press. He [Sastri] replied—at first disappointing, but as he warmed to it, very good indeed; but forty minutes rather long for an after-dinner speech': Iris Butler, ed., *The Viceroy's Wife* (London, 1968), p. 87. The actual speech is included in *Speeches and Writings of the Rt. Hon. V. S. Srinivasa Sastri*, Vol. I (Madras, 1969) and is a good example of what the editor describes as 'such giddy mental gyrations, such logical finesse' (xvii).
21. Making preparations for the tour, Bajpai urged Sastri (10 April 1922) to discount the opposition: 'I confess that I don't scour the columns of the Indian newspapers for all the venom that they spout every day'.
22. Copies of Coryndon's secret telegrams are located in the Secretary of

State's Private Office papers. The correspondence relating to Kenya down to August 1923 which follows is taken from the same source.

23. The Cabinet meeting was held on Friday (20th); Devonshire signed the White Paper (Cmd. 1922) on Monday (23rd), and the policy was announced in parliament on Wednesday (25th). Reading's speech to the legislative assembly was made on Saturday (28th).

24. Although, on 2 May 1923, Reading had told Peel: 'I believe in caution in the forward march to the promised Indian ultimate goal of self-government.'

25. Robert Gregory in *India and East Africa* (Oxford, 1971) provides a very detailed account of the many reactions and responses to the Kenya White Paper; but he does not mention Reading's speech, even when he discusses the debate in the Indian legislative assembly (op. cit., p. 252).

26. The draft reply which India Office officials supplied to Lord Peel added this qualification: 'At the same time, the Viceroy did not regard the decision of H.M.G. as binding the Government of India to abandon completely, forthwith, and for all time the causes which the Government of India had advocated.' The easy-going Peel cut out this sentence which might, so very likely, lead to trouble in parliament.

27. *Communique*, dated 10 August 1923: 'Lord Winterton felt that it would place both Mr Sastri and himself in an embarrassing position if they met for a discussion without Mr Sastri having first had an opportunity of seeing Lord Peel.'

28. Bajpai adopted a supercilious attitude to most of those with whom he worked, whether British or Indian. But he retained a touching devotion to Sastri, and right to the end he began his letters to Sastri with 'My dear Chief', in recognition of their first association in 1921.

29. Peel's recollections of the 1923 conference were contained in a letter to Irwin, 29 November 1928.

30. Cmd. 1988, *Imperial Conference, 1923. Appendices to the Summary of Proceedings*, 1923. The speeches of the delegates take up 133 pages, and of these 60 pages are devoted to the Indian question.

31. Although Sapru made the most of his lonely position, it is not right to suggest, as Sir Keith Hancock does (*Smuts: the Fields of Force*, p. 147), that Sapru was 'far more formidable' than Sastri. Professor Hancock had access to Sapru's private papers, but not to the unpublished details of the 1921 proceedings, and this may have affected his assessment.

32. Sastri commented (perhaps a little peevishly) to S. G. Vaze, one of his colleagues in the Servants of India Society: 'It is useless now to speculate whether on the whole it would not have been better for Sapru to have withdrawn at first, as I repeatedly pressed him in London' (4 November 1923).

33. Minute by A[rthur] H[irtzel] dated 2 February 1924, on the Class Areas Bill (File 1 & O 88/21, 'Indians in the Union of South Africa', 1921-25).

34. Governor-General, South Africa (the Earl of Athlone), to Secretary of State for the Colonies (J. H. Thomas), 22 February 1924.

35. *Speeches and Writings of the Right Honourable V. S. Srinivasa Sastri*, Vol. I (Madras, 1969) pp. 62-7.

CHAPTER 3, THE SEPARATION OF WHITE, BLACK AND BROWN

1. Margaret Cole, ed., *Beatrice Webb's Diaries, 1924-1932* (London, 1956), p. 30.
2. The Sastri papers in the Indian National Archives contain several notes about the 1924 visit addressed to A. V. Patwardhan. Elsewhere, Sastri told his friend: 'Lansbury says he [Olivier] is a log of wood'.
3. India Office to Government of India, telegram, 23 May 1924.
4. CP 375 (24), July 1924, 'Position of Indians in Kenya', memorandum by the Secretary of State for the Colonies.
5. Geoffrey Dawson to Lord Irwin, 1 November 1927: from the Viceroy's 'Correspondence with Persons in England and Abroad'. Dawson's comments were occasioned by a complaint to him from Irwin (3 October 1927): 'I keep seeing pictures of F. E. at Deauville, or somewhere, in the illustrated papers, which no doubt accounts for the difficulty I am experiencing in getting work through with the India Office.' Irwin went on: 'Eddie Winterton hasn't the drive to get things through if there is inertia at the top.' Long after, Irwin told R. A. Butler: 'I remember so well how bloody it was serving under F. E.': Lord Butler, *The Art of the Possible* (London, 1971) p. 36.
6. W. K. Hancock, *Smuts: the Fields of Force, 1919-1950* (Cambridge, 1968) p. 223. If it appears ironic that Kruger's former State Attorney should extol the expansionist policies of Cecil Rhodes, it has to be remembered that Smuts always carefully considered his audience in composing his message.
7. Private Office Papers, 'Indians in Africa'; Winterton recorded a minute on a paper by Sir Louis Kershaw (2 October 1925).
8. G. F. Paddison, Confidential Memorandum submitted by the Government of India Deputation to South Africa (Reading Papers).
9. CP 22(26), 'Indians in South Africa', Memorandum by the Secretary of State for India.
10. The duties were defined in a letter from the Viceroy to the Secretary of State, 7 April 1927: he was 'To interpret the wishes of the Indian community to the Union Government and thus obviate the misunderstandings which in the past have been a fruitful source of trouble; (2) to give that Government every possible help in carrying out the policy of upliftment of the resident Indian population which has now been officially affirmed; and (3) to watch the progress of the new scheme of assisted emigration, on the satisfactory working of which a great deal will depend'. He was expected to 'gradually educate [white] opinion . . . to regard the Indians as a permanent element of the population'. The appointment was to run for three years (i.e. the post, not Sastri's tenure) and the Agent was to be assisted by a clerical staff of three. Actually Sastri was given a British official as secretary — J. D. Tyson, ICS.

A simplified description of the duties of the Agent was communicated by Irwin to Athlone in an official telegram of 18 May 1927.
11. T. N. Jagadisan, ed., *Letters of the Rt. Hon. V. S. S. Sastri*, 1944 (2nd. edn. London, 1963), p. 170.
12. *Fiji Royal Gazette*, No. 13 of 1927 (supplement), 'Position of the Indian Community in Fiji', also *Emigration Proceedings*, Government of India, 1925, '26, '27.
13. *Report by Kunwar Maharaj Singh on his deputation to Mauritius*, Delhi, 1925, and *Report by Kunwar Maharaj Singh on his deputation to British Guiana in 1925.*
14. Irwin told Birkenhead (10 February 1927) that the Indian representatives at the Cape Town conference had strongly received this impression.
15. *Imperial Conference, 1926; Summary of Proceedings*, Cmd. 2768, 1926, p.39.
16. *Selected Works of Jawaharlal Nehru*, Vol. 2 (Delhi, 1972) pp. 353-62.
17. Benarsi Das was not over-impressed by his assignment. He told the General Secretary of the AICC, B. Raja Rau, (29 October 1929) that Congress had appointed a committee in 1924 to investigate the conditions of returned emigrants, but it had done nothing: 'This will give you an idea of the inefficient way we have tackled the problem'. On 19 February 1930 the Working Committee of the AICC sanctioned expenditure up to Rs.25 per month (about £2) on work connected with Indians overseas.
18. Irwin to E. Hilton Young, 24 August 1927.
19. *East Africa: Report of the East Africa Commission*, Cmd. 2387, 1925.
20. The 'Women of Kenya' (i.e. the white women) sent a telegram to Queen Mary protesting against 'the Indian Menace'.
21. *Future Policy in Regard to Eastern Africa*, Cmd. 2904, 1927.
22. *House of Commons Debates*, Vol. 209.
23. Birkenhead to R. P. Paranjpye and others, 3 October 1927 (Private Office Papers).
24. During the years 1926-31, when Andrews was constantly writing to Irwin, he was abroad most of the time and his letters are therefore contained in the Viceroy's series 'Correspondence with Persons in England and Abroad', but during the first half of 1928 Andrews returned to his home (if such a restless soul ever had a home) at Santiniketan: so this letter (19 March 1928) is reproduced in 'Correspondence with Persons in India': Irwin Papers, India Office Records.
25. *Report of the Commission on Closer Union of the Dependencies in Eastern and Central Africa*, Cmd. 3234, 1929.
26. This telegram, and much of the correspondence reproduced below, is taken from a file in the Private Office Papers, 'East Africa, 1928-1929'.
27. A personal letter, Peel to Amery, 5 December 1928: in his original draft, Peel added to the passage quoted 'and not impossibly expose them to actual danger', but in his matter-of-fact way he cut this out.
28. Brigadier Sir Samuel Wilson succeeded Sir James Masterton Smith as

head of the Colonial Office in 1925. He was a former West Indian governor, and a commanding figure.
29. Reddi to Habibullah, 21 February 1929, and Athlone to Irwin, 5 May 1929: both in the Viceroy's 'Correspondence with Persons in England and Abroad'.
30. In March, it seems that Peel was adopting all Amery's arguments and trying to dissuade Irwin from asking for Sastri's deputation. R. G. Gregory, *India and East Africa*, emphasises this aspect of the controversy: pp. 317-330, especially p. 325.
31. Telegrams to Secretary of State for the Colonies: from Governor of Tanganyika, 29 March; from Governor of Uganda, and Officer Administering the Government of Kenya, 30 March.
32. Kershaw's memorandum, dated 9 April, is in the Private Office Papers.
33. Telegram, Viceroy to Secretary of State, 13 June 1929.
34. Sastri to Gandhi, 27 July 1929, *Letters of... Sastri*, pp. 180-81. Although Sastri's report to the Government of India was not immediately published, it was issued later in 1930.

CHAPTER 4, SEPARATION QUESTIONED AND AFFIRMED

1. *Beatrice Webb's Diaries, 1924-1932*, p. 225.
2. The memorandum by Norman Leys was presented to the Labour Party's Advisory Committee on Imperial Questions in February 1939. Leonard Woolf's letter to Leys was dated 22 February 1939. Both items are in the Creech Jones Papers. See also Leonard Woolf, *Downhill all the Way: an autobiography of the years 1919-1930* (London, 1968); references to Webb are on pp. 236-7. Woolf was a leading member of Labour's International and Imperial Committees during the inter-war years.
3. R. Gregory, *Sidney Webb and East Africa: Labour's Experiment with the Doctrine of Native Paramountcy* (Berkeley, 1962). Dr. Gregory wrote this study, having received access to the private papers of Sidney and Beatrice Webb (London School of Economics) long before other related papers were made available under the Thirty Year Rule. He fell a victim to their persuasive presentation of the Webb view of the world. When Dr. Gregory came to publish his *India and East Africa* (Oxford, 1971), he wanted to restate his favourable interpretation of Webb's role as Secretary for the Colonies but found this more difficult in the light of the additional evidence. His last reference was, therefore, to 'Passfield's dilatory and irresolute performance' (p. 421). Webb's performance may be judged in the following pages, but an interim judgment can be found in Margaret Cole's Introduction to the *Diaries*. Mrs. Cole was very close to the Webbs, but she does not shrink from speaking of 'the failure of Sidney as a Minister'. He was 'too much in the hands of his officials.... Sidney's innate trust in the "expert" served him ill' (*Diaries*, xiii).
4. *Report of Sir Samuel Wilson on his visit to East Africa, 1929*, Cmd. 3378.

5. Telegrams: Benn to Irwin, 11 November, and Irwin to Benn, 16 November 1929.
6. The committee consisted of Lord Sankey (chairman), Lord Passfield, Wedgwood Benn, and Lord Thomson, Secretary for Air. Thomson, a former regular soldier, had been born in India but had no special Indian interests.
7. CP 65(30), 'Cabinet Committee on Policy in East Africa, Report', signed by Sankey, 4 April 1930.
8. *Statement of the Conclusions of His Majesty's Government as regards Closer Union in East Africa, presented by the Secretary of State for the Colonies to Parliament, June 1930,* Cmd. 3574, and *Memorandum on Native Policy in East Africa.* Cmd. 3573, 1930.
9. The Rt Hon Earl Winterton, *Orders of the Day* (London, 1953), p. 164.
10. Azim Husain, *Fazl-i-Husain: a political biography* (Bombay, 1946), pp. 203-4.
11. Kenneth Robinson, *The Dilemmas of Trusteeship: aspects of British colonial policy between the Wars* (London, 1965), p. 51.
12. *House of Lords Debates,* 3 July 1930 (vol. 78). Passfield's motion was eventually accepted on 12 November 1930 (Debates, Vol. 79), when there was a pedestrian debate in which Lord Cranworth insisted that there was already sufficient evidence for a decision to be taken. Lord Delamere spoke on this occasion — his first and last speech in the House of Lords. The Peers appointed to the committee were named on 20 November 1930 (with Cranworth among them).
13. The evidence of Beatrice Webb's Diaries suggests that Sidney had already washed his hands of Kenya the year before. The entry for November 28, 1929 records him as saying: 'I have done my best to get a workable scheme of reform — but it is so uncertain how things will work out that I'm quite ready to leave the final decision to the Joint Committee.' Beatrice added: 'It is just possible that the eventual decision will be made by another Secretary of State — which S[idney] will not altogether regret.' (p. 229)
14. A speech reproduced in the *East African Standard,* 12 July 1929, may be regarded as Delamere's political testament:

> As to the political future of the natives, there is ample scope for such development within the boundaries of the reserves, without bringing the natives within the field of the white man's politics. If that last safeguard is undermined there will go with it in its fall the right of British people to claim that with their race, and their race alone, whether as settlers or as officials, must lie the responsibility for . . . the development of the Empire in Africa.

15. As he told Professor W. H. Macmillan (Macmillan to Roden Buxton, 30 June 1937: Creech Jones Papers).
16. R. Gregory, *India and East Africa,* p. 363. Gregory gives a very full summary of the proceedings of the committee.
17. R. Gregory, *Sidney Webb and East Africa,* p. 136.
18. *Joint Select Committee, Evidence* and *Report,* H. C. 156, 1931.

19. *Beatrice Webb's Diary*, p. 215.
20. *Report of the Special Commission on the Ceylon Constitution*, Cmd. 3131, 1928, p. 18: 'Working of the Existing Constitution'.
21. Irwin to Sir Malcolm Hailey, 22 August 1928 (Correspondence with Persons in India).
22. The Commission actually recommended manhood suffrage, together with votes for all females over thirty years. Webb decided to enlarge this into universal adult suffrage.
23. E. F. C. Ludowyk, *The Modern History of Ceylon* (London, 1966) pp. 164-5.
24. *Correspondence Regarding the Constitution of Ceylon*, Cmd. 3419, 1929. Despatch from Governor Stanley to the Secretary of State, 2 June 1929; Secretary of State to Stanley, 10 October 1929.
25. CP 174 (30), 'Franchise Proposals in Ceylon', Memorandum by the Secretary of State for the Colonies, dated 26 May 1930.
26. N. R. Chakravarti, *The Indian Minority in Burma: the rise and decline of an immigrant community* (London, 1971) pp. 126-7. See Chapter IX: 'Indians Under Dyarchy, 1923-1936'.
27. S. Arasaratnam, *Indians in Malaysia and Singapore* (London, 1970) pp. 85-6.
28. *Report . . . on a Visit to Malaya*, by Sir Samuel Wilson, Cmd. 4276, 1933.
29. Note by Dominions Office: see file 'Imperial Conference, 1930' (Private Office Papers). See also *Imperial Conference, 1930*, Cmd. 3717.
30. The very detailed account given by Bridglal Pachai, *The South African Indian Question, 1860-1971* (Cape Town, 1971), states that the Bill was introduced by the Minister of the Interior (p. 132).
31. Hoare did read a long India Office memorandum, 'Indians Overseas', and initialled it on 8 October 1931, soon after his appointment.
32. At the end of his viceroyalty, Willingdon explained to Zetland (13 July 1935): 'The policy of my government ever since I have been here has been in the main to make Gandhi realise that we are the government, that he is only the head of a political party.'
33. Azim Husain, *Fazl-i-Husain; a political biography* (Bombay, 1946), pp. 204-5. His chapter 'Indians in South Africa' provides an intimate account of the second Cape Town conference based upon the personal diary of Fazl-i-Husain.
34. Azim Husain, op. cit., p. 312.
35. Irwin to Wedgwood Benn, private telegram, 3 January 1931.
36. Maharaj Singh to Sastri, 20 February 1933. He signed himself 'Guruwali Maharaj', meaning that he acknowledged Sastri as his mentor.
37. The full history of the liquidation of the Cape native franchise is given by W. K. Hancock, *Smuts: the Fields of Force, 1919-1950:* see Ch. 14, 'A New Unsettlement'. The Africans who possessed the vote in Cape Province (a dwindling minority) were transferred to a separate role and were given token representation by Whites. The measure was passed by the Hertzog-Smuts coalition in 1936.
38. *Rand Daily Mail*, 21 August 1933.

39. These letters from Naidoo to Sastri were dated 10 September and 15 September 1933 and 17 February 1934.
40. Professor Monica Wilson (as she later became) wrote to Sastri on 7 January 1934 to declare her suspicion that Indians were to be 'dumped' in the British protectorates in South Africa: she feared that they would 'join the European in keeping in his position the true heir to Africa' (i.e. the African).
41. Maharaj Singh to Philip Liesching of the British High Commissioner's Office, Pretoria, 18 September 1934.
42. These measures were the Alienation of Land (Restriction and Evidence) Decree, Clove Growers Association Decree, Agricultural Export Decree, Clove Exporters Decree, Adulteration of Produce Decree, Moneylenders Amendment Decree.
43. Confidential Report by K. P. S. Menon to the Government of India, 10 September 1934.
44. *Report of the Kenya Land Commission, September 1933*, p. 485. Printed in Kenya and issued as Cmd. 4556 in May 1934, 618 pp and many maps. That equivocal document, the Devonshire Report (*Indians in Kenya*, 1923) was the authority for Sir Morris Carter and his colleagues in their categorical assumption that the highlands were reserved for Europeans only. Yet the Devonshire Report merely referred to 'past practice', and 'present practice', and stated (p. 17) that 'It would be possible for the Executive Government to grant land in the Highlands to an Asiatic, or to approve of the transfer of land from a European to an Asiatic, without any alteration of the existing Law.' The Carter Report sought to ensure that the law would make any such transfer legally impossible.
45. *Kenya Land Commission Report: Summary of Conclusions Reached by His Majesty's Government . . . May 1934*, Cmd. 4580.
46. Azim Husain, op. cit., pp. 212-15.

CHAPTER 5, A PATTERN OF INEQUALITY

1. The occasion for Linlithgow's comment was the publication of the Donoughmore Report which, he told Irwin (23 September 1928) 'has fairly put the wind up me'.
2. As Zetland told Linlithgow in a private letter of 2 August 1935.
3. K. P. S. Menon, *Many Worlds: an autobiography* (Bombay, 1965), pp. 134-5.
4. Bajpai's caustic comment came in a letter to Sastri(20 February 1938). This was one of Fazl-i-Husain's appointments: he wanted a Muslim as Agent in South Africa. Sir Abdul Kadir was invited in 1932, but he declined the post. In 1934 Fazl-i-Husain pressed hard for Raza Ali's appointment in the face of India Office opposition. W. D. Croft told the Secretary of State that Raza Ali was 'quite good-natured but only second-rate, if that, in intelligence. He is rather hot-headed and excitable and very clumsy and tactless'. The choice was questioned

(telegram, Secretary of State to Viceroy, 17 November 1934) but the appointment went through.
5. On Willingdon's shilly-shallying, see K. P. S. Menon, op. cit., pp. 131-2, and on the split in the Congress see G. H. Calpin, *A. I. Kajee, his work for the South African Indian Community* (Durban, n.d.) pp. 32-9.
6. UK High Commissioner in South Africa to Secretary of State for the Dominions, 14 April 1937. This followed a telegram sent to the High Commissioner (12 April) in which a message was conveyed from Baldwin to Hertzog expressing 'anxiety' at the private member's Bill. It was still considered helpful to invoke the prestige of the prime minister of the United Kingdom in a matter which concerned South Africa — and India — but not Britain.
7. Government of India Act, 1935, Part V, Chapter III, and Government of Burma Act, 1935, Part V.
8. The St Germaine Convention was signed in 1919 on behalf of the United States, France, Italy, Japan, Portugal, and Belgium: with a representative of Great Britain signing on behalf of the British Empire, which had the largest stake in the area. In addition, the Dominions and India signed separately.
9. In the preliminary exchange of letters, the most important were those of Zetland to Thomas, 19 December 1935, and Thomas to Zetland, 7 January 1936. Their Cabinet papers were: CP 18 (36) 'The Highlands Question in Kenya; Memorandum by the Secretary of State for India' dated 30 January 1936, and CP 43 (36) 'Kenya; Reservation of the Highlands Question; Memorandum by the Secretary of State for the Colonies' dated 13 February 1936.
10. Presumably this was a reference to Beharilal Anantari, editor of *Zanzibar Voice*, who was then living in Hampstead.
11. Aga Khan to W. D. Croft, 19 July 1937 (Private Office Papers).
12. S. K. Patil to the President of the Congress, 15 May 1938 (AICC Papers).
13. *Review of Important Events Relating to or Affecting Indians in Different Parts of the British Empire, during the Year 1939-40*. This useful annual survey was first issued for the year 1936-7, and it continued to appear until the issue 1944-5 (January 1946) when it was discontinued.
14. *Report by the Right Hon. V. S. Srinivasa Sastri regarding his Mission to East Africa*, Delhi, 1930.
15. Kenya Immigration Restriction (Amendment) Ordinance: *Kenya Gazette*, 29 November 1938.
16. The fiction was that there was a separate Secretary of State for Burma—who also happened to be Secretary of State for India. Likewise there was a Burma Office—accommodated in the India Office—with Sir John Walton (after a lifetime of service in the India Office) at the head of the new department.
17. *House of Commons Debates*, Vol. 317, 17 November 1936.
18. Correspondence relating to Nehru's three visits to neighbouring countries (Burma, Malaya, Ceylon) is on file with the AICC Papers. The

Burma material contains unique information about Aung San's early career.
19. *Kala Htoon Thin* may be translated as 'Bash the Indian' or 'Bash the Foreigner', as *kala* is a term applied to all foreigners except the Chinese (known as *pauk-paw*, 'cousin') though it seems to have a special intensity when used about Indians. Learned opinion derives *kala* from 'caste people' (i.e.Indians) though the obvious derivation might appear to be *kāla* ('black man').
20. *Report on the Immigration of Indians into Burma*, Rangoon, 1941. For a more detailed account of these events see N. R. Chakravarti, *The Indian Minority in Burma*, Ch. X, 'Indians in Separated Burma, 1937-1942'.
21. R. H. Hutchings to the Private Secretary to the Viceroy (G. Laithwaite) 12 September 1939.
22. Bajpai to Sastri, 23 March 1937. The Bajpai-Sastri correspondence of the 1920s and '30s is among the papers of Indian leaders deposited at the Jawaharlal Nehru Memorial Library.
23. Sastri was still Vice-Chancellor of Annamalai University, but he withdrew from active public affairs. Soon he was writing to Bajpai (6 May 1938) 'An occasional letter from you is a welcome assurance to me that I am alive still and remembered'.
24. These quotations from Nehru and Lohia are taken from a report prepared by the Malayan CID and enclosed with a despatch from Sir Shenton Thomas to the Secretary for the Colonies, dated 14 July 1941, Appendix A.
25. Memorandum, 'Plantation Labour in Ceylon', by S. A. Wickremasinghe, June 1937 prepared for a Socialist conference on India and Ceylon (Creech Jones Papers).
26. *Correspondence Regarding the Constitution of Ceylon*, Cmd. 15910, 1938.
27. CP 254(38) 'Ceylon Constitution; Memorandum by the Secretary of State for the Colonies', November 1938. There is one unexplained difference between Caldecott's analysis and that of MacDonald: in his despatch, Caldecott wrote of the need to re-draw certain constituencies so that the Kandyan voters would not be 'swamped' [sic] by the Indian labour vote. MacDonald advised an increase of ten seats for the Kandyans *and* the Indians (together) in his paper.
28. Private and personal telegram, Linlithgow to Zetland, 28 May 1939.
29. C. F. Andrews, *India and the Pacific* (London, 1937), pp. 11, 15.
30. The price of raw sugar, per hundred-weight, in London was 11s. in 1910, 58s. in 1920, 6s. 7d in 1930 and 4s. 8d in 1935. Noel Deerr, *The History of Sugar* (London, Vol. II, 1950), p. 531.
31. The *Rose Hall* conflict of 1913 is treated in detail in the author's *A New System of Slavery*, pp. 229-30. The events of 1935 were communicated by the Governor of British Guiana, Sir Geoffrey Northcote, to the Colonial Office in a series of telegrams dated 17 October, 20 October, 23 October (two) and a despatch, Northcote to J. H. Thomas, 7 December 1935.
32. *Report of the Commissioners Appointed to Enquire Into and Report on the Labour Disputes*... Georgetown, 1936.
33. The colonies with laws permitting trade unions were: British Guiana,

Ceylon, Jamaica, Kenya, Northern Rhodesia, Tanganyika, Trinidad, Uganda, Zanzibar.

34. The officers of the MPCA, besides A. E. Edun as President, were Edward Pile, Vice-President, H. Barron, General Secretary (Indian), and Committee: R. N. Persaud, O. A. Ashby, O. N. Persaud, Seemangal Maharaj, T. R. King, J. B. Singh.
35. The largest amount taken back on the *Ganges* was owned by Ramnarain Singh who had arrived in Guiana in 1901 and who brought back $1,345 (about £270) while Budhoo who had arrived in 1909 brought back $1,200 (£250) and Sahebdin who arrived in 1896 brought $1,050 (£215).
36. *British Guiana: Report of the Leonora Enquiry Commission, dated 23 March 1939* (a sessional paper of the Legislative Council).
37. *Report on the Condition of Indians in Jamaica, British Guiana and Trinidad*, by J. D. Tyson, Delhi, 1939.
38. *Report of the West India Royal Commission*, Cmd. 6607, 1945. Copies of the report were sent to India early in 1940, but they were recalled and returned in their sealed covers.
39. *Proconsul: being incidents in the life and career of the Honourable Sir Bede Clifford* ((London, 1964), p. 235. Throughout his autobiography, Clifford portrays his thoughts and actions as those of 'C'.
40. 'Odd Man Out: the Loneliness of the Indian Colonial Politician: the career of Manilal Doctor' by the present author; *Journal of Imperial and Commonwealth History*, January 1974.
41. Despatch from the Officer Administering the Government, E. W. Evans, to the Secretary of State for the Colonies, 24 August 1937.
42. *Report of the Committee of Inquiry into Unrest on Sugar Estates in Mauritius*, 1937 (dated 30 March 1938), Port Louis, 1938.
43. The Creech Jones Papers include a file on Mauritius, 1936-39, which provides very full documentation for these years. The present work does no more than skim over the surface of these papers. Among his regular Mauritian correspondents were Dr J. M. Curé, R. Jomadar, Dr H. Joomye, and J. E. Anquetil.
44. Clifford treats the strikes summarily in his autobiography, *Proconsul*, pp. 233-5. Curé was an 'outstanding trouble maker'; Anquetil, 'an eloquent stump orator'. It is alleged that on his return from banishment, Anquetil 'thanked the Governor for his kindness'.
45. *House of Commons Debates*, Vol. 348, 6 June and 21 June 1939.
46. Indians in Mauritius were very conscious that they were neglected by the national movement, by contrast to Indians in East Africa. Thus, J. B. Roy of Phoenix, Mauritius, wrote to complain to Dr Rajendra Prasad (future President of India) that no attention was paid to their grievances: 'Pandit Kunzru came to our doorstep in Kenya, but in spite of our entreaties he did not consider it worth his while to pay us a visit'. Mr Roy concluded: 'Are we the depressed classes of the overseas Indians that we should be relegated to the limbo of oblivion and left to fight our battles unaided and alone?' (19 February 1946). Prasad forwarded the letter to K. R. Kripalani, then secretary of the AICC,

observing rather vaguely: 'I believe you have a department in your office which deals with Indians abroad' (AICC Papers).
47. However, there were examples of British practice which demonstrated an acceptance of Indian (and African) equality as citizens of the empire. A Foreign Office directive of 12 October 1933 was headed 'Circular: Consular Instructions', and this laid down rules for the registration of British subjects at British consulates in foreign countries: 'The procedure to be followed is identical whether the persons concerned are of white or coloured race. Births and deaths of British protected persons should not be recorded in the Consular registry'. This is one of the rare occasions on which British citizenship law is directly linked to the skin shade of a citizen: and it was then pronounced irrelevant.
48. U. K. High Commissioner in Canada to Secretary for the Dominions (MacDonald), 2 March 1936.

CHAPTER 6, COERCION AND CONFLICT

1. Foreign Office to Colonial Office, 4 April 1941.
2. Lord Lloyd lasted nine months, Lord Moyne twelve months, Cranborne another nine months, and Stanley for nearly three years.
3. Confidential 'Report on the Condition of Indians in Mauritius' by S. Ridley, printed (but not published) in Delhi, 1941. The Mauritius government asked for many references to people and events to be removed, and with these deletions the report was published in January 1944.
4. Subsequently, the *Report of the Commission of Enquiry into the Disturbances which occurred in the North of Mauritius in 1943*, London, 1943, showed (p. 8) that in 1938-9 there were 260 cases of victimisation: eight were taken to Court by the Labour Department, and six were dismissed. It would appear that two victims of the employers obtained redress.
5. The Ridley report also showed that among the ten magistrates appointed to each of the districts of the island, only one was an Indian; the fourteen medical officers included two Indians; 63 of the 205 clerks in government offices were Indian—though almost all the office peons were Indians! Of the teachers, 167 of the total of 406 were Indians. The only prominent Indian official was the Post Master General F. E. Perombelon, but Ridley discovered that having attained prominence he was no longer regarded as an Indian.
6. For the constitutional significance of the 'Mooloya Incident' see Sir Charles Jeffries, *Ceylon: the Path to Independence* ((London, 1962) pp.85-6. Jefferies provides a full account of the years 1920-48, derived from his own intimate connection with the island's affairs at the Colonial Office.
7. This was the third Confidential despatch on the Indian question which Caldecott had sent to the Secretary of State within four months; it followed despatches dated 23 February and 17 May 1940.
8. A public statement on the conference was issued by the Government of India on 11 February 1941 after accounts of the proceedings had

appeared in Ceylon; the quotation relating the case of the Ceylon ministers comes from this statement. A report on the conference was transmitted by telegram to the India Office, 13 November 1940; this referred to repatriation on the South African model. The two documents are virtually identical.

9. Bajpai's 'Note on Ceylon Visit' was given to the Private Secretary to the Viceroy, 24 January 1941.
10. *Revision of Electoral Regulations 1940: Interim Report by the Legal Secretary, January 1941.* See also Government of India letter to Secretary of State for India, 15 March 1941. Mr Dibdin of the India Office noted that there was no need 'to exercise ourselves unduly over the precise details of the controversy. It will settle itself'.
11. The Chief Secretary of Ceylon informed the Government of India on 26 August 1940 that the Ministers had completed their proposals. On 15 November 1940 a telegram from the Colonial Office was sent to warn the ministers that if the bills were passed by the State Council they would not be given the Royal assent.
12. J. Norman Parmer, 'Chinese Estate Workers' Strikes in Malaya in March 1937', C. D. Cowan, ed. *The Economic Development of South-East Asia* (London, 1964) see especially p. 169: 'Indians had been regarded as easygoing, tractable and respectful of authority'.
13. The correspondence relating to this sequence of events is accumulated on file C. O. 51574/1 and 2, 'Labour Conditions: Disturbances on Klang Rubber estates'. The main source is the despatch by Shenton Thomas dated 14 July 1941, which extended to 16 pages, with 123 pages of appendices (a colonial record?). This includes reports from the C.I.D. which was watching all the Indian leaders (including the Agent of the Government of India). The flow of telegrams reporting the drama begins with a telegram dated 10 May 1941 from the High Commissioner of the Federated Malay States to the Secretary for the Colonies, and continues almost daily: 12, 20, 22, 30 May.
14. *House of Commons Debates*, Vol. 371, 28 May 1941.
15. George Hall, or his private secretary, wrote: 'I am grateful to Sir C. Parkinson for drawing attention to... the general question of the appointment of commissions of enquiry—views with which [sic] I do not dissent (29.5.41)'.
16. The information was conveyed by Linlithgow to Amery in a personal telegram of 31 August; he enlarged on the subject in his weekly personal letter of 2 September 1941.
17. Telegrams from Orde Browne to the Colonial Office, dated 9 and 26 August. Orde Browne eventually produced an official report, *Labour Conditions in Ceylon, Mauritius and Malaya*, Cmd. 6423, 1942 which is a masterpiece of under-statement and omission. There had been serious industrial unrest in each of the three territories he visited, but scarcely a hint of the measures taken by the colonial authorities against the strikers is mentioned in the report. Orde Browne admitted that the forty-five days he spent in Malaya were 'far from adequate' for assessing the situation, though this did not prevent him giving immediate advice

to the Colonial Office. His report includes twenty-eight lines on trade unions in Malaya, but there is no mention of strikes, and he gives the impression that there were no Indian unions in Malaya.
18. The despatch from Sir Shenton Thomas, dated 14 July, arrived at the Colonial Office on 30 August 1941.
19. See file 717/147 'Indians in Malaya; Commission of Inquiry'.
20. In his usual meticulous way, Bajpai immediately recorded a full account of the negotiations, dated 8 July 1941.
21. R. Hutchings to G. Laithwaite (private secretary to the Viceroy), 4 July 1941.
22. The terms were cabled by the Governor of Burma, Sir Reginald Dorman-Smith, to Amery on 30 June 1941. Their substance was as follows, though not in these exact words:

(1) From 1 October 1941, all Indians entering Burma would have to carry Indian passports and possess Burma immigration permits.
(2) Four classes of immigrants were defined; those with previous links enjoyed certain privileges; long-term new immigrants must be 'on some financial standing'.
(3) Overall numbers would be limited.
(4) Indians in Burma without passports, or means of subsistence might be expelled. Indians who cohabit with a female of the indigenous races might have their permits cancelled: though the Burma Government could sanction such a marriage, providing that the immigrant first made adequate financial provision for his intended wife.
(5) There would be an Immigration Board to advise on quotas.
(6) Each immigrant must deposit Rs. 20 on arrival, to cover the cost of his return.
(7) Indians in Burma on 22 July 1941 could submit claims to Burma domicile; such claims to be submitted to a tribunal within two years.
(8) Anyone with seven years' previous residence in Burma between 1932 and 1941 would have a right of residence and employment and a right to re-entry; these rights would be forfeit after an absence of over a year.
(9) All Indians resident in Burma other than those above (8) could stay, but would be treated as new immigrants if they left the country.
(10) The immigration of unskilled Indian labour was to be suspended completely from 15 July 1941, except for seasonal labourers, who would receive short-stay permits.

23. Kunzru advised the committee that 'The agreement was very satisfactory and the committee should not repudiate it; Raza Ali agreed; it was 'The best that could be arrived at in the circumstances. The Committee endorsed this opinion' (Minutes: meetings, 14-15 July, Aney papers).
24. The Department of Indians Overseas kept a file of protest letters and

telegrams: it is over two inches thick. By contrast, the protests against the Ceylon agreement, a few weeks later, form a file only half an inch thick.

25. Dorman-Smith to Linlithgow, 6 November 1941: Dorman-Smith wanted Hutchings to be made a High Commissioner, to give him proper diplomatic status, but Linlithgow wanted to 'go a little slowly' on this proposal.

26. In his report to Amery, cabled on 12 November 1941, Linlithgow did not give the exact number of votes for and against repudiation, but it would appear that seven members voted to reject the agreement and five voted in favour.

27. R. Hutchings: 'Report on Evacuation from Burma', signed 4 September 1942. This immensely long report, written while the memory of these dreadful days still burned in Hutchings' mind, is one of the most vivid documents of the second World War.

28. Telegram, Bajpai to Government of India, 17 September, and 'Note' by Bajpai, enclosed by Linlithgow in his weekly personal letter to Amery, 30 September 1941.

29. Details of the evacuation of Indians from Malaya were reported by M. S. Aney to the National Defence Council at their meeting in April 1942. This account is taken from the Minutes of the Council. Information about Malaya was sparse, though Aney's statement about the evacuation from Burma was in great detail.

30. A file of the Department of Indians Overseas, 'Burma, Malaya and Ceylon, Evacuation of Indians' surveyed the figures and arrived at totals which indicated a final figure of 425,000 refugees.

31. Beside the report by Hutchings, cited above (note 27) an important source is *Report on the Evacuation of Refugees from Burma to India (Assam), January to July 1942 by Major-General E. Wood, Administrator-General of Eastern Frontier Communications*, Calcutta, 1 October 1942. There was also a report by J. S. Vorley, controller of the Indian refugee camps at Rangoon and Mandalay; the India Office noted that 'criticisms of government and government officers occur all through' Mr Vorley's report, which appears not to be available either in London or New Delhi. The trek of the Indians out of Burma deserves to be the subject of a full-length book. For a longer account by the present author, see 'A Forgotten Long March; the Indian exodus from Burma', *Journal of South East Asian Studies* (Singapore, March 1975).

32. A total of 14,354 persons were evacuated from north Burma by air before all flights stopped on 9 May; of these 3,863 were Europeans 2,869 were Anglo-Indians, 548 were Anglo-Burmans, 126 were Burmans and 4,801 were Indians.

33. A. V. Pai answered a question on this subject in the Legislative Assembly on 21 September 1942. Eventually, the refugees were expected to reimburse the British Government for costs incurred in their evacuation, and for their maintenance; the file is thick with correspondence from the Accounts Department.

34. Ba Maw, *Breakthrough in Burma* (New Haven, 1968), also Thakin Nu,

Burma Under the Japanese (London, 1954) and Hugh Tinker, *The Union of Burma: a Study of the First Years of Independence* (London, 1957, 4th edn. 1967).

35. *Burma During the Japanese Occupation*, a 'Confidential' publication 'under the authority of the Governor of Burma', Vol. I, 1943, Vol. II, 1944. See sections on 'Non-Official Organisation' Part IV, (6.f) and 'The Chettiars', Part VI, (B.3)
36. Philip Toye, *The Springing Tiger* (London, 1959), provides a lifelike and searching account of Bose as wartime leader. Several of the INA leaders wrote bombastic accounts of the experience. A verdict on the INA recorded by an Indian witness before the mythmaking began may be of interest. Visaka Kasi Chettiar, a former merchant in Burma, wrote to the AICC on 24 September 1945: 'A microscopic minority might have been actuated by patriotic motives but generally speaking a vast majority of them had inflicted many difficulties on Indians who were left behind in Burma, sometimes associating with the Japanese and at other times with the brutal Burmese' (AICC Papers). See also Usha Mahajani, *The Role of Indian Minorities in Burma and Malaya* (Bombay, 1960) Ch. V, 'The Japanese Occupation of Burma and Malaya'.
37. S. Arasaratnam, *Indians in Malaysia and Singapore* (London, 1970), p. 30.
38. Besides Malaya, the Dutch East Indies and French Indo-China were lost to the Anglo-American alliance. Ceylon's output now represented 85 per cent of the rubber production under allied control.
39. The reader who desires to follow the controversy through in complete detail can do so by referring to the *Proceedings of the Council of State* (India), 'Statements Laid on the Table'; 22 February 1943, which includes the whole official correspondence from the beginning of 1942 to February 1943.
40. Because there are so many accounts of the events leading up to the partition of India, the subject is merely touched upon in passing in this work; but a knowledge of the events leading to the 'Transfer of Power' helps to explain the pressures developing in relation to the overseas Indians. The present writer's interpretation is contained in *Experiment with Freedom: India and Pakistan 1947* (London, 1967). At this time (1943) Churchill told George VI that 'He felt that they had already been talked into giving up India', J. W. Wheeler-Bennett, *King George VI: his life and reign* (London 1958). See also Lord Butler, *The Art of the Possible*, and conversations at Chequers at this time, when Churchill declared that it was not worth holding on to India at the expense of damage to the British army.
41. WP (43) 129, 'Ceylon Constitution: Memorandum by the Secretary of State for the Colonies' dated 27 March 1943.
42. Croft's note was dated 22 March 1943. Amery, who always enjoyed constitutional theorising, advised Stanley that he should speak of 'full self-government' not 'full responsible government': 'Responsible government of the British type is ... not feasible', it had led to the demand for a separate Muslim state, he said (24 March 1942); but the

more pragmatic Stanley brushed this aside, observing that the Ceylon politicians were 'wedded to the clichés' (26 March 1942).
43. WP (43) 204, 'Ceylon Constitution: Memorandum by the Secretary of State for the Colonies', dated 15 May 1943. The Cabinet accepted this draft, and cabled to Churchill to obtain his 'concurrence'.
44. Caldecott to Stanley, telegram of 4 July 1943.
45. The next entry is taken from the collection of documents, edited by Nicholas Mansergh and E. W. R. Lumby, *The Transfer of Power, 1942-7*, Vol. III, p. 502: Linlithgow to Amery, 13 January, 1943. These volumes are focussed upon the constitutional debate leading to partition, and in the first three volumes this is the only direct reference to Indians overseas.
46. Indian emigration to Fiji fell away to a trickle before the war. The numbers of Indians entering Fiji in 1936 were 650, 151 in 1937, 859 in 1938, 611 in 1939, and 80 in 1940. Thereafter there were no Indians arriving until 1945 when 36 were admitted into Fiji.
47. Telegram, Fiji Government to Government of India, 15 June 1943 and 8 October 1943. A debate in the Fiji legislature was reported in the *Fiji Times and Herald*, 19 May 1943, in which Indian members explained why the community had not responded to military recruiting. One member of the legislature, K. B. Singh, became a lieutenant in the Fiji forces.
48. Colonial Office to India Office, 30 August 1943, enclosing telegram from Mitchell dated 5 August 1943.
49. Adrian C. Mayer, *Indians in Fiji* (London, 1963), Ch. VI 'The Second World War'. Mayer's account of the 1943 conflict is somewhat brief.
50. *Report of the Commission of Enquiry into the Disturbances which occurred in the North of Mauritius in 1943*, London, 1944.
51. Where he began to sum up the situation in mordant terms. He told Dr Khare that the local Indian Congress organisation was 'riddled with faction' (7 September 1943) and only the president, Aziz, wanted to work with the Ceylonese leaders. Among these leaders he described Senanayake as 'a sober, quiet and strong man'; Bandaranaike as 'intensely ambitious and an unabashed opportunist', and Kotelawala as 'impulsive and rather unbalanced': 'not only extremely anti-Indian but often unscrupulous' (demi-official letters to Khare, 13 October and 17 December 1943).
52. WP (42) 544 'Colonial Policy', Memorandum by the Deputy Prime Minister, Secretary of State for Foreign Affairs, Lord Privy Seal, and Secretary of State for the Colonies, dated 5 December 1942; WP (42) 'Colonial Policy', Memorandum by the Secretary of State for India and Burma, dated 10 December 1942; WP (42) 614, 'Colonial Policy', Memorandum by the Lord Privy Seal, dated 30 December 1942; WP (43) 9, 'Telegram from the Viceroy to the Secretary of State for India' dated 5 January 1943. All these papers came before the War Cabinet on 7 January 1943.
53. Cabinet Ministers seem to have been in some doubt as to what they had discussed on 7 January; Amery gave Stanley his impression of what

had gone on (8 January 1943) and Stanley replied with his version (9 January).
54. Churchill used this phrase at the annual banquet given by the Lord Major of the City of London, 11 November 1942: C.E. Carrington, *The Liquidation of the British Empire* (London, 1961) p. 11.

CHAPTER 7, EQUALITY: THE CLAIM ASSERTED

1. Information and quotations contained in letter from Bhawani Dayal Sannyasi of Natal to D. Y. Dev, Secretary, Department of Indians Overseas, AICC, dated 27 April 1940.
2. *Report of the Indian Penetration Commission, 1941,* published 1942.
3. The Instructions issued to Shafa'at Ahmad Khan later acquired significance. He was informed that the South African Government had taken exception to speeches made by Raza Ali towards the end of his term. The High Commissioner should 'act with restraint'. He should not attempt to act as spokesman for the local Indian community. Because none of the current South African Indian leaders exercised influence 'in the direction of moderation', he must 'educate' opinion. His speeches should avoid 'embarrassment' to the Government. Any demands should be put in confidential form to Ministers, 'the public presentation of the standpoint of the Indian community being left to the spokesmen of the Indian community'. Among the local organisations, the South African Indian Congress was pronounced 'the most reliable and influential', though it had been inactive since 1935. The High Commissioner should try to promote better relations between Europeans and Indians in South Africa; he should also 'quicken ... a sense of social duty [by middle class Indians] towards their less fortunate compatriots. Unless this moral duty is recognised ... by prosperous and educated Indians, the improvement from within ... will not receive impetus or make appreciable headway' (3 November 1941).
4. *Report of the Second Indian Penetration (Durban) Commission,* 1943. Broome's findings were corroborated by Shafa'at Ahmad Khan. In a demi-official letter to Dr Khare (19 July 1943) he wrote that 'The [Natal Indian] Association did no solid work but went on purchasing property in European areas. Many of the members of the association — such as Sorabjee, Ashwin Choudree and others — were the greatest culprits'. He returned to the charge in his Monthly Report to the Government of India (December 1943) where he declared that Ashwin Choudree, a house agent was 'responsible for the conditions which brought about the Pegging Act'.
5. UK High Commissioner to Dominions Office, 15 April 1943. Harlech was sending a stream of telegrams to London at this time. He was asked to provide a channel of communication between Amery and the South African Ministers, as well as acting on behalf of Attlee, who was in charge of the Dominions Office while Deputy Prime Minister.
6. Polak wrote to Mackenzie King on 18 September 1943; he received a reply from King sent on 12 October. It was not entirely clear whether

King meant that the Indian question in Canada or South Africa was so complex; probably the latter.

7. Some writers have inferred that Pather went to jail (cf. Bridglal Pachai, *The South African Indian Question, 1860-1971*, p. 175). He was given the alternative of a fine or seven days' imprisonment (suspended for six months). The fine was paid anonymously. Next year (28 June 1944) Pather announced that he was vacating the house: 'In an atmosphere which is already charged with anti-Indian feeling it is not my purpose further to embarrass the Government' in its efforts 'to settle amicably the Indian question'.

8. At first, Sir Shafa'at Ahmad had backed Rustomjee against Kajee, who he alleged was 'exploiting rich Muslim merchants for his personal ends' (demi-official, to Khare, 5 June 1943). He then decided that though 'there is little to choose between Sorabjee and Kajee from the point of view of honesty' it was impossible to work with the former, who was 'mischievous, vindictive, unscrupulous and factious' (19 July 1943). Within six months he was telling Khare that Kajee 'has done brilliantly as Chairman' (20 December 1943). This assessment did not last long.

9. The reader who wishes to follow the correspondence between the Indian and South African governments can find the details in the *Legislative Assembly Debates*, Vol. III, 30 July, 1943.

10. Linlithgow's telegram to Amery of 16 August 1943 announced unanimous support for the boycott; his telegram of 20 August notified the postponement. The Supply Department memorandum showed that India's exports to South Africa for 1941-2 were worth Rs. 6,04,00,000 and imports Rs. 1,24,00,000, giving a surplus of Rs. 4,80,00,000 (about £3,500,000).

11. Harlech to Sir Eric Machtig, Permanent Under Secretary of State for the Dominions, 29 December 1943.

12. The story of the leak via Dr Khare was given by Wavell in his weekly letter to Amery, 15 February 1944. An entirely different version appears in *My Political Memoirs or Autobiography* by N. B. Khare (Nagpur, n.d. 1960), pp. 158-9. Khare tries to suggest that Wavell wrote his letter to Smuts *now*, in February 1944, as the price required by Khare for getting the adjournment debate put off. Presumably when Khare compiled his memoirs he relied upon his own memory. This raises questions about the authenticity of his other recollections of his three years as Member for Indians Overseas: which is a pity, as he tells some good stories.

13. Wavell saw many of the telegrams from Shafa'at Ahmad to Khare and must have been astonished at some of them. On 19 July 1943, the High Commissioner wrote: 'Smuts is ruthless, cruel, unscrupulous and vain', and thereafter accused him of Mephistophelean practices. But perhaps his furthest flight of fancy came when he cabled Khare: 'I am now convinced that Broome was instrumental in fostering agitation in favour of Pegging Act through his misleading report' (20 September 1944).

14. UK High Commissioner to South Africa, telegram to Dominions Office, 15 April 1944.

15. G.H. Calpin, A.I. Kajee, *His Work for the South African Indian Community* (Durban, n.d.) p. 139. Calpin had been editor of the *Natal Witness*.
16. Amery to Wavell, 11 May 1944.
17. Heaton Nicholls arrived in London at the end of 1944 as High Commissioner for South Africa; he had a conversation with Amery about the Natal ordinances, which Amery related to Wavell: 24/25 January 1945.
18. This news was given by the UK High Commissioner in South Africa to the Dominions Office in telegrams dated 20, 23, and 27 June 1944.
19. When Nicholls came to write his reminiscences he gave a rather different account in which he suggested that Douglas Mitchell led the revolt against the original ordinance in June 1944: see G. Heaton Nicholls, *South Africa in My Time* (London, 1961) p. 317. It appears as though Nicholls also wrote his reminiscences largely from his own memory, and though the question could only be finally established by reference to the papers of Natal politicians (not attempted by this author) the charge is not corroborated by Shafa'at Ahmad Khan. His suspicions of the South African leaders had become almost hysterical at this time, but he excludes Mitchell from those he accuses of selling out. Finally, in a telegram dated 25 October 1944 he did inform Khare that Mitchell 'Who had so far supported the Pretoria Agreement has also gone over to the other camp, and unanimity of opposition to Indians among Europeans is complete'.
20. Wavell to Amery, personal and private telegram of 3 November and letter of 8 November 1944. A very different version of this encounter is given by Dr Khare in *My Political Memoirs*, pp. 160-1. According to this version, it was Wavell who proposed that a delegation of Council Members should go to London, and the Council rejected the Viceroy's proposal, at the instance of Dr Khare. There seem to be good reasons for preferring Wavell's immediate contemporary account; though he may have minimised the extent of the pressures put upon him.
21. UK High Commissioner to Secretary for the Dominions, 9 November 1944.
22. On 29 October 1944 he cabled to Khare: 'Kajee is most unreliable and has been corrupt all his life'.
23. J. H. Basson was Commissioner for Immigration and Asiatic Affairs in Natal.
24. See Note 3 above.
25. WP (44) 632, 'Indians in South Africa', Memorandum by the Secretary of State for India, dated 10 November 1944, and WP (44) 653, with the same title, dated 15 November 1944. Subsequently, the Cabinet were given WP (44) 694, 'Indians in South Africa', Memorandum by the Secretary of State for India, dated 27 November 1944.
26. A copy of Wavell's letter was shown to a few senior officials at the India Office, and an unknown hand has written 'Shades of Lord Allenby' in the margin. Wavell's terse and minatory language in private communication is revealed in *Wavell: the Viceroy's Journal*, edited by Penderel Moon (London, 1973).

27. In the *Viceroy's Journal* (p. 33), Wavell recorded, 'Linlithgow's view of Amery was the same as mine, he admired his qualities but said he was quite unable to get his stuff across in Cabinet, or I think in Parliament'. When Wavell attended a Cabinet committee on India in May 1945, Amery was 'prolix and unconvincing and was shot down from all sides' (p. 129).
28. UK High Commissioner to Secretary for the Dominions, 23 November 1944.
29. This account of the meeting is taken partly from the *Review of Important Events Affecting Indians Overseas . . . 1944-45*, and partly from a telegram from the UK High Commissioner to the Dominions Office, 29 November 1944. But according to Baring's account (source not indicated) at the meeting Smuts re-affirmed his 'adherence' to the Pretoria Agreement. This is not in accordance with the next account by Baring of a conversation with Smuts, when he said that the Agreement had been 'dropped'; it was 'of no further effect'. Bridglal Pachai in *The South African Indian Question, 1860-1971* gives a very brief account of the meeting, and states that afterwards Smuts announced that the Agreement was 'stone dead' (p. 177). Sir Keith Hancock (*Smuts, The Fields of Force*) does not mention this meeting.
30. Telegram, UK High Commissioner to Dominions Secretary, 22 December and 23 December 1944.
31. Despite his stormy record as High Commissioner, Sir Shafa'at Ahmad Khan was invited to be a member of the Secretary of State's Council of India in London. He declined, stating that he wished to enter public life. He was to serve, briefly, as a member of Nehru's interim government in 1946.
32. Baring to Lord Cranborne, 26 September 1944. Baring also produced some detailed and percipient studies of living conditions among the South African Indians when he became High Commissioner, especially a 'Confidential' letter dated 20 November 1944 to Sir Eric Machtig. Concerning Durban, he wrote 'The neglect of housing has been scandalous' contrasting the efforts of the Salisbury Council in providing hospital, school, swimming bath and football ground for the Indians. For Durban, a post-war scheme was planned to cost £10 million, but the city council refused to accept it.
33. Hancock, *Smuts, The Fields of Force*, p. 411.
34. Governor of Kenya to Secretary for the Colonies, 30 May 1942.
35. Minute by R. N. Gilchrist, India Office specialist on Indians overseas, dated 11 May 1945.
36. At the India Office, when correspondence was to be presented for consideration by the Secretary of State or an Under Secretary, it was the custom for a Minute to be prepared by the official responsible, stating the background to the case, and (usually) putting up a suggested draft reply. A few other officials might see the file, and would record 'I agree' or otherwise, but the ascent of the file was strictly *vertical*. At the Colonial Office, with its many departments and sections, it was the practice to revolve the file in a *circular* direction, and while the

main correspondence was tagged to the right-hand file cover, a series of long minutes, as well as casual observations, were affixed to the left-hand cover. The observations by Edmunds and Seel are in this category: the remarks on the left-hand side are usually considerably more frank than those on the right-hand side.

37. N. B. Khare, *My Political Memoirs*, p. 169.
38. See N. B. Khare, op. cit., p. 167. Khare was one of the first politicians in power at the centre to consolidate his position by using his ministerial patronage to appoint his own former regional *bhai-band* (brethren) to key positions. Every one of his important appointments went to somebody from the Central Provinces or to a Maharashtrian. Madhao Shrihari Aney and Sir R. P. Paranjpye, appointed as India's representatives in Ceylon and Australia were Maharashtrians, and so was R. V. Deshmukh. Jamnadas Mehta, chosen as India's representative with the Burma Government, was — despite his Gujarati-sounding name — a man of Maharashtra, and a firm political ally of Khare. Even R. N. Banerjee, the official head of Khare's department (who presumably originated from Bengal) had been in the Central Provinces throughout his ICS career and was Secretary (head) of a department of the Central Provinces government while Khare was Premier.
39. Baring to Machtig, 3 February 1945.
40. Deshmukh kept the Department of Commonwealth Relations informed in a series of telegrams, dated 30 March, and 4, 5, 10 and 11 April.
41. Telegram, Mudaliar (London) to Khare, 18 April 1945, and Khare to Mudaliar (San Francisco) 23 April 1945: with message for Smuts.
42. Telegram, Deshmukh to Khare, 28 May 1945.
43. *Interim Report of the Commission of Enquiry into Matters Affecting the Indian Population of the Province of Natal*, Cape Town, 1945.
44. Telegrams from the Governor, Mauritius, to Secretary for the Colonies, 20, 22 and 28 January 1944.
45. Government of Burma (Reconstruction Department) to Government of India, 13 March 1944; 'Notes on Discussion at Delhi, 24 and 25 April 1944', by Tin Tut; *Report of the Conference of the Members of the Standing Emigration Committee and Representatives of Indian Interests in Burma*, Secret, November 1944.
46. For an account of this operation from the technical viewpoint, see F. S. V. Donnison, *British Military Administration in the Far East, 1943-46* (London, 1956) especially Ch. XVII, Section i, 'Labour'.
47. Burma Office (London) to War Office, 14 November 1944.
48. The speech was delivered on 19 August 1943 and was reported by Aney to Khare on 27 November 1943. The Government of India instructed Aney to see the Governor of Ceylon to ask for a postponement of constitutional discussions until after the end of the war (minute by G. S. Bozman, 12 December 1943). This, of course, was impossible.
49. WP (44) 299, 'Ceylon' memorandum by the Secretary of State for the Colonies, dated 13 June 1944.
50. *Ceylon: Report of the Commission on Constitutional Reform*, Cmd. 6677, 1945.
51. 'Report on Investigation into Conditions of the Coloured Population

in a Stepney Area', March 1944, by Phyllis Young (Anti-Slavery Papers).
52. Both were published as paperbacks by Kitabistan, Allahabad, 1944. From internal evidence it appears as though 'An Onlooker' was probably H. N. Kunzru.
53. *The British Commonwealth and World Society: Proceedings of the Third Unofficial Conference on British Commonwealth Relations, London, 12 February to 3 March 1945*, ed. Richard Frost (London, 1947). Part II 'The Work of the Conference', 'Race and Migration'; the quotations which follow in the text come from pp. 109-113.
54. The Indian viewpoint was impressed upon the Canadians who, perhaps for the first time, realised the implications of their immigration policy upon Commonwealth relations. Edgar Tarr, the Canadian vice-chairman of the conference, told the Ministry of External Affairs in Ottawa that 'The Indians felt very keenly the stamp of inferiority which we have placed upon them by reason of our discrimination'. James Eayrs, *In Defence of Canada: Peacemaking and Deterrence* (Toronto, 1972), p. 242. There is a full account of the Chatham House conference from the Canadian point of view by Eayrs, pp. 211-16.

CHAPTER 8, EQUALITY: THE CLAIM VINDICATED

1. The present writer remembers his puzzlement on reading in the Allahabad *Leader* the statement by the Labour M.P. Professor Robert Richards, on arriving in India with a parliamentary delegation in January 1946, that they wanted India to get Home Rule.
2. Two authors have written detailed and scholarly studies of the Colonial Office and its policies, with Creech Jones as the central figure: J. M. Lee, *Colonial Development and Good Government: a study of the ideas expressed by the British official classes in planning decolonisation, 1939-1964* (Oxford, 1967) and David Goldsworthy, *Colonial Issues in British Politics, 1945-1961; from 'colonial development' to 'wind of change'* (Oxford, 1971). Neither seems conscious of the paradox of Creech Jones' almost Pauline conversion to the Colonial Office view. Thus, Goldsworthy (p. 20), 'Creech Jones always detested the idea of political and racial domination by settlers over natives ... But equally ... settler communities had to be kept reasonably contented: indeed augmented by immigration ... It is difficult to see what other courses were open to him'.
3. Cf. *Wavell: the Viceroy's Journal*, p. 180. Penderel Moon as editor decided to omit almost all references to Indians in South Africa, though this topic 'bulked largely' in Wavell's deliberations (xv).
4. The continuity of an Indian in charge of the department (begun in 1925) was thus maintained.
5. Mitchell to Secretary for the Colonies (Stanley 5 June 1945), enclosing draft white paper 'Proposals for the Reorganisation of the Administration of Kenya'. Mitchell wrote subsequently to Stanley (3 July) about Indian and African resettlement.
6. Sir Henry Moore as Governor had justified the extension of the terms of both Cavendish-Bentinck and Lord Francis Scott beyond the eight

years laid down in a Colonial Office circular (22 May 1941) on the grounds that there was a 'Gentleman's Agreement' between the Governor and the European members of the Legislative Council that the Governor would accept two members of his Executive Council recommended by the European elected members: and they still wanted Bentinck and Scott to serve (demi-official letter, Moore to Gerald Creasey, 16 May 1944). The Colonial Office hastened to sanction this breach of its own rules in favour of the Gentleman's Agreement (Colonial Secretary to Rennie, acting governor, 29 June 1944).

7. Secret telegram (no. 555) from Governor to Secretary for the Colonies, 21 July 1945.
8. Demi-official letter, Rennie (acting governor) to Cohen, 22 January 1946.
9. Rennie (acting governor) to Secretary for the Colonies, 22 December 1945: Rennie announced that Mitchell had asked him to acquaint the Secretary of State with his opinion on African representation in the legislature in the words quoted.
10. The Asiatic Civil Service formally came into being on 1 April 1909, though its origin was much earlier. In 1935, a Kenya European Civil Service was created on 1 January and a Local Asiatic Civil Service on 1 May: both were instituted for economy purposes, to recruit officers at lower salaries than in the (European) Colonial Service and the Asiatic Civil Service. An Arab and African Clerical Service was formed on 1 September 1927, and the African Civil Service was created on 1 January 1945. Details from 'Report to Governor of Kenya', by L. C. Hill.
11. Government of Kenya, *Land Utilisation and Settlement: a Statement of Government Policy*, (Sessional Paper No. 8 of 1945).
12. Subsequent exchanges between Creech Jones and the Fabians during 1947 and 1949 are reproduced in Goldsworthy, op cit., p. 142.
13. *Colonial Office: Inter-Territorial Organisation in East Africa*, Colonial No. 191, 1945, and *Colonial Office: Inter-Territorial Organisation in East Africa: Revised Regulations*, Colonial No. 210, 1947.
14. *Report of the Government of India Delegation to East Africa on the Proposed Immigration Restrictions in Kenya, Uganda, Tanganyika and Zanzibar, 1946*, 30 November 1946, classified as 'Confidential'.
15. This quotation is from the *Report of the ... Delegation* ... (p. 19) and it has not been possible to verify the words from the Creech Jones Papers. However, in quoting Creech Jones' speech to the Fabian Colonial Bureau in London, the *Report* is substantially accurate, and it seems probable that they would not have erred in reproducing a statement made on the spot a few days previously.
16. *The Crown Colonist*, October 1946, 'Face to Face with East African Problems'.
17. Mitchell: Despatch No. 44 to Secretary for the Colonies, 17 April 1946, and speech to the Caledonian Society, Nairobi, 30 November 1946.
18. The Colonial Office belatedly informed the India Office on 5 December 1946 that the constitution had been presented to the Council of Government; it was 'regretted' that information about the constitution had not

been supplied to the Government of India. It is clear that the Colonial Office made sure India did not see the terms in advance in case a fuss was raised similar to the objections to the Ceylon constitution.
19. *Ceylon: Statement of Policy*, Cmd. 6690, 1945.
20. Charles Jeffries, *Ceylon—The Path to Independence* (London, 1962). This admirable personal account is suspect only because Jeffries attributes to all the other participants the same degree of goodwill as he himself undoubtedly genuinely felt.
21. For a much fuller account of these events, see the author's *The Union of Burma: a Study of the First Years of Independence*, Chapter 1, 'British Rule and Independence'.
22. Government of India to India Office, 18 October 1945, and Wavell to Pethick-Lawrence (Private and Secret), 29 October 1945.
23. India Office to Government of India, Food Department, 8 March 1946.
24. It was quite possible that Aung San had been flown to Delhi by military aircraft without the knowledge of the Burma Government or the Government of India. Mountbatten decided as early as April 1945 that Aung San was the Burmese leader of the future, and promoted his cause: see my *Union of Burma*, pp. 16-17.
25. *The Malayan Union and Singapore*, Cmd. 6724, 1946.
26. Government of India to India Office, 22 November 1945.
27. *Wavell: the Viceroy's Journal*, p. 222.
28. Help was given to 76,000 Indians between April 1946 and June 1947; the Committee arranged repatriation for 3,622 to India; the balance left—$52,143 was available as loans for Indians: *Straits Times*, 23 March 1948 and 14 September 1948.
29. Nehru on nationality in *Malaya Tribune*, 27 March 1946; enclosed by Sir Edward Gent in forwarding to the Secretary for the Colonies (16 April 1946) reports by the Director of Intelligence, Headquarters, Supreme Commander, South-East Asia Command (dated 30 March 1946) and by F. V. Duckworth (4 April 1946) on the Nehru visit.
30. Comparative figures for children at school in February 1946 were:

    English schools: 80,000+ 19,000 in 1941
    Chinese schools : 128,000+ 7,000 ,, ,,
    Malay schools : 125,000− 3,000 ,, ,,
    Indian schools : 16,000−10,000 ,, ,,

31. These details were given by A. V. Pai to the Council of State, 7 November 1946. For a more detailed account of the Indians' post-war conditions, see M. R. Stenson, *Industrial Conflict in Malaya* (London, 1970).
32. In these pages the portrait of Smuts which emerges is rather like that political caricature which his opponents continually presented—'Slim Jannie'—and there seem to be good reasons for presenting this view. But people are always complex, and Smuts was more complex than most. In this letter we see a glimpse of the noble warrior, the philosopher statesman that Sir Keith Hancock has presented as the truth. If one reads the letters of Smuts these qualities appear as very much part of the truth. During late 1945, Smuts was very concerned about his old

friend Leo Amery, dismissed with ignominy from the political stage and sorely grieved over the trial of his son, John, as a traitor to his country. On 4 November, Smuts wrote to comfort his friend, concluding: 'It is in the domain of personal relations that we must look for the fundamental reform of human society'. How tragic that, for Smuts, across the colour line the racial dimension always overruled the personal, human dimension!

33. Baring cabled the Dominions Office on 19 January 1946 that Smuts made his announcement on the 16th. The 'Memorandum on the Position of Indians in the Union of South Africa' submitted by the Government of India on 26 August 1946 states that Smuts made his announcement on 21 January, and Bridglal Pachai (who, as always, gives a lucid and detailed account of the question) follows the Memorandum (*The South African Indian Question, 1860-1971*, p. 185). It makes no difference, which day it was.
34. Wavell: *the Viceroy's Journal*, p. 219.
35. Legislative Assembly Debates, 12 November 1946, answer to a question by Jawaharlal Nehru.
36. Heaton Nicholls told the U.N. on 25 November 1946 'No Indian had been imprisoned for contravening the Asiatic Land Tenure and Indian Representation Act, although on account of the policy of passive resistance, organised and financed by the Indian Congress [sic] some Indians had been arrested for common trespass and jailed when they refused to pay a fine'.
37. *Question of Treatment of Indians in the Union of South Africa before the United Nations: Documents and Proceedings*, Government of India, 1947. See also G. Heaton Nicholls, *South Africa in my Time*, for one personal account, and K. P. S. Menon, *Many Worlds, an autobiography*, for another—distinctly more light-hearted.
38. The final vote *for* the resolution was: *Communist Bloc*: U.S.S.R., Ukraine, Byelorussia, Czechoslovakia, Poland, Yugoslavia; *Afro-Asians*: Afghanistan, China, Egypt, Ethiopia, India, Iran, Iraq, Lebanon, Liberia, Philippines, Saudi Arabia, Syria; *Latin Americans*: Chile, Colombia, Cuba, Dominica, Guatemala, Haiti, Honduras, Mexico, Panama, Uruguay, Venezuela; *West Europeans*: France, Iceland, Norway. Smuts said later that the U.N. was dominated by coloured peoples. It is not easy to classify the Latin Americans into 'coloured' and 'white' but it might appear that at least 11 of India's 32 supporters were 'white'. Among those who voted *against* the resolution there were countries with a 'coloured' majority (beside South Africa), viz., almost all the Latin American allies of the U.S.A., though Argentina is 'white'. The supporters of South Africa were: *White Commonwealth*: Britain, Canada, New Zealand, South Africa; *West Europeans*: Belgium, Luxemburg, Netherlands, Greece; *U.S.A. and Latin Americans*: United States, Argentina, Costa Rica, El Salvador, Nicaragua, Paraguay, Peru. Smuts ought to have taken notice of the defectors from Western Europe who renounced the South African cause. Apart from the Afrikaners' traditional Dutch-speaking friends—Netherlands and Belgium—there

was little Luxemburg, and Greece, the home of Smuts' dear 'Queen Freddy'. The drawing back of Scandinavia—the small, anti-imperial countries Smuts liked to regard as his own kind of people—ought to have been particularly disturbing.
39. The document submitted by the Government of India to the U.N. in August 1947, *Treatment of Indians in the Union of South Africa: Report by the Government of India on the Resolution passed by the United Nations General Assembly on December 8, 1946,* contains a chronological account of events in South Africa after the U.N. debate.
40. W. K. Hancock, *Smuts: The Fields of Force, 1919-1950,* p. 481 in his Ch. 27, 'Colour'.
41. As recently as January, Amery had written to tell Smuts he would visit India (in fact, the plan fell through). 'Remind them that I have ever been a friend to India and her aspirations' replied Smuts (14 January 1947).
42. This letter from Kajee was addressed to Henry Cooper, private secretary to Smuts. It was a sign of the nature of the Smuts-Kajee relationship that he did not feel able to approach the Prime Minister directly. The letter is undated, but there is a reference to a meeting on 12 August 1947 as imminent. Kajee's letter is included among the letters *to* Smuts, in the Collected Smuts Papers, but in the separate series of letters *from* Smuts (including letters from his secretary) there is no communication to him. A. I. Kajee died in January 1948.
43. As Sir Henry Moore told Smuts, 25 April 1947.
44. Jeffries, op. cit., p. 114.
45. There are many of Lady Moore's entertaining letters from Ceylon in the Collected Smuts Papers, and it is a temptation to quote from more of them. But in a work of this kind it is questionable how far they are admissible as evidence. Lady Moore set out to entertain an old gentleman; she told him the gossip, but she also passed on information that he might wish to know as senior Commonwealth statesman. Her comment on Dominion status seems to show that the two aspects sometimes got a little mixed up.
46. Governor of Burma to Secretary of State for Burma, 19 June 1947.
47. United Kingdom High Commissioner, Delhi, to Cabinet Office, 3 July 1947.
48. Government of India to India Office, 9 May 1947.
49. During the months of his appointment before India became Independent, the UK High Commissioner corresponded with the Cabinet Office; presumably the Prime Minister was personally in charge.
50. Telegram, Cabinet Office to UK High Commissioner, 19 July 1947: the text reproduced the terms laid down by the Colonial Office.

CHAPTER 9, THE TEST OF INDEPENDENCE

1. Other countries outside the Commonwealth with important Indian communities were Indonesia 40,000, Thailand 11,000, Nepal 10,441 (1941), Madagascar 9,995 (1950), Mozambique 5,000, Bahrain 3,000,

Kuwait 2,500, Saudi Arabia 2,400, Reunion 2,200. These communities are outside the scope of the present survey.
2. Indian representatives in Commonwealth countries, 1948-9: *Australia* Lieut. Colonel D. S. Bedi (succeeded by Prince Duleepsinjhi); *Burma* (outside Commonwealth from January 1948) Dr M. A. Rauf, Labour Welfare Officer, P. S. Moses; *Canada* S. K. Kripalani; *Ceylon* V. V. Giri, Agent, I. P. M. Menon; *East Africa* Apa B. Pant; *Fiji* S. A. Waiz; *Malaya* J. A. Thivy, Agent, T. V. Ramakrishna Rao, *Mauritius* D. Y. Dev, *Pakistan* Dr Sitaram, *South Africa* vacant, Secretary, R. T. Chari, *West Indies* (headquarters, Trinidad) Satya Charan (succeeded by D. B. Desai.)
3. *Question of Treatment of Indians in the Union of South Africa before the United Nations, Documents and Proceedings, General Assembly Session, September-December 1947*, Government of India, 1948.
4. Mountbatten's remarks were contained in an interview given to the *Sunday Express*, 23 November 1947. Reuters sent the story to Smuts and asked for his comment. There are two exclamation marks (!!) in the margin of the Reuters letter. There is no reply on file. Among the letters in the Collected Correspondence for 1947 and 1948 there are no letters to or from Mountbatten, though there is a letter from Lady Mountbatten congratulating Smuts upon the conferment of an honour.
5. *Wavell: the Viceroy's Journal*, p. 440.
6. O. A. Oosthuizen, General Secretary, United Party: draft policy statement: 'South Africa and the Government of Natives and Coloured Races; the Indians' Place in South African Life'.
7. *Report of the Commission of Enquiry into Riots in Durban*, 1949.
8. UK High Commissioner in Canada to Secretary of State for Commonwealth Relations, 18 November 1949.
9. *The Hindu* (Madras), 29 November 1950.
10. For example *The Daily Mail*, 3 February 1949, 'Will the Indians Swamp Africa?'; *Cape Times*, 18 March 1949, 'How East Africa Views the Indian Problem' ('High time steps were taken to check the growth of the Asiatic community on the African continent'); *Sydney Morning Herald*, 16 May 1949, calling for 'complete ban on immigration from India'. By contrast, *The Times*, 7 September 1951, in a leading article 'Racial Needs in East Africa', stated that the Europeans in Tanganyika had increased by two-thirds since the 1948 Census, though of 410 European farmers only 89 were English-speaking, with 163 Greeks and 60 Afrikaners. One thousand Italians were said to be admitted to Kenya each year.
11. Speaking in reply to a question by Brigadier Payne, 2 June 1948; *House of Commons Debates*, Vol. 451.
12. 'Note on Land Policy in Kenya', by I. D. Robertson (19 January 1949).
13. *Colonial Office: Report on the Colony and Protectorate of Kenya for the Year 1950*, p. 2, 1951.
14. Hostility to Apa B. Pant reached the point where a question was put in the House of Commons by C.J.M. Alport (Lord Alport) to the Secretary of State for the Colonies, concerning 'the contribution made to the

prevailing condition of tension and unrest in Kenya by the staff of the Indian Commissioner's office': Alport demanded that the Government of India should be asked to withdraw their staff from Kenya. The Secretary for the Colonies (Lyttelton) agreed that there were 'a number of complaints from responsible sections of opinion' in Kenya, and he promised that he would make representations to the Government of India 'if there were grounds for doing so'. It was a clear warning. *House of Commons Debates*, Vol. 518, 29 July 1953.

15. His real name was Hazara Singh Rajput but as a renowned hunter of big game he received a nickname which ought to be given as 'Machan Singh', as a *machan* is the hunter's platform, whereas *makkan* is butter (both are Hindustani words, assimilated into the Swahili lingua-franca). Among the colonial Indians the spelling of Indian names was crude and even misleading. The Mauritius leader known as Bissoondayal was, properly, Basudeo Bishan Dayal, but this form was never used.
16. The information that Makhan Singh was deported comes from *Report on the Colony and Protectorate of Kenya for the Year 1950*, p. 15, though J. S. Mangat, *History of the Asians in East Africa c. 1886 to 1945* (Oxford 1969) states (p. 177) that 'Makhan Singh was to spend over ten years in jail after his arrest in 1950'.
17. Sir Charles Woolley to Lord Listowel, Minister at the Colonial Office, 2 September 1948.
18. *Commission to Report on the Possibility of Settlement in British Guiana and British Honduras*, Cmd. 7533, 1947.
19. *Legislative Council of Fiji, Council Paper 34 of 1959, Report of the Committee on Immigration*.
20. I. Watts, Colonial Office, to F. H. Cleobury, C.R.O., 2 December 1948.
21. *Revision of the Constitution of Mauritius: Correspondence between the Governor and the Secretary of State for the Colonies*, Cmd. 7228, 1947.
22. J. D. Harford, Officer administering the Government of Mauritius, to the Secretary for the Colonies, 8 and 27 July 1949.
23. Admiralty to Commonwealth Relations Office, 25 August 1949.
24. So rudimentary was the U.N.P. party organisation that early in 1948 Senanayake invited a former Labour M.P. George Shephard (Lord Shephard) to visit Ceylon in order 'to advise government leaders there on the organisation of their political party', as Malcolm MacDonald informed Creech Jones (19 May 1948). It was all very hush-hush, he wrote; asking whether the Colonial Office would commission Shephard to visit Malaya also to help organise political parties of the Centre, or Left of Centre, to check the drift 'towards association with the Communists'.
25. *Correspondence Relating to the Citizenship Status of Indians Resident in Ceylon*, Ceylon Parliament Sessional Paper 22 of 1948. See S. U. Kodikara, *Indo-Ceylon Relations Since Independence* (Colombo, 1965), for a detailed account of the subject from a Sinhalese point of view.
26. *The Constitution of the Union of Burma* (Rangoon, 1947), Chapter II, 'Fundamental Rights'. See also B. N. Rau *India's Constitution in the*

Making (Bombay, 1960) Chapter 29, 'The Constitution of Burma'. This includes a section (pp. 446-7) on the legal position of Indians in Burma after independence.
27. This estimate is given by N. R. Chakravarti, *The Indian Minority in Burma*, p. 178. Usha Mahajani, *The Role of Indian Minorities in Burma and Malaya*, p. 183, states that 150,000 Indians opted for citizenship immediately after independence. This estimate is not confirmed by any other source and seems quite improbable.
28. It is a feature of Burmese political life that so many of the national leaders are said to be of foreign or mixed descent. Ba Maw was said to be partly Armenian; Tin Tut was supposed to be of Chin (tribal) origin; General Ne Win, Burma's leader in the 1960s and early 1970s, certainly a Sino-Burman. All are known by Burmese names except for M. A. Raschid.
29. British High Commissioner, Delhi, to C.R.O., 1 July 1948 (telegram).
30. These events are treated in much greater detail in the author's *The Union of Burma: a Study of the First Years of Independence*, Chapter 2, 'The Background of Civil War, 1948-60'.
31. S. Arasaratnam, *Indians in Malaysia and Singapore*, p. 119.
32. *The Federation of Malaya: summary of revised constitutional proposals, July 1947*, Cmd. 7171.
33. 'Labour and Trade Union Organisation in the Federation of Malaya and Singapore', a report by S. S. Awberry, M.P., and F. W. Dalley, Kuala Lumpur, 1948.
34. Krishna Menon gave Creech Jones an aide memoire from the Government of India which stated that political unrest was due to economic causes: this was forwarded by telegram to the Federation Government on 17 September 1948.
35. The High Commissioner of Malaya replied to the telegram above by a telegram to the Secretary for the Colonies, 28 October 1948.
36. Note for the Secretary of State for the Colonies by O. H. Morris, dated 1 November 1948. Mr Morris noted that the total numbers banished (Chinese and Indians) numbered 193 in 1947 and 472 in 1948 (up to that date) (Creech Jones Papers).
37. Telegram, British High Commissioner to C.R.O., 1 July 1948.
38. *House of Commons Debates*, Vol. 452: written reply by D. Rees-Williams, Under Secretary for the Colonies, 30 June 1948.
39. *Straits Times*, 19 December 1948, 'The View from Inside', an account of Indian detainees in Malaya, stating that most were arrested for being members of unions affiliated to the P.M.F.T.U. Also *Straits Times*, 28 December 1948, and interview with Narajan Pillai, Agent of the Government of India.
40. At the same time a general warning against payment of protection money was given to the Malayan Chettyars. The guerrillas were said to be receiving $250.000 per annum from all sources. The Chettyar investment in Malaya was calculated at Rs. 20,00,00,000 or £15,000,000. *The Statesman*, 24 September 1949.

41. J. D. Higham, Colonial Office to J. P. Gibson, C.R.O., 24 December 1948.
42. *The Hindu*, 17 February 1949.
43. *The Hindu*, 10 April 1950 and 25 June 1950; *The Statesman*, 27 October 1950. See also 'Background Note on Economic and Social Policy in Malaya' [1950?] (Creech Jones Papers).
44. An account of the whole case of Ganapathy was given by O. H. Morris, Colonial Office, to J. P. Gibson, C.R.O., 5 May 1949.
45. *The Statesman*, 7 May 1949.
46. Telegrams, British High Commissioner, Delhi to Secretary for Commonwealth Relations, 9, 12 and 14 May 1949.
47. *1950, Law Reports, House of Lords: Judicial Committee of the Privy Council, A.C. 1950*, pp. 458-480.
48. *The Hindu*, 1 and 9 June 1950.
49. *The Statesman*, 19 July 1948.
50. *Straits Times*, 3 August 1949.
51. *Straits Times*, 1 April 1949. During 1946 there had been preliminary negotiations between the governments of Malaya and India about the possible resumption of labour emigration. The Malayan Indians strongly opposed further migration, and Thivy made personal representations to Nehru. See M. R. Stenson, *Industrial Conflict in Malaya* (London, 1970) pp. 82-3.
52. *Straits Times*, 28 December 1949.
53. The reorganisation of the procedure by which the Government of India handled the affairs of Indians overseas went through a number of phases between 1946 and 1949. As we have seen, the Department of Commonwealth Relations (formerly the Department of Indians Overseas) was amalgamated with the External Affairs Department in 1946. It then became the 'Commonwealth Relations Wing' of the Department—subsequently Ministry—of External Affairs and Commonwealth Relations. But in March 1949 the two wings were amalgamated as the Ministry of External Affairs. Under the Secretary-General (Bajpai) there was a Foreign Secretary and a Commonwealth Secretary. The sections included under the supervision of the second Secretary included the United Kingdom, Africa, South East Asia, Burma and Ceylon, Indo-China, the Afro-Asian Conference, and Emigration. The Emigration Establishment included a Controller-General and ten Protectors of Emigrants (some of whom were part-time) at various Indian ports. Indian Institute of Public Administration, *The Organisation of the Government of India* (Bombay, 1958).
54. F. K. Roberts, British High Commission, Delhi, to F. Turnbull C.R.O., 22 October 1949.
55. R. W. Selby, British High Commission, Delhi, to F. H. Cleobury, C.R.O., 4 November 1949.

CHAPTER 10, THE MOMENT OF EQUALITY

1. Creech Jones preserved in his papers a memorandum presented to the Labour Party's Advisory Committee on International Questions on 'Migration' by Charles Roden Buxton, M.P. The memorandum is undated, probably relating to 1939 or 1940. Buxton asked that his 'emphatic dissent' be noted when his draft was modified by the Committee. There is no indication that Creech Jones dissented.
2. *Canada: An Act Respecting Citizenship, Nationality, Naturalisation and the Status of Aliens*, published November 1945.
3. CP (46) 236, 'Memorandum by the Home Secretary and the Secretary of State for the Dominions', dated 20 June 1946.
4. CP (46) 331, 'Memorandum of the Committee on British Nationality; Chairman, the Home Secretary', dated 30 August 1946.
5. This schedule was replaced in the Bill in its final form by Clause 1 (3) which listed the member countries of the Commonwealth—beside the United Kingdom and Colonies. Ceylon appears on the list. Eire and Burma are omitted.
6. At the India Office, when the plea by Creech Jones was noticed, E.W.R. Lumby minuted 'Do we care?', to which R. N. Gilchrist replied 'India is strong enough to take care of Indians in Ceylon' (4 January 1947). An unexplained aspect of this matter is the interval of four and a half months which elapsed between the Colonial Office pressing the case for Ceylon, and the moment when the India Office took cognizance of the invitation.
7. At the first, formal meeting, Chuter Ede was in the chair; thereafter Sir Alexander Maxwell was chairman. The various delegations were: *United Kingdom:* Sir John Stephenson, W. E. Beckett, L. S. Brass, Sir Charles Dixon, Sir Keith Kemp, Sir Ernest Holderness, N. E. Archer, A. B. Acheson, W. L. Dale (most of the Whitehall departments were represented); *Canada:* N. A. Robertson, Dr E. H. Coleman, M. H. Wershof, J. Delauté, H. R. Horne; *Australia:* J. Horgan, T. D. Lyons, T. G. Glasheen; *South Africa:* Dr Louis Wessels, L. J. Fouché, J. T. R. Gibson; *Eire:* F. H. Boland, Dr M. Rynne, D. Costigan, Miss S. Murphy; *New Zealand:* H. D. C. Adams, C. C. Aikman; *Newfoundland:* J. S. Neils; *Southern Rhodesia:* R. J. Morton; *Ceylon:* L. M. D. de Silva; *Burma:* Justice E Maung.
8. *British Commonwealth Conference on Nationality and Citizenship, London, February 1947 Minutes* and *Report* (dated 26 February 1947). See *Report*, Appendix A, 'Scheme...proposed by the United Kingdom representatives', Appendix B, 'Scheme revised by the Conference'.
9. Draft Brief in respect of India for the Secretary of State [for India] on the British Nationality Bill, 7 August 1947.
10. Under the 1948 Act, British Protected Persons could acquire naturalisation through residence in a Protectorate from the Governor of the territory in which they resided, though the approval of the Secretary of State was required; also, Protected Persons were exempt from the Aliens Restrictions Acts, 1914 and 1919.

11. A. B. Acheson, Colonial Office, to Sir Ernest Holderness, 5 November 1947.
12. *Home Office, British Nationality Bill, 1948 summary of main provisions;* Cmd.7326, 1948.
13. B. N. Rau, *India's Constitution in the Making*, Ch.17, 'A Visit to U.S.A., Canada, Eire and Britain', p. 304.
14. Just before August 1947, when Mountbatten was urging the princes to accede to the new Indian Union, Sir C. P. Ramaswamy Aiyar, Dewan of Travancore, asked the Viceroy what would happen if his state joined the Indian Union, and if India later left the Commonwealth, would Travancore have the right to secede from India and remain in the Commonwealth? 'Lord Mountbatten told him that he could give no official opinion, but that he thought it would not be difficult for His Highness to disentangle himself...and that whereas His Majesty's Government would never agree to the Maharajah's entering the Commonwealth as a separate Dominion...Travancore would have a different case in demanding not to be thrown out once it was in'. H. V. Hodson, *The Great Divide: Britain—India—Pakistan* (London, 1969) p. 379. Mr Hodson comments that awareness that certain princely states might demand to cancel their adherence to the Indian Union on departure from the Commonwealth 'may have been a makeweight in determining India's policy of seeking continued Commonwealth membership'.
15. In his paper 'India and the Commonwealth' (Ch. 22 of *India's Constitution in the Making*) Rau evokes Indian history to demonstrate that kingship and republicanism had co-existed in India's past. He passes rather hastily over the legal aspects of allegiance to the Crown.
16. UK High Commissioner to Secretary for Commonwealth Relations, Despatch No. 658, 16 March 1948.
17. The *nuances* of Commonwealth protocol in the correspondence of members in the late 1940s may be of interest to the specialist. The Australian telegram to the C.R.O. (23 April) was repeated to New Zealand only; the New Zealand telegram of 24 April was repeated to all the Dominions except India and Pakistan. The Canadian reply, when at last it was sent on 10 May, was repeated only to the white Dominions. No Dominion government repeated any message to Southern Rhodesia, which was regarded as outside the club by everybody except Britain.
18. Minute to Philip Noel-Baker, 3 May 1948.
19. CP (48) 120, 'British Nationality Bill: Memorandum by the Home Secretary and the Secretary of State for Commonwealth Relations' dated 4 May 1948.
20. When New Zealand brought in legislation, the measure was given the title of the British Nationality and New Zealand Citizenship Act, 1948. Under this Act the status of a British subject and a New Zealand citizen were synonymous. As late as 1974, a New Zealand passport described the holder as a 'British subject and New Zealand citizen', though British subjects from the United Kingdom entering New Zealand now (1974) require visas. Australia also passed a Nationality and Citizenship

Act in 1948 which made for interchangeability between British subjects and Australian citizens. C. Parry, 'Plural Nationality and Citizenship, with special reference to the Commonwealth', *British Year Book of International Law, 1953*, pp. 244–292.
21. *Parliamentary Debates, House of Lords*, Volumes 155 and 156. *The Round Table* (June 1948) conceded that 'Commonwealth status or Commonwealth citizen are good enough pseudonyms for British subjecthood' but urged of the new terminology: 'Let it come gradually and naturally'.
22. *Parliamentary Debates, House of Commons*, Volume 453.
23. Rau, op. cit., p. 341, Ch. 21, 'Citizenship in the Commonwealth of Nations'. See also B. N. Rau, 'Reciprocity in Citizenship Rights', a paper for the 1949 unofficial Commonwealth Conference, Canada.
24. *The Times*, 17 November 1960, Charles Carrington, 'Republics in the Commonwealth'.
25. Government of India, *Jawaharlal Nehru's Speeches, Volume One, September 1946-May 1949:* 'A New Atmosphere of Cooperation', London, 26 October 1949.
26. James Eayrs, *In Defence of Canada: Peacemaking and Deterrence*, (Toronto, 1972), p. 243. This account of Canada's external policy (the third in a trilogy) is based upon access to the papers of the prime minister and the files of the Ministry of External Affairs. Chapter 4, 'Composing the Commonwealth', includes what is probably the most detailed day-by-day account of the London conference of April 1949.
27. Durga Das, ed., *Sardar Patel's Correspondence, 1945-50* (Ahmedabad, 1973) Vol. 8, p. 2. Chapter I, 'New Commonwealth Emerges', provides full and detailed documentation of the negotiations leading up to the Declaration of London from the viewpoint of the Government of India.
28. Patrick Gordon-Walker set down his own account in *The Commonwealth* (London, 1962). Another background version of these events is given in J. W. Wheeler-Bennett, *King George VI: his life and reign* (London, 1958) though there is undue emphasis upon the King's preoccupation with the Royal style and titles. Perhaps the most complete and coherent account is that by H. Duncan Hall, *Commonwealth: a history of the British Commonwealth of Nations* (London, 1971) Ch. XXVII, 'The Crossing of the Watershed'.
29. Durga Das, op. cit. pp. 8–9.
30. Durga Das, op. cit. On the opening day (23 April) Patel advised Nehru to accept the 'Head of the Commonwealth' formula: 'We can justify acceptance... as consistent with our objectives and past commitments and in no sense derogatory to our republican sovereign status' (p. 15). Nehru agreed to relegate the question of Commonwealth citizenship to a separate minute on 26 April, after registering Patel's supportive position (pp. 17–18).
31. James Eayrs, op. cit., concludes 'Pearson's gifts as a conciliator had been deployed again to good effect' (p. 256). V. K. Krishna Menon himself claimed the credit for inventing the formula which reconciled the opposing viewpoints: see Michael Brecher, *India and World Politics: Krishna Menon's View of the World* (London, 1968). When Sir Ivor

Jennings was Vice-Chancellor of the University of Cambridge he gave his personal account of how agreement was reached in a letter to the author of this book (11 October 1961). Observed Jennings: 'Several of us tried our hands at drafting a document', but without success; 'Sir Stafford Cripps took all the drafts home for the weekend and produced what became the Commonwealth Declaration'. Unfortunately, Dame Isobel Cripps is unable to discover any materials which would amplify this claim, which, on the face of it, is the most convincing.

32. Jean van der Poel, ed., *Selections from the Smuts Papers*, Vol. VII, *August 1945-October 1950* (Cambridge, 1973) p. 296.
33. *Jawaharlal Nehru's Speeches*, pp. 274–88. Apart from a speech on non-alignment (8 March 1948) this seems to have been the longest speech by Nehru during the three years 1946-8. It took over an hour to deliver.
34. Rau, op. cit., p. 355, 'India and the Commonwealth–II'.
35. The Influx from Pakistan (Control) Act of 1949 laid down that no person could enter India from any place in Pakistan unless, in addition to a passport, he was in possession of a permit issued by the Government of India. The Act was repealed in 1952.
36. The original schedule of Commonwealth countries comprised an 'A' list, which included all the seven countries which, with India, were independent in 1955 (among them South Africa) and also the then Federation of Rhodesia and Nyasaland. The 'B' list covered one country: the Republic of Ireland.
37. Down to 1962, the only Commonwealth country to admit all immigrants from anywhere in the Commonwealth for all purposes, including settlement and employment, was the United Kingdom. India restricted the entry of all Christian missionaries, while other persons might freely enter India but might not take up employment except upon carefully defined terms.
38. *The Hindu*, 24 March 1952. Under Section 9 of the Citizenship Act (India) 1955, an Indian 'who by naturalisation, registration or otherwise voluntarily acquires...the citizenship of another country...shall cease to be a citizen of India'. According to the advice given by the U. K. Community Relations Commission (August 1973) this has effect automatically, and according to the C.R.C. there is no longer dual citizenship as between Britain and India for Indians residing in Britain. Before 1962 this issue was never raised.
39. For example, in an analysis of Indian foreign policy prepared for the enlightenment of the Colonial Office: R. W. D. Fowler, C.R.O. writing to M. R. J. Huisjman, C.O., 10 September 1949.

A Personal Note

On being appointed Director of the Institute of Race Relations at the end of 1969 I began to plan a programme which would bring together research work on the Indians overseas within an overall framework, providing a panoramic view of these communities in their historical and contemporary setting. There was a sizeable literature on aspects of the subject, and a number of scholars, mainly Indians, were already at work and expressed interest in a cooperative venture. My own contribution to this series of studies would be a history of the forms of controlled labour supply—of which the indenture system was the most notorious—under which Indians were transported across the seas as coolies.

For various reasons, the idea of a number of studies, moving forward simultaneously, could not be turned into a reality within the time-scale in which it was necessary to function. Yet the importance of presenting a complete picture of the Indians overseas was given added impetus by ominous events in East Africa, especially the pressure exerted upon the Uganda Asians, culminating in their expulsion in 1972. I pushed on with my own study, under increasing difficulties and distractions arising out of the controversies occupying the Institute of Race Relations and everyone working there throughout 1971. As differences intensified with the group who then formed a majority on the Council of the Institute, I decided I must move away and I determined to put together a comparative study which would (though probably in a less comprehensive form) provide a synthesis such as it was originally hoped would emerge from different people's research. Officers of the Ford Foundation expressed interest and encouragement, especially Craufurd Goodwin, in charge of the Foundation's work in relation to Europe.

This was the situation when in March and April 1972 the differences at the I.R.R. reached a climax. The members of the Institute were asked to endorse the policy outlined by the then Chairman of the Council, involving my removal. Instead, the members chose to pass a vote of confidence in my record as Director. I had already told the members that I wanted to leave, but in the changed circumstances I stayed on. In the following months it became even more difficult to try to maintain my writing and research—which I felt represented my real contribution to the debate on race; it was clear that in the 1970s the Director of I.R.R. could not expect to function as a scholar. By October 1972, the I.R.R. had adequate funds to weather the next twelve months while its vast deficit had been cleared. It was the time to go.

When I had become Director of the I.R.R. I was repeatedly told that I was cutting myself off from the academic world. This seemed all too likely, but when Peter Lyon, the Secretary of the Institute of Commonwealth Studies in the University of London, was told about my project he talked to the Director of the I.C.S., W. H. Morris-Jones, and I was invited to join them. At this moment my academic lamp seemed to be burning low (many former colleagues thought that it had gone out). It was heartening to find that some old friends were friends indeed. It was specially agreeable to be a member of the I.C.S., with which I had been associated ever since its beginnings under Keith Hancock.

My next move was to spend several weeks at the rather fabulous Villa Serbelloni at Bellagio. The invitation was intended to give me an opportunity to think out an approach to the subject, after the hectic events of the previous months. I drafted a number of tentative schemes; and then one day I decided to refresh my memory of Sir Keith Hancock's biography of Smuts (which he had worked upon at the Villa). It was while reading Hancock's second volume: *Smuts: the Fields of Force*, that the theme of the present book was thrust upon me. Hancock had first seized upon the theme of equality and inequality, as one of the most crucial questions the Commonwealth had to resolve, as far back as the 1930s. So, from Sir Keith Hancock I derived the approach which shapes this book.

It is a pleasure to acknowledge my debt to the man who more than anyone has given me whatever insight I have into contemporary history. When I was well launched into the research I corresponded with Professor Hancock and was guided by him towards the collected Smuts correspondence: an immense treasury, into which I have only dipped. In return for this kindness I have presented a portrait of Smuts in this book which is almost directly contrary to that which Hancock has portrayed with such nobility and power. Doubtless Hancock (and Smuts) will survive my re-examination.

In carrying out the research for this book I have worked at the Public Record Office, the India Office Library and Records, the former Colonial Office Library (now part of the Foreign and Commonwealth Office), the Library of the High Commission of India, the Chatham House Press Library, and the Institute of Historical Research (all in London) as well as Rhodes House Library at Oxford and the Cambridge University Library. Subsequently, at Delhi, I worked in the Indian National Archives and the Nehru Memorial Library. I was treated with the greatest courtesy and consideration by almost all to whom I went with my requests. If I do not mention names it is only because so many gave me help and guidance: the list is long. However, the assistance of Miss Keswani at the National Archives was so crucial in gaining access for me to important materials which I would not otherwise have seen that I must, as an exception, record my special thanks to her.

It has been a great advantage to be at the I.C.S. while working on this subject, and I ought to mention the undertaking by a colleague, Michael Twaddle, historian of modern Africa, who has successfully brought together different kinds of specialists to investigate the problems of the overseas Indians, especially those in East Africa. I have also had the benefit of discussion with Professór K. L. Gillion, completing his exhaustive study of the Indians in Fiji.

The present work is not quite what the Ford Foundation were led to expect when they generously agreed to support the project financially. Instead of an 'overview' this is a somewhat specialised analysis of one phase of the story. When I began, I did intend to cover the whole period from 1920 to the present day within one volume. I had not reckoned with the almost embarrassing wealth of material which was to emerge. The decision taken by Mr Wilson as Prime Minister to change the 'Fifty Year Rule' regarding access to public documents into a 'Thirty Year Rule' (which by subsequent administrative decisions has permitted access to the documents until after the Second World War) has not yet made its full impact upon contemporary history. Now, we can really begin to understand the end of empire.

The years between the wars were the last era of leisurely written correspondence — the lengthy despatch, the detailed confidential letter — before we entered the present age of instant communication and instant decision. Politicians and officials justified their decisions or their refusal to take decisions at length. Because this book is intended to describe the British ruling caste as much as the Indians who were under their rule the process of decision-making and decision-faking has been explored in detail.

An analysis of the present-day conditions of the overseas Indians will be presented in another book in a somewhat shorter, analytical form, I very much hope that these books will contribute to a growing literature concerning the Indian communities overseas, as was the original intention. This emigration is one of the most important movements of peoples in modern times: and it has not yet attracted the attention which is its due.

It remains for me to record my warm thanks to W.H. Morris-Jones, Peter Lyon and James Kimber for reading the first draft of this book and offering comments which may have helped to make the present text more precise. Anne Barnes and Sonja Jansen typed it out in their impeccable style: I am grateful. My wife, Elisabeth, scrutinised the text at every stage from rough draft to final proof: once again, I hope she knows how grateful I am.

H.T.

A Note on Sources

Rather than lay out a conventional list of sources, it may be more useful to discuss the kinds of documentary materials used, to describe their nature, and how they contributed to this book.

The main work of research was upon the India Office Records; three kinds of material were consulted; the 'private' papers of the viceroys, the 'private office' papers of the Secretary of State for India, and the departmental correspondence.

The papers of the viceroys, now available for this period, were officially classified as private letters to the Secretary of State, private and personal telegrams to the Secretary of State, letters to persons in India, and letters to persons in England and abroad. These documents are located with the India Office Records as regards Lord Reading, Lord Irwin, Lord Linlithgow, and Lord Wavell: thus, the correspondence of Lord Willingdon is absent, though the private letters to Willingdon from the Secretary of State, Sir Samuel Hoare, and then the Marquess of Zetland, are in the Records. The Willingdon period was the least important in the story of the overseas Indians; there was a lull in events during his viceroyalty, so the absence of the papers he retained is not vital.

The weekly 'private' letter between the Viceroy and Secretary of State was the means whereby the Viceroy was kept in touch with political developments in Britain — the deliberations of the Cabinet, events in parliament, party politics, etc. Similarly the Viceroy used his letters to describe political events and attitudes in India; but because the political climate was much more administrative and official than in England, the tone of his letters often reflects a preoccupation with immediate decisions. As the affairs of the overseas Indians almost always involved another Secretary of State, and often another government, they feature in this correspondence much more than some internal problems which the Viceroy could settle without reference to any outside authority.

As the years passed, the confidential, intimate character of this correspondence diminished somewhat. Excerpts from the letters were transmitted to senior officials, and they often tried to 'feed' the Viceroy or the Secretary of State with tricky problems which they wanted to have discussed at the topmost level. Wavell adopted the practice of alternating his weekly letters; one week would be a 'round-up' communication, reviewing the more pressing problems in which the Secretary of State was required to take action, and then the following week he would present his own reflections and conclusions. It remained the convention that this correspondence was not part of the corpus of the official correspondence, and the Viceroy and Secretary of State were free to remove their letters when they left office. As we see, most have been returned to the India Office Records.

The nature of the correspondence varied, depending upon the personal relationships between the two sides. Montagu and Reading were close to each other; Reading was an old friend and rival of Birkenhead, at the Bar and in politics. Irwin and Birkenhead had little in common, and it was not until Wedgwood Benn became Secretary for India that Irwin warmed to his colleague and constitutional superior. Indeed, the feeling towards Benn and his policies which Irwin developed led him to doubt for a little while — High Tory though he was — whether he could continue as an active Conservative politician. Linlithgow had a kind of majestic intimacy with his secretaries of state. Amery attempted to get onto pally terms with Wavell (he was a great hobnobber with persons of quality) but though he began his correspondence to the Viceroy with 'Dear Archie', Wavell remained aloof, and it was 'Dear Amery' until almost the end of their partnership.

The telegraphic correspondence, private and personal, was concerned with immediate questions requiring answers. The convention was that by this method problems could be assessed, and preliminary decisions reached, without either party becoming fully committed, or down on record as committed. When a decision was hardened up, the private cable was sometimes made official: otherwise there might be unexplained gaps in the decision-making process. Again, because of imperial and international repercussions, the subject of the Indians overseas featured frequently in these exchanges.

The Viceroy's correspondence with persons in India and in England and elsewhere is chiefly important because it brings in people who are not officials, and it involves the high and lowly. The correspondence with Indian public men is, perhaps, somewhat stilted, with obvious reservations on both sides, but it provides some indication of different shades of public opinion.

The 'private office' papers of the Secretary for India include all the matters on which he was personally required to correspond and communicate. There are Cabinet memoranda — his own, and those of other ministers, with the records of the accompanying bargaining which went on before the conclave in the Cabinet room. There are a great many other letters to Ministers — again, upon a personal and confidential basis, with the purpose of trying to solve some problem which had reached a stalemate at the official level. There is a handlist of the private office papers which indicates their different subjects. East Africa is represented by a continuing series of files throughout the 1920s and 1930s; Ceylon became an issue at Cabinet level on occasion, but the Caribbean, Mauritius, and Fiji with their Indian communities, scarcely ever assumed sufficient inter-departmental importance to involve the Secretary of State. The distinction between private office papers and departmental papers often appears thin and unreal; correspondence drifts from one set of files into the other. Usually, the private office papers represent the climactic points in inter-departmental controversies, but this is not always so, and in the 1940s they are of less importance than at an earlier period. Included among these series there are letters to and from Indian public men (the Aga Khan was an assiduous correspondent) and occasionally there are surprises: such as communications from Saklatvala, the Communist M.P.

For most aspects of the subject the materials are in the departmental files. For a few years in the early 1920s, responsibility for supervising the affairs of the Indians overseas was assigned to the Industry and Overseas Department, but for the greater part of the period the responsibility fell to the Public and Judicial Department, which had handled Indian emigration and settlement long before.

Each year a register was kept in which the details of letters received was recorded, with an indication of the file to which they were allocated. It is from these registers that the research worker identifies the number of the file (always initially P and J) which contains information relating to the overseas Indians. During the 1920s, the India Office maintained the traditional practice of binding up files in series — not according to subject, but according to numerical progression, with little relevance to subject. These bound volumes were fine examples of the binder's craft, and all the papers, however flimsy or fleeting, are bound in. It was India Office practice to keep a file open as long as a particular correspondence continued; thus a file begun in 1919 might not be closed until 1925. Sometimes one file is so bulky that it makes up an entire bound volume.

The practice of binding up the files was discontinued in 1930, presumably as an economy measure because of the depression. Also at this time a different kind of register was instituted, and this volume (Z/L/P & J/8/1) provides references to all subsequent correspondence during the 1930s and 1940s down to the closure of the India Office and even beyond. Perhaps because the files relating to Indians Overseas were not referred to so frequently as other kinds of correspondence, many of them fell into poor condition. During the 1940s, R. N. Gilchrist was required to undertake a good deal of research into these files in order to compile surveys of the different problems which were then attaining critical dimensions. Gilchrist had started his career in the Indian Education Service, he had written a book, and he liked things to be in order. When he was compiling a 'Note on Indians in the Dominions' he recorded vexatiously 'One has to search through an incredible jungle before reaching one's objective'; the files 'shocked me to a very high degree', he recorded, adding that they were kept much more systematically in any Indian Secretariat (18 April 1944). It appears unlikely that anybody has touched the files in the intervening thirty years, and although they are kept in meticulous order, externally, by the custodians of the India Office Records their internal condition is certainly very uneven.

During the 1940s, under the conditions of wartime, the correspondence was allocated to files in a somewhat rough and ready manner. As all these files have the title 'Indians Overseas' upon them, this may have contributed to an occasional act of random filing.

Perhaps because the files were no longer periodically inspected to determine whether they were ready for binding, many of them cover immensely long periods of time. In general, they are divided up geographically — South Africa, Ceylon, Malaya, etc. Only occasionally are there subject files: one of the most important series being concerned with the appointment of Agents of the Government of India in East Africa and other Colonies. There is also a significant series concerned with the status of a British subject in relation to the overseas Indians— corporately, and as individuals.

During the period under review, the formal despatch, signed by the Viceroy and all his Council — which had been the standard form of communication in Victorian and Edwardian times — largely fell into desuetude. It was replaced by the departmental letter, signed by the Secretary or Under Secretary. There was also a certain amount of correspondence in the 'demi-official' category, at a less exalted level. Like the

Viceroy's private and personal communications, these letters did not commit the sender, officially. Correspondence tended to go back and forth between Britain and India in this way until an issue reached a critical point, and had to be referred by the official in routine charge of the subject to his superiors: to an assistant Under Secretary of State, or even the Under Secretary or Secretary of State. At this point, the originating official would write a long minute, summarising the previous correspondence, giving a brief history of the problem, and probably appending a draft letter which would answer the question. The file would then ascend upwards, gathering notes and comments, until the decision-taking level was reached. These milestones are very helpful to the researcher, in case he has nodded over some important document which he should have considered more carefully.

Even in its new, faceless office block, the India Office Library and Records still retains something of the air of the old India Office Library, situated at the top of Sir Gilbert Scott's Italianate edifice, which used to be a kind of very special and secret club. By contrast, the section of the Public Record Office concerned with Colonial Office records, situated in the Land Registry, is rather like a Labour Exchange of a singularly drab description. The Colonial Office records are classified according to the different Colonies to which they refer: Kenya, Malaya, British Guiana, etc. The original correspondence is located in boxes according to the years of origin. There are registers listing the various subjects dealt with in the different files, but the P.R.O. system is so slow and cumbersome that it is probably quicker to go through all the boxes relating to the different Colonies, year by year, rejecting all those which are irrelevant. Unlike the India Office, the Colonial Office went in for relatively short files, covering an episode, rather than a series of years. Frequently one subject will be treated in several files, all of which were circulating at the same time. In the colonial empire the practice of sending long, formal despatches continued into the 1940s. The Colonial Office became a much bigger organisation than the India Office, and the process of decision-making was more complicated.

A hundred yards or so from the P.R.O. there is the Library of the High Commission of India, which supplements the India

Office records for the period 1920-50 to a considerable extent. Most useful is the collection of *Proceedings* of the debates in the various houses of the Indian central legislature, from the 1920s onwards, but there are also large numbers of reports and periodical publications relating to Indians overseas.

The former Colonial Office library in Great Smith Street also contains materials essential to this study. There are volumes of sessional papers of the various Colonial legislatures for the 1940s and afterwards, and there are important collections of colonial pamphlets, some being official publications and others the product of chambers of commerce, societies, and other non-official colonial bodies. These are bound together in series by titles such as *Far Eastern Pamphlets*, and they provide a wealth of background material from the 1920s onwards. This library is also a convenient place for reference to parliamentary papers — Blue Books and White Papers — and to the series of Colonial papers issued by the Colonial Office.

Two university libraries provided valuable materials for this study. At Rhodes House, Oxford, two collections were consulted, the Anti-Slavery Papers, and the Creech Jones Papers. During the 1920-50 period, the Anti-Slavery Society, under its Secretaries, Sir John Harris and C. W. W. Greenidge, was assiduous in contesting white dominance in Kenya, as well as maintaining its traditional concern with the sugar colonies in the West Indies and Mauritius. The correspondence includes many items from staunch anti-colonialists like Henry Polak and Reginald Sorensen, and also frequent communications with Indian and other organisations in the colonies. There is also correspondence with Whitehall departments (mostly leading nowhere) and certain communications with business interests.

The Creech Jones Papers represent a kind of scholar's lucky dip. Arthur Creech Jones seems to have preserved every communication he ever received, and as socialist, humanitarian and educationalist his mail was enormous. His life and career fell into two sharply separated parts — before he took office, and during and after his time as a Minister. In many ways, the first period is the most interesting, in which he built up a wide and varied range of correspondents in Colonial opposition circles; though when he became an Establishment figure, Creech Jones relaxed none of his energies in corresponding with people of power and influence. The papers are beautifully catalogued by Rhodes House library, and there is no need to attempt an itemised description here. First as their friend, and then as their castigator, Creech Jones occupied an important place in the fortunes of the overseas Indians in the late 1930s and throughout the 1940s.

At Cambridge there is a complete microfilm duplicate set of the original correspondence of Jan Christiaan Smuts. Selections have been published by the Cambridge University Press, but most of the material relating to this study has not been included.

The Smuts papers are arranged quite simply, year after year, as letters to Smuts and letters from Smuts (and his secretary) in alphabetical order. There are hundreds (or thousands) of items and without any kind of sub-division or classification by subject, the task of the research worker is laborious. For myself, I only went through the years 1945-8, the last years in which Smuts was prime minister. The range of his correspondents was extraordinary, and Smuts replied to most of them first by writing out a draft in his own angular hand. Several more books are waiting to be written out of the Smuts correspondence.

The National Archives of India in New Delhi complement the India Office records by providing the departmental files of the Government of India in which questions were thrashed out before a letter or telegram was despatched to Whitehall. For the purpose of this study, only those files relating to the years of the second World War were consulted; for it was during this period that the Department of Indians Overseas assumed the initiative, and responded to Indian nationalist pressures in raising greater demands on behalf of the overseas Indians. Their activity was specially concentrated upon Ceylon, South Africa, Burma and — to a lesser extent — Fiji. For these countries, the New Delhi material supplements the India Office papers in important respects. Perhaps the most illuminating series are the demi-official letters between India's representatives overseas and the Member of the Viceroy's Council in charge of the department. Even greater interest attaches to the private papers of Indian national leaders now on deposit in the National Archives. Benarsi Das Chaturvedi systematically collected correspondence concerning the overseas Indians from 1915 onwards, and the letters of C. F. Andrews, Srinivasa Sastri and their correspondents in South Africa, East Africa and Fiji reveal the difficulties experienced by the overseas communities and their dilemmas in attempting to organise for their own defence.

The leisured atmosphere of other days lingers within the National Archives, and although the building was erected in the 1920s a sense of timelessness pervades its ample halls and corridors. The Jawaharlal Nehru Memorial Library and Museum is situated in another monument of the Raj, the former residence of the British Commander-in-Chief (which became Nehru's residence as Prime Minister). Yet past grandeurs give way to present-day efficiency and simplicity in its important, expanding archive. The main collection consists of the entire correspondence of the central organisation of the Indian National Congress down to 1947. The All-India Congress Committee established a foreign or overseas department in 1929 and in 1936 started a separate department to communicate with Indians overseas. The correspondence of these departments actually reveals how slender were the connections between the AICC and the Indians in the Dominions and Colonies; even when local Congress organisations existed, as in South and East Africa (the main correspondence was with Indians in Britain and North America). The J. N. Memorial Library is also creating a collection of the private papers of Indian public men which rivals that deposited in the National Archives. There is another Sastri collection together with the papers of other leaders of the Servants of India Society. Others concerned with Indians overseas, such as Maharaj Singh and G. A. Natesan of Madras are represented. The papers of M. S. Aney, Member of the Viceroy's Council in charge of Indians overseas, and subsequently India's representative in Ceylon, had only recently been received at the time of my visit (November-December 1973) but I was permitted to rummage through the tin trunks in which the papers had arrived and significant documents emerged (though many had been consumed by the white ants).

Select Bibliography

Both parts of this bibliography are restricted to works which make a sizable contribution to some aspect of this study. Certain works mentioned in the preceding Notes have been excluded because they offer only an incidental commentary on the subject. Even so, many of the items listed concentrate upon a specialised part of the subject, and only about a dozen of the books mentioned provide surveys in breadth. The official reports do include several which provide a wide conspectus, though the exigencies of policy often influenced the selection of the facts as well as their presentation.

Printed Official Reports
(chronological order)

Asiatic Enquiry Commission, Interim Report . . . , Cape Town, 1920.
Recommendations of the Asiatic Enquiry Commission, Cape Town, 1921.
Conference of Prime Ministers and Representatives of the United Kingdom, the Dominions and India held in June, July and August 1921, Cmd. 1474, 1921.
West Indies: Report by the Hon. E. F. L. Wood MP . . . on his visit to the West Indies and British Guiana, December 1921, — February 1922, London, 1922.
Indians in Kenya: Memorandum by the Secretary of State for the Colonies, Cmd. 1922, 1923.
Imperial Conference, 1923, Appendices to the Summary of Proceedings [speeches]. Cmd. 1988, 1923.
Ruimveldt Inquiry: [British Guiana] *Minutes of an Inquiry into the deaths of thirteen persons . . . on 3 April 1924* printed by the Government of India, 1925.
Report by Kunwar Maharaj Singh on his Deputation to Mauritius, Delhi, 1925.
Report by Kunwar Maharaj Singh on his Deputation to British Guiana in 1925, Delhi, 1926.
Interim Report of the Indian Deputation to South Africa, Delhi, 1926.
'Position of the Indian Community in Fiji', *Fiji Royal Gazette* No. 13, 1927.
Report of the Special Commission on the Ceylon Constitution, Cmd. 3131, 1928.
Report of the Commission on Closer Union of the Dependencies in Eastern and Central Africa, Cmd. 3234, 1929.
Correspondence Regarding the Constitution of Ceylon, Cmd. 3419, 1929.
Report by the Rt. Hon. V. S. S. Sastri regarding his visit to East Africa, Delhi, 1930.
Report of the Kenya Land Commission, September 1933, Cmd. 4556, 4580, 1934.
Report of the Indian Colonisation Enquiry Committee, 1933-34, Cape Town, 1934.
Report of the Commissioners appointed to enquire into and report on the labour disputes [in British Guiana] . . . , Georgetown, 1936.
Report on the conditions of Indian labour in Malaya by the Rt. Hon. V. S. S. Sastri, Delhi, 1937.
Report of the Commission of Inquiry into unrest on sugar estates in Mauritius, 1937, Port Louis, 1938.

Report of a Commission on Immigrants into Ceylon, by Sir E. St. J. Jackson, Ceylon Sessional Paper No. III, 1938.
Correspondence Relating to the Constitution of Ceylon, December 1938, Cmd. 1591, 1938.
Report of the Leonora Enquiry Commission, dated 23 March 1939, Legislative Council paper, Georgetown, 1939.
Report on the Condition of Indians in Jamaica, British Guiana and Trinidad, by J. D. Tyson, Delhi, 1939.
Statement by the Government of India, dated 11 February 1941, on the India-Ceylon conference, Delhi, 1941.
Report of the Ceylon delegation, February 1941, Ceylon Sessional Paper No. VIII, 1941.
Statement addressed by the Ministers to HE the Governor and his reply, Ceylon Sessional Paper No. XIV, 1941 ('Undertakings given to the Government of India').
Report on the condition of Indians in Mauritius, by S. Ridley (Confidential), Delhi, 1941.
Report on the immigration of Indians into Burma [by J. Baxter], Rangoon, 1941.
Report on the evacuation of refugees from Burma to India (Assam) January to July 1942, by Major-General E. Wood, Calcutta, 1942.
Indians in South Africa: restrictions on Indians acquiring land and property; Report of the Indian Penetration Commission, 1941, Pretoria, 1942.
Report of the 2nd Indian Penetration (Durban) Commission, Pretoria, 1943.
Labour Conditions in Ceylon, Mauritius and Malaya: report by Major Orde Browne, Cmd. 6423, 1943.
Report of the Commission of Enquiry into the disturbances which occurred in the north of Mauritius in 1943, London, 1943 (published, Mauritius, 1944).
Burma Under the Japanese Occupation, 2 vols., Simla, 1943-4.
Interim Report of the Commission of Enquiry into matters affecting the Indian population of the Province of Natal, Cape Town, 1945.
Ceylon: Report of the Commission on Constitutional Reforms, Cmd. 6677, 1945.
Colonial Office: Inter-Territorial Organisation in East Africa, Colonial No. 191, London, 1945.
Land Utilisation and Settlement: a statement of government policy, Kenya Government, Sessional Paper No. 8, 1945.
Report of the Government of India Delegation to East Africa on the proposed immigration restrictions in Kenya, Uganda, Tanganyika and Zanzibar (Confidential), Delhi, 1946.
The Malayan Union and Singapore, Cmd. 6724, 1946.
Colonial Office: Inter-Territorial Organisation in East Africa, Revised Proposals, Colonial No. 210, London, 1947.
Question of treatment of Indians in the Union of South Africa before the United Nations: Documents and Proceedings, Delhi, 1947.
Treatment of Indians in the Union of South Africa: report by the Government of India on the Resolution passed by the United Nations General Assembly on December 8, 1946, Delhi, 1947.
Federation of Malaya: summary of revised constitutional proposals, July 1947, Cmd. 7171, 1947.

Revision of the Constitution of Mauritius: Correspondence, Cmd. 7228, 1947.
Correspondence Relating to the Citizenship Status of Indians resident in Ceylon, Ceylon Sessional Paper No. XXII, 1948.
British Nationality Bill, 1948: summary of main provisions, Cmd. 7326, 1948.
Report of the Commission of Enquiry into riots in Durban, Cape Town, 1949.
Immigration Policy, Kenya Government, Sessional Paper No. 78, 1956.
Report of the Committee on Immigration, Fiji, Legislative Council, Paper No. 34, 1959.

Review of Important Events affecting Indians in different parts of the British Empire, Delhi, annual, from 1936-7 to 1944-5.
Annual Reports of the Government of India Agents in Malaya and Ceylon, Delhi, from 1922 onward.

Books, Pamphlets

Aiyer, K. A. N., *Indian Problems in Malaya: a brief survey in relation to emigration*, Kuala Lumpur, 1938.
Andrews, C. F., *The Indian Question in East Africa*, Nairobi [1921].
────── *The New Asiatic Bill and the Alleged Breach of Faith*, Cape Town, 1926.
────── *An Interim Statement concerning East Indian conditions in British Guiana*, Georgetown [1929].
────── *The Zanzibar Crisis*, Allahabad, 1934.
────── *India and the Pacific*, London, 1937.
Anstey, Vera, *The Economic Development of India*, London, 1929.
Arasaratnam, Sinnapah, *Indians in Malaysia and Singapore*, London, 1970.
Asian Relations Organisation, *Report of Proceedings and Documentation of first Asian Relations Conference*, Delhi, 1948.
Bahadoorsingh, Krishna, *Trinidad Electoral Politics: the persistence of the race factor*, London, 1968.
Bailey, Sydney D., *Ceylon*, London, 1952.
Beejadhur, Aunath, *Les Indiens à l'Ile Maurice*, Mauritius, 1935.
Bell, H. H., *Glimpses of a Governor's Life*, London, 1946.
Benedict, Burton, *Indians in a plural society: a report on Mauritius*, London, 1961.
──────, *Problems of Smaller Territories*, London, 1967.
Birkenhead, Earl of, *Halifax: a life of Lord Halifax*, London, 1965.
Bhatt, J. R., *Ceylon: a second South Africa?* Allahabad, 1951.
Bissoondayal, B., *The Truth About Mauritius*, Bombay, 1968.
Bose, Subhas Chandra, *India Calling* (ed. R. I. Paul), Lahore [1945].
Calpin, G. H., *Indians in South Africa*, Pietermaritzburg, 1949.
────── (ed.), *A. I. Kajee: his work for the South African Indian Community*, Durban, n.d.
Chakravarti, N. R., *The Indian Minority in Burma: the rise and decline of an immigrant community*, London, 1971.
Chaturvedi, Benarsi Das and Sykes, Marjorie, *Charles Freer Andrews: a narrative*, London, 1949.

Cheng, Siok-Hwa, *The Rice Industry of Burma, 1852-40*, Kuala Lumpur, 1968.
Chettur, S. K., *Malayan Adventure*, Mangalore, 1948.
Christian, J. L., *Modern Burma*, Berkeley, 1942.
Clifford, Bede, *Proconsul: being incidents in the life of the Hon. Sir Bede Clifford*, London, 1964.
Coulter, J. W., *Fiji: little India of the Pacific*, Chicago [1942].
Dayal, Bhawani and Chaturvedi, B. D., *A Report on the Emigrants Repatriated to India under the Assisted Emigration Scheme from South Africa . . .*, Khargarh, 1931.
Deerr, Noel, *The History of Sugar*, London, 1949, Vol. I; 1950, Vol. II.
Desai, W. S., *India and Burma*, Delhi, 1954.
Despres, L. A., *Cultural Pluralism and Nationalist Politics in British Guiana*, Chicago, 1967.
Donnison, F. S. V., *British Military Administration in the Far East, 1943-46*, London, 1956.
Dotson, Floyd and Lillian, *The Indian Minority of Zambia, Rhodesia and Malawi*, New Haven, 1968.
Durga Das (ed.), *Sardar Patel's Correspondence, 1945-50*, Ahmedabad, 1973, Vol. 8.
Farmer, B. H., *Ceylon: a divided nation*. London, 1963.
Frost, Richard (ed.), *The British Commonwealth and World Society: proceedings of the third unofficial conference on British Commonwealth relations*, London, 1947.
Furnivall, J. S., *Colonial Policy and Practice: a comparative study of Burma and Netherlands India*, Cambridge, 1948.
Gamba, Charles, *The Origins of Trade Unionism in Malaya*, Singapore, 1962.
Gangulee, N., *Indians in the Empire Overseas: a Survey*, London, 1947.
Glasgow, R. A., *Guyana — Race and Politics among Africans and East Indians*, The Hague, 1970.
Gregory, R. G., *Sydney Webb and East Africa; Labour's Experiment with the doctrine of native paramountcy*, Berkeley, 1962.
_____*India and East Africa: a history of race relations within the British Empire, 1890-1939*, Oxford, 1971.
Gupta, Anirudha (ed.), *Indians Abroad: Asia and Africa; report of an international seminar*, Delhi, 1971.
Hancock, W. K., *Survey of British Commonwealth Affairs*, Vol. I, 'Problems of Nationality', London, 1937.
_____*Smuts: the Fields of Force, 1919-50*, Cambridge, 1968.
_____and Poel, Jean van der (eds.), *Selections from the Smuts Papers*, Vols. 5-7 (1919-50), Cambridge, 1973.
Hazareesingh, K., *History of Indians in Mauritius*, London, 1975.
Hinden, Rita, *Empire and After: a study of British imperial attitudes*, London, 1949.
Hunter, Guy, *South-East Asia: race; culture and nation*, London, 1966.
Husain, Azim, *Fazl-i-Husain: a political biography*, Bombay, 1946.
Husain, Fazl-i-, *Indians Abroad . . . Statement on the position of Indians in Africa*, Bombay, 1930.

Huxley, Elspeth, *White Man's Country: Lord Delamere and the making of Kenya*, London, 1935.
Jagadisan, T. N. (ed.), *The letters of the Rt. Hon. V. S. S. Sastri, 1944* (2nd edn., London, 1963).
Jagan, Cheddi, *The West on Trial: my fight for Guyana's freedom*, London, 1966.
Jain, R. K., *South Indians on the Plantation Frontier in Malaya*, New Haven, 1970.
Jayawardena, Chandra, *Conflict and Solidarity in a Guyanese Plantation*, London, 1963.
Jayawardene, V. K., *The Rise of the Labor Movement in Ceylon*, Durham, North Carolina, 1972.
Jeffries, Charles, *Ceylon: the path to independence*, London, 1962.
Joshi, P. S., *The Tyranny of Colour*, Durban [1942].
Karnik, V. B., *Indian Trades Unions: a survey*, Bombay, 1966.
Khan, Shafa'at Ahmad, *The Indian in South Africa*, Allahabad, 1946.
Khare, N. B., *My Political Memoirs, or autobiography*, Nagpur [1960].
Khushwant Singh, *A History of the Sikhs, Vol. 2, 1839-64*, Princeton, 1966.
Klass, Morton, *East Indians in Trinidad: a study in cultural persistence*, New York, 1961.
Kodikara, S. U., *Indo-Ceylon Relations since Independence*, Colombo, 1965.
Kondapi, C., *Indians Overseas, 1838-49*, Bombay, 1951.
Kotelawala, John, *An Asian Prime Minister's Story*, London, 1956.
Krishnan, R. B., *Indians in Malaya: a pageant of Greater India*, Singapore, 1936.
Kuczynski, R. R., *Demographic Survey of the British Colonial Empire*, London, 1949, Vol. II, 'East Africa' (including Mauritius), 1953, Vol. III, 'The West Indies and American Territories'.
Kuper, Hilda, *Indian People in Natal*, Durban, 1960.
Kuper, Leo, *Passive Resistance in South Africa*, London, 1956.
Lohia, Rammanohar, *Indians in Foreign Lands*, Allahabad, 1938.
Lowenthal, David, *West Indian Societies*, London, 1972.
Ludowyk, E. F. C., *The Modern History of Ceylon*, London, 1960.
Mahajani, Usha, *The Role of Indian Minorities in Burma and Malaya*, Bombay, 1960.
Malik, Y. K., *East Indians in Trinidad: a study in minority politics*, London, 1971.
Mangat, J. S., *A History of Asians in East Africa, c. 1886-1945*, Oxford, 1969.
Mayer, Adrian, *Peasants in the Pacific: a study of Fiji Indian rural society*, London, 1961 (2nd edn., Berkeley, 1973).
——*Indians in Fiji*, London, 1963.
Mehrotra, S. R., *India and the Commonwealth, 1885-1929*, London, 1965.
Menon, K. N., *Passive Resistance in South Africa*, Delhi, 1952.
Menon, K. P. S., *Many Worlds: an autobiography*, Bombay, 1965.
Minority Rights Group Reports: *The Asian Minorities of East and Central Africa* (by Yash Ghai and Dharam Ghai), *East Indians of Trinidad and Guyana* (by Malcolm Cross)
Mitchell, Philip, *African Afterthoughts*, London, 1974.
Moon, Penderel (ed), *Wavell, the Viceroy's Journal*, London, 1973.
Morris, H. S., *The Indians in Uganda*, London, 1968.
Mukerjee, Radhakamal, *Population Problems in South-East Asia*, Allahabad, 1944.

Nair, M. N., *Indians in Malaya*, Madras, 1937.
Narain, Iqbal, *The Politics of Racialism: a study of the Indian minority in South Africa*, Agra, 1962.
Nehru, Jawaharlal, *An Autobiography*, London, 1936 (revised edn., 1942).
———*Nehru on Africa*, Delhi [1954].
Nicholls, G. Heaton, *South Africa in My Time,* London, 1961.
Niehoff, A. and J., *East Indians in the West Indies*, Milwaukee, 1960.
'Onlooker, An', *The Status of Indians in the Empire*, Allahabad, 1944.
Pachai, Bridglal, *The International Aspects of the South African Indian Question, 1860-1971*, Cape Town, 1971.
Palmer, G. E. H., *Consultation and Cooperation in the British Commonwealth*, London, 1934.
Palmer, Mabel, *The History of Indians in Natal*, Cape Town, 1957.
Panikkar, K. M., *An Introduction to the Problems of Greater India*, Madras, 1916.
———*India and the Indian Ocean*, 2nd edn., London, 1951.
Parmer, J. Norman, *Colonial Labor Policy and Administration*, Locust Valley, New York, 1960.
Parry, Clive, *Commonwealth Citizenship with special reference to India*, Delhi, 1954.
———*Nationality and Citizenship Laws of the Commonwealth and of the Republic of Ireland*, London, 1957.
Pillai, P. P., (ed.), *Labour in South-East Asia*, Delhi, 1947.
Raghavan, N., *India and Malaya: a study*, Bombay, 1954.
Rajkumar, N. V., *Indians Outside India*, Delhi [1951].
Rao, A. Narayan, *Indian Labour in Burma*, Madras, 1933.
Rao, P. R. Ramachandra, *India and Ceylon: a study*, Bombay, 1954.
Ratnam, K. J., *Communalism and the Political Process in Malaya*, Kuala Lumpur, 1965.
Rau, B. N., *India's Constitution in the Making*, Bombay, 1960.
Reading, Marquess of, *Rufus Isaacs, First Marquess of Reading*, London, 1945, 2 vols.
Rothchild, Donald, *Racial Bargaining in Independent Kenya: a study of minorities and decolonization*, London, 1973.
Rothermund, Indira, *Die Politische und Wirtschaftliche rolle der asiatischen minderheit in Ostafrika*, Berlin, 1965.
Roy, Jay Narain, *Mauritius in Transition*, Allahabad, 1960.
Sandhu, K. S., *Indians in Malaya: some aspects of their immigration and settlement, 1786-1937*, Cambridge, 1969.
Sastri, S. R., *Congress Mission to Malaya*, Tenali, 1947.
Sastri, V. S. S., *Speeches and Writings of the Rt. Hon. V. S. S. Sastri*, Vol. I, Madras, 1969.
Smith, M. G., *The Plural Society in the British West Indies*, Berkeley, 1965.
Smith, R. T., *British Guiana*, London, 1962.
Stenson, M. R., *Industrial Conflict in Malaya: prelude to the Communist revolt of 1948*, London, 1970.
Sundaram, Lanka, *Indians Overseas; a study in economic sociology*, Madras, 1933.
Thompson, Virginia, *Labor Problems in Southeast Asia*, New York, 1947.
———and Adloff, Richard, *Minority Problems in Southeast Asia*, Stanford, 1955.

Tinker, Hugh, *The Union of Burma; a study of the first years of independence.* London, 1957 (4th edn., 1967).
—— *Experiment With Freedom: India and Pakistan, 1947,* London, 1967.
—— *A New System of Slavery; the export of Indian Labour overseas, 1830-1920,* London, 1974.
Toye, Philip, *The Springing Tiger,* London, 1959.
Vatuk, V. P., *British Guiana,* New York, 1963.
—— *Thieves in My House,* Banaras, 1969.
Waiz, S. A., (ed), *Indians Abroad* . . . . Bombay [1927].
Waley, S. D., *Edwin Montagu: a memoir* . . . . London, 1964.
Wilson, Christopher, *Kenya's Warning: the challenge to white supremacy in our British colonies,* Nairobi, n.d.
Earl Winterton, *Orders of the Day,* London, 1955.
Wriggins, W.H., *Ceylon: dilemmas of a new nation,* Princeton, 1960.

Index

Indian and Ceylonese names are listed like European names, under the last name, unless the name is hyphenated (Shams-ud-Deen). Burmese names are listed under the first part of the name, ignoring the prefix, U (Ba Maw, Nu, U).

ACHARIAR, S., 94
Addison, Lord, 292, 297-8, 379
Aden, 275, 314, 353-4
Aga Khan, 79, 133, 145, 148, 273, 297, 438
Agents of the Government of India, 79-80, 88-9, 90-1, 95, 100-1, 118-19, 127, 141-6, 162-3, 165-6, 169, 171, 177, 186-7, 194, 202, 217, 233, 253-4, 282, 289-90, 308-11, 352, 399-400, 414, 424
Ahmed, Sir Sultan, 232
Aiyer, K. A. Neelakandha, 153
Alexander, A. V. (Lord Alexander), 264, 360
Ali, Sir Raza, 85, 132, 137, 177, 221, 226, 256, 404
All-India Congress Committee, *see* Indian National Congress
All-India Muslim League, *see* Muslim League
Altrincham, Lord, 378-9
Ambedkar, Dr B. R., 371, 374
Amery, L. S., 24, 81-3, 86, 90, 94-7, 100-5, 112, 162, 175, 178, 181, 187-9, 192, 195-6, 202, 205, 212, 218, 219, 222, 224, 225, 228, 230, 233, 237, 246-7, 253-7, 264, 417, 422, 437
Andrews, C. F., 11, 24, 35-6, 42, 54, 64, 85, 87-9, 91, 93, 94, 98-9, 102, 128, 132, 162, 166, 318, 390, 397, 400, 442
Aney, M. S., 188-9, 191, 194-200, 205, 212, 217, 221, 258, 285, 338, 413, 418, 443
Anti-Fascist Peoples Freedom League, 257, 286, 288

Anti-Segregationist Council, 251, 292
Anti-Slavery Society, 24, 216, 278, 441
Arya Samaj, 331
Asian Relations Conference (Delhi), 301-2, 307
Athlone, Earl of, 83, 84, 85-6, 88, 101-2
Attlee, C. R. (Lord Attlee), 222-3, 239, 264-5, 288, 298, 301, 302, 306, 349, 373, 374-5, 385-6
Auchinleck, General Sir Claude, 226, 264
Aung San, *Bogyoke*, 151, 286-8, 305, 308, 366-7, 406, 421
Australia, 21-2, 37, 39, 51-2, 61-2, 228, 261-2, 299, 322, 356, 357, 359, 361-3, 370, 372, 374-5, 376, 378, 387, 429-30

BAILEY, Sir Abe, 33, 55
Bajpai, Sir G. S., 46, 48, 50-1, 52, 61, 70, 85, 86-7, 108, 111, 128, 137, 142, 143-6, 154-5, 160-2, 165, 176, 179, 183, 192, 193-5, 198, 316-17, 341-2, 346, 350, 372, 385-6, 387, 397, 427
Baldwin, Stanley (Lord Baldwin), 66, 71, 73, 76, 81, 105, 136
Ba Maw, Dr, 151, 152, 206-7, 257, 426
Bandaranaike, S. W. R. D., 157, 179-80, 182, 259, 307
Banerjee, R. N., 242, 254-5, 286, 296, 309, 360, 362, 418
Banishment, deportation, 185, 187-8, 330, 344-5

451

INDEX

Ba Pe, U, 122
Baring, Sir Evelyn, 233-4, 237-40, 248, 250-1, 292-3
Ba U, Justice, 305
Baxter, James, 152, 193
Beejadhur, Aunath, 335
Benn, Wedgwood (Lord Stansgate), 11, 62, 106-10, 113, 180, 437
Bewoor, Sir Gurunath, 266
Bhore, Sir Joseph, 133
Birkenhead, Lord, 81, 83, 86, 91, 92, 95, 107, 437
Bissoondayal, B., 254-5, 284, 335, 425
Boland, F. H., 363, 369, 428
Bose, Rash Behari, 206
Bose, Subhas Chandra, 208, 290
Bottomley, Arthur, 304
Bozman, G. S., 147, 192, 193, 242
Braund, Justice H. B. L., 151-2, 204
British Columbia, 28, 228, 304, 325-6
British Guiana, 39-40, 42, 91-2, 129, 131, 163-5, 168-9, 253, 313, 332-3 440
British nationality, 74, 92-3, 155, 173, 311, 338, 353-4, 359, 367-8, 374, 376-82, 408
British Nationality Act, 1948, 354-6, 370, 372-83, 428
British protected persons, 93, 365-6, 369, 381, 428
Broome, Justice F. N., 220, 221-2, 228, 233-4, 238, 248, 252, 294
Browne, G. St J. Orde, 165, 190-2, 254, 409-10
Burma, 40, 121-3, 150-2, 193-8, 202-8, 212, 255-7, 261-2, 266, 286-9, 305, 307-8, 313, 337, 340-2, 359-63, 366-7, 369, 371, 392, 410-11
Butler, R. A. (Lord Butler), 150-1, 174, 195
Buxton, C. R., 112, 114, 428

CALDECOTT, Sir Andrew, 158, 160-1, 179-82, 199, 209-10, 244, 259
Cameron, Sir Donald, 96, 100

Canada, 22, 28-9, 37-8, 39, 52, 61, 127, 173, 177, 228, 262, 304, 325-6, 356-8, 361-3, 368-70, 372, 374, 376-7, 378, 386, 419, 429, 430
Canadian Citizenship Act, 1946, 356-7, 377-8
Cape Town Conference, and Agreement, 87-8, 92, 95, 102, 128-31, 234, 296
Carter, Sir Morris, 134-5, 139-40, 278, 404
Cavendish-Bentinck, Major F. W., 243, 270-2, 276, 329
Central Indian Association (Malaya), 153, 186-7
Ceylon, 40, 80, 100, 115-21, 152, 156-61, 170, 178-83, 186, 198-201, 209-12, 244, 257-60, 262, 264-5, 284-6, 289, 305-7, 313, 337-40, 359, 362-4, 367, 374-5, 386, 392, 428, 430
Chagla, M. C., 297-8
Chamberlain, Neville, 148, 175
Charan, Satya, 317-18, 331-3, 335
Chaturvedi, Benarsi Das, 29-30, 69, 80, 94, 400, 442
Chelmsford, Lord, 30, 44, 65-6, 67
Chettiar, R. N. Annamalai, 346
Chettiar, V. K., 412
Chettur, S. K., 289, 308
Chettyars, 193-4, 207, 287, 343, 346-7, 426
Chifley, J. B., 385
Chinese, 183-4, 246, 304, 308, 342-3, 347
Choudree, Ashwin, 414
Christopher, Albert, 131, 251
Churchill, W. S., 10, 25-6, 35, 41, 46-50, 57-62, 99, 175, 205, 211, 218, 237, 298, 388
Citizenship, 339, 340-1, 353-4, 391-3
Civil Affairs Service (Burma), 256-7, 286
Clarendon, Lord, 128
Clarkson, Senator C. F., 226-7, 233-5, 237, 250

Clifford, Sir Bede, 169-72
Clifford, Sir Hugh, 116, 124
Clow, Sir Andrew, 197, 204
Cohen, Sir Andrew, 265, 269, 274-5, 276
Colonial Sugar Refining Company (Fiji), 60-1, 162, 212-13
Colonies Committee, 78-80, 90
Commissioners of the Indian Government in the Colonies, 315-18, 331-6
Common roll, see Votes, franchise
Commonwealth citizenship, 354-6, 360, 371-3, 387, 392
Commonwealth Conference, (1946) 358, (1948) 348, 384-5, (1949) 386-8
Commonwealth Immigration Act, 1962, 356, 431
Commonwealth Relations, Department of Government of India, 228, 266, 427,
——, Office, in London, 311
Congress, see Indian National Congress
Connaught, Prince Arthur of, 54, 55, 65, 85
Constituent Assembly, of India, 319, 348, 371, 383, 388-90
Constitution of India, 391-2
Corbett, Sir G. L., 60-1, 87, 129
Corea, Claude, 181, 198
Coryndon, Sir Robert, 59, 62-3, 64, 81, 82, 99
Cranborne, Lord, 175, 230
Creech Jones, Arthur, see Jones, Arthur Creech
Crewe, Lord, 26, 27
Cripps, Sir Stafford, 200-1, 207, 210, 264, 385, 387, 431
Croft, Sir W. D., 143, 211
Cunliffe-Lister, Sir Philip, 121, 134
Cure, Dr J. M., 170, 172
Curtis, Lionel, 24-5, 30, 261

DADOO, Y. M., 174, 302
Dass, Isher, 114, 146
Dawson, Geoffrey, 24, 81, 128

Dayal, Basudeo Bishen, see Bissoon dayal, B.
Delamere, Lord, 26, 62, 64, 65-6, 70, 95, 98, 105, 112, 402
Deo, Visnu, 162
Deportation, see Banishment
Deshmukh, G. V., 139, 221, 232-3, 248
Deshmukh, R. V., 247, 249, 294, 302, 418
Desai, Bhulabhai, 233
Desai, Manilal, 34, 94
Desai, P. K., 128
Dev, D. Y., 318, 335-6
Devonshire, Duke of, 62-7, 72-3, 110, 404
Doctor, Manilal, 169-70
Dominion status, 44, 52, 86, 111-12, 125-6, 305-7, 357-9, 379-80
Donoughmore, Lord, and Ceylon's constitution, 116-17, 157-8, 179, 182, 212
Dorman-Smith, Sir Reginald, 195, 197, 203, 255, 286-8
Duckworth, F. V., 290-1
Duncan, Sir Patrick, 24, 55, 75, 87, 97, 129, 231
Durban riots, 324
Dutt, Subimal, 187-90, 314, 352, 367

EAST AFRICA: federation and 'closer union', 94-6, 99-100, 109-10, 113, 114, 149, 279
East African Indian National Congress, 80, 93-4, 104, 146, 177, 243
Ede, Chuter, 359, 366, 376, 379-80, 428
Edun, Ayube, 165, 167, 332
Eire, see Ireland
Elgin, Lord, 25-6
Eritrea, 246
Erskine-Crum, V. F. E., 370-1, 385

FABIAN COLONIAL BUREAU, 266, 272, 277-8, 280, 333

INDEX

Fazl-i-Husain, 111, 128-30, 132, 133, 135, 137
Feetham, Justice R., 220-1, 234
Fiji, 29-30, 40, 60-1, 80, 90-1, 142, 162-3, 1 7, 212-14, 311, 314, 318, 333-4, 361, 392, 438
Fitzgerald, Desmond, 73, 92
Franchise, *see* Votes, franchise
Frontier Force Rifles, 185, 201
Furnivall, J. S., 8
Fyfe, Sir D. Maxwell, 380

GANAPATHY, S. A., 302, 343, 347-8
Gandhi, Manilal, 90, 131, 251
Gandhi, Mohandas K., 23-4, 27, 31, 32, 35-6, 70, 76, 89-90, 91, 102, 105, 111, 113, 122, 146, 174, 195, 207, 224, 247, 293, 295, 390
Gent, Sir Edward, 191, 289, 308, 343-4
George, David Lloyd, 43-4, 47-8, 51, 59, 62, 77, 82
Ghadr, 29, 34, 206
Ghaznavi, Sir A. H., 196
Ghetto Act, 296, 298, 302, 304
Ghoshal, H. N. (Thakin Ba Tin), 341
Giri, V. V., 338-9
Glyn, Sir Ralph, 381-2
Gokhale. G. K., 23, 27, 76
Goonesinha, A. E., 160
Goonetilleke, Sir Oliver, 285, 306-7
Gopalan, A.K., 155
Gordon-Walker, Patrick, 330, 334, 372-3, 385
Greenidge, C. W. W., 216, 441
Gregory, Robert G., 398, 401
Grigg, Sir Edward, 82, 95-8, 100-1, 103, 139, 148; *see also* Altrincham, Lord
Group Areas Act, 325
Gujadhar, R., 170
Gurney, Sir Henry, 348, 350, 352

HABIBULLAH, Sir Muhammad, 82, 87, 101, 102, 108, 111
Hailey, Lord, 261

Haldane, Lord, 47
Hall, George (Lord Hall), 185-6, 191-2, 265, 270, 272, 283, 409
Hall, Sir John, 282
Hancock, Sir Keith, 398, 421, 433
Haque, Sir Azizul, 232
Hardinge, Lord, 27, 67, 68, 147
Harford, Sir James, 335-6
Harlech, Lord, 176, 222-4, 227, 233
Hasan, K. Sarwar, 281
Hasluck, Sir Paul, 299
Hertzog, General J. B. M., 75-6, 83-6, 88, 92, 111, 128, 131, 138, 174, 222
Hilton Young, Sir Edward, *see* Young, Sir Edward Hilton
Hinchingbrooke, Lord, 261, 380
Hinden, Rita, 333
Hoare, Sir Samuel, 128, 133, 136, 436
Hofmeyr, J. F. H., 138, 174, 223, 235, 239, 249-50, 292, 297, 323
Hope-Simpson, Sir John, 78, 80, 81
Htoon Aung Gyaw, Sir, 193, 287
Hughes, W. M., 46-9, 50-2
Hutchings, Sir Robert, 152, 193-4, 197-8, 202-5
Hydari, Sir Akbar, 197

IMAM, Hossain, 132, 166
Immigration restrictions, 22, 28-9, 37-8, 63, 79-81, 148-9, 155, 158, 160-1, 183, 199-200, 209, 240, 241-2, 275, 281-2, 327-8, 334, 378, 391-2, 410
Imperial Conferences, (1911) 27-8, (1918) 31-2, (1921) 11, 44-53, 54, 60, (1923) 70-4, 78, 355, (1926) 92-3, (1930) 127, (1937) 173, 380, (1944) 229
Imperial Indian Citizenship Association (Bombay), 34, 53-4, 146-7, 318
Indenture system, 21, 40, 292
Indian Army, 30-1, 185-6, 189, 201, 207, 223, 288
Indian Independence League, 206-8, 341

Indian National Army (Azad Hind Fauj), 207-8, 290-1, 412
Indian National Congress, 36, 43, 70, 93-4, 144, 147, 154-5, 159-60, 190, 207, 248, 266, 287, 318, 359, 384, 400, 443
Indian Opinion, 90, 251
Indian population overseas, (1921) 36, (1947) 313-14, 423-4
Indian Statutory Commission, 100
Indians in Kenya (White Paper), 67, 97, 404
Indians Overseas Association, 24
Indo-Caribbean Cultural Institute, 332
Indonesia, 266
Innes, Sir Charles, 123
Ireland, 37, 71-3, 133, 173, 357, 360-3, 369, 374, 382-3, 431
Irish Nationality and Citizenship Act, 1935, 357
Irwin, Lord, 11, 87, 94-5, 97, 98-100, 103-4, 108, 116, 128, 399, 436-7
Ismail, Sir Mirza, 198, 221
Ismailis, 8, 133-4, 273
Ispahani, M. A. H., 195, 320

JACKSON, Sir Edward, 152, 157-9
Jagan, Cheddi, 333
Japanese conquest, 197, 199, 201-9, 253, 264
Jayakar, M. R., 102, 225
Jayatilaka, Sir Baron, 157, 159, 182-3, 210
Jeevanjee, A. M., 66
Jeffries, Sir Charles, 265, 276-7, 285, 306, 421
Jennings, Sir Ivor, 212, 386, 430-1
Jha, C. S., 281, 309
Jinnah, M. A., 64, 225, 303
Johore, Sultan of, 289, 350
Jones, Arthur Creech, 10, 137, 144-5, 157, 165, 171, 172, 186, 216, 256, 261, 265-70, 277-8, 280-3, 289, 305-7, 309-11, 314, 328, 330-1, 335-6, 338, 344-5, 347-8, 356, 359, 366, 419, 441-2

Jowitt, Lord, 375, 377-9, 385-6

KAJEE, A. I., 54, 89, 130, 137, 174, 219-20, 225, 228-30, 234-5, 237-8, 248, 292-5, 301, 302-3, 415, 423
Kajee, A. S., 323
Kalkar, V. V., 280
Kathrithamby, V., 120
Kennedy, Sir D. M., 255, 283-4
Kenya, 26, 34-5, 38, 46-7, 56-9, 62-7, 70-1, 78-81, 94, 97-9, 99-100, 107-10, 114-15, 134-5, 139-41, 148-9, 240-5, 267-83, 313-14, 318-19, 326-30, 361, 419-20, 425, 440
Kerr, Philip (Lord Lothian), 24-5
Kershaw, Sir Louis, 95-6, 103-4, 108, 120, 180
Keskar, Dr B. V., 347-8, 350
Khan, Sir Muhammad Zafrullah, 143-5, 165, 261-3, 320
Khan, Sir Shafa'at Ahmad, 221, 223, 224-5, 226-7, 230-6, 238-9, 246, 248, 414-17
Khan, Zafar Ali, 248
Khare, Dr N. B., 217, 225-6, 230-2, 234-6, 239, 246, 247-50, 255-6, 258-9, 266, 281, 295, 415, 418
King, W. L. Mackenzie, 70-1, 92, 127, 224, 228, 229, 303-4, 357-8, 378
Kotelawala, Sir John, 160
Krishna Menon, V. K., *see* Menon, V. K. Krishna
Kunzru, Pandit H. N., 11, 43, 60, 104, 108, 166, 192, 225, 242, 256, 271, 280, 290, 301, 319, 325, 389-90, 401

LAITHWAITE, Sir Gilbert, 177, 193, 372-3, 377
Lalljee, Hooseinbhoy, 233
Latif, Abdul (Khin Maung Lat), 341
Lawrence, Senator H. G., 220, 221-2, 223, 229, 249-50, 320
League of Nations, 55-6, 72, 95, 133, 263

Lewis, Professor Arthur, 277
Linlithgow, Lord, 11, 136, 141, 143, 145, 160-1, 175, 176, 181, 187-9, 192, 195-7, 201, 204-5, 212, 217-18, 224-6, 231, 436-7
Listowel, Lord, 310-11, 348, 385
Lloyd, Lord, 179-82
Lloyd George, David, *see* George, David Lloyd
Lohia, Rammanohar, 154-5
Louw, Eric, 324-5
Luckhoo, J. A., 168

MACDONALD, Malcolm, 136, 158, 160, 161, 172, 176, 179, 289, 345, 425
MacDonald, J. Ramsay, 78, 105, 111-12, 136
Machtig, Sir Eric, 250, 292-3, 303
Mackenzie King, W. L., *see* King, W. L. Mackenzie
McNeill, Hector, 242, 321-2
Maharaj, A. B., 292
Maharaj, Badri, 91
Mahn Ba Khaing, 307
Malan, Dr D. F., 83, 84-7, 128-31, 301, 322-3, 387
Malaya, 80, 123-6, 152-6, 165, 183-92, 201-2, 206-7, 208-9, 261, 265, 266, 289-92, 308, 313-14, 342-52, 409-10, 440
Malayan Communist Party, 344-5
Malayan Indian Congress, 292, 308, 342-3, 352
Man-Power Citizens Association, 165, 167, 332-3
Maraj, Seemongat, 166
Mathu, Eliud, 271-2
Mau Mau, 326, 329
Mauritius, 39-40, 91-2, 165, 169-73, 178-9, 214-17, 254-5, 283-4, 309, 311, 313, 318, 334-7, 392, 407-8, 438
Maxwell, Sir Alexander, 358-9, 428
Medh, S. B., 128
Mehd, P. V., 148
Mehta, Jamnadas, 196, 287, 305, 418

Menon, K. P. S., 134, 137, 297
Menon, U. K., 184-5
Menon, V. K. Krishna, 205, 317-18, 330-1, 343-4, 347-50, 373, 385, 387, 430
Menon, V. P., 371
Menzies, Sir Robert, 387
Milner, Lord, 10, 24, 32-5
Mitchell, Douglas, 229-30, 237-8, 249-50, 416
Mitchell, Sir Philip, 214, 244, 269-76, 279, 283, 318-19, 326-7
Montagu, E. S., 11, 31-3, 42-53, 57-9, 62, 69, 77, 139, 397, 437
Moore, Sir Henry, 244-5, 285, 305, 338
Moore, Lady, 306-7, 423
Morley, Lord, 23, 27
Mountbatten, Lord Louis (Earl Mountbatten of Burma), 257, 266, 286, 289-90, 311, 322, 367, 369, 370-1, 385, 429
Moyne, Lord, 168-9, 172, 175, 186-92, 199, 254
Mudaliar, Sir Ramaswamy, 226, 232, 249, 285, 296
Mukerjee, Radhakamal, 261-2
Murray, Gilbert, 55-6
Muslim League, 194-5, 248, 266, 287, 359

NAICKER, Dr G. M., 292, 302
Naidoo, H. A., 251
Naidoo, M. D., 292
Naidoo, S. R., 131-2, 224, 228, 238, 248
Naidoo, Mrs Sarojini, 129, 301
Natal Indian Congress, 32, 83, 219-20, 224, 229, 230, 235, 238-9, 247-8, 251, 292-3, 303
Natal Indian Organisation, 302, 323
Natesan, G. A., 131, 338, 443
Nathan, R. H., 184-5, 190-1
Nehru, Jawaharlal, 11, 93, 151-2, 154-5, 159-60, 178-9, 205-6, 266-7, 288, 290-1, 297, 301-3, 305,

307-8, 309-12, 319, 325, 337, 339-40, 342, 347, 369, 371, 384-90, 393, 430-1, 443
Nehru, Motilal, 70, 108
Newfoundland, 37, 71, 357, 361-2, 374-5
Ne Win, General, 426
New Zealand, 21-2, 37, 39, 52, 61, 73, 262, 299, 321, 357, 361-3, 372, 374-5, 376-7, 387, 429
Nicholls, G. Heaton, 129, 131-2, 229-31, 248, 297-9, 416
Noel-Baker, Philip, 316, 319, 375-6
Noon, Sir Firoz Khan, 195, 229
Northey, Sir Edward, 35, 57, 58-9
Nu, U, 341-2, 367
Nye, Sir Archibald, 348, 350

OLDHAM, J. H., 97, 99
Olivier, Lord, 76, 78, 399
Ormsby-Gore, W. G. A., 40-1, 62, 65, 80, 82, 94, 96, 98, 101, 103, 110, 112, 134, 136, 140-6, 157, 162, 165, 176; *see also* Harlech, Lord

PADDISON, Sir G. F., 85-7
Pai, A. V., 159, 212, 213-14, 275-6, 285, 304
Pakistan, 260, 263, 267, 314, 320-1, 367, 370, 391-2, 429, 431
Pandit, Mrs Vijaya Lakshmi, 297, 320-2
Paranjpye, Sir R. P., 43, 97, 101-2, 228, 418
Parkinson, Sir Cosmo, 176, 186, 189, 409
Panikkar, K. M., 261
Pant, Pandit Govind Ballabh, 138-9, 221, 318
Paroo, K. R., 273
Passfield, Lord, 107-10, 112-14, 118-20, 165, 180, 401
Passive Resistance Council, 296, 301
Patel, A. B., 271-3, 330
Patel, Ambalal, 213
Patel, Sardar Vallabhbhai, 144, 346, 385-6, 387, 430

Pather, P. R., 131, 224, 229, 237, 415
Patil, S. K., 144
Pan-Malayan Federation of Trade Unions, 302, 343
Pant, Apa B., 318-19, 329, 333, 393, 424-5
Pearson, Lester B., 304, 385-7, 430
Peel, Lord, 59, 62, 64-9, 70-2, 81, 103-4, 107, 398
Pegging Act, 222, 224, 228, 238, 240, 249, 292, 294
Perera, I. X., 212
Pethick-Lawrence, Lord, 264-5, 285, 286, 288, 310
Pickthorne, Kenneth, 381
Pillai, T. G. N., 202
Pirow, Oswald, 111, 129
Polak, H. S. L., 24, 58, 65, 157, 165, 171, 174, 224, 243-4, 265-6, 277, 441
Prakasa, Sri, 295-6
Prasad, Sir Jagdish, 132, 137, 225
Prasad, Dr Rajendra, 383, 407-8
Pretoria Agreement, 229-30, 237-8, 250, 416-17
Pritt, D. N., 346

QUEENSLAND, 127

RAGHAVAN, N., 184-5, 190, 192
Rajput, Hazara Singh, 425, *see* Singh, Makhan
Ramakrishna Mission, 213
Ramgoolam, Dr S., 255, 335
Ramnarain, H. P., 215-16, 254-5
Rance, Sir Hubert, 288, 305, 367
Rao, Kodananda, 290
Rao, B. Shiva, 301, 319-20
Raschid, M. A., 305, 340, 426
Rau, Sir Benegal Narsinga, 355, 366, 369-72, 382-3, 385-6, 390-1
Rau, Sir Benegal Rama, 177, 219-21
Rauf, Dr M. A., 151, 256, 305, 308
Razak, Abdul, 340
Reading, Lord, 44-6, 47, 50, 52, 53, 58, 64-5, 67-70, 78, 83-4, 87, 147, 397, 436

Reciprocity Act, 222, 225, 230, 232-3, 236, 248
Reddi, Sir V. K., 102, 128, 130
Republican status, for India, 369-70, 372, 374, 382-3, 385, 388
Rennie, Sir Gilbert, 244-5, 269
Repatriation, 53, 60, 63, 84, 87-8, 93-4, 181, 190, 223, 241, 323
Rhodes, Cecil, 57, 59, 81, 327
Ridley, S., 178
Robertson, Sir Benjamin, 33, 53, 65, 79, 80
Round Table, The, 24-5, 37, 62, 81, 82, 104, 107, 221, 379, 430
Roy, J. N., 335
Roy, K. C., 79
Royal Institute of International Affairs (Chatham House), 11, 260-3, 301, 356
Rozemont, Guy, 335-6
Rudranand, Swami, 213-14
Runganadhan, Sir Samuel, 362
Rustomjee, Sorabjee, 137, 225, 301, 414-15

SADR ANJUMAN-E-ISLAM, 332
Sahadeo, Pandit, 172
St Germaine Convention, 139, 405
St Laurent, Louis, 304, 386
Saklatvala, Shapurji, 39, 438
Saksena, S. L., 350
Salisbury, Lord (1830-1903), 22, 296
Sankey, Lord, 108-9
Sambasivam, 347-51
Sanatan Dharma Maha Sabha, 331, 332
Sapru, P. N., 192, 254
Sapru, Sir Tej Bahadur, 11, 43, 70-5, 200, 390
Sarvadhikary, Sir D. P., 84-5
Sastri, V. S. Srinivasa, 11, 34, 43, 46-53, 56, 60-2, 64, 65, 69-70, 72, 73, 76-7, 82, 87-90, 94, 97, 100, 101-5, 111-13, 119, 120, 128-32, 146, 147, 148, 153-4, 224-5, 236, 390, 397, 398, 403, 406, 442-3

Satyamurti, S., 135
Saw, U, 151-2, 193-7
Schuster, Sir George, 97, 99, 100
Scott, Lord Francis, 112, 243, 379-80
Scullin, J. H., 127
Segregation policy, 35, 57-8, 75-6, 222-3, 228-9, 230-1, 240, 250, 294, 304; *see also* White Highlands
Selborne, Lord, 25, 67-8
Senanayake, D. S., 118, 121, 157, 179, 181-3, 198, 199, 210, 212, 257-60, 284-5, 305-6, 337-9, 426
Shafi, Sir Muhammad, 127
Shakespeare, Sir Geoffrey, 242, 246-7
Shams-ud-Deen, 80-1, 114, 273
Shaw, Sir John, 331-2
Shawcross, Sir Hartley, 298, 381-2
Shepstone, Senator D. G., 228, 237, 249, 252, 303
Shiels, Dr Drummond, 107, 112, 115, 116, 118-19
Shone, Sir Terence, 309, 311, 316, 367
Sikhs, 28-9, 207, 282, 314, 325, 393
Silva, George de, 181
Simla Conference, 263, 272-3
Simon, Sir John (Lord Simon), 100, 378-9
Singapore, 290, 308, 342-4
Singh, Dr J. B., 164, 332
Singh, Jenarine, 332
Singh, Lachman, 332
Singh, Sir Maharaj, 11, 92, 97-8, 101-2, 130-2, 137, 149-50, 224-5, 261, 271, 281-2, 327, 390, 403, 443
Singh, Makhan, 330
Singh, Zora, 291, 340
Sinha, Lord, 31-2, 43
Sitaramayya, Dr P., 348
Slade, Humphrey, 279
Smuts, Field-Marshal J. C., 25, 33, 44-51, 53-5, 65, 70-6, 82, 87, 131, 138, 174, 177, 219, 222-3, 224, 227-31, 233-40, 247-50, 253, 263, 279-80, 292-5, 297-9, 302, 307,

322-3, 375, 378, 387-8, 421-3, 433, 442
Sorensen, Reginald (Lord Sorensen), 186, 224, 441
Soulbury, Lord, 259-60, 284-5, 337
South Africa, 26-7, 32-4, 38, 45-6, 49-50, 53-6, 62, 65, 75-7, 83-90, 127-33, 137, 173-4, 218, 219-39, 247-53, 263, 267, 292-303, 313, 320-6, 357, 361-4, 370, 372, 374-5, 376, 389, 392, 399, 414-17
South African Indian Congress, 93-4, 128-30, 138, 294
South East Asia Command, 256-7, 266
Southern Rhodesia, 38-9, 56, 98, 149-50, 239-40, 246, 303-4, 357, 361-3, 365, 374-5, 397, 429
Stanley, Sir Herbert, 118-20
Stanley, Colonel Oliver, 175-6, 210-12, 218, 245, 254, 258-9
Strachey, John, 306
Strikes, 91, 123, 163-5, 170-2, 179, 183-5, 213-17, 254, 291-2, 308, 330
Symon, A. C. B., 316, 371-2

TANGANYIKA, 95, 96, 129, 133, 148, 241-3, 271, 313-14, 318
Tarr, Edgar, 419
Thivy, John, 292, 308, 343, 347-51
Thivy, Louis, 124
Thomas, J. H., 76, 78, 80, 96, 136, 139-40
Thomas, Sir Shenton, 153, 155, 184-7, 190-1, 201, 343
Thondaman, S., 286
Times, The, 104, 271
Times of India, 213
Tin Tut, U, 193, 195, 206, 255-6, 286, 305, 426
Trade boycott, 226, 233, 236, 249, 295
Trade unions, 162-5, 171, 178-9, 184-6, 215, 253, 283, 302, 305, 330, 349, 426
Trinidad, 39-40, 41, 163, 165, 169, 253, 283, 313-14, 331-2

Tyabji, S. A. S., 122, 194, 197, 256, 341
Tyson, J. D., 168-9, 399

UGANDA, 147-48, 241, 243, 271, 282, 313-14, 18, 326
United Nations, 237, 249, 263, 267, 296-301, 303-4, 307, 320-2, 370, 391, 422-3
United Planting Association of Malaya, 123, 155, 187, 190, 192

VAZE, S. G., 94, 398
Veeraseenam, P., 347
Venkatachar, C. S., 154, 184
Votes, franchise, 34-5, 38-9, 46, 49, 52, 57, 59, 60, 88, 90-1, 98-9, 100, 104-5, 116-19, 159, 162, 180-3, 198, 226-7, 252, 284, 294, 321, 323, 335, 339

WADDINGTON, Sir John, 333
Waiz, S. A., 318, 334
Walton, Sir John, 33-4, 195, 405
Wavell, Field-Marshal Lord, 11, 176, 196-7, 217, 219, 226-8, 230-3, 236-9, 246-9, 258, 263, 266, 285, 293, 301, 323, 415-16, 434-7
Webb, Beatrice, 78, 107, 115, 121, 401
Webb, Sidney, see *Passfield*, Lord
Wedgwood, Josiah, 69, 78
Wershof, M. H., 369, 386, 428
West Indies, 39, 41-2, 142, 163-9, 253-4, 311, 313-14, 318, 392, 438
White Highlands, 26, 35, 57-8, 67, 79, 134-5, 136, 137-40, 243, 268, 270, 277-8, 328-9
Willingdon, Lord, 128, 130, 136, 137, 139, 147, 436
Wilson, Sir Samuel, 101-2, 103-5, 107-9, 120, 126
Winterton, Lord, 40, 49, 62, 54, 66-9, 81, 85, 96, 110-11, 144-5, 150, 398
Wood, Major-General E., 203
Wood, Edward, 40-2, 57, 59, 62, 64, 66, 87; see also Irwin, Lord

Woolf, Leonard, 107
Woolley, Sir Charles, 332

YOUNG, Sir Edward Hilton, 94, 96-7, 98-101, 103

ZANZIBAR, 79, 134, 143-7, 160, 256, 314
Zerbadis (Indo-Burmans), 314
Zetland, Marquess of, 136, 139-40, 147-8, 160, 175, 179, 436